DE MISERIA CONDICIONIS HUMANE

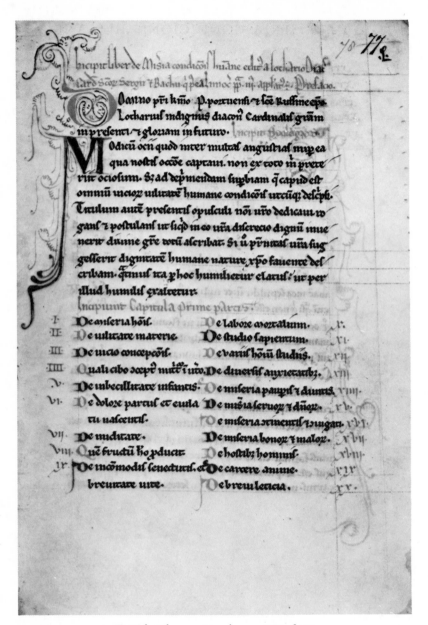

Incipit liber de miseria condicionis humane editus a Lothario Dia-
cono Sancte Sergii et Bachi qui postea uocatus est papa Innocencius tercius. Prologus.

Domino patri karissimo P. portuensi et sancte Ruffine episcopo,
Lotharius indignus diaconus Cardinalis, graciam
in presenti et gloriam in futuro. Incipit Prologus.

Modicum ocii quod inter multas angustias mihi ea
qua nostis occasione captaui, non ex toto in preteritum ociosum. Sed ad deprimendam superbiam que caput est
omnium uiciorum uilitatem humane condicionis utcumque descripsi.
Titulum autem presentis opusculi non uobis dedicaui rogans et postulans ut siquid in eo uestra discrecio dignum inue-
nerit, diuine gracie uestri ascribat. Si uero presumat uestra suggesserit dignitate humane nature, xpo fauente describam. Fiat nam ita per hoc humilietur clarus, ut per
illud humilis exaltetur.

Incipiunt Capitula prime partis.

LOTARIO DEI SEGNI
(POPE INNOCENT III)

DE MISERIA
CONDICIONIS HUMANE

EDITED BY
ROBERT E. LEWIS

THE CHAUCER LIBRARY

THE UNIVERSITY OF GEORGIA PRESS
ATHENS

Library of Congress Catalog Card Number: 75-26119
International Standard Book Number: 0-8203-0395-X

The University of Georgia Press, Athens 30602

Set in VariTyper Bembo
Printed in the United States of America

TO NEIL KER

CONTENTS

FOREWORD

Shortly after the publication of *Sources and Analogues of Chaucer's Canterbury Tales*, edited by W. F. Bryan and Germaine Dempster (Chicago, 1941), the Chaucer Group of the Modern Language Association of America created a committee to suggest a new project for the group to sponsor. Under the chairmanship of Margaret Schlauch, the committee explored several possibilities, was particularly impressed by the investigations that Karl Young had been making in British libraries on the learning of Chaucer, and finally recommended "that the Group sponsor publication of a series of texts, based on primary sources, to constitute a Chaucer's Library" to be prepared under the direction of an editorial committee. It was stressed that "each volume should present the results of labors on original manuscripts, glosses, early editions, etc."

The Chaucer Group approved this proposal at the December meeting of 1945; the Editorial Committee was appointed, and held its first meeting in Washington, D. C., on December 27, 1946. The original members of the committee were Albert C. Baugh, Germaine Dempster, Fred N. Robinson, Robert K. Root, J. Burke Severs (chairman), Margaret Schlauch, and J. S. P. Tatlock. All but the last two were present at the 1946 meeting. It was agreed that the name of the series should be "The Chaucer Library." "Glosses and commentaries which accompanied the texts will be presented; even scribal perversions which may explain Chaucer's text will be recorded. . . . Such a faithful reproduction of Chaucer's books as he knew them is of course essential if we are accurately and adequately to understand their influence upon him."

About twenty years later Paul M. Clogan edited *The Medieval Achilleid of Statius* for the Chaucer Library; he then arranged for its publication by E. J. Brill (Leiden, 1968).

In 1969 and 1970 the committee took steps to find a press to be the official publisher of the series. At the suggestion of the Executive Secretary of the Modern Language Association, John H. Fisher, the Mediaeval Academy of America was invited to cooperate in the publication of the series; and on October 24, 1969, its Executive Committee voted "that the Mediaeval Academy sponsor the publication of the Chaucer Library . . . with the understanding that the Mediaeval Academy could assume no financial responsibility." Finally during December 1970 an agreement for publication was ratified by the Chaucer Library Committee, the Executive Committee of the

Chaucer Group of the Modern Language Association, the Executive Council of the Modern Language Association, the Executive Committee of the Mediaeval Academy, and the University of Georgia Press. The agreement begins, "The Chaucer Library is a series of the classical and medieval works that Chaucer knew, so edited from the medieval manuscripts as to provide texts most nearly like those that Chaucer used. Each text will be accompanied by a translation." It is a pleasure to welcome both the present text and translation, and the participation of the University of Georgia Press in the presentation of the Chaucer Library.

Robert A. Pratt
Chairman, The Chaucer Library Committee

The Committee:
  Albert C. Baugh
  Morton W. Bloomfield
  Martin M. Crow
  Ruth J. Dean
  John H. Fisher
  Albert C. Friend
  Siegfried Wenzel
  Robert E. Lewis, General Editor

PREFACE

The English poet Geoffrey Chaucer (ca. 1343-1400), like most other medieval writers at a time when the notion of "authority" was quite different from the current notion, made use of the works of classical and earlier medieval authors, but there are no editions of these works in versions that would have been available to Chaucer and his contemporaries in the late Middle Ages. Present editions, unless they are facsimiles, attempt to reconstruct an author's original, but before the invention of printing, when texts were reproduced by hand, a classical or medieval work would have been altered, often greatly, by each successive copying. The purpose of the Chaucer Library, therefore, is to present the works that Chaucer knew, translated, or made use of in his writings in versions that are as close as possible to those that were in existence, circulating, and being read by Chaucer and his contemporaries. These versions were, of course, not critical editions—they were filled with readings that the original authors did not write, with additions and omissions, and sometimes with glosses and commentaries—and to have a true understanding of the way in which classical and medieval texts were perceived by medieval readers, it is necessary to reproduce such nonoriginal material. This the Chaucer Library has done, and will continue to do, while at the same time striving to present readable texts, with punctuation and capitalization modernized, abbreviations expanded, some letters regularized, and accompanied by English translations.

Lotario dei Segni's extremely popular treatise *De Miseria Humane Conditionis* is a particularly good one for this kind of treatment because parts of his presumed original did not circulate widely, and to present a reconstruction of that original would have given a misleading picture of what was actually being read in the late Middle Ages. I considered emending the very small number of clearly meaningless (as opposed to ungrammatical or consistently misspelled) readings in my base text for the convenience of the reader, but even that raised more problems than it solved, and I decided against it (the correct readings are, however, marked with an asterisk in the critical apparatus). Emendation makes sense only if one is trying to recover an author's original or an earlier stage of a text, and neither of these is the purpose of the Chaucer Library. Though this edition is not therefore a critical one in the traditional sense, certain sections of it constitute authoritative statements, based as they are on an examination of all but four of the 672 known manuscripts, about aspects of Lotario's treatise; and these sections would need to be incorporated into any critical edition: the study of the nature and evolution of the titles (Introduction, pp. 19-29), the reconstruction of the typical *De Miseria* as it circulated in the Middle Ages (Introduction, pp. 51-54), and the study of its transmission and circulation in medieval Europe (Appendix II). In deciding how much documentation to include in support of my general conclusions in these and other sections, I have tried to steer a middle course between the principle, stated in another connection by Paul Maas in his *Textual Criticism*, that "to present what is doubtful as certain is to remain farther from the goal than if one were to confess one's doubt," and his warning that "an over-conscientious weighing of probabilities is liable eventually to stifle the germ of progress." I hope I have succeeded, for, to quote Maas again, "texts are the foundation of all philological investigation and should be so treated that the least possible doubt prevails as to how far they are reliable" (trans. Barbara Flower, Oxford: Clarendon Press, 1958, p. 17).

I have incurred many debts during the years I have been working on this edition. With very few exceptions, librarians and owners of manuscripts have been unfailingly courteous and patient in answering my questions about manuscripts and related matters and in arranging to have microfilms made for me. The list would be too long if I acknowledged all of them by name, but I must mention a few who helped me far more than duty required: Professor J. A. W. Bennett and Mr. D. Pepys-Whiteley of Magdalene College, Cambridge; Mr. and Mrs. H. W. Edwards of Newbury, for their kindness in letting me examine Mr. Edwards's manuscript of the *De Miseria* in their home; Miss Suzanne Eward of the Gloucester Cathedral Library; Mme H. LeGoff of the Institut de Recherche et d'Histoire des Textes in Paris, for many courtesies over a long period of time; Mrs. M. R. Ormerod of Reading and Mr. W. E. Ormerod of the London School of Hygiene and Tropical Medicine, for arranging to have Mrs. Ormerod's manuscript of the *De Miseria* microfilmed; Mr. William O'Sullivan of Trinity College, Dublin; Mr. A. E. B. Owen of the Cambridge University Library, for sharing his wealth of knowledge with me, both in person and by letter; Mr. R. W. Page of Corpus Christi College, Cambridge; Professor Julian G. Plante of the Hill Monastic Manuscript Library, Collegeville, Minnesota; and the librarians and staffs of the Archivo de la Corona de Aragón in Barcelona, Durham Cathedral, the Real Biblioteca in El Escorial, the British Library, the Biblioteca Nacional in Madrid, the Stadtbibliothek in Mainz, the Bayerische Staatsbibliothek in Munich, the Stiftsbibliothek in Sankt Florian, and the Biblioteka Uniwersytecka in Wroclaw.

Libraries have been very generous in permitting me to examine and to quote from manuscripts in their possession, and here I particularly want to thank the authorities of Corpus Christi College, Cambridge; Magdalene College, Cambridge; Pembroke College, Cambridge; Peterhouse, Cambridge; the Cambridge University Library; the Edinburgh University Library; the British Library; the Bodleian Library; the Biblioteca Vallicelliana in Rome; and the Biblioteca Apostolica Vaticana. I also wish to thank the University of North Carolina Press for permission to quote from my article, "Glosses to the *Man of Law's Tale* from Pope Innocent III's *De Miseria Humane Conditionis*," in *Studies in Philology*, 64 (1967), 1–16, and Professor Robert W. Frank, Jr., for permission to quote from my article, "What Did Chaucer Mean by *Of the Wreched Engendrynge of Mankynde*?" in *The Chaucer Review*, 2 (1968), 139–58, published by the Pennsylvania State University Press.

For help with various foreign-language problems I am indebted to my friends and colleagues (present and former) Ernest and Eva Bernhardt, Shirley L. Guthrie, James W. Halporn, David Sigsbee, Jon Strolle, and especially John H. Wright for his careful reading of my translation of the *De Miseria;* I am also happy to acknowledge the earlier English translations of the *De Miseria* by Margaret Mary Dietz (Indianapolis: Bobbs-Merrill, 1969) and George Gascoigne (London, 1576), which I have consulted from time to time and which have helped me considerably in translating difficult or ambiguous passages. Many people have typed versions of parts of the edition, but I particularly want to thank Suzanne Brown, Maureen McLean, and Sue Rasmussen for their help over long periods of time. I have been generously supported for various aspects of my work on the *De Miseria* with research grants by the American Philosophical Society in 1965 and 1970 (Penrose fund No. 4080 and No. 5403) and with research grants and faculty summer fellowships by the Office of Research and Advanced Studies at Indiana University in 1963, 1965, 1966, 1968, and 1970; and I am very grateful for this support.

Finally, I owe special debts of thanks to Professor Donald R. Howard, Professor Paul O. Kristeller, the late Dr. A. N. L. Munby, and the late Sir Francis Wormald, for assistance in locating and describing manuscripts; to Professor Marie-Thérèse d'Alverny, for calling my attention to the *Correctorius Correctorii* of Nicholas Eymerich; to Dr. Robert Bultot, for information about the French translations of the *De Miseria;* to Professor Sigmund Eisner, for checking manuscripts for me in London; to Mr. Edward Wilson, for helpful discussions on editorial matters; to Professor David C. Fowler and the University of Washington, for putting microfilms of many of the British and American manuscripts of the *De Miseria* at my disposal; to the staff of the University of Georgia Press (including Mr. Moreland Hogan and Mr. Kenneth Cherry, who were formerly with the Press), for their patience and cheerful yielding to most of my wishes; to Professors Ruth J. Dean, John H. Fisher, and J. Burke Severs, for their careful reading and constructive criticism of parts of the edition; to Dr. Neil R. Ker, for his expert paleographical help, references to uncatalogued manuscripts, encouragement through the years, and many other kindnesses; and to Professor Robert A. Pratt, for the example of his careful, thorough scholarship and for his support over a longer period of time than either of us cares to remember.

INTRODUCTION

DATE, AUTHORSHIP, AND CONTENTS
OF THE *DE MISERIA*

Early in 1195 Cardinal Lotario dei Segni, later Pope Innocent III, wrote a short treatise that was to become one of the most popular and influential works of the Middle Ages—the *De Miseria Humane Conditionis* (or *De Miseria Condicionis Humane,* as in the title of the manuscript used for the text of the present edition).[1] The treatise is organized into three parts, called books in the original: the first concerns the wretchedness of man's conception, the disgusting physical aspects of humans, especially old ones, and the various miseries man must endure in his life; the second deals with the three goals for which man strives—riches, pleasures, and honors—with exempla and vivid descriptions used to illustrate the various forms of each; the third concerns the putrefaction of the body, the pains of hell, and the coming of God on the Day of Judgment. The primary source is the Bible: the author either presents an idea and then quotes a biblical passage or two in support of it or presents the biblical passage first and then expands on it. But his learning is not confined to the Bible. He also shows a familiarity with the works of a number of medieval Latin authors, including, among others, Gregory, Isidore of Seville, Peter Lombard, John of Salisbury, pseudo-St. Bernard, and Robert of Melun, and even occasionally with the works of such classical authors as Ovid, Horace, and Juvenal.[2]

The author, Lotario dei Segni, was born into a noble Italian family in 1160 or 1161. As a young man he studied theology at Paris with Peter of Corbeil and law at Bologna with Huguccio of Pisa. On his return to Rome he was ordained a subdeacon and a little later, probably in 1189 before he was thirty, he was made a cardinal-deacon by his uncle, Pope Clement III. It was during the reign of the next pope, Celestine III (1191-98), that Lotario wrote the *De Miseria,* as well as two other works, the *De Sacro Altaris Mysterio* and the *De Quadripartita Specie Nuptiarum.* Though we know precisely the date of the *De Miseria* (the winter of 1195), we know little about the occasion for the writing of it. Apparently Lotario was able to find a bit of leisure ("modicum ocii," as he says in the prologue) among his many duties and cares as cardinal[3] and expected to write two complementary works—one on the vileness of the human condition ("vilitatem humane condicionis") and another on the dignity of human nature ("dignitatem humane naturo"). The first, the *De Miseria,* was completed and dedicated to Cardinal Peter Galloccia, Bishop of Porto and St. Rufina; so far as we

2

know, the second was never written, perhaps because Lotario was never able to find time between 1195 and his election to the papacy three years later.

The author of the standard biography of Pope Innocent III calls the *De Miseria* an "Exercice d'écolier, thèse de théoricien frais émolu de la scolastique,"[4] and it cannot be denied that it has characteristics of the medieval classroom, both in its rhetorical flourishes and in its piling up of quotations: Lotario's highly specialized education at Paris and Bologna would have prepared him well for this kind of writing. But it would be a mistake to dismiss the *De Miseria* as just an exercise. During the one hundred years before Lotario wrote his treatise the subject of contemptus mundi had been a popular one, engaging the minds and pens of such well-known figures as Peter Damian, Anselm of Canterbury, and Hugh of St. Victor,[5] and it would be perfectly natural for Lotario to choose a subject in the mainstream of current ascetic thought. Certainly his contemporaries thought so: his biographer reports that "le prestige de Lothaire de Segni, comme théologien, moraliste et écrivain, n'a pas été étranger à son avènement."[6] It may even be, as Maccarrone suggests,[7] that Lotario had a burning desire to examine divine and human affairs, which would help to explain why he hoped to write about both the *vilitatem* of the human condition and the *dignitatem* of human nature.

THE POPULARITY AND INFLUENCE
OF THE *DE MISERIA*

But whatever the reason for writing it, from the late eleventh century to the seventeenth century, when the influence of the contemptus mundi idea began to wane, the *De Miseria* was the most popular work on the subject, in part because the author was regarded as one of the greatest of the medieval popes and in part because it brought together nearly every cliché of earlier works on contemptus mundi. The popularity of the *De Miseria* can be seen in the number of extant manuscripts in which it appears (some 672),[8] in the number of printed editions it went through by the middle of the seventeenth century (52),[9] and in the number of languages into which it was translated by the end of the same century (Dutch, English, Flemish, French, German, Irish, Italian, Spanish).[10]

The popularity of the *De Miseria* can also be seen in the enormous extent and variety of its influence on other writers during the Middle Ages. On the continent, for example, Guillaume le Clerc, in *Le Besant de Dieu* (ca. 1226), borrowed several passages from the work.[11] Alexan-

3

der of Hales, working in Paris, used it in his *Summa Theologica* (1234-45).[12] Albertano of Brescia quoted twice from the *De Miseria* in his *Liber Consolationis et Consilii* (1246), a work known to Chaucer at least in French translation.[13] The German poet Hugo von Langenstein paraphrased the first book of the *De Miseria* in his poem *Martina* (1293).[14] Chaucer's contemporary and admirer, the French poet Eustache Deschamps, in 1383 made a verse condensation of the whole *De Miseria* entitled *Double lay de la fragilité humaine*.[15] The French poet Christine de Pisan quoted from the *De Miseria* Book II, chapter 6, in her *Epître d'Othéa* (ca. 1400).[16] Two other French works, probably of the fifteenth century, are indebted to the *De Miseria*: a *Miroir de l'âme* makes use of Book I in its first chapter (of seven); a *Miroir d'humilité* paraphrases Book I.[17] St. Bernardine of Siena used the *De Miseria* in his sermons in the fifteenth century.[18] The German Geiler von Keisersberg (1445-1510), in a poem *Das Buoch Arbore Humana von dem menschlichen Baum,* made use of the famous metaphor of man as an upside-down tree from Book I, chapter 8, of the *De Miseria*.[19] The Italian humanists of the fifteenth century read and imitated the treatise,[20] and quotations from it appeared in collections of exempla throughout the Middle Ages.[21] In fact, the ideas in the *De Miseria* had such currency in medieval Europe that two hundred years after it was written, Nicholas Eymerich, a Spanish theologian and Inquisitor General of Aragon, felt called upon to attack its errors and "heresies" in a work entitled *Correctorius Correctorii* (1396),[22] and during the first half of the following century Gianozzo Manetti (1396-1459) could write a refutation of Book I of the *De Miseria* in his *De Dignitate et Excellentia Hominis* Book IV.[23]

In Britain the influence of the *De Miseria* was, if anything, greater than on the continent. Over one-sixth of the extant manuscripts were probably written in Britain, and there must have been at least twice that number in circulation during the Middle Ages. Forty-five of the extant manuscripts have been assigned specific British provenances or locations in the Middle Ages,[24] and though there are none from Scotland or Wales, all parts of England are represented: Cockersand, Durham, Rievaulx, Staindrop, and York in the north; Bardney, Bury St. Edmunds, Cambridge, Ely, Lincoln, Peterborough, Spalding, and Stamford in East Anglia and Lincolnshire; Bodmin, Chester, Crediton, Lanthony, Oxford, Reading, Salisbury, Wenlock, and Worcester in the west and southwest; and Ashridge, Battle, Canterbury, Sheen, Sompting, Syon, Waltham, Westminster, and Windsor in the southern and London areas.

As on the continent, the *De Miseria* was widely read and quoted in Britain, by both religious and secular writers, during the Middle Ages. For example, in a Latin poem, *De Miseria Humana,* written in England in the thirteenth century, during Henry III's reign, the anonymous writer paraphrases portions of Book I of the *De Miseria*.[25] Early in the next century Thomas Hibernicus, in his compilation *Manipulus Florum* (1306), quotes extensively from Books I and especially II of the *De Miseria*.[26] A short time later William of Pagula, Vicar of Winkfield, included a series of extracts from the *De Miseria* at the end of Part I of his widely read *Oculus Sacerdotis* (ca. 1320–28).[27] Two English Dominicans writing during the first half of the fourteenth century, John Bromyard (d. 1352?) in his *Summa Predicantium*[28] and Robert Holkot (d. 1349) in his *Super Librum Sapientie*,[29] quote from the *De Miseria*. The most popular English poem of the Middle Ages (to judge from the number of extant manuscripts, 117), the *Pricke of Conscience* (mid-fourteenth century), is heavily indebted to the *De Miseria*: Book I is based almost entirely on the *De Miseria* Book I, chapters 2–10, and Book III, chapter 1; and the anonymous author appears to be acquainted with the rest of Lotario's treatise.[30] Another popular work of the fourteenth century, the *Speculum Christiani* (compiled in the 1360s or 1370s), contains a quotation from Book II, chapter 1, of the *De Miseria* in a series of wise sayings at the end of the eighth *tabula*.[31] The same passage from the *De Miseria* appears, again incorporated in a series of wise sayings, in *Contemplations of the Dread and Love of God*, a work for a time wrongly attributed to Richard Rolle.[32] John Wyclif quotes at length from Book I of the *De Miseria* in one of his works, *Tractatus de Mandatis Divinis*.[33] In *Piers Plowman* there are two possible quotations from the *De Miseria*, and other passages may be indebted to it as well.[34] There appear to be correspondences between the *De Miseria* and passages in two of John Gower's works, the *Mirour de l'Omme* and *Vox Clamantis*.[35] In the famous sermon preached at Paul's Cross about 1388, "Redde Rationem Villicationis Tue," Thomas Wimbledon quotes the examples against *cupiditas* given by Lotario in chapter 9 of the second book of the *De Miseria*.[36] Toward the end of the century Richard Lavynham, a Carmelite friar, quotes Lotario on gluttony and lechery in *A Litil Tretys on the Seven Deadly Sins*, a short treatise that enjoyed a measure of popularity, appearing in fourteen manuscripts.[37] In the first half of the fifteenth century the anonymous author of *Jacob's Well* incorporates a fairly close translation of Book II, chapter 17, of the *De Miseria* into his discussion of gluttony.[38]

CHAUCER'S INDEBTEDNESS TO THE *DE MISERIA*

When Chaucer decided to translate from the *De Miseria*, therefore, he was choosing a treatise in the mainstream of medieval thought, one of the most popular and widely read works of the Middle Ages;[39] his use of the *De Miseria* in his own writings was part of a literary tradition that had begun before his time and, at the end of the fourteenth century, was flourishing all around him. Chaucer's major indebtedness to the *De Miseria* can be seen in the Man of Law's Prologue and Tale.[40] In the long passage on poverty in the Man of Law's Prologue, Chaucer translates Lotario's lines on the subject generally in the order in which they appear in the original though not exactly word for word:[41]

Man of Law's Prologue 99–121; *De Miseria* I.14.1–14

> O hateful harm, condicion of poverte!
> With thurst, with coold, with hunger so confoundid!
> To asken help thee shameth in thyn herte;
> If thou noon aske, with nede artow so woundid
> That verray nede unwrappeth al thy wounde hid!
> Maugree thyn heed, thou most for indigence
> Or stele, or begge, or borwe thy despence!
>
> Thou blamest Crist, and seist ful bitterly,
> He mysdeparteth richesse temporal;
> Thy neighebor thou wytest synfully,
> And seist thou hast to lite, and he hath al.
> "Parfay," seistow, "somtyme he rekene shal,
> Whan that his tayl shal brennen in the gleede,
> For he noght helpeth needfulle in hir neede."
>
> Herkne what is the sentence of the wise:
> "Bet is to dyen than have indigence";
> "Thy selve neighebor wol thee despise."
> If thou be povre, farwel thy reverence!
> Yet of the wise man take this sentence:
> "Alle the dayes of povre men been wikke."
> Be war, therfore, er thou come to that prikke!
>
> If thou be povre, thy brother hateth thee,
> And alle thy freendes fleen from thee, allas![42]

Pauperes enim premuntur inedia, cruciantur erumpna, fame, siti, frigore, nuditate . . . O miserabilis condicio mendicantis! Et si petit, pudore confunditur, et si non petit, egestate consumitur, set ut mendicet necessitate compellitur. Deum causatur iniquum quod non recte dividat; proximum criminatur malignum quod non plene subveniat; indignatur, murmurat, inprecatur. Adverte super hoc sentenciam sapientis: "Melius est mori quam indigere." "Eciam proximo suo pauper odiosus erit." "Omnes dies pauperis mali." "Fratres hominis pauperis oderunt eum, insuper et amici procul recesserunt ab eo."[43]

In five passages in the Man of Law's Tale Chaucer again takes the lines in the order in which they appear in the original but does not translate exactly word for word:

Man of Law's Tale 421-27; *De Miseria* I.21.1-5, 13-14

> O sodeyn wo, that evere art successour
> To worldly blisse, spreynd with bitternesse!
> The ende of the joye of oure worldly labour!
> Wo occupieth the fyn of oure gladnesse.
> Herke this conseil for thy sikernesse:
> Upon thy glade day have in thy mynde
> The unwar wo or harm that comth bihynde.

Semper enim mundane letitie tristicia repentina succedit . . . Mundana quippe felicitas multis amaritudinibus est respersa . . . extrema gaudii luctus occupat . . . Salubre consilium: "In die bonorum ne immemor sis malorum."

Man of Law's Tale 771-77; *De Miseria* II.19.1-4

> O messager, fulfild of dronkenesse,
> Strong is thy breeth, thy lymes faltren ay,
> And thou biwreyest alle secreenesse.
> Thy mynde is lorn, thou janglest as a jay,
> Thy face is turned in a newe array.
> Ther dronkenesse regneth in any route,
> Ther is no conseil hyd, withouten doute.

Quid turpius ebrioso, cui fetor in ore, tremor in corpore; qui promit stulta, prodit occulta; cui mens alienatur, facies transformatur? "Nullum enim secretum ubi regnat ebrietas."

Man of Law's Tale 925-31; *De Miseria* II.21.5-8, 12-13[44]

> O foule lust of luxurie, lo, thyn ende!
> Nat oonly that thou feyntest mannes mynde,
> But verraily thou wolt his body shende.
> Th'ende of thy werk, or of thy lustes blynde,
> Is compleynyng. Hou many oon may men fynde
> That noght for werk somtyme, but for th'entente
> To doon this synne, been outher slayn or shente!

O extrema libidinis turpitudo, que non solum mentem effeminat, set corpus enervat; non solum maculat animam, set fedat personam.

. . . semper secuntur dolor et penitencia.

Man of Law's Tale 1132-34; *De Miseria* I.20.10-11, 12-13

> But litel while it lasteth, I yow heete,
> Joye of this world, for tyme wol nat abyde;
> Fro day to nyght it changeth as the tyde.

De Brevi Leticia [the title to Book I, chapter 20][45]

"A mane usque ad vesperam mutabitur tempus."
"Tenent tympanum et cytharam et gaudent ad sonitum organi."

Man of Law's Tale 1135–38; *De Miseria* I.20.1–7

Who lyved euere in swich delit o day
That hym ne moeved outher conscience,
Or ire, or talent, or som kynnes affray,
Envye, or pride, or passion, or offence?

Quis unquam vel unicam diem totam duxit in sua delectacione
iocundam, quem in aliqua parte diei reatus consciencie vel impetus ire vel motus concupiscencie non turbaverit? Quem livor
invidie vel ardor avaricie vel tumor superbie non vexaverit?
Quem aliqua iactura vel offensa vel passio non commoverit?

These passages from the Man of Law's Prologue and Tale are
clearly translations: for each of the six Chaucer uses only a single
chapter from the *De Miseria* and translates Lotario's lines in the order in
which they appear in the original. With the words themselves he is
fairly literal, although he often omits lines and phrases that are in the
Latin original. In his borrowings from the *De Miseria* in the Pardoner's
Tale, however, his method is quite different. There he makes use of
four consecutive chapters (Book II, chapters 17–20), but instead of
translating lines in order, he paraphrases, condenses, and chooses ideas
and lines from each of the four chapters in an order quite unlike that of
the original, introducing them into the tale as they fit his artistic plan. I
list all the possible parallels:

Pardoner's Tale 467–69; *De Miseria* II.18.11–12[46]

They daunce and pleyen at dees bothe day and nyght,
And eten also and drynken over hir myght,
Thurgh which they doon the devel sacrifise

"Sedit populus manducare et bibere, et surrexerunt ludere." (Ex.
32:6 and 1 Cor. 10:7)

Pardoner's Tale 481–82; *De Miseria* II.19.11–12[47]

To kyndle and blowe the fyr of lecherye,
That is annexed unto glotonye.

Et Osee: "Fornicacio et vinum et ebrietas auferunt cor." (Osee
4:11)

Pardoner's Tale 483–84; *De Miseria* II.19.12–13

The hooly writ take I to my witnesse
That luxurie is in wyn and dronkenesse.

Propterea dicit Apostolus: "Fugite vinum, in quo est luxuria."
(Eph. 5:18)

Pardoner's Tale 485-87; *De Miseria* II.20.1[48]

> Lo, how that dronken Looth, unkyndely,
> Lay by his doghtres two, unwityngly;
> So dronke he was, he nyste what he wroghte.

Ebrietas verenda Noe [*Noe* omitted in many MSS] nudavit, incestum commisit. . . .

Pardoner's Tale 505-7, 488-91; *De Miseria* II.18.5-7[49]

> Adam oure fader, and his wyf also,
> Fro Paradys to labour and to wo
> Were dryven for that vice, it is no drede.
>
> Herodes, whoso wel the stories soghte,
> Whan he of wyn was repleet at his feeste,
> Right at his owene table he yaf his heeste
> To sleen the Baptist John, ful giltelees.

Gula paradisum clausit . . . decollavit Baptistam.

Pardoner's Tale 513-16, 521-23; *De Miseria* II.17.21-26[50]

> O, wiste a man how manye maladyes
> Folwen of excesse and of glotonyes,
> He wolde been the moore mesurable
> Of his diete, sittynge at his table.
>
> Of this matiere, o Paul, wel kanstow trete:
> "Mete unto wombe, and wombe eek unto mete,
> Shal God destroyen bothe," as Paulus seith.

. . . inde non salus et sanitas, set morbus et mors. Audi super hoc sentenciam sapientis: "Noli avidus esse in omni epulacione, et non te effundas super omnem escam; in multis enim escis erit infirmitas, et propter crapulam multi obierunt." "Esca ventri et venter escis: Deus autem et hunc et has destruet." (Ecclus. 37:32-34; 1 Cor. 6:13)

Pardoner's Tale 517-20; *De Miseria* II.17.2-5, 14[51]

> Allas! the shorte throte, the tendre mouth,
> Maketh that est and west and north and south,
> In erthe, in eir, in water, men to swynke
> To gete a glotoun deyntee mete and drynke!

Nunc autem gulosis non sufficiunt fructus arborum, non genera leguminum, non radices herbarum, non pisces maris, non bestie terre, non aves celi. . . .

Ceterum tam brevis est gule voluptas. . . .

Pardoner's Tale 534-36; *De Miseria* II.18.2-5

> O wombe! O bely! O stynkyng cod,
> Fulfilled of dong and of corrupcioun!
> At either ende of thee foul is the soun.

9

. . . quia quanto sunt delicaciora cibaria, tanto fetidiora sunt stercora. Turpius egerit quod turpiter ingerit, superius et inferius horribilem flatum exprimens, et abominabilem sonum emittens.

Pardoner's Tale 537–46; *De Miseria* II.17.5–14[52]

> How greet labour and cost is thee to fynde!
> Thise cookes, how they stampe, and streyne, and grynde,
> And turnen substaunce into accident,
> To fulfille al thy likerous talent!
> Out of the harde bones knokke they
> The mary, for they caste noght awey
> That may go thurgh the golet softe and swoote.
> Of spicerie of leef, and bark, and roote
> Shal been his sauce ymaked by delit,
> To make hym yet a newer appetit.

. . . set queruntur pigmenta, comparantur aromata, nutriuntur altilia, capiuntur obesa, que studiose coquuntur arte cocorum, que laute parantur officio ministrorum. Alius contundit et colat, alius confundit et conficit, substanciam vertit in accidens, naturam mutat in artem, ut saturitas transeat in esuriem, ut fastidium revocet appetitum; ad irritandam gulam, non ad sustentandum naturam; non ad necessitatem supplendam, set ad aviditatem explendam.

Pardoner's Tale 547–48; *De Miseria* II.17.19–21[53]

> But, certes, he that haunteth swiche delices
> Is deed, whil that he lyveth in tho vices.

Set inde gravatur stomachus, turbatur sensus, opprimitur intellectus; inde non salus et sanitas, set morbus et mors.

Pardoner's Tale 549–50; *De Miseria* II.19.14[54]

> A lecherous thyng is wyn, and dronkenesse
> Is ful of stryvyng and of wrecchednesse.

"Ebriosa res vinum et tumultuosa ebrietas." (Prov. 20:1)

Pardoner's Tale 551–52, 560–61; *De Miseria* II.19.1–4[55]

> O dronke man, disfigured is thy face,
> Sour is thy breeth, foul artow to embrace, . . .
>
> In whom that drynke hath dominacioun
> He kan no conseil kepe, it is no drede.

Quid turpius ebrioso, cui fetor in ore, tremor in corpore; qui promit stulta, prodit occulta; cui mens alienatur, facies transformatur? "Nullum enim secretum ubi regnat ebrietas." (Prov. 31:4)

Pardoner's Tale 583–87; *De Miseria* II.19.3–4[56]

And over al this, avyseth yow right wel
What was comaunded unto Lamuel—
Nat Samuel, but Lamuel, seye I;
Redeth the Bible, and fynde it expresly
Of wyn-yevyng to hem that han justise.

"Nullum enim secretum ubi regnat ebrietas." (Prov. 31:4)

In these passages from the Pardoner's Tale it is often impossible to know exactly where Chaucer got his material, whether from the *De Miseria*, from St. Jerome's *Epistola Adversus Jovinianum*, from John of Wales's *Communiloquium*, from the Vulgate (directly or indirectly), from another source,[57] or simply from his personal knowledge. Chaucer seems to have assimilated the relevant material from books he had just recently read or translated and then to have paraphrased that material, according to his own artistic plan, as the Pardoner's "sermon" on gluttony. For a few of the passages the parallels with other works seem closer; for a few others the parallels with the *De Miseria* are not exclusive ones. It would be a mistake to claim that all the passages are indebted to the *De Miseria*—the ideas expressed, after all, are medieval commonplaces—but what seems striking is that the ideas can be found in four consecutive chapters that, depending on the size of Chaucer's manuscript of the *De Miseria,* could all have been written on one page or on one two-page opening and could have been seen by him at a glance.

In the Man of Law's Prologue and Tale, where Chaucer translates fairly literally from the *De Miseria,* there is no apparent use of the treatise beyond the six passages cited earlier, but in the Pardoner's Tale, where Chaucer's use of the *De Miseria* is more paraphrastic, it would not be surprising if there were to be found further indebtedness to this treatise. John M. Steadman has pointed out some possible parallels,[58] for example, Pardoner's Tale 745–47 and *De Miseria* I.9. 30–33:

"Ne dooth unto an oold man noon harm now,
Namoore than that ye wolde men did to yow
In age, if that ye so longe abyde."

Porro nec senes contra iuvenem glorientur, nec insolescant iuvenes contra senem, quia quod sumus iste fuit, erimus quandoque quod hic est.

Chaucer's description of the Old Man and the Old Man's words to the three "riotoures" (720–67) may be indebted, according to Steadman, to the *De Miseria* II.12.1–3:

Omnis cupidus contra naturam nititur et molitur. Natura namque pauperem adducit in mundum; natura pauperem reducit a mundo,

11

or perhaps to these lines (II.13.1-2) not noted by Steadman:

> Cur ad congregandum quis instet cum stare non possit ille qui congregat?

Perhaps even the allusions to covetousness in the following lines (and elsewhere in the tale) may owe something to Book II of the *De Miseria,* in which fifteen out of forty-one chapters are given over to this topic, especially the equating of gold and death:

> "Now, sires," quod he, "if that yow be so leef
> To fynde Deeth, turne up this croked wey,
> For in that grove I lafte hym, by my fey,
> Under a tree, and there he wole abyde;
> Noght for youre boost he wole him no thyng hyde.
> Se ye that ook? Right there ye shal hym fynde." (760-65)

Also, the allusion to the "three temptations" in the *De Miseria* (II.1.7-12) may have given rise to the same three in connection with the "riotoures" in the Pardoner's Tale: the lust of the flesh (463-84, 663, 705, 795-97), the lust of the eyes (773-74, 838-39), and the pride of life (716):[59]

> Concupiscencia carnis ad voluptates, concupiscencia oculorum ad opes, superbia vite pertinet ad honores. Opes generant cupiditatem et avariciam, voluptates pariunt gulam et luxuriam, honores nutriunt superbiam et iactanciam.

None of these examples, however, is persuasive as a verbal parallel, and I do not offer them as direct evidence of Chaucer's indebtedness to the *De Miseria:* they remain possibilities only.

Besides the Man of Law's Prologue and Tale and the Pardoner's Tale, other passages hint at possible correspondences between Chaucer's works and the *De Miseria,* but none of them can definitely be traced, by means of verbal parallels, to Lotario's treatise. It is worth examining some of these passages, however, to see the difficulties involved in trying to determine accurately where a medieval writer gets his source material. For example, Koeppel and J. S. P. Tatlock point out that in Chaucer's Monk's Tale the description of Adam as having been created by God "And not bigeten of mannes sperme unclene" (B² 3299) reflects the *De Miseria.* For Koeppel the passage is Book I, chapter 1, 24-26: "Formatus est homo de pulvere, de luto, de cinere: quoque vilius est, de spurcissimo spermate"; while for Tatlock it is Book I, chapter 3, 1-4: "Adam . . . fuit formatus de terra, set virgine; tu vero procreatus de semine, set immundo."[60] But this is a dubious correspondence: in either case the idea Chaucer expresses is a

12

very common one, not necessarily needing a written source; and at least for Koeppel's parallel the context is quite different from that in the Monk's Tale. The same is true of a similar passage, Parson's Tale 333:

> "Of thilke Adam tooke we thilke synne original; for of hym flesshly descended be we alle, and engendred of vile and corrupt mateere."

For this passage Beatrice Daw Brown believes that Book I, chapter 2, of the *De Miseria* "supplied the verbal basis, presumably such lines as 'Formavit igitur Dominus Deus hominem de limo terre, que ceteris est indignior elementis'" (1–2).[61] Again the idea is a commonplace, and the verbal parallels are not persuasive.

Another passage noted by Koeppel (pp. 413–14) is the Wife of Bath's Prologue 278–80:

> "Thow seyst that droppyng houses, and eek smoke,
> And chiding wyves maken men to flee
> Out of hir owene hous; a! *benedicitee!*"

which he believes is based on the *De Miseria* I.16.33–34: "Tria sunt enim que non sinunt hominem in domo permanere: fumus, stillicidium, et mala uxor." In a subsequent article, Koeppel designates Albertano of Brescia's *Liber Consolationis et Consilii* as Chaucer's source,[62] but it is impossible to know from which of the two sources Chaucer took the quotation, if in fact he took it from either one: the sentiment is proverbial, appearing often in medieval English writings,[63] and could have reached Chaucer through oral tradition. Moreover, if the quotation were from the *De Miseria*, one would expect to find further influence of the *De Miseria* elsewhere in the Wife of Bath's Prologue, but there is none.[64]

George R. Coffman suggests in his article on old age in the Middle Ages that the Reeve's words in his own Prologue may ultimately derive from the *De Miseria*,[65] especially such lines as these:

> "The sely tonge may wel rynge and chymbe
> Of wrecchednesse that passed is ful yoore;
> With olde folk, save dotage, is namoore!" (3896–98)

Coffman is well aware of the difficulties involved in trying to pin down such allusions as these, and he concludes (p. 277) that "the Reeve's elegiac outburst is the final essence of much reflecting and much reading on old age by Chaucer" in the *De Miseria*, Maximianus's *Elegie*, probably Vincent of Beauvais's *Speculum Doctrinale*, perhaps Horace's *Ars Poetica*. It is tempting to view Chaucer as having assimi-

13

lated ideas from the *De Miseria* so thoroughly as to make them his own when writing the Reeve's Prologue, but the verbal parallels are not at all persuasive.

In *Troilus and Criseyde,* lines 1504-5 of Book IV read: "And thynk that folie is, whan man may chese, / For accident his substaunce ay to lese." This is the same pattern of words that appears at Pardoner's Tale 539, which is a translation of the *De Miseria* Book II, chapter 17: "substanciam vertit in accidens." Two considerations, however, militate against the influence of the *De Miseria* at this point in *Troilus and Criseyde.* First, the context of the phrase in the *De Miseria* is entirely different. In *Troilus and Criseyde* Troilus is speaking to Criseyde, trying to persuade her to go away with him; in the *De Miseria* Lotario is talking about the abilities of cooks. Second, "substance" and "accident" were philosophical terms known in Chaucer's time, and probably also applied to the current controversy over the Eucharist;[66] it is therefore unlikely that Chaucer would need a written source for the terms.

In the Manciple's Prologue the Manciple describes the Cook's drunken condition in these words:

> "For, in good feith, thy visage is ful pale,
> Thyne eyen daswen eek, as that me thynketh,
> And, wel I woot, thy breeth ful soure stynketh:
> That sheweth wel thou art nat wel disposed.
> Of me, certeyn, thou shalt nat been yglosed.
> See how he ganeth, lo! this dronken wight,
> As though he wolde swolwe us anonright.
> Hoold cloos thy mouth, man, by thy fader kyn!
> The devel of helle sette his foot therin!
> Thy cursed breeth infecte wole us alle.
> Fy, stynkyng swyn! fy, foule moote thee falle!
> A! taketh heede, sires, of this lusty man." (30-41)

And the Host responds:

> "By cause drynke hath dominacioun
> Upon this man, by my savacioun,
> I trowe he lewedly wolde telle his tale.
> For, were it wyn, or oold or moysty ale,
> That he hath dronke, he speketh in his nose,
> And fneseth faste, and eek he hath the pose." (57-62)

These words seem reminiscent of some of the passages from the *De Miseria* that Chaucer used for the Pardoner's Tale, especially 534-36, 551-52, 560-61. The *verbal* parallels are not persuasive, however, and it is probably best to say either that Chaucer was making use of com-

14

monplaces regarding gluttony or that he was echoing the Pardoner's Tale which he had written earlier.

A large number of references to the alternation of joy and woe appear in Chaucer's works and may ultimately derive from the *De Miseria* I.21.1–5:

> Semper enim mundane letitie tristicia repentina succedit, et quod incepit a gaudio desinit in merore. Mundana quippe felicitas multis amaritudinibus est respersa. Noverat hoc ille qui dixerat: "Risus dolore miscebitur, et extrema gaudii luctus occupat."

Representative of these references, which may be discussed as a group, is this one from *Troilus and Criseyde* IV.834–36:

> "Endeth thanne love in wo? Ye, or men lieth!
> And alle worldly blisse, as thynketh me.
> The ende of blisse ay sorwe it occupieth;"[67]

Here again it is difficult to know where Chaucer gets an idea, but I am inclined to think that, except for the passage in the Man of Law's Tale, the *De Miseria* is not the source. The idea was a common one in the Middle Ages,[68] probably originating in Proverbs 14:13, which Lotario quotes in I.21. Because it appears also in Boethius's *De Consolatione Philosophiae,* Book II, prose 4, and was therefore translated by Chaucer,[69] and because at least two of Chaucer's works that contain the idea are heavily indebted to the *De Consolatione Philosophiae* (*Troilus and Criseyde* and the Knight's Tale), Boethius appears to be a more likely source than Lotario, if in fact any is needed, for the references in question.

Another group of quotations that may be from the *De Miseria*—those that derive ultimately from the Bible—can also be discussed together. The most recent study of Chaucer's use of the Bible, by W. Meredith Thompson, concludes that Chaucer "got most of his [biblical] texts from his immediate sources, some from his general knowledge."[70] For biblical quotations not directly from the immediate sources, one would expect that Chaucer would have gone to one of the five repositories of biblical passages at his disposal—the French translation of Albertano of Brescia's *Liber Consolationis et Consilii,* St. Jerome's *Epistola Adversus Jovinianum,* the *De Miseria,* the source(s) of the Parson's Tale, and John of Wales's *Communiloquium*—but at least with the *De Miseria* that is not the case. Discounting those biblical quotations derived from immediate sources, I cannot find any verbal parallels shared exclusively by the remaining quotations and the relevant passages in the *De Miseria.*[71] As an example take Palamon's set speech to Arcite in Knight's Tale Part I, 1303–12:

> "O crueel goddes that governe
> This world with byndyng of youre word eterne,
> And writen in the table of atthamaunt
> Youre parlement and youre eterne graunt,
> What is mankynde moore unto you holde
> Than is the sheep that rouketh in the folde?
> For slayn is man right as another beest,
> And dwelleth eek in prison and arreest,
> And hath siknesse and greet adversitee,
> And ofte tymes giltelees, pardee."

F. N. Robinson notes (p. 672) that the biblical passage in question here is Ecclesiastes 3:18ff. but then adds, gratuitously I believe, that the passage is quoted in the *De Miseria* I.2. It is certainly true that Lotario quotes this particular passage from Ecclesiastes, but the Knight's Tale is surely not indebted to the *De Miseria* for it. Aside from the fact that there are no verbal parallels between the two works, the context is different: the idea of man's guiltlessness at Knight's Tale 1312 is not in the *De Miseria* but is in Boethius's *De Consolatione Philosophiae* Book I, meter 5, which Robinson cites as a source for the passage. Probably the passage is indebted to both Boethius and the Bible, but there is nothing peculiar to Chaucer and Lotario that would argue for Chaucer's dependence on the *De Miseria* at this point.

In short, outside of Chaucer's clear indebtedness to the *De Miseria* in the Man of Law's Prologue and Tale and his very likely indebtedness to the *De Miseria* in the Pardoner's Tale, there is no other passage in his works that can definitely be traced to Lotario's treatise, and if this were the only evidence that Chaucer knew the treatise, one would be tempted to add it to the list of works that he had dipped into, or had a secondhand acquaintance with, like Alanus de Insulis's *De Planctu Nature* or Boccaccio's *De Casibus Virorum Illustrium* or Seneca's *Letters*, either for general knowledge or for useful quotations. There is, however, a direct reference to the *De Miseria* in Chaucer's works which at once confirms the influences already noted and compounds the difficulties. In the revised Prologue to the *Legend of Good Women* Queen Alceste, in making a catalogue of Chaucer's works, says:

> He hath in prose translated Boece,
> And of the Wreched Engendrynge of Mankynde,
> As man may in pope Innocent yfynde;
> And mad the lyf also of Seynt Cecile.
> He made also, gon is a gret while,
> Orygenes upon the Maudeleyne. (413–18)

Lines 414–15 are generally assumed to mean, coming as they do between two accepted translations (of Boethius's *De Consolatione Philosophiae* and of the legend that the Second Nun tells), that Chaucer made a translation (now lost) of the *De Miseria* with the title "of the Wreched Engendrynge of Mankynde" (henceforth italicized), but those who have examined the lines in greatest detail have come to quite different conclusions.

DID CHAUCER TRANSLATE
THE *DE MISERIA*?

In the mid-1930s, during a scholarly controversy between Carleton Brown and Beatrice Daw Brown on one side and J. S. P. Tatlock and Germaine Dempster on the other over whether or not a poem usually attributed to Lydgate, "An Holy Medytacion," was the lost translation that Chaucer calls *Of the Wreched Engendrynge of Mankynde*, both sides came to the conclusion that *Of the Wreched Engendrynge of Mankynde* was not intended to refer to the *De Miseria*.[72] Brown and his wife argued that the passage from the Prologue to the *Legend of Good Women* meant only that Chaucer had translated a work similar to or based on material from Lotario's treatise; that *Of the Wreched Engendrynge of Mankynde* was "An Holy Medytacion," which is a verse paraphrase of a thirteenth-century Latin *De Miseria Humana*, itself a paraphrase of the first nine chapters of Lotario's treatise;[73] that the poem was an early work of Chaucer's that he had forgotten about until his reading of Lotario's original later in life called it to mind; and that he then inserted it into the revised Prologue to the *Legend of Good Women* with a title (perhaps borrowed from the first chapter of Lotario's treatise) that seemed appropriate to the earlier work. Tatlock and Dempster argued that Chaucer's words must be taken at face value, even though lines 414–15 are a later addition; that therefore "An Holy Medytacion" could not be by Chaucer because the passage refers to a genuine prose translation either taken from Lotario's treatise or containing a portion of it; and that, because *Engendrynge* means 'conception' or 'gestation,' *Of the Wreched Engendrynge of Mankynde* in fact refers not to the whole *De Miseria* but only to the first five chapters of Book I of the treatise because only those chapters deal with man's conception.[74]

The conclusions of all four writers, insofar as they concern Chaucer's intention and choice of title, seem to me to be the result of special pleading either for or against Chaucerian authorship of "An Holy Medytacion": the Browns' verse paraphrase of a work based on part of Lotario's treatise is too great a distortion of Chaucer's words; Tatlock and Dempster's prose translation of only the first five chapters of the treatise is too narrow an interpretation of the same words. We will of course never know exactly what *Of the Wreched Engendrynge of Mankynde* meant to Chaucer until something by that name comes to light—and that is highly unlikely at this advanced stage in the cataloguing of European manuscript collections, especially in the British Isles—but I think that we can come to some conclusions, based on a careful examination both of Chaucer's own words and of the various possibilities open to him in choosing *Of the Wreched Engendrynge of Mankynde*, about his probable intention when he inserted this title into the revised Prologue to the *Legend of Good Women*.

The key to Chaucer's intention is of course the meaning of the title, *Of the Wreched Engendrynge of Mankynde*, but this cannot be determined without first resolving the verbal difficulties of the passage containing *Of the Wreched Engendrynge of Mankynde*. First, there is the problem caused by Chaucer's insertion of two new lines into an old framework. In the earlier version of the Prologue to the *Legend of Good Women* only these lines appear: "He hath in prose translated Boece, / And maad the lyf also of Seynt Cecile" (Prologue F 425-26). Between them, in the revised version, Chaucer has added "And of the Wreched Engendrynge of Mankynde, / As man may in pope Innocent yfynde" (414-15). Carleton Brown believed that because "in prose" was already in the earlier version, it did not necessarily apply to the medium of the work added to the revised version.[75] On the same grounds it would be possible, I suppose, to say that *translated* also does not apply to the work added to the revised version, but no one has ever made this suggestion. The fact is that the added lines need a verb, and the only possible verb is *translated*. Furthermore, "in prose" precedes *translated* and syntactically applies to both *Boece* and "of the Wreched Engendrynge of Mankynde." There is no reason not to take Chaucer's words at face value here. We must assume that Chaucer would not have added "of the Wreched Engendrynge of Mankynde" at this point unless it were fitting and that "in prose" and *translated* are fitting also.[76]

Second, *As,* in the line "As man may in pope Innocent yfynde," has caused some confusion. Brown believed that it meant that Chaucer had translated a work similar to or based on material in the *De Miseria*—not the *De Miseria* itself.[77] Germaine Dempster was not sure whether *As* meant "translation, imitation, or simply treatment of the same question" as in the *De Miseria*.[78] Both Brown and Dempster have made an unnecessarily difficult problem out of this word. There would seem to be only two possibilities for the use of *As*. The first is as a conjunction used in a parenthetical clause (*MED, as,* sense 7); that is, Alceste mentions that Chaucer translated *Of the Wreched Engendrynge of*

18

Mankynde and then as a comment or explanation says that it can be found "in pope Innocent." The second is as a relative with the meaning 'which' (*OED, as,* sense B, VI, 24), so that the lines would read "And of the Wreched Engendrynge of Mankynde, / [which] man may in pope Innocent yfynde."[79] The second fits the situation, which calls for an object of *yfynde,* better than the first and seems the more likely possibility to me. But whichever of the two uses of *as* one chooses, the meaning is essentially the same and very clear: that Chaucer translated *Of the Wreched Engendrynge of Mankynde* and that this work may be found "in pope Innocent."

Third, what precisely did Chaucer mean by "in pope Innocent"? Neither the Browns nor Tatlock and Dempster ever allude to this phrase specifically, but it is clear from their conclusions that they have assumed the phrase to mean "in the *De Miseria.*" This seems an unlikely assumption to me, but one cannot be too dogmatic about Chaucer's intended meaning. To understand exactly what the phrase means, one would need to find other examples of a well-attested title followed by an "in an author" phrase, and to my knowledge there are none of these in Chaucer.[80] But some observations can be made concerning Chaucer's use of titles and authors in other situations which may point to the probable meaning of "in pope Innocent." (1) It is true that Chaucer often uses "in an author" to stand for "in a particular work by that author" but only when the work is not actually mentioned in the same passage.[81] (2) Never does Chaucer give a title to part of a work and then in the same passage say that it can be found in the whole work, whether represented by the actual title or by an "in an author" phrase. (3) Nor in fact is he in the habit of giving a title to part of a work.[82] (4) Moreover, there is no evidence in the manuscripts of the *De Miseria* to indicate that part of the treatise ever stood by itself with a title different from the main title. (5) Other works by Pope Innocent III were known in the Middle Ages and in fact often appeared in manuscript with the *De Miseria* (especially the *De Sacro Altaris Mysterio*), so that "in pope Innocent" would have been ambiguous if applied only to a single work. (6) Chaucer himself was aware that Pope Innocent had written more than one treatise (*Melibee* B[2] 2758: "and the same seith Innocent in oon of his bookes"). Chaucer's intended meaning of "in pope Innocent" will never be known for certain, but on the basis of these observations—admittedly "circumstantial" evidence—I am inclined to believe that the phrase means "in, or among, the works of Pope Innocent III" rather than "in the *De Miseria.*"

With these verbal difficulties resolved as satisfactorily as they can be, we can go on to examine the title itself, *Of the Wreched Engendrynge of Mankynde.* I have been assuming all along that *Of* is part of the title.

19

When Chaucer uses the verb *translate* in the sense of 'turn from one language into another', it is always transitive, and there is no reason to assume that he is using the word differently with *Of the Wreched Engendrynge of Mankynde*; he has in fact just used it transitively in the preceding line with *Boece*.[83] *Of* is no doubt a translation of *De* 'about, concerning', which appears in nearly every title in the manuscripts of the *De Miseria* that I have examined, whether applied to the whole work, to one of the three books, or to a separate chapter. It is well known that titles to Latin works begin with prepositions. Chaucer himself knew this: there are plenty of such titles, untranslated, in his own writings.[84] Furthermore, when he translates a Latin title into English, he often retains the introductory preposition;[85] the same is no doubt true of *Of* in *Of the Wreched Engendrynge of Mankynde*.

The meaning of Chaucer's title, as the Browns, Tatlock, and Dempster recognized, depends on *Engendrynge*, and it is essential to try to discover exactly what Chaucer meant by it. The *Middle English Dictionary* (*MED*) has three definitions for the word *engendring*. The first and by far the most common, with copious examples from Chaucer and others, is: (a) 'The act of begetting, procreating, childbearing, or giving birth'; (b) 'the action of creating, producing, growing; the fact of being produced'. The second, similar to the first and perhaps derived from it, is 'A thing produced by natural process', with two citations, one of which is from Chaucer's *House of Fame*. The third, somewhat different from the other two, is: 'Natural endowment, nature, character'. Of the two citations for this last definition, one is line 414 from the revised Prologue to the *Legend of Good Women*, the line under discussion here. But it will be obvious to anyone who examines this line and the passage from which it is taken that there is absolutely no context from which to derive a meaning—whether this one or any other—of the word *Engendrynge*, and one wonders how the editors of the *MED* decided that the word meant 'natural endowment, nature, character' in this situation.

The original and most popular title of Lotario's treatise was *De Miseria Humane Conditionis* (with various permutations, as in the title of the manuscript used for the present edition),[86] and this was probably also the title in Chaucer's manuscript of the treatise.[87] *Of the Wreched Engendrynge of Mankynde* may very possibly be a translation of this title. The most likely definition of *Conditionis* in this context, or in any context, is 'external position, situation, condition, rank, place, circumstances';[88] a literal translation of the title would therefore be something like "Of the Misery of the Human Situation." This is probably the meaning that Lotario intended, since his treatise is about the whole of man's life—at birth, through life, and after death—in other words, man's whole set of circumstances, or his whole "condition" as we have come to use that word in the phrase "the human condition." But neither the Middle English noun *engendring* nor the related nouns *engendre, engend(r)ure, gendrer, gendringe, gendrure* are ever given this meaning by the *MED*, and Chaucer's *Engendrynge* is surely not a translation of *Conditionis* in this sense.

Often, however, in both Classical and Medieval Latin, when *conditio* is used with reference to animate objects, its meaning is 'nature', as in the phrase *humana conditio*, "human nature," and this is a possible definition of *Conditionis* in Lotario's title.[89] Because, as I have emphasized, there is no context from which to derive a meaning of Chaucer's word *Engendrynge*, I think that the editors of the *MED* must have assumed that Chaucer intended *Of the Wreched Engendrynge of Mankynde* to be a translation of Lotario's title; having assumed this, must then have reconciled *Engendrynge* with the corresponding word *Conditionis* by understanding the latter to mean 'nature'; and finally must have rendered *Engendrynge* by the nearly identical 'natural endowment, nature, character', which was a possible definition for the word in Middle English, and listed it accordingly as a citation for this definition in the *MED*. Whether or not this hypothesis explains the inclusion of *Engendrynge* as a citation for the *MED*'s definition 'natural endowment, nature, character', the definition itself provides a possible solution to the problem of Chaucer's title: *Of the Wreched Engendrynge of Mankynde* could be a translation of *De Miseria Humane Conditionis*, with *Of the Wreched* a rendering of *De Miseria* and *Engendrynge of Mankynde* a rendering of *Humane Conditionis*, using a definition of *conditio*— 'nature'—that is similar to a possible one for Middle English *engendring*.

The only difficulty with this solution is that the *MED*'s definition of *Engendrynge* is never the one that the word has elsewhere in Chaucer's writings. In forty instances (not counting the one under discussion here) in which Chaucer uses this and related words, he is always talking about begetting, procreating, producing, originating, etc., either literally or figuratively.[90] Nor, except in a very few instances, do Middle English *engendring, gendringe*, and related words ever have the meaning 'natural endowment, nature, character'—or, for that matter, any meaning other than Chaucer's. Because, in the absence of a context, there is no a priori reason for *Engendrynge* to mean 'natural endowment, nature, character', the likelihood is very great that the word means 'begetting, procreating, producing, originating', its nearly universal meaning in Middle English and the one that Chaucer always uses elsewhere in his writings.

The problem may lie in the definition of *conditio*. So far I have been discussing its most widely known meaning—'situation', the one that

21

Lotario probably intended and the one that remains to this day in our word *condition*; and an alternate meaning—'nature'—that could possibly fit *Conditionis* in Lotario's title. But *conditio* has still another meaning in Classical Latin and especially in Medieval Latin—'creation, procreation', both in the sense of the 'act of creating' and in the sense of 'the thing procreated or made'.[91] This definition is not so well known as the others but will be found in the standard dictionaries of Medieval Latin and is well attested by copious citations.[92] The reason for the different meanings lies in the fact that they come from two originally different words: *condicio* (from *condico*) for 'situation' and 'nature' and *conditio* (from *condo*) for 'creation'.[93] In medieval manuscripts, however, *c* replaced *t* when followed by *i* plus a vowel long before Chaucer's time, so that it is impossible to determine, except by context, whether *condicio* or *conditio* is the word intended by a given writer. But because *conditio* 'creation' and related words were current in the British Isles throughout the Middle Ages,[94] it is reasonable to assume that Chaucer knew 'creation' along with 'situation', 'nature', and others as meanings of a single word spelled either *conditio* or *condicio*. And it is also reasonable to assume that he would have translated this word, when it meant 'creation', by *engendring* (or a related word), which, to judge from the number of times that he uses it in his writings, was the most common word for this notion at his disposal.[95]

It is therefore possible that *Of the Wreched Engendrynge of Mankynde* is an exact translation of *De Miseria Humane Conditionis*, with *Engendrynge* in the sense always used by Chaucer—'begetting, procreating', etc.—a rendering of *Conditionis*. But since this meaning of *Conditionis* is probably not the one intended by Lotario, would it have been possible for Chaucer to have translated the word by *Engendrynge* 'begetting, procreation'? Perhaps the following hypothetical course of events may provide an explanation: when Chaucer came upon the work, he did not know its contents, or knew them imperfectly, perhaps only by reputation, and found the word *Conditionis* in the title *De Miseria Humane Conditionis* ambiguous; after reading, or perhaps translating, a few pages (the first seven chapters of Book I are about the wretchedness of man's birth), he was satisfied that *Conditionis* was to be understood in its sense of 'creation, procreation' and translated the title accordingly; later on, for one reason or another, perhaps because he forgot to change it, perhaps because he found it satisfactory, perhaps even because he thought that it represented the meaning that Lotario intended, he inserted it in its original form into the revised Prologue to the *Legend of Good Women*. This solution to the problem of Chaucer's title, though identical to the first in that *Of the Wreched* translates *De Miseria* and *Engendrynge of Mankynde* translates *Humane Conditionis*, is more plausible because *Engendrynge*, translating as it does a possible and well attested medieval sense of *Conditionis*, is in accord with Chaucer's use of this and related words elsewhere in his works. But in both solutions the important point is that, because *De Miseria Humane Conditionis* is the title to the whole of Lotario's treatise, *Of the Wreched Engendrynge of Mankynde* would have been Chaucer's title for the whole treatise also.

What light can the manuscripts of the *De Miseria* throw on Chaucer's choice of title? In looking at the manuscripts one is immediately struck by the number and variety of the titles to the treatise. Without counting variant spellings and changes in word order, I have found more than 60 different titles in the manuscripts;[96] in addition, 60 manuscripts have no title, 39 have neither title nor colophon, and 78 have a title different from the colophon. But in spite of this chaotic situation, one thing is clear: *De Miseria Humane Conditionis*, Lotario's original title, is the most popular single title, appearing in 248, or over 35 percent, of the manuscripts. In addition, there are 49 manuscripts in which *De Miseria Humane Conditionis* is combined with other words or with another title. The closest competitors are *De Contemptu Mundi* (83 plus 26 combinations), *De Vilitate Humane Conditionis* (68 plus 40 combinations), and *De Miseria Hominis* (50 plus 19 combinations).[97] It would therefore be the title most likely to have been seen by Chaucer in manuscripts of the *De Miseria* and in fact was probably the title in Chaucer's own manuscript.[98]

I have already shown that it is possible for *Of the Wreched Engendrynge of Mankynde* to be a translation of *De Miseria Humane Conditionis*— and this would also be true of *De Vilitate Humane Conditionis*, another popular title—with *Engendrynge* a rendering of *Conditionis* either in the sense of 'nature' or in the sense of 'creation', even though Lotario probably intended the word to mean 'situation'. The manuscripts give evidence that *Conditionis* must also have been ambiguous to the scribes and that they may have understood it to mean something other than 'situation'.[99] To take *Conditionis* in the sense of 'nature' first, we find, for example, *De Miseria Conditionis Humane Nature, De Vilitate Conditionis Humane Nature*, and *De Fragilitate Conditionis Humane Nature*, where *Nature* may have been added to clarify the meaning of *Conditionis*.[100] More important, we find the combined titles *De Contemptu Mundi et Miseria Humane Nature* and *De Miseria et Vilitate Humane Nature*, where *Nature* may be a scribal substitution for *Conditionis*;[101] recognizing the ambiguity of *Conditionis*, the scribes may have read into the work, satisfied themselves that it was about human nature, and for the sake of clarity made the appropriate substitution in the titles. To take *Conditionis* in the sense of 'creation', we find, for example, *De Miserabili*

Conditione Humani Generis, where *Generis*, if it is understood to mean 'birth, descent, origin', may have been added to clarify the meaning of *Conditione*, perhaps under the influence of the first seven chapters of the treatise, which are about man's birth.[102] We also find *De Miseria Humane Conditionis* used as the title to chapter 1 of Book I in manuscripts that have a different main title;[103] the importance of such a configuration of titles is that the original main title has been given to only a portion of the treatise that concerns man's birth, indicating that *Conditionis* may have been understood in the sense of 'creation'. There would thus seem to be precedent for Chaucer's confusion over *Conditionis* if he had decided to translate *De Miseria Humane Conditionis* by *Of the Wreched Engendrynge of Mankynde*.

If Chaucer's manuscript did not have the title *De Miseria Humane Conditionis*, there are a number of other main titles in the manuscripts that could have provided an original for *Of the Wreched Engendrynge of Mankynde*. I list them in order of increasing closeness to Chaucer's title.

1. *De Vilitate Humane Materie et de Contemptu Mundi*.[104] The word *Materie* probably means 'matter, stuff', but it could also mean 'natural abilities' or 'natural disposition'. With the latter meaning—and perhaps even with the former—the title could have been paraphrased by *Of the Wreched Engendrynge of Mankynde*, with *Materie* rendered by *Engendrynge* in the sense of 'natural endowment, nature, character'. The *de Contemptu Mundi* would of course have been omitted in the paraphrase.

2. *De Miserabili Statu Conditionis Humane*.[105] The word *Statu* is nearly identical in meaning to *Conditionis* if the latter is understood in the sense probably intended by Lotario—'state, circumstances, situation'. A title like this one would easily lend itself to interpretation with one of the other meanings of *conditio*, perhaps chosen from a knowledge of the contents of the work or from a reading of the first few chapters. This title could have been paraphrased by *Of the Wreched Engendrynge of Mankynde*, with *Engendrynge* a rendering of *Conditionis* either in the sense of 'nature' or in the sense of 'creation'.

3. *De Miserabili Conditione Humani Generis*.[106] If *Generis* in this title is understood to mean 'birth, descent, origin', then *Of the Wreched Engendrynge of Mankynde* could be a paraphrase of it, with *Generis* rendered by *Engendrynge* in Chaucer's usual sense of 'begetting, procreating, producing, originating'.

4. *De Miseria Humani Ingressus*.[107] This title literally translated means "Of the Misery of the Human Beginning." Because, for Chaucer, *engendring* and related words are very similar in meaning to *Ingressus*—are in fact identical to it in a few instances[108]—*Of the Wreched Engendrynge of Mankynde* could easily be a paraphrase of *De Miseria Humani Ingressus*.

5. *De Miserabili Humane Conditionis Ingressu.*[109] *Of the Wreched Engendrynge of Mankynde* would be quite an adequate translation of this title, with *Ingressu* 'beginning' rendered by *Engendrynge* as in the previous example, *De Miserabili* by *Of the Wreched*, and *Humane Conditionis* by *Mankynde*.

Any one of these five titles, as well as *De Miseria Humane Conditionis* and *De Vilitate Humane Conditionis*—all of them titles to the whole treatise—could have provided an original for *Of the Wreched Engendrynge of Mankynde.* The manuscripts, however, present another possibility in the origin and development of *De Miseria Hominis,* one of the four most popular main titles to Lotario's treatise. The original title to both Book I and chapter 1 of Book I was *De Miserabili Humane Conditionis Ingressu,* but it appears in only 99 manuscripts. In the course of transmission a new title, *De Miseria Hominis,* takes its place and in time becomes the most popular of all the titles to Book I and to chapter 1 of Book I (291, or over 43 percent of the manuscripts). At the same time, the distinction between a separate title to Book I and a separate title to chapter 1 of Book I is lost—understandably when the two titles are identical. In the great majority of manuscripts only one title is retained, sometimes called the title to Book I but more often called the title to chapter 1 of Book I, and this is true whether the title is *De Miserabili Humane Conditionis Ingressu, De Miseria Hominis,* or any of the other titles used in this position. The reasons for the development of *De Miseria Hominis* and its displacement of *De Miserabili Humane Conditionis Ingressu* are not entirely clear. What may have happened is that, at an early stage in the transmission of Lotario's treatise, a scribe decided that, because the titles to Book I and to chapter 1 of Book I were identical (the same thing is true in Books II and III), a new one was needed for chapter 1, and for the purpose he created *De Miseria Hominis* because of its appropriateness to the first part of chapter 1—a complaint about man's misery over having been born. At a later stage, perhaps, a separate title to Book I was thought superfluous, and *De Miseria Humane Conditionis Ingressu* was thereby dropped, leaving only *De Miseria Hominis;* or perhaps, when the table of contents to Book I immediately followed the main title, as so often happened, *De Miseria Hominis*—the first item—would be taken as the title to Book I, whether or not *De Miserabili Humane Conditionis Ingressu* actually appeared before Book I later in the text.

The next stage in the development of *De Miseria Hominis* is that from its position as the title to Book I or to chapter 1 of Book I it is elevated to the main title of the whole treatise. This happens in no less than fifty manuscripts.[110] In twenty others it appears as the main title in combination with another title, as for example in *De Contemptu Mundi et de Miseria Hominis* or *De Vilitate Conditionis Humane et de Miseria*

Hominis. Furthermore, in fully thirty-seven others it would have worked its way into the position of title to the whole work. The ways in which this happened are worth enumerating. Sixteen manuscripts have no main title, so that *De Miseria Hominis*, the title to chapter 1 of Book I, becomes the main title by default.[111] Three manuscripts have no titles anywhere in the text but have *De Miseria Hominis* as the first item in the table of contents, where it would be the first thing seen by a reader looking for a title.[112] Five manuscripts have *De Miseria Hominis* as the title to chapter 1 of Book I as well as a main title, but the main title appears to be a later addition, so that *De Miseria Hominis* would have been the main title by default in the original versions of the manuscripts.[113] In two manuscripts the table of contents comes first, without a preceding main title, and *De Miseria Hominis* is the first title that a reader would see.[114] Ten manuscripts have an inadequate main title like *Incipit Liber Lotharii Diaconi* or *Incipit Tractatus*, so that *De Miseria Hominis,* the title to chapter 1 of Book I, becomes the main title by default.[115] In one manuscript the first few words of the prologue and probably a main title are missing; in the table of contents, which follows the prologue, *De Miseria Hominis* is the first title that a reader would see.[116]

The importance of this discussion of *De Miseria Hominis* is the principle at work: that a title to Book I or chapter 1 of a medieval work could become the main title to the whole work, either intentionally or by default.[117] The principle is well documented by the progress of *De Miseria Hominis* during the course of transmission of Lotario's treatise: from its probable origin as a substitute for the original title to Book I or chapter 1 of Book I, *De Miseria Hominis* became the most popular single title in this position (291 manuscripts out of 668) and from there was elevated, either intentionally or by default, to the main title in 103—or nearly one-sixth—of the manuscripts. The absence of an adequate title in the scribe's exemplar is probably the main reason why he elevates the first title in the text to the head of the work; in 34 out of the 36 manuscripts in which *De Miseria Hominis* would have worked its way into the position of title for the whole work, the main title is either inadequate or added later or omitted entirely. Another reason is the occasional omission of Lotario's prologue; in such a situation the main title is just above the title to chapter 1, and the scribe would take in both with the same glance, reproducing a combination of the two such as *De Contemptu Mundi et de Miseria Hominis* or *De Vilitate Conditionis Humane et de Miseria Hominis*. A third reason is that contemptus mundi was a very popular subject in the Middle Ages and had many titles associated with it. A scribe would have felt free to modify the existing title according to his notion of what the work was about, especially if the title was *De Contemptu Mundi*, the name of the genre itself,[118] or to change the title entirely, perhaps substituting another one that he had heard for the same subject, perhaps choosing one from the early part of the work itself.[119] These scribal tendencies would have been especially in evidence in a work that was copied as often as the *De Miseria*.

The principle illustrated by *De Miseria Hominis* may have been at work in Chaucer's manuscript of the *De Miseria* if it did not contain *De Miseria Humane Conditionis* as the main title: of the five titles that I listed earlier as possible originals for *Of the Wreched Engendrynge of Mankynde*, the first four show the probable influence of the principle,[120] and with the last, *De Miserabili Humane Conditionis Ingressu*, the title to the first chapter has clearly been elevated to the main title. More important, the principle may have been at work in Chaucer's own choice of title; as the scribes did before him, so Chaucer himself may have used the title to the first chapter as the main title to his translation, either because there was no main title in his manuscript of the *De Miseria* or because he found the title given there, whether *De Miseria Humane Conditionis* or another, inadequate or ambiguous.[121] One of the following possibilities, listed in order of increasing closeness to *Of the Wreched Engendrynge of Mankynde*, may explain Chaucer's choice of title. I illustrate only from manuscripts in which the title to Book I or chapter 1 of Book I could have been elevated to the main title with some degree of probability.

1. *Incipit Liber Primus de Contemptu Mundi Quem Edidit Innocentius Pape Tertius Continens ad Quod Homo Nascitur* appears in one manuscript as the title to Book I, but the prologue preceding Book I is missing, and there is no main title.[122] The title to Book I would thus become the main title by default. If Chaucer's manuscript were similar to this one, he might have paraphrased *de Contemptu Mundi . . . Continens ad Quod Homo Nascitur* by *Of the Wreched Engendrynge of Mankynde*.

2. The title to chapter 1 of Book I in one manuscript is *De Miseria Hominis Nascentis* (listed as *De Miseria Nativitatis Hominis* in the table of contents).[123] This manuscript has a main title, but it is ambiguous: *Incipit Liber de Miseria et Utilitate Humane Conditionis . . . .* If the same configuration of titles had been in Chaucer's manuscript, he might have been puzzled by *Utilitate* and decided to use *De Miseria Hominis Nascentis* (or *De Miseria Nativitatis Hominis*) as more accurately describing the contents of the work. *Of the Wreched Engendrynge of Mankynde* could be a paraphrase of either title.

3. In a number of manuscripts *De Miserabili Humane Conditionis Ingressu*, the original title to Book I and to chapter 1 of Book I, could easily have been elevated to the main title. In these manuscripts the

main title is omitted altogether, and *De Miserabili Humane Conditionis Ingressu*, whether it is the title to Book I, the title to chapter 1, or the first item in the table of contents at the beginning of the treatise, would become the main title by default.[124] As I pointed out earlier, *Of the Wreched Engendrynge of Mankynde* would be quite an adequate rendering of this title, with *Of the Wreched Engendrynge* a translation of *De Miserabili . . . Ingressu,* and *Mankynde* a paraphrase of *Humane Conditionis.*

4. As the title to chapter 1 one manuscript has *De Miseria et Feditate Conceptus Hominis.*[125] In this manuscript the main title is ambiguous—*Ad Clementissimum Virum Dominum Petrum Episcopum Portuensem Lotarii Diaconi Prefatio Libri Secundum Bernardum de Miseria Condictionis Humane*—both because of the phrase *Secundum Bernardum* and because of the word *Condictionis,* which can mean 'announcement' or 'declaration'. If Chaucer's manuscript of the *De Miseria Humane Conditionis* were similar to this one, he would have been puzzled by the words of the main title and might have decided that the title to chapter 1 would be a more accurate title for the whole work. *De Miseria et Feditate Conceptus Hominis* is very close to *Of the Wreched Engendrynge of Mankynde: Of the Wreched* could easily be a paraphrase of *De Miseria et Feditate,* and *Engendrynge of Mankynde* is an accurate translation of *Conceptus Hominis.*

5. One manuscript has *De Miserabilis Ingressu Hominis* as the title to chapter 1 of Book I, but the main title is missing,[126] and the title to chapter 1 of Book I would have become the main title by default. *Of the Wreched Engendrynge* is an adequate translation of *De Miserabilis Ingressu,* and *of Mankynde* is an accurate translation of *Hominis.*

6. One manuscript has *De Vili Conceptione Hominis* as the title to chapter 1 of Book I.[127] This title is in the margin of the first page of text and would have been the first item to catch a reader's attention, probably even before the long main title, which is only partially in the margin: *Incipit Prologus Libri Domini Lotharii Diaconi Cardinalis Sanctorum Sergii et Bachii. Compositus Anno Quarto Pontificatus Domini Celestini III Pape Indictione Tercia Decima. De Contemptu Mundi.* If this configuration of titles had been in Chaucer's manuscript, he might have decided that *De Contemptu Mundi,* because it was the name of the genre to which Lotario's treatise belonged, was neither particularly descriptive nor particularly individualizing and might have chosen the easily available *De Vili Conceptione Hominis* as more accurately describing the contents of the treatise. *Of the Wreched Engendrynge of Mankynde* is an exact translation of *De Vili Conceptione Hominis.*

Though in the absence of a work entitled *Of the Wreched Engendrynge of Mankynde* there can be no certain conclusions about Chaucer's intention, all the available evidence—the manner in which Chaucer introduces the words "of the Wreched Engendrynge of Mankynde" into the revised Prologue to the *Legend of Good Women*; the ease with which it could be a translation of *De Miseria Humane Conditionis,* the original and most popular title to Lotario's treatise and the one most likely to have been in Chaucer's own manuscript; the many possibilities available in manuscript for Chaucer to have chosen *Of the Wreched Engendrynge of Mankynde* as a main title if *De Miseria Humane Conditionis* were not the title in his manuscript—leads to the only probable conclusion that, when Chaucer revised the Prologue to the *Legend of Good Women,* he intended to indicate that he had translated the whole *De Miseria.* I think we can be almost certain about this.

The question of course is: Do we believe Chaucer? Koeppel and Lounsbury, who were the first to discuss Chaucer's debt to the *De Miseria,* did not: they believed that the translation was never completed, that it remained a fragment.[128] But they were writing at a time when it was believed that Prologue G was the earlier version and Prologue F the later, and their conclusion was a perfectly natural one: if Chaucer had said in an earlier work that he had translated the *De Miseria* and then in a later work had withdrawn the reference, it would be reasonable to assume that he had, for some reason, abandoned the work. Now that Prologue F is considered the earlier,[129] there is no reason to argue for a partial translation on the basis of the order of the Prologues alone. Tatlock, Dempster, and Brusendorff also believed, on the basis of the words "of the Wreched Engendrynge of Mankynde," that Chaucer had made only a partial translation—namely, of the first five to seven chapters of Book I.[130] But in view of my findings regarding Chaucer's title—and the additional fact that, though Chaucer has translated passages from two books and at least eight chapters of the *De Miseria,* not a single one is from the first five to seven chapters of the treatise—their conclusion does not hold.

It is difficult not to agree with Tatlock when he says, "With all the literary cribbing that went on in the middle ages, if a poet admits translating we had better believe him";[131] and I am inclined to believe that Chaucer's words should be accepted at face value: that he made a prose translation of the *De Miseria.* It does seem strange, however, that if Chaucer actually translated the treatise, it did not exert more influence on his own writings. With other works that he translated— particularly Boethius's *De Consolatione Philosophiae* and the *Roman de la Rose,* perhaps also pseudo-Origen's homily *De Maria Magdalena*[132]—or even with works that he did not translate but knew well, like St. Jerome's *Epistola Adversus Jovinianum,* we find a pervasive influence in his writings throughout his career. On the other hand, one might argue that Chaucer's translation of the *De Miseria,* like his translation of Renaud de Louens's *Livre de Mellibee et Prudence,* was an occasional piece which, perhaps because it was less congenial to him than other works he translated, he used very little or not at all after making his translation, or that it was made too late in life to have had much influence on his works. Another possibility, however, might be worth considering: that, when Chaucer inserted lines 414-15 into the revised Prologue to the *Legend of Good Women,* he had only partially completed his translation of the *De Miseria* and wanted to make sure that it was included among his other translations but that for one reason or another (for example, he could not find the time, or he tired of Lotario's treatise, having mined it already for the most interesting portions), he never completed it. This would at least explain why Chaucer does not use the *De Miseria* again after writing the Man of Law's Prologue and Tale and the Pardoner's Tale, but it is at best only a possibility. The most reasonable assumption, in the absence of more conclusive evidence, is that Chaucer made a prose translation of the whole *De Miseria* and that he records that fact in the revised Prologue to the *Legend of Good Women.*[133]

THE DATE OF CHAUCER'S TRANSLATION

If this is so, when would he have made the translation? Prologue F to the *Legend of Good Women,* which is now accepted as the earlier of the two versions,[134] probably written in 1384-86,[135] does not contain the two-line allusion to the *De Miseria,* and it is reasonable to assume that 1384-86 is the terminus a quo for the translation. Prologue G provides a terminus ad quem of 1394-95.[136]

It is possible, I think, to be more precise. Similarities between Chaucer's Man of Law's Tale and John Gower's story of Constance in the *Confessio Amantis* have long been recognized, and most scholars believe that Chaucer borrowed from Gower rather than the other way around;[137] indeed, it is even possible that Chaucer chose the tale to see if he could outdo Gower at his own game, as a response to Gower's displeasure at the tales of the Miller, Reeve, and Cook.[138] The generally accepted date for the first "edition" of the *Confessio Amantis* is 1390, though with such a long poem, parts of which must have been written earlier, it is possible that because Chaucer was a friend of Gower's, he could have seen the story of Constance before 1390 (if in fact it had been written by then), perhaps in 1385-86 just before he presumably moved to Kent, or—more likely—in 1389 when he returned to London as Clerk of the King's Works.[139] But the manner of Chaucer's reference to the stories of Canace and Appollonius, also in the *Confessio Amantis,* in the Introduction to the Man of Law's Tale assumes a knowledge of Gower's poem on the part of Chaucer's audience, and this would argue for a date for the Man of Law's Tale *after* the *Confessio Amantis* was made available to the public, or 1390 at the earliest. In fact, the Man of Law's Tale is usually dated ca. 1390.[140]

By itself a date for the Man of Law's Tale, which incorporates five passages from the *De Miseria,* indicates nothing about the date of Chaucer's translation of the *De Miseria,* as it is possible that the passages from the *De Miseria* could have been taken from an earlier translation of his or could have been inserted in the Man of Law's Tale, in revision, long after 1390.[141] Another important item must be considered along with the date. For the five passages from the *De Miseria* in the Man of Law's Tale there are Latin glosses in the margins of many manuscripts of the *Canterbury Tales.* As I will demonstrate,[142] these glosses were almost certainly written by Chaucer himself or by a scribe copying from Chaucer's own manuscript of the *De Miseria.* It seems unlikely, if Chaucer had been paraphrasing from an earlier translation, that he would have added these marginal glosses in his copy of the Man of Law's Tale or would have instructed a scribe to add them. Their appearance there makes sense only if he were occupied with the Latin original at the time. It would therefore seem to me that Chaucer's translation of the *De Miseria* ought to be dated no earlier than 1390.

Chaucer's use of the *De Miseria* in the Pardoner's Tale provides very little evidence for dating the translation, but a few observations may be worth making in this connection. First, because the translated passages from the *De Miseria* are more in the nature of a paraphrase, more at random, more assimilated into his own thought than they are in the Man of Law's Prologue and Tale, it is possible to think that Chaucer was reworking lines from an earlier translation. Second, if the appearance of marginal glosses indicates a coterminous relationship with a source, as I believe it does with the *De Miseria* in the Man of Law's Tale, then the absence of marginal glosses from the *De Miseria* in the Pardoner's Tale may indicate, especially because the tale is rather heavily glossed, that Chaucer is not working with Lotario's treatise at the time. Finally, Chaucer's use of St. Jerome's *Epistola Adversus Jovinianum,* including the marginal glosses taken directly from it,[143] in the Pardoner's Tale connects that tale with the so-called Marriage Group (usually dated mid-1390s), in which St. Jerome's *Epistola* is a primary source, and with the revised Prologue to the *Legend of Good Women* (1394-95), which contains a list of books, including St. Jerome's *Epistola,* that Chaucer had probably been working with in the recent past (Prologue G 268-312). The conclusion that suggests itself from these observations is that Chaucer's translation of the *De Miseria* was probably completed after 1390 and before 1394-95, and this conclusion is in line with the evidence from the Man of Law's Tale.

THE GLOSSES TO THE MAN OF LAW'S TALE

In order to determine the text of the *De Miseria* from which Chaucer made his translation, I turn first to the marginal glosses in the manuscripts of the Man of Law's Tale. For each of the five passages in this tale translated from the *De Miseria* there are corresponding Latin glosses in representative manuscripts of all four groups of Manly and Rickert's classification of the tale, including Hengwrt and Ellesmere.[144] If it could be shown that these glosses were written either by Chaucer from his own manuscript of the *De Miseria* or by a scribe copying from that same manuscript, either under Chaucer's supervision or shortly after his death, then they would provide the primary evidence for determining Chaucer's text of the *De Miseria*.

Very little has been written about the glosses to the *Canterbury Tales*. Manly and Rickert, who should speak more authoritatively than anyone else by virtue of their extensive study of the manuscripts, are not very explicit on the subject. The only ones they are willing to attribute definitely to Chaucer are the lines from Statius's *Thebaid* at the beginning of the Knight's Tale, but they believe that "perhaps" Chaucer added the glosses from Petrarch to the Clerk's Tale, that he may have written the glosses to the Second Nun's Tale, and that "possibly" he may have added the glosses from the *De Miseria* to the Man of Law's Tale.[145] On the Man of Law's Tale, however, Manly and Rickert are uncertain because if Chaucer had added the lines from the *De Miseria*, "one would expect his debt to Pope Innocent in the Proem [B¹ 99–121] to be acknowledged by a gloss."[146]

Other scholars, however, are more convinced that Chaucer wrote the glosses himself, although their opinions, made before Manly and Rickert's edition of the *Canterbury Tales* appeared, are not based on a systematic study of the manuscripts either of the *Canterbury Tales* or of the works cited in the glosses. Aage Brusendorff, for instance, believes that all, or at least most, of the glosses in the tales of the Man of Law, Clerk, Merchant, Franklin, and Pardoner, and in the Wife of Bath's Prologue are by Chaucer: "This can be definitely proved in cases where the quotations are found in a form corresponding with the version in the *Tales*, but not with the original text."[147] This is a very perceptive statement but is unfortunately not substantiated with manuscript evidence. J. S. P. Tatlock in "The *Canterbury Tales* in 1400"[148] agrees with Brusendorff, presumably because the glosses are much more common in the Hengwrt and Ellesmere manuscripts, two of the oldest and most authoritative manuscripts of the *Canterbury Tales*.

32

Since Manly and Rickert's edition there have been few studies of the authorship of the glosses, and they have been confined to a comparison of individual tales and their sources. Germaine Dempster, in an article supplementing and correcting J. Burke Severs's conclusions in his *Literary Relationships of Chaucer's "Clerkes Tale"* (1942), concludes that the glosses from Petrarch in the Clerk's Tale are by Chaucer or at least from Chaucer's own manuscript: "For the glosses were first written either by Chaucer, who, of course, would use only one manuscript, or by a scribe, whose use, so soon after Chaucer's death, of a manuscript sharing with that of Chaucer so many rare variants strongly suggests that the copy, along with other papers, came to him from Chaucer's own library."[149] Daniel S. Silvia, Jr., on the basis mainly of the unevenness of the glossing and the memorandalike nature of the glosses, has made a very strong case for attributing the glosses from St. Jerome's *Epistola Adversus Jovinianum* in the Wife of Bath's Prologue and the Franklin's Tale to Chaucer himself.[150]

It is clear from the past work on the glosses of the *Canterbury Tales* that future studies of their origin must consider individual tales because the nature of the glossing varies from tale to tale; must involve a close comparison of Chaucer's text and the glosses themselves; and must be based on the evidence of the relevant manuscripts, both of the *Canterbury Tales* and of the sources used. Following these principles, the first step in determining the origin of the glosses from the *De Miseria* in the manuscripts of the Man of Law's Tale is to find out how close the glosses actually are to Chaucer's paraphrase, and that can most easily be done by setting forth, examining, and comparing the differences in the relevant passages from Lotario's original, the glosses, and the Man of Law's Tale. For the sake of clarity, in each of the following five groups of texts every difference between the original and the gloss is italicized in the gloss, and every difference between the original and the gloss that is reflected in Chaucer's paraphrase is italicized at the appropriate place in the passage from the Man of Law's Tale.[151]

De Miseria I.21.1–5, 13–14; Gloss[152]; Man of Law's Tale 421–27

Semper enim mundane letitie tristicia repentina succedit . . .
Mundana quippe felicitas multis amaritudinibus est respersa . . .
"extrema gaudii luctus occupat" . . . Salubre consilium: "In die bonorum ne immemor sis malorum."

Semper ——— mundane leticie tristicia repentina succedit Mundana *igitur* felicitas multis amaritudinibus est respersa extrema gaudii luctus occupat *Audi ergo* salubre consilium In die bonorum ne immemor sis malorum

O sodeyn wo, that evere art successour
To worldly blisse, spreynd with bitternesse!

33

The ende of the joye of oure worldly labour!
Wo occupieth the fyn of oure gladnesse.
Herke this conseil for thy sikernesse:
Upon thy glade day have in thy mynde
The unwar wo or harm that comth bihynde.

Since the nature of a gloss is generally a condensation of a text that
the author has used, the omission of *enim* is not surprising; words like
ergo, enim, autem, et were often omitted or added indiscriminately by
scribes. It is impossible to determine from Chaucer's paraphrase
whether or not *enim* was in his source manuscript. The same is true of
the substitution of *igitur* for *quippe*; the meaning of *igitur* is slightly
weaker than *quippe*, but because Chaucer translates neither word, it is
again impossible to decide which was in Chaucer's source manuscript.
It is safe to say, however, that the third change—the addition to the
gloss of "Audi ergo"—was in Chaucer's source manuscript because it is
reflected in *Herke* at Man of Law's Tale 425.

De Miseria II.19.1–4; Gloss; Man of Law's Tale 771–77

> Quid turpius ebrioso, cui fetor in ore, tremor in corpore; qui
> promit stulta, prodit occulta; cui mens alienatur, facies transfor-
> matur? "Nullum enim secretum ubi regnat ebrietas."

> Quid turpius ebrioso cui fetor in ore tremor in corpore qui promit
> stulta prodit occulta *cuius* mens alienatur facies transformatur
> Nullum enim *latet* secretum ubi regnat ebrietas

>> O messager, fulfild of dronkenesse,
>> Strong is thy breeth, thy lymes faltren ay,
>> And thou biwreyest alle secreenesse.
>> Thy mynde is lorn, thou janglest as a jay,
>> Thy face is turned in a newe array.
>> Ther dronkenesse regneth in any route,
>> Ther is no conseil *hyd*, withouten doute.

The substitution of the genitive *cuius* for the dative of possession *cui*
is a common enough scribal correction; no matter which form was in
his source manuscript, Chaucer would have translated it as a posses-
sive, as he does, in the process changing third person singular to second
person singular, with *Thy*. Furthermore, many manuscripts of the
Canterbury Tales in three out of four of Manly and Rickert's classificatory groups for the Man of Law's Tale have *cui*, including Hengwrt and
many of the manuscripts closest to Ellesmere. The second change in
the gloss—the addition of *latet*—was without doubt in Chaucer's
source manuscript because it is reflected in *hyd* at Man of Law's Tale
777.[153]

De Miseria II.21.5–8, 12–13; Gloss; Man of Law's Tale 925–29

O extrema libidinis turpitudo, que non solum mentem effeminat, set corpus enervat . . . semper secuntur dolor et penitencia.

O extrema libidinis turpitudo que non solum mentem effeminat set *eciam* corpus enervat semper sequntur dolor et penitencia *post* et cetera

> O foule lust of luxurie, lo, thyn ende!
> Nat oonly that thou feyntest mannes mynde,
> But *verraily* thou wolt his body shende.
> Th'ende of thy werk, or of thy lustes blynde,
> Is compleynyng.

The addition of *eciam* appears to be reflected in Chaucer's *verraily* at Man of Law's Tale 927. The addition of *post* is somewhat redundant, duplicating *sequntur,* and because Chaucer paraphrases the whole notion of "following after" simply by *ende,* it is impossible to know whether or not *post* was in his source manuscript.

De Miseria I.20.10-11, 12-13; Gloss; Man of Law's Tale 1132-34

"A mane usque ad vesperam mutabitur tempus." "Tenent tympanum et cytharam et gaudent ad sonitum organi."

A mane usque ad vesperam mutabitur tempus tenent tympanum
— ——— et gaudent ad *sonum* organi

> But litel while it lasteth, I yow heete,
> Joye of this world, for tyme wol nat abyde;
> Fro day to nyght it changeth as the tyde.

The omission of a phrase—here, "et cytharam"—is to be expected in a gloss. Chaucer's translation in these three lines is more paraphrastic than the preceding three passages; "tenent tympanum et gaudent ad sonum organi" is represented by "Joye of this world." Because "et cytharam" is superfluous to the translation, it is impossible to determine whether or not the phrase was in Chaucer's source manuscript. The words *sonum* and *sonitum* are interchangeable in meaning, but since neither one is reflected directly in Chaucer's paraphrase, it is again impossible, as with the previous phrase, to come to any definite conclusions about the appearance of the word in Chaucer's source manuscript.

De Miseria I.20.1-7; Gloss; Man of Law's Tale 1135-38

Quis unquam vel unicam diem totam duxit in sua delectacione iocundam, quem in aliqua parte diei reatus consciencie vel impetus ire vel motus concupiscencie non turbaverit? Quem livor invidie vel ardor avaricie vel tumor superbie non vexaverit? Quem aliqua iactura vel offensa vel passio non commoverit?

Quis unquam — unicam diem totam duxit in sua *dileccione* iocun-

dam quem in aliqua parte diei reatus consciencie vel impetus ire vel
motus concupiscencie non turbaverit quem livor invidie vel ardor
avaricie vel tumor superbie non vexaverit Quem aliqua iactura
vel offensa vel passio non commoverit et cetera

> Who lyved euere in swich delit o day
> That hym ne moeved outher conscience
> Or ire, or talent, or som kynnes affray,
> Envye, or pride, or passion, or offence?

This passage from the Man of Law's Tale, like the preceding one, is
more paraphrastic than the first three. The omission of the insignificant *vel* is common enough, although, like the other omissions in the
glosses, it is impossible, on the basis of Chaucer's paraphrase, to
determine whether or not it was omitted in his source manuscript.
Originally the word *dileccione* was probably a mistake for the *delectacione*
'delight' of the original, arising from confusion in the abbreviation,[154]
and in fact many manuscripts of the *Canterbury Tales* in two out of four
of Manly and Rickert's classificatory groups for the Man of Law's Tale
(although not Hengwrt or Ellesmere) have *delectacione*. If Chaucer's
source manuscript had *dileccione,* he may have recognized that it was a
mistake for *delectacione*. On the other hand, it is possible that Chaucer
would have known the word *dilectio* 'love'[155] and that *dileccione* was
intended to be a form of *dilectio*. The phrase "love o day" is not very
different from "delit o day," however, and I think it is impossible to
say for certain from the word *delit* which word was in Chaucer's source
manuscript; if this one word were the only basis for determining the
manuscript, the evidence is probably in favor of *delectacione*.[156]

On the basis of the preceding evidence, the following list of
changes from the original in Chaucer's glosses can be drawn up. The
items are arranged according to their importance in determining
Chaucer's source manuscript. Each item is noted by its book and
chapter in the *De Miseria*:

(1) II.19 addition of *latet*; (2) I.22 addition of "Audi ergo"; (3) II.21
addition of *eciam*; (4) I.21 substitution of *dileccione* for *delectacione*; (5) II.21
addition of *post*; (6) I.22 substitution of *igitur* for *quippe*; (7) I.21
substitution of *sonum* for *sonitum*; (8) II.19 substitution of *cuius* for *cui*;
(9) I.20 omission of "et cytharam"; (10) I.20 omission of *vel*; (11) I.21
omission of *enim*.

As the discussion of each gloss indicates, it is very difficult to
determine the nature of Chaucer's source manuscript because of the
paraphrastic character of the translation, and not every change from
the original in the gloss is of equal value. Omissions are least valuable.
Since the nature of these glosses or, for that matter, of any gloss that is
presumably translated in the author's text is a condensation of a work

36

that the author has translated, usually reproducing only those parts of the work that are actually reflected in the translation, it is impossible to make very much of omissions in determining the source manuscript. Of the three omissions in the glosses, two are insignificant—the omissions of *vel* and *enim*—and a third—the omission of "et cytharam"—is impossible to detect in Chaucer's paraphrase.

Substitutions are more important than omissions, for if a substitution of a word or phrase in the gloss for one in the original is reflected in Chaucer's paraphrase, then it can prove something about the nature of his source manuscript. Of the four substitutions in the gloss, however, only one may give a clue to Chaucer's source manuscript: *dileccione* for *delectacione*. But it is difficult to build a case on this one word for two reasons: first, because of possible confusion in the abbreviation, *dileccione* could be a mistake for *delectacione*—a mistake that Chaucer may have recognized and corrected mentally, translating it *delit*; second, there is very little difference in meaning between "love o day" and "delit o day."[157]

Additions to the gloss are the most important kind of change in determining the source manuscript; if they are reflected in the paraphrase, they can be detected without much trouble. Of the four additions to the glosses, three are either certainly or probably reflected in Chaucer's paraphrase. The gloss's "Audi ergo" is clearly reflected in *Herke* at Man of Law's Tale 425; the gloss's *latet* is clearly reflected in *hyd* at Man of Law's Tale 777; the gloss's *eciam* is probably reflected in *verraily* at Man of Law's Tale 927, although one cannot insist on this last because *verraily* is not an exact translation of *eciam* and may have been added by Chaucer either to emphasize the evils of lechery or to fill out the line. Even the fourth addition, *post,* may have been in Chaucer's source manuscript, although it is impossible to detect in Chaucer's paraphrase because, as noted above, *post,* by partially duplicating *sequntur,* is unnecessary to the meaning of the line.

The evidence therefore points to the conclusion that, except for the substitution of *dileccione* for *delectacione,* which is inconclusive, Chaucer's paraphrase must have been based on a manuscript of the *De Miseria* that was practically identical to the one used for the glosses. From such a conclusion Brusendorff would doubtless have said that Chaucer wrote the glosses himself because they appear "in a form corresponding with the version in the *Tales,* but not with the original text,"[158] and it is tempting to agree with him here. But Brusendorff's opinions were not based on evidence of the relevant manuscripts, and by itself the conclusion that Chaucer's paraphrase is based on a manuscript practically identical to the one used for the glosses indicates nothing about the origin of the glosses, for if it were found that all, or even some, of the manuscripts of the *De Miseria* had the additions "Audi ergo," *latet,* probably *eciam,* and possibly *post,* then the glosses could have been inserted later, from a different manuscript, by someone other than Chaucer or a scribe copying from Chaucer's manuscript of the work. But this is not the case. Only one manuscript—British Library, MS. Royal 8 F.xiv—has the most important addition: *latet.* Only one manuscript—Royal 8 F.xiv—has the addition of "Audi ergo" (another manuscript, Uppsala, Universitetsbiblioteket C 226, has *Audi,* but it has none of the other changes in the glosses). The same manuscript has the addition of *eciam.* Many other manuscripts have *eciam* also, but as mentioned earlier, the addition of an unimportant word like *eciam* is a common scribal alteration: the important element here is that Royal 8 F.xiv has *eciam* in addition to *latet* and "Audi ergo." No manuscript has the addition of *post.* Eight manuscripts have *dileccione* for *delectacione,* but none of them has any of the important additions in the glosses.

Because the text of the glosses is almost unique among the extant manuscripts of the *De Miseria* that I have examined, it is therefore extremely likely, and in fact the only reasonable conclusion, that not only is the manuscript used for Chaucer's paraphrase practically identical to the one used for the glosses, but they are one and the same manuscript. And if this is so, then the glosses were written either by Chaucer in his autograph copy of the Man of Law's Tale or by a scribe under Chaucer's supervision from Chaucer's own manuscript of the *De Miseria* or by a scribe shortly after Chaucer's death from that same manuscript found among Chaucer's papers.[159] What we know of the external details of the glosses corroborates such a conclusion. According to Manly and Rickert, the origin of two of the most authoritative manuscripts of the *Canterbury Tales,* Hengwrt and Ellesmere, is quite different. Hengwrt derives from a pre-1400 copy of a considerable number of the *Canterbury Tales* made during Chaucer's lifetime for one of his friends;[160] Ellesmere, in Germaine Dempster's words, "is apparently the only surviving manuscript believed to derive its text of most C[anterbury] T[ales] pieces from the copies in Chaucer's house at his death."[161] Hengwrt and Ellesmere, however, have the glosses in nearly identical form where Hengwrt is not defective, which is only at Man of Law's Tale 1132–38, and both manuscripts have the additions *latet,* "Audi ergo," and *eciam.* It is extremely unlikely, not to say impossible, that two manuscripts of such different origin would contain glosses with the same additions to the original text when those additions appear together in only one manuscript out of all the manuscripts of the *De Miseria,* unless the additions actually came from Chaucer's own copy of the *De Miseria.*[162]

The available evidence, therefore, strongly supports the conclusion that the glosses from the *De Miseria* were written either by Chaucer himself from his own manuscript of the work or by a scribe copying from that same manuscript, either under Chaucer's supervision or shortly after his death. It is more plausible, I think, that the glosses were written during Chaucer's lifetime than after his death in 1400. If the glosses had been inserted by a scribe after Chaucer's death, from Chaucer's manuscript of the *De Miseria,* with the intention of giving the tale a learned or dignified appearance, one of two situations would have been involved: either that Chaucer left definite instructions for the glossing of the Man of Law's Tale, and there is no evidence in the manuscripts of the *Canterbury Tales* that he did;[163] or that the scribe, somehow recognizing exactly which lines were translated from the *De Miseria,* leafed through Chaucer's copy of the work to find the appropriate passages, which appear in four different chapters and two different books, and this is a task which, to judge from contemporary comments on scribal habits,[164] one would expect only a very intelligent and conscientious scribe to be willing or able to perform. If, however, Chaucer wrote the glosses himself, or if they were done under his supervision, they would doubtless be intended either as notes to himself, against which to check his translation when he returned to revise the Man of Law's Tale, or as an expression, to use Tatlock's words, of the "genuine medieval love of precedent and authority, especially in Latin, sincerely shared by Chaucer,"[165] and these are both plausible reasons for adding glosses. But this is of course speculation. Whether inserted during Chaucer's lifetime or afterwards, the glosses from the *De Miseria* in the Man of Law's Tale take their place beside the glosses from Statius in the Knight's Tale, from Petrarch in the Clerk's Tale, and from St. Jerome's *Epistola Adversus Jovinianum* in the Wife of Bath's Prologue and the Franklin's Tale as having been written either by Chaucer himself or by a scribe copying from his manuscript.[166]

CHAUCER'S TEXT OF THE *DE MISERIA*

As will be clear from the preceding section, the glosses constitute the primary evidence for determining Chaucer's text of the *De Miseria.* Returning to the list of changes in the glosses given earlier, I add to it here the manuscripts that contain each of the eleven readings, with those having two or more of the readings italicized.[167]

1. II.19 addition of *latet* (L^{31})
2. I.21 addition of *Audi ergo* (L^{31}; *Audi* in U^4)

3. II.21 addition of *eciam* (60 manuscripts, including $BwBz^1C^{19}Es^3FGL^{31}$
$M^1MnMu^6Pa^{15}Pr^1S^2StU^7V^1V^3Vi$)

4. I.20 substitution of *dileccione* for *delectacione* ($C^3C^{11}Du^4Ma^1O^{23}Pa^5S^2S^3$)

5. II.21 addition of *post* (none)

6. I.21 substitution of *igitur* for *quippe* (none)

7. I.20 substitution of *sonum* for *sonitum* (64 manuscripts, including
$BaBz^1CcE^2EgL^6L^{37}MoMu^3Mu^6Pa^2Pa^3Pa^{15}Ph^1PoPr^1Pr^2Pr^3Pr^5Pr^6Re^1Re^2SuUt^2Vi$)

8. II.19 substitution of *cuius* for *cui* ($M^2Ma^4Ph^3Wr^2$)

9. I.20 omission of *et cytharam* (U^7)

10. I.20 omission of *vel* (145 manuscripts, including $AdAuBaBl^1BwC^{19}$
$CcDu^4E^2EgEr^1Es^3FGGiGrL^{37}Ma^4MeMnMoMu^2Mu^3Pa^1Pa^2Pa^3Ph^1PoPr^2Pr^3Pr^4Pr^5Pr^6$
$Re^1S^2StSuUt^2V^1V^3V^4ViWWr^1$)

11. I.21 omission of *enim* (64 manuscripts, including $AdAuBl^1C^{11}Er^1Es^1$
$GiGrL^6M^1MeMu^2Pa^1Pa^5Pr^4Re^2V^4WWr^1$)

The secondary evidence for determining Chaucer's text of the *De Miseria* consists of the passages in the Man of Law's Prologue and the Pardoner's Tale for which there are no Latin glosses. Because Chaucer's translations are not absolutely literal, however, especially in the Pardoner's Tale, the information provided by a comparison of these passages with the *De Miseria* is bound to be somewhat ambiguous and not nearly so valuable as the evidence from the glosses. Nevertheless, it is important to determine on the basis of the limited evidence whether Chaucer's unglossed passages reflect Lotario's original and, if not, in what ways they differ from it. I use only passages that are literal enough to provide a reasonably close textual comparison.

De Miseria I.14.1–14; Man of Law's Prologue 99–121

> Pauperes enim premuntur inedia, cruciantur erumpna, fame, siti, frigore, nuditate . . . O miserabilis condicio mendicantis! Et si petit, pudore confunditur, et si non petit, egestate consumitur, set ut mendicet necessitate compellitur. Deum causatur iniquum quod non recte dividat; proximum criminatur malignum quod non plene subveniat; indignatur, murmurat, inprecatur. Adverte super hoc sentenciam sapientis: "Melius est mori quam indigere." "Eciam proximo suo pauper odiosus erit." "Omnes dies pauperis mali." "Fratres hominis pauperis oderunt eum, insuper et amici procul recesserunt ab eo."

> O hateful harm, condicion of poverte!
100   With thurst, with coold, with hunger so confoundid!
> To asken help thee shameth in thyn herte;
> If thou noon aske, with nede artow so woundid
> That verray nede unwrappeth al thy wounde hid!
> Maugree thyn heed, thou most for indigence
105   Or stele, or begge, or borwe thy despence!

Thou blamest Crist, and seist ful bitterly,
He mysdeparteth richesse temporal;
Thy neighebor thou wytest synfully,
And seist thou hast to lite, and he hath al.
110 "Parfay," seistow, "somtyme he rekene shal,
Whan that his tayl shal brennen in the gleede,
For he noght helpeth needfulle in hir neede."

Herkne what is the sentence of the wise:
"Bet is to dyen than have indigence";
115 "Thy selve neighebor wol thee despise."
If thou be povre, farwel thy reverence!
Yet of the wise man take this sentence:
"Alle the dayes of povre men been wikke."
Be war, therfore, er thou come to that prikke!

120 If thou be povre, thy brother hateth thee,
And alle thy freendes fleen from thee, allas!

De Miseria II.18.4-5; Pardoner's Tale 534-36

. . . superius et inferius horribilem flatum exprimens, et abominabilem sonum emittens.

O wombe! O bely! O stynkyng cod,
Fulfilled of dong and of corrupcioun!
At either ende of thee foul is the soun.

De Miseria II.17.8-14; Pardoner's Tale 538-46

Alius contundit et colat, alius confundit et conficit, substanciam
vertit in accidens, naturam mutat in artem, ut saturitas transeat in
esuriem, ut fastidium revocet appetitum; ad irritandam gulam,
non ad sustentandum naturam; non ad necessitatem supplendam,
set ad aviditatem explendam.

Thise cookes, how they stampe, and streyne, and grynde,
And turnen substaunce into accident,
To fulfille al thy likerous talent!
Out of the harde bones knokke they
The mary, for they caste noght awey
That may go thurgh the golet softe and swoote.
Of spicerie of leef, and bark, and roote
Shal been his sauce ymaked by delit,
To make hym yet a newer appetit.

Of these three groups of passages, only in the first are the differences between the original and Chaucer's translation worth examining
in detail. In the second "At either ende of thee foul is the soun" is
accurate enough for "superius et inferius . . . abominabilem sonum
emittens." It might be argued that Chaucer has omitted "horribilem

41

flatum exprimens," but it would be difficult to make a case on the basis of the omission because of the paraphrastic nature of the passage; besides, Chaucer may have intended to represent these three words by "Fulfilled of dong and of corrupcioun!" In the last group Chaucer's translation is an expansion of the Latin, again too much in the nature of a paraphrase to warrant any definite conclusions about the Latin source; where Chaucer is literal—in "turnen substaunce into accident" for "substanciam vertit in accidens"—his translation is close to the original Latin.

In the first group, however, the passage from the Man of Law's Prologue is more literal than the passages from the Pardoner's Tale, and it may be possible to detect some differences between Chaucer's translation and the original *De Miseria*. In the interest of clarity, the lines from the Man of Law's Prologue are discussed in order:

Line 99: The word *harm* is not represented in the Latin original, and possibly a Latin equivalent was in Chaucer's source manuscript, but it is more likely that Chaucer either thought that *miserabilis* was a noun and translated it "hateful harm" or added *harm* for the meter. Chaucer's *poverte* does not represent *mendicantis*, and it may be that Chaucer's manuscript had something like *mendicitatis* or *paupertatis*; however, none of the manuscripts that I have collated definitely has either of these forms (though one probably has an abbreviation for the former), and it is possible that Chaucer intended to discuss poverty as a comment on the Man of Law's character and that "of a beggar," the accurate translation of *mendicantis*, would not fit his purpose.

100: Here *nuditate* is omitted, and possibly Chaucer's source manuscript also omitted it, but it would be dangerous to try to determine Chaucer's Latin source manuscript from omissions in his translation, especially since elsewhere it is clear that portions of the *De Miseria* are deliberately omitted (see the passages from the Man of Law's Tale and the corresponding glosses). The order "thurst . . . coold . . . hunger" does not correspond to the original "fame siti frigore," and Chaucer's manuscript may have had a different order; on the other hand, none of the manuscripts that I have collated inverts *fame* and "siti frigore," and Chaucer may have put *hunger* where he did for the meter.

101: Here and elsewhere *thee* and *thyn* are substituted for the third person singular pronouns of the original; this does not necessarily reflect a change in Chaucer's source manuscript but is rather an adaptation of the passage for his artistic purposes. The *et* of the original is not translated, but again it is difficult to determine Chaucer's source manuscript on the basis of an omission; since a number of the manuscripts omit *et*, it seems at least possible that Chaucer's manuscript may also have omitted it, but the omission is by no means a certainty.

102: The *et* of the original is again omitted, and again a number of manuscripts omit it, so that it is possible that Chaucer's source manuscript also omitted it.

103: Chaucer's translation has the active voice instead of the passive, but it is doubtful that any conclusions can be reached about the source manuscript on the basis of this change.

104-5: These lines do not correspond to anything in the Latin original and are no doubt Chaucer's own addition to the text.

106: The change from passive to active is again probably not indicative of the source manuscript. The word *bitterly* may be a misreading on Chaucer's part for *iniquum*, or it may just be Chaucer's addition for the sake of the meter.

107: The phrase "richesse temporal" is not in the original. It is possible that it was in Chaucer's manuscript, although it must be said that Chaucer could have added it on his own to clarify the Latin "quod non recte dividat."

108: The change from passive to active is again probably not indicative of Chaucer's source manuscript.

109-11: These lines do not correspond exactly to anything in the Latin; Chaucer no doubt meant them to be an expansion of "indignatur murmurat inprecatur."

112: Chaucer's *needfulle* has no equivalent in the Latin original; no manuscript that I have collated, however, has anything to correspond to it, and it is probably Chaucer's own addition for the sake of clarification. Chaucer's phrase "in hir neede" is not an accurate translation of *plene* and may reflect a different reading in Chaucer's source manuscript; or it may be his way of making a colorless and ambiguous word more definite; or he may simply have duplicated the meaning of the verb *subveniat*.

113: Here Chaucer omits the "super hoc" from the original; the omission may have been in Chaucer's source manuscript, but again it is uncertain.

115: The change from passive to active is again probably not indicative of Chaucer's source manuscript.

116: This line is added by Chaucer and is no doubt his own. It is not in the original and was probably not in Chaucer's source manuscript.

117: This line is not in the original. I doubt that it was in Chaucer's source manuscript, but it may be either Chaucer's translation of the rubric *Salomon*, which appears in various forms either before or after the sentence "Omnes dies pauperis mali" in some of the manuscripts that I have collated, or a repetition of the earlier "sentenciam sapientis," or simply an indication that Chaucer knew the source of the following quotation.

119: This is Chaucer's addition, perhaps to characterize the Man of

Law. I doubt that anything corresponding to it was in Chaucer's source manuscript.

120: Here "If thou be povre" does not correspond to the original, but is probably Chaucer's own addition for the sake of either clarity or meter. It seems strange that Chaucer has *brother* (singular) for the original *Fratres* since the added *-s* would not change the meter; it is possible, though not imperative, that the singular was in Chaucer's source manuscript.

121: Chaucer's *alle* is not represented in the original and may have corresponded to an addition in the source manuscript; on the other hand, "insuper et amici" means "in addition, even friends," and Chaucer may have wanted to capture the emphasis of the phrase by using *alle*. Latin *procul* is not represented in Chaucer's translation, though it may in conjunction with *recesserunt* have called forth *fleen*; since it is redundant, I doubt that it is possible to say for certain that it was omitted in Chaucer's source manuscript.

It will be noticed immediately that the evidence from this comparison is extremely ambiguous and, in fact, nowhere argues conclusively that Chaucer's source manuscript differed from the original *De Miseria*. I list here some readings that might have been in Chaucer's source manuscript and that differ from the original, but they are not nearly so important as the readings from the glosses in determining Chaucer's text of the *De Miseria*. Following each item are the manuscripts in which it is found; the manuscripts having two or more of the readings are italicized. Because so many manuscripts have readings 4 and 5, I list only those that have at least one other reading.[168]

1. Line 99: addition of a word meaning *harm* (none)
2. Line 99: substitution of a word meaning *poverte* for *mendicantis* (Er^2 probably has the abbreviation for *mendicitatis*; others: *Bs* has *mendacitatis*—an error for *mendicitatis?*—and *Mi* has *pauperis*)
3. Line 100: change in word order (none)
4. Line 101: omission of *et* (64 manuscripts, including $BsL^{11}U^5$)
5. Line 102: omission of *et* (82 manuscripts, including $D^5L^{12}O^{25}U^8Ut^2$)
6. Line 107: addition of a phrase meaning "richesse temporal" (none)
7. Line 112: addition of a word meaning *needfulle* (none)
8. Line 112: substitution of a phrase meaning "in hir neede" for *plene* (none)
9. Line 113: omission of "super hoc" (none; omission of *hoc* only: $C^7L^{43}S^4Wo^1$)
10. Line 117: addition of *Salomon* or something like it (*Salomon*: $Bv^2C^{12}L^{12}Ma^3MiMoO^{25}Ph^1RlT^1U^5U^8Ut^2$; "Salomon in Proverbiis": $L^{41}O^9$; "Unde dicitur in Proverbiis": Bz^2)
11. Line 120: substitution of *Frater* (?) for *Fratres* (none)
12. Line 121: addition of a word meaning *alle* (none)
13. Line 121: omission of *procul* ($Bl^3Bm^1BsD^5Er^1L^{11}O^{18}O^{27}$)

With the primary evidence from the comparison of the glosses with the original and the secondary evidence from the comparison of the unglossed passages with the original, it is now possible to come to some conclusions about the manuscript closest to Chaucer's source manuscript. In the evidence from the glosses it can be seen that only three manuscripts (L^{31}S^{2}Vi) have more than two of the eleven readings and that only five manuscripts (C^{11}Du^{4}Ma^{4}Pa^{5}U^7) have two readings when one is not the very common item 10 or the relatively common items 3, 7, 11. S^2 and Vi have the addition of *eciam* and the omission of *vel*, both of which are common scribal errors. In addition, S^2 has *dileccione* for *delectacione*, which may have been caused by confusion in the abbreviation, and Vi has *sonum* for *sonitum*, which may have been caused either by the similarity in meaning of the two words or by confusion in the abbreviation. The other five manuscripts each have one of the common readings 3, 10, 11. In addition, C^{11}, Du^4, and Pa^5 have *dileccione* for *delectacione*; Ma^4 has *cuius* for *cui*, a substitution that cannot be detected in Chaucer's translation; and U^7 omits "et cytharam," which may or may not reflect Chaucer's source manuscript. By themselves the readings in all these manuscripts are insignificant in determining Chaucer's text of the *De Miseria*: in order to be significant, they would need to accompany one or more of the important readings.

Of the eleven differences between the glosses and the original *De Miseria*, the first three are the most important ones because they are reflected in Chaucer's translation, and any manuscript, in order to qualify as close to Chaucer's source manuscript, would need to have these three at least, regardless of how many other readings it had. Only 1 of the 668 manuscripts that I have examined has the addition of *latet* (L^{31}); only 1 has the addition of "Audi ergo" (L^{31}), though U^4 has *Audi*; and 60 have the addition of *eciam* (including L^{31}), which would have been a fairly common scribal addition. L^{31}, or British Library, MS. Royal 8 F.xiv, is the only manuscript to have all three of the gloss variants that are reflected in Chaucer's translation. That L^{31} has all three, and not just one or two, is of great importance, since it is only by the greatest coincidence that such readings could appear by accident in a single manuscript. It does not, however, have any of the other readings from the glosses.

As might have been expected, the ambiguous evidence from the comparison of the unglossed passages with the *De Miseria* does not shed much light on Chaucer's source manuscript. Only ten manuscripts have two or more of the possible readings (Bs, which has three, and D^{5}Er^{1}L^{11}L^{12}MiO^{25}U^{5}U^{8}Ut^2, which have two). All of these manuscripts except Mi have either the omission of an *et* (items 4 and 5) or the omission of *procul* (item 13), and it is extremely doubtful that Chaucer's source manuscript can be determined only on the basis of omissions.

More interesting is the addition of *Salomon* (item 10), but as I pointed out earlier when discussing line 117, there are other possible explanations for the line. The most interesting reading is the probable substitution in Er¹, and possibly in Bs, of *mendicitatis* for *mendicantis* (item 2), which may have been in Chaucer's source manuscript; Mi has *pauperis*, which is not quite the same thing as *poverte*, though it could have called the English word to Chaucer's mind. There are, however, other possible explanations for the word *poverte,* and, in addition, Er¹, Bs, and Mi (as well as the other seven manuscripts with two or more readings) have against them, as possible source manuscripts, the fact that they have no more than one of the gloss readings and none of the important ones.

THE RELATIONSHIP OF L³¹ TO CHAUCER'S SOURCE MANUSCRIPT

Because it has the three important gloss readings, L³¹ therefore appears to be the closest extant manuscript to Chaucer's source manuscript. It is not, however, the manuscript that Chaucer used, as a comparison of it with the glosses to the Man of Law's Tale, presented earlier, makes clear. In the following all differences between the glosses and L³¹ are italicized.

L³¹, I.21 (Man of Law's Tale 421-27)

> Semper *enim* mundane leticie tristicia repentina succedit . . . Mundana *quippe* felicitas multis amaritudinibus est respersa . . . "extrema gaudii luctus occupat." . . . Audi ergo salubre consilium: *ut* "in die bonorum *non* inmemor *sit* malorum."

L³¹, II.19 (Man of Law's Tale 771-77)

> Quid turpius ebrioso, cui fetor in ore, tremor in corpore; qui *promittit* stulta, prodit occulta; *cui* mens alienatur, facies transformatur? "*Malum* enim latet secretum ubi regnat ebrietas."

L³¹, II.21 (Man of Law's Tale 925-29)

> O extrema libidinis turpitudo, que non solum mentem effeminat, set eciam corpus enervat . . . *pena et dolor secuntur semper* ———.

L³¹, I.20 (Man of Law's Tale 1132-34)

> "A mane usque ad vesperam mutabitur tempus." "Tenent tympanum . . . et gaudent ad *sonitum* organi."

L³¹, I.20 (Man of Law's Tale 1135-38)

> Quis unquam *vel* unicam diem totam *deduxit* in sua *delectacione* iocundam, *quam* in aliqua parte diei *reate* consciencie vel impetus

ire vel motus *concupiscen* non turbaverit? *Que* livor invidie vel ardor avaricie vel tumor superbie non vexaverit? Quem *alia* iactura vel offensa vel *compassio* non commoverit?

The results of the comparison can be classified as follows:

1. Identical variants in Gloss and L[31]: I.21 addition of "Audi ergo"; II.19 addition of *latet*; II.21 addition of *eciam*.

2. Variants in L[31] against original readings in Gloss: I.21 *ut* L[31], omission in Gloss; I.21 *non* L[31], *ne* Gloss; I.21 *sit* L[31], *sis* Gloss; II.19 *promittit* L[31], *promit* Gloss; II.19 *Malum* L[31], *nullum* Gloss; II.21 "pena et dolor secuntur semper" L[31], "semper sequntur dolor et penitencia" Gloss; I.20 *deduxit* L[31], *duxit* Gloss; I.20 *quam* L[31], *quem* Gloss; I.20 *reate* L[31], *reatus* Gloss; I.20 *concupiscen* L[31], *concupiscencie* Gloss; I.20 *Que* L[31], *quem* Gloss; I.20 *alia* L[31], *aliqua* Gloss; I.20 *compassio* L[31], *passio* Gloss.

3. Variants in Gloss against original readings in L[31]: I.21 *igitur* Gloss, *quippe* L[31]; I.21 omission in Gloss, *enim* L[31]; II.19 *cuius* Gloss, *cui* L[31]; II.21 "post et cetera" Gloss, omission in L[31]; I.20 *sonum* Gloss, *sonitum* L[31]; I.20 omission in Gloss, *vel* L[31]; I.20 *dileccione* Gloss, *delectacione* L[31].

It is clear from this list that L[31] has the three most important variants in the glosses, but that it also differs from the readings in the glosses in a number of places. Many of these are careless errors (*non* for *ne*, *sit* for *sis*, *quam* for *quem*, *Que* for *quem*), probably peculiar to the scribe of L[31] and therefore not important. A few readings, however, appear to be important because they do not coincide with Chaucer's translation. The word *nullum* in the gloss is translated *no*, whereas L[31] has *Malum*, which does not fit Chaucer's translation. The word *passio* in the gloss (I.20) is translated *passion* at Man of Law's Tale 1138, whereas L[31] has *compassio*, which does not fit the translation. Other differences in L[31] that may not coincide with Chaucer's translation are the addition of *ut* (I.21), which is not translated at Man of Law's Tale 425: "Herke this conseil for thy sikernesse"; and possibly the word order of "penitencia et dolor secuntur semper" (II.21), which may not be reflected at Man of Law's Tale 928-29: "Th'ende of thy werk, or of thy lustes blynde, / Is compleynyng," although this example is admittedly a dubious one.

A comparison of L[31] with Chaucer's translations in those passages for which there are no marginal glosses also reveals disparities between the two. I give L[31]'s versions of the same three passages that I used earlier, including Chaucer's translation of the first for comparison.

L[31], I.14; Man of Law's Prologue 99-121

Pauperes —— *cruciantur* inedia, *premuntur* erumpna, fame, siti, frigore, *et* nuditate . . . O miserabilis condicio mendicantis! ——

si petit, pudore *confurditur*, —— si non ——, egestate consumitur, sed ut mendicet necessitate compellitur. Deum *causeatur* iniquum, *proximum Deum eo* quod non recte dividat, *iniquum quod non recte dividicat;* proximum *criminanatur* malignum *quia* non plene *subvenit;* indignatur, murmurat, *et* inprecatur. *Audi* super hoc sentenciam sapientis: "Melius est mori quam indigere." "Eciam proximo suo *odiosus erit pauper."* "Omnes dies pauperis mali." Fratres hominis pauperis oderunt eum, insuper —— *amcii* procul recesserunt ab eo."

> O hateful harm, condicion of poverte!
> *With thurst, with coold, with hunger so confoundid!*
> *To asken* help thee shameth in thyn herte;
> *If thou noon aske,* with nede artow so woundid
> That verray nede unwrappeth al thy wounde hid!
> Maugree thyn heed, thou most for indigence
> Or stele, or begge, or borwe thy despence!
>
> Thou blamest Crist, and seist ful bitterly,
> He mysdeparteth richesse temporal;
> Thy neighebor thou wytest synfully,
> And seist thou hast to lite, and he hath al.
> "Parfay," seistow, "somtyme he rekene shal,
> Whan that his tayl shal brennen in the gleede,
> For he noght helpeth needfulle in hir neede."
>
> *Herkne* what is the sentence of the wise:
> "Bet is to dyen than have indigence";
> "Thy selve neighebor wol thee despise."
> If thou be povre, farwel thy reverence!
> Yet of the wise man take this sentence:
> "Alle the dayes of povre men been wikke."
> Be war, therfore, er thou come to that prikke!
>
> If thou be povre, thy brother hateth thee,
> And alle thy freendes fleen from thee, allas!

L[31], II.18 (Pardoner's Tale 534–36)

. . . superius et inferius horribilem flatum exprimens, et abominabilem sonum emittens.

L[31], II.17 (Pardoner's Tale 538–46)

Alius contundit et colat, alius confundit et conficit, substanciam vertit in accidens, naturam mutat in artem, ut *satietas transit* in esuriem, *et* fastidium revocet appetitum, ad *irritandum* gulam, non ad *sustendandam* naturam; non ad necessitatem supplendam, sed ad aviditatem explendam.

In the second passage there are no differences between L[31] and the original. In the third there are five differences between L[31] and the original, but because none of them changes the meaning of the passage, it is impossible to say for certain which readings were in Chaucer's source manuscript.

Only in the first group are the differences worth examining. A few of the readings peculiar to L³¹ may be reflected in Chaucer's translations. L³¹'s *Audi* for the original *Adverte* may be reflected in *Herkne* because the primary meanings of the word (*MED, herkenen*) refer in some way to an act involving the ear.[169] Possibly the omission of the two *et*'s may be reflected at Man of Law's Prologue 101-2, "To asken help . . . / If thou noon aske," but this is highly uncertain. On the other hand, there are peculiarities in L³¹ that are not reflected in Chaucer's translation. The two most obvious are the additions "proximum Deum eo" and "iniquum quod non recte dividicat." In the first of these it appears that the scribe looked ahead four words and copied *proximum*; realizing his mistake, he then repeated *Deum* to retain the meaning of the original. In the second addition the scribe repeated *iniquum* instead of writing *proximum* and then repeated the phrase in the original, "quod non recte dividat," but realizing when he came to *dividat* for a second time that he had made a mistake, wrote *dividicat* in order to vary *dividat*. Neither of these additions is reflected in Chaucer's translation, either because they did not appear in Chaucer's source manuscript or because Chaucer, puzzled by them, understood the Latin well enough to disregard them in his translation: the first explanation seems more likely. The reversal of *premuntur* and *cruciantur* may not have been in Chaucer's source manuscript because *cruciantur* should probably be as close as possible to "fame siti frigore." The omission of *petit* may not be reflected in Chaucer's translation; at Man of Law's Prologue 102 Chaucer has "If thou noon aske." But it is possible that Chaucer, in changing the third person singular verb *petit* to ·the second person singular "thou . . . aske," felt obliged to repeat the verb to make his meaning clear. In short, very little, if any, of the evidence presented here is conclusive. *Audi* may be in favor of L³¹; the two additions may be against L³¹. The rest is uncertain.

CHAUCER'S MANUSCRIPT OF THE *DE MISERIA*

It is clear from the preceding evidence that Chaucer's manuscript of the *De Miseria* no longer exists. Of the extant manuscripts L³¹ is the closest to it in the important readings from the glosses—in fact, uniquely so—and perhaps close in some minor readings, but it differs in a number of other readings. If one is to recover Chaucer's manuscript, therefore, one must reconstruct it, and in Appendix II I have presented data on which such a reconstruction could be made. My conclusions there are (1) that L^{31} belongs to a large group of manuscripts, primarily British, that exhibit a textual tradition consistently different from either Lotario's original or Chaucer's manuscript; (2) that, within this group of manuscripts, L^{31} is most closely related to C^{18} (Cambridge University Library MS. Dd.1.21), which itself forms a genetic group with C^{14} (Cambridge Peterhouse MS. 219); (3) that L^{31} is a contaminated member of the large group of manuscripts, with its base strain similar to that in C^{18} and C^{14} and with the contamination deriving from a group manuscript; and (4) that the contamination, along with the carelessness of the scribe of L^{31} (or the scribe of his exemplar), can account for the differences and similarities between it and Chaucer's manuscript. The following partial stemma illustrates the relationship between L^{31} and Chaucer's manuscript:

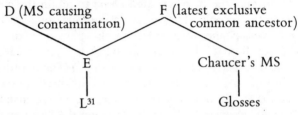

If one were attempting to reconstruct Chaucer's manuscript, therefore, one would do so by using L^{31} as the base manuscript but purged of the group readings, certainly those in the list at the end of Appendix II and probably most of the corroborative readings, though this could only be determined after a careful analysis of the individual items. In addition, one should examine the misreadings caused by the carelessness of the scribe (or by the scribe of his exemplar) to see whether the purging of certain patterns from L^{31} might bring us closer to Chaucer's manuscript: I am thinking here particularly of *Malum* for *Nullum,* which was clearly not in Chaucer's version of Book II, chapter 19, and some of the readings in Appendix II, p. 259, but doubtless many of the other peculiarities in L^{31} were also not in Chaucer's manuscript. However, because L^{31} breaks off towards the end of Book II, chapter 36 (at line 14, with *homo*), the kind of reconstruction that I have outlined could only be applied for the first two thirds of the text. From Book II, chapter 36 on, the only possible way to recover what was in the base strain of L^{31} (and therefore in Chaucer's manuscript) would be to use C^{18} as the base manuscript, purged of group readings, both those in Appendix II and, where applicable, those used as corroboration for the group; in addition, a very careful and skeptical eye should be cast at the readings in which C^{14} and C^{18} agree against the other manuscripts: some of these readings might reflect the base strain of Chaucer's manuscript (on the grounds that L^{31} has some similarities to C^{14}–C^{18} until it breaks off), but because of the extensive evidence for C^{14}–C^{18} as a genetic group, most of them would not.

THE TEXT OF THIS EDITION

In the case of the *De Miseria*, the limited evidence does not warrant printing this kind of reconstructed text, nor is it in line with the purpose and policies of the Chaucer Library. I have therefore chosen as text a manuscript of the *De Miseria* that is typical of the kind in existence and circulating in Britain during the Middle Ages, putting the information necessary for reconstructing Chaucer's manuscript, as well as readings from other textual traditions, into the critical apparatus. Such a text brings us much closer to the *De Miseria* as it was read in the Middle Ages than a reconstruction of either Chaucer's manuscript or Lotario's original, and it should therefore be of value and use to anyone who is interested in the transmission and influence of the *De Miseria* in the Middle Ages. The criteria of typicality on which the manuscript was chosen are the following:

1. TITLE. As I pointed out earlier (p. 23), the most popular title to the *De Miseria* was *De Miseria Humane Conditionis,* which appears, either by itself or in combination, in over 44 percent of the manuscripts. Among British manuscripts,[170] 46 percent have *De Miseria Humane Conditionis,* either by itself or in combination. The nearest competitor is *De Contemptu Mundi,* which is the characteristic title of group manuscripts. Omitting group manuscripts from the total number of British manuscripts, I find that nearly 60 percent have *De Miseria Humane Conditionis;* the remaining 40 percent have either *De Contemptu Mundi* (16 percent) or no title (12 percent) or *De Miseria Hominis* (11 percent) or another title. *De Miseria Humane Conditionis* is therefore the typical title to Lotario's treatise and was probably in Chaucer's manuscript as well, for as I pointed out earlier (pp. 20–23), "Of the Wreched Engendrynge of Mankynde" could easily be a translation of it.[171]

2. CONTENTS. The great majority of manuscripts, when they contain a complete *De Miseria,* exhibit all the chapters (and no extra chapters) in Lotario's original as reconstructed by Maccarrone except three. The three in question are the original chapters 2, 3, and 8 of Book III, the first two of which would go between Book II, chapter 41 and Book III, chapter 1 of the present edition and the last of which would go between chapters 4 and 5 of Book III (see Appendix III).

Over two-thirds of all manuscripts, and over 90 percent of the British manuscripts, omit these three chapters. They would therefore not appear in a typical manuscript of the *De Miseria*.

The prologue is the only other section of the text over which the manuscripts show some hesitation, nearly 10 percent of all manuscripts, though just over 5 percent of the British manuscripts, omitting it, perhaps because the first part (entitled *Prefacio* in the present edition) so often duplicated information in the title and the second was considered superfluous to the contemptus mundi genre of which the work was a part. Clearly, however, the prologue was a characteristic feature of the *De Miseria* as it circulated in the Middle Ages.

Finally, only 24 percent of the British manuscripts (nearly 30 percent when the group manuscripts are omitted) have a table of contents, either complete at the beginning or end or partial before each book. (Though I have not taken a count of the non-British manuscripts for this feature, I suspect that they would exhibit the table of contents rather more often than the British manuscripts but that it would not appear in a majority of them.) The reason for the omission of a feature that was doubtless in Lotario's original was probably that the scribes considered it superfluous, duplicating as it always did the titles to the individual titles within the text, and therefore too space-consuming. In any case, a table of contents is not typical of the *De Miseria* as it circulated in Britain in the Middle Ages.

3. DIVISION OF CHAPTERS. The vast majority of the manuscripts has the chapter divisions that were in Lotario's original and that are represented in the present edition. In only three cases do the manuscripts deviate from these divisions to any significant degree or with any consistent pattern. First, Book I, chapter 2 in Lotario's original includes the first twelve lines of chapter 3 in this edition, the original chapter 3 beginning with "Est autem duplex" at line 13 and entitled *De Conceptione Infantis*. However, nearly 80 percent of all manuscripts, and over 90 percent of the British manuscripts, have the division in this edition, and of the six British manuscripts to retain the chapter 3 beginning as in Lotario's original, four have in addition another chapter beginning with "An illud" (chap. 3, line 1 in this edition).

Second, in Lotario's original Book I, chapter 9 of this edition is divided into two chapters, the second beginning with "Si quis autem" at line 17 and entitled *De Incommodo Senectutis*, making a total of thirty chapters in the original Book I. However, three quarters of all manuscripts, and over 90 percent of the British manuscripts, combine the two chapters into one, entitled either *De Incommodis Senectutis et Brevitate Vite* (with variations) or, less often, just *De Incommodis Senectutis*, as in this edition.

Finally, there is considerable hesitation in the manuscripts as to where Book III should begin. The original chapter 1 to Lotario's Book III (as reconstructed by Maccarrone) is Book II, chapter 41 in the present edition, and its original affiliations can be seen in its content, which is closer to the matters in Book III than to those in Book II.[172] Only 27 percent of all manuscripts (and only 7 percent of the British manuscripts) begin Book III with this chapter. 70 percent of all manuscripts (and all but three of the manuscripts that omit the original chapters 2, 3, and 8), and 90 percent of the British manuscripts (with no exceptions among those that omit the original chapters 2, 3, and 8), begin Book III with the original chapter 4 (Book III, chap. 1, in this edition).

4. VARIANT READINGS. In making my collations for this edition, I discovered 394 readings in which a majority of the 208 collated manuscripts differed from Lotario's original as reconstructed by Maccarrone. Though among these 394 readings there are more nonstriking ones (minor additions, short omissions, transpositions of words, etc.) than striking, their persistence is important and qualifies them as typical features of the De Miseria—typical, that is, at least of British manuscripts, since the manuscripts in British libraries and of British provenance amount to over half of the collated manuscripts. I have, however, collated a number of continental manuscripts, both group and nongroup, and I would judge, on the basis of the evidence from them, that the majority of the 394 readings would be typical of continental manuscripts as well. In any case, because I am interested primarily in presenting a manuscript typical of the kind that Chaucer could have seen, these variant readings constitute very important evidence for choosing that manuscript.

5. PROVENANCE. Everything else being equal, the manuscript should be of demonstrably or presumably British provenance.

Omitting all condensations and fragments, all manuscripts containing excerpts or otherwise incomplete texts,[173] and all group and contaminated manuscripts, and then applying the five criteria to the remaining manuscripts, I could easily eliminate all but nineteen: $(AC^3C^7C^{15}C^{16}L^1L^3L^{10}L^{20}L^{27}L^{30}L^{42}L^{44}L^{46}O^3O^{11}O^{22}O^{27}O^{29})$. Of these nineteen, none emerged as the perfect choice, but on balance L^{20} (British Library, Lansdowne 358) seemed the best. It conforms to all the criteria in the second and third categories except that it contains a table of contents, which is not a typical feature of the De Miseria as it circulated in Britain in the Middle Ages. Unlike the other features of these two categories, however, the presence or absence of a table of contents would not affect a reader's perception of the text, and as there is no pattern to the manuscripts that contain a table of contents, apparently scribes felt freer to keep or discard this feature than to omit a portion of the text or to tamper with chapter divisions. As for the fourth category, L[20] has 87 percent (342 out of 394) of the typical variant readings; it has the most common title to Lotario's treatise; and it has a specific British provenance (Battle Abbey).[174]

The closest competitors are L[1] (British Library, Arundel 332) and C[3] (Cambridge, Corpus Christi College 459). L[1] conforms to all the criteria in the first, second, third, and fifth categories but falls down in the important fourth category (with only 323, or 80 percent, of the readings). More importantly, L[1] has a number of textual omissions that are not characteristic of the great majority of the manuscripts. Moreover, L[31], the manuscript whose base strain is closest to the gloss readings, is remarkably free of omissions (whether this freedom is due to its group strain or its nongroup strain is impossible to know). It therefore seems best, in order to represent a typical manuscript of the *De Miseria* and also to bring us close to Chaucer's text, to choose a manuscript that is as free of omissions, especially atypical ones as in L[1], as possible.

C[3] has the highest number of typical variant readings (363 out of 394, or 92 percent) and conforms to all the criteria in the first, second, and fifth categories, but it has two deviations from the typical divisions of chapters: it combines chapters 3 and 4 of Book II into a single chapter entitled *De Acceptione Personarum* (the usual title to chapter 3) and chapters 40 and 41 of Book II into a single chapter entitled *De Fuscatione Colorum* (the usual title to chapter 40). These two combinations appear often enough in British manuscripts (25 percent and 28 percent respectively; omitting group manuscripts, 34 percent and 36 percent respectively) to constitute a persistent tradition—a tradition that, because it is reinforced by readings in common among many of the manuscripts that have the combinations, may even have the status of a variational group. I decided against using C[3], however, because these two combinations are more important deviations from the typical *De Miseria* than the inclusion of a table of contents in L[20], and the slightly higher percentage of typical variant readings in C[3] did not tip the scales in its favor.[175]

EDITORIAL PRINCIPLES

The text of this edition is an unemended transcription of L[20], including marginalia, except that capitalization and punctuation have been modernized according to English usage,[176] abbreviations (including numbers) silently expanded according to the scribe's usage, and *u* and *v*

54

regularized (with *u* for vowels and *v* for consonants); in the joining or separation of parts of words, primarily compounds, I have followed the scribe's usual practice except where he produces forms that are clearly abnormal or impossible. In certain passages from the Bible (and in one place in the *Prefacio*), where the scribe appears to know his text so well that he omits all but the initial letters of the words, I have used italics to indicate the missing letters, but as the scribe is very clear in his use of abbreviations, I have not felt the need to use italics elsewhere: the occasional ambiguity is recorded in the critical apparatus. I would have preferred, in accordance with the scribe's usage, to use *u* for all occurrences of modern *u* and *v*, as I have used *i* for all occurrences of modern *i* and *j*, but whereas *i* seldom produces confusion when written for *j* because it usually appears in well-known proper nouns (*Iob, Ierusalem*, etc.) or in common words (*iustus, iudicii*, etc.), *u* appears so frequently and in so many kinds of words in Medieval Latin that to reproduce it everywhere would impede the reader's understanding of the text. My aim throughout has been to preserve as much as I could of the final appearance of the manuscript, as intended by the scribe or by his supervisor, without making the text inaccessible to readers who are not specialists in Medieval Latin.

The only changes I have made in the text of L[20] are to omit the tables of contents that appear before each book on the grounds that they would not have appeared in the typical manuscript of the *De Miseria* circulating in the Middle Ages[177] and to add chapter numbers (and one title) in brackets where L[20] does not have them, using Arabic numbers rather than Roman (as appear in the tables of contents) for clarity of reference when discussing book and chapter together.[178] A few corrections appear in L[20], and these I have incorporated into the text, with entries in the critical apparatus noting the nature of the correction: they take the form either of scrapings in the text, with corrections written over, or of marginal and occasional above-line additions and appear to be in the same hand as that of the text. I would judge that the corrections in the text, both those over scrapings and those above the line, are from the manuscript used in the copying of the text but that probably the marginal additions are from another manuscript.

L[20] London, British Library, Lansdowne 358, ff. 78–109v.[179] Vellum, 199 ff. of which 1–5 and 195–199 are flyleaves, 7″ by 5″; British Museum binding (1970). Consists of two manuscripts bound together, the first (ff. 6–147v) in one hand of the first half of the thirteenth century, the second in one hand of the late twelfth century. The *De Miseria* is one of three items in the first manuscript (collation: i–v[10], vi[12], vii–viii[10], ix[12], x–xii[10], xiii[8]).

Contents of the first manuscript: (1) St. Bernard, *De Consideratione* (no title in the manuscript), ff. 6–77v; (2) *De Miseria Condicionis Humane* (as in manuscript), ff. 78–109v; (3) Anonymous treatise in Latin on the Office of the Mass (no title in the manuscript), beginning "[T] ria sunt in quibus lex precipue anima consistit Mandata Promissa Sacramenta," ff. 110–147v, ending imperfectly at the bottom of f. 147v with "misterium plenius explicare" (cf. the same treatise in British Library, Royal 5 A.i, ff. 43–63, 13th c.).

The second manuscript contains three works by Peter of Blois (*Compendium in Iob, De Conversione Sancti Pauli,* and *De Transfiguratione Domini*) and also ends imperfectly.

The initials in the *De Miseria* are, with very few exceptions, alternating red and green, beginning with red for *D* in *Domino* at the beginning of the *Prefacio;* all titles, all numbers in tables of contents, and all marginal references are in red. The marginal references are correlated with quotations in the text by means of a mark over or by a flourishing in red of the first letter of the first word in the quotation.

Provenance: Battle, Benedictine Abbey of St. Martin, Pressmark FX.

The critical apparatus to this edition is as important and as interesting as the text because it presents the evidence necessary for reconstructing Chaucer's text of the *De Miseria*, a generous sampling of readings from various textual traditions and of the kinds of alterations made by scribes during the transmission of the text, and ample evidence for reconstructing, except for minor readings (e.g., *enim* for *autem*, or the omission or addition of words like *et, eciam,* etc.), the text of Lotario's original. The main manuscripts to be found in the critical apparatus are the following:

L[31] London, British Library, Royal 8 F.xiv, ff. 180v–183v. Vellum, 204 ff. of which ff. 1–6 are flyleaves, 11″ by 7.75″; binding: vellum of the nineteenth century. Consists of a number of manuscripts from the thirteenth and fourteenth centuries bound together. The *De Miseria* is one of three items in a manuscript of one gathering of twelve leaves in double columns in an English hand of the second quarter of the thirteenth century (after 1237).

Contents: various Latin works, primarily theological (twenty-seven items in all), including Pope Gregory's *Libri Dialogorum*, Hugh of St. Victor's *De Arca Noe, Didascalicon,* and *De Institutione Noviciorum,* Richard of Bury's *Philobiblon,* Bishop Martin of Braga's *Formula Honeste Vite,* St. Bernard's *De Dispensatione et Precepto,* the Rule of St. Francis, the *Ymago Mundi*, and a life of St. Edmund of Canterbury. The items in the manuscript containing the *De Miseria* are: (1) *De Interpretacione Nominum Ebreorum* (title apparently in later hand), an abridged form of a work by Bede or more likely Remigius of Auxerre, ff. 172ra–178va; (2) *Constituciones Othonis Legati* (as in table of contents on f. 6v; no title in manuscript), promulgated at the Council of London in 1237, ff. 178vb–180rb; (3) *Innocencius de Miseria Hominis et de Contemptu Mundi* (as in table of contents; no title in manuscript), ff. 180va–183vb; the text of the *De Miseria* breaks off in Book II, chapter 36, at line 11, but there are the catchwords "si deus" in the lower right hand corner of f. 183v, and originally the text may have continued. For further details of the contents of the other manuscripts bound with the one containing the *De Miseria*, see Sir George F. Warner and Julius P. Gilson, *British Museum. Catalogue of Western Manuscripts in the Old Royal and King's Collections* (London: Oxford University Press, 1921), 1, 270–272.

The initials in the manuscript containing the *De Miseria* are red and flourished in red, though not consistently. In the *De Miseria* only the prologue and Book I, chapter 1 have red initials; for most of the other chapters initials are written lightly in the margins.

Provenance: Bury St. Edmunds, Benedictine Abbey of St. Edmund, Pressmark G.15. One of the manuscripts "acquired" for Bury by Henry of Kirkestede and "in all probability . . . intended for the instruction of novices," for "Its contents [are] an introduction to ecclesiastical literature and the monastic ideal."[180] Not necessarily written at Bury, but the table of contents is in Kirkestede's hand, and there are annotations by him throughout, including a brief work in his own hand on ff. 138v–139, *De Septem Gradibus Contemplacionis*. The latest work in the manuscript is the *Philobiblon* (ca. 1344), which provides the terminus a quo for the putting together of the collection; Kirkestede's death, probably a few years after 1378, provides the terminus ad quem.[181]

For L[31], which is the most important manuscript for reconstructing Chaucer's text of the *De Miseria*, I have recorded all deviations from L[20], including transpositions, except minor spelling differences (including the variation of t/d in *sed*, n/m, c/t, and the doubling of single consonants and the singling of double consonants) and obvious misreadings (e.g., *Tutulum* for *Titulum* in the prologue, or *spurcssimo* for *spurcissimo* in Book I, chapter 1). I have followed the same principles in recording corrections, of which there are very few in this manuscript: those in the text and above the line are in the same hand as the text; those few in the margins are in another hand. In addition, in order to keep the size of the critical apparatus reasonably small, I do not record the fact at the beginning of each chapter that L³¹ has no titles anywhere in the text of the *De Miseria*.

C¹⁴ Cambridge, Peterhouse, 219, ff. 1–20v. Vellum, iv + 161 + iii ff., 10.75″ by 7.5″; binding: eighteenth-century vellum, made from an old title deed. In various hands of the fourteenth century. Double columns. Catchwords.

Contents: various Latin works, almost exclusively theological, of which the *De Miseria* (entitled *De Vilitate Humane Materie et de Contemptu Mundi* in the manuscript) is the first of nineteen items, followed by the *Speculum Peccatoris* attributed to St. Augustine, the *Meditationes* of St. Anselm, Hugh of St. Victor's *De Anima*, the *Homilia de Maria Magdalena* by pseudo-Origen, the *Meditationes* of pseudo-St. Bernard, etc. For further details of the contents of this manuscript see M. R. James, *A Descriptive Catalogue of the Manuscripts in the Library of Peterhouse* (Cambridge: Cambridge University Press, 1899), pp. 267–270.

Titles occasionally tipped in red; all initials (except in table of contents) are red, beginning with the capital *D* in *Domino* in the prologue.

Provenance: on last leaf is "Liber Will . . . ," but it is erased. At Peterhouse by 1600 but probably not written there; not listed in the catalogue of 1418.

C¹⁸ Cambridge, University Library, Dd.1.21, ff. 147v–151v. Vellum, i + 213 ff. (out of 218: 130–132, 205–206 cut out), 16.75″ by 10.75″; binding: speckled calf, blind tooled (rebacked) of the sixteenth century. In several clear fourteenth-century English hands; the *De Miseria* (item 10) is in a hand of the early fourteenth century along with items 2 through 9 and part of 1. Double columns, 100 lines per column in the *De Miseria*.

Contents: thirty-one items, primarily St. Augustine's *De Civitate Dei* (ff. 1–127v) and works by or attributed to St. Anselm, including *Cur Deus Homo*, the *Proslogion*, *In Casu Diaboli*, *Meditatio I*, *Oratio VII*, etc., among which appears the *De Miseria Condicionis Humane* (as in manuscript) on ff. 147v–151v. For a detailed description of the contents see the unpublished description by M. R. James revised by H. L. Pink at the Cambridge University Library.

In the *De Miseria* the capital *D* in *Domino* in the prologue is gold, blue, and red on a reddish background. Most initials are blue on a red-lined background; a few are red on a blue-lined background. Titles from beginning through I.10 and from II.5 to 30 are in red; titles to I.11 and from I.14 through II.4 are in black; no titles after II.30. Marginalia in now brownish ink.

Provenance: England, though the manuscript cannot be assigned a specific location. Two sixteenth-century English notes on f. i, including the name of a former owner (?) in an early sixteenth-century hand: "Roberte Wodward."

For C^{14} and C^{18}, the two manuscripts closest to L^{31} (especially C^{18}), I have recorded all substantive readings (that is, all readings that substantially change the meaning: additions, substitutions, and most omissions of nouns, verbs, adjectives, and adverbs; changes in tense, number, and voice of verbs; changes in number of nouns, and in case except after prepositions); all readings, no matter how insignificant, shared by C^{14} and C^{18}; and nonsubstantive readings in one of the manuscripts if they are shared by other manuscripts, if they shed any light on readings in L^{31}, or if they illustrate certain scribal habits that might be used from Book II, chapter 36 on in reconstructing Chaucer's text. I have not recorded transpositions in one manuscript only, minor spelling differences, obvious misreadings, and minor additions, substitutions, and omissions. For C^{14}, which is a heavily corrected manuscript (in the text and above the line in both the same and another hand, in the margins always in another hand, in all cases from a manuscript different from the exemplar of the main text), I have cited only those corrections that are of interest to the transmission of the *De Miseria* in the Middle Ages or that shed some light on the readings in L^{31}. For C^{18} I have recorded simplifications of compound verbs (a common characteristic in this manuscript) and examples of homeoteleuton (that is, omissions produced by the eye's jumping from one word to an identical or very similar one later on) only when they shed some light on the readings in L^{31} or are shared by other manuscripts; for corrections, which are either in the text or above the line, written in a hand different from that of the text but probably from the same manuscript, I have followed the same principles as for the corrections in C^{14}.

C^3 Cambridge, Corpus Christi College, 459, ff. 1-22v. Vellum, iii + 159 ff., 6.5″ by 4″; binding: eighteenth-century, boards with leather spine. In a number of thirteenth-century hands. The *De Miseria* is written all in one hand, which does not return again, and is complete in two gatherings, one of ten and one of twelve.

Contents: various theological works in Latin, of which the *De Miseria Humane Condicionis* (as in manuscript) is the first item of twenty-five, followed by the Rule of St. Basil, Robert Grosseteste's treatise (or sermon) on Confessors, the *De Spiritu et Anima* attributed to St. Augustine, works by St. Bernard and St. Anselm, etc., for further details of which see M. R. James, *A Descriptive Catalogue of the Manuscripts in the Library of Corpus Christi College Cambridge* (Cambridge: Cambridge University Press, 1912), vol. 2, 383-388.

Titles to the *De Miseria* are in red, with initials in red, blue, or black. Initials to chapters are, with a few exceptions, alternating red and blue, beginning with blue for *D* in *Domino* in the prologue. Marginalia in red. A few corrections, both in text and above the line.

Provenance: Peterborough, Benedictine Abbey of Sts. Peter, Paul, and Andrew, item X.11 in late fourteenth-century catalogue.

For C[3], which contains a few more majority readings than L[20] and which illustrates another British textual tradition, I have recorded all substantive variants but only those nonsubstantive variants that shed some light on the readings in L[31] or are shared by other manuscripts.

C[10] Cambridge, Magdalene College, F.4.15, ff. 1-22. Vellum, i + 208 ff., 9.5″ by 6.3″; binding: late eighteenth or early nineteenth-century plain marbled cloth, rebacked. In many hands of the twelfth to fourteenth centuries. The *De Miseria* is in a thirteenth-century hand, in double columns of thirty-two lines (collation: i-ii[8], iii[6]).

Contents: various theological works in Latin, of which the *De Miseria* (entitled *De Contemptu Mundi* in the manuscript) is the first item of thirteen, followed by the *Scintille* by Defensor of Ligugé, the *Speculum Ecclesie* by Hugh of St. Victor, various sermons, etc., for further details of which see M. R. James, *A Descriptive Catalogue of the Manuscripts in the College Library of Magdalene College Cambridge* (Cambridge: Cambridge University Press, 1909), pp. 40-43.

The initials in the *De Miseria* are, with a few exceptions, alternating red and blue, beginning with blue for *D* in *Domino* in the prologue. All titles and marginalia in red. Some corrections both in text and in margins, probably from a nongroup manuscript, in same hand as text, often apparently based on lightly written corrections made in the margins in another hand (the proofreader's?).

Provenance: Stamford, Franciscan Convent, given by John, Rector of the Church of Allenton.

E[1] Edinburgh, University Library, 107, ff. 1-28v. Vellum, ii + 192 + i ff., 7″ by 4.75″; binding: modern, blue morocco, with gold tooling. The first part of the manuscript (ff. 1-166v), including the *De Miseria*, is in late thirteenth-century gothic script, double columns; the second part (ff. 167-end) is in a fourteenth-century English hand, single columns.

Contents: various works, primarily theological and in Latin, with a few in French and one in English, of which the *De Miseria* (entitled *De*

Contemptu Mundi in the manuscript) is the first of twenty-one, followed by Bishop Martin of Braga's *Formula Honeste Vite*, works by Hugh of Folieto, various tales, legends, prayers, meditations, including five meditations in English from Richard Rolle's *Form of Perfect Living*, for further details of which see Catherine R. Borland, *A Descriptive Catalogue of the Western Mediaeval Manuscripts in Edinburgh University Library* (Edinburgh: Edinburgh University Library, 1916), pp. 168-170.

The initials in the *De Miseria* are, with a few exceptions, alternating blue and red; the capital *D* in *Domino* in the prologue is red and blue. All titles are in red.

Provenance: probably England because of the "unmistakably English script" of ff. 167-end, though the manuscript cannot be assigned a specific location.

As it would increase the size of the critical apparatus immensely and unnecessarily to give sigils of every group or contaminated manuscript for every group reading, I have chosen one manuscript, C^{10}, as the representative of the group because, from the figures at the end of Appendix II, it has the group readings more often than any other manuscript. From C^{10} I have recorded only the group readings from Appendix II and the corroborative readings for the group that I have discovered in my collations (that is, all evidence in which all, or nearly all, group manuscripts and very few, or no, nongroup manuscripts have certain readings). To do otherwise—that is, to present all the features of C^{10} or of any group manuscript—would be very misleading for anyone who was attempting to decide what readings to purge from L^{31} in order to reconstruct Chaucer's text of the *De Miseria*. In the few places where C^{10} does not have the group reading, I have used E^1, another group manuscript, in its place. Whenever C^{10} or E^1 appears in the critical apparatus, therefore, it indicates a group reading.

Ro Rome, Biblioteca Vallicelliana, F. 26, ff. 66-86v. Vellum, 126 ff., 8.25″ by 5.3″. Consists of four manuscripts bound together, of various dates. The *De Miseria*, in the second manuscript, is in a hand of the late twelfth century.

Contents of second manuscript: (1) *De Miseria* (no title in manuscript originally; a postmedieval hand adds *De Miseria Humanae Vitae . . . de Contemptu Mundi*), followed by an additional chapter entitled *De Proprietatibus Romanorum*, taken from Book IV of St. Bernard's *De Consideratione*, ff. 66-86v; (2) anonymous treatise, *De Mortalitate* (no title in manuscript), in a hand different from that of the *De Miseria*, ff. 87-87v; (3) f. 96r-v, blank.

Contents of the other manuscripts: The first contains Peter Damian, *Expositio Historiarum Veterii Testamenti,* ff. 2–65v; the third, anonymous sermons and epistles in Latin, ff. 88–95v, on much smaller leaves inserted in the second manuscript; and the fourth, Arator, *Actus Apostolorum,* two metrical books, ff. 97–126v.

In the *De Miseria* the initials, titles, and biblical additions above the line are in red. Some corrections, both in same hand as the text and in another hand.

Provenance: probably Rome or in the Roman region.

V² Vatican City, Biblioteca Apostolica Vaticana, Regin. lat. 71, ff. 1–33v. Vellum, 65 ff., 6.7″ by 4.8″; seventeenth-century binding. Consists of two manuscripts bound together, the first (ff. 1–33v) in a hand of the beginning of the thirteenth century, the second (ff. 34–65v) primarily in one English hand of the thirteenth–fourteenth century (ff. 34–62), with ff. 62–64v in another hand probably of the same date.

Contents of the first manuscript: the *De Miseria* alone (entitled *Liber Lotharius ab Actoris Nomine Vocatus,* which may mean that it is descended from a manuscript written before Lotario's elevation to the papacy in 1198), followed by an additional chapter entitled *De Proprietatibus Romanorum* as in Ro. The second manuscript contains two works by Gérard of Liège on ff. 34–62, followed by miscellaneous items on ff. 62–65v, for further details of which see Andreas Wilmart, *Codices Reginenses Latini,* I (Vatican: Biblioteca Vaticana, 1937), 156–158.

In the *De Miseria* the initials and titles are in red. A few corrections, in a fourteenth-century hand.

Provenance: unknown.

Ro and V² are the two manuscripts judged by Maccarrone to have been closest to Lotario's original, either having come from the original or from a copy of the original, with Ro the more authoritative of the two because it seems to have been written in Rome or in the Roman region probably between 1195 (the date of composition of the *De Miseria*) and 1198 (the date of Lotario's elevation to the papacy as Pope Innocent III).[182] Ro is not the original itself: its scribe (or the scribe of its exemplar) was very erratic (or ignorant, or careless) and produced (or preserved) readings that are clearly not original and that appear in very few, if any, of the other manuscripts.[183] I have recorded only substantive readings from Ro that are closer to Lotario's presumed original, based on my examination and collations of the manuscripts, than those in L²⁰. The only nonsubstantive readings that I have recorded are in the chapters that Chaucer made use of and in places where I have had occasion to record nonsubstantive variants from other manuscripts. In places where Ro does not have the original reading, I have used V^2 in its place if it preserves the original reading. Whenever Ro or V^2 appears in the critical apparatus, therefore, it indicates a reading closer to Lotario's presumed original than the one in L^{20}.[184]

In addition to these eight manuscripts, I have recorded selectively, from a number of other manuscripts,[185] readings that illuminate readings, or the origin of readings, in L^{20} and L^{31}; readings from other textual traditions; certain scribal changes in words and forms that shed some light on the transmission of the text; and readings that are interesting or important in interpreting parts of the text. I have given rather more variants for chapters that Chaucer used (Book I, chapters 14, 20, 21; Book II, chapters 17–20) than for others and in general rather more in Books I and II than in III: I and II seem to have called forth more scribal change and embellishment than the more conventional III. When other manuscripts accompany L^{31} in its striking readings, the list of manuscripts is complete for the 208 that I have collated; in general, however, I have been selective both in the readings I have recorded and in the manuscripts given for each reading: my main interest has been to give examples of readings that illuminate the meaning, context, and transmission of the *De Miseria* as it comes down to and is read by Chaucer and others during the later Middle Ages.

In the critical apparatus the line number is given first, followed by the lemma (that is, the reading in L^{20}) in boldface type, the variant(s), and finally the manuscript sigil(s), which can be found in Appendix I, for each variant. Separate variants are set off by semicolons, and all variants for a given lemma by a period; a comma is used only within an entry for a given variant, to indicate that a particular manuscript has a peculiarity that sets it apart from the other manuscripts exhibiting the same variant. In recording the variants themselves I have followed the same general editorial principles as for L^{20} except that occasionally I italicize abbreviations or retain the abbreviations themselves where there is ambiguity. In both lemma and variants I retain the capitalization of the base text. I do not, however, retain the punctuation of the base text because it would cause confusion with the commas, semicolons, and periods used for specific purposes in the critical apparatus, nor do I use a period after single-letter abbreviations of whole words for the same reason (thus, *n*, for example, would stand for the abbreviation *n.* in L^{31} at I.14.14–15).

Variants from the main manuscripts are listed according to the alphabetical order of their sigils ($C^3C^{10}C^{14}C^{18}E^1L^{31}RoV^2$) unless, for clarity of presentation, it seemed appropriate to deviate slightly from this order (see, for example, *operantur* at I.12.16); the only fixed exception is that when I have occasion to comment on a correction in L[20], that comment always comes before the variants. The variant is always an accurate representation of the reading in the manuscript in question or, where more than one manuscript has it, in the first manuscript in the list; in a list of main manuscripts the reading will always be the same in all manuscripts except for minor differences in spelling. The order of sigils after a variant is always alphabetical except when, for clarity, I use a manuscript other than the alphabetically first one for a reading (see, for example, *insompnes* at I.15.26). Variants from manuscripts other than the main manuscripts follow the main manuscripts and conform to the same general principles except that they are listed according to my sense of their relative importance rather than their alphabetical order, and in a list of such manuscripts the reading in subsequent manuscripts will always be the same as that in the first except for minor differences in spelling and occasional additions or omissions of insignificant words (*et, enim,* etc.).

Some refinements are inevitable. For variants that are additions to the base text, in which it is necessary to repeat the lemma, the addition follows the lemma except when, in order to keep related units together, the addition precedes the lemma. For additions above the line or in the margins, which are especially prevalent in C[14], the form "**sepulchrum** sepulcrum vel tumulus *above line* C[14]" at I.1.11 means that only the addition "vel tumulus" is above the line; in ambiguous cases, of which there are very few, I have resorted to circumlocutions to clarify the situation in the manuscript. Occasionally L[20] has group readings, and to indicate these I have put the C[10] sigil immediately after the square bracket, before giving any variants (for example, **torquetur** at I.9.28–29). For transpositions, which I consider of greater importance than most editors do, primarily because they so often follow patterns set by substantive readings, I have used the following formula wherever possible in order to save space: "**aqua . . . panis** *trans*," which means that only the two words given are transposed and that the transposition does not involve the intervening word or words.

Most abbreviations used in the critical apparatus are self-explanatory: *om* for *omitted, incl* for *including, MS(S)* for *manuscript(s), trans* for *transposed.* Those that are not self-explanatory are *many MSS* and *most MSS.* One of the purposes of Appendix II and the only reason for using a single manuscript, C[10], as the representative of the group is to keep the critical apparatus to a manageable size: it would be superfluous to list all the group and contaminated manuscripts each time I gave a group variant, and the same is true of some of the nongroup readings in the critical apparatus. I therefore use the designations *many MSS* and *most MSS* to indicate patterns involving large groups of manuscripts: *most MSS* means over half of the 208 manuscripts that I have collated, and *many MSS* means more than 20 (i.e., at least 10 percent of the collated manuscripts) when the reading is a nongroup reading. Occasionally, also to save space, I use the designations *some MSS* and *a few MSS* when there are no persistent textual similarities among the manuscripts exhibiting a particular reading or when the reading sheds no light on readings in the main manuscripts: *a few MSS* means up to 10, and *some MSS* means from 10 to 20 when the reading is a nongroup reading.

A NOTE ON THE TRANSLATION

In my translation of the text in L[20] I have tried to be as literal as possible, within the limits of what I conceive to be acceptable and comprehensible English; in only a few cases, where the Latin simply resisted literal translation, have I paraphrased or added words for the sake of clarity. L[20] has a few clearly meaningless readings, and for these I have translated the most likely originals, which are asterisked in the critical apparatus.[186] For quotations from the Vulgate I have used the Douai-Rheims-Challoner translation rather than my own in order to convey the traditional character that Vulgate Latin had for both Lotario and the scribe of L[20];[187] where L[20]'s morphology and vocabulary differ from the Vulgate's, however, I have made the necessary changes in the translation.

NOTES TO INTRODUCTION

1. The date is from Michele Maccarrone's introduction to the most recent edition, *Lotharii Cardinalis (Innocentii III) De Miseria Humane Conditionis* (Lugano: Thesaurus Mundi, 1955), p. xxxvii; the treatise could have been written any time between 25 December 1194 and 13 April 1195. Maccarrone's edition is not a critical edition, as he himself says (p. xxxi), and is based on a study of fewer than 30 percent of the extant manuscripts. Moreover, the edition must be used with caution, for it has many errors, primarily in the critical apparatus but also occasionally in the text; it incompletely (and often incorrectly) represents, in the critical apparatus, substantive readings in MS. F. 26 in the Biblioteca Vallicelliana in Rome, the manuscript Maccarrone considers the most important for reconstructing Lotario's original and on which he says he leans most heavily in his edition (p. xlii); and the reconstruction of Lotario's quotations from the Bible, which comprise a considerable portion of the text, is, I believe, made on indefensible grounds (see Maccarrone's discussion, p. xxxii). When quoting passages from "Lotario's original" in the

Introduction, therefore, instead of using Maccarrone's text I have used the text of the present edition but emended, whenever it does not represent Lotario's presumed original, according to the readings from MS. F. 26 (supplemented by MS. Regin. lat. 71 at the Vatican) that are given in the critical apparatus. For further details see pp. 62–63.

2. See Anselm Nagy, *De Tractatu de Miseria Humanae Conditionis Innocentii Papae III* (Budapest: Monasterium B. M. V. de Zirc in Hungaria, 1943), pp. 22–44, chap. 4 passim; also Maccarrone, pp. xxxix–xlii.

3. This is the standard, authoritative view; see especially Maccarrone, who is the leading authority on the life and works of Lotario, in his study "Innocenzo III prima del pontificato," *Archivio della R. Deputazione romana di Storia patria,* 66 (1943), 86–89. There is no evidence for another view that has gained some currency: that Lotario's career suffered a setback in 1191 when Celestine III became pope (Celestine was from a family, the Orsini, that later became enemies of the Scotti, the family of Lotario's mother)—in its most extreme form, that he was relieved of his duties as cardinal—and that the *De Miseria* may have been written in response to this change of fortune.

4. Achille Luchaire, *Innocent III: Rome et l'Italie,* 3rd ed. (Paris: Librairie Hachette et Cie., 1907), p. 10.

5. The history of the pervasive contemptus mundi tradition has yet to be written, but good starts have been made by Robert Bultot, who has projected a six-volume work carrying the tradition from its origins through the *De Miseria* and then into medieval French literature, and by Donald R. Howard, who is planning a study of the tradition after the *De Miseria.* Thus far only one volume of Bultot's work has appeared: *La Doctrine du mépris du monde, en occident, de S. Ambroise à Innocent III,* 4: *Le XIᵉ siècle:* pt. 1: *Pierre Damien* and pt. 2: *Jean de Fécamp, Hermann Contract, Roger de Caen, Anselme de Canterbury* (Louvain: Editions Nauwelaerts, 1963 and 1964). Howard's preliminary work can be found in his unpublished dissertation, "The Contempt of the World: A Study in the Ideology of Latin Christendom with Emphasis on Fourteenth-Century English Literature" (University of Florida, 1954), chaps. 2–3, 5–6; see also his book, *The Three Temptations: Medieval Man in Search of the World* (Princeton: Princeton University Press, 1966), especially pp. 68–72, and his introduction to Margaret Mary Dietz's translation, *On the Misery of the Human Condition* (Indianapolis: Bobbs-Merrill Co., 1969), pp. xxiv–xxxiii.

6. Luchaire, p. 12.

7. In his edition, p. xxxvii ("ductus illo divinas et humanas res indagandi incenso studio").

8. See the list in Appendix I. Nearly all of these have been listed before: see Maccarrone's edition, pp. x–xx; Maccarrone, "Altri Manoscritti del 'De Miseria'," *Italia medioevale e umanistica,* 4 (1961), 172–73; Donald R. Howard, "Thirty New Manuscripts of Pope Innocent III's *De Miseria Humanae Conditionis* 'De contemptu mundi'," *Manuscripta,* 7 (1963), 31–35; and my lists: "More New Manuscripts of Pope Innocent III's *De Miseria Humanae Conditionis,*" *Manuscripta,* 8 (1964), 172–75; 10 (1966), 160–64; 12 (1968), 25–28; and 19 (1975), 119–22.

9. Maccarrone lists forty-five editions in his edition, pp. xx–xxii; Robert Bultot adds one in his "Mépris du monde, misère et dignité de l'homme dans la pensée d'Innocent III," *Cahiers de civilisation médiévale,* 4 (1961), 441, n. 1; and Donald R. Howard supplies the other six in his introduction to *On the Misery of the Human Condition,* p. xiii, n. 2.

10. The list could probably be enlarged, especially for the first 300 years of printing. For the medieval period I have not made a systematic survey, but the manuscripts I know of will indicate the variety and the extent: for the Dutch, one manuscript (Leiden, Rijksuniversiteit, BPL 2231, fragment, 15th c.); for the German, three (West Berlin, Staatsbibl. der Stiftung Preuss. Kulturbesitz, germ. 4° 1133, 15th c., formerly in Leipzig; Schloss Harburg, Fürstlich Oettingen-Wallerstein'sche Bibl. und Kunstsammlung, III, 1, 8°, 8, fragment, 15th c.; Heiligenkreuz, Stiftsbibl., 165, 15th c.); for the Irish, five (London, British Library, Egerton 91 and 1781, both 15th c.; Oxford, Bodleian, Rawl. B. 512, 14th–15th c.; Paris, Bibl. Nat., Celtique 1, 15th c.; and Rennes, Bibl. Mun., 598, 15th c.—for all of which see James A. Geary's edition, *An Irish Version of Innocent III's De Contemptu Mundi* [Washington, D.C.: Catholic University of America, 1921]); for the Italian, two (Florence, Bibl. Naz. Centrale, Palat. 37, 16th c.; Florence, Bibl. Riccardiana, 1742, 15th c., for Book I of which see Arrigo Levasti, ed., *Mistici del duecento e del trecento* [1935; rptd. Milan: Rizzoli Editore, 1960], pp. 81–105); for the Spanish, four (Madrid, Bibl. Nac., 10,201, and 11,357, both 15th c.; Montserrat, Abadia, 1025, 15th c.; and Santander, Bibl. Menéndez y Pelayo, R-I-10-28, 15th c., for which see Miguel Artigas's edition, "Un nuevo poema por la cuaderna via," in *Boletín de la Biblioteca Menéndez y Pelayo,* 1 [1919], 31–37, 87–95, 153–61, 210–16, 328–38, and 2 [1920], 41–48, 91–98, 154–63, 233–54).

For French there is a 5310-line verse translation by Guillaume Alexis (1480) entitled *Le Passe Temps de tout homme et de toute femme,* in *Oeuvres poétiques de Guillaume Alexis, Prieur de Bucy,* 2, ed. Arthur Piaget and Emile Picot, SATF (Paris: Librairie de Firmin Didot et Cie., 1899), 71–291; and a verse condensation by Eustache Deschamps, for which see p. 4 and n. 15. There are at least three prose translations, one or all of which will be edited by Robert Bultot of the University of Louvain: one, probably dating from the thirteenth century, appears in fourteen manuscripts (Paris, Bibl. de l'Arsenal, 5201, of the 13th c.; Besançon, Bibl. Mun., 434, Paris, Bibl. de l'Arsenal, 2071, Paris, Bibl. Nat., lat. 19271, lat. 22921, lat. 24432, and nouv. acq. fr. 10237, all of the 14th c.; and Lyon, Bibl. Mun., 1234, Nantes, Bibl. Mun., 212, Paris, Bibl. Nat., lat. 461, lat. 916, lat. 918, lat. 957, and Rouen, Bibl. Mun., 941, all of the 15th c.); another, containing portions of the Latin text and parallel French translations, in two (Lyon, Bibl. du Palais des Arts, 28 and Vienna, Nationalbibl., 2627, both of the 15th c.); and a third, a partial condensation, in one (Paris, Bibl. Ste-Geneviève, 792, 13th–15th c.).

11. Ed. by Ernst Martin (Halle: Verlag der Buchhandlung des Waisenhauses, 1869), with a discussion of the influence of the *De Miseria* on pp. xvi–xviii.

12. Noted by Maccarrone in his edition, pp. ix, xxxiv.

13. Ed. by Thor Sundby for the Chaucer Society (London: N. Trübner and Co., 1873). The first passage (p. 29, ll. 2-10) is from Book I, chap. 2; the second (p. 100, ll. 8-14), from Book I, chap. 14.

14. Ed. by Adelbert von Keller in *Bibliothek des litterarischen Vereins in Stuttgart,* 38 (1856); the paraphrase is on pp. 290ff.

15. In *Oeuvres complètes de Eustache Deschamps,* 2, ed. le Marquis de Queux de Saint-Hilaire, SATF (Paris: Librairie de Firmin Didot et Cie., 1880), 239-305.

16. There is no modern edition of *L'Epître.* I found the quotation in Curt Bühler's edition of Stephen Scrope's translation, EETS o.s. 230 (London: Oxford University Press, 1970), pp. 111-12.

17. The *Miroir de l'âme* exists in at least two manuscripts (Lille, Bibl. Mun., 127, ff. 37-108v, and 128, ff. 3-95v); the *Miroir d'humilité* in at least one (Valenciennes, Bibl. Mun., 240, beginning to f. 272).

18. Noted by Maccarrone in his edition, p. ix.

19. Noted by Reinhold Köhler, "Quellennachweise zu Richard Rolle's von Hampole Gedicht '*The Pricke of Conscience*'," *Jahrbuch für romanische und englische Literatur,* 6 (1865), 200.

20. Noted by Maccarrone in his edition, p. ix. See also Charles E. Trinkhaus, *Adversity's Nobleman: The Italian Humanists on Happiness* (New York: Columbia University Press, 1940), especially chaps. 3ff., and *In Our Image and Likeness: Humanity and Divinity in Italian Humanist Thought* (London: Constable, 1970), I, pt. 2.

21. See J.-Th. Welter, *L'Exemplum dans la littérature religieuse et didactique du moyen âge* (Paris: Occitania, 1927), passim.

22. See Paris, Bibliothèque Nationale, lat. 3171, ff. 50-58, end of 14th c. For a brief mention of the work, see Marie-Thérèse d'Alverny's article, "Un sermon d'Alain de Lille sur la misère de l'homme," in *The Classical Tradition: Literary and Historical Studies in Honor of Harry Caplan* (Ithaca: Cornell University Press, 1966), p. 517, n. 12.

23. See Trinkhaus, *Adversity's Nobleman,* pp. 72-76 et passim, and *In Our Image and Likeness,* vol. 1, 253-58.

24. Nearly all these assignments are from Neil R. Ker's *Medieval Libraries of Great Britain: A List of Surviving Books,* 2nd ed. (London: Royal Historical Society, 1964); a few are from the modern manuscript catalogues. There are at least 86 manuscripts listed in published medieval library catalogues, as a survey of these catalogues in Ker's headnotes indicates, and they come from such additional places as Crowland, Dover, Glastonbury, Leicester, London (St. Paul's Cathedral), Meaux, Titchfield, Winchester, and Witham. At St. Augustine's, Canterbury alone, for example, there were at least 16 copies (out of a total of 1837 manuscripts) in the late fifteenth century, and 10 at Peterborough Abbey (out of 346 manuscripts) in the late fourteenth century.

25. Printed by M. Esposito, *EHR,* 32 (1917), 400-405. See Carleton Brown, "Chaucer's *Wreched Engendring,*" *PMLA,* 50 (1935), esp. 1000-1002, for connections between the poem and the *De Miseria.*

26. The edition I have used is *Flores Omnium Pene Doctorum Qui Tum in Theologia, Tum in Philosophia Hactenus Claruerunt per Thomam Hibernicum . . .* (Paris: Cenomani, 1887).

27. The *Oculus Sacerdotis* has never been printed. The version I have used is British Library, MS. Royal 6 E.i, of the late fourteenth century; the extracts from the *De Miseria,* which are on ff. 21-23, might better be described as a condensation of the whole work, though with many chapters omitted entirely. The fullest study of the *Oculus Sacerdotis* is by Father L. E. Boyle, O.P., "The *Oculus Sacerdotis* and Some Other Works of William of Pagula," *Transactions of the Royal Historical Society,* 5th Series, 5 (1955), 81-110. So far as I know, W. A. Pantin, in *The English Church in the Fourteenth Century* (Cambridge: Cambridge University Press, 1955), p. 198, was the first to point out that part of the *Oculus Sacerdotis* was based on the *De Miseria.*

28. In the section on "Avaricia," according to Ione Kemp Knight, ed., *Wimbledon's Sermon Redde Rationem Villicationis Tue: A Middle English Sermon of the Fourteenth Century,* Duquesne Studies, Philological Series, 9 (Pittsburgh: Duquesne University Press, 1967), p. 132, n. to ll. 485-510; and in the section on "Senectus," according to George R. Coffman, "Old Age from Horace to Chaucer. Some Literary Affinities and Adventures of an Idea," *Speculum,* 9 (1934), 267-68. There are probably other passages indebted to the *De Miseria,* but I have not had an opportunity to consult a copy of the *Summa Predicantium.*

29. Kate O. Petersen first suggested that Holkot used the *De Miseria* in *On the Sources of the Nonne Prestes Tale,* Radcliffe College Monographs, no. 10 (Boston: Ginn and Co., 1898), p. 115, n. 4. The edition of Holkot that I have consulted is *Robertus Holkot Super librū Sapientiae . . .* (Venice: Octauiani Scoti per Bonetum Locatellus, 1509), filmed by *Manuscripta* (List 27, no. 26).

30. Edited by Richard Morris, *The Pricke of Conscience (Stimulus Conscientiae) a Northumbrian Poem by Richard Rolle de Hampole* (Berlin: A. Asher and Co., for the Philological Society, 1863). Reinhold Köhler, in "Quellennachweise zu Richard Rolle's von Hampole Gedicht *'The Pricke of Conscience'*"(see n. 19), pp. 196-212, was the first to point out the correspondences between the *Pricke* and the *De Miseria,* though his list is not complete. See also Arnold Hahn, *Quellenuntersuchungen zu Richard Rolles englischen Schriften* (Halle: Inaugural Dissertation, 1900), pp. 16-40.

31. Edited by Gustaf Holmstedt, EETS o.s. 182 (London: Oxford University Press, 1933); see especially pp. xv, xvi-xviii, clxxvi, clxxx-cxci.

32. In Carl Horstmann, ed., *Yorkshire Writers,* 2 (London: Swan Sonnenschein and Co., 1896), 81.

33. Edited by J. Loserth and F. D. Matthew for the Wyclif Society (London: C. K. Paul and Co., 1922); see pp. 235-41.

34. The possible quotations in the B text, Passus IV, ll. 143-44 and Passus XVIII, l. 388, are from Book III, chap. 14, ll. 37-38, though this passage is a fairly well known one in the Middle Ages, appearing also in Peter Lombard's *Sententie,* Peter of Poitiers's *Sententie,* and other works (see *Sententiae Petri Pictaviensis,* 2, ed. P. S. Moore, J. N. Garvin, and M. Dulong [Notre Dame: University of Notre Dame, 1950], 54-55, note to ll. 182-183). Some passages (among others) that may also be indebted to the *De Miseria* are B V.304-91 (Book II, chaps. 17-19); B XIII.355-99, and XIV.201-23 (II.4); B XIV.145-59 (II.16); and B XVII.315-27 (I.15). See the edn. by W.W. Skeat, EETS o.s. 38 (London: N. Trübner and Co., 1869).

35. Edited by G. C. Macaulay, *The Complete Works of John Gower, 1: The*

French *Works* and *4: The Latin Works* (Oxford: Clarendon Press, 1899, 1902). The correspondences are *Mirour* 7825-48, 7945-56 with the *De Miseria* II.17; and *Vox* III.119-26, 821-32 and IV.67-70 with the *De Miseria* II.17.25-26. The ideas on gluttony contained in these lines are commonplaces, but the appearance of the lines so close together in the *De Miseria* and their similarity of expression especially to the *Vox Clamantis* may indicate that they are derived from Lotario's treatise.

36. Edited by Ione Kemp Knight (see n. 28 above); the passage in question is on pp. 92-93, ll. 492-503.

37. Edited by J. P. W. M. van Zutphen (Rome: Institutum Carmelitanum, 1956); the relevant passages are on pp. 21-22, 25.

38. *Jacob's Well* has been partially edited by Arthur Brandeis, EETS o.s. 115 (London: Kegan Paul, Trench, Trübner and Co., Ltd., 1900); the passage is on p. 145. The author of *Jacob's Well* seems to have borrowed some of his material from Lavynham's treatise, though not the passage in question.

39. The preceding lists of works that quote the *De Miseria*—which by the way could be expanded—give very little indication of the variety of ways a classical or medieval work could be used in the Middle Ages. This is an important subject that deserves further study, especially—in conjunction with a study of the extent of popularity—for the information it can provide on how to measure literary influence. See, for example, L. D. Reynolds, *The Medieval Tradition of Seneca's Letters* (Oxford: Oxford University Press, 1965), especially chap. 9, for the variety of ways a classical work was used in the twelfth century. For extent of popularity one should look not only at firsthand quotations but also at secondhand quotations: in the case of the *De Miseria,* not only at the works listed above but also at, for example, the *Cursor Mundi,* which quotes passages from the *Pricke of Conscience* that are based on the *De Miseria; Peter Idley's Instructions to His Son,* which quotes a passage from Albertano of Brescia's *Liber Consolationis et Consilii* that is in turn based on the *De Miseria;* some of the poems in Horstman's *Yorkshire Writers* based on portions of the *Pricke of Conscience* that are indebted to the *De Miseria;* the English translations by Stephen Scrope and Anthony Babyngton of Christine de Pisan's *Epître d'Othéa,* which quotes from the *De Miseria.*

40. The fullest discussion of Chaucer's indebtedness to the *De Miseria* is by Emil Koeppel, "Chaucer und Innocenz des Dritten Traktat *De Contemptu Mundi sive De Miseria Conditionis Humanae,*" *Archiv für das Studium der neueren Sprachen und Litteraturen,* 84 (1890), 405-18. Apparently A. von Düring in 1886 was the first to recognize Chaucer's debt to the *De Miseria* (in *Geoffrey Chaucers Werke,* 3 [Strassburg: Karl J. Trübner, 1886], 352, 385), but both Koeppel (see *Archiv,* 85 [1890], 48) and Thomas R. Lounsbury ("Chaucer's Sources," *Nation,* 49 [July 4, 1889], 10-11) came to the same conclusion independently. A fuller statement by Lounsbury can be found in his *Studies in Chaucer* (New York: Harper and Brothers, 1892), vol. 2, 329-34.

41. Cf. Chaucer's translation of some of the same lines at *Melibee* B² 2758-61, via Renaud de Louens' French translation of Albertano of Brescia's *Liber Consolationis et Consilii:* "the same seith Innocent in oon of his bookes. He seith that 'sorweful and myshappy is the condicioun of a povre beggere; for if

70

he axe nat his mete, he dyeth for hunger; and if he axe, he dyeth for shame; and algates necessitee constreyneth hym to axe'. And seith Salomon that 'bet it is to dye than for to have swich poverte'." Though there is no way to prove it, the French original of this passage may have been what led Chaucer to delve into the *De Miseria* in the first place. *Melibee* is usually assigned to the later 1380s or early 1390s, about the time Chaucer was working on the *De Miseria* (see pp. 30-31 below); the poverty passage from the *De Miseria* is used in both *Melibee* and the Man of Law's Prologue; the following tale of Custance relies more heavily on the *De Miseria* than any other work of Chaucer's; and there are connections (primarily thematic) between *Melibee* and the Man of Law's performance that have even led to the suggestion that *Melibee* was the tale originally assigned to the Man of Law. All quotations from Chaucer's works are from F. N. Robinson's second edition, *The Works of Geoffrey Chaucer* (Boston: Houghton Mifflin Co., 1957).

42. For 110-11 Chaucer may have translated either Book II, chap. 18, ll. 15-16 ("Dives ille qui 'epulabatur cotidie splendide' 'sepultus est in inferno'") or Book II, chap. 37, ll. 14-15 ("Dives ille 'qui induebatur purpura et bisso, sepultus est in inferno'"), but the idea is proverblike, and I am inclined to think that Chaucer simply expanded "indignatur, murmurat, inprecatur."

43. R. P. Miller suggests that Chaucer adapted the rest of chap. 14 for ll. 122-30, but there are no verbal parallels; see "Constancy Humanized: Trivet's Constance and the Man of Law's Custance," *Costerus,* n.s. 3 (1975), 53-58.

44. The last two and one-half lines of Chaucer's translation do not reproduce any of the Latin exactly. They may be a paraphrase of "non solum maculat animam," or they may be a paraphrase of the idea expressed in Lotario's next chapter—that lechery has the power to ruin any person, high or low, male or female, young or old.

45. That Chaucer may have been indebted to the title to Book II, chap. 21 for 1133 was first suggested by Carleton Brown, in "The Man of Law's Head-link and the Prologue of the Canterbury Tales," *SP,* 34 (1937), 15.

46. Some of Lotario's words appear in Chaucer, but the same passage appears in John of Wales's *Communiloquium,* and it may offer a more persuasive parallel because the word *dyabolus* (cf. Chaucer's *devel*) appears in the line following. See Robert A. Pratt, "Chaucer and the Hand That Fed Him," *Speculum,* 41 (1966), 631-32.

47. Koeppel does not mention this parallel, and of course the joining of gluttony and lechery was common in medieval treatises on the seven deadly sins (cf. Parson's Tale 836: "After Glotonye thanne comth Lecherie, for thise two synnes been so ny cosyns that ofte they wol nat departe"), but in view of the fact that in the following lines of the Pardoner's Tale (483-84) Chaucer translates the following line of the *De Miseria* (13), it seems very likely that the immediate inspiration for 481-82 came from Lotario's treatise. As corroboration, the following two chapters in the *De Miseria* (Book II, chaps. 20 and 21) treat, in passing, the sins of lechery that come from gluttony and drunkenness. On the other hand, the *Communiloquium* offers a more persuasive verbal parallel in that it has "prohibetur libido luxurie et gule que est ei annexa" (cf. Chaucer's *annexed*). See Pratt, p. 635.

71

48. This passage is probably taken from the *Communiloquium,* where *Loth* is mentioned by name (see Pratt, p. 635), though it is possible that the phrase "incestum commisit" in the *De Miseria*—the first line of the chapter following the one Chaucer has just used—may have given him the idea for 485-87. Petersen, *On the Sources of the Nonne Prestes Tale,* p. 113, offers a parallel with a passage from Lectio 21 of Robert Holkot's *Super Librum Sapientie* (Lectio 20 in the edition I have used), but it is only an allusion to the "exemplum de Loth" and has nothing about the story itself.

49. 505-7ff. are probably from St. Jerome's *Epistola Adversus Jovinianum* Book II, chap. 15, because of the marginal gloss at 508: "Ieronimus contra Iouinianum Quamdiu ieiunauit Adam in Paradiso fuit comedit et eiectus est statim duxit vxorem" (see John M. Manly and Edith Rickert, *The Text of the Canterbury Tales* [Chicago: University of Chicago Press, 1940], vol. 3, 516).

50. 521-23 may not be based on the *De Miseria.* Paul's name is not mentioned in connection with the quotation in Lotario's work, and the exact place in the Bible is not given. If Chaucer knew that the quotation was from Paul, he may have known it by heart, or he may have taken it from another source that included Paul's name. There is a Latin gloss at 522 with the Bible verse—1 Cor. 6:13—in a form that is probably from St. Jerome's *Epistola:* "Esca ventri et venter escis deus autem et hunc et illam destruet" (Manly and Rickert, vol. 3, 516). The Vulgate has *has* for *illam,* but as Daniel S. Silvia, Jr. points out, St. Jerome has *illam* in Book II, chap. 6 of the *Epistola* (see his unpublished dissertation, "Chaucer's Use of Jerome's *Adversus Jovinianum,* with an Edition of Book I, Chapters 40-49, Based on a Study of Medieval Manuscripts," University of Illinois, 1962, p. 125).

51. For the source of these lines W. W. Skeat, *The Complete Works of Geoffrey Chaucer* (Oxford: Clarendon Press, 1894), vol. 5, 278, gives a quotation from St. Jerome's *Epistola,* Book II, chap. 8—"Propter breuem gulae uoluptatem, terrae lustrantur et maria: et ut mulsum uinum preciosusque cibus fauces notras transeat, totius uitae opera desudamus"—as well as the relevant line from the *De Miseria* (and see Silvia, pp. 124-25). It is, of course, impossible to know which of the two works was the immediate source. Jerome seems closer, but he has nothing corresponding to "est and west and north and south, / In erthe, in eir, in water." Lotario is not so close, but he has something that corresponds to "In erthe, in eir, in water." Perhaps Skeat is right when he says that Chaucer was probably using both Lotario and Jerome for this passage.

52. Henry Morgan Ayres, in "Chaucer and Seneca," *RR,* 10 (1919), 1-15 (esp. 5-7), compares the Pardoner's words with relevant passages from Seneca's Epistles and finds that 513-16 and 534-48 reflect portions of certain epistles, especially Epistle 95. Professor Ayres is certainly right to point out these passages as reminiscences from Seneca, but they are closer to Lotario than to Seneca. Moreover, as Pratt has shown in "Chaucer and the Hand That Fed Him," many of Chaucer's Senecan quotations probably came to him through the *Communiloquium;* it is even possible that he never consulted Seneca at first hand (p. 638). The passage from the *De Miseria* is quoted in full by Holkot, *Super Librum Sapientie* Lectio 118 (see Petersen, p. 115, n. 4).

53. Koeppel does not mention this parallel, but it is at least possible that it

reflects the *De Miseria*, especially because the preceding lines (537–46) are also from Book II, chap. 17. There is, however, a marginal gloss at 547 that reproduces 1 Tim. 5:6, a passage that is not found in the *De Miseria*, and Chaucer may have taken the passage directly from the Vulgate.

54. I point out the correspondence because the Latin passage is found in the *De Miseria* in the sections that Chaucer used for the Pardoner's Tale. However, Chaucer must certainly have used St. Jerome's *Epistola* Book II, chap. 10 here. The marginal gloss to this line is "luxuriosa res vinum et contumeliosa ebrietas" (Manly and Rickert, vol. 3, 516) and appears in this form (with *contumeliosa* for *tumultuosa*) in the *Epistola* but not in the *De Miseria*. If it were not for the gloss, it would be impossible to know which of the two works Chaucer used. See Silvia, p. 126.

55. Joseph E. Grennen, in "'Sampsoun' in the *Canterbury Tales:* Chaucer Adapting a Source," *NM*, 67 (1966), 117–22, says that 549–61 may be from *Le Livre de la Chevalier de la Tour-Landry* because the chapter in question is devoted mainly to the story of Samson. The verbal parallels are not convincing, but the allusion to Samson and the connection between his abstinence and the Pardoner's Tale are interesting and could probably be pursued further with profit. The passage from the *De Miseria* is quoted in full by Holkot, *Super Librum Sapientie* Lectio 20 (see Petersen, p. 115, n. 4).

56. Though it is possible that Chaucer knew Prov. 31:4 well enough to be reminded that the words preceding the passage from the *De Miseria* concerned the commands given to Lamuel by his mother (apparently the scribe of the Selden manuscript of the *Canterbury Tales* was so reminded because he added *Lamuel* before the marginal gloss "Noli vinum dare," Manly and Rickert, vol. 3, 516), the parallels between 583–87 and the *Communiloquium* are so persuasive, as Pratt has shown (p. 634), that Chaucer must have used that work as his source here.

57. Perhaps from Chaucer's own Parson's Tale (see Skeat, vol. 5, 275, who points out parallels that continue through 650 of the Pardoner's Tale); or Seneca's *Epistles* (but see n. 52 above); or Holkot's *Super Librum Sapientie* (see Petersen, pp. 113–15, and nn. 52 and 55 above), though what militates against this work as a possible source, it seems to me, is that the quotations are so far apart (Lectio 20 and Lectio 118).

58. In "Old Age and *Contemptus Mundi* in *The Pardoner's Tale*," *MAE*, 33 (1964), esp. 125–29.

59. The joining of these three sins was very common in medieval writings, as Donald R. Howard makes clear in *The Three Temptations*, esp. pp. 43–75.

60. Koeppel, "Chaucer und Innocenz des Dritten Traktat," pp. 416–17; Tatlock, "Has Chaucer's *Wretched Engendering* Been Found?" *MLN*, 51 (1936), 282, n. 9.

61. In "Chaucer's *Wreched Engendrynge*," *MP*, 35 (1937–38), 331.

62. "Chaucer und Albertanus Brixiensis," *Archiv für das Studium der neueren Sprachen und Litteraturen*, 86 (1891), 31. Cf. the corresponding passage at *Melibee* B² 2276: "men seyn that thre thynges dryven a man out of his hous,—that is to seyn, smoke, droppyng of reyn, and wikked wyves," with its French original:

"'Trois chois sont qui gettent l'omme hors de sa maison: la fumiere, la goutiere, et la mauvaise femme'" (Renaud de Louens, *Le Livre de Mellibee et Prudence*, ed. J. Burke Severs in *Sources and Analogues of Chaucer's Canterbury Tales*, ed. W. F. Bryan and Germaine Dempster, Chicago: University of Chicago Press, 1941, p. 575).

63. See B. J. Whiting, *Proverbs, Sentences, and Proverbial Phrases From English Writings Mainly Before 1500* (Cambridge, Mass.: Belknap Press, 1968), item T 187 (nine citations).

64. Koeppel (p. 415) mentions a second passage from the Wife of Bath's Prologue only as suggestive of a passage in the *De Miseria:* "And after wyn on Venus moste I thynke" (464), perhaps reflecting the *De Miseria* II.21.4-5: "Venter enim opipare satur libenter Venerem amplexatur." But this too is a very doubtful correspondence, and Koeppel does not insist on it. The joining of gluttony and lechery was common in medieval treatises on the sins and occurs in Chaucer's works as well, in both the Parson's Tale and the Pardoner's Tale. See n. 47 above.

65. "Old Age from Horace to Chaucer," esp. pp. 273-77. And see Pratt, pp. 636-37, for possible parallels with the *Communiloquium*.

66. Robinson, p. 730, note to Pardoner's Tale 537.

67. The others are: *Troilus and Criseyde* I.952 and III.813-33, Knight's Tale 2841 and 3068, Nun's Priest's Tale B² 4395-96, Merchant's Tale 2055, Physician's Tale 221-22, and of course Man of Law's Tale 421-27, which is definitely based on the *De Miseria* (see p. 7). For Chaucer's thematic use of the alternation of joy and woe, see my "Chaucer's Artistic Use of Pope Innocent III's *De Miseria Humane Conditionis* in the Man of Law's Prologue and Tale," *PMLA,* 81 (1966), 488-92 and Robert A. Pratt's "'Joye after Wo' in the *Knight's Tale,*" *JEGP,* 57 (1958), 416-23.

68. Whiting, items J 58 and J 61.

69. The Latin is "Quam multis amaritudinibus humanae felicitatis dulcedo respersa est!" (see the edition of Ludwig Bieler, Turnhout: Typographi Brepols Editores Pontificii, 1957, p. 24), which Chaucer translates as "The swetnesse of mannes welefulnesse is spraynd with many bitternesses" (118-19).

70. "Chaucer's Translation of the Bible," in *English and Medieval Studies Presented to J. R. R. Tolkien on the Occasion of His Seventieth Birthday,* ed. Norman Davis and C. L. Wrenn (London: George Allen and Unwin, Ltd., 1962), p. 192.

71. Outside of the biblical passages cited earlier in this discussion of Chaucer's debt to the *De Miseria,* I can find only twelve passages that Chaucer might have taken from the *De Miseria: House of Fame* 514, Knight's Tale 1303-12, Man of Law's Tale 286 and 488, Squire's Tale 518, Franklin's Tale 880, stories of Sampson, Nabugodonosor, and Balthasar from the Monk's Tale, Nun's Priest's Tale B² 4320-25, Pardoner's Prologue 334, and Manciple's Tale 344. My figures are based on W. W. Skeat's list of biblical citations in *The Complete Works of Geoffrey Chaucer* (Oxford: Clarendon Press, 1894), vol. 6, 381-84, and on the biblical citations in Robinson's notes. There are, of course, difficulties in taking a count of Chaucer's quotations from the Bible using such

lists and notes, as Grace W. Landrum discovered long ago when she was doing her study of "Chaucer's Use of the Vulgate," *PMLA,* 39 (1924), 75–100, esp. 98—Skeat, for instance, had acknowledged only 285 passages in his list, but there are nearly 300 more in his annotations—but probably no passages have been overlooked that would reveal *verbal* parallels.

72. The relevant studies, in chronological order, are: Carleton Brown, "Chaucer's *Wreched Engendring*" (1935); Tatlock, "Has Chaucer's *Wretched Engendering* Been Found?" (1936); Dempster, "Did Chaucer Write *An Holy Medytacion?*" *MLN,* 51 (1936), 284–95; Carleton Brown, "An Affirmative Reply," ibid., pp. 296–300; Dempster, "Chaucer's *Wretched Engendering* and *An Holy Medytacion,*" *MP,* 35 (1937–38), 27–29; Beatrice Daw Brown, "Chaucer's *Wreched Engendrynge,*" ibid., pp. 325–33. For similar conclusions see Tatlock, *The Development and Chronology of Chaucer's Works,* Chaucer Society, 2nd series, 37 (London: Kegan Paul, Trench, Trübner, and Co., 1907), pp. 181–82n.; Aage Brusendorff, *The Chaucer Tradition* (London: Humphrey Milford, 1925), p. 427; and Victor Langhans, "Chaucers angebliche Übersetzung des Traktates 'De Contemptu Mundi' von Innocenz III," *Anglia,* 52 (1929), 325–49. Langhans (pp. 342–46) does not even believe that Chaucer wrote ll. 414–15 of the revised Prologue to the *Legend of Good Women* (he believes a later scribe did) because the meaning of *Engendrynge* is so unclear, the meter of 414 is so defective, and the insertion of 414–15 into the original version of the Prologue is so awkward; but cf. J. Burke Severs, "Author's Revision in Block C of the *Canterbury Tales,*" *Speculum,* 29 (1954), 525, who argues that the addition of 414–15 parallels Chaucer's method of revision elsewhere.

73. See pp. 4–5 and n. 25.

74. I have summarized the arguments only insofar as they touch upon the meaning of Chaucer's title, as it is unnecessary here to review the whole problem of Chaucerian authorship of "An Holy Medytacion." Tatlock and Dempster's arguments against Chaucerian authorship, however, are decidedly more convincing than those of the Browns in favor of it.

75. "Chaucer's *Wreched Engendring,*" p. 1004.

76. In addition to Brown, only W. W. Skeat has questioned Chaucer's use of "in prose," and he does it obliquely. Believing that Chaucer made a complete translation, he argues for a verse original on the grounds that, because the passages from the *De Miseria* appear in seven-line stanzas in the Man of Law's Prologue and Tale, Chaucer's original must also have been in seven-line stanzas (see *The Complete Works,* vol. 3, 307 and vol. 5, 142, though Skeat contradicts himself in vol. 3, 445). This is not a convincing argument, mainly because the passages from the *De Miseria* in the Pardoner's Tale are in rhyming couplets. Chaucer would of course have given the material from the *De Miseria* the verse form of the work into which he inserted it. If Chaucer translated the *De Miseria,* all indications are that he would have done it in prose.

77. "Chaucer's *Wreched Engendring,*" p. 1003.

78. "Did Chaucer Write *An Holy Medytacion?*" pp. 285–86.

79. The *MED* does not list this use of *as,* but there is precedent for it both in Chaucer and in other Middle English writers. For Chaucer see *Troilus and*

Criseyde II.859–60: "'for swich manere folk, I gesse, / Defamen Love, as nothing of him knowe'," where *who* can be substituted for *as*; Knight's Tale 1857–58: "'wheither he or thow / May with his hundred, as I spak of now'," where *which* can be substituted for *as*, and this is reinforced by the preposition *of*; probably Knight's Tale 2472; perhaps Merchant's Tale 2024; cf. also a similar situation in Knight's Tale 2810, where *as* corresponds to the relative adverb *where*. For Middle English writers, see the *OED*'s three citations; also Tauno F. Mustanoja, *A Middle English Syntax,* Part I (Helsinki: Société néophilologique, 1960), 202, for two citations and a short discussion. According to Otto Jespersen, *A Modern English Grammar on Historical Principles,* 3 (Heidelberg: Carl Winters Universitätsbuchhandlung, 1927), 168–79, *as* was used as a relative from the twelfth century on.

80. The closest I have found is "But who wol al this letter have in mynde, / Rede Ovyde, and in hym he shal it fynde" (*Legend of Good Women* 1367–68). But it is not relevant because, though *Ovyde* no doubt stands for the *Heroides*, *hym* is merely a substitution for *Ovyde*: what one is, the other is also. Nor is "'In Stace of Thebes'" (Knight's Tale 2294) really relevant: like other phrases of this sort in Chaucer (*Parliament of Fowls* 31, Retraction 1088, etc.; see below, n. 85), the whole phrase no doubt stands for "in the book," in this case "in the *Thebaid*" (i.e., "in the book by Statius on the subject of Thebes," as opposed to "in the book on the subject of Achilles"; cf. *House of Fame* 1460–63). Phrases with the author's name, uninflected, followed by the title of the work are common as titles in Medieval Latin (cf. Chaucer's "'Tullyus of the Drem of Scipioun'," *Parliament of Fowls* 31).

81. For example, *House of Fame* 449, *Troilus and Criseyde* I.146, *Legend of Good Women* 928, Merchant's Tale 2232. On the other hand, there are examples of "in the particular work" without mention of the author (*Legend of Good Women* 928, Monk's Tale B^2 3769, Nun's Priest's Tale B^2 4502). In general, Chaucer is quite clear, given the requirements of the metrical line, and, more often than not, gives both the name of the author and the name of the book (for example, Prologue G to the *Legend of Good Women* 281, 305, 307; Wife of Bath's Prologue 182–83, 324–25, 674–75, 679–80; Canon's Yeoman's Tale 1428–29).

82. "'Tullyus of the Drem of Scipioun'" (*Parliament of Fowls* 31) is not really an exception: though usually appended (or prefixed) to Macrobius's *Commentary* on it, it is clearly a separate work, and a reader would have had plenty of opportunity in the early part of the *Commentary* (or possibly even in a title) to find both Cicero's name and the name of his work. Moreover, Chaucer may have seen the work by itself. Though the old myth persists that the *Somnium Scipionis* was preserved during the Middle Ages only by Macrobius, I know of five manuscripts from before the fourteenth century (there are no doubt others) that contain the *Somnium Scipionis* separately and at least twenty-eight from the fifteenth century.

Nor are the "'lyf . . . of Seynt Cecile'" (Prologue F to the *Legend of Good Women* 426) and single letters from the *Heroides* (*Legend of Good Women* 1366, 1678, 2220) really exceptions. For the legend of St. Cecilia Chaucer may have used one of the separate versions that were in circulation during the Middle

76

Ages, or he may have used the *Legenda Aurea*, a compilation of earlier legends that was transmitted in various states of completeness. Ovid's *Heroides* was known to Chaucer as *Epistles* or *Epistle* (*House of Fame* 379, Prologue G to the *Legend of Good Women* 305, *Legend of Good Women* 1465, Man of Law's Introduction 55), from its probable original title *Heroidum Epistolae*; the work is a series of clearly separate letters, and it too was transmitted in various states of completeness.

83. Besides the example already cited, there are at least four others: Prologue F to the *Legend of Good Women* 329, 370; Prologue G (only) 341; *Treatise on the Astrolabe* 62–63. A fifth is *Romaunt* 5666, but it is from Part B and should probably not be counted.

84. *De*: Monk's Tale headnote, Merchant's Tale 1811, Parson's Tale 754, Retraction 1098; also many examples in subheadings to the Parson's Tale. *Ad*: Parson's Tale 598, 634, 739, 748. *In*: *Boece* III, pr. 9.192. *Contra*: many examples in subheadings to the Parson's Tale.

85. Prologue G to the *Legend of Good Women* 281: "'Jerome agayns Jovynyan'" and Wife of Bath's Prologue 675: "'agayn Jovinian'," both translations of St. Jerome's *Epistola Adversus Jovinianum; Parliament of Fowls* 31: "'Tullyus of the Drem of Scipioun'," a translation of Cicero's *De Somnio Scipionis*; and Prologue F to the *Legend of Good Women* 428: "'Origenes upon the Maudeleyne'," perhaps a translation of *Origenis de Maria Magdalena*. Cf. *Romaunt* 4884: "'Of Age'," Cicero's *De Senectute*, though the line is probably not by Chaucer.

86. See Maccarrone, in his edition, pp. xxxii–xxxv; and see n. 118.

87. See p. 51.

88. The definition is from Charlton T. Lewis and Charles Short, *A Latin Dictionary* (Oxford: Clarendon Press, 1879), p. 407; cf. *MED, condicioun*, sense 1a.

89. See *Thesaurus Linguae Latinae*, 4 (Leipzig: B. G. Teubner, 1946–49), col. 131; cf. *MED, condicioun*, senses 3a and 3b, and *OED, condition*, senses 11–13. And cf. the ambiguity produced by Lotario's own words at the beginning of Book I, chap. 8: "O vilis humane condicionis indignitas, indigna vilitatis humane condicio!"

90. In thirty-six out of forty instances the word refers to the act itself; in the other four (*House of Fame* 968; Parson's Tale 562, 621, 939) the word refers to the thing begotten or produced. The forty may be found in J. S. P. Tatlock and Arthur G. Kennedy's *Concordance to the Complete Works of Geoffrey Chaucer* (Washington, D.C.: Carnegie Institution, 1927), under *Engender* (5), *Engendered* (15), *Engendereth* (4), *Engendring* (5), *Engendrure* (10), *Engendrures* (1), although the three examples from Part B of the *Romaunt* should probably not be counted. See especially Chaucer's translation of Boethius IV, pr. 6.42, where *engendrynge* is a rendering of *generatio*, and II, m. 3.22, where *engendred* is a rendering of *genitum*.

91. The definitions are translated from the *Thesaurus Linguae Latinae*, 4, col. 145: "creatio, procreatio; actus creandi; de rebus procreatio vel effectis i. q. creatura."

92. Albert Blaise, *Dictionnaire latin-français des auteurs chrétiens* (Strasbourg:

"Le Latin chrétien," 1954), p. 192; Charles DuF. DuCange, *Glossarium Mediae et Infimae Latinitatis*, new ed. by Léopold Favre, 2 (Niort: L. Favre, 1883), 488; J. F. Niermeyer, *Mediae Latinitatis Lexicon Minus*, fasc. 3 (Leiden: E. J. Brill, 1956), 240; Alexander Souter, *A Glossary of Later Latin to 600 A. D.* (Oxford: Clarendon Press, 1949), p. 69.

93. I follow the *Thesaurus Linguae Latinae*'s etymological separation of the three meanings; but cf. Blaise, p. 192, who lists 'nature' under *conditio*. See also the discussion by John E. B. Mayor, "On Condicio and Conditio," *Journal of Philology*, 8 (1879), 265–68.

94. The word *conditio* 'creation, procreation' appears as early as the tenth century in a Latin–Old English glossary in MS. Harley 3376 (see T. Wright and R. P. Wülcker's *Anglo-Saxon and Old English Vocabularies*, 2nd ed. [London: Trübner and Co., 1884], 1, col. 213: "*Conditio, i. status, iudicio, procreatio, natura, sors, regula, lex, rectitudo*, gescæp, gewyrd, gescæft, gebyrd"). It is well attested in its figurative sense of 'founding, foundation' all through the Middle Ages in the British Isles (see R. E. Latham, ed., *Revised Medieval Latin Word-List from British and Irish Sources*, London: Oxford University Press, 1965, p. 104: citations from seventh, eighth, twelfth centuries, and from ca. 1400). The derivative *conditor* 'creator' was known by British writers (see Latham, p. 104: citations from ca. 730, twelfth century, ca. 1504), including Chaucer himself, who renders the word by either *creatour* or *makere* in his translation of Boethius (I, m. 5.1; II, pr. 5.50, 138; IV, m. 6.41; V, m. 2.7). Various forms of *condo* 'create' can be found in Latin–Old English glossaries (in MS. Cotton Cleopatra A. III, of the eleventh century, as printed in Wright and Wülcker, 1, col. 367: "*Conderunt*, gesettan"; also *The Corpus Glossary* of the late eighth century, ed. W. M. Lindsay, Cambridge: Cambridge University Press, 1921, p. 42, ll. 540–41: "i Condidit: *gesette" and p. 44, l. 644: "i Condita: composita") and in Latin written in the British Isles (see Latham, p. 104: the adjective *conditivus* 'able to establish', ca. 1260). Some forms of *condo* were in fact known to Chaucer through the *De Consolatione Philosophiae* (see Chaucer's translation II, pr. 2.37: *condere*, "to make"; V, pr. 6.55: *conditori*, "makid").

95. Chaucer uses the words *conceive* (in various forms) and *conception* only twenty-one times, in comparison with the forty-one for *engendring* and related words (see n. 90); other words like *creation, procreation, begotten* (and their various forms) appear less often.

96. The following will indicate the variety: *De Miseria; De Contemptu Mundi; De Miserabili Ingressu, Progressu, et Egressu Hominis; De Miseria Hominis et Fragilitate Humane Conditionis; De Vilitate Conditionis Humane Incipit Speculum Ecclesie vel Contemptus Mundi; De Miserabili Humane Conditionis Egressu de Contemptu Mundi et de Multis et Diversis Aliis Conditionibus.* For the sake of clarity, both here and in the following discussion of manuscript titles, I have normalized spelling, capitalization, and word order and omitted nonessential words; in doing so, I have been careful not to distort the meanings of the titles in any way. All manuscripts can be found listed in Appendix I.

97. Only two patterns that may have some relevance to Chaucer's choice of title are discernible in these four main titles. First, *De Contemptu Mundi* is far more common as a title, either by itself or in combination, in British

manuscripts than in non-British manuscripts: 34 of 115 versus 78 of 553. Second, and by contrast, *De Vilitate Humane Conditionis* is almost nonexistent as a title, either by itself or in combination, in British manuscripts: only 3 of 115 versus 107 of 553. For another pattern see n. 110, and for the way in which I have determined "British" manuscripts, see n. 170.

98. See p. 51.

99. Cf. *De Libro Miserie Conditionis* (Würzburg, Universitätsbibl., ch. f. 193, 14th c., and p. th. f. 127b, 14th c.; Vatican, Ottob. lat. 128, 13th c.), *De Miseria seu Conditione Vilitatis Humane* (West Berlin, Staatsbibl., lat. qu. 64, 15th c.), and *De Conditione Humane Miserie* (West Berlin, Staatsbibl., theol. lat. fol. 240, 15th c.), where there is no way of telling from the titles alone exactly what *Conditione* or *Conditionis* means.

100. For *De Miseria Conditionis Humane Nature,* Munich, Staatsbibl., Clm 21103, 15th c., Prague, Nar. Muz., XIII D 28, 15th c., and, at the end, Prague, Univ., adlig. 40. G. 8, 15th c.; for *De Vilitate Conditionis Humane Nature,* Rodez, Bibl. Mun., 60, 15th c., Sankt Florian, Stiftsbibl., XI. 126, 14th c., and, at the end, Madrid, Bibl. Nac., 8854, 15th c.; for *De Fragilitate Conditionis Humane Nature,* Wolfenbüttel, Herz.-Aug.-Bibl., Gud. lat. 233, 15th c.

101. For *De Contemptu Mundi et Miseria Humane Nature,* Worcester, Cathedral, F. 152, 14th c. For *De Miseria et Vilitate Humane Nature,* Braunschweig, Stadtbibl., 163, 14th-15th c.; Paris, Bibl. Nat., lat. 3697, 14th c., lat. 14444, late 12th c., lat. 15737, 13th c., lat. 16331, 13th c.; and Vatican, Ottob. lat. 33, 15th c.

102. Brussels, Bibl. Royale, 1138-59, 15th c. The word *genus* usually means 'race', 'class', 'species', 'kind', etc.

103. In at least eleven manuscripts: Cambridge, Peterhouse, 219, 14th c.; London, British Library (B. L.), Harley 3923, 14th c.; Amiens, Bibl. Mun., 481, 14th c.; Krakow, Bibl. Jag., 1422, 14th c.; Munich, Staatsbibl., Clm 21103, 15th c.; Prague, Univ., XIV D 7, 15th c.; Salzburg, Universitätsbibl., M II 143, 15th c.; Torino, Bibl. Naz., D vi 45, 14th c.; Überlingen, Leopold-Sophien-Bibl., 18, 15th c.; Vatican, Vat. lat. 1248, 13th c.; Wroclaw, Bibl. Uniw. Milich 12,88/9421, 15th c. In another three manuscripts, because of possible confusion in the main title, a reader would have assumed that *De Miseria Humane Conditionis* was the title to Book I or to chap. 1: London, B. L., Harley 337, 14th c.; Munich, Staatsbibl., Clm 21576, 13th c.; Vienna, Nationalbibl., 12538, 14th c.

104. Cambridge, Peterhouse, 219, 14th c.

105. Oxford, Bodleian, Laud Misc. 527, 14th c.

106. Brussels, Bibl. Royale, 1138-59, 15th c.

107. Erlangen, Universitätsbibl., 546, 15th c. The title is probably in a later hand; below it there is *De Miseria Humane Conditionis* in the same hand as the text of the treatise.

108. General Prologue 421, Nun's Priest's Tale B[2] 4113, *Boece* IV, pr. 6.42.

109. Durham, Cathedral, B. III. 18, 15th c.; Florence, Bibl. Laur., Plut. 89 sup. 90, 16th c.; Florence, Bibl. Naz. Cent., Conv. soppr. D. 8. 119, 15th c.; Krakow, Bibl. Jag., 1398, 15th c.; Prague, Univ., XIV D 23, 14th c.; Reims, Bibl. Mun., 456, 14th c. This possibility was also noted by Koeppel, in "Zur

Chronologie von Chaucer's Schriften," *ES,* 17 (1892), 199–200, and Beatrice Daw Brown, "Chaucer's *Wreched Engendrynge,*" p. 332.

110. *De Miseria Hominis* as a main title is most popular in manuscripts now found in French libraries, whère, out of 109 possible manuscripts, 14 have it by itself, 5 have it in combination with another title, and in 6 it would have become the main title by default. The first French prose translation of the *De Miseria* mentioned in n. 10 above must have been made from a manuscript having the main title *De Miseria Hominis* because its title is *La Livre de la misère de* (or *à*) *l'omme.*

111. Bristol, Roman Catholic Bishopric of Clifton, 6, 15th c.; Oxford, Bodleian, Selden Supra 74, 13th c.; Alba Julia, Bibl. Batth., I 64, 15th c.; Arras, Bibl. Mun., 456, 14th c.; Cambrai, Bibl. Mun., 260, 14th–15th c.; Carcassonne, Bibl. Mun., 30, 15th c.; Lucca, Bibl. Stat., 2110, 13th c.; Madrid, Bibl. Nac., 501, 13th c.; Munich, Staatsbibl., Clm 14243, 15th c.; Naples, Bibl. Naz., VII. G. 58, 14th c.; Pavia, Bibl. Univ., Aldini 167, 15th or 16th c.; Prague, Met. Kap., C. XLVI, 14th c.; Prague, Univ., I G 2, 14th c., IX B 9, 15th c., and XIV F 5, 14th c.; Wroclaw, Bibl. Uniw., I O 23, 15th c.

112. Cambridge, Corpus Christi College, 518, 14th c.; Leipzig, Karl-Marx-Univ., 439, 13th c.; Sankt Florian, Stiftsbibl., XI. 228, 15th c.

113. Cambridge, Univ. Library, Ll.1.15, 14th c.; London, B. L., Royal 4 B.viii, 13th c., and Royal 5 A.viii, 13th c.; Oxford, Christ Church, 91, 14th–15th c.; Vatican, Vat. lat. 2206, 13th c.

114. London, B. L., Harley 337, 14th c.; Munich, Staatsbibl., Clm 21576, 13th c. Both manuscripts have a main title later, before Book I, but the manner in which it is introduced is ambiguous, and it could have been understood as the title to Book I only.

115. London, B. L., Harley 4736, 15th–16th c.; Oxford, Bodleian, Rawlinson C.269, 15th c.; Auxerre, Bibl. Mun., 7, 13th c.; West Berlin, Staatsbibl., lat. qu. 70, 14th c.; Jena, Fried.-Schiller-Universitätsbibl., El.q.7, 15th c.; Munich, Staatsbibl., Clm 6808, 15th c.; Namur, Bibl. de la Société Archéologique, 24, 15th c.; Nantes, Musée Dobrée, VI, 13th c.; Paris, Bibl. Nat., lat. 14444, late 12th c.; Vatican, Rossiano 647, 15th c.

116. Oxford, Bodleian, Rawlinson A.363, 13th c.

117. The manuscripts of the *De Miseria* show that one cannot, and should not, assume that a classical or medieval work was known, during its transmission in manuscript, only by the title that appears in a modern printed edition. If one knew more about how original titles were lost, for what reasons titles were changed, where new titles came from, etc., one would have a clearer understanding of textual transmission in general, and in particular of the possibilities open to a medieval author like Chaucer in choosing a title by which to refer to a work in his own writings. Paul Lehmann's "Mittelalterliche Büchertitel," *Erforschung des Mittelalters,* 5 (Stuttgart: A. Hiersemann, 1962), 1–93, is the closest thing to a discussion of the problem that I have seen, but he is not concerned with changes in specific titles. Because the age of a work, its degree of popularity, the importance of its author, etc. can vary so greatly, probably the only way to approach the problem is to examine each work separately, as I have done here with the *De Miseria.*

118. See Maccarrone's discussion in his edition, pp. xxxii–xxxv. There are works called *De Contemptu Mundi* by, among others, St. Augustine, St. Anselm, St. Bonaventura, and Bernard of Morlais. I have found thirteen different combinations containing *De Contemptu Mundi*. The following title seems to indicate an awareness on the scribe's part that the genre was called contemptus mundi: *De Miseria sive Vilitate Conditionis Humane Qui Contemptus Mundi Dicitur* (Prague, Univ., XII F 18, 15th c.).

119. As with *De Miserabili Humane Conditionis Ingressu* and *De Miseria Hominis*. Another of the popular titles, *De Vilitate Humane Conditionis*, must have originated in the actual text of the prologue 3–5: "set ad deprimendam superbiam, que capud est omnium viciorum, vilitatem humane condicionis utcumque descripsi."

120. In the first one the choice of *Materie* was probably influenced by the title to chap. 2 of Book I—*De Vilitate Materie*; in the second and third *Miserabili* was probably borrowed from *De Miserabili Humane Conditionis Ingressu*, the original title to chap. 1; *Ingressus* in the fourth was probably taken from the same title.

121. Of importance in this connection is the fact that 15 out of 115—or 13 percent—of the British manuscripts have either no title or an inadequate title: 6 manuscripts have no titles anywhere at the beginning, 6 have no main title, and 3 have an inadequate title such as *Incipit Liber* or *Incipit Prologus*.

122. Angers, Bibl. Mun., 403, 14th c.

123. Vatican, Regin. lat. 261, 15th c.

124. Fifteen manuscripts altogether: Baltimore, Walters Art Gallery, W. 348, 15th c.; Besançon, Bibl. Mun., 208, 14th c.; Bonn, Univ. Bibl., 730, 15th c.; Florence, Bibl. Ricc., 824, 15th c.; Graz, Univ., 704, 14th c.; Montserrat, Abadia., 1075, 15th c.; Paris, Bibl. Nat., lat. 16490, 14th c.; Prague, Met. Kap., E. LXV, 1436; Prague, Univ., V G 10, 14th–15th c.; Reims, Bibl. Mun., 564, 15th c.; St. Omer, Bibl. Mun., 297, 15th c.; Vatican, Ottob. lat. 22, 15th c., Ottob. lat. 1472, 14th c., and Vat. lat 2590, 14th c.; Vienna, Nationalbibl., 13822, 15th c. The elevation of *De Miserabili Humane Conditionis Ingressu* would have occurred in at least nine others: Milan, Bibl. Ambros., D 46 sup., 13th c., Paris, Bibl. Nat., lat. 16331, 13th c., Rome, Bibl. Vall., F. 26, 12th–13th c., and Vatican, Vat. lat. 1042, 13th–14th c., where the main title is a later addition; Munich, Staatsbibl., Clm 19130, 14th c., and Clm 21075, 15th c., where *De Miserabili Humane Conditionis Ingressu* is part of the main title; Gdansk, Bibl. Gdańska P. A. N., 1963, 15th c., Milan, Bibl. Ambros., + 48 sup., 13th c., and Wroclaw, Bibl. Uniw., I F 309, 14th c., where the main title is inadequate.

125. London, B. L., Addl. 11760, 15th c. There is a stroke, perhaps added later, between the *c* and the *e* in *conceptus*, making the word appear to be either *condeptus* or *concleptus*.

126. Sankt Pölten, Diöcesanbibl., San Hippolytensis 27, 15th c.

127. London, B. L., Harley 325, 13th c.

128. Koeppel, "Chaucer und Innocenz des Dritten Traktat," pp. 405–6. Even after Prologue F was shown to be earlier by Ten Brink (see n. 134 below), Koeppel did not change his mind about the fragmentary nature of Chaucer's translation (see his "Zur Chronologie von Chaucer's Schriften," pp. 199–200). Lounsbury in fact believed (*Studies in Chaucer,* vol. 1, 426–27 and

vol. 2, 334) that the passages in the Man of Law's Prologue and Tale and the Pardoner's Tale were all Chaucer translated and that he later "struck out the lines containing the reference, because he came to see that they conveyed an impression that something had been done which he had not really attempted" (vol. 1, 427).

129. See p. 30 and n. 134.

130. See references in n. 72.

131. "Has Chaucer's *Wretched Engendering* Been Found?" p. 284.

132. See the tables in B. L. Jefferson's *Chaucer and the Consolation of Philosophy of Boethius* (Princeton: Princeton University Press, 1917), chap. 5; Dean S. Fansler, *Chaucer and the Roman de la Rose* (New York: Columbia University Press, 1914), passim; and John P. McCall's "Chaucer and the Pseudo Origen *De Maria Magdalena*," *Speculum*, 46 (1971), 501-4.

133. By "whole *De Miseria*" I assume also a complete manuscript. It is not impossible that Chaucer could have used a condensed version or a series of extracts, but very few of the extant ones contain all of the chapters from which Chaucer translated in the *Canterbury Tales*, and in those that do there are no textual similarities with the glosses to the Man of Law's Tale. The extant fragments are precisely that, usually containing only the beginning of the treatise. I have compared Chaucer's translations with the French prose and verse translations and find no evidence that would argue for his dependence on any of them. I have also compared Chaucer's translations with the relevant passages in other works, written before his time, that quote from the *De Miseria* and find no persuasive textual similarities. As for commentaries as a possible channel of transmission, to my knowledge there are none, probably because the *De Miseria* is itself a kind of commentary on various passages from the Bible; and there are almost no explanatory glosses. See further, n. 173.

134. It was so accepted as early as 1892, by Bernhard Ten Brink in "Zur Chronologie von Chaucer's Schriften," *ES*, 17 (1892), 13-23. J. L. Lowes documented the priority of F more extensively in "The Prologue to the *Legend of Good Women* as Related to the French *Marguerite* Poems, and the *Filostrato*," *PMLA*, 19 (1904), 593-683, primarily by showing that F is closer to the sources than G. Subsequent publications have given additional evidence, both historical and aesthetic, for the priority of F. See Tatlock, *Development and Chronology*, pp. 86-121; Lowes, "The Two Prologues to the *Legend of Good Women*: A New Test," *Anniversary Papers by Colleagues and Pupils of George Lyman Kittredge* (Boston: Ginn and Co., 1913), pp. 95-104; D. D. Griffith, "An Interpretation of Chaucer's *Legend of Good Women*," in *The Manly Anniversary Studies in Language and Literature* (Chicago: University of Chicago Press, 1923), pp. 32-41; James R. Hulbert, "A Note on the Prologues to the *Legend of Good Women*," *MLN*, 65 (1950), 532-35; Kemp Malone, *Chapters on Chaucer* (Baltimore: Johns Hopkins Press, 1951), pp. 85-99.

135. See especially: Lowes, "The Prologue to the *Legend of Good Women* Considered in Its Chronological Relations," *PMLA*, 20 (1905), 749-71, who bases his date of late 1386 on Chaucer's indebtedness to Deschamps's *Lai de Franchise* (written for May Day, 1385) and the probability that Chaucer did not see the poem until the spring of 1386; Marian Lossing, "The Prologue to the *Legend of Good Women* and the *Lai de Franchise*," *SP*, 39 (1942), 15-35, who

makes it appear unlikely that Chaucer used the *Lai de Franchise*; and Carleton Brown, "The Date of Prologue F to the *Legend of Good Women*," *MLN*, 58 (1943), 274–78, who argues for a date before 7 August 1385 (and presumably after 14 September 1384).

136. See, for example, Lowes, *PMLA*, 20 (1905), 780–801, for the date 1394, based on the omission in G of a reference to Queen Anne, presumably because she had died (7 June 1394). Robert D. French is probably correct in arguing for a terminus ad quem of 1395 when he says that "the modification of some of the more ardent expressions of devotion to the daisy make it appear likely that Chaucer's revision of the Prologue was undertaken at a time when such pointed references to his 'lady sovereyne' would not have been acceptable to the king" (*A Chaucer Handbook*, 2nd ed., New York: Appleton-Century-Crofts, Inc., 1947, p. 128). See also Tatlock, *Development and Chronology*, p. 122.

137. Edward A. Block, in his exhaustive "Originality, Controlling Purpose, and Craftsmanship in Chaucer's *Man of Law's Tale*," *PMLA*, 68 (1953), 614, finds that Chaucer borrowed forty words from Gower: see his pp. 600–602 (including n. 78) and 609–11 for a discussion of the specific passages. See also Margaret Schlauch's chapter on the Man of Law's Tale in *Sources and Analogues of Chaucer's Canterbury Tales*, pp. 155–56, 181–206.

138. See John H. Fisher's *John Gower: Moral Philosopher and Friend of Chaucer* (New York: New York University Press, 1964), p. 290: "If Chaucer had been influenced by Gower [at the end of Group A of the *Canterbury Tales*] to desist in his cultivation of naturalism and return to more 'moral' literature, and if he were even slightly annoyed at the implication that, by finishing the *Confessio*, Gower had somehow surpassed him in poetic achievement, what would have been more natural than that he demonstrate both his return to the strait and narrow and his poetic superiority by outdoing Gower at one of his own stories?" Some of the implications of this possibility are explored by Alfred David in "The Man of Law vs. Chaucer: A Case in Poetics," *PMLA*, 82 (1967), 220–21 et passim.

139. For the date of the *Confessio Amantis* see G. C. Macaulay in his edition, *The Complete Works of John Gower, 2: The English Works* (Oxford: Clarendon Press, 1901), xxi–xxii, and Fisher, p. 116; for the other dates see Fisher, pp. 249–50, 286, et passim.

140. Robinson's note on p. 692 provides the consensus. The fullest discussion is by Tatlock in *Development and Chronology*, pp. 172–88, who believes that the tale was probably written after 1390, the date of the first "edition" of the *Confessio Amantis*.

141. For the view that the passages are later additions see, for example, Skeat (vol. 3, 408), Lowes (*PMLA*, 20 [1905], 795–96), and Brown ("The Man of Law's Head-link," pp. 14–17), but there is no concrete evidence for it.

142. See pp. 32–39.

143. See nn. 49, 50, 54.

144. *The Text of the Canterbury Tales*, vol. 3, 492, and, for the classification itself, vol. 2, 174. The glosses to the Man of Law's Tale are the most widely distributed of all the glosses to the *Canterbury Tales*.

145. Ibid., vol. 3, 525–27. Such noncommittal conclusions are not sub-

stantially different from those made twelve years earlier by Robert L. Campbell, who, in working over much the same material that Manly and Rickert used, came to the conclusion that many of the marginal glosses to the *Canterbury Tales* were of scribal origin and that there was no proof that any of them were written by Chaucer himself ("Extra-Textual Data for a Classification of the Manuscripts of the *Canterbury Tales*," *Abstracts of Theses: Humanistic Series,* 5, Chicago: University of Chicago Press, 1928. 453-56).

146. Ibid., p. 527. There is no reason why one should expect consistency in the glossing, even when it is all from the same work. If a reason is desirable, however, it is probably to be found in the chronology of composition of the Man of Law's Tale. The Man of Law's Introduction was written for a prose tale (possibly the Tale of Melibee) because of the line "I speke in prose, and lat him rymes make" (B^1 96), and it has long been recognized that the Man of Law's Prologue seems out of place, forming only an artificial transition between Introduction and Tale. It may be that Chaucer wrote the Man of Law's Tale with glosses, that he then decided to give it to the Man of Law, and that he needed a transition to the Tale, which he found at hand in a work that he was translating at the time. This is speculation, of course, but would account for the absence of a gloss at B^1 99-121.

147. *The Chaucer Tradition,* p. 127; see also p. 82 and n. 2 on same page. It would seem that Manly and Rickert agree with Brusendorff's statement of the way to determine Chaucerian authorship of a gloss; the reason they presumably give for believing in possible Chaucerian authorship of the glosses to the Clerk's Tale from Petrarch is that "the text of the Latin agrees with Chaucer in several particulars, especially 'alto stilo' for 'alio stilo'" (vol. 3, 527).

148. *PMLA,* 50 (1935), 103.

149. "Chaucer's Manuscript of Petrarch's Version of the Griselda Story," *MP,* 41 (1943-44), 10.

150. "Glosses to the *Canterbury Tales* from St. Jerome's *Epistola Adversus Jovinianum,*" *SP,* 62 (1965), 28-39. In a recent article, "Reflections on a Gloss to the *Prioress's Tale* from Jerome's *Adversus Jovinianum,*" *SP,* 70 (1973), 243-51, John P. Brennan has made a case for Chaucer as the writer of the Latin glosses at Prioress's Tale ll. 1770 and 1773. See also my "Glosses to the *Man of Law's Tale* from Pope Innocent III's *De Miseria Humane Conditionis,*" *SP,* 64 (1967), 1-16, from which the next few pages are quoted in revised form.

151. I have noted every difference between the original and the glosses except the unimportant variations *in-/im-, c/q,* and *d/t* in *sed/set.* The glosses can be found in Manly and Rickert, vol. 3, 494-95. I have checked them, and the variant readings, against the photographs of the manuscripts at the University of Chicago Library and have found them to be admirably accurate. The text of the glosses presented here is my corrected version of Manly and Rickert, with *c/t, u/v,* and capitalization (though not punctuation) regularized according to the usage of the present edition. In three readings in which the four classificatory groups split evenly (*cuius/cui* at Man of Law's Tale 771-77, *dileccione/delectacione* and *tumor/timor* at Man of Law's Tale 1135-38), Manly and Rickert seem to have given priority to the readings contained in Ellesmere. Though I have retained their readings in my text, it is possible that the

alternate readings were in the manuscript originally used for the glosses. See the discussions following Man of Law's Tale 771-77 and 1135-38 and n. 156 and 157 below.

152. Preceding *Semper* in the gloss in some manuscripts, including Hengwrt and Ellesmere, is "Nota de inopinato dolore," the last three words of which are the title to Book I, chap. 21 in the *De Miseria*. They may have been translated by Chaucer as "O sodeyn wo," though it seems more likely to me that this phrase is a translation of "tristicia repentina."

153. The word *latet* may be reflected in *kepe* at Pardoner's Tale 560-61— "In whom that drynke hath dominacioun / He kan no conseil kepe, it is no drede"—which is also a translation from the *De Miseria*, but this correspondence cannot be insisted on. Cf., however, the Tale of Melibee B^2 2384—"Ther is no privatee ther as regneth dronkenesse"—a translation of the French "Nul secret n'est la ou regne yvresse" (*Sources and Analogues of Chaucer's Canterbury Tales*, p. 581), ultimately Vulgate, Prov. 31:4: "Quia nullum secretum est ubi regnat ebrietas," where a French word corresponding to *latet* is not present and therefore not reflected in Chaucer's translation.

154. Adriano Cappelli, *Dizionario di abbreviature latine ed italiane*, 3rd ed. (Milan: U. Hoepli, 1929), pp. 94, 99.

155. See *Thesaurus Linguae Latinae*, 5, pt. 1 (Leipzig: B. G. Teubner, 1909-34), cols. 1166-67. In the specifically Medieval Latin dictionaries the word is defined additionally as 'love of God', 'Christian love', 'charity'; see, for instance, Blaise, p. 273; Du Cange, vol. 2, 171; Niermeyer, fasc. 4 (Leiden: E. J. Brill, 1956), 333; Souter, p. 104.

156. There is the interesting variant *timor* for *tumor* in group 3 and in most manuscripts of group 1 of Manly and Rickert's classificatory groups for the Man of Law's Tale (though not Hengwrt or Ellesmere). Chaucer has translated the phrases and words in the original as follows: [*reatus*] *consciencie*, "conscience"; [*impetus*] *ire*, "ire"; *motus concupiscencie*, "talent" (in its now obsolete sense of 'desire', 'appetite', 'passion'); [*livor*] *invidie*, "envy"; [*tumor*] *superbie*, "pride"; *offensa*, "offence"; *passio*, "passion." The English word in the same series for which there is apparently no corresponding Latin word is *affray*, which I take to mean, following the *MED*, 'fear, consternation, dismay', its primary meaning in Chaucer's works. Neither the untranslated "ardor avaricie" nor the untranslated *iactura* appears to correspond to *affray*, and it is possible that Chaucer's source manuscript contained *timor* for *tumor*, which he would have translated by *affray* (he may have read the phrase "timor superbie," "affray . . . pride"). On the other hand, *affray* might mean 'outcry, uproar, disturbance', which could possibly be a translation of *iactura*; or it might be a translation of *tumor* in its sense of 'excitement of the mind'; or Chaucer might have chosen *affray* to rhyme with *day* because even though a Latin equivalent did not appear in his manuscript, it fit the sense conveyed by Lotario's passage. It is probably best, given the ambiguity of the evidence, to leave open the question of what reading appeared in Chaucer's source manuscript.

157. It is also possible, as I indicate in the preceding note, that *timor* (for *tumor*) may have been in Chaucer's source manuscript, but the evidence is

ambiguous. On the basis of the 208 manuscripts that I have collated, I would judge that approximately one-quarter of all the manuscripts have *timor* for *tumor*.

158. Brusendorff, p. 127.

159. Brusendorff came to a different conclusion, but it is certainly incorrect. Having noticed the rendering of *latet* by *hyd* (pp. 127'–28), he then examined eight editions of the *De Miseria* and, because none of them had *latet*, came to the conclusion that "Chaucer quoted from memory here, unwittingly inserting a word which he duly rendered in his paraphrase" (p. 128). Quoting from memory, I suppose, is a possible way of writing glosses but not for those in the Man of Law's Tale, because *latet* actually appears, along with the other important additions, in a copy of the *De Miseria*—Royal 8 F.xiv.

160. Manly and Rickert, vol. 2, 490; see vol. 2, 36–39 for the reasons behind such a conclusion.

161. "Manly's Conception of the Early History of the *Canterbury Tales*," *PMLA*, 61 (1946), 396. Manly and Rickert never explicitly make this statement, but they do make a number of allusions which, taken together, point to it, as Dempster makes clear (esp. vol. 1, 159; vol. 2, 151, 385, 490, 498–99). One cannot be too grateful for Dempster's collection, organization, and clear presentation of the assumptions on which Manly and Rickert based their edition and which they so often left either obscured or understood.

162. Even if it could be demonstrated that a few more manuscripts of the *De Miseria* had the important readings in the glosses, it is still extremely unlikely that the glosses in Hengwrt and Ellesmere would have had the same text unless they were from Chaucer's manuscript, and even more unlikely—in fact it could happen only by the strangest coincidence—that a learned scribe, in adding the glosses after Chaucer's death, would have had a manuscript so similar to Chaucer's unless it were Chaucer's own.

163. The only remotely possible instruction may be "Nota de inopinato dolore" at Man of Law's Tale 421 (see above, n. 152). But this note refers neither to a specific work nor, even if the work were known, to a specific place in the work; it would still have been necessary for the scribe to hunt through the *De Miseria* to find it.

164. See Chaucer's own comments in "Chaucers Wordes unto Adam, His Owne Scriveyn" and *Troilus and Criseyde* 5.1793–96; Petrarch's complaints about scribes are recorded by Robert K. Root in "Publication Before Printing," *PMLA*, 28 (1913), 425–26. Part of the 1403 "Ordinance of the Writers of Text-Letter, Limners, and Others Who Bind and Sell Books" (in Edith Rickert's *Chaucer's World*, ed. C. C. Olson and M. M. Crow, 1948; rptd. New York: Columbia University Press, 1962, pp. 197–98) is concerned with provisions for the punishment of those members who do not obey the rules of the trade; one suspects that such provisions would not have been necessary unless there had been previous offenders.

165. "The *Canterbury Tales* in 1400," p. 103. These two reasons, expressed in various ways, are the ones usually given for Chaucer's use of glosses in general; see Brusendorff, pp. 82, 127; Campbell, p. 455; Manly and Rickert, vol. 2, 526.

166. There are also three biblical glosses to the Pardoner's Tale that might have been taken from the *De Miseria*: (1) at 483-84: "Nolite inebriari vino in quo est luxuria" (Eph. 5:18); (2) at 522-23: "Esca ventri et venter escis, Deus autem et hunc et illam destruet" (1 Cor. 6:13); and (3) at 549-50: "luxuriosa res vinum et contumeliosa ebrietas" (Prov. 20:1). But as I have indicated, nn. 50 and 54, (2) and (3) appear in a form similar to that in St. Jerome's *Epistola Adversus Jovinianum* and were therefore almost certainly taken from that work. In (1) the gloss appears in a form different from that in Lotario's original, in most of the extant manuscripts, and therefore probably in Chaucer's manuscript ("Fugite vinum" for "Nolite inebriari vino").

167. From this point on I use sigils in place of manuscript titles. They can be found in Appendix I. I have tried to use sigils that would suggest the cities and libraries in question, but because of the large number of manuscripts and the desirability of preserving the alphabetical arrangement, this has not always been possible. In only one case are the sigils slightly out of alphabetical order: in the L's, where, in the interest of space, I have used L rather than Lo to accommodate the large number of London manuscripts. For the gloss readings—as well as for the readings peculiar to British Library, MS. Royal 8 F.xiv and for the large group of manuscripts discussed in Appendix II—I have examined all of the 672 extant manuscripts except those marked with † in Appendix I.

168. The information about manuscripts for this list of readings and for the discussion of the relationships of Royal 8 F.xiv (L^{31}) which follows is based on my collations of 208, or approximately 30 percent, of the 672 extant manuscripts. These manuscripts are asterisked in Appendix I.

169. In corroboration of this possible similarity between L^{31} and Chaucer's translation, it may be of some interest that a number of manuscripts of the *Canterbury Tales*, including Ellesmere and Hengwrt, have *Herke* for *Herkne* at Man of Law's Prologue 113 and that Chaucer translates *Audi* as *Herke* at Man of Law's Tale 425. On the other hand, it is also possible that Chaucer translated *Adverte* by *Herkne*, for in some cases he uses the word in contexts that, at least from a postprinting point of view, do not call for the act of hearing, for example, Clerk's Tale 1141: "And herkneth what this auctour seith therfoore"; *Troilus and Criseyde* 2.31: "That herkneth, as the storie wol devise"; *Troilus and Criseyde* 2.94-95: "But I am sory that I have yow let / To herken of youre book ye preysen thus." Because, in all three cases, Chaucer is thinking of writing in terms of hearing, it may be that he was thinking of the written phrase from Ecclesiastes at Man of Law's Prologue 113-14 in the same way. Or perhaps dramatic considerations may have caused him to translate *Adverte* 'pay attention to' with *Herkne* 'listen to': 'pay attention to' naturally means 'listen to' when one pilgrim is speaking to the others.

170. My discussion of "British" manuscripts in this section is based on all manuscripts in British libraries that are not demonstrably of non-British origin (that is, all but $Bm^1Bm^2BnBv^1Bv^2C^{22}C^{23}E^2L^{33}L^{39}L^{41}O^7O^8O^9O^{12}O^{15}O^{16}$ O^{25}) and on those manuscripts in non-British libraries that are demonstrably or presumably British in origin (that is, $BeD^3D^4D^5D^6Es^2Pa^{10}Ph^1Sa$)—a total of 115. Though there may be some objections to such a procedure—for example,

two Laud manuscripts of the *De Miseria* have no *assigned* provenance, but we know that many manuscripts in the Laud collection came to England from the continent during the Thirty Years' War—it is as close as we can come to a list of "British" manuscripts and therefore to a typical "British" manuscript of the *De Miseria*. The percentages given for each feature, both of all the manuscripts and of the British manuscripts, are based on the number of manuscripts exhibiting or not exhibiting each feature, not on the total number of manuscripts, which would give a misleading picture because of the fragmented, excerpted, and incomplete state of many of them.

171. If L[31] had a title, it might bring us a little closer to the title in Chaucer's manuscript, but unfortunately there is no title anywhere in the text. In the main table of contents to the volume (f. 6v), however, there is the title "Innocencius de miseria hominis et de contemptu mundi," but I am convinced that it has no necessary connection with the text of the *De Miseria* in L[31]. L[31] is one of the volumes that Henry of Kirkestede "acquired" for the Abbey of Bury St. Edmunds, and the table of contents to the whole volume is in his hand (see Richard H. Rouse, "Bostonus Buriensis and the Author of the *Catalogus Scriptorum Ecclesiae*," *Speculum,* 41 [1966], 483, pl. 6, et passim). However, there are a number of differences between the titles given in this table of contents and the actual titles to the individual works in the manuscript, and I suspect that Kirkestede reproduced the titles either from his own extensive bibliographical knowledge or, more likely, from his *Catalogus Scriptorum Ecclesiae*. In the case of the *De Miseria* this is confirmed by the entry in the only surviving copy of the *Catalogus,* Cambridge University Library, Additional 3470, a transcript made by Thomas Tanner in the seventeenth century, on p. 90: "De miseria hominis sive de contemptu mundi." Moreover, Kirkestede seems to have been working on L[31] at the same time as he was compiling the *Catalogus,* for on f. 132, at the beginning of an abridged version of Richard of St. Victor's *Beniamin Maior,* he notes that the work "est perfectus et integre scriptus apud hulmum [St. Benet Hulme, Norfolk] et apud babewell [Babwell, Suffolk] cum raby moyse."

172. See Maccarrone's discussion of these matters, pp. xxv–xxvii.

173. See n. 133 for the reasons for omitting the condensations, excerpts, and fragments. It is possible that Chaucer had a manuscript that omitted some chapters or that broke off before the end (since he translates nothing after Book II, chap. 21), but there is no textual evidence for choosing one of the extant abbreviated manuscripts, and if my analysis of his title is correct (pp. 19–29 above), he intended to make a translation of the whole *De Miseria*. Moreover, nearly all the manuscripts that are not condensations, excerpts, or fragments continue to the end of the work, and very few omit chapters other than the original 2, 3, and 8 of Book III, so that a typical manuscript of the *De Miseria* is a complete one.

174. The three main deviations in L[20] from the typical *De Miseria,* as will be apparent from the critical apparatus to this edition, are in the verbs, the biblical quotations, and transpositions of words. The scribe often produces— and produces very accurately—verb forms that differ from all or most of the other manuscripts that I have collated, especially by substituting the passive

for the active voice; he often abbreviates, and sometimes even omits, biblical passages that appear in most of the other manuscripts; and he transposes two words more often than usual. This scribe (or the scribe of his exemplar) is clearly a good Latinist and knows his Bible thoroughly; he is also very accurate, and is able to catch and correct his own inaccuracies.

175. Only 7 of the possible manuscripts other than C^3 have a larger number of typical variant readings than L^{20} ($AC^{15}L^3L^{27}L^{30}L^{42}O^{22}$): of these, 5 have both and 2 have one of the combinations in C^3; and all have some of the readings characteristic of this possible group. I have also compared the typical variant readings in L^{31} with the possible manuscripts: L^{20} has the same pattern of readings 219 times, or nearly 80 percent, out of a possible 276, with only 4 manuscripts having higher totals ($AC^3L^{30}O^{22}$, with O^{22} the highest with 223, or 81 percent). None of the possible manuscripts has more than 7 of the 195 readings peculiar to L^{31} mentioned in Appendix II, p. 259, so that they cannot be used as criteria for choosing a manuscript.

176. By "English usage" I mean of course my own usage in the accompanying translation. In order to avoid the excessive use of quotation marks in passages from the Vulgate, I have indicated quotations within quotations only when they are called for by the text of the *De Miseria*. I have not followed the customary practice, which seems to me awkward, of capitalizing the first letter of personal, relative, and interrogative pronouns whose antecedent is "God", "the Lord", "Jesus", or "Christ"; I capitalize the first letter of *apostolus* only when it refers to Paul, whose Christian name is never used by either Lotario or the scribe of L^{20}.

177. The tables of contents to the three books can be found on the following folios in L^{20}: Book I, ff. 78-78v; Book II, ff. 89v-90; Book III, f. 103. See the Frontispiece for the placement of the table of contents to Book I in relation to the text. There are few differences between the titles in the text and the titles in the tables of contents. I list them all here: I.9—*De Incommodis Senectutis et Brevitate Vite*; I.25—*De Speciebus Egritudinum;* I.6—*Insaciabili* omitted; II.13—*De Superflua Sollicitudine Cupidorum*; II.15—*Cur Avaricia Dicatur Servitus Ydolorum*; II.27—*De Nimia Concupiscencia Ambicionis*; II.29—*De Brevi et Misera Vita Magnatum*; III.10—*Supplicibus* for *Suppliciis*; III.12—*Precedenti* for *Precedente*; III.13—*Item de Die Iudicii*.

178. The scribe of L^{20} does not list Book II, chap. 1, as a separate chapter in the table of contents to II, perhaps because it was not so listed in his exemplar or perhaps because he, like the scribe of C^{18} (or of his exemplar), considered it a kind of prologue, or introduction, in which the main topics of the book were outlined. I have, however, numbered it as a separate chapter to conform to the practice of the majority of the manuscripts (as well as of Lotario's original).

179. In this and the following descriptions I give only information that seems to me relevant to the *De Miseria* as it appears in each manuscript. For fuller descriptions see the printed catalogues for $C^3C^{10}C^{14}E^1L^{31}V^2$ and the unpublished description for C^{18}, listed after each summary of contents; for L^{20} and Ro the catalogues are inadequate, and the descriptions given here are the fullest now available.

180. Rouse, p. 483.

181. See Rouse, p. 494, though Kirkestede probably "acquired" the collection for Bury somewhat earlier than 1378, because L[31] is not one of the manuscripts that illustrates the noticeable tremor of his hand in the late 1370s.

182. Maccarrone, in his edition, p. xxix.

183. I do not record these, but they can be found throughout the manuscript and include such obvious misreadings as "enim liphas" for *Eliphat* or *Eliphaz* (I.23.10) or *v.* (an abbreviation for *quinque*) for *quique* (II.23.13); in fact, the scribe was so careless that he could not even get the well known "O vanitas vanitatum" right on the first try, producing instead "O vanitas vanitas," which he then corrected to the original by changing *s* to *t* and adding *-um* (II.39.10-11).

184. In some cases neither Ro nor V[2] preserves Lotario's probable original reading. Thus, if neither Ro nor V[2] appears in the critical apparatus, it should be assumed that the reading in L[20] is also the original reading unless there is a variant for it found in "*most MSS*," which in nearly every case will be the probable reading in Lotario's original.

185. Some 155 manuscripts in all, though the great majority of them appear only a few times in the critical apparatus. Those on which I have relied most heavily (more than ten readings) are Ar, Au, Bu, C[9], D[1], Ev, Go, I, L[17], L[40], Lm, Mu[5], O[21], O[31], Pa[5], Pa[9], Pa[11], Re[3], Ru[2], and T[2].

186. Specifically, *si* for *si si* at I.14.15; *insidiantur* for *insidiaitur* at I.18.2; *convivii* for *convii* at I.21.13; *ossa* for *ossia* at I.23.12; *relinquunt* for *relinquntit* at I.28.45-46; *contempta* for *contentpta* at I.29.7; and *deviet* for *deivet* at II.41.20. Occasionally the scribe of L[20] gives an ungrammatical reading or consistently misspells a word, and where these occur, I have translated according to what I assume he intended.

187. The edition I have used is *The Holy Bible*, with preface by the Cardinal Archbishop of Westminster (1914; rptd. London: Burns and Oates, 1964).

DE MISERIA
CONDICIONIS HUMANE

Here Begins the Book of the Misery of the Human Condition Published by Lotario, Cardinal-Deacon of Saints Sergius and Bachius, Who Was Afterwards Called Pope Innocent the Third.

PREFACE

For my dearest lord Father Peter, Bishop of Porto and Saint Rufina, Lotario, unworthy cardinal-deacon, prays for grace in the present and glory in the future.

HERE BEGINS THE PROLOGUE

A bit of leisure, which I caught among many difficulties recently on that occasion which you know of, did not pass for me completely in leisure, but to put down pride, which is the chief of all vices, I described the vileness of the human condition in one way or another. Nevertheless I have dedicated the title of the present little work to your name, asking and requesting that if your judgment shall find anything worthy in it, it ascribe all to divine grace. Indeed if your reverence shall advise, I will describe, with Christ's aid, the dignity of human nature, so that just as in this book the haughty man is humbled, so in the next the humble man may be exalted.

[HERE BEGINS THE FIRST PART]

[1] OF THE MISERY OF MAN

"Why came I out of my mother's womb to see labor and sorrow and that my

Title Condicionis Humane *trans many MSS incl* C³; Incipit Tractatus . . . de Contemptu Mundi C¹⁰; Hic Incipit Tractatus Domini Pape Innocencii de Vilitate Humane Materie et de Contemptu Mundi C¹⁴; Incipit Prologus Libri Innocencii Pape Tercii de Miseria Condicionis Humane C¹⁸; *no title in* L³¹, *but* spiritus assit nobis gracia *is in top margin in same hand; for others see Introduction, pp. 23–25 and n. 96.*
Prefacio: *the present* Prefacio *and* Prologus *are normally combined into a single section known as the* Prologus, *with separate title om, as in* C¹⁰C¹⁴C¹⁸L³¹Ro; Prologus *in margin in hand of rubricator* C³. 1 **Petro** Petro Dei gracia *most MSS incl* C¹⁴C¹⁸L³¹V²; Petro divina dignacione Er²Wo². 1–2 **et . . . Ruffine** *om most MSS incl* C³C¹⁰C¹⁴C¹⁸L³¹; et Sancte Rufine ecclesie Ro. 3 **cardinalis** *om most MSS incl* C³C¹⁰C¹⁴C¹⁸L³¹; cardinalis Sanctorum Sergi et Bachi Ro.
Prologus: 1 **multas** multas diuturnasque C¹⁸. 2 **qua** quam *most MSS incl* C¹⁰ C¹⁴C¹⁸V²; que L³¹. **nostis** nosti *most MSS incl* C³C¹⁰C¹⁴; *om* C¹⁸. **michi** me C¹⁰C¹⁸L³¹. 5 **utcumque** utrumque C³C¹⁸; interim C¹⁰. 6 **nomini vestro** *trans most MSS incl* C³C¹⁰C¹⁴C¹⁸L³¹. 7 **postulans** expostulans C¹⁸. **si quid** quod C¹⁰L³¹; sicut C¹⁸. 10 **quatinus** *om* C¹⁰L³¹. **ita** ita ut C¹⁰C¹⁸; ut L³¹. 11 **ut** ut et C³; et C¹⁴C¹⁸L³¹. **exaltetur** *a table of contents to Book I follows the* Prologus *in many MSS incl* L²⁰ *(on ff. 78–78v) and* Ro, *entitled* Incipiunt Capitula Prime Partis L²⁰, Incipiunt Capitula Libri Primi Ro; *table of contents om most MSS incl* C¹⁰C¹⁴C¹⁸L³¹ *(see Introduction, p. 52); table of contents also om* C³, *but one to the whole treatise added in an early fourteenth-century hand on flyleaf iiir–v.*

Incipit Liber de Miseria Condicionis Humane Editus f. 78 a Lothario, Diacono-Cardinali Sanctorum Sergii et Bachii, Qui Postea Innocencius Papa Tercius Appelatus Est.

PREFACIO

Domino Patri karissimo *Petro,* Portuensi et Sancte Ruffine Episcopo, Lotharius, indignus diaconus-cardinalis, graciam in presenti et gloriam in futuro.

INCIPIT PROLOGUS

Modicum ocii, quod inter multas angustias nuper ea qua nostis occasione captavi, non ex toto michi preteriit ociosum, set ad deprimendam superbiam, que capud est omnium viciorum, vilitatem humane
5   condicionis utcumque descripsi. Titulum autem presentis opusculi nomini vestro dedicavi, rogans et postulans ut si quid in eo vestra discrecio dignum invenerit, divine gracie totum ascribat. Si vero paternitas vestra suggesserit, dignitatem humane
10 nature, Christo favente, describam, quatinus ita per hoc humilietur elatus, ut per illud humilis exaltetur.

[INCIPIT PRIMA PARS]

[1] DE MISERIA HOMINIS   f. 78v

"Quare de vulva matris mee egressus sum ut vide- Ieremias
rem laborem et dolorem et consumerentur in confu-

days should be spent in confusion?" If he whom God sanctified in the womb spoke such things about himself, what things shall I say of myself, whom my mother brought forth in sin? Ah me, I might say, my mother, why did you bear me, the son of bitterness and sorrow? "Why did I not die in the womb? Having come out of the belly, why did I not perish at once? Why received upon the knees, suckled at the breasts," born "for burning and for fuel for the fire"? If only I had been destroyed in the womb, so "that my mother might have been my grave and her womb an everlasting conception." "For I should have been as if I had not been, carried from the womb to the grave." Who therefore will give my eyes a fountain of tears so that I may bewail the miserable beginning of the human condition, the culpable progress of human behavior, the damnable ending of human dissoluteness. With tears I might consider what man is made of, what man does, what man will be. Man is indeed formed from earth, conceived in sin, born to pain. He does depraved things that are unlawful, shameful things that are indecent, vain things that are unprofitable. He becomes fuel for the fire, food for worms, a mass of putridness. I shall show this more clearly; I shall analyze more fully. Man is formed of dust, of clay, of ashes: what is more vile, from the filthiest sperm. He is conceived in the heat of desire, in the fervor of the flesh, in the stench of lust: what is worse, in the blemish of sin. He is born to labor, fear, sorrow: what is more miserable, to death. He does depraved things by which he offends God, offends his neighbors, offends himself. He does vain and shameful things by which he pollutes his fame, pollutes his person, pollutes his conscience. He does vain things by which he neglects serious things, neglects profitable things, neglects necessary things. He will become fuel for the inextinguishable fire that always flames and burns; food for the immortal worm that always eats and consumes; a mass of horrible putridness that always stinks and is filthy.

I.1: *Title* De Miseria Hominis Ieremias C[10]; De Miseria Condicionis Humane Capitulum Primum C[14]; Finito Prologo Incipit Capitulum Primum C[18]; Incipit Primus Liber de Miserabili Humane Conditionis Ingressu Primum Capitulum Primi Libri Ro. 1 **mee** *om* C[3]C[14]V[2]. 4 **Deus sanctificavit** Dominus sanctificavit *most MSS incl* C[3]C[10]C[14]L[31]V[2]; sanctificavit Dominus C[18]. 7 **vulva** vulva conceptus L[31]. **sum** sive C[18]. 8 **de** C[10]; ex *most MSS incl* C[14]Ro. **exceptus** conceptus L[31]. 9 **genibus** genibus cur L[31], *above line* C[14]. 10 **cibum** in cibum C[18]; cibus L[31]. 11 **ut** et C[10]C[18]. **michi** *om* C[18]L[31]. **sepulchrum** sepulcrum vel tumulus *above line* C[14], *in margin* O[24]. 12 **enim** *om* C[10]C[14]C[18]L[31]. 13 **qui** *om most MSS incl* C[3]C[10]C[14]C[18]L[31]V[2]. **de utero** *om* L[31]. 14 **det ergo** *trans most MSS incl* C[3]C[10]C[14]C[18]L[31]V[2]. 15 **fleam** defleam C[10]C[18]L[31]. 16 **culpabilem humane** hunc BuGoPa[9]Pa[11]. 17–18 **Consideraverim** Consideramini C[18]; Considerabam L[31]; *many variants incl* Considerabo, Consideram, Considerans, Consideraverunt. 18 **ergo** *om* L[31]. **est** sit C[3]. 19 **futurus** facturus C[14]. 20 **est homo** *om most MSS incl* C[3]C[10]C[18]L[31]; homo C[14]. 22 **Fit** Fiet *most MSS incl* C[3]C[10]C[14]C[18]L[31]Ro. 22–23 **cibus ignis** cinis BuGoPa[5]Pa[9]Pa[11]. 24 **planius . . . plenius** plenius edisseram planius C[3]; planius edisseram plenius *most MSS incl* C[14]V[2]; brevius sive planius C[18]; brevius sive planius edisseram planius L[31]. 25 **luto de cinere** cinere de luto C[10]C[18]; cinere et luto L[31]. **quodque** et quod C[18]L[31]. 26 **spurcissimo** purissimo C[2]; vilissimo AuBuGoILmPa[9]Pa[11]. **Conceptus** Conceptus est C[3]. 27 **quodque** et quod C[14]C[18]L[31]. 28–29 **timorem** timorem et *most MSS incl* C[3]C[10]C[14]C[18]L[31]. 29 **quodque** et quod L[31]. 31 **vana et** *om most MSS incl* C[3]C[10]C[14]C[18]L[31]Ro. 36 **qui** que *most MSS incl* C[3]C[10]C[14]C[18]L[31]Ro.

sione dies mei?" Si talia locutus est ille de se quem
Deus sanctificavit in utero, qualia loquar ego de me,
quem mater mea genuit in peccato? Heu me, dixerim, mater mea, quid me genuisti, filium amaritu-
dinis et doloris? "Quare non in vulva mortuus sum?
Egressus de utero, non statim perii? Cur exceptus
genibus, lactatus uberibus," natus "in combus-
tionem et cibum ignis"? Utinam interfectus fuissem
in utero, "ut fuisset michi mater mea sepulchrum et
vulva eius conceptus eternus." "Fuissem enim quasi
qui non essem, de utero translatus ad tumulum."
Quis det ergo oculis meis fontem lacrimarum, ut
fleam miserabilem humane condicionis ingressum,
culpabilem humane conversacionis progressum,
dampnabilem humane dissolucionis egressum? Consideraverim ergo cum lacrimis de quo factus est
homo, quid faciat homo, quid futurus sit homo. Sane
formatus est homo de terra, conceptus in culpa,
natus ad penam. Agit prava que non licent, turpia
que non decent, vana que non expediunt. Fit cibus
ignis, esca vermis, massa putredinis. Exponam id
planius; edissera plenius. Formatus est homo de
pulvere, de luto, de cinere: quodque vilius est, de
spurcissimo spermate. Conceptus in pruritu carnis,
in fervore libidinis, in fetore luxurie: quodque deterius / est, in labe peccati. Natus ad laborem, ti-   f. 79
morem, dolorem: quodque miserius est, ad mortem.
Agit prava quibus offendit Deum, offendit proximum, offendit seipsum; agit vana et turpia quibus
polluit famam, polluit personam, polluit conscien-
ciam. Agit vana quibus negligit seria, negligit utilia,
negligit necessaria. Fiet cibus ignis qui semper ardet
et urit inextinguibilis; esca vermis qui semper rodit
et commedit immortalis; massa putredinis qui semper fetet et sordet horribilis.

"Therefore the Lord God formed man of the slime of the earth," which is inferior to other elements. He made the planets and the stars from fire, made the breezes and the winds from air, made the fish and the birds from water, made men and beasts from earth. If man therefore considers the creatures of the water, he will discover that he is vile; if he considers the things of the air, he will know that he is more vile; if he considers the things of fire, he will consider that he is most vile. He will neither be able to make himself equal to the stars nor dare to prefer himself to earthly things, because he will discover that he is equal to the beasts, will know that he is similar. "Therefore the death of men and of beasts is one, and the condition of them both is equal, and man hath nothing more than beast. Of earth they were made, and into earth they return together." The words are not those of just any man, but of wisest Solomon. What therefore is man but clay and ashes? For man says to God: "Remember, I beseech, that thou hast made me as the clay, and thou wilt bring me into dust again." And God replies to man: "Dust thou art, and into dust thou shalt return." "I am compared," he says, "to dirt and am likened to embers and ashes." Clay is made from water and dust, both remaining; ashes, however, are made from fire and wood, both disappearing. A mystery expressed, but to be explained at another time. Therefore, mud, what are you proud of? Dust, what are you puffed up about? Ashes, why do you boast?

[3] OF THE FLAW OF CONCEPTION

But perhaps you will reply that Adam himself was made from the slime of the earth but that you were created from human seed. On the contrary, he was

I.2: *Title* De Vilitate Materie dè Qua Formatus Est Homo Ro. 1 **Formavit** F *in another hand in margin* L³¹. **Dominus . . . hominem** Dominus Deus Adam C¹⁰C¹⁸; Adam Dominus L³¹. 3 **Stellas** terre stellas C³. 3-4 **ex (*all three*)** de C¹⁸. 4 **homines** hominem C¹⁸. 5 **igitur aquatiqua** ergo homo aquatica C¹⁰L³¹. 5-6 **igitur . . . considerans** *om* C¹⁸. 6 **aerea** *om in text but* aera *added in margin in another hand* L³¹. 8 **valebit . . . celestibus** se parificare celestibus C³; audebit se parificare celestibus C¹⁰C¹⁸; se celestibus valebit parificare L³¹. 9 **iumentis inveniet** *trans* L³¹; iumentis inveniet et Ro. 10 **recognoscet** se agnoscet C¹⁸L³¹Bs; se recognoscet Bv¹Er²O¹³. **enim** *om* C¹⁴C¹⁸L³¹. 11 **utriusque** utrius L³¹. 12 **nichil** nichil aut parum L³¹BeDu³O⁵U⁴U⁶U⁷. **iumento . . . amplius** homo iumento amplius *most MSS incl* C³C¹⁰C¹⁴C¹⁸Ro; homo amplius iumento L³¹. 12 **De . . . orta** Dum de terra C¹⁸. 13 **revertentur** revertuntur Ro. 14 **hominis** *om* L³¹. 15 **igitur** ergo C³C¹⁸Ro; *om* L³¹. **cinis** cinis Lutum . . . deficiente *(trans of lines 20–22)* C¹⁰; cinis Lutum efficitur ex aqua ex cinere utroque . . . igne in ligno utroque deficiente C¹⁸; cinis Lutum confiscitur ex aqua . . . fit ex ligno et igne utroque deficiente L³¹. 16 **dicit homo** *trans most MSS incl* C³C¹⁰C¹⁴C¹⁸L³¹V². **Deum** Dominum memento quod cinis es et in cinerem reverteris L³¹. 17 **reduxisti** reduces *most MSS incl* C¹⁰C¹⁴Ro; red' C³C¹⁸; re L³¹. 18 **et** *om* C¹⁴; eciam L³¹. **inquid** dicit *most MSS incl* C³C¹⁴C¹⁸L³¹V². 19 **ait** ait Iob C¹⁸L³¹. 20 **sum** *om* C¹⁰C¹⁸. 20-22 **Lutum . . . deficiente** *om* C¹⁰C¹⁸L³¹. 24 **De** Vel C¹⁰C¹⁸. **pulvis** *om* L³¹.

I.3: 1-12 **An . . . alienis** *included in I.2 in many MSS incl* Ro, *with a new chapter beginning at line 13 with* Est enim duplex, *entitled* De Conceptione Infantis (*see Introduction, p. 52*). 1 **An** verum V². **forsitan** forsan C¹⁰L³¹. **respondebis** respondebit C¹⁰C¹⁴. **Adam ipse** *trans* L³¹. 1-2 **fuit . . . formatus** fuit formatus de limo terre C¹⁰C¹⁸; formatus est de limo terre C¹⁴. 2 **semine** corpore C¹⁰. 3 **fuit formatus** *trans*

[2] DE VILITATE MATERIE

"Formavit igitur Dominus Deus hominem de limo
terre," que ceteris est indignior elementis. Planetas
et stellas fecit ex igne, flatus et ventos fecit ex aere,
pisces et volucres fecit ex aqua, homines et iumenta
5 fecit de terra. Considerans igitur aquatiqua, se vilem
inveniet; considerans aerea, se viliorem agnoscet;
considerans ignea, se vilissimum reputabit. Nec
valebit se parificare celestibus nec audebit se pre-
ferre terrenis, quia parem se iumentis inveniet,
10 similem recognoscet. "Unus est enim hominum et
iumentorum interitus, et equa utriusque condicio, et
nichil habet iumento homo amplius. De terra orta
sunt et in terram pariter revertentur." Verba sunt
ista non cuiuslibet hominis, sed sapientissimi Salo-
15 monis. Quid est igitur homo nisi lutum et cinis?
Hinc enim dicit homo ad Deum: "Memento, queso,   Iob
quod sicut lutum feceris me et in pulverem reduxisti
me." Hinc et Deus inquid ad hominem: "Cinis es, et   Genesis
in cinerem reverteris." "Comparatus sum," ait,   Iob
20 "luto et assimilatus sum faville et cineri." Lutum
efficitur ex aqua et pulvere, utroque manente; cinis,
autem, fit ex igne et ligno, utroque deficiente.
Expressum misterium, set alias exprimendum. Quid
ergo, lutum, superbis? De quo, pulvis, extolleris?
25 Unde, cinis, gloriaris?

[3] DE VICIO CONCEPCIONIS /

An illud forsitan respondebis quod Adam ipse fuit de   f. 79v
limo terre formatus, tu autem ex humano semine

97

made from earth, but virgin; you were created from seed, but unclean. "Who can make him clean that is conceived of unclean seed?" "What is man that he should be without spot and he that is born of a woman that he should appear just?" "For behold I was conceived in iniquities, and in sins did my mother conceive me." Not in one such sin, not in one such transgression, but in many sins and in many transgressions: in her own transgressions and sins, in the transgressions and sins of others. There is, however, a double conception, one of seeds and the other of natures. The first is in the commission, the second in the fulfillment. In the first the parents commit; in the second the offspring fulfill. Who does not know that copulation, even conjugal, is never performed entirely without the heat of desire, without the fervor of the flesh, without the stench of lust? Because of this conceived seeds are made filthy, defiled, and spoiled, from which seeds the soul ultimately imparted contracts the blemish of sin, the stain of guilt, the filth of iniquity, just as an infused liquid is spoiled by a tainted vessel and, touching the polluted item, is polluted by the contact. For the soul has three natural powers or three natural forces: the rational to distinguish between good and evil, the irascible to reject evil, the appetitive to desire good. These three powers are originally corrupted by three opposite vices: the rational force by ignorance, so that it cannot distinguish between good and evil; the irascible force by anger, so that it rejects good; the appetitive force by lust, so that it desires evil. The first begets transgression, the last produces sin, and the middle one engenders transgression and sin. For it is a transgression not to do what ought to be done, and a sin to do what ought not to be done. These three vices are contracted from the corrupt flesh through three fleshly enticements. For in fleshly intercourse the clarity of

C³C¹⁴C¹⁸L³¹. **set** *om* L³¹. 4 **vero** autem C¹⁸L³¹. **de** ex C¹⁰C¹⁸L³¹. 6 **semine** semine Nonne tu qui solus es GoBuLmPa⁵Pa⁹Pa¹¹. **Quid** Quis C³C¹⁴L³¹Ro. 7 **quod** et *most MSS incl* C³C¹⁰C¹⁴C¹⁸L³¹Ro. 8 **enim** *om* C³C¹⁰C¹⁸L³¹. 9 **peccatis** delictis *many MSS incl* C¹⁰L³¹. **concepit** peperit *many MSS incl* L³¹V²; percepit *or* precepit *many MSS*. **me** *om* C¹⁴ C¹⁸. 9–10 **tantum iniquitate** *trans* C¹⁰C¹⁸L³¹. 10 **non** nec C³C¹⁴L³¹. **tantum** *om* C³C¹⁸ L³¹. **in** cum L³¹. **multis** mulieribus C¹⁸. 11 **iniquitatibus . . . multis** *om* C¹⁰L³¹. **in** *(1st)* *om* C¹⁴C¹⁸. 12 **propriis** propriis videlicet C¹⁰C¹⁸L³¹. 13 **alia** altera *most MSS incl* C³C¹⁰C¹⁴C¹⁸L³¹V². 14 **Prima** Prima fit *most MSS incl* C³C¹⁰C¹⁴C¹⁸L³¹Ro. **fit** *om* C³C¹⁸ Ro. 15 **enim** *om* C¹⁰C¹⁸L³¹. 19–20 **maculantur . . . viciantur** *trans* C¹⁰C¹⁸L³¹. 20 **ex** de L³¹. 21 **culpe** quippe C¹⁸. 23–24 **contactu** tactu C³. 24–25 **anima . . . vires** homo tres naturaliter vires GoIPa⁹Pa¹¹. 24 **naturales** *om* L³¹. 25 **racionalem** scilicet racionalem C¹⁸. **ut** unde L³¹. 27 **respuat** respuiat L³¹. 29 **racionabilis** racionalis *most MSS incl* C³C¹⁰C¹⁴C¹⁸L³¹Ro. 33–34 **delictum generat** *trans* C¹⁴L³¹. 35 **facere faciendum** *trans* L³¹. **agere non agendum** non agendum agere L³¹. **agendum** agendum delictum et peccatum respuere bonum C¹⁰C¹⁸L³¹. 37 **carnales** carnales tres C³; carnales vel naturales *above line* C¹⁴. **quippe** quidem C¹⁰C¹⁴L³¹; quoque C¹⁸. 39 **propagetur** propagetur vel

procreatus. At ille fuit formatus de terra, set virgine; tu vero procreatus de semine, set immundo.
"Quis enim potest facere mundum de immundo Iob
conceptum semine?" "Quid est homo ut immacula-
tus sit quod iustus appareat natus de muliere?"
"Ecce enim in iniquitatibus conceptus sum, et in Psalmus
peccatis concepit me mater mea." Non in una tantum
iniquitate, non in uno tantum delicto, set in multis
iniquitatibus et in multis delictis: in delictis et iniquitatibus propriis, in delictis et iniquitatibus alienis.
Est enim duplex concepcio, una seminum et alia
naturarum. Prima in commissis, secunda fit in con-
tractis. Parentes enim committunt in prima; proles
contrahit in secunda. Quis enim nesciat concubitum,
eciam coniugalem, nunquam omnino committi sine
pruritu carnis, sine fervore libidinis, sine fetore
luxurie? Unde semina concepta fedantur, maculantur, et viciantur, ex quibus anima tandem infusa
contrahit labem peccati, maculam culpe, sordem
iniquitatis, sicut ex vase corrupto liquor infusus
corrumpitur, et, pollutum contingens, ex ipso contactu polluitur. Habet enim anima tres naturales
potencias sive tres naturales vires: racionalem ut
discernat inter bonum et malum, irascibilem ut
respuat malum, concupiscibilem ut appetat bonum.
Iste tres vires tribus oppositis viciis originaliter
corrumpuntur: vis racionabilis per ignoranciam, ut
non discernat inter bonum et malum; vis irascibilis
per iracundiam, ut respuat bonum; vis concupiscibi-
lis per concupiscenciam, ut appetat malum. Prima
gignit delictum, ultima parit peccatum, media delictum generat et peccatum. Est enim delictum non
facere faciendum, peccatum agere non agendum.
Hec tria vicia / contrahuntur ex carne corrupta per f. 80
tres carnales illecebras. In carnali quippe commercio

reason is lulled to sleep, so that ignorance is begotten; the heat of desire is stimulated, so that anger is propagated; the desire for pleasure is satiated, so that lust is produced. This is the tyrant of the flesh, the law of the bodily members, the kindling wood of sin, the weakness of nature, the nourishment of death, without which no one is born, without which no one dies. But if at any time it passes away in terms of culpability, it still remains in terms of potentiality. "For if we say that we have no sin, we deceive ourselves, and the truth is not in us." O grievous necessity and unhappy condition: before we sin, we are bound by sin; and before we transgress, we are held fast by transgression. "By one man sin entered into this world, and by sin death passed upon all men." "Have the fathers not eaten a sour grape, and are the teeth of the children not set on edge?"

[4] WITH WHAT KIND OF FOOD THE FETUS IS FED IN THE WOMB

But notice with what food the fetus is fed in the womb; with menstrual blood of course, which ceases in the woman after conception so that with it the fetus is fed inside the woman. This blood is said to be so detestable and unclean that "on contact with it crops do not germinate, orchards wither, plants die, trees drop their fruit; if dogs eat of it, they are transported into madness." Conceived fetuses contract the defect of the seed, so that lepers and elephantiacs are born from this corruption. Because of this according to the Mosaic law a woman who is undergoing her monthly period is considered unclean, and if anyone comes near a menstruous woman, it is commanded that he be killed. Because of the uncleanness of menstruous women it is also commanded that a woman stay away from the entrance to the temple for forty days if she bears a male child and for seventy days if a female child.

provocetur *above line* C[14]; provocetur Es[2]. 40–41 **contrahatur** carnis irritetur BuGoI Mu[5]Pa[11]; provocatur Au. 42 **nature** vero L[31]. 43 **nemo** nullus C[10]C[18]L[31]. **Quid** Qui C[14]Ro; Quod C[18]L[31]. **si** *om* C[18]. 44 **quando** quandoque C[14]C[18]L[31]. **remanet actu** manet actu C[14]; remanet actus C[18]. 45 **quia** quod C[14]C[18]; quoniam L[31]. 45–46 **nos ipsos** nosmetipsos C[3]C[14]L[31]. 48 **constringimur** astringimur C[18]. 49–50 **in hunc** *om* C[18]; in L[31]. 51 **Annon** Antiqui C[3]. **patres** patres nostri *many MSS incl* C[10]C[18]L[31].

I.4: *Title* in Utero *om* C[3]; Corpore *for* Utero C[10]; Quo Cibo Conceptus Nutriatur in Corpore C[18]. 1 **utero** corpore C[10]C[18]L[31]. 2 **menstruo** menstruoso C[18]. 3 **ut** ut ex *most MSS incl* C[3]C[10]C[14]C[18]L[31]Ro. **femina** corpore C[10]C[18]. 6 **moriantur herbe** *om* C[10]. **fetus** fructus C[14]. 7 **canes** canis L[31]. 8 **fetus . . . seminis** fetus ex semine et cibo vicium C[10]C[14]; fetus ex semine vicium seminis C[18]; fetus ex semine vicium L[31]. **contrahant** contrahunt *most MSS incl* C[3]C[14]C[18]L[31]V[2]. 11 **ruputatur** reputatur *nearly every MS incl* C[3]C[10]C[14]C[18]L[31]Ro. 11–12 **menstruatam** menstruam C[10]. 12 **accesserit** accederet *many MSS incl* Ro. **iubetur** iuberetur C[14]. 13 **precipitur** iubetur C[10]L[31]; iubetur in Levitico precipitur C[18]. **ut** *above line* L[31]. 14 **quadraginta** quadraginta diebus C[10]C[14]C[18]. **vero** *om* L[31]. 14–15 **septuaginta** octoginta C[18]Ro; sexaginta BuGoIMu[5]Pa[9]Pa[11]Wo[2].

racionis sopitur intuitus, ut ignorancia seminetur;
libidinis irritatur pruritus, ut iracundia propagetur;
40 voluptatis saciatur affectus, ut concupiscencia contrahatur. Hic est tyrannus carnis, lex menbrorum,
fomes peccati, languor nature, pabulum mortis, sine
quo nemo nascitur, sine quo nullus moritur. Quid si
quando transit reatu, semper tamen remanet actu.
45 "Si enim dixerimus quia peccatum non *habemus, nos
ipsos seducimus,* et *veritas* in *nobis* non est." O gravis
necessitas et infelix condicio: antequam peccemus,
peccato constringimur; et antequam delinquamus,
delicto tenemur. "Per unum hominem peccatum in
50 hunc mundum intravit, et per peccatum in omnes
homines mors pertransit." Annon "patres comme-
derunt uvam acerbam, et dentes filiorum obstupes-
cunt"?

Iohannes in
Epistola Ca-
nonica

Apostolus ad
Romanos

Ezechiel

[4] QUALI CIBO CONCEPTUS NUTRIATUR IN UTERO

Sed attende quo cibo conceptus nutriatur in utero:
profecto sanguine menstruo, qui cessat ex femina
post conceptum ut eo conceptus nutriatur in femina.
Qui fertur esse tam detestabilis et immundus ut "ex
5 eius contactu fruges non germinent, arescant ar-
busta, moriantur herbe, amittant arbores fetus; si
canes inde commederint, in rabiem efferantur."
Concepti fetus vicium seminis contrahant, ita ut
leprosi et elefantici ex hac corrupcione nascantur.
10 Unde secundum legem Mosaicam mulier que men-
strua patitur ruputatur immunda, et si quis ad menstruatam accesserit, iubetur interfici. Ac propter
immundiciam menstruorum precipitur ut mulier si
masculum pareret quadraginta, si vero feminam
15 septuaginta diebus a templi cessaret ingressu.

In Levitico

101

"Why is light given to him that is in misery and life to them that are in bitterness of soul?" Happy are those who die before they are born, experiencing death before knowing life. For some are born so deformed and unnatural that they seem to be not human beings, but rather abominations; perhaps they would have been better provided for if they had never appeared in the sight of men, because these monsters are pointed out and held up for display. Many are born with stunted limbs and impaired senses, a sadness to friends, a humiliation to parents, a disgrace to relatives. Why should I say this about these in particular, when in general all are born without knowledge, without speech, without strength? Weeping, frail, weak, differing very little from dumb animals, in fact having less in many things: for they walk as soon as they are born; but we do not only not walk upright on our feet, we do not even crawl bent over on our hands.

[6] OF THE PAINS OF CHILDBIRTH AND THE CRYING OF THE CHILD

All are born crying in order to express the misery of nature. For the newly born male says "Ah," the female "E." "All are born of Eve saying 'E' or 'Ah'." What is "Eve" therefore? Either syllable is the interjection of one in pain, expressing the magnitude of the pain. Hence she deserved to be called virago ("made from man") before sin, "Eve" after sin, because of which she heard said to her: "In sorrow shalt thou bring forth children." There is no pain like that of a woman in labor: thus Rachel died from the excessive pain of

I.5: 1 **data est misero** misero data est *most MSS incl* C³C¹⁰C¹⁸L³¹V². 1-2 **sunt . . . anime** in amaritudine anime sunt C³L³¹. 5-6 **abominaciones pocius** abhominabiles pocius C³; pocius abhominabiles C¹⁰C¹⁸L³¹. 7 **quoniam** quam L³¹. **ut** *om* C¹⁴; ad L³¹. 8 **monstrantur** monstrantui C³. 8-9 **Plurimique** Plerique *most MSS incl* C³C¹⁰C¹⁴ C¹⁸L³¹Ro. 9-10 **corrupti nascuntur** *trans* C¹⁰C¹⁸L³¹. 12 **dixerim de quibusdam** de quibusdam dixerim C¹⁰C¹⁸L³¹. 13 **nascantur** nascimur C³; nascamur *most MSS incl* C¹⁰C¹⁴ C¹⁸L³¹Ro. 15 **in multis** *om* C¹⁰. **ut statim** *trans most MSS incl* C³C¹⁰C¹⁴C¹⁸L³¹Ro. **sunt** sint C¹⁸. 16 **erecti** erectis C³. 17 **curvati** curvatis L³¹.

I.6: *Title* Infantis *for* Nascentis C¹⁰C¹⁸; et . . . Nascentis *om* C¹⁴; Labore et Partu *for* Dolore Partus E¹. 2-3 **femina** femina dicit C³C¹⁴C¹⁸; femina vero V². **Dicentes** Unde versus Et dicent V². 4 **Quid . . . Eva** Quid . . . Eva nisi heu a *most MSS incl* C³ C¹⁰C¹⁴C¹⁸L³¹Ro. **Utrum** Utrumque *most MSS incl* C³C¹⁰C¹⁴C¹⁸L³¹Ro. 4-5 **dolentis . . . interiectio** est interiectio dolentis C¹⁰C¹⁸L³¹. 6 **enim** *om* C¹⁴; est quod C¹⁸L³¹LeO¹⁴; est enim quod O¹⁹. **peccatum (1st)** peccatum prima parens nostra dicebatur C¹⁰C¹⁸L³¹; post parens Pa¹⁴. 7 **sibi dictum** *trans* C¹⁸L³¹. 8 **sicut** sicut dolor *many MSS incl* C¹⁰C¹⁴C¹⁸L³¹. 10

[5] DE INBECILLITATE INFANTIS

"Quare ergo data est misero lux et vita hiis qui sunt
in amaritudine anime?" Felices illi qui / moriuntur   f. 80v
antequam oriantur, prius mortem sencientes quam
vitam scientes. Quidam enim tam deformes et pro-
5 digiosi nascuntur ut non homines, set abominaciones
pocius videantur; quibus forte melius fuisset provi-
sum si nunquam prodiissent ad visum, quoniam ut
monstra monstrantur et ostenduntur ostentui. Plurimique vero diminuti menbris et sensibus corrupti
10 nascuntur, amicorum tristicia, parentum infamia,
verecundia propinquorum. Quid hoc particulariter
dixerim de quibusdam, cum generaliter omnes sine
sciencia, sine verbo, sine virtute nascantur? Flebiles,
debiles, inbecilles, parum a brutis distantes, immo
15 minus in multis habentes: nam illa ut statim orta sunt
gradiuntur; nos autem non solum erecti pedibus non
incedimus, verum eciam curvati manibus non rep-
tamus.

[6] DE DOLORE PARTUS ET EIULATU NASCENTIS

Omnes nascimur eiulantes ut nature miseriam expri-
mamus. Masculus enim recenter natus dicit "A," femina "E." "Dicentes 'E' vel 'A' quotquot nascuntur
ab Eva." Quid est igitur "Eva"? Utrum dolentis est
5 interiectio, doloris exprimens magnitudinem. Hinc
enim ante peccatum virago, post peccatum "Eva"
meruit appellari, ex quo sibi dictum audivit: "In   In Genesi
dolore paries." Non est dolor sicut parturientis:
unde Rachel pre nimio dolore partus interiit et,

childbirth and, dying, "called her son's name Benoni, that is, son of pain." The wife of Phinees, when sudden pains seized her, gave birth just as she died, and at the very moment of death named her son Ichabod. "A woman, like a person shipwrecked, when she is in labor indeed hath sorrow; but when she hath brought forth the male child, she remembereth no more the anguish for joy that a man is born into the world." Thus she conceives with uncleanness and stench, gives birth with sorrow and pain, feeds with difficulty and labor, and protects with constancy and fear.

[7] OF NAKEDNESS

Naked he comes forth and naked he goes back; poor he comes and poor he goes. "Naked," he says, "came I out of my mother's womb; naked shall I return thither." "For we brought nothing into this world; certainly we can carry nothing out." If, however, anyone comes forth clothed, let him consider what kind of clothing he wears. Filthy to speak of, filthier to hear of, filthiest to see: a loathsome skin stained with blood. This is that partition of which Thamar spoke in childbirth: "Why is the partition divided for thee? And for this reason she called his name Phares."

[8] WHAT FRUIT MAN PRODUCES

O vile unworthiness of the human condition, unworthy condition of human vileness! Investigate the plants and the trees: they produce flowers, foliage, and fruit from themselves, and you nits and lice and worms from yourself. They bring forth oil, wine, and balsam from themselves, you spittle, urine, and excrement from yourself. They emit a sweetness of smell from them-

Bennoni Beniamin C[18]. 11 **Fhinees** *corrected from* Phinees L[20]. 12 **ac** *corrected from* et L[20]. **et** et in *most MSS incl* C[3]C[10]C[14]C[18]L[31]Ro. 13 **filium** filium suum *most MSS incl* C[10]C[14]L[31]; nomen filii sui C[18]U[4]; nomen filium L[15]O[21]. **Hichaboth** Nicaboth C[10]; Nachabot id est cecidit gloria L[31]; Ycaboth id est filium meroris Ro; Hichabeth id est filius meroris *in margin* C[14]; Ichaboth id est inglorius Sa; Hychabot id est inglorius vel filium meroris CiH[1]; Iacob L[40]. **autem** *om* C[10]C[18]. 14 **vero** autem C[18]; *om* L[31]. 15 **masculum** filium L[31]BeBoC[23]CaD[5]Du[2]L[4]L[10]L[25]L[37]Ma[3]Mu[4]Pa[5]U[1]; puerum *a few MSS.* 15-16 **propter gaudium** pre gaudio C[18]GoLmPa[9]Pa[11]. 16 **mundum** mundo C[18]; m L[31]. 17 **Concipit** Concepit L[31]. **cum** in L[31]. 18 **angustia** angustia et dolore C[3].

I.7: **Title** De Nuditate Infantis C[14]; De Nuditate et Vestitu Nascentis V[2]. 1 **ingreditur** regreditur *most MSS incl* C[3]C[14]C[18]L[31]Ro. 2 **inquid** inquid Iob L[31]C[18]. **egressus** gressus L[31]. 3 **ex** de *most MSS incl* C[3]C[10]C[14]C[18]L[31]Ro. 4 **hunc mundum** hanc mundum C[18]; *trans* L[31]. 5 **quia** *an additional, preceding* quia *expunged in* L[20]; *om* C[10]C[18]L[31]. **auferre** afferre L[31]. 6 **indutus** non nudus C[10]C[18]L[31]. **egreditur** ingreditur C[14]Ro. **attendat** attende C[10]C[18]L[31]. 8 **fedam** fedam scilicet Ro. **cruentatem** cruentatis C[18]. 9 **Thamar** Thamar in Genesi C[10]L[31]; Terra mar in Genesi C[18]. **inquit** dixit C[3]. 10 **propter** pro C[10]L[31]. **Et** *om* C[10]C[18]L[31]. **vocavit** vocatum est C[3]. **eius** filii sui C[10]C[18]L[31]. **Phares** Phares id est divisio L[31]L[37]Sa, *in margin* C[14]; Phares quod interpretatur divisio V[2].

I.8: **Title** Qualem *for* Quem Ro. 1 **O** *om* L[31]. **humane** *om* C[18]L[31]. 1-2 **vilitatis** vilitas *many MSS incl* C[10]C[18]. 2 **condicio** condicionis C[10]C[18]. 4-5 **de se fundunt** defundunt C[10]L[31]. 5 **vinum** vinum thus C[14]. **tu** et tu *most MSS incl* C[3]C[14]C[18]E[1]L[31]Ro. 6

10 moriens, "vocavit nomen filii sui Bennoni, id est,
filius doloris." Uxor Fhinees subitis doloribus irru-
entibus peperit simul ac periit, et ipso mortis arti-
culo vocavit filium Hichaboth. "Mulier autem, ut Iohannes in Ewangelio
naufragus, cum parit tristiciam habet; cum vero
15 peperit masculum, iam non meminit pressure propter gaudium quia natus est homo in mundum."
Concipit ergo cum inmundi- / -cia et fetore, parit f. 81
cum tristicia et dolore, nutrit cum angustia et labore, custodit cum instancia et timore.

[7] DE NUDITATE

Nudus egreditur et nudus ingreditur; pauper accedit et pauper recedit. "Nudus," inquid, "egressus Iob
sum ex utero matris mee; nudus revertar illuc."
"Nichil intulimus in hunc mundum; haut dubium Apostolus ad Timotheum
5 quia nec auferre quid possumus." Si quis, autem,
indutus egreditur, attendat quale proferat indumen-
tum. Turpe dictu, turpius auditu, turpissimum visu:
fedam pelliculam sanguine cruentatam. Hec est illa
macheria de qua Thamar inquit in partu: "Quare In Genesi
10 divisa est propter te maceria? Et ob hanc causam
vocavit nomen eius Phares."

[8] QUEM FRUCTUM HOMO PRODUCIT

O vilis humane condicionis indignitas, indigna vilitatis humane condicio! Herbas et arbores investiga:
ille de se producunt flores, frondes, et fructus, et tu
de te lendes et pediculos et lumbricos. Ille de se
5 fundunt oleum, vinum, et balsamum, tu de te spu-
tum, urinam, et stercus. Ille de se spirant suavitatem

selves, and you give out an abomination of stench from yourself. As the tree is, so is the fruit, "for an evil tree cannot bring forth good fruit." For what is man in his shape but a tree turned upside down? Its roots are the hair, its base is the head along with the neck, its trunk is the chest along with the belly, its branches are the arms along with the legs, its foliage is the fingers and toes along with the joints. This is the leaf that is carried away by the wind and the straw that is dried by the sun.

[9] OF THE DISCOMFORTS OF OLD AGE

In the beginning of the human condition men are reported to have lived for nine hundred years and more. But as the life of man gradually decreased, God said to Noah: "My spirit shall not remain in man forever because he is flesh, and his days shall be a hundred and twenty years." This can be understood as well of the end of life as of the period of repenting. For very rarely since then are men reported to have lived longer, but because human life was shortened more and more, it was said by the psalmist: "The days of our years in themselves are threescore and ten years—if, however, in the strong, fourscore years; most of them are labor and sorrow." "Now the fewness of my days is ended shortly." "Our days have passed more swiftly than the web is cut by the weaver." "Man born of a woman, living for a short time" et cetera. Few now reach forty years, very few sixty. If, however, one does reach old age, his heart weakens straightaway and his head shakes, his spirit fails and his breath stinks, his face wrinkles and his back bends, his eyes dim and his joints falter, his nose runs and his hair falls out, his touch trembles and his competence fails,

stercus stercora L[31]. **se** *om* L[31]. 8 **enim** *om* L[31]. 8-9 **potest . . . bonos** potest arbor mala bonos fructus C[3]; arbor mala fructus bonos potest C[10]; arbor mala potest bonos C[18]. 9 **facere** facere neque arbor bona fructus malos facit Ro. **enim** igitur C[10]; ergo C[18]L[31]. 10 **eversa** eversa Unde dicitur Antropos C[18]. 11 **crines** *corrected probably from* cineres L[20]. 14 **rapitur** movetur C[18].

I.9: **Title** De Incommodis Senectutis et Brevitate Vite C[14]C[18]E[1]; De Brevitate Huius Vite Ro. 1 **primordio** principio C[14]. 2 **homines** *om* C[3]. 5 **eruntque** Erunt L[31]. **illius** eius L[31]. 6 **potest** *om* C[3]. 7 **tunc** hoc C[3]. 8 **plus vixisse** vixisse C[10]; vivere plus L[31]. 8-9 **ac magis** *om* C[18]. 9 **vita recideretur** abbreviatur vita C[18]; recideretur vita L[31]; vita recidatur Ro; *many variants for* recideretur *incl* decideretur, desideretur, eradetur, procederet, redditur, tradetur. **humana** hominis L[31]. 9-10 **dictum . . . psalmista** unde dictum est a psalmista C[18]; unde psalmista L[31]; unde *(above line)* dictum est in psalmo C[6]. 10 **nostrorum** meorum C[10]L[31]; *om* C[18]. 12 **plurimum eorum** plurimum erit C[10]; amplius C[14]; amplius e C[18]; et amplius et plurimum erit L[31]; et amplius eorum *many MSS incl* V[2]. **autem** *om* L[31]. 13 **finitur** finietur *most MSS incl* C[3]C[10]C[14]C[18]L[31]V[2]. **nostri** mei L[31]. 15-16 **et cetera** repletur multis miseriis Qui quasi flos egreditur et conteritur et fugit velut umbra et nunquam in eodem statu permanet *most MSS incl* C[3]C[10]C[14]Ro, *except for the omission of* et *after* umbra L[31]; repletur . . . miseriis *only* C[18]. 16 **quadraginta** sexaginta C[18]; quadraginta pauciores ad quinquaginta O[14]O[26]; quinquaginta O[7]; septuaginta C[1]L[4]; octoginta Es[2]. 17 **sexaginta** quinquaginta C[10]; 1 vel xlx L[31]; quinquaginta vel sexaginta D[1]Pa[8]; septuaginta Bn; octoginta C[1]C[23]D[5]Es[2]L[37]O[9]. **Si** *a new chapter begins here in many MSS incl* Ro, *entitled* De Incommodo Senectutis *(see Introduction, p. 52); in margin of* C[14] Nota *is added, followed by* 10[m] *and the title* De Incomodis Senectutis. 18 **processerit** pervenerit *many MSS incl* C[14]C[18]; perveniunt L[31]. **eius** *om* C[10]L[31]. **et** *om* C[14]C[18]. 19 **capud** capillus L[31]. **et** *om* C[14]C[18]. 20 **facies** cutis C[18]. **curvatur** *above* cur- *a superfluous abbreviation for* -ur- *expunged* L[20]. **et** *om* L[31]. 23 **Senex** Senex ad iram

odoris, et tu de te reddis abominacionem fetoris.
Qualis est arbor, talis est fructus, "non enim potest
arbor mala fructus bonos facere." Quid est enim
10 homo secundum formam nisi quedam arbor eversa?
Cuius radices sunt crines, truncus est capud cum
collo, stipes est pectus cum alvo, rami sunt ulne cum
tibiis, frondes sunt digiti cum articulis. Hoc est
folium quod a vento rapitur et stipula que a sole
15 siccatur.

[9] DE INCOMMODIS SENECTUTIS

In primordio condicionis humane nongentis annis et
amplius homines vixisse leguntur. Set paulatim vita
hominis declinante, dixit Dominus ad Noe: "Non
permanebit spiritus meus in homine in eternum quia
5 caro est, eruntque dies illius centum viginti an- / -no-
rum." Quod intelligi potest tam de termino vite
quam de spacio penitendi. Ex tunc enim rarissime
leguntur homines plus vixisse, set cum magis ac
magis vita recideretur humana, dictum est a psal-
10 mista: "Dies annorum nostrorum in ipsis septuaginta
annis—si, autem, in potentatibus, octoginta anni;
plurimum eorum labor et dolor." "Nunc autem
paucitas dierum meorum finitur brevi." "Dies nostri
velocius transeunt quam a texente tela succiditur."
15 "Homo natus de muliere, brevi vivens tempore" et
cetera. Pauci nunc ad quadraginta, paucissimi ad
sexaginta annos perveniunt. Si quis, autem, ad se-
nectutem processerit, statim cor eius affligitur et
capud concutitur, languet spiritus et fetet anhelitus,
20 facies rugatur et statura curvatur, caligant oculi et
vacillant articuli, nares effluunt et crines defluunt,
tremit tactus et deperit actus, dentes putrescunt et

his teeth rot and his ears become dirty. An old man is provoked easily and restrained with difficulty, believes quickly and disbelieves slowly, is stingy and greedy, dejected and complaining, quick to speak and slow to listen, but not slow to anger; he praises the things of old and spurns modern things, disparages the present and commends the past, sighs and is anxious, is tormented and enfeebled. Hear the poet: "Many discomforts beset an old man" et cetera. But neither should the old man glory against the young person nor the young be insolent to the old person, for we are what he was, someday will be what he is.

[10] OF THE LABOR OF MORTALS

"The bird is born to fly, and man is born to labor." "All his days are full of labors and miseries, and even in the night he doth not rest his mind. And is not this vanity?" There is nothing without labor under the sun, there is nothing without defect under the moon, there is nothing without vanity in time. For time is the period of motion of mutable things. "Vanity of vanities, says Ecclesiastes, and all is vanity." O how various are the endeavors of men, how diverse are their efforts! Yet there is one end and the same consequence for all: "labor and vexation of spirit." "Great labor is created for all men, and a heavy yoke is upon the sons of Adam from the day of their coming out of their mother's womb until the day of their burial into the mother of all."

[11] OF THE ENDEAVOR OF WISE MEN

Let wise men examine and investigate the heights of the sky, the expanses of the earth, the depths of the sea. Let them dispute about each, inquire into all, always learn or teach. And what do they find from this pursuit but labor and

C¹⁸Er²LeSa, *added two words later* H¹L⁴⁰O¹⁸Pa¹³. 25 **tristis** tristis est C³. **et (2nd)** *om many MSS incl* L³¹Ro. 26 **set . . . iram** set non ad iram C¹⁴; *om* C¹⁸; et non tardus ad iram L³¹. 27 **presens** presentes C¹⁰C¹⁸. 28 **commendat** laudat L³¹. **preteritum** preteritos C¹⁸. **suspirat** suspicatur C¹⁰. 28–29 **torquetur** C¹⁰; torpet *most MSS incl* C³C¹⁴V². 29 **poetam** poetam dicentem V²; philosophum Au; prophetam GoIMu⁵Pa⁵Pa⁹; poetam vel prophetam Bu. 30 **et cetera** *om most MSS incl* C¹⁰C¹⁸L³¹; vel quod querit et inventis miser abstinet et timet uti vel quod res onis timide gelide que ministrat C¹⁴Er²L²² O²¹. 30-31 **nec senes** senex nec C¹⁰; nec senex C¹⁴C¹⁸. 31 **iuvenem** iuvenes C³; iuniorem *many MSS incl* C¹⁴E¹; minorem L³¹L⁹L⁴⁰O²³. **glorientur** gloriantur L³¹. **nec** *probably* ñ *expanded to* nec L²⁰.
    I.10: 1 **volatum** volandum *most MSS incl* C¹⁴C¹⁸L³¹Ro. **nascitur** *om* C¹⁸L³¹. 2 **laborem** laborandum C¹⁸. **dies eius** *trans* C¹⁸L³¹. 3 **noctem** noctem nec per diem C¹⁰L³¹, *before* nec per noctem *in some group MSS incl* C¹⁸. 4 **hec** hoc C¹⁸Ro. 5 **non est** *om* C¹⁰L³¹. **quicquam** *added in margin of* L²⁰; *om most MSS incl* C³C¹⁰C¹⁴C¹⁸L³¹Ro. 6 **non est** *om* C¹⁰C¹⁸L³¹. **quicquam** *added in margin of* L²⁰; *om most MSS incl* C³C¹⁰C¹⁴C¹⁸L³¹Ro. 7 **enim** *om many MSS incl* C¹⁰C¹⁸. 8 **dicit** inquid *most MSS incl* C³C¹⁰C¹⁸L³¹Ro. 9 **varia** vana *many MSS incl* C³. **hominum studia** hominis studia C¹⁰C¹⁸L³¹; studia hominum Ro. 10 **sunt** sunt hominum C³; sint L³¹. **exercicia** exteriora Es²GoIL²⁴L⁴⁰LaSa, *though it is often corrected to the reading in* L²⁰. **est** *om* C¹⁰. 10-11 **idem effectus** idem est effectus C¹⁴; *trans* C¹⁸L³¹. 13 **grave . . . Adam** grave super filies Adam C¹⁴; grave filiis Ade C¹⁸; filiis Ade grave L³¹; Ade *for* Adam *many MSS incl* C¹⁰. 14 **et** *in most MSS incl* C³C¹⁴ C¹⁸E¹L³¹Ro.
    I.11: *Title* De Diverso Studio Sapientum Ro. 2 **profunda** profunditas L³¹. **disputent** displicent L³¹. 3 **pertractent** proficent L³¹. 4 **nisi** *om* L³¹. 5 **hoc** *om* C¹⁰; hec

aures surdescunt. Senex facile provocatur et difficile
revocatur, cito credit et tarde discredit, tenax et
cupidus, tristis et querulus, velox ad loquendum et
tardus ad audiendum, set non tardus ad iram; laudat
antiquos et spernit modernos, vituperat presens et
commendat preteritum, suspirat et anxiatur, torquetur et infirmatur. Audi poetam: "Multa senem   Oracius
circumveniunt incommoda" et cetera. Porro nec
senes contra iuvenem glorientur, nec insolescant
iuvenes contra senem, quia quod sumus iste fuit,
erimus quandoque quod hic est.

[10] DE LABORE MORTALIUM

"Avis ergo nascitur ad volatum, et homo nascitur ad
laborem." "Cuncti dies eius laboribus et erumpnis
pleni sunt, nec per noctem requiescit mens eius. Et
hec nonne vanitas?" Non est quicquam sine labore
sub sole, non est quicquam / sine defectu sub luna,   f. 82
non est quicquam sine vanitate sub tempore. Tempus enim est mora motus rerum mutabilium. "Vanitas vanitatum, dicit Ecclesiastes, et omnia vanitas."
O quam varia sunt hominum studia, quam diversa
sunt exercicia! Unus est tamen omnium finis et idem
effectus: "labor et afflictio spiritus." "Occupacio   In Ecclesias-
tico
magna creata est omnibus hominibus, et iugum
grave super filios Adam a die exitus de ventre matris
eorum usque in diem sepulture et matrem omnium."

[11] DE STUDIO SAPIENTUM

Perscrutentur sapientes et investigent alta celi, lata
terre, profunda maris. De singulis disputent, de
cunctis pertractent, discant semper aut doceant. Et

sorrow and vexation of spirit? He knew this by experience who said: "I have given my heart to know prudence and learning, errors and folly, and I have perceived that this was labor and vexation of spirit, because in much wisdom there is much indignation, and he that addeth knowledge addeth sorrow." For though it behooves an investigator to toil through many vigils and to keep vigil through toils, still there is hardly anything so worthless, or so simple, that one understands it in full, comprehends it with certainty, unless perhaps it is fully known that nothing is known fully, though from this an insoluble contradiction follows. Why not? "For the corruptible body is a load upon the soul, and the earthly habitation presseth down the mind that museth upon many things." Hear what Solomon observes on this: "All things are hard; man cannot explain them by word." "For there is man, that day and night taketh no sleep with his eyes and can find no reason of all these works of God, and the more he shall labor to seek, so much the less shall he find." "The searchers have failed in their search, because man shall come to a deep heart, and God shall be exalted." "He that is a searcher of majesty shall be overwhelmed by glory." The more he understands the more he doubts, and the more he considers himself to know the more foolish he acts. Part of knowledge, therefore, is to know what you do not know. "God made man right, and he hath entangled himself with an infinity of questions."

[12] OF THE VARIOUS PURSUITS OF MEN

Mortals rush and run about through fences and paths, climb mountains, cross hills, ascend cliffs, fly over the Alps, step over pits, go into caves; they explore

---

C[18]L[31]. 6 **scirem** scrutem L[31]. 7 **atque . . . stulticiam** errores et stulticiam et doctrinam C[10]C[18]L[31]. 8 **hoc** *above line* L[20]; *om most MSS incl* C[3]C[10]C[18]Ro; in his C[14]; hec L[31]. 10 **dolorem** et dolorem *many MSS incl* C[10]C[14]; et laborem C[18]; et dolorem et laborem L[31]. **oporteat** oportet L[31]. 11 **indagantem** indagare C[14]; indagari L[31]. **multis** *added in margin* L[20]; *om* C[10]C[18]L[31]; multa C[14]. 12 **sudoribus** laboribus vel sudoribus *many MSS incl* C[3]; laboribus C[18]L[31]. **est** *om* L[31]. **quicquam** *om* C[10]C[18]. **vix est** *om* C[10]C[14]L[31]. 13 **intelligat** intelligatur *many MSS incl* C[10]C[14]C[18]; intelligat homo et *a few MSS.* 13-14 **comprehendat ad liquidum** ad liquidum comprehendatur C[10]C[14]C[18]; ad liquidum comprehendat *many MSS incl* L[31]. 14 **illud** id L[31]. **perfecte sciatur** *trans most MSS incl* C[10]C[18]L[31]Ro. **quod** quia C[10]. 15 **scitur perfecte** perfecte scitur *marked for trans* L[20]; sciatur perfecte *most MSS incl* C[3]C[10]C[18]L[31]Ro; perfecte sciatur C[14]. 16 **Quid ni** Quoniam C[10]C[18]L[31]; Quid mirum C[14]O[24]; Quod mirum Mo. 18 **multa** plura C[18]L[31]C[9]; plurima L[40]. 20 **potest** potest plura cogitarem *but marked for expunction* L[31]. **eas homo** *trans many MSS incl* C[10]L[31]; homo ea C[14]; eas *after* explicare *in* C[18]. **sermone** sermonem L[31]. 21 **qui** cuius C[10]; cuius oculus C[18]. **diebus . . . noctibus** *trans* C[10]C[18]L[31]. **sompnum** sompnium L[31]. 22 **oculis** oculus *many MSS incl* C[10]C[14]; *om* C[18]. **invenire** venire L[31]. 23 **querendum** inquirendum C[18]. 24 **Deficiunt** Deficiant C[14]Ro. 25 **scrutinium** scrutinio *many MSS incl* C[3]. **accedit** accedet *most MSS incl* C[10]C[18]L[31]V[2]; ascendit C[14]. 26 **enim** igitur C[18]L[31]. 27 **opprimetur** opprimitur *many MSS incl* C[18]L[31]. **Qui** Et qui C[10]L[31]. 28 **videtur sibi** *trans* L[31]; videtur *many MSS incl* C[10]V[2]. 29 **desipit** despiat C[18]; desipitur L[31]. **nescias** nesciat L[31]Ro. 30 **autem** ergo L[31]. **Deus** Dominus C[10]C[18]L[31]. 30-31 **se . . . immiscuit** im- *above line* L[20]; se . . . miscuit C[3]C[14]Ro; inmiscuit se infinitis C[10]; miscuit se infinitis C[18]; se miscuit infinitis L[31]. 31 **questionibus** doloribus O[19].

I.12: *Title om* C[18]. 1 **Currunt** C *in another hand in margin* L[31]. 2 **transcendunt** et transeunt C[10]; et transcendunt C[14]C[18]L[31]. 3 **rupes** alpes et C[10]C[18]L[31]. **Alpes** rupes C[10]C[18]L[31]. 3-4 **foveas ingrediuntur** foveas et ingrediuntur C[10]L[31]; *om* C[18]. 5 **fluminis**

quid ex hac occupacione nisi laborem et dolorem et
affliccionem spiritus invenient? Noverat hoc experimento qui dixerat: "Dedi cor meum ut scirem Ecclesiastes
prudenciam atque doctrinam, errores et stulticiam,
et agnovi quod hoc esset labor et affliccio spiritus, eo
quod in multa sapiencia multa sit indignacio, et qui
addit scienciam addit dolorem." Licet enim oporteat
indagantem multis insudare vigiliis et invigilare
sudoribus, vix tamen est quicquam tam vile, vix est
tam facile, quod ad plenum intelligat, comprehendat
ad liquidum, nisi forsan illud perfecte sciatur quod
nichil scitur perfecte, quamquam ex hoc insolubilis
redargucio consequatur. Quid ni? "Corpus quod In Libro Sapiencie
corrumpitur aggravat animam, et deprimit terrena
inhabitacio sensum multa cogitantem." Audi quid
super hoc senciat Salomon: "Cuncte res difficiles;
non potest eas homo explicare sermone." "Est
homo, qui diebus ac noctibus sompnum non capit
oculis et nullam operum Dei potest invenire racionem, et quanto plus laboraverit ad querendum,
tanto / minus inveniet." "Deficiunt ergo scrutantes f. 82v
In Psalmo
scrutinium, quoniam accedit homo ad cor altum, et
ex*altabitur* Deus." "Perscrutator enim maiestatis Salomon
opprimetur a gloria." Qui magis intelligit magis
dubitat, et ille videtur sibi plus sapere qui plus
desipit. Pars, ergo, sciencie est scire quod nescias. Salomon
"Fecit autem Deus hominem rectum, et ipse se
infinitis immiscuit questionibus."

[12] DE VARIIS HOMINUM STUDIIS

Currunt et discurrunt mortales per sepes et semitas,
ascendunt montes, transcendunt colles, transvolant
rupes, pervolant Alpes, transgrediuntur foveas, in-

the inner parts of the earth, the depths of the sea, the uncertainties of the water, the shadows of the forest, the inward way of solitude; they expose themselves to winds, to rains, to thunders and lightnings, to floods and storms, to disasters and dangers. They hammer and melt metals, cut and polish stones, cut down and chop wood, spin and weave fabrics, cut and stitch clothes, build houses, plant gardens, cultivate fields, grow vines, fire ovens, erect mills, fish, hunt, and catch birds. They meditate and cogitate, consult and arrange, complain and dispute, rob and steal, cheat and trade, contend and fight, and do countless things of such sort in order to accumulate riches, to multiply profits, to pursue wealth, to acquire honors, to raise their ranks, to extend their powers. And this also is labor and vexation of mind. If this is not believed of me, let it be believed of Solomon: "I made my works great," he says: "I built me houses and planted vineyards, made gardens and orchards and set them with trees of all kinds. I made me ponds of water to water therewith the wood of the young trees, got man-servants and maid-servants, and had a great family, and herds of oxen and great flocks of sheep, above all that were before me in Jerusalem. I heaped together for myself silver and gold and the wealth of kings and provinces. I made me singing men and singing women and the delights of the sons of men, cups and vessels to serve to pour out wine, and surpassed in riches all that were before me in Jerusalem. And when I turned myself to all the works which my hands had wrought and to the labors wherein I had labored in vain, I saw in all things vanity and vexation of mind, and that nothing was lasting under the sun."

fluminum C^{10}C^{18}. **nemoris** nemorum C^{10}C^{18}L^{31}. 6 **ymbribus** et imbribus *most MSS incl* C^{3}C^{10}C^{14}C^{18}; imbribus et L^{31}. 7 **et fulminibus** et C^{10}; *trans* L^{31}. **et procellis** *trans* C^{10}C^{18}L^{31}. **et** *om* C^{10}. 8 **lapides sculpiunt** lapides sculpunt *many MSS incl* C^{3}C^{10}C^{14}C^{18}; sculpunt lapides L^{31}. 9 **ligna** lingna L^{31}; lingua CiD^{3}Du^{4}L^{14}L^{39}L^{41}LmO^{14}Pa^{5}RlU^2. **succidunt** scindunt C^{10}C^{18}L^{31}. **ordiuntur** toneunt L^{31}. 11 **plantant** et plantant *most MSS incl* C^{10}C^{18}L^{31}Ro. **pastinant** et pastinant C^{10}C^{18}L^{31}. 12 **clibanos** libanos L^{31}. 13 **Meditantur** Et meditantur L^{31}. 14 **querelantur** querelant C^{10}L^{31}. 15 **diripiunt** dirumpunt C^{10}. 15–16 **et** *(2nd)* . . . **contendunt** contendunt mechantur L^{31}C^{10}. 16 **innumera** in miseria C^{18}. **operantur** *in margin* L^{20}; *om most MSS incl* C^{3}C^{10}C^{14}Ro; agunt Quare L^{31}; agunt *one word earlier* C^{18}L^{36}; agunt EvH^{2}L^{37}Mu^{5}NeRu^2; faciunt *nineteen MSS*. 17–18 **ut** *(1st)* . . . **sectentur** *om* C^{10}. 19 **ut** et C^{3}C^{10}L^{31}. **hoc** hec L^{31}V^2. 20 **mentis affliccio** *trans* C^{10}C^{14}C^{18}L^{31}; afflictio spiritus BuC^{9}GoL^{17}LmO^{31}Pa^{5}Pa^{9}Pa^{11}Pa^{15}. **creditur** credatur L^{31}. 22 **feci** feci michi C^{3}C^{10}C^{18}L^{31}. 23 **pomoria** pomeria *most MSS incl* C^{3}C^{10}C^{14}C^{18}L^{31}. **et** *om many MSS incl* L^{31}V^2. **ea** *om most MSS incl* C^{10}C^{14}C^{18}L^{31}. **cuncti generis** cunctis generibus C^3. **arboribus** arborum C^{3}L^{31}; arbores C^{14}. 24 **irrigarem** irrigarent *most MSS incl* C^{10}C^{18}L^{31}Ro. 24–25 **silvam lignorum** silvas lignorum C^{18}; lingna silvarum L^{31}, *with* ligna AuL^{23}O^{14}Wo^1; silvam agrorum MoO^{16}. 25 **possedi** possedi filios et filias C^{10}C^{18}L^{31}. 26 **multamque** et multam C^{10}C^{18}. **multamque** . . . **armenta** habui L^{31}. **quoque** *om* C^{10}L^{31}. 27 **magnas** magnos *most MSS incl* C^{3}C^{10}C^{14}C^{18}Ro; multos L^{31}. 28–29 **argentum** . . . **aurum** *trans most MSS incl* C^{3}C^{14}C^{18}L^{31}. 29 **et** *(2nd) om* L^{31}. 30 **cantores** cantatores *many MSS incl* C^{3}C^{14}C^{18}L^{31}. 31 **ministerio** ministeria *many MSS incl* C^{10}C^{14}C^{18}L^{31}. 32 **fundenda** infundenda C^{14}C^{18}. 33 **me** *om* E^1. 34 **universa** omnia C^3; universa opera C^{10}; omnia opera L^{31}D^{3}Pa^{14}; cunta opera C^2. 34–35 **que** . . . **labores** *om* C^{10}L^{31}. 34 **fecerant** fecerunt C^3; fecissent C^{14}. 35 **sudaveram** sudaveram que fecerant manus mee C^{10}; suaderam C^{18}; sudaram que fecerant manus mee L^{31}. 36 **affliccionem** . . . **et** *om* C^{10}L^{31}. 37 **sole** sole quod non sit labor at afflictio spiritus Ro.

grediuntur cavernas; rimantur viscera terre, profunda maris, incerta fluminis, opaca nemoris, invia
solitudinis; exponunt se ventis, ymbribus, tonitruis
et fulminibus, fluctibus et procellis, ruinis et precipi-
ciis. Metalla cudunt et conflant, lapides sculpiunt et
poliunt, ligna succidunt et dolant, telas ordiuntur et
texunt, vestes incidunt et consuunt, edificant domos,
plantant ortos, excolunt agros, pastinant vineas,
succendunt clibanos, extruunt molendina, piscantur,
venantur, et aucupantur. Meditantur et cogitant,
consiliantur et ordinant, querelantur et litigant,
diripiunt et furantur, decipiunt et mercantur, contendunt et preliantur, et innumera talia operantur ut
opes congregent, ut questus multiplicent, ut lucra
sectentur, ut honores adquirant, ut dignitates extol-
lant, ut potestates extendant. Et hoc quoque labor et
mentis affliccio. Si michi non creditur, Salomoni
credatur: "Magnificavi," inquid, "opera mea: edifi-   Salomon
cavi michi domos et plantavi vineas, feci ortos et
pomoria et consevi ea / cuncti generis arboribus.   f. 83v
Extruxi michi piscinas aquarum ut irrigarem silvam
lignorum germinancium, possedi servos et ancillas,
multamque familiam habui, armenta quoque et
magnas ovium greges, ultra omnes qui fuerunt ante
me in Ierusalem. Coacervavi michi argentum et
aurum et substancias regum et provinciarum. Feci
michi cantores et cantatrices et delicias filiorum
hominum, cyphos et urceolos in ministerio ad vina
fundenda, et supergressus sum opibus omnes qui
fuerunt ante me in Ierusalem. Cumque me conver-
tissem ad universa que fecerant manus mee et ad
labores quibus frustra sudaveram, vidi in omnibus
vanitatem et affliccionem animi, et nichil permanere
sub sole."

O how much anxiety troubles mortals, how much care afflicts, disquiet molests, fear terrifies, terror strikes, dread diverts, pain afflicts, sadness confuses, confusion saddens! Poor and rich, servant and master, married and celibate, good and bad—all are afflicted with worldly tortures and are tortured with worldly afflictions. Believe the experienced teacher: "If I be wicked," he says, "woe unto me, and if just, I shall not lift up my head, being filled with affliction and misery."

[14] OF THE MISERY OF THE POOR AND THE RICH

The poor are indeed oppressed by starvation, tortured by need, hunger, thirst, cold, nakedness; they become worthless and waste away, are despised and confounded. O miserable condition of a beggar! If he begs, he is confounded with shame, and if he does not beg, he is consumed with want, and indeed is compelled by necessity to beg. He maintains that God is unjust because he does not dispense properly; he accuses his neighbor of being evil because he does not help fully; he is offended, he complains, he curses. Consider the opinion of the wise man on this subject: "It is better to die than to want." "The poor man shall be hateful even to his own neighbor." "All the days of the poor are evil." "The brethren of the poor man hate him, and even his friends have departed far from him." "When you are happy, you will count many friends. If times are dark, you will be alone." O shame! A person is valued according to his wealth, when wealth should be valued according to the

I.13: *Title om* C[18]. 1 **angit** agit C[10]. 2 **sollicitudo molestat** *trans* C[10]C[14]C[18]L[31]. **tremor** timor C[10]C[14]C[18]. 3 **abducit** obducit C[10]C[14]C[18]. 4 **contristat turbacio** tristatur turbatio V[2]. **et** *(1st) om* L[31]. 5-6 **denique . . . malus** *om* C[10]. 6 **cruciatibus affliguntur** *trans* L[31]. 7 **cruciantur affliccionibus** *trans most MSS incl* C[3]C[10]C[14]C[18]L[31]Ro. 8 **ve** *corrected (from* va?*)* L[20]. 9 **et** *(1st) om* C[10]C[14]C[18]L[31].

I.14: 1 **enim** *om many MSS incl* C[3]C[10]C[14]C[18]L[31]. **premuntur . . . cruciantur** *trans* L[31]. 2 **frigore** frigore et C[14]C[18]L[31]. 4 **mendicantis** mendicitatis Er[2]; mendacitatis Bs; pauperis Mi; miserantis D[1]; medicantis Mu[5]; indicantis C[9]. **Et** *om* C[10]C[14]C[18]L[31]. **pudore** *om* C[14]C[18]. 5 **et** *om* C[10]C[14]C[18]L[31]. **petit** *om* C[10]C[14]C[18]L[31]. 6 **causatur** causeatur L[31]; accusat BuGoIPa[9]Pa[11]; accusatur LmPa[5]. 7 **iniquum** iniquum proximum criminatur malignum Deum eo C[10]C[18]; iniquum proximum criminatur malignum Deum causatur C[14]; iniquum proximum Deum eo L[31]; iniquum eo AuH[1]L[11]Pa[8]Wo[2]; iniquum esse C[4]C[5]. **dividat** dividat iniquum quod non recte dividicat L[31]; dividicat L[40]NO[26]. 7-8 **criminatur malignum** *om* C[14]C[18]; criminanatur malignum L[31]. 8 **quod** quia C[10]C[14]C[18]L[31]. **plene** bene Bn. **subveniat** subvenit C[10]L[31]. 9 **inprecatur** et imprecatur *many MSS incl* C[10]C[14]C[18]L[31]. **Adverte** Audi C[10]C[14]C[18]L[31]. 10 **hoc** *om* C[7]L[43]S[4]Wo[1]. 11-12 **pauper . . . erit** odiosus erit pauper C[10]C[14]C[18]L[31]. 12 **Omnes** Salomon Omnes Bv[2]C[12]L[12]Ma[3]Mi MoO[25]Ph[1]RlT[1]U[5]U[8]Ut[2]; Salomon in Proverbiis Omnes L[41]O[9]; Unde dicitur in Proverbiis Bz[2]. 13 **et** *om* C[10]C[14]C[18]L[31]. **amici** amcii *corrected from* amca L[31]. **procul** *om* Bl[3]Bm[1]BsD[5]Er[1]L[11]O[18]O[27]; procul eius Au. 14-15 **numerabis** n L[31]; numerabilis C[4]; vulnerabis Ev; nuntiabis O[10]. 15 **si si** *one* si *in margin* L[20], *the other in text probably corrected from* cum; cum *many MSS incl* C[18]L[31]; quo C[14]; *si most MSS.* 16 **pudor** dolor *many MSS incl* C[3]C[10]C[14]C[18]L[31]. **estimatur** existimatur C[3]. 17 **sit estimanda** *trans many MSS incl*

[13] DE DIVERSIS ANXIETATIBUS

O quanta mortales angit anxietas, affligit cura,
sollicitudo molestat, metus exterret, tremor con-
cutit, horror abducit, dolor affligit, conturbat tristicia, contristat turbacio! Pauper et dives, servus et
5 dominus, coniugatus et continens, denique bonus et
malus—omnes mundanis cruciatibus affliguntur et
mundanis cruciantur affliccionibus. Experto crede
magistro: "Si impius," inquit, "fuero, ve michi est,   Iob
et si iustus, non levabo capud, saturatus affliccione et
10 miseria."

[14] DE MISERIA PAUPERIS ET DIVITIS

Pauperes enim premuntur inedia, cruciantur e-
rumpna, fame, siti, frigore, nuditate; vilescunt et
contabescunt, spernuntur et confunduntur. O miserabilis condicio mendicantis! Et si petit, pudore
5 confunditur, et si non petit, egestate consumitur, set
ut mendicet necessitate compellitur. Deum causatur
iniquum quod non recte dividat; proximum criminatur malig- / -num quod non plene subveniat;   f. 83
indignatur, murmurat, inprecatur. Adverte super
10 hoc sentenciam sapientis: "Melius est mori quam   In Ecclesias-
indigere." "Eciam proximo suo pauper odiosus   tico
erit." "Omnes dies pauperis mali." "Fratres hominis   In Proverbiis
pauperis oderunt eum, insuper et amici procul recesserunt ab eo." "Cum fueris felix, multos nume-
15 rabis amicos. Tempora si si fuerint nubila, solus eris."
Proh pudor! Secundum fortunam estimatur persona,
cum pocius secundum personam sit estimanda for-

115

person. He is considered as good as he is rich, as bad as he is poor, when rather he should be considered as rich as he is good, as poor as he is bad. The rich man, however, is untied by superfluity and unbridled by boasting, he flies away to his pleasure and falls into unlawfulness, and they become the instruments of his punishments that had been the pleasures of his sins. Labor in acquiring, fear in possessing, sorrow in losing always tires, disturbs, and afflicts his mind. "Where thy treasure is, there is thy heart also." But of this more in the following.

[15] OF THE MISERY OF SERVANTS AND MASTERS

The servant is terrified by threats, worn out with duties, afflicted by beatings, robbed of his money. If he does not have money, he is compelled to have it, and if he has it, he is constrained not to have it. The wrongdoing of the master, the punishment of the servant; the wrongdoing of the servant, the profit of the master. "Whatever folly the kings commit, the Greeks are punished." "The wild ass is the lion's prey in the desert: so also the poor are the food of the rich." O outrageous condition of servitude! Nature bore free men, but fortune created servants. The servant is forced to suffer and is not allowed to suffer with anyone; he is compelled to undergo pain and no one is permitted to undergo pain with him. While he is not his own man no one is his. Miserable are those who are camp followers, because it is miserable "to live from another's table." But if the master is cruel, it is necessary for him to fear because of the profligacy of his subjects; if he is gentle, it happens that he is despised because of the insolence of his subordinates. Fear therefore afflicts the one who is severe, and scorn belittles the one who is mild; for cruelty produces hate, and familiarity produces contempt. Family care tires him out, and domestic responsibility annoys him. It is necessary for him to be prepared always, to be protected everywhere so that he can guard against the plots of

C³C¹⁰C¹⁴C¹⁸L³¹. 19 **dives** dives est C¹⁸. **sit reputandus** *trans* C¹⁴C¹⁸; sit reprobandus O¹⁹. 20 **malus** bonus L³¹. **autem** *om* C¹⁴C¹⁸. 20–21 **superfluitate** gravitate C¹⁴. 21 **effrenatur** refrenatur AuBuD⁶L¹⁷L²⁵O³¹. 22 **corruit** cadit C¹⁴. **in** ad *many MSS incl* C¹⁴C¹⁸V². **instrumenta** et instrumenta L³¹. 23 **Labor** Labor eciam C¹⁰C¹⁴C¹⁸L³¹. 24 **in adquirendo** ad inquirendo L³¹; inquirendo C⁹. 25 **eius** *om* C¹⁴C¹⁸. 26 **est** vero L³¹. **tuus** suus *many MSS incl* C³C¹⁸E¹. **ibi** ubi C¹⁸. **tuum** tuus *many MSS incl* C³C¹⁰C¹⁸. 27 **Set** *om* C¹⁴C¹⁸. **sequentibus** consequentibus C¹⁰C¹⁴C¹⁸; sequentibus dicemus *many MSS incl* V².

I.15: 2 **Quod** Quos *many MSS incl* C³C¹⁰C¹⁴C¹⁸; Qui *most MSS incl* L³¹. 2–3 **habere compellitur** *trans* C¹⁰C¹⁴C¹⁸L³¹. 7 **O** *om* L³¹. **Natura** Natura namque C¹⁰C¹⁴C¹⁸L³¹. 9 **non** nemo *most MSS incl* C³C¹⁰C¹⁴C¹⁸L³¹Ro. 10 **et** set C¹⁴C¹⁸L³¹. **ei** *above line* L²⁰; *om most MSS incl* C³C¹⁰C¹⁴C¹⁸L³¹Ro. 10–11 **ipse . . . sibi** homo est ut non homo BuGoLmPa⁹Pa¹¹. 11 **suus est** *trans* C¹⁰; est servus C¹⁴C¹⁸. **ut** *a following* et *expunged* L²⁰; ut et L³¹. **nemo sit sibi** memor sit sui C¹⁴C¹⁸E¹. **Miseri** Miseri sunt C³. 12 **quadra** quadra id est expensa *in margin* C¹⁴; quam ora L³¹. 13 **oportet** contingat C¹⁰; continget C¹⁴; contingit C¹⁸. **illum** eum C¹⁸. 14–15 **contingit** contingat *many MSS incl* C¹⁰L³¹; continget C¹⁴C¹⁸. 15–16 **subditorum** subiectorum *many MSS incl* V². 17 **vilitas** multa cura BuGoLm Pa⁹Pa¹¹. **parvipendit** impendit C¹⁸. **et** *om* C¹⁴C¹⁸. 18 **parit** vero C¹⁴; autem C¹⁸. **enim** *above line* L²⁰; *om* C³; autem C¹⁴C¹⁸L³¹. **eum** *om most MSS incl* C³C¹⁰C¹⁴C¹⁸L³¹Ro. 19 **fatigat** semper fatigat C¹⁰C¹⁴C¹⁸L³¹. 21 **possit . . . insidias** malignancium insidias

tuna. Tam bonus reputatur ut dives, tam malus ut
pauper, cum pocius tam dives sit reputandus ut
20 bonus, tam pauper ut malus. Dives, autem, superfluitate resolvitur et iactancia effrenatur, currit ad
libitum et corruit in illicitum, et fiunt instrumenta
penarum que fuerant oblectamenta culparum. Labor
in adquirendo, timor in possidendo, dolor in amit-
25 tendo mentem eius semper fatigat, sollicitat, et
affligit. "Ubi est thesaurus tuus, ibi est et cor tuum."
Set de hoc plenius in sequentibus.

[15] DE MISERIA SERVORUM ET DOMINORUM

Servus minis terretur, angariis fatigatur, plagis affligitur, opibus spoliatur. Quod si non habet, habere
compellitur, et si habet, cogitur non habere. Culpa
domini, servi pena; culpa servi, domini preda.
5 "Quicquid delirant reges, plectuntur Achivi." "Ve-   In Ecclesias-
nacio leonis onager in heremo: sic pascua divitum   tico
pauperes." O extrema condicio servitutis! Natura
liberos genuit, set fortuna servos constituit. Servus
cogitur pati et non sinitur compati; dolere compelli-
10 tur et nemo ei condolere permittitur. Sic ipse non
suus est ut nemo sit sibi. / Miseri qui castra sequn-   f. 84
tur, quia miserum est "aliena vivere quadra."
Dominus autem si crudelis est, oportet illum vereri
propter nequiciam subiectorum; si mitis est, contin-
15 git illum contempni propter insolenciam subditorum. Severum ergo metus affligit, et mansuetum
vilitas parvipendit; nam crudelitas parit odium, et
familiaritas parit contemptum. Familiaris enim eum
cura fatigat, et domestica sollicitudo molestat.
20 Oportet eum semper esse paratum, ubique munitum
ut possit malignancium insidias precavere, oppug-

117

the malicious, repulse the assaults of attackers, destroy his enemies, protect his people. Nor is the evil of the day sufficient thereto, but day sends forth the labor of the day and night discloses the anxiety of the night. The days are therefore spent in labor, and the nights are passed without sleep.

[16] OF THE MISERY OF THE MARRIED AND THE CELIBATE

If fire cannot burn, flesh cannot lust, because as much as it is fought, that Jebusite can still never be expelled completely. "You may expel nature with a pitchfork, but she will always return." "All men," he says, "take not this word, but let him take who can." When God himself commanded regarding the priestly vestments that Moses should clothe Aaron and his sons, he did not give orders about the breeches alone, but said that they themselves should make use of the breeches when they entered the tabernacle of the testimony. But the Apostle says: "Defraud not one another, except perhaps by consent for a time, that you may give yourselves to prayer and return together again, lest Satan tempt you for your incontinency." "It is better to marry than to be burnt." Therefore the angel of Satan fights continence. He stimulates carnally and buffets violently, kindles the fire of nature with a breath of suggestion, provides the occasion, furnishes the ability, affords the opportunity. He fights, and the outward appearance as well, which, seen unexpectedly, is easily desired. When "David after noon walked on the roof of the king's house, seeing Bethsabee washing herself opposite, and the woman was very beautiful, he sent and took her and slept with her." "But he that is with a wife is solicitous for the things of the world and is divided." For he is distracted by many needs and is divided among various cares, such as to search for and

possit $C^{10}C^{14}C^{18}L^{31}$. 24 **eructuat laborem** *trans* C^3; laborem eructat *most MSS incl* $C^{10}C^{14}C^{18}V^2$; eructat laborem L^{31}. 24-25 **indicat** indicit $C^{14}C^{18}$. 25 **ducuntur** dura*n*tur C^{14}; dicuntur C^{18}. 25-26 **expenduntur** expediuntur C^3C^{18}Ro. 26 **insompnes** in sompnis C^3; in sompnos $C^{18}L^{31}$, *corrected to* in sompnes C^{14}.

I.16: 2 **quia** et $C^{10}C^{14}C^{18}$. 2-3 **tamen . . . expelli** tamen potest ille Iebuseus expelli $C^{14}C^{18}$; tamen potest Iebuseus ille expelli E^1; tamen ex toto potest ille Iebuzeus expelli L^{31}; Iebuseus ille penitus expugnatur Ro. 4 **expellas** licet expellas C^3; expellens L^{31}. **tamen . . . recurret** et cetera $C^{14}C^{18}$. 5 **inquit** *om* $C^{10}C^{14}C^{18}L^{31}$. 6 **cum . . . ipse** cum Dominus ipse C^3; ipse Dominus cum $C^{10}C^{14}C^{18}L^{31}$. **de** de ceteris *most MSS incl* $C^3C^{10}C^{14}C^{18}L^{31}$Ro. 7 **ut Moyses** ut Moyses et C^3L^{31}; Moysi ut $C^{10}C^{14}C^{18}$. 8 **feminalibus** femoralibus C^{14}; femorabus *corrected to* feminalibus *above line* L^{31}. 9 **ut . . . uterentur** *om* C^{10}. **ut ipsi** facies L^{31}. **feminalibus** *in margin* C^{14}; femoralibus $C^{18}L^{36}$; feminalia L^{31}. **uterentur** linea ut operiant carnes turpidinis sue arenibus usque ad femora L^{31}Bs. **ingrederentur** ingrederetur Moyses L^{31}. 10 **testimonii** testimonii et cetera $C^{14}C^{18}$. **Set** Sed et *most MSS incl* C^3Ro; Et $C^{14}C^{18}$. **inquit** inquit ad Corinthios $C^{14}C^{18}$; dicit *many MSS*. 11 **fraudare** fraudari ad $C^{10}C^{14}C^{18}$; fraudari *many MSS*. 13 **tempnet** temptet *many MSS incl* $C^{10}C^{14}C^{18}L^{31}$. **Sathanas** diabolus $C^{10}C^{14}C^{18}L^{31}$. 14 **est enim** *trans* C^{18} L^{31}. 15 **continenciam** continenciam vestram C^{10}. 18-19 **ministrat** subministrat $L^{31}O^{21}$. 19 **Pugnat** Pungit $C^{14}C^{18}$. **visa** visa est *many MSS incl* $C^3C^{14}L^{31}$. 20 **concupiscitur** concupiscatur C^3. **cum . . . meridiem** David post meridiem cum $C^{10}C^{14}C^{18}L^{31}$. 21 **solario** solio $C^{14}C^{18}$. **domus** domus sue C^3. **videns** vidit L^{31}. 22 **se** *om* L^{31}. **autem** enim *most MSS incl* $C^{10}L^{31}V^2$. **mulier** *om* $C^{10}C^{14}C^{18}L^{31}$. 23 **valde** nimis V^2. 24 **illa** ea *most MSS incl* C^3V^2. **sollicitus** sollicitus earum C^3; sollicitus circa ea C^{14}. 26 **et in** in C^{10}; et

nancium iniurias propulsare, hostes conterere, cives
tueri. Nec sufficit diei malicia sua, set dies diei
eructuat laborem et nox nocti sollicitudinem indi-
25 cat. Dies ergo laboriosi ducuntur, et noctes expenduntur insompnes.

[16] DE MISERIA CONTINENTIS ET CONIUGATI

Si potest ignis non urere, potest caro non concupis-
cere, quia quantumcumque pugnetur, nunquam tamen ex toto Iebuseus ille potest expelli. "Naturam
expellas furca, tamen usque recurret." "Non   In Matheo
5 omnes," inquit, "capiunt verbum istud, set qui potest capere capiat." Unde cum Deus ipse de pontifi-
calibus indumentis iussisset ut Moyses Aaron et filios   In Exodo
eius vestiret, de solis feminalibus non precepit, set
ait ut ipsi feminalibus uterentur cum ingrederentur
10 tabernaculum testimonii. Set Apostolus inquit: Ad Corinthi-
"Nolite fraudare invicem, nisi forte ex consensu ad   os
tempus, ut vacetis oracioni et iterum revertimini in
idipsum, ne tempnet vos Sathanas propter inconti-
nenciam vestram." "Melius est enim nubere quam
15 uri." Pugnat ergo contra continenciam angelus Sa-
thane, qui carnaliter stimulat et graviter colafizat,
ignem nature suggestionis flatu succendit, materiam
apponit, facultatem tribuit, / et oportunitatem mi-   f. 84v
nistrat. Pugnat, et species, que, subito visa, facile
20 concupiscitur. Unde cum "David post meridiem   In Regum
deambularet in solario domus regie, videns ex adverso Bersabee se lavantem, erat autem mulier
pulcra valde, misit et tulit eam et dormivit cum
illa." Porro "qui cum uxore est sollicitus est que   Apostolus
25 sunt mundi et divisus est." Distrahitur enim per
multas angustias et in varias sollicitudines disse-

provide the necessities for his male and female servants. "Such shall have tribulation of the flesh." The wife strives to have precious apparel and a diverse wardrobe, so that the wife's clothing may often be of greater value than her husband's pay; otherwise she sighs and wails, jabbers and mutters day and night. For there are three things that do not permit a man to stay at home: smoke, the dripping of rain, and a wicked wife. "That one," she says, "appears better dressed in public, this one is honored by everybody. Poor me, I alone am despised in a meeting of the women, scorned by all." She wishes to be honored alone, to be praised alone. She declares his love of one an offense; she believes his praise of another a disgrace. All that she values is to be loved, and all that she despises is to be hated. She wishes to rule if she cannot be ruled. She does not tolerate being a servant, but strives to be master. She wishes to have influence in all things, not to have influence in none. If she is beautiful, she is easily loved; if ugly, she is easily desired. But what is esteemed by many is kept with difficulty, and what no one deigns to have is annoying to possess. One man is enticed by her figure, one by her cleverness, one by her humor, one by her generosity; and thus what was attacked on all sides is captured from any side. A horse and an ass, an ox and a dog, clothing and a bed, a cup and pitchers are inspected first and bought afterwards! But a bride is scarcely exhibited so much, lest she displease before she is led home; whatever misfortune occurs, she will be endured of necessity. If ugly, if foul, if sick, if foolish, if proud, if wrathful, however vicious, a wife can be divorced by a man only on account of fornication. But the one divorcing cannot marry another, nor can the one divorced be joined to another. For "whosoever shall put away his wife, excepting for the cause of fornication, and shall marry another, commits adultery; and he that shall marry her that is put away commits adultery." "But if the wife depart from her husband, she must remain unmarried or be reconciled to her husband; and likewise the man if he depart

C¹⁴C¹⁸. 28 **Tribulacionem** Iubilacionem C¹⁸; Tribulationes V². 29 **habent huiusmodi** huius habent C¹⁴C¹⁸. **contendit** enim contendat C³. 30 **ornatum** ornamentum C³. 33 **non** om L³¹. 34 **manere** permanere V². **fumus stillicidium** trans C¹⁴; stillicidium fluⱱius C¹⁸. 35-36 **omnibus** hominibus many MSS incl C¹⁰L³¹. 39 **suspicatur** suspiratur L³¹. 41 **si** sed most MSS incl C³C¹⁰C¹⁴C¹⁸L³¹Ro. **vinci** vincere L³¹. 43 **nulla** et nichil C¹⁰; set et non vult nichil C¹⁸; et nulla L³¹. 44 **concupiscitur** contempnitur C³; concupiscit most MSS incl C¹⁰C¹⁴C¹⁸Ro; concupis L³¹; despicitur Pa¹¹; concupiscitur vel despicitur Bu. 46 **possidere** custodire C¹⁴. 47 **liberalitate** libertate some MSS. 47-48 **sollicitatur** sollicitat most MSS incl C¹⁰C¹⁴C¹⁸L³¹Ro. 48 **ex** om C¹⁰C¹⁴C¹⁸L³¹. **undique** multis modis C¹⁴; tot modum C¹⁸. 49 **incessitur** inpeditur C¹⁴C¹⁸; incersitur E¹; corrected from inceditur L³¹; inceditur O²⁴; many variants incl appetitur, intenditur, invaditur, lacessitur. **et** (1st) om many MSS incl C¹⁴C¹⁸Ro. 50 **urceoli** urceolus nearly every MS incl C³C¹⁰C¹⁴C¹⁸L³¹Ro. 51 **vero** tamen C¹⁰; om C¹⁴C¹⁸. **tantum** tandem most MSS incl C³L³¹Ro; om C¹⁰; prius C¹⁴C¹⁸. 53 **advenerit** obvenerit most MSS incl C¹⁰C¹⁴C¹⁸L³¹Ro. **Si . . . fetida** om C¹⁰C¹⁸; Si fetida si feda C¹⁴; Si . . . fetida si racunda L³¹. 54 **si iracunda** om C¹⁰C¹⁸. **si** (5th) set L³¹. **quamlibet** quantumlibet many MSS incl C¹⁰C¹⁸; quoquo modo C¹⁴Er²O²⁴; qualibet macula Ro. 56 **Set** om C¹⁰C¹⁴C¹⁸. **non** nec most MSS incl C³C¹⁰C¹⁴C¹⁸L³¹Ro. **aliam potest** trans C³L³¹. 57 **alii potest** C¹⁰; trans most MSS incl C³C¹⁸Ro. 58 **dimiserit uxorem** dimiserit uxorem suam most MSS incl C¹⁰C¹⁴C¹⁸Ro; uxorem suam dimiserit L³¹. **fornicacionem** fornicationis causam many MSS incl V². 59 **mechatur** corrected above line from inchoatur C¹⁴. 59-60 **et . . . mechatur** om many MSS incl C¹⁰C¹⁴C¹⁸L³¹. 60 **Quod** Et C¹⁴C¹⁸. 61 **debet** det C¹⁴C¹⁸. 62 **nimis** enim C¹⁰C¹⁸; n

catur, ut filiis et uxori, famulis et ancillis necessaria
querat et subministret. "Tribulacionem ergo carnis
habent huiusmodi." Uxor contendit habere precio-
30 sum ornatum et variam superlectilem, ut pluris sit
sepe cultus uxoris quam census mariti; alioquin per
dies et noctes suspirat et plangit, garrit et murmurat. Tria sunt enim que non sinunt hominem in domo   Salomon
manere: fumus, stillicidium, et mala uxor. "Illa,"
35 inquit, "ornacior procedit in publicum, hec ab omnibus honoratur. Ego misera in conventu feminarum
sola despicior, a cunctis contempnor." Sola vult
diligi, sola laudari. Alterius amorem suum asserit
odium; alterius laudem suum dedecus suspicatur.
40 Amandum est omne quod diligit, odiendum est
omne quod spernit. Vincere vult si vinci non valet.
Famulari non patitur, set dominari molitur. Cuncta
vult posse, nulla non posse. Si pulchra fuerit, facile
adamatur; si feda, facile concupiscitur. Set difficile
45 custoditur quod a multis diligitur, et molestum est
possidere quod nemo dignatur habere. Alius forma,
alius ingenio, alius faceciis, alius liberalitate sollicitatur; et sic ex aliqua parte capitur quod undique
incessitur. Equus et asi- / -nus, bos et canis, vestis et   f. 85
50 lectulus, calix et urceoli prius probantur et postea
comparantur! Sponsa vero vix tantum ostenditur, ne
prius displiceat quam ducatur; qualiscumque casus
advenerit, necessario est habenda. Si feda, si fetida,
si egra, si fatua, si superba, si iracunda, si quamlibet
55 viciosa, propter solam fornicacionem potest uxor a
viro dimitti. Set non dimittens aliam potest ducere,
nec dimissa alii potest copulari. Nam "quicumque   Matheus
dimiserit uxorem, nisi ob fornicacionem, et aliam
duxerit, mechatur; et qui dimissam duxerit me-
60 chatur." "Quod si uxor a viro discesserit, manere   Ad Corinthios
debet innupta aut viro suo reconciliari; similiter et

from his wife." The burden of marriage is extremely heavy, for "he that keepeth an adulteress is foolish and wicked," and he is the patron of disgrace who conceals the crime of his wife. But if he puts away the adulteress, he is punished without fault of his own, because with her living he is forced to be continent. Because of this the disciples said to Christ: "If the case with his wife be so, it is not expedient to marry." Who could ever tolerate a rival calmly? Mere suspicion strongly distresses the jealous man, for even though it is written, "They shall be two in one flesh," still the jealousy of man does not endure two men in one flesh.

[17] OF THE MISERY OF THE GOOD AND THE BAD

It is not for the sinful to rejoice, says the Lord, because "by what things a man sinneth, by the same also is he tormented." For the truth of conscience never dies, and the fire of reason is never quenched. "I have seen those who work iniquity and sow sorrows and reap them perishing by the blast of God and consumed by the spirit of his wrath." Pride inflates and envy gnaws, avarice stimulates, anger inflames, gluttony chokes, lechery destroys, lying binds, murder corrupts. So also the other signs of vices, so that what are pleasures to the man who sins are instruments to the God who punishes. "The envious man grows thin at the sizable possessions of another." Indeed "the Sicilian tyrants have not invented a greater torment than envy." For vice corrupts nature, as is shown by the Apostle, who says: "Because they became vain in their thoughts, their foolish heart was darkened. Wherefore God gave them up to the desires of their heart, unto uncleanness, to inflict their own bodies with abuses, and as they liked not to have God in their knowledge, God delivered them up to a reprobate sense, to do those things which are not convenient."

L³¹. **est pondus** iugum C¹⁸. 64 **est turpitudinis** *trans* C¹⁴C¹⁸L³¹. 65 **Set et si** Et qui C³; Si C¹⁰C¹⁸L³¹; Nisi *corrected above line to* Set si C¹⁴; Set si *most MSS incl* V². 67 **Propter** Ob C¹⁴C¹⁸. **et** *om many MSS incl* C¹⁰C¹⁴C¹⁸L³¹. **Christo dixerunt** *trans* C¹⁰C¹⁸L³¹; duxerunt Christo C¹⁴. 67-68 **ita est** *om* C¹⁰C¹⁸L³¹. 68 **causa** causa hominis *most MSS incl* C³C¹⁴Ro; causa hominis est talis super terram C¹⁰C¹⁸; causa hominis talis est super terram L³¹. **uxore** muliere C¹⁴O²⁴. **non . . . nubere** nubere non expedit C¹⁰C¹⁸. 69 **equanimiter . . . rivalem** potuit rivalem sustinere equanimiter C¹⁰C¹⁴C¹⁸L³¹. 71 **scriptum** strepitum L³¹. **tamen** cum C¹⁸. 72 **duos** duo C¹⁰L³¹.

I.17: 1 **Dominus** Deus L³¹. 2 **Veritas** Vermis *nearly every MS incl* C³C¹⁰ C¹⁴C¹⁸L³¹Ro; ceriiciis *in margin next to this word* L³¹. 3 **enim** autem C¹⁰C¹⁴C¹⁸L³¹. **consciencie** et sciencie L³¹. **nunquam** non C¹⁰C¹⁴C¹⁸. 4 **nunquam** non C¹⁰C¹⁴C¹⁸. **extinguitur** extinguetur *many MSS incl* C¹⁰C¹⁸. **Vidi** Vidi enim C³C¹⁰C¹⁴C¹⁸L³¹. 6 **ire** oris C¹⁰C¹⁴C¹⁸. 7 **Superbia** Superbiat L³¹. **et** *om most MSS incl* C³C¹⁰C¹⁸L³¹Ro. **rodit** redit L³¹; corrodit L⁹. 9 **cetera** alia C¹⁰C¹⁴C¹⁸. 10 **portenta** portenta naturam corrumpunt L³¹. **peccanti** peccandi *most MSS incl* C³C¹⁰C¹⁴C¹⁸V²; peccati L³¹. 11 **sint** sunt *nearly every MS incl* C³C¹⁰Ro. **punienti** puniendi *most MSS incl* C³C¹⁰C¹⁴C¹⁸L³¹V². 12 **macrescit rebus** marcescit rebus C³C¹⁰C¹⁴; rebus m C¹⁸; ma rebus L³¹; *trans many MSS incl* Ro. 12-13 **Set . . . tormentum** *om* C¹⁰C¹⁸L³¹; *in margin* C¹⁴. 13 **enim** *om* C¹⁴C¹⁸. 14 **testante** attestante C³. 15 **Quia** Qui L³¹. 16 **eorum** illorum L³¹. 17 **in (1st)** in reprobum sensum et C¹⁰L³¹; in reprobum sensum et in C¹⁴C¹⁸. **eorum** illorum L³¹. 18 **contumeliis** incontumeliis L³¹; contumeliosa BuD¹GoILmPa⁵Pa⁹Pa¹¹. **afficiant** afficient L³¹; efficiant BuGoILmPa⁵Pa⁹, *corrected to* afficiant *in* Pa¹¹. **sua** eorum C¹⁴. **et . . . non** et sic C¹⁰; sic eciam C¹⁴L³¹; sicut eciam C¹⁸. 19 **probaverunt** reprobaverunt *many MSS incl* C³V². **habere** non habere C¹⁰C¹⁴C¹⁸L³¹. **sua** *om most MSS incl* C³C¹⁴Ro. **tradidit** ideo tradidit

vir si discesserit ab uxore." Grave nimis est pondus
coniugii, nam "stultus et impius est qui tenet adul- Salomon
teram," et patronus est turpitudinis qui celat crimen
65   uxoris. Set et si dimittit adulteram, absque sui culpa
punitur, quoniam illa vivente cogitur continere.
Propter quod et discipuli Christo dixerunt: "Si ita Matheus
est causa cum uxore, non expedit nubere." Quis
unquam equanimiter potuit sustinere rivalem? Sola
70   suspicio zelotipum vehementer affligit, nam licet
scriptum sit, "Erunt duo in carne una," zelus tamen
viri duos in una carne non patitur.

[17] DE MISERIA BONORUM ET MALORUM

Non est impiis gaudere, dicit Dominus, quia "per
que peccat homo, per hec et torquetur." Veritas
enim consciencie nunquam moritur, et ignis racionis
nunquam extinguitur. "Vidi eos qui operantur ini-
5   quitatem et seminant dolores et metunt eos flante
Deo perisse et spiritu ire eius esse consumptos."
Superbia inflat et invidia rodit, avaricia stimulat, ira
succendit, angit gula, dissolvit luxuria, ligat menda-
cium, maculat homicidium. / Sic et cetera viciorum f. 85v
10   portenta, ut que sunt homini oblectamenta peccanti
Deo sint instrumenta punienti. "Invidus alterius
macrescit rebus opimis." Set "invidia Siculi non
invenere tyranni maius tormentum." Vicium enim
corrumpit naturam, Apostolo testante, qui ait:
15   "Quia evanuerunt in cogitacionibus suis, obscura- Ad Romanos
tum est insipiens cor eorum. Propter quod tradidit
illos Deus in desideria cordis eorum, in immundicia,
ut contumeliis afficiant corpora sua, et sicut non
probaverunt Deum habere in noticia sua, tradidit
20   illos Deus in reprobum sensum, ut faciant ea que non

123

But also "those that intend to live godly in Christ shall suffer persecution." "The saints had trial of mockeries and stripes, moreover also of bands and prisons; they were stoned, they were cut asunder, they were put to death by the sword for the Lord. They wandered about in sheepskins, in goatskins, being in want, distressed, afflicted, of whom the world was not worthy, wandering in deserts and in mountains and in dens and in caves of the earth." "In perils of waters, in perils of robbers, in perils from the nation, in perils from the gentiles, in perils in the city, in perils in false brethren. In labor and painfulness, in much watchings, in cold and nakedness, in many difficulties, in hunger, in thirst, in many fastings." For the just man "denies himself," crucifying his limbs in vices and concupiscences, so that the world is crucified to him and he to the world. "He hath not here a lasting city, but seeketh one that is to come." He endures the world as a place of exile, confined in the body as in a prison. "I am," he says, "a sojourner on the earth," "and a wayfarer as all my fathers were. Forgive me that I may be refreshed, before I go hence and be no more." "Woe is me that my sojourning is prolonged; I have dwelt with the inhabitants of Cedar; my soul hath been long a sojourner." "Who is weak, and I am not weak? Who is scandalized, and I am not on fire?" For this is the watery ground that Caleb gave his daughter Axa as dowry.

[18] OF THE ENEMIES OF MAN

"The life of man upon earth is a warfare." Is it not indeed warfare when many enemies lie in wait on all sides in order to capture, pursue in order to kill—the

C10C14C18L31. 20 **faciant** faciantur C18. **ea** *om* C10C14C18L31. 21 **et** *om* C10C14C18L31. 22 **Sancti** Sunt L31. **vero** namque *most MSS incl* C3C10C14C18L31V2. 23 **et . . . experti** experti et verbera C14; experti sunt C18. 23-24 **vincula et carceres** vincti et carcerati C18; **vinc'** et car C14. 24 **secti . . . sunt** temptati sunt secti sunt C10C18L31. 25 **pro Domino** pro Christo C10C14; in Christo C18L31. 27 **afflicti** *om* C14C18. 28 **et (1st)** *om many MSS incl* C10C14C18L31. 29 **cavernis** *a superfluous* er *above line expunged* L20. 30 **genere . . . gentibus** *trans* C10; gentibus C14C18; gen . . . genere L31. 31 **civitate** civitate periculis in solitudine periculis in mari *some MSS*. **in falsis** ex falsis *many MSS incl* Ro. 32-33 **in frigore . . . multis** in fame et siti in ieiuniis multis in frigore et nuditate in angustiis multis *most MSS incl* C3Ro, *with* in ieiuniis multis *and* in frigore et nuditate *trans* C18; in fame . . . ieiuniis multis *om* C10; *the whole passage om* L31. 35 **in** cum *most MSS incl* C3C10C14C18L31Ro. **viciis . . . concupiscenciis** *trans* C10C14C18L31. 37 **manentem civitatem** *trans* C10. 39 **carcere** corde C3. **Incola inquit** Incola *many MSS incl* C10L31; unde ait C14C18. 40 **in terra** apud te C3. 41-42 **ut . . . ero** et cetera C14; refrigerer et cetera C18. 42 **eam** abeam *most MSS incl* C3C10V2; habeam *many MSS incl* L31. **me** michi *many MSS incl* L31Ro. 43-44 **prolongatus . . . mea** et cetera C14C18; prolongatus est L31. 46-47 **frixoria sunt** refrixorium sunt C3; *trans* L31; frixorium sunt *most MSS incl* Ro. 47 **enim** C10; *om most MSS incl* C3C14Ro.

I.18: 1 **Annon** An nonne *many MSS incl* C3Ro. **vere** nature C18; vera *many MSS incl* Ro. 2 **milicia** milicia est *many MSS incl* C18. **insidiaitur undique** insidiaitur (*insidian*tur *intended*) *corrected from* insiduntur L20; undique insidientur C3; undique semper insidientur *many MSS incl* C10Ro; fuit videlicet qui insidiantur semper C14, *with* sint *for* fuit C18; undique quod insidientur semper L31; semper undique insidientur *most MSS*. 3 **persequantur** persecuntur C18L31. **perimant** pertinent L31. **demon et** demon scilicet et C3; hii scilicet C14C18. 4 **et caro . . . viciis** Demon caro C14C18. 4-5 **homo . . .**

124

conveniunt." Set et "qui pie volunt vivere in
Christo persecucionem paciuntur." "Sancti vero Ad Hebreos
ludibria et verbera experti, insuper et vincula et
carceres; lapidati sunt, secti sunt, temptati sunt, in
25 occisione gladii mortui sunt pro Domino. Circum-
ierunt in melotis, in pellibus caprinis, egentes, an-
gustiati, afflicti, quibus dignus non erat mundus, in
solitudinibus errantes et in montibus et in speluncis
et in cavernis terre." "Periculis fluminum, periculis Ad Corinthios
30 latronum, periculis ex genere, pe*riculis* ex gentibus,
pe*riculis* in civitate, pe*riculis* in falsis fratribus. In
labore et erumpna, in vigiliis multis, in frigore et
nuditate, in augustiis multis, in fame, in siti, in
ieiuniis multis." Iustus enim "abnegat semetipsum,"
35 crucifigens menbra sua in viciis et concupiscenciis,
ut sibi mundus crucifixus sit et ipse mundo. "Non
habet hic manentem civitatem, set futuram
inquirit." Sustinet seculum tanquam exilium, clau-
sus in corpore tanquam in carcere. "Incola," inquit, In Psalmo
40 "ego sum in terra," "et peregrinus sicut omnes
patres mei. Remitte michi ut refrigerer, priusquam
eam et *amplius* non ero." "Heu me quia incolatus
meus prolongatus est; ha*bitavi* / cum ha*bitantibus* f. 86
Cedar; *multum incola fuit anima mea*." "Quis infir- Apostolus
45 matur, et ego non infirmor? Quis scandalizatur, et
ego non uror?" Nam peccata proximorum frixoria
sunt iustorum. Hoc est enim irriguum quod Caleph
Axe filie sue dedit in dotem.

[18] DE HOSTIBUS HOMINIS

"Milicia est vita hominis super terram." Annon vere Iob
milicia cum multiplices hostes insidiaitur undique ut
capiant, persequantur ut perimant—demon et

devil and man, the world and the flesh, the devil together with the vices, man together with the beasts, the world together with its elements, the flesh together with the senses? "For the flesh lusteth against the spirit, the spirit against the flesh." Yet "our wrestling is not so much against flesh and blood, but against the spirits of wickedness in the high places, against the rulers of these darknesses." "For our adversary the devil goeth about as a roaring lion seeking whom he may devour." The flaming weapons of the most wicked one are ignited. Death comes in through the windows. The eye plunders the soul. "The whole world shall fight against the unwise." "Nation against nation, and kingdom against kingdom, there shall be great earthquakes in divers places, pestilences and famines, and terrors from heaven and tempests." Earth produces thorns and thistles; water, storms and floods; air, tempests and thunders; fire, flashings and lightnings. "Cursed is the earth," he says, "in thy work; thorns and thistles shall it bring forth to thee. In the sweat of thy face shalt thou eat thy bread till thou return to the earth, for dust thou art and into dust thou shalt return." "The boar out of the wood layeth it waste, and a singular wild beast devoureth it." The wolf and the bear, the panther and the lion, the tiger and the wild ass, the crocodile and the griffon, the serpent and the snake, the lizard and the asp, the horned serpent and the dragon, scorpions and vipers; but also nits and fleas and lice, insects and flies, hornets and wasps, fish and birds. For we who were created to "rule over the fishes of the sea and the fowls of the air and all living creatures that move upon the earth" now are given to them as prey, now are given to them for food. For it is written: "I will send the teeth of beasts upon them, with the fury of creatures that trail upon the ground" et cetera.

elementis homo . . . elementis demon cum viciis C¹⁴C¹⁸; mundus cum elementis homo cum elementis L³¹. 6 **namque** aut L³¹. **spiritum** spiritum et *most MSS incl* C³Ro. 7 **Verum** Unde C¹⁴L³¹. 8 **tantum** *om most MSS incl* C¹⁰L³¹Ro; *after* carnem *in* C¹⁴C¹⁸. **et sanguinem** *om* C¹⁰C¹⁴C¹⁸. 9 **spirituales** spiritualia *most MSS incl* C³C¹⁰C¹⁴C¹⁸Ro. **nequicias** nequicie *most MSS incl* C³C¹⁰C¹⁴C¹⁸Ro. **adversus** et adversus C¹⁰C¹⁴C¹⁸ L³¹. 10 **harum** *om* C¹⁰L³¹. **enim** *om* C¹⁴C¹⁸L³¹. 11–12 **querens . . . devoret** querens et cetera C¹⁴; et cetera C¹⁸. 12 **nequissimi** nequissimi hostis C¹⁰C¹⁴C¹⁸L³¹. 13–14 **depredatur** depredatur et L³¹. 16 **regnum** regnum et *most MSS incl* C¹⁰C¹⁴C¹⁸L³¹. **erunt** *om most MSS incl* C³C¹⁰C¹⁴C¹⁸L³¹Ro; factus est O¹⁹. **magni** magnus *many MSS incl* C³C¹⁸; m L³¹. **loca** loca et C¹⁰C¹⁴C¹⁸. 17 **et tempestates** tempestates et tonitrua *many MSS incl* C¹⁰C¹⁴L³¹; tempestates que et tonutrua C¹⁸; et signa multa erunt O⁷. 18–19 **Terra . . . tonitrua** *om* C¹⁴. 20 **inquit** inquit Dominus C¹⁴C¹⁸. 21–22 **spinas . . . tuo** *om* L³¹. 22 **vertaris** revertaris *nearly every MS incl* C³C¹⁰C¹⁴C¹⁸L³¹Ro. 23 **quia** *om* C¹⁴C¹⁸L³¹. **Insidiatur** Ingrediatur C¹⁰; Egrediatur C¹Es²La, *and* E¹ *but not a group reading.* 24 **et . . . depascitur** et cetera C¹⁴C¹⁸. **depascitur** depascetur C³. 25 **pardus** lapardus L³¹D²Ut². 26 **aspis** apes C¹⁰; apes et L³¹; aspis serpens cornutus Re³T². 27–28 **set . . . pulices et** sed . . . pulices punices et C³; *om* C¹⁰C¹⁴C¹⁸L³¹; sed eciam lendes et pulices cimices et *most MSS, with* formices *for* cimices Re³T². 28 **cyniphes et** *trans* C¹⁰C¹⁴C¹⁸; et semifes L³¹. **musce** musce et C¹⁰C¹⁴C¹⁸L³¹. **crabones** scrabones *most MSS incl* C³C¹⁰C¹⁴C¹⁸L³¹Ro. 29 **et wespe** *trans* C¹⁰C¹⁴C¹⁸; vespe L³¹. **et volucres** et eciam volucres nobis insidiantur C¹⁴C¹⁸. **fuimus** sumus *most MSS incl* C¹⁰C¹⁴C¹⁸. 32 **damur (1st)** *om* L³¹. **in . . . escam** in escam damur in predam C¹⁰; in escam et in predam C¹⁸, *with* in *om* C¹⁴; in escam damur et in predam L³¹; in predam damur in escam *most MSS incl* Ro, *with* illis *after* damur *in* C³. 33–34 **Scriptum . . . eos** Scriptum est enim *trans to follow* eos C¹⁰; ut scriptum est C¹⁴C¹⁸. 34 **eos** eis C¹⁰L³¹. **et cetera** *om* C³C¹⁰C¹⁴L³¹.

homo, mundus et caro, demon cum viciis, homo cum
bestiis, mundus cum elementis, caro cum sensibus?
"Caro namque concupiscit adversus spiritum, spiri- Apostolus
tus adversus carnem." Verum "non est nobis colluc-
tacio tantum adversus carnem et sanguinem, set
adversus spirituales nequicias in celestibus, adversus
rectores tenebrarum harum." "Adversarius enim Petrus
noster diabolus tanquam leo rugiens circuit querens
quem devoret." Accenduntur ignea tela nequissimi.
Mors ingreditur per fenestras. Oculus animam de- Ieremias
predatur. "Pugnat orbis terrarum contra insensa- Salomon
tos." "Gens contra gentem, et regnum adversus Matheus
regnum, terremotus erunt magni per loca, pestilencie et fames, terroresque de celo et tempestates."
Terra producit spinas et tribulos; aqua, procellas et
fluctus; aer, tempestates et tonitrua; ignis, chorusca-
ciones et fulgura. "Maledicta," inquit, "terra in In Genesi
opere tuo; spinas et tribulos germinabit tibi. In
sudore vultus tui vesceris pane tuo donec vertaris in
terram, quia terra es et in terram ibis." "Insidiatur
aper de silva, et singularis ferus depascitur." Lupus
et ursus, pardus et leo, tigris et onager, corcodrillus
et griphes, serpens et coluber, basiliscus et aspis,
cerastes et draco, scorpiones et vipere; set et lendes
et pulices et pediculi, cyniphes / et musce, crabones f. 86v
et wespe, pisces et volucres. Nam qui creati fuimus
ut "dominaremur piscibus maris et volatilibus celi et
universis animantibus que moventur in terra" nunc
damur illis in predam, nunc damur illis in escam.
Scriptum est enim: "Dentes bestiarum inmittam in
eos, cum furore trahencium super terram" et cetera.

"Who shall deliver me, unhappy man, from the body of this death?" Of course he who does not wish to escape from the body does not wish to escape from prison, for the prison of the soul is the body. Of this the psalmist says: "Bring my soul out of prison that I may praise thy name." Nowhere is there quiet and tranquillity, nowhere peace and security; everywhere there is fear and trembling, everywhere labor and sorrow. "His flesh shall have pain while he shall live, and his soul shall mourn over him."

[20] OF BRIEF JOY

Who indeed has ever spent one whole delightful day in his own pleasure, whom the guilt of conscience or an attack of anger or the agitation of concupiscence has not disturbed in some part of the day? Whom the spite of envy or the burning of avarice or the swelling of pride has not vexed? Whom some loss or offense or passion has not upset? Whom finally any sight or sound or contact has not offended? "A rare bird on the earth and very similar to a black swan." Hear the opinion of the wise man on this: "From the morning until the evening the time shall be changed." "Vain thoughts succeed one another, and the mind is hurried away to different things." "They take the timbrel and the harp and rejoice at the sound of the organ. They spend their days in wealth, and in a moment they go down to hell."

I.19: *Title* Quod Corpus Dicitur Carcer Anime V². 1 **Infelix** Infelix ego *most MSS incl* C³L³¹Ro; Infelix ergo C¹⁰; Infelix ergo ego C¹⁴C¹⁸. **corpore mortis** morte corporis C¹⁰. 2 **exire** educi *nearly every MS incl* C³C¹⁰C¹⁴C¹⁸L³¹Ro. **carcere** corpore C¹⁰. 3 **exire** educi C¹⁰L³¹. **corpore** carcere C¹⁰. 4 **dicit** *om* C¹⁰C¹⁴C¹⁸L³¹. 5 **ad . . . tuo** C¹⁰; *om most MSS incl* C³Ro; ut confitendum nomini tuo Domine L³¹. **Nusquam** Nunquam L³¹. 6 **ubique** ubi L³¹. **est** *om most MSS incl* C³C¹⁰C¹⁴C¹⁸L³¹Ro. 7 **ubique** ibi L³¹. 8 **super** semper L³¹. **lugebit** dolebit et lugebit L³¹; dolebit H¹S³.
I.20: *Title* Scintilla *for* Leticia Re³T². 1 **vel** *om* Gloss *and many MSS incl* C¹⁴C¹⁸. **duxerit totam** totam duxit *most MSS incl* C³Ro; totam deduxit C¹⁰C¹⁴C¹⁸L³¹. 2 **delectacione** dileccione Gloss *and* C³C¹¹Du⁴Ma¹O²³Pa⁵S²S³; del*e*ctacione L³¹. **quem** quam L³¹. 3 **reatus** reate L³¹. 4 **turbaverit** turbavit C³. **Quem** Que L³¹. 5 **avaricie** consciencie L¹⁷L⁴⁵. **tumor** timor *many MSS incl* C¹⁴. 6 **aliqua** alia L³¹. **iactura vel** naturalis Bu; iacturalis Go. **passio** compassio C¹⁴C¹⁸E¹L³¹. 7 **denique** decor L³¹. 8 **tactus** actus *most MSS incl* C³C¹⁰C¹⁴C¹⁸L³¹Ro; odoratus vel tactus BuGoLmPa⁵Pa⁹Pa¹¹. **quilibet** aliquis *most MSS incl* C³C¹⁰C¹⁴C¹⁸L³¹Ro. **terris** terra avis in terra L³¹. 9 **nigroque . . . cigno** et cetera C¹⁸; nigro . . . cingno L³¹. **super hoc** *om* L³¹. 11 **vane sibi** varie C³; sibi mane, C¹⁰; vane C¹⁸; *trans* L³¹. **succedunt** succedunt vel secuntur C¹⁴; secuntur vel succedunt C¹⁸. 12–13 **et cytharam** *om* Gloss *and* U⁷. 13 **ad** ob C³. **sonitum** sonum Gloss *and* C²³L¹L⁶L¹⁸L³⁷MoMu⁶O¹⁷Pa¹⁵S⁴T¹Ut¹Ut²; vocem *a few MSS.* 14 **infernum** inferna *many MSS incl* C¹⁴C¹⁸V².

[19] DE CARCERE ANIME

"Infelix homo, quis me liberabit de corpore mortis huius?" Certe non vult exire de carcere qui non vult exire de corpore, nam carcer anime corpus est. De quo dicit psalmista: "Educ de carcere animam m*eam* 5 ad conf*itendum* n*omini tuo.*" Nusquam est quies et tranquillitas, nusquam pax et securitas; ubique est timor et tremor, ubique labor et dolor. "Caro dum   Iob vivit dolebit, et anima super semetipsam lugebit."

[20] DE BREVI LETICIA

Quis unquam vel unicam diem duxerit totam in sua delectacione iocundam, quem in aliqua parte diei reatus consciencie vel impetus ire vel motus concupiscencie non turbaverit? Quem livor invidie vel 5 ardor avaricie vel tumor superbie non vexaverit? Quem aliqua iactura vel offensa vel passio non commoverit? Quem denique visus vel auditus vel tactus quilibet non offenderit? "Rara avis in terris nigroque simillima cigno." Audi super hoc senten-10 ciam sapientis: "A mane usque ad vesperam mutabi-   In Ecclesias-tur tempus." "Cogitaciones vane sibi succedunt, et   tico mens rapitur in diversa." "Tenent tympanum et cytharam et gaudent ad sonitum organi. Ducunt in bonis dies suos, et in puncto ad infernum descen-15 dunt."

Sudden woe always follows worldly joy, and what begins with gladness ends in sorrow. Worldly happiness is indeed sprinkled with many bitternesses. He knew this who said: "Laughter shall be mingled with sorrow, and mourning takes hold of the ends of joy." The children of Job also experienced this: when they "were eating and drinking wine in the house of their eldest brother," "a violent wind came on a sudden from the side of the desert, and shook the four corners of the house, which in falling crushed them all." The father said justly: "My harp is turned to mourning and my organ into the voice of those that weep." "It is better to go to the house of mourning than to the house of feasting." Sound counsel: "In the day of good things be not unmindful of evils." "In all thy works remember thy last end, and thou shalt never sin."

[22] OF THE PROXIMITY OF DEATH

The last day is always the first, and the first day is never thought to be the last, although it is nevertheless appropriate always to live as if it might always be necessary to die. It is written: "Remember that death is not slow." Time passes, and death approaches. "A thousand years in the eyes of a dying man are as yesterday, which is past." For the future is always being born, the present is always dying, and whatever is past is utterly dead. We are therefore always dying while we live, and we only stop dying at such time as we stop living. It is better to die for life than to live for death, because mortal life is nothing but a living death. Solomon: "I praised the dead rather than the living, and I

I.21: **Title** Labore *for* Dolore C³; De Mundana Leticia IMu⁵. 1 **Semper** Gloss *and seventeen MSS*; Semper enim *most MSS incl* C³C¹⁰C¹⁴C¹⁸L³¹Ro. **mundane** humane vel mundane C³. 2 **incipit** incepit *most MSS incl* C¹⁰L³¹Ro. **a** in C³C¹⁴; *om* C¹⁸. **merore** merrorem L³¹. 3 **quippe** igitur Gloss; vero D⁴. 4 **Noverat** Nam novit C¹⁴C¹⁸; Non erat *some MSS.* **hoc** *om* C¹⁰C¹⁴C¹⁸L³¹. 5-6 **Experti . . . hoc** Experti sunt hoc et C³; hoc *om most MSS incl* C¹⁰; Hec enim experti sunt C¹⁴C¹⁸; Experti L³¹. 6 **comederent** commederent panem D¹O²³Pa⁸. 7 **vinum** *om* C¹⁴C¹⁸L³¹. **fratris sui primogeniti** primogeniti sui fratris C¹⁴C¹⁸. 8 **vehemens ventus** *trans most MSS incl* C³Ro; ventus vehementer C¹⁰; ventus C¹⁸L³¹; ventus *originally in* C¹⁴, *but corrected to the reading in* L²⁰. 9 **angulos** angelos O¹⁰O³¹. **corruens** corruit et C¹⁴C¹⁸. 10 **Merito** Merito ergo *many MSS incl* C¹⁴C¹⁸L³¹V². **pater** pater eorum C¹⁴C¹⁸. **aiebat** ait C³. 11 **mea** *corrected probably from* mei L²⁰. **vocem** lucem *some MSS.* 12 **Melius** Unde Salomon Melius C¹⁴C¹⁸. **igitur** enim C¹⁰; *om* C¹⁴C¹⁸; michi L³¹. 13 **convii** *convivii *nearly every MS incl* C³C¹⁰C¹⁴C¹⁸L³¹Ro. **Salubre** Audi ergo salubre Gloss *and* L³¹; Audi salubre U⁴; Attende salubre Sy. **consilium** consilium est ut C¹⁴C¹⁸; consilium ut L³¹C⁹L⁴⁰. 13-14 **bonorum** beatorum O¹⁰. 14 **ne** non *many MSS incl* C³C¹⁰C¹⁴C¹⁸L³¹; ut non D¹O²³. **immemor sis** *trans* C¹⁴C¹⁸; inmemor sit L³¹. **malorum** malorum in omnibus Re³T². 15 **tua** *om* L³¹. **et . . . peccabis** et cetera C¹⁸; et non peccabis in eternum L³¹.

I.22: **Title** De in Civitate Mortis C³Es². 1 **dies (2nd)** *om nearly every MS incl* C³C¹⁰C¹⁴C¹⁸L³¹Ro. 2 **dies** *om* C¹⁰C¹⁴C¹⁸L³¹. **semper** *om* C¹⁰C¹⁴C¹⁸L³¹. 4 **quia** quoniam C¹⁴C¹⁸L³¹. **mors non tardat** non tardat mors C¹⁰C¹⁴C¹⁸L³¹. 5 **anni** *om* L³¹. 6 **sicut** tamquam *most MSS incl* C³C¹⁰C¹⁴C¹⁸L³¹. 7 **enim** *om* C¹⁴C¹⁸L³¹. **semper** et C¹⁰C¹⁴C¹⁸. 8-9 **et . . . mortuum** *om* C¹⁰. 8 **est** *om* L³¹. 9 **Morimur . . . semper** Morimur ergo C¹⁰C¹⁴C¹⁸; Semper ergo morimur L³¹. 10 **cum . . . vivere** vivere cum desinimus C¹⁰L³¹; cum vivere desinimus C¹⁸. 11 **est** est ergo *most MSS incl* C³C¹⁰C¹⁴C¹⁸L³¹Ro. 12 **Salomon** Unde Salomon *most MSS incl* C¹⁰C¹⁴C¹⁸L³¹V². 13 **mortuum** mortuos *most*

[21] DE INOPINATO DOLORE

Semper mundane letitie tristicia repentina succedit,
et quod incipit a gaudio desinit in merore. Mundana
quippe felicitas multis / amaritudinibus est respersa. f. 87
Noverat hoc ille qui dixerat: "Risus dolore miscebi- Salomon
5 tur, et extrema gaudii luctus occupat." Experti sunt
et hoc liberi Iob: qui cum "comederent et biberent Iob
vinum in domo fratris sui primogeniti," "repente
vehemens ventus irruit a regione deserti, et concus-
sit quatuor angulos domus, que corruens universos
10 oppressit." Merito pater aiebat: "Versa est in luctum
cythara mea et organum meum in vocem flencium."
"Melius est igitur ire ad domum luctus quam ad Ecclesiastes
domum convii." Salubre consilium: "In die bo- Ecclesiasti-cus
norum ne immemor sis malorum." "Memorare no-
15 vissima tua, et in eternum non peccabis."

[22] DE VICINITATE MORTIS

Semper ultimus dies primus, et nunquam dies primus
dies ultimus reputatur, cum tamen ita semper vivere
deceat tanquam mori semper oporteat. Scriptum est
enim: "Memor esto quia mors non tardat." Tempus In Ecclesias-tico
5 preterit, et mors appropinquat. "Mille anni ante
oculos morientis sicut dies hesterna, que preteriit."
Semper enim futura nascuntur, semper presencia
moriuntur, et quicquit est preteritum totum est
mortuum. Morimur ergo semper dum vivimus, et
10 tunc tantum desinimus mori cum desinimus vivere.
Melius est mori vite quam vivere morti, quia nichil
est vita mortalis nisi mors vivens. Salomon: "Lau- In Ecclesiaste

131

judged him happier in both ways that is not yet born." Life flees quickly and cannot be detained; but death attacks vehemently and is unable to be checked. The miracle is this, that life decreases by as much as it increases, because it moves near to death by as much as it moves forward.

[23] OF THE TERROR OF DREAMS

The time that has been allowed for rest is not allowed to be restful, for dreams frighten, visions perturb. And even though what dreamers dream are not actually sad or frightening or troublesome, still dreamers are actually sad, frightened, and troubled, so much so in fact that in sleeping they sometimes cry and on waking are often perturbed. But if what they dream is pleasing, they are no less sad on waking because they have lost it. Observe what Eliphaz the Themanite says about this: "In the horror of a vision by night, when deep sleep is wont to hold men, fear seized upon me and trembling, and all my bones were affrighted, and when a spirit passed in my presence, the hairs of my flesh stood up." Consider the saying of Job: "If I say my bed shall comfort me and I shall be relieved speaking with myself on my couch, he will frighten me with dreams and terrify me with visions." King Nabuchodonosor had a dream that terrified him exceedingly, and the visions of his head perturbed him. Many cares follow dreams, and where there are many dreams, there are many vanities. Dreams have caused many to go astray and have destroyed those who trust in them. For in dreams shameful images often appear, through the nocturnal deceits of which not only is the flesh contami-

MSS incl C³C¹⁰C¹⁴C¹⁸L³¹Ro. **viventem** viventes *nearly every MS incl* C³C¹⁰C¹⁴C¹⁸L³¹ Ro. 15 **potest** valet C¹⁰C¹⁸L³¹. 16 **valet** potest C¹⁰C¹⁸. 18 **plus vita** *trans* L³¹. 19 **mortem** C¹⁰; finem *most MSS incl* C³Ro.

    I.23: 3 **tristia** tristicia L³¹. 4 **sompniant** sompniantur L³¹. 6 **et** *(1st) om most MSS incl* C¹⁰C¹⁴C¹⁸L³¹V². **aliquando** *om* L³¹. **lacrimentur** lacrimantur L³¹. 7 **evigilantes** *corrected above line from* eiulantes L²⁰; vigilantes C¹⁰C¹⁴C¹⁸L³¹. **conturbentur** turbentur C³. 8 **viderint** videtur L³¹. **evigilantes** et vigilantes C¹⁰; vigilantes C¹⁴C¹⁸L³¹. 10 **horrore** honore L³¹. 12 **ossia** *ossa *nearly every MS incl* C³C¹⁰C¹⁴C¹⁸L³¹Ro. 15 **lectulus** lectus *most MSS incl* C³C¹⁰C¹⁴C¹⁸L³¹. 16 **terrebit** terrebis *most MSS incl* V². 17 **per** *om* C¹⁸; *above line* C¹⁴. **horrore** horrores C³; horror C¹⁴C¹⁸E¹L³¹. **concuciet** concuties *most MSS incl* C³Ro; concuciens C¹⁸C¹⁰, *but corrected to* concucies C¹⁴; concuciens et L³¹. 18 **rex** *om most MSS incl* C³C¹⁰C¹⁴C¹⁸L³¹Ro. **vidit sompnium** *trans most MSS incl* C³C¹⁰C¹⁴C¹⁸L³¹Ro. 19 **et** *om* C¹⁰C¹⁴C¹⁸L³¹. **conturbaverunt** turbaverunt C¹⁴C¹⁸; perturbaverunt L³¹D¹. 21 **plurime** ibi plurime C¹⁴; plures C¹⁸L³¹O¹¹Pa⁵; plura O¹⁶. **fescerunt** s *above line* L²⁰; fecerunt *nearly every MS incl* C³C¹⁰C¹⁴C¹⁸L³¹Ro. 22 **sompnia** *om* C¹⁰C¹⁸L³¹. 23 **sepe** frequenter *most MSS incl* C³C¹⁰Ro; *om* C¹⁴C¹⁸L³¹. **sompniis** sompnia *many MSS incl* C¹⁰; sompno C¹⁸. **ymagines** ymaginaciones C¹⁴. 24 **per illusiones** pollutiones C¹⁰C¹⁸L³¹; per polluciones C¹⁴. **nocturnas** nocturne ex quibus C¹⁰C¹⁸L³¹; nocturne fiunt ex quibus D¹O²³PPa⁸; perveniunt ex quibus La. **per . . . nocturnas** nocturnis pollucionibus BuGoLmPa⁹Pa¹¹. **caro** corpus C¹⁰C¹⁸L³¹. 25 **et** *om many MSS incl*

davi magis mortuum quam viventem, et utroque
feliciorem iudicavi qui necdum natus est." Vita
velociter fugit et retineri non potest; mors autem
instanter occurrit et impediri non valet. Hoc est
illud mirabile, quod quanto plus crescit tanto magis
decrescit, quia quanto plus vita procedit tanto magis
ad mortem accedit.

[23] DE TERRORE SOMPNIORUM

Tempus quod quieti concessum est non conceditur
esse quietum, / nam terrent sompnia, visiones con- f. 87v
turbant. Et licet non sint in veritate tristia vel
terribilia seu laboriosa que sompniant sompniantes,
tamen in veritate tristantur, terrentur, et fatigantur,
in tantum ut et dormientes aliquando lacrimentur et
evigilantes sepissime conturbentur. Si vero iocun-
dum quid viderint, nichilominus evigilantes tristantur tanquam illud amiserint. Adverte quid super hoc
dicat Eliphat Themanites: "In horrore visionis noc- In Iob
turne, quando solet sopor occupare homines, pavor
tenuit me et tremor, et omnia ossia mea perterrita
sunt, et cum spiritus, me presente, transiret, inhor-
ruerunt pili carnis mee." Considera Iob dicentem:
"Si dixero consolabitur me lectulus meus et releva-
bor loquens mecum in stratu meo, terrebit me per
sompnia et per visiones horrore concuciet." Nabu- In Daniele
godonosor rex vidit sompnium quod eum valde
perterruit, et visiones capitis eius conturbaverunt
eum. Multas curas sequuntur sompnia, et ubi multa In Ecclesiaste
sompnia, plurime vanitates. Multos errare fescerunt In Ecclesias-
sompnia et exciderunt sperantes in illis. Apparent tico
enim sepe in sompniis turpes ymagines, ex quibus
per illusiones nocturnas non solum caro polluitur,

133

nated but also the soul is defiled. God in Leviticus concerning this: "If there be among you," he says, "any man that is defiled in a dream by night, he shall go forth out of the camp and shall not return before he be washed with water in the evening, and after sunset he shall return into the camp."

[24] OF COMPASSION

O with how much sorrow we are troubled, with how much trembling we are disturbed, when we observe the injuries of friends, when we fear the perils of relatives! Sometimes a healthy person is more troubled by fear than a sick person by illness. The former is more distressed by the feeling of anguish of his own free will than the latter is by the result of infirmity against his will. For the poetic saying is true: "Love is a thing full of anxious fear." Whose breast is so hard, whose heart so stony that he does not emit sighs, does not shed tears, when he looks upon the sickness or death of a neighbor or friend, that he does not feel pity for the one who suffers and suffer with those who are in pain? Jesus himself, when he saw Mary and the Jews who had come with her weeping to the tomb, groaned in his spirit, troubled himself, and wept, but more for the reason that he called a dead man back to the miseries of life. But let him who laments the corporeal death of his friend and does not bewail the spiritual death of his soul understand that he is culpably stubborn and stubbornly culpable.

[25] THAT THERE ARE COUNTLESS KINDS OF SICKNESSES

Medical activity through the ages has not yet been able to investigate as many kinds of sicknesses, as many species of sufferings, as human frailty can tolerate. Should I say the tolerable intolerance of diseases, or should I say the

C^{10}C^{18}L^{31}; eciam frequenter C^{14}; et frequenter L^{22}O^{24}. **Unde** *possibly corrected from* uns L^{20}. 26 **inquit . . . vos** inter vos inquid L^{31}. 26–27 **polluitur** pollutus sit *most MSS incl* C^{10}C^{14}C^{18}L^{31}Ro. 27 **sompnio** sompno *many MSS incl* C^{10}C^{14}C^{18}L^{31}. 28 **ad vesperam** *om* C^{10}C^{14}. **et** *om* L^{31}. 29 **regrediatur** revertatur C^{14}C^{18}. **in** ad C^{3}; *om* L^{31}.

  I.24: *Title* De Sancto Passione C^{2}. 1 **quanto** *(2nd)* et C^{14}C^{18}. 2 **amicorum dampna** *trans* C^{10}C^{18}L^{31}. 5 **hic** hic operatur C^{14}C^{18}. **affectu** affectus C^{10}C^{14}; affectum C^{18}. **is** *om* C^{10}; ibi C^{14}C^{18}. 6 **effectu** affectus C^{10}C^{14}; affectum C^{18}; affectu L^{31}. **languoris** *om* L^{31} *but space left for it.* 8 **ferreum** frigidum C^{10}; secretum L^{31}. 11 **ut** et L^{31}. **pacienti** compacienti C^{10}. **dolentibus non** dolenti non *most MSS incl* C^{10}C^{14}; dolencium C^{18}; doleum L^{31}. 13 **ea** ipsa C^{14}C^{18}. **plorantes** *om* C^{10}L^{31}. 14 **seipsum** semetipsum *most MSS incl* C^{3}C^{10}L^{31} Ro. 15 **est** *om* L^{31}; est Forsitan non quia mortuus est *a few MSS.* 16 **revocabat** revocavit L^{31}. **autem** enim C^{10}C^{18}L^{31}; *om* C^{14}. **durum** et durum L^{31}.

  I.25: *Title* De Innumerabilibus Speciebus Egritudinis C^{3}C^{14}; De Innumere Sunt Egritudines C^{18}. 1 **Nondum** Nondum enim C^{10}L^{31}; Nondum autem C^{14}. **seculis** senibus L^{31}. 2 **potuit industria** *trans most MSS incl* C^{3}Ro; industria poterit C^{10}L^{31}; industria poterat C^{14}C^{18}. 3 **tolerare** sustinere C^{10}C^{14}C^{18}L^{31}. 4 **dixerim** dixerunt E^{1}. **morborum intoleranciam** *trans most MSS incl* C^{10}C^{14}C^{18}L^{31}V^{2}. 5 **dixerim** *om* C^{14}C^{18}; dixerunt E^{1}.

25 set et anima maculatur. Unde Dominus in Levitico:
"Si sit," inquit, "inter vos homo qui nocturno polluitur sompnio, egrediatur extra castra et non revertatur priusquam ad vesperam lavetur aqua, et post
solis occasum regrediatur in castra."

[24] DE COMPASSIONE

O quanto dolore turbamur, quanto tremore concuti-
mur, cum amicorum dampna sentimus, cum parentum pericula formidamus! Plus interdum sanus for-
midine quam infirmus egritudine perturbatur. Plus
5 hic voluntarius affectu doloris / quam is invitus   f. 88
effectu languoris affligitur. Verum est enim illud
poeticum: "Res est solliciti plena timoris amor."
Cuius pectus tam ferreum, cuius cor tam lapideum
ut gemitus non exprimat, lacrimas non effundat,
10 cum proximi vel amici morbum vel interitum intu-
etur, ut pacienti non compaciatur et dolentibus non
condoleat? Ipse Iesus, cum vidisset Mariam et Iudeos   In Iohanne
qui cum ea venerant ad monumentum plorantes,
infremuit spiritu, turbavit seipsum, et lacrimatus
15 est, set eo pocius quod mortuum ad vite miserias
revocabat. Sciat autem se culpabiliter durum et dure
culpabilem, qui corporalem amici sui mortem de-
plorat et spiritualem anime sue mortem non deflet.

[25] QUOD INNUMERE SUNT SPECIES EGRITUDINUM

Nondum a seculis tot egritudinum genera, tot species passionum phisicalis potuit industria indagare
quot humana fragilitas potuit tolerare. Tolerabilem
dixerim morborum intoleranciam, aut intolerabilem

intolerable tolerance? I should better join both together, for it is intolerable because of the severity of the suffering and tolerable because of the necessity of suffering. From day to day human nature is corrupted more and more, so much so that many things were formerly healthy experiences that are today deadly things because of the failing of human nature itself. Each world has already grown old, the màcrocosm and the microcosm, and the longer the old age of each is extended, the more severely the nature of each is disturbed.

[26] OF SUDDEN MISFORTUNES

Suddenly, when it is not suspected, misfortune strikes, calamity rushes in, disease invades, death, which no one escapes, snatches away. Therefore "boast not for tomorrow; for thou knowest not what the day to come may bring forth." "Man knoweth not his own end, but as fishes are taken with the hook, and as birds are caught with the snare, so men are taken in the evil time when it shall suddenly come upon them."

[27] OF VARIOUS KINDS OF TORMENTS

What may I say about the miserable people who are destroyed by countless kinds of torments? They are beaten with clubs and slain with swords, burned with flames and overwhelmed with stones, torn to pieces with claws and suspended with yokes, tortured with nails and whipped with scorpions, restrained with chains and bruised by fetters, subdued by prisons and made thin by fastings, thrown down and submerged, flayed and torn apart, cut up and pierced through. "Such as are for death, to death; and such as are for the

---

toleranciam toleranciam et intollerabilis est propter *but expunged* L31. 5–6 **coniunx-erim** dixerim C14. 6 **nam** *om* C10C18. 6–7 **intolerabilis . . . acerbitatem** *om* C10C14C18L31; intolerabile . . . acerbitatem V2. 7 **et** *om* C14L31; quia C18. **tolerabilis** tolerabilis est C10C14L31; tolerabile V2. **necessitatem** necessitatem et intollerabilis propter passionis acerbitatem C10C14C18, *with* est *before* propter L31. 9 **quod** quodque L31. 9–10 **experimenta** meditamenta et experimenta C14. 10 **que** *om* L31. **ipsius** ipsius nature C14U4. 11 **mortifera** instrumenta mortifera AuBuGoILmMu5Pa9Pa11; mortifera secundum instrumenta Pa5. **iam** autem C14; enim iam L31. 11–12 **megacosmus . . . microcosmus** microcosmus C18; *trans* L31; id est maior et minor mundus megacosmus et microcosmus Pa10L35; id est maior mundus et minor *after* microcosmus Au. 13 **deterius utriusque** *trans* L31. 14 **natura** natura vel corpore *in margin* C14.

I.26: 1 **suspicatur** speratur C3. 4 **ignoras** ignorans C18. **enim** *om* C18L31. **super-ventura . . . dies** pariat superventura dies C10; superventura dies pariat tibi C18; parit superventura dios L31. 5 **homo** *om* L31. **sic** ita C10C14C18L31. 7 **extemplo** extermina-tio C3, *in margin* C14; exemplo C9L40.

I.27: 1 **miseris** miseriis C3; miseriis eorum L31. **innumera** innumera vel inmania *above line* C14; immani L10; diversa et innumera O23O33; multa innumera T2; diversa Le. 2 **perimuntur** puniuntur *many MSS.* 3 **flammis** *om* C14C18. 4 **discerpuntur** discrepuntur C18; discerpunt L31. 5 **unguibus** unguibus vel iurgis *above line* C14; tigribus V2; iurgis Mo. 6 **detrunduntur** detentuntur *many MSS.* **et ieiuniis** ieiunii C18. **macerantur** flagellantur L31. 7–8 **precipitantur et** distrahuntur et precipitantur C10C18L31. 8–9 **excoriantur . . . secantur** excecantur et secantur C10; excecantur secantur C18; et excoriantur excetantur secantur L31; exortantur secantur L40; execran-tur et distrahuntur sectantur BuGoIPa9Pa11. 9 **suffodiuntur** suffocantur EvRu2; effodiuntur suffodiuntur D1O23. **Qui** Repetatur qui L31. 10 **ad mortem** *om* L31. **et *(1st)***

136

5 dixerim toleranciam? Melius utrumque coniunx-
erim, nam intolerabilis est propter passionis acerbitatem et tolerabilis propter paciendi necessitatem.
De die in diem magis ac magis humana natura
corrumpitur, ita quod multa fuerunt olim experi-
10 menta salubria que propter defectum ipsius hodie
sunt mortifera. Senuit iam mundus uterque, megacosmus et microcosmus, et quanto prolixius utriusque senectus producitur, tanto deterius utriusque
natura turbatur.

[26] DE SUBITIS INFORTUNIIS

Subito, cum non suspicatur, infortunium accidit,
calamitas irruit, morbus invadit, mors intercipit,
quam nullus evadit. Ergo "ne glorieris / in cras-   f. 88v
tinum; ignoras enim quid superventura pariat dies."
5 "Nescit homo finem suum, set sicut pisces capiuntur
hamo, et sicut aves comprehenduntur laqueo, sic
capiuntur homines tempore malo cum eis extemplo
supervenerit."

[27] DE DIVERSIS GENERIBUS TORMENTORUM

Quid dicam de miseris qui per innumera tormentorum genera perimuntur? Ceduntur fustibus et
gladiis iugulantur, cremantur flammis et lapidibus
obruuntur, discerpuntur ungulis et patibulis suspen-
5 duntur, torquentur unguibus et scorpionibus flagellantur, artantur vinculis et laqueis sugillantur,
detruduntur carceribus et ieiuniis macerantur, precipitantur et submerguntur, excoriantur et distrahuntur, secantur et suffodiuntur. "Qui ad mortem,   Ieremias

sword, to the sword; and such as are for famine, to famine; and such as are for captivity, to captivity." Cruel judgment, monstrous punishment, sad spectacle! They are given as food to the birds of the sky, the beasts of the earth, the fish of the sea. Alas, alas, alas, miserable mothers, who have borne such unhappy children!

[28] OF A CERTAIN DREADFUL CRIME

Let me insert here that horrible crime that Josephus describes from the Jewish siege. A certain woman, noble in riches and in birth, suffered the misfortune of the siege common to all along with the rest of the multitude that had crowded Jerusalem. The tyrants took complete possession of her remaining riches that she had brought from home into the city. If there was anything left of the great riches with which she provided for her meager daily sustenance, the followers of the robbers, rushing in for brief periods of time, carried it off. On account of these things a certain extraordinary insanity as it were, from indignation, kept tormenting the woman, so that she sometimes urged the robbers with curses and insults to kill her. But, when either out of irritation or out of pity no one would kill her, and if by chance anything to eat was obtained by her, it was demanded by others, nor was there at the time an opportunity of searching anywhere. Moreover a terrible hunger pressed upon her bowels and innermost parts, and starvation now goaded her to fury; having adopted the worst counsel, she herself was now armed against the laws of nature. For there was at her breasts a baby boy, holding whom before her eyes she said, "O more unhappy son of an unhappy mother, in war, and famine, and the plundering of robbers, for whom shall I save you? For though

om many MSS incl C³C¹⁴C¹⁸L³¹Ro. **et** *(2nd) om* many MSS incl C¹⁰C¹⁴L³¹Ro. 11 **ad famem** *(2nd) om* L³¹. **et** *om* many MSS incl C¹⁴L³¹Ro. 11-12 **ad captivitatem** *om* L³¹. 12 **immane** terribile C¹⁸L³¹, *with* vel inmane *above line* C¹⁴. 14 **heu** *(3rd) om* most MSS incl C³C¹⁰C¹⁴C¹⁸L³¹. 15 **infelices** infideles L³¹.

I.28: *Title* De Quodam Horribili Facinore de Quadam Muliere Que Comedit Infantem Suum Ro. 1 **inserere** inferre L³¹. 4 **confluxerat** confluebat C¹⁴; fluxerat C¹⁸. **Ierusalem** Ierosolimis *most MSS incl* C³C¹⁰C¹⁴Ro; Ierosolimam C¹⁸L³¹. 4-5 **communem cum omnibus** communem omnibus C³; communem cum omnibus vel cum ceteris C¹⁴, *with* cum *marked for expunction and last three words in margin;* convencionibus C¹⁸. 5 **obsidionis** obsidionem L³¹. **casum ferebat** *trans* C¹⁰C¹⁸L³¹. **Huius** *om* C¹⁰C¹⁸L³¹. **reliquas** reliquas vero C¹⁰C¹⁸L³¹; vero reliquas C¹⁴. 7 **invaserunt** invaserant C¹⁸. **relictum** reliquiarum *most MSS incl* C³C¹⁰L³¹Ro, *with* vel relictum *in margin* C¹⁴; *om here but added after* opibus C¹⁸. 8-9 **victum . . . pertenuem** cotidianum per tenue victum L³¹. 10 **rapiebant** capiebant C¹⁸. 11 **ex . . . quedam** velud ex indignacione quadam C³; indignatio quasi quedam C¹⁰C¹⁴C¹⁸L³¹. 12 **fatigabat** vexabat C¹⁴C¹⁸, *with* vel fatigabat *above line* C¹⁴. **predones** precones L³¹L²⁵. **necem** necesse L³¹. 13 **et** *om* L³¹. 14 **miseratus** insensatus *(in margin)* miseratus C¹⁴. **perimeret** pertineret C¹⁸. 15 **cibi** tibi C¹⁸L³¹. **quesitum** quesitum et C¹⁴C¹⁸. **aliis** ab aliis *many MSS incl* C¹⁴C¹⁸V². 16-17 **perquirendi** requirendi *most MSS incl* C³C¹⁰C¹⁴C¹⁸L³¹Ro. 17 **instaret** insisteret *nearly every MS incl* C³C¹⁰C¹⁴C¹⁸L³¹Ro. 18 **furorem . . . inedia** famem iam fames instans C¹⁸. **perurgeret** perurgeret eam C¹⁸; eam perurgeret *with* eam *above line* C¹⁴. 19 **ipsa iam** iam ipsam C¹⁰; ipsa C¹⁴C¹⁸; *trans* L³¹. 19-20 **armatur iura nature** iura nature armatur C¹⁴C¹⁸. 20 **ei** *om many MSS incl* C³C¹⁰. **filius** *om* C¹⁰L³¹. 21 **Infelicis inquit** Inquit O infelicis C¹⁰C¹⁸; *trans* C¹⁴; Inquid O infelices L³¹. **matris** *corrected from* matres L³¹. 22 **o** *om* C¹⁰C¹⁸L³¹. **et** *om most MSS incl* C³C¹⁰C¹⁴C¹⁸L³¹Ro. **direpcione** discerptione *many MSS incl* C¹⁰; in direp-

10 ad mortem; et qui ad gladium, ad gladium; et qui
ad famem, ad famem; et qui ad captivitatem, ad
captivitatem." Crudele iudicium, immane supplicium, triste spectaculum! Dantur in escam volatilibus celi, bestiis terre, piscibus maris. Heu, heu, heu,
15 misere matres, que tam infelices filios genuistis!

[28] DE QUODAM HORRENDO FACINORE

Illud hic horribile facinus libet inserere quod Iosephus de Iudaica obsidione describit. Mulier quedam,
facultatibus et genere nobilis, cum cetera multitu-
dine que confluxerat Ierusalem communem cum
5 omnibus obsidionis casum ferebat. Huius reliquas
facultates quas de domo in urbem convexerat tyranni penitus invaserunt. Si quid vero relictum ex
magnis opibus fuerat quibus victum cotidianum
pertenuem duceret, irruentes per momenta, pre-
10 donum satellites rapiebant. Pro quibus ingens mulierem, ex indignacione, / velud quedam insania   f. 89
fatigabat, ita ut interdum predones in necem sui
maledictis et conviciis instigaret. Verum, cum nec
irritatus quisquam nec miseratus illam perimeret, et
15 si quid forte cibi fuisset ab illa quesitum, id aliis
quereretur, nec iam usquam fieret copia perquirendi. Fames autem dira visceribus instaret ac medul-
lis, et ad furorem iam famis inedia perurgeret;
pessimis usa consiliis, contra ipsa iam armatur iura
20 nature. Erat enim ei sub uberibus parvulus filius,
quem ante oculos ferens, "Infelicis," inquit, "matris
o infelicior fili, in bello, et fame, ac direpcione
predonum, cui te reservabo? Nam etsi possit vita

139

your life could be hoped for, we would be oppressed by the yoke of Roman slavery. Come now therefore, o my son, be food for your mother, madness for the robbers, a tale for the ages of what alone was lacking in the defeats of the Jews." And when she had said this, she immediately killed her son. Thereupon she roasted him superposed over the fire, and she ate half, kept half concealed. And behold, the robbers immediately rushed in, having recognized the aroma of burned flesh; they threatened death unless she would without delay produce the food that they assumed to have been prepared. Then she: "I have saved the best part for you," and she immediately revealed the members that remained of the child. But suddenly a great horror seized them, and, frozen though their monstrous souls were, their voice was cut off in their throats. But she with a fierce look and more savage now than the robbers themselves: "My son," she said, "he is my offspring, and it is my crime. Eat what I brought forth, for I ate first; do not be shown either more scrupulous than a mother or softer than a woman. But if scrupulousness does overcome you and you denounce my means of nourishment, I, who have already fed on such, I will feed on it again." After this these terrified and trembling men ran off, and of all her riches they left behind only this food for the miserable mother.

[29] OF THE PUNISHMENT OF THE INNOCENT

Let no one believe that he is free from punishment because he knows that he is exempt from guilt. Let him who stands "take heed lest he fall." For often the

cione L^{31}; diceptacione I; redemptione Au. 23 **cui** om C^{10}L^{31}. 23–24 **possit . . . sperari** vita possit sperari C^{10}C^{3}C^{14}C^{18}; vita possit seperari L^{31}. 24 **urgebimur** urgemur *nearly every MS incl* C^{3}C^{10}L^{31}Ro; perurgemur C^{14}C^{18}. 25 **nunc** om *many MSS incl* C^{3}C^{10}C^{18}L^{31}. **o** om C^{10}C^{18}L^{31}. 26 **cladibus** claudibus L^{31}; gladibus C^9. 27 **Et** om C^{14}C^{18}. **cum hec** *trans* C^{10}C^{14}; hoc cum C^{18}. **protinus** proximus C^{18}. **filium** filium suum C^{10}C^{18}L^{31}. 28 **iugulavit** vigilavit C^{18}. **Tum** om C^3; Cum C^{14}C^{18}; Tunc L^{31}. **deinde** demum C^{3}C^{14}C^{18}L^{31}; denique *many MSS incl* V^2. **superpositum** suppositum *many MSS incl* C^{3}C^{10}C^{14}L^{31}. **torret** torreret C^{14}C^{18}. **et** om *many MSS incl* C^{14}C^{18}V^2. 29 **consumit** consumit et C^{10}C^{14}C^{18}L^{31}. **servat** conservat C^{14}C^{18}; observavit L^{13} Mu^6. 29–30 **obtectum** obesum C^{14}C^{18}; obiectum *some MSS.* 30 **predones confestim** *trans most MSS incl* C^{3}C^{10}C^{14}C^{18}L^{31}Ro. **irruunt** irruerunt C^{10}C^{14}C^{18}L^{31}. **combuste** aduste V^2; obuste *some MSS.* 31 **nidore** odore *most MSS incl* C^{3}V^2; nidore *corrected to* odore C^{14}. **concepto** precepto C^{14}C^{18}. **minantur** minaverit C^{18}. 33 **optimam** om C^{10}L^{31}. 34 **superfuerant** superaverant L^{31}Sa; supererant L^{40}. **retexit** detexit *many MSS incl* C^{10}C^{14}C^{18}L^{31}. 35 **horror ingens** *trans nearly every MS incl* C^{3}C^{10}C^{14}C^{18}L^{31}Ro. 36 **quamvis animi** et quamvis animi C^{10}L^{31}; et interim ora eorum C^{14}C^{18}. **diriguere** irriguere C^3; dirriguerunt C^{10}L^{31}; dirriguerunt quod C^{14}C^{18}. **est faucibus** *trans* C^{14}C^{18}. 37–38 **predonibus truculencior** *trans* C^{10}C^{14}C^{18}L^{31}. 38 **inquit** inquit est *most MSS incl* C^{3}C^{10}L^{31}Ro; est inquit C^{14}C^{18}. **filius** hic filius C^3; filius et C^{10}C^{18}L^{31}; hic filius et C^{14}; partus *many MSS incl* V^2. **est** om L^{31}. 38–39 **partus** hic partus C^{3}C^{14}; filius *many MSS incl* V^2. 39 **est** om *many MSS incl* C^{10}C^{14}C^{18}L^{31}. **Edite** Edite vel commedite *above line* C^{14}; Commedite L^{31}; Edite et commedite H^1; Edicite et edite O^{22}. **prior** primo L^{31}C^{9}L^{17}Mu^6 O^{10}O^{31}T^2. 40 **que** quem *many MSS incl* C^{10}C^{14}C^{18}L^{31}. **matre** mirum L^{31}. 41 **molliores** meliores L^{31}O^{13}. 42 **vincit** vivere C^{18}; inficit L^{31}. **execramini** execrarium L^{31}. **ego** om *many MSS incl* C^{14}C^{18}L^{31}. 43 **his iterum** *trans* C^{3}C^{10}C^{14}C^{18}L^{31}. 44 **trementesque discedunt** trementes recedunt L^{31}. **et** C^{10}; qui *most MSS incl* Ro. **solum** solum matri misere C^{14}C^{18}L^{31}. 45 **misere . . . cibum** om C^{14}C^{18}, *though* cibum *added above line* C^{14}; cibum L^{31}; cibum misere matri *many MSS incl* V^2. 45–46 **relinquntit** *corrected probably*

sperari, iugo tamen Romane servitutis urgebimur.
25 Veni ergo nunc, o mi nate, esto matri cibus, predonibus furor, seculis fabula que sola deerat cladibus
Iudeorum." Et cum hec dixisset, protinus filium
iugulavit. Tum deinde igni superpositum torret, et
medium quidem consumit, medium servat obtec-
30 tum. Et ecce, predones confestim irruunt, combuste
carnis nidore concepto; mortem minantur nisi sine
mora cibos quos paratos senserant demonstraret.
Tunc illa: "Partem vobis optimam reservavi," et
continuo que superfuerant menbra retexit infantis.
35 At illos repente horror ingens invasit, et, immanis
quamvis animi diriguere, vox est faucibus inter-
clusa. Illa vero truci vultu et ipsis iam predonibus
truculencior: "Meus," inquit, "filius, meus est partus, et meum est facinus. Edite, nam ego prior
40 comedi, que genui; nolite vos effici aut matre reli-
giosiores aut femina molliores. Quod si vos pietas
vincit et meos execramini cibos, / ego, que iam f. 89v
talibus pasta sum, ego his iterum pascar." Post hec
illi territi trementesque discedunt, et hunc solum ex
45 omnibus facultatibus misere matri cibum relinquntit.

[29] DE PENA INNOCENTIS

Nemo se confidat expertem a pena quia se novit
immunem a culpa. Qui stat "videat ne cadat." Nam
sepe dampnatur innocens et nocens absolvitur, puni-

from *relinquunt L20; reliquerunt *many MSS incl* C3L31; reliquerant *most MSS incl* C10Ro;
relinqunt C14; reliqunt C18.
  I.29: *Title* Quod Quandoque Punitur Innocens et Nocens Absolvitur Ro. 1 **se
confidat** *trans* C14C18L31. **expertem** expertem esse L31. **quia** qui *most MSS incl* C3C18Ro;
quia nemo C10L31, *above line* C14. **se novit** si non novit C18; *trans* L31. 2 **immunem**
inimicum C18. 3 **dampnatur innocens** dampnantur innocentes C10L31. **absolvitur**

innocent is condemned and the guilty set free, the pious punished and the impious honored, Jesus crucified and Barabbas freed. Today a quiet man is considered useless, a religious man considered a hypocrite, a simple man considered foolish. "For the simplicity of the just man is laughed to scorn, the lamp despised in the thoughts of the rich."

absolvetur C³. **3-4 punitur pius** *trans most MSS incl* C³C¹⁰C¹⁴C¹⁸L³¹Ro. **5 vir *(2nd)*** *om* C¹⁴C¹⁸. **7 simplicitas** simplicitas et C¹⁴C¹⁸; simplicitas quare L³¹L¹⁵; simplicitas scilicet D¹O²³. **contentpta** *contempta most MSS incl* C³C¹⁰C¹⁴C¹⁸L³¹Ro; contenta *some MSS*. **8 divitum** *followed by table of contents to Book II in* L²⁰ *(on ff. 89v-90), entitled* Incipiunt

tur pius et impius honoratur, Iesus crucifigitur et
5 Barrabas liberatur. Hodie vir quietus inutilis, vir
religiosus ypocrita, vir simplex fatuus reputatur.
"Deridetur enim iusti simplicitas, lampas contentpta
apud cogitaciones divitum."

Capitula Secunde Partis; divitum Explicit Primus Liber Ro, *followed by table of contents to*
Book II entitled Incipiunt Capitula Secundi Libri; hominum Au.

HERE BEGINS THE SECOND PART

[1]

Men are accustomed to strive for three things in particular: riches, pleasures, and honors. From riches come perverse things, from pleasures shameful things, from honors vain things. Hence John the apostle says: "Love not the world, nor the things which are in the world, for whatever is in the world is the concupiscence of the flesh and the concupiscence of the eyes and the pride of life." The concupiscence of the flesh pertains to pleasure, the concupiscence of the eyes to riches, the pride of life to honors. Riches engender covetousness and avarice, pleasures bring forth gluttony and lechery, honors nourish pride and boasting.

[2] OF COVETOUSNESS

"Nothing is more wicked than the covetous man and nothing more wicked than to love money." That is the word of the wise man, which the Apostle confirms, saying: "They that will become rich fall into temptation and the snare of the devil and many unprofitable and hurtful desires, which drown men into destruction and perdition. For the desire of money is the root of all evils." It brings sacrileges and thefts, works robberies and plunderings, brings forth wars and homicides, sells and buys simoniacally, seeks and takes back unfairly, trades and lends unjustly, menaces with deceits and threatens with frauds, dissolves an agreement and violates an oath, corrupts testimony and subverts judgment.

II: *Title* Incipit Secundus Liber de Cupiditate C^3; Secunda Pars C^{10}C^{14}; *om* C^{18}; Liber Secundus de Culpabili Humane Conversationis Progressu Ro.

II.1: *Title no separate title to II.1 in* L^{20}C^{3}C^{10}C^{14}Ro; Prologus Secundi Libri C^{18}. 1 **solent homines** *trans* C^{10}. 3 **turpia** concupiscencia AuBuGoILmMu^{5}Pa^{5}Pa^{9}Pa^{11}. **vana** vana gloria Au. **enim** *om* C^{14}C^{18}. 4 **Iohannes . . . ait** ait apostolus C^{18}; ait Iohannes apostolus L^{31}. 5 **in . . . sunt** sunt in mundo C^{10}. **quia** *om* C^{3}L^{31}. 7 **oculorum** oculorum est C^{18}. **carnis** carnis est E^1. 8 **voluptatem** voluptates *nearly every MS incl* C^{3}C^{10} C^{14}C^{18}L^{31}Ro; voluntates Au. 10–11 **pariunt . . . honores** *om* E^1. 11–12 **iactanciam** vanam gloriam C^{14}C^{18}.

II.2: *Title* De Iniquis Muneribus C^3. 1 **nichil** nichil est L^{31}. 2 **est** *om* L^{31}. 3 **fieri** fieri in hoc seculo C^{14}C^{18}. 4 **temptacionem** temptationes C^{3}C^{14}C^{18}. **laqueum** lacum *many group MSS*; lacum *corrected to* laqueum C^{18}. 5 **et nociva** *om* C^{10}L^{31}. 6 **homines** *om* C^{10}; hominem C^{14}C^{18}Ro. **in** in infernum vel in C^3; ad C^{14}C^{18}L^{31}. 7 **malorum** viciorum C^{10}C^{14}C^{18}L^{31}. 8 **furta** furta et C^{10}C^{18}L^{31}. **predas** predas et C^{10}C^{14}C^{18}L^{31}. 9 **symoniace** simoniaco L^{31}. 10 **iniuste** iuste C^3; et iuste C^{18}. 11 **et (*1st*)** *om* C^{18}L^{31}. **imminet** immanet *many group MSS*; inmat L^{31}; remanet in Mu^5.

[1]

Tria maxime solent homines affectare: opes, voluptates, honores. De opibus prava, de voluptatibus
turpia, de honoribus vana procedunt. Hinc enim
Iohannes apostolus ait: "Nolite diligere mundum, In Epistola
5 neque ea que in mundo sunt, quia quicquid est in Canonica
mundo concupiscencia carnis est et concupiscencia
oculorum et superbia vite." Concupiscencia carnis
ad voluptatem, concupiscencia oculorum ad opes,
superbia vite pertinet ad honores. Opes generant
10 cupiditatem et avariciam, voluptates pariunt gulam
et luxuriam, honores nutriunt superbiam et iactanciam.

[2] DE CUPIDITATE

"Nichil est avaro scelestius et nichil iniquius quam In Ecclesias-
amare pecuniam." Verbum est sapientis, quod con- tico
firmat Apostolus, dicens: "Qui volunt divites fieri
incidunt in temptacionem et laqueum diaboli et
5 desideria multa et inutilia et nociva, que mergunt
homines in interitum et perdicionem. Radix enim
omnium malorum est cupiditas." Hec sacrilegia
committit et furta, rapinas exercet et predas, bella
gerit / et homicidia, symoniace vendit et emit, ini- f. 90v
10 que petit et recipit, iniuste negociatur et feneratur,
instat dolis et imminet fraudibus, dissolvit pactum et
violat iuramentum, corrumpit testimonium et pervertit iudicium.

Consult the evangelical prophet Isaias: "They all," he says, "love bribes, they run after rewards, they judge not for the fatherless; the widow's cause cometh not in to them." They themselves are not above rewards, because they judge with the love of money. For they always run after a gift or a promise or a hope, and therefore do not judge for the fatherless, from whom nothing is given or promised or hoped for. O faithless princes, you companions of thieves who love bribes, run after rewards! You will never force your hand away from a bribe unless you eliminate covetousness from your heart. The prophet speaks about you: "Her princes are like wolves ravening the prey, and more greedily running after gains." "Her princes have judged for bribes, and her priests have taught for hire, and her prophets have divined for money." On the other hand, the Lord commanded through Moses in the law: "Thou shalt appoint judges and magistrates in all thy gates, that they may judge the people with just judgment, and not go aside to either part. They shall accept neither person nor gifts, for gifts blind the eyes of the wise and change the words of the just. But let them follow justly after that which is just that they may live." He says two things—"just" and "justly": for some justly follow after what is just, others unjustly what is unjust; on the other hand some unjustly follow after what is just, others justly after what is unjust.

II.3: *Title* De Acceptione Personarum C³; De Iniquis Muneribus vel Donis C¹⁸. 1 **evangelicum** *om* L³¹. 3-4 **pupillo . . . retribuciones** *om* C¹⁴C¹⁸. 3 **causa** et causa L³¹. 4 **Non ipsi** *trans* C¹⁰L³¹. 5 **quia** *a following* non *expunged* L²⁰; quia non iudicant amore institie sed retributiones precedunt ipsos quia *most MSS incl* C³C¹⁰L³¹Ro; quia non iudicant amore iusticie unde ipsi non precedunt retribuciones set retribuciones precedunt eos quia C¹⁴, *second* precedunt *om* C¹⁸. 5-6 **sequuntur** sequntur retribucionis L³¹BoBsBt²Bz²C⁴C⁵Er²L²³L⁴¹O¹²O¹⁶Ph¹. 6 **ideo** ideo causa vidue non ingreditur ad eos C¹⁴, *three words later in* Re³T² *but without* non *and with* ipsos *for* eos. 7 **aut** vel C¹⁴C¹⁸; nichil *a few MSS.* 8 **speratur** pervertitur L³¹. **infideles** infelices *a few MSS.* **socii** sociique C¹⁰C¹⁸L³¹. 9 **qui** quicumque *most MSS incl* C³C¹⁰C¹⁴C¹⁸L³¹Ro; quia omnes O²⁵Re³T¹ T². 11 **excludatis** excluditis C¹⁸. **pectore** *probably corrected from* peccator L²⁰. **De** Ve C¹⁰C¹⁸L³¹. 12 **eius** vestri C¹⁰C¹⁴C¹⁸L³¹. **quasi** *om* C¹⁰C¹⁸L³¹; *above line* C¹⁴. **rapientes** rapaces C¹⁰C¹⁸L³¹, *corrected to* rapientes *above line* C¹⁴. **predam** *om* C¹⁰C¹⁸L³¹; *above line* C¹⁴. 13 **et** *om* C¹⁰C¹⁴C¹⁸L³¹. **sectantes** sectando C³. **eius** vestri C¹⁴C¹⁸L³¹. 14 **iudicabant** iudicant C¹⁴C¹⁸. **et** *om* C¹⁰C¹⁴C¹⁸. **eius** *om* C¹⁰C¹⁴C¹⁸. 15 **eius** vestri C¹⁴; *om* C¹⁸L³¹. 15-16 **E contra** Ecce C³. 16 **per . . . lege** Dominus precepit in lege per Moysen C³; Dominus per Moysen precepit in lege *most MSS incl* C¹⁰C¹⁴C¹⁸; precepit Deus per Moysen in lege L³¹. 18 **iudicent** iudicunt C¹⁸. 19 **Nec** Non *most MSS incl* C³C¹⁴Ro. **accipiant** accipies *most MSS incl* C³C¹⁰L³¹Ro; accipias C¹⁴C¹⁸. 20 **excecant** obcecant C¹⁴. **oculos sapientum** sapientes C¹⁸. 20-21 **et mutant** commutant L³¹C¹²Du⁴L¹²MoPh¹T¹; et mutant vel vincant L⁴⁰. 21 **iuste** inde L³¹. 22 **persequantur** persequeris *most MSS incl* C³Ro; prosequaris C¹⁰C¹⁴; persequaris C¹⁸L³¹. **ut vivant** et vives C³; ut vivas *most MSS incl* C¹⁰C¹⁴C¹⁸L³¹Ro. **Duo** Ideo *many MSS incl* Ro. **dicit** dicit et C¹⁸L³¹. 22-23 **iustum et iuste** iuste quod iustum est *many MSS incl* Ro; iustum et iuste quod iustum est, *with last three words marked for expunction* L³¹. 23 **quidam . . . iuste** *om* C¹⁸. **enim** *om* L³¹. 24 **iniuste . . . est** quod est iniustum iuste C³; quod est iniustum iniuste *most MSS incl* C¹⁰C¹⁴; quod iustum est iniuste C¹⁸L³¹; quod iniustum est iniuste *many MSS incl* Ro. **iniuste** *(2nd)* iuste L³¹.

[3] DE INIQUIS MUNERIBUS

Consule prophetam evangelicum Ysaiam: "Omnes," inquit, "diligunt munera, sequuntur retribuciones, pupillo non iudicant; causa vidue non ingreditur ad eos." Non ipsi precedunt retribuciones,
5 quia iudicant amore pecunie. Semper enim sequuntur largicionem vel promissionem vel spem, et ideo pupillo non iudicant, a quo nichil largitur aut promittitur aut speratur. O principes infideles, socii furum qui diligitis munera, sequimini retribuciones!
10 Nunquam excucietis manum a munere nisi prius excludatis cupiditatem a pectore. De vobis inquit propheta: "Principes eius quasi lupi rapientes predam, et avare sectantes lucra." "Principes eius in muneribus iudicabant, et sacerdotes eius in mercede
15 docebant, et prophete eius in pecunia divinabant." E contra per Moysen precepit Dominus in lege: "Iudices et magistros constitues in omnibus portis tuis, ut iudicent populum iusto iudicio, nec in alteram partem declinent. Nec accipiant personam nec mu-
20 nera, quia munera excecant oculos sapientum et mutant verba iustorum. Set iuste quod iustum est persequantur ut vivant." Duo dicit—"iustum" et "iuste": quidam enim iuste quod iustum est, alii iniuste quod iniustum est; rursus quidam iniuste
25 quod iustum est, alii iuste quod iniustum est persequuntur.

Ysaias

Ezechiel

In Deuteronomio

147

Woe to you who, corrupted by entreaty or reward, who, led by love or hatred, "call good evil or evil good, putting darkness for light and light for darkness," "killing souls that do not die and saving souls alive that do not live." Moreover you do not heed the merits of cases, but of persons; not laws, but bribes; not justice, but money; not what reason dictates, but what the will desires; not what the law desires, but what the mind longs for. You do not incline your intellect to justice, but incline justice to your intellect, not that what is lawful may be pleasing but that what is pleasing be lawful. The eye in you is never so clear that the whole body is full of light, but you always mix some yeast with which you corrupt all the dough. You neglect the case of the poor with delay, you promote the case of the rich with urgency; with the former you show harshness, with the latter you dispense out of mildness; you respect the former with difficulty, you treat the latter with favor; you listen to the former inattentively, you heed the latter minutely. The poor man calls and no one hears; the rich man speaks and everyone applauds. "The rich man spoke, and all held their peace, and what he said is extolled even to the clouds; the poor man spoke, and they say: 'Who is this?', and if he stumble, they will overthrow him." "The person suffering violence calleth and there is none that heareth; he crieth aloud and there is none that judgeth." If by chance you take on the case of the poor, you assist them negligently; but when you take up the case of the rich, you help them perseveringly. You despise the poor, you honor the rich; you stand up respectfully for the latter, you trample the former disdainfully. "If there shall come into your assembly a man having a

II.4: *Title om* C³ *because this chapter is included in the preceding one.* 1 **corrupti** corrupti estis *many MSS incl* C¹⁴C¹⁸L³¹Ro. 2 **amore** amore dolore C³, *in margin* C¹⁴. **dicitis** dictus C³. **bonum malum** *trans* C¹⁰C¹⁴C¹⁸L³¹. **vel** et *most MSS incl* C³C¹⁰C¹⁴C¹⁸L³¹Ro. 2–3 **malum bonum** *trans* C¹⁰C¹⁴C¹⁸L³¹. 3–4 **tenebras lucem . . . lucem tenebras** *trans* C¹⁴C¹⁸L³¹. 4 **mortificantes animas** vivificantes vitas C¹⁰C¹⁸L³¹. **moriuntur** vivunt C¹⁰C¹⁸L³¹. 5 **vivificantes** mortificantes C¹⁰C¹⁸L³¹. **vivunt** moriuntur C¹⁰C¹⁸L³¹. 6 **personarum** merita personarum *most MSS incl* C³C¹⁰C¹⁴C¹⁸L³¹Ro. 7–8 **non quod** *trans* L³¹. 8 **dictet** dictat C¹⁰C¹⁴C¹⁸; dicat L³¹. **voluntas** voluptas L³¹Lm. **affectet** affectat *many MSS incl* C¹⁰C¹⁴C¹⁸L³¹. 9 **sanctiat** sanciat *many MSS incl* C¹⁴; senciat *many MSS incl* L³¹. 9–11 **inclinatis . . . animum** *2nd* inclinatis *om many MSS incl* C¹⁰C¹⁴L³¹; *2nd* inclinatis *om and* dominum *for second* animum C¹⁸; iusticiam inclinatis ad animum sed animum ad iusticiam V². 11 **non ut** *trans* C¹⁴C¹⁸; nonne L³¹. **quod . . . hoc** licet hoc quod L³¹. 12 **hoc** *om* C³L³¹. 12–13 **est oculus** *trans* L³¹. 13 **semper** semper sit *many MSS, with* sit *marked for expunction* L³¹. 16 **instancia** magna instancia *most MSS incl* V², *above line* C¹⁴. 18 **difficultate** difficilitate L³¹. 20 **nullus** nemo C¹⁰C¹⁴C¹⁸L³¹. 23 **producitur** perducent *most MSS incl* C³Ro; producent C¹⁰; producunt C¹⁴C¹⁸; perducunt L³¹. **est** *om* L³¹. **dicunt** dicunt omnes C¹⁰C¹⁴C¹⁸L³¹. 24 **subvertent illum** subvertent eum C¹⁴; subvertet illum C¹⁸. 25 **Clamat** Clamat pauper L³¹. **paciens** patieris L³¹. **non . . . exaudiat** nullus exaudit *most MSS incl* C³C¹⁰C¹⁴L³¹Ro; nemo exaudit C¹⁸. 27 **suscipitis** accipitis C¹⁴. **illos** illos et L³¹. **autem** *om* C¹⁴C¹⁸L³¹. 28 **divitum causam** *trans* C¹⁰. 29 **despicitis** despicitis et C¹⁰C¹⁸L³¹. 29–30 **reverenter** libenter C¹⁴. 30 **conculcatis** conculcatis vel oculatis *above line* C¹⁴. 31 **vir** unus C¹⁰L³¹. 31–32 **aureum . . . anulum** *trans most*

[4] DE ACCEPCIONE PERSONARUM

Ve vobis qui, corrupti prece vel precio, qui, tracti
amore vel odio, "dicitis bonum malum vel malum
bonum, ponentes tenebras lucem et lucem tenebras," "mortificantes animas / que non moriuntur et f. 91
5 vivificantes animas que non vivunt." Vos autem non
attenditis merita causarum, set personarum; non
iura, set munera; non iusticiam, set pecuniam; non
quod racio dictet, set quod voluntas affectet; non
quod lex sanctiat, set quod mens cupiat. Non incli-
10 natis animum ad iusticiam, set iusticiam inclinatis ad
animum, non ut quod licet hoc libeat, set ut liceat
hoc quod libet. Nunquam in vobis ita simplex est
oculus ut totum corpus sit lucidum, set semper
aliquid admiscetis fermenti quo totam massam cor-
15 rumpitis. Pauperum causam cum mora negligitis,
divitum causam cum instancia promovetis; in illis
rigorem ostenditis, cum istis ex mansuetudine dis-
pensatis; illos cum difficultate respicitis, istos cum
favore tractatis; illos negligenter auditis, istos sub-
20 tiliter ascultatis. Clamat pauper et nullus exaudit;
loquitur dives et omnis applaudit. "Dives locutus   In Ecclesias-
tico
est, et omnes tacuerunt, et verbum illius usque ad
nubes producitur; pauper locutus est, et dicunt:
'Quis est hic?', et si offenderit, subvertent illum."
25 "Clamat vim paciens et non est qui exaudiat; vo-
ciferatur et non est qui iudicet." Si forte pauperum
causam suscipitis, illos remisse fovetis; cum autem
divitum causam assumitis, illos pertinaciter adiuva-
tis. Pauperes despicitis, divites honoratis; istis reve-
30 renter assurgitis, illos despicabiliter conculcatis. "Si   Iacobus
Apostolus
introierit in conventu vestro vir aureum habens

golden ring in fine apparel, and there shall come in also a poor man in mean attire, and you have respect for him that is clothed with the fine apparel and shall say to him: 'Sit here well', but say to the poor man: 'Stand thou here', or 'Sit under my footstool', do you not judge within yourselves and are become judges of unjust thoughts?" For the prophet says about you and against you: "They are become great and enriched, they are grown gross and fat; they have not managed the cause of the fatherless, they have not judged the judgment of the poor." But it is commanded in the law: "There shall be no difference of persons. You shall hear the little as well as the great. Neither shall you respect any man's person, because it is the judgment of God." "For there is no respect of persons with God."

[5] OF THE SELLING OF JUSTICE

But you neither give a favor gratis nor dispense justice justly, because where it does not come forth, it does not grow, nor is it given unless it is sold. Often you defer justice so long that you take away from the litigants more than the total, because the amount of your fee is greater than the value of the judgment. But what will you be able to respond at the last judgment to him who commanded: "Freely have you received; freely give"? A profit in the coffer, a loss in the conscience: you chase money, but you take your soul captive. Truly "what doth it profit a man if he gain the whole world but suffer the loss of his own soul? Or what exchange shall a man give for his soul?" "If a brother shall not redeem, shall man redeem? He shall not give to God his ransom, nor the price of the redemption of his soul; he shall labor forever and shall live unto the end." Hear, rich men, what James says against

MSS incl C³C¹⁰C¹⁸Ro; anulum aureum habens L³¹. 32–33 **pauper . . . habitu** in sordido habitu pauper C¹⁰C¹⁸L³¹. 33 **indutus** vestitus C¹⁴; inductus Pa¹⁰Re³T². 34 **veste preclara** *trans* L³¹. **ei** *om* C¹⁰C¹⁸L³¹. **Sede** Tu sede *most MSS incl* C³C¹⁰C¹⁴L³¹Ro; Sedete C¹⁸. 35 **vero** *om* C¹⁰. **illic** illuc C¹⁰C¹⁴C¹⁸L³¹. **aut** vel C¹⁴C¹⁸; sive L³¹. 37 **iniquarum** iniquitatum Set L³¹. 38 **enim** *om* C¹⁰C¹⁴C¹⁸L³¹. 39 **ditati** ditati et C³; ditati sunt C¹⁰C¹⁸L³¹; dilatati Ro. **sunt** *(2nd)* *om most MSS incl* C³C¹⁴Ro. **inpinguati** inpinguati sunt C¹⁰C¹⁸. 40 **dixerunt** dixerunt et *most MSS incl* C³C¹⁸L³¹Ro; direxerunt et C¹⁰C¹⁴; voluerunt ducere nec L⁴⁰. **iudicium** iudicium sunt C¹⁸. **pauperum** pauperis C¹⁰C¹⁴C¹⁸L³¹. 41 **in lege** in Deuteronomio C¹⁴; in detero nomen C¹⁸. 41–42 **precipitur . . . erit** precipitur scilicet in Deuteronomio Non erit tibi C¹⁰L³¹; precipitur Non erit tibi C¹⁴C¹⁸. 42 **parvum audietis** pauperem audies ut divitem parvum C¹⁴C¹⁸; parvum audiens L³¹. 43 **Nec** Non C¹⁴C¹⁸L³¹. **accipietis** accipies C¹⁰C¹⁴; accipiens C¹⁸; accipias L³¹. 44 **iudicium est** *trans* C¹⁰C¹⁴C¹⁸L³¹. 44–45 **Non . . . Deum** *in margin* C¹⁴; Non enim personarum accepcio est aput Deum C¹⁸; Non enim personarum est accepcio apud Deum L³¹.

II.5: 1 **Vos autem** Ve vobis dicitur qui Ma²Pa¹²Pa¹³. **gratis datis** *trans* L³¹. 2 **ubi non** ubi C³; nisi *most MSS incl* C¹⁰C¹⁴C¹⁸Ro; quod L³¹. **non provenit** non pervenit C¹⁰C¹⁴; non percievit C¹⁸; *om* L³¹. 3 **nisi vendatur** ubi venditur C³. **Sepe** Se C¹⁸. 5 **est** *om* L³¹. **sentencie** sentencie vel anime *above line* C¹⁴; semine BuGoILmPa⁹Pa¹¹; ex semine Mu⁵; sciencie *some MSS*. 6 **autem** *om* C¹⁰C¹⁴C¹⁸L³¹. 6–7 **respondere** reddere L³¹S³. 7 **precipit** precepit C¹⁸; precepit quod E¹. 8 **archa** archa set L³¹. 8–9 **pecuniam** lucrum C¹⁰C¹⁸L³¹. 9 **captatis** capitis C³; captatis vel capitis *above line* C¹⁴. **set** et C¹⁴L³¹; *om* C¹⁸. **animam** animas L³¹. 10 **proficit** prodest C¹⁰C¹⁴C¹⁸L³¹. **mundum universum** *trans many MSS incl* C¹⁰C¹⁴L³¹; totum mundum C¹⁸. 12 **dabit . . . commutacionem** commutacionem dabit homo C¹⁴C¹⁸L³¹. 12–13 **Frater** Super C¹⁸. 13 **redimet** *(1st)* redimit *most MSS incl* C³C¹⁰V²; *om* C¹⁸; redimit L³¹. **redimet** *(2nd)* redimit *(same abbreviation as in preceding word)* L³¹. 13–15 **Non . . . finem** *om* C¹⁰C¹⁸L³¹. 15 **vivet** vivet adhuc *most MSS*

anulum in veste candida, introierit et pauper in
sordido habitu, et intendatis in eum qui indutus est
veste preclara et dixeritis ei: 'Sede hic bene', pauperi vero dicatis: 'Tu sta illic', aut 'Sede sub scabello
pedum meorum', nonne iudicatis apud vosmetipsos
et facti estis iudices cogitacionum iniquarum?" De
vobis / enim et contra vos dicit propheta: "Magni-
ficati sunt et ditati, incrassati sunt et inpinguati;
causam pupilli non dixerunt, iudicium pauperum
non iudicaverunt." Set in lege precipitur: "Nulla
erit distancia personarum: ita parvum audietis ut
magnum. Nec accipietis cuiusquam personam, quia
Dei iudicium est." "Non est enim personarum accepcio apud Deum."

f. 91v
Ieremias

In Deutero-
nomio

[5] DE VENDICIONE IUSTICIE

Vos autem nec graciam gratis datis nec iusticiam
iuste redditis, quia ubi non venit, non provenit, nec
datur nisi vendatur. Sepe iusticiam tantum differtis
quod litigantibus plusquam totum aufertis, quia
maior est sumptus expense quam fructus sentencie.
Quid autem illi poteritis in districto iudicio respondere qui precipit: "Gratis accepistis; gratis date"?
Lucrum in archa, dampnum in consciencia: pecuniam captatis, set animam captivatis. Verum "quid
proficit homini si mundum universum lucretur
anime vero sue detrimentum paciatur? Aut quam
dabit homo commutacionem pro anima sua?" "Frater non redimet, redimet homo? Non dabit Deo
placacionem suam, nec precium redempcionis anime
sue; laborabit in eternum et vivet in finem." Audite,

Matheus

In Psalmo

151

you: "Go to now, ye rich men; weep howling in your miseries which shall happen to you. Your riches are corrupted, and your clothes are motheaten; your gold and silver is cankered, and the rust of them shall be for a testimony against you and shall eat your flesh like fire. You have stored up to yourselves wrath against the last days. Behold, the hire of the laborers who have reaped down your fields, which by fraud has been kept back by you, crieth, and the cry of them hath entered into the ears of the Lord of Sabaoth." Therefore Truth says: "Lay not up to yourselves treasures on earth, where the rust and moth consume, where thieves break through and steal."

[6] OF THE INSATIABLE DESIRE OF COVETOUS MEN

Insatiable covetousness is an inextinguishable fire! What covetous man was ever contented with his first wish? When he obtains what he wished for, he always desires to possess more and never sets a limit on things possessed. "The eye of the covetous man is insatiable; in his portion of iniquity he will not be satisfied." "A covetous man shall not be satisfied with money, and he that loveth riches shall reap no fruit from them." Hell and perdition are never filled up, in like manner also the insatiable eyes of men. "There are two daughters of the horseleech saying: 'Bring, bring'." For "the love of money increases as much as the money itself increases."

[7] WHY THE COVETOUS MAN CANNOT BE SATISFIED

Do you want to know, o covetous man, why you are always empty and are never full? Observe: no measure is full, however much it contains, that is yet

incl C³V². 16 **Iacobus** Iacobus apostolus *most MSS incl* C³C¹⁰C¹⁸L³¹Ro; apostolus Iacobus C¹⁴. **ait** dicit C¹⁴; dicat C¹⁸. 17 **ululantes** eiulantes C¹⁸E¹L³¹. 18 **evenient** advenient *most MSS incl* C³C¹⁰C¹⁴C¹⁸L³¹V². 20 **eruginavit** eriginavit C¹⁸; eruginavit id est rubiginem prodiit T²Re³. **eorum** *om* L³¹. 22 **ignis** tygris C¹⁸. **Thesaurizastis** Thesaurizate Ro. 23 **qui** quam C¹⁰L³¹; quam qui C¹⁸. 24 **regiones vestras** cogitaciones vestre C¹⁰L³¹. **fraudata** defraudata C¹⁰C¹⁴C¹⁸L³¹. **clamat et** *trans* L³¹. 25 **ipsorum** *om* C¹⁰C¹⁸L³¹. **aures Domini** auribus Dei C¹⁴C¹⁸L³¹; ore Domini *some MSS.* **introivit** intonuit L³¹. 26 **dicit** precipit *most MSS incl* C³C¹⁴Ro; precepit C¹⁰C¹⁸L³¹. 28 **ubi . . . furantur** *om* C¹⁰C¹⁴L³¹; et cetera C¹⁸.

II.6: *Title* Cupidorum *om* C¹⁴C¹⁸. 1 **Ignis** O ignis *many MSS incl* C³C¹⁰C¹⁴C¹⁸. 2 **contentus** contemptus C³; contento C¹⁴; *corrected from* contemptus L³¹. 3 **adipiscitur** adeptus fuerit C¹⁸. **optaverat** captaverat C¹⁰C¹⁸; optaverit L³¹. 4 **in (1st)** inhiat C¹⁰C¹⁴C¹⁸. **et** *om* L³¹. **habitis** hiatis C¹⁸; habitis L³¹. 6 **non (2nd)** numquam C³; *om* C¹⁸; vix EvL²⁹LaO²⁶Pa¹⁰Pa¹⁴Ru². 6-7 **inplebitur pecunia** pecunia non ad implebitur C¹⁸. 7 **et** *om* C¹⁰C¹⁴C¹⁸. **pecunias** pecuniam C¹⁰C¹⁸; pecunia *corrected to* divicias *above line* C¹⁴; divicias L³¹. **fructus** fructum C¹⁴C¹⁸V². 8 **eis** ea C¹⁰, *corrected to* eis C¹⁴L³¹. **replentur** implebitur C³C¹⁰; repellentur C¹⁸; implentur *most MSS incl* L³¹Ro. 10 **affer (2nd)** affer quoquomodo vis C¹⁴. 11 **nummi** mimi *(sic)* C¹⁴; numerum L³¹; mundi L²⁹O²⁶; minimi D¹. **ipsa** *om many MSS incl* C³; *above line* C¹⁴.

II.7: *Title* De Siti Cupidi C¹⁴C¹⁸. 1 **o** *om* C¹⁰C¹⁸. 3 **adhuc . . . est** semper est capax

divites, quid contra vos Iacobus ait: "Agite nunc, In Epistola Canonica
divites; plorate ululantes in miseriis vestris que
evenient vobis. Divicie vestre putrefacte sunt, et
vestimenta vestra a tineis comesta sunt; aurum et
20 argentum vestrum eruginavit, et erugo eorum erit
vobis in testimonium et manducabit carnes vestras
sicut ignis. Thesaurizastis vobis iram in novissimis
diebus. Ecce, merces operariorum qui messuerunt
regiones vestras, que fraudata est a vobis, clamat, et
25 clamor ipsorum in aures Domini Sabaoth introivit."
Propterea Veritas dicit: "Nolite thesaurizare vobis Matheus
thesauros in terra, ubi erugo / et tinea demolitur, f. 92
ubi fures effodiunt et furantur."

[6] DE INSACIABILI DESIDERIO CUPIDORUM

Ignis inextinguibilis cupiditas insaciabilis! Quis
unquam cupidus primo fuit voto contentus? Cum
adipiscitur quod optaverat, desiderat ampliora
semper in habendis et nunquam in habitis finem
5 constituit. "Insaciabilis est oculus cupidi; in partem In Ecclesias-tico
iniquitatis non saciabitur." "Avarus non inplebitur
pecunia, et qui amat pecunias fructus non capiet ex
eis." Infernus et perdicio nunquam replentur, similiter et oculi hominum insaciabiles. "Sanguisuge due In Parabolis
10 sunt filie dicentes: 'Affer, affer'." Nam "crescit
amor nummi, quantum ipsa pecunia crescit."

[7] QUARE CUPIDUS SACIARI NON POTEST

Vis, o cupide, scire quare semper es vacuus et
nunquam impleris? Adverte: non est plena mensura
que, quantumcumque contineat, adhuc capax est

capable of more. But the human soul is capable of God, because what adheres to God is one spirit with him. However much it contains therefore, it is never full unless it has God, of whom it is always capable. If you wish therefore, covetous man, to be satisfied, cease to be covetous, for as long as you are covetous you will not be able to be satisfied. For there is no meeting of light with darkness, or of Christ with Belial, because no one can serve God and mammon.

[8] OF THE FALSE NAME OF RICHES

O false happiness of riches, which truly makes the rich man unhappy! For what is more false than the treasures of the world? Are they called riches? To be rich and to be poor are opposites. But yet the treasures of the world do not remove but bring on poverty. For a little is more sufficient to the poor man than a great deal to the rich man, since "where there are many riches, many eat them." In how many and in what great ways magnates are in need, I myself frequently experience. And thus treasures do not make a man rich, but poor.

[9] EXAMPLES AGAINST COVETOUSNESS

How many men covetousness has seduced! How many more avarice has ruined! The little ass refuted Balaam and bruised the feet of the rider because, overcome by longing for the things promised, he had determined to curse Israel. The people stoned Achan because he took gold and silver away from cursed Jericho. Naboth was slain so that Achab might possess his vineyard. Leprosy covered Giezi because he asked for and received silver and garments in the name of Eliseus. Judas hanged himself with a halter because he sold and betrayed Christ. Sudden death destroyed Ananias and Saphira because they

---

C^{10}C^{18}L^{31}; est capax C^{14}. 4-5 **quoniam** quare L^{31}. 5 **est** efficitur C^{14}C^{18}. 6 **ergo** *om* L^{31}. 7-8 **vis . . . cupide** ergo vis C^{10}C^{14}C^{18}L^{31}; ergo tu vis AuGoIMu^{5}Pa^{15}. 9 **enim** *om many MSS incl* C3L^{31}.

    II.8: 1 **que** qui L^{31}. **veraciter** *om* C^{10}L^{31}; *above line* C^{14}. 2 **efficit** facit C^{14}C^{18}; *om* L^{31}. **enim** est enim C^{3}C^{14}; *om* C^{18}L^{31}. **falsius** fallacius C^3; falsius sive fallacius *in margin* C^{14}. 2-3 **opes mundi** quod opes mundi C^3; mundi opes que C^{10}C^{14}C^{18}L^{31}; opes mundi que *most MSS incl* Ro. 3-4 **Divicie . . . mundi** *om* C^{10}L^{31}; divitie nuncupantur Oppositi sunt dives et egenus At opes mundi V^2. 6 **plurimum** multum C^{10}C^{14}C^{18}L^{31}. 7 **comedent eas** que illas comedunt C^3; qui comedunt illas *most MSS incl* C^{10}L^{31}Ro; qui sunt comedunt illas C^{14}C^{18}. 8 **magnates** magnatos L^{31}. **indigeant** indigent L^{31}. **experior** te*m*perior L^{31}. 9 **Opes itaque** Opposita sunt esse divitem et egenum ast opes mundi C^{10}C^{18}L^{31}. **non** et non L^{31}. **egenum** egenum Unde quidam versificator ait Cui satis est quod habet satis illum constat habere Cui non est quod habet satis illum constat egere Ergo facit virtus non copia sufficientem et non paupertas sed mentis hiatus egentem V^2, *in margin* C^{14}.

    II.9: *Title* De Exemplo Contra Cupiditatem in Numero C^3. 1 **Quam** O quam C^{10}C^{14}C^{18}. **seduxit** seducit L^{31}. 2 **pedes** C^{10}; pedem *most MSS incl* C^{3}Ro. 3 **cupiditate** cupidine *most MSS incl* C^{10}C^{18}L^{31}Ro, *with* vel cupiditate *above line* C^{14}. 4 **disposuerat** disposuit C^{10}C^{14}C^{18}L^{31}. **Israeli** populo Israeli D^{1}L^{47}O^{21}O^{30}Pa^8. 5 **lapidavit** lapidabat L^{31}. 6 **interemptus** interfectus C^{18}. 7 **vineam** veniam *corrected to* vineam C^{14}; uxorem L^{30}. **perfudit** percussit C^{10}C^{18}, *corrected in margins to* perfudit vel percussit C^{14}. 7-8 **peciit et** *om* C^{18}; *above line* C^{14}. 8 **argentum** aurum C^{14}O^{13}; *om* C^{18}; aurum et argentum L^{31} ArC^{12}Du^{4}L^{4}L^{12}MoO^{25}Ph^{1}Re^{3}T^{1}T^2. **vestes** vestem L^{31}Bn. 9 **vendidit . . . tradidit** *trans* C^{10}L^{31}; vendidit C^{14}C^{18}. 10 **Christum** iustum id est Christum L^{31}. **subitanea** subita

154

amplioris. Set humanus animus capax est Dei, quo- Apostolus
5 niam qui adheret Deo unus spiritus est cum eo.
Quantumlibet ergo contineat, nunquam est plenus
nisi Deum habeat, cuius semper est capax. Si vis
ergo, cupide, saciari, desinas esse cupidus, quia dum
cupidus fueris saciari non poteris. Non est enim Apostolus
10 convencio lucis ad tenebras, neque Christi ad Belial,
quia nemo potest Deo servire et mammone. Matheus

[8] DE FALSO NOMINE DIVICIARUM

O falsa diviciarum felicitas, que divitem veraciter
efficit infelicem! Quid enim falsius quam opes
mundi? Divicie nuncupantur? Opposita sunt esse
divitem et egenum. At opes mundi non auferunt set
5 afferunt egestatem. Magis enim sufficit modicum
pauperi quam plurimum diviti, quoniam "ubi multe Salomon
divicie, mul- / -ti comedent eas." Quot et quantis f. 92v
magnates indigeant, ipsemet frequenter experior.
Opes itaque non faciunt divitem, set egenum.

[9] EXEMPLA CONTRA CUPIDITATEM

Quam multos seduxit cupiditas! Quam plures per-
didit avaricia! Balaam asella redarguit et pedes In Libro Numerum
sedentis attrivit quia, captus cupiditate promis-
sorum, disposuerat maledicere Israeli. Achor popu- In Iosue
5 lus lapidavit quia tulit aurum et argentum de ana-
themate Iericho. Naboth interemptus est ut Achab In Libro Regum
vineam possideret. Gyezi lepra perfudit quia peciit
et recepit argentum et vestes sub nomine Helysei.
Iudas laqueo se suspendit quia vendidit et tradidit Matheus In Actibus Apostolorum
10 Christum. Ananiam et Saphiram subitanea mors

defrauded the apostle of the price of the land. "Tyre hath built her stronghold and heaped together silver as earth and gold as the mire of the streets. But behold, the Lord shall possess her and shall strike her strength in the sea and shall devour them with fire."

[10] OF THE INJURIOUS POSSESSION OF RICHES

What the wise man declares is true: "Gold and silver hath destroyed many." "He that loveth gold shall not be justified." Woe to those who chase it: "Behold, these are sinners, and abounding in the world they have obtained riches." Hence Truth himself admonished the apostles: "Do not possess gold or silver or money in your purses," because "just as the camel is not able to enter through the eye of the needle, so is it difficult for a rich man to enter into the kingdom of heaven." For the way is narrow and the gate strait through which one goes and enters into life. The apostle therefore, following the rule of Truth, said: "Silver and gold I have none." "Woe therefore to you that join house to house and lay field to field even to the end of the place." "The land is filled with gold and silver, and there is no end of their treasures." "Because of the iniquity of her covetousness I was angry and struck her."

[11] OF LAWFUL WEALTH

But Abraham was rich, Job wealthy, David opulent. And yet scripture says of Abraham that he "believed in God and it was reputed to him unto justice"; and of Job that "there is none like him in the earth, a simple and upright man

C^{10}C^{14}C^{18}L^{31}. 11 **quia** quoniam C^{10}C^{18}L^{31}. **defraudaverunt** fraudaverunt C^{14}Ro. 12 **municionem suam** municiones sues C^{14}. 12-13 **coacervavit** coarcebant C^{18}; coacerbavit L^{31}. 13 **argentum** argenteum acervum L^{31}; aurum et argentum L^{12}O^{11}. **argentum . . . aurum** *trans many MSS incl* C^3. **ut** quasi *many MSS incl* C^{3}C^{10}C^{14}C^{18}L^{31}. 15 **percuciet** percussit C^{18}. **igni** igne L^{31}. 15-16 **devorabit** devorabitur *most MSS incl* C^{3}C^{10}C^{14}C^{18}L^{31}Ro.

II.10: ***Title*** Passione *for* Possessione EvRu^2. 1 **protestatur** testatur C^{14}C^{18}L^{31}. 2 **aurum . . . argentum** *trans* C^{10}. **aurum diligit** *trans* C^{10}C^{18}L^{31}. 3 **sectantur** secuntur C^{10}C^{18}L^{31}. **et habundantes** *om* C^{10}C^{18}L^{31}. 5 **Hinc** Hinc etiam C^{10}L^{31}; et C^{18}. 6 **aurum . . . argentum** *trans* C^{10}. **neque** *(1st) in margin* L^{20}; et C^{18}. 6-7 **neque pecuniam** *om* C^{10}C^{14}C^{18}L^{31}. 8 **introire** intrare C^{18}; transire L^{36}. 9 **est enim** est C^{18}; *trans* L^{31}. 10 **via** via que ducit ad vitam D^{6}Er^{2}L^{3}O^{13}O^{21}. **porta** est porta C^{18}; *om* L^{31}. **intratur** intratur in regnum L^{31}D^{3}Pa^{15}. 11 **secutus** secutus est C^{18}L^{31}. **regulam** viam *many MSS*. 12 **aiebat** qui ait C^{18}; dum aiebat L^{31}. 13 **ergo** ergo vobis *many MSS incl* C^{10}C^{18}L^{31}. 13-14 **ad agrum** *om most MSS incl* C^{3}C^{10}C^{14}C^{18}L^{31}Ro. 14 **loci** loci immo potius usque ad sui terminum loci E^1. 15 **auro . . . argento** *trans most MSS incl* C^{3}C^{10}C^{18}L^{31}Ro. 16 **avaricie eius** thesaurorum et avaricie eius C^{10}C^{14}L^{31}; eius et avariciam C^{18}. 16-17 **iratus sum et** *om* L^{31}. 17 **percussi eam** percussi eum *most MSS incl* C^{3}C^{10}L^{31}Ro; percussi eum dicit Dominus C^{14}; dicit Dominus C^{18}.

II.11: ***Title*** De Illicitis Opibus C^{10}. 1 **Ceterum** Et enim C^3; *om* C^{14}C^{18}L^{31}. 2 **Et** *om* C^{14}C^{18}; *probably om* L^{31}, *but MS impossible to read at this point because of a stain.* **inquit scriptura** dicit scriptura *many MSS incl* C^{3}C^{14}C^{18}; scriptum est L^{31}Au. 3 **et** *om* C^{10}L^{31}. **reputatum** *a superfluous* e *expunged above* re- L^{20}. 4 **et** *om* C^{18}L^{31}. **Iob** Iob vero L^{31}. **ei**

extinxit quia de precio agri defraudaverunt aposto-
lum. "Edificavit Tyrus municionem suam et coacer- Zacharias
vavit argentum quasi humum et aurum ut lutum
platearum. Set ecce, Dominus possidebit eam et
15 percuciet in mari fortitudinem eius et hec igni devorabit."

[10] DE INIQUA POSSESSIONE DIVICIARUM

Verum est quod sapiens protestatur: "Multos per- In Ecclesias-
didit aurum et argentum." "Qui aurum diligit non tico
iustificabitur." Ve illis qui sectantur illud: "Ecce,
ipsi peccatores, et habundantes in seculo optinuerunt
5 divicias." Hinc Veritas ipsa precipiebat apostolis:
"Nolite possidere aurum neque argentum neque Matheus
pecuniam in zonis vestris," quia "sicut camelus non
potest introire per foramen acus, ita difficile est
divitem intrare in regnum celorum." Arta est enim
10 via et angusta porta per quam itur et intratur ad
vitam. Apostolus ergo, secutus regulam Veritatis, In Actibus
aiebat: "Argentum et aurum non / est michi." "Ve Apostolorum
ergo qui coniungitis domum ad domum et agrum ad f. 93
Ysaias
agrum copulatis usque ad terminum loci." "Repleta
15 est terra auro et argento, et non est finis thesaurorum eius." "Propter iniquitatem avaricie eius
iratus sum et percussi eam."

[11] DE LICITIS OPIBUS

Ceterum Abraham dives fuit, Iob locuplex, David
opulentus. Et tamen de Abraham inquit scriptura
quia "credidit Deo et reputatum est ei ad iusti- In Genesi
ciam"; et de Iob quia "non erat ei similis in terra,

and also fearing God and avoiding evil"; and indeed of David that the Lord found a man after his own heart. And these were also "as if having nothing and possessing all things," according to the saying of the prophet: "If riches abound, set not your heart upon them." But we possess all things as if having nothing, according to the saying of the psalmist: "The rich have wanted and have suffered hunger." For you will more easily find one who loves riches and does not have them than one who has riches and does not love them, because it is difficult to be in fire and not burn, more difficult to possess riches and not love them. Hear the prophet: "From the least of them even to the greatest, all are given to covetousness, and from the prophet even to the priest, all practice deceit."

[12] OF THE UNCERTAINTY OF RICHES

Every covetous and avaricious man strives and struggles against nature. For nature brings a man into the world poor; nature takes him back from the world poor. Indeed the earth received him naked, and the earth will receive him naked. But the covetous man desires and takes care to become rich in the world. "I will pull down my barns," he says, "and will build greater, and into them will I gather all things that are grown to me and all my goods." But "o fool, this night is thy soul required of thee, and whose shall those things be which thou hast provided?" "You store up, and you know not for whom you gather." "They have slept their sleep, and all the men of riches have found nothing in their hands." "The rich man, when he shall sleep, shall take away nothing with him; he shall open his eyes and find nothing." "Therefore be not thou afraid when a man shall be made rich and when the glory of his house shall be increased; for, when he shall die, he shall not take all these things, nor shall his glory descend with him." But "they shall leave their riches to

similis *trans* C¹⁴L³¹; ei *above line* C¹⁸. 5 **rectus** iustus C¹⁰L³¹; *om because part of an* et cetera C¹⁸. **ac** et L³¹; *om because part of an* et cetera C¹⁸. 6 **invenerit** invenit *most MSS incl* C³C¹⁰C¹⁴C¹⁸L³¹Ro. 7 **secundum cor suum** ad cor eius C¹⁰; secundum cor eius L³¹; secundum cor meum D⁴L¹⁵LmO⁷O²⁶. **isti** illi *many MSS incl* C³C¹⁰C¹⁴L³¹. 9 **prophete** propheticum C³; *om* L³¹; *in margin* C¹⁴. 11 **psalmiste** prophete C¹⁰C¹⁴C¹⁸L³¹. 13 **diligat divicias** diligunt C¹⁸E¹L³¹; diligunt divicias C¹⁴. **habeat (both)** habent C¹⁰C¹⁴C¹⁸ L³¹. 13–14 **divicias** *om many MSS incl* C¹⁰C¹⁴C¹⁸L³¹Ro. 14 **diligat** diligunt C¹⁰C¹⁴C¹⁸L³¹. **quia** quia sicut *many MSS incl* Ro, *above line* C¹⁴. **est** *om* L³¹. 15 **difficilius** ita difficilius *many MSS incl* Ro, ita *above line* C¹⁴. 16–17 **maiorem** minimum L³¹; minorem EvLaRu² *(but with* maiore *earlier).* 17 **avaricie student** *trans* L³¹. 18 **sacerdotem** sacerdotes C¹⁰L³¹.

II.12: 1 **et avarus** *om most MSS incl* C¹⁰C¹⁸L³¹Ro. 2 **adducit** ducit L³¹. 3 **natura** et C¹⁰C¹⁸L³¹. **a** de C¹⁴C¹⁸. 4 **suscepit** *corrected from* suscipit L²⁰; suscipit C¹⁰C¹⁸L³¹. **nudum** mundum C⁹C²²L¹². 5 **fieri dives** *trans* C¹⁰C¹⁸L³¹. **mundo** hoc mundo C¹⁸. 6 **inquit . . . mea** orrea mea inquid L³¹. **maiora faciam** faciam ea maiora C¹⁸E¹L³¹; maiora horum faciam *many MSS incl* Ro. 7 **illuc** illic C³C¹⁴. 8 **Set** *om* C¹⁰C¹⁸L³¹. **hac** si hac C¹⁰. **nocte** nocte demones exactores Bo, *above line* C¹⁴. 8–9 **repetetur** repetent *most MSS incl* C³L³¹Ro; recederet C¹⁰; rapient C¹⁴; repetam C¹⁸. 9 **anima tua** C¹⁰; animam tuam *most MSS incl* C³C¹⁴C¹⁸L³¹Ro. **autem** ante C¹⁰L³¹. 10 **Thesaurizas** Thesaurizat L³¹. **ignoras** ignorat L³¹. **congreges** congregabis ea *many MSS incl* C¹⁴C¹⁸; congregabit ea L³¹. 11–12 **et . . . suis** et cetera C¹⁸L³¹. 14 **timueris** terminus C¹⁸. **ergo** *om most MSS incl* C³C¹⁰C¹⁸ L³¹. 15–16 **fuerit (2nd) . . . eius** et cetera L³¹. 16 **non . . . accipiet** quoniam cum interierit non sumet LaBz²C¹²Re³T². 16–17 **non . . . eius** *om* C¹⁰C¹⁸L³¹; *in margin* C¹⁴. 17 **eius** domus eius C³. **Set** Ecce C¹⁰C¹⁴C¹⁸L³¹. 17–18 **relinquent** relinquet *many MSS incl*

vir simplex et rectus ac timens Deum et recedens a malo"; de David autem quia Dominus invenerit In Regum virum secundum cor suum. At isti fuerunt "quasi nichil habentes et omnia possidentes," secundum illud prophete: "Divicie si affluant, nolite cor ap- In Psalmo ponere." Nos autem sumus omnia possidentes quasi nichil habentes, secundum illud psalmiste: "Divites eguerunt et esurierunt." Facilius enim invenies qui diligat divicias et non habeat quam qui habeat divicias et non diligat, quia difficile est esse in igne et non ardere, difficilius est possidere divicias et non amare. Audi prophetam: "A minore usque ad maio- Ieremias rem, omnes avaricie student, et a propheta usque ad sacerdotem cuncti faciunt dolum."

[12] DE INCERTITUDINE DIVICIARUM

Omnis cupidus et avarus contra naturam nititur et molitur. Natura namque pauperem adducit in mundum; natura pauperem reducit a mundo. Nudum enim terra suscepit, et nudum terra suscipiet. Cupidus autem cupit et curat fieri dives in mundo. "De- Lucas struam," inquit, "horrea mea, et maiora faciam, et illuc congregabo omnia que nata sunt michi et omnia bona mea." Set "o stulte, hac nocte repetetur anima tua a te, que autem parasti cuius erunt?" "Thesaurizas, et / ignoras cui congreges." "Dor- f. 93v mierunt sompnum suum, et nichil invenerunt omnes viri diviciarum in manibus suis." "Dives, cum dor- Iob mierit, nichil secum afferet; aperiet oculos suos et nichil inveniet." "Ne timueris ergo cum dives factus In Psalmo fuerit homo et cum multiplicata fuerit gloria domus eius; non enim, cum morietur, accipiet hec omnia, neque descendet cum eo gloria eius." Set "relin-

159

strangers, and their sepulchers shall be their houses forever." And hence the wise man confirms: "He that gathereth together by wronging his own soul gathereth for others, and another will be wanton in his goods." O sadness, he leaves behind as heir him whom he considered an enemy.

[13] OF THE ANXIETY OF THE COVETOUS

Why would anyone insist on accumulating when he who accumulates is unable to survive? For he "cometh forth like a flower and is destroyed and fleeth as a shadow and never continueth in the same state." Why would one desire many things when a few suffice? "Having food and clothing," he says, "with these we are content." Why would one seek the necessities with great anxiety when they present themselves without great difficulty? Hear what Truth says about this: "Be not solicitous, saying: 'What shall we eat' or 'What shall we drink' or 'Wherewith shall we be clothed?' For your Father knoweth that you have need of all these things. Seek ye therefore first the kingdom of God and his justice, and all these things shall be added unto you." "I have never seen the just forsaken nor his seed seeking bread."

[14] OF AVARICE

"Tantalus is thirsty among the waves, and the avaricious man is needy among his riches." To him what he has is as great as what he has not, because he never uses the things acquired, but always gapes at the things to be acquired. Solomon: "One is as it were rich when he hath nothing, and another is as it were poor when he hath great riches." The avaricious man and hell as well eat and do not digest, receive and do not return. The avaricious man has neither compassion for those suffering nor pity for those in misery, but offends God,

C³V². 18 **eorum** *om* L³¹. 19 **illorum** eorum *most MSS incl* Ro; *om* C¹⁸. **eciam** enim C¹⁸L³¹; *om* C¹⁴. 20 **animo suo** animo *many MSS incl* V²; alieno ArRe³T². **iniuste** iniusto L³¹. **et** *om* C¹⁰C¹⁴C¹⁸. 21 **alius** alienus C¹⁸. **Proh dolor** *om* L³¹. 22 **habebat** habuit C¹⁸; habebit L³¹; habet Ro. **dimittit** habebit C¹⁴; dives dimittit C¹⁸.

II.13: **Title** De Superflua Sollicitudine Cubitorum Ydolorum C³; De Superflua Sollicitudine Cupidorum C¹⁰; De Superflua Solicitudine Dicitur Cupidorum C¹⁴; De Contempnenda Possessione Divitiarum Ro. 2 **possit** possit nam C¹⁰C¹⁴; possit namque L³¹. **Nam** *om* C¹⁰C¹⁴L³¹. 3 **et** *(3rd)* *om* L³¹. 4 **desideret** desiderant C¹⁸. 5 **sufficiant** sufficiunt L³¹. **inquit** inquit apostolus C³, *above line* C¹⁴; *om* C¹⁸L³¹. 6 **contenti** contempti *some MSS*. **sitis** simus C³; sitis *corrected to* simus C¹⁴; *other variants incl* es *and* sumus. 7 **multa** magna C¹⁸; multa ex incertitudine L³¹. **magna** *om* C¹⁰C¹⁸L³¹; *in margin* C¹⁴. 9 **solliciti** sollite L³¹. 10–11 **Scit . . . indigetis** *om* C¹⁰C¹⁸L³¹; *in margin* C¹⁴, *with* celestis *after* vester. 11–12 **Querite . . . primum** Primum querite C¹⁰C¹⁸L³¹; Primum ergo querite C¹⁴, *with* ergo *above line.* 12 **et . . . eius** *in margin* C¹⁴. 12–13 **iusticiam . . . hec** *om* L³¹. 13 **enim** *om* C¹⁸; *in margin* C¹⁴.

II.14: **Title** De Avaro et Cupido Ro. 1 **undis** media unda C¹⁰C¹⁴C¹⁸L³¹. **opibus** medius opibus C¹⁸. 2 **est** *(2nd)* *om* L³¹. 5 **habeat** habebat C¹⁰. 7 **Avarus nec** Nec C¹⁰C¹⁴; *trans* L³¹. 8 **pacientibus** compacientibus C¹⁰C¹⁸. **miseretur** subvenit vel miseretur

quent alienis divicias *suas, et sepulchra eorum domus illorum* in eternum." Hinc eciam sapiens attestatur: "Qui acervat ex animo suo iniuste aliis congregat, et in bonis suis alius luxuriabitur." Proh dolor, quem habebat hostem dimittit heredem.

In Ecclesiastico

[13] DE SOLLICITUDINE CUPIDORUM

Cur ad congregandum quis instet cum stare non possit ille qui congregat? Nam "quasi flos egreditur et conteritur et fugit velut umbra et nunquam in eodum statu permanet." Cur multa desideret cum pauca sufficiant? "Habentes," inquit, "victum et vestitum, his contenti sitis." Cur necessaria cum multa sollicitudine querat cum ipsa sine magna difficultate se offerant? Audi quid super hoc Veritas dicat: "Nolite solliciti esse, dicentes: 'Quid manducabimus' aut 'Quid *bibemus*' aut 'Quo *operiemur?*' Scit enim Pater vester quia his omnibus indigetis. Querite ergo primum regnum Dei et iusticiam eius, et hec omnia adicientur vobis." "Nunquam enim vidi iustum derelictum nec *semen eius querens panem.*"

Iob

Apostolus

Matheus

In Psalmo

[14] DE AVARICIA

"Tantalus sitit in undis, et avarus eget in opibus." Cui tantum est quod habet quantum est quod non habet, quia nunquam utitur adquisitis, set semper inhiat adquirendis. Salomon: "Est quasi dives cum nichil habeat, et est quasi pauper cum in multis diviciis sit." Avarus et infernus uterque comedit et non digerit, recipit et non reddit. / Avarus nec pacientibus compatitur nec miseris miseretur, set

In Parabolis

f. 94

offends his neighbor, offends himself. For he withholds his debt from God, denies the necessities to his neighbor, takes away useful things from himself. Ungrateful to God, disrespectful to his neighbor, cruel to himself. "Wealth is not comely for a covetous man and a niggard, and of what use is gold to an envious man?" "He that is evil to himself, to whom will he be good? He shall not take pleasure in his goods." "He that hath the substance of this world and shall see his brother in need and shall shut up his bowels from him, how doth the charity of God abide in him?" For he does not love his neighbor as himself—he lets him be destroyed by hunger, consumed by need; nor does he love God above all things—he prefers gold to him, values silver above him.

[15] WHY AVARICE IS CALLED THE SERVICE OF IDOLS

The Apostle defines accurately: "Avarice is the service of idols." For as the idolater serves the image, so the avaricious man serves his treasure. For the one diligently extends the cultivation of idolatry, and the other willingly increases the quantity of his money. The one protects the image with all diligence, and the other guards his treasure with all care. The one puts his hope in idolatry, and the other places his hope in money. The one is afraid to disfigure the image, and the other is afraid to diminish his treasure.

[16] OF CERTAIN CHARACTERISTICS OF THE AVARICIOUS MAN

The avaricious man is quick to demand, slow to give, bold to refuse. If he spends anything, he loses all. Sad, complaining, and morose, anxious, he sighs; doubting, he holds fast; reluctant, he spends. He praises a gift, but deprecates

C³. 9 **offendit (2nd)** . . . **offendit** om L³¹. 10 **retinet** detinet *most MSS incl* C¹⁰C¹⁴L³¹Ro; detinet se C¹⁸. **denegat** negat C¹⁰C¹⁴C¹⁸. 11 **opportuna** optima C¹⁸. 12 **impius** om C¹⁸. **sibi** sibi existit C³. 14 **quid** quis L³¹. **cui** quomodo *many MSS incl* Ro. **alii** om C¹⁴C¹⁸ L³¹. 15 **Non** C¹⁰; Et non *most MSS incl* C³Ro. **Non** . . . **suis** Non dimidiabit in bonis dies suos C¹⁰, *also in* C¹⁴ *but with the* L²⁰ *reading in the margin*; Non dimidiabunt in bonis dies suos C¹⁸; Non dimidiabitur in bonis dies suos L³¹. 16 **huius** om L³¹. **videt** viderit *most MSS incl* C¹⁰C¹⁴C¹⁸L³¹Ro. 17 **habere** habentem C¹⁰C¹⁴C¹⁸L³¹. **clauserit** *a preceding* el *expunged* L²⁰; claudit C³C¹⁸. 18 **manet** est L³¹D²U⁴. **ipso** eo *most MSS incl* C¹⁰C¹⁸L³¹V²; illo C¹⁴. 20 **sinit perimi** perimit *most MSS incl* C³C¹⁰C¹⁴C¹⁸Ro; permit L³¹. **egestate** et egestate C¹⁰; egestas *many MSS incl* C¹⁴V²; et egestas C¹⁸L³¹. **consumi** consumit *most MSS incl* C³C¹⁰C¹⁴C¹⁸L³¹Ro. **neque** neque enim L³¹. 21 **cui** qui C³. **prefert** prescit L³¹; presunt L²³.

II.15: *Title* Cur *for* Quod C³C¹⁸Ro; Quare *for* Quod C¹⁰; Quare Avaricia Dicitur Ydolorum Servitus C¹⁴. 1 **Recte** Avariciam itaque C¹⁸; Recte C¹⁴ *but* Avariciam *in margin.* 2 **servitus** servitus quia C¹⁴C¹⁸. **enim** om C¹⁰C¹⁴C¹⁸L³¹. **sic** ita C¹⁴C¹⁸E¹L³¹. 3 **servit** om *many MSS incl* C¹⁴C¹⁸V². 4-5 **cumulum** . . . **libenter** pecuniam studiose C¹⁰C¹⁸L³¹, *with* cumulum *in margin and* pecuniam *corrected to* pecunie C¹⁴. 5-6 **symula-chrum** simulacra C¹⁴C¹⁸. 7 **spem constituit** om C¹⁸; *in margin* C¹⁴; spem ponit *many MSS incl* V². 8 **et** om L³¹. 9 **timet** om L³¹.

II.16: *Title* Quibusdam om C³Ro; Thesauri *for* Avari C¹⁴. 1 **petendum** penitendum C¹⁸. 2-3 **Si** . . . **morosus** om C¹⁰. 2 **Si** Et si C¹⁴C¹⁸. **expendit** expedit C¹⁴C¹⁸, *with* n *in margin in* C¹⁴. 3 **morosus** murmurosus C¹⁴C¹⁸. **suspirat** supputat *many MSS incl* C³C¹⁰; supputat *corrected to* suspirat C¹⁴; superpetat C¹⁸; suspirat et anxiatur *some MSS.* 4

offendit Deum, offendit proximum, offendit seipsum. Nam Deo retinet debita, proximo denegat
necessaria, sibi subtrahit opportuna. Deo ingratus,
proximo impius, sibi crudelis. "Viro cupido et te-
naci sine racione est substancia, et homini livido ad
quid aurum?" "Qui sibi nequam est, cui alii bonus
erit? Non iocundabitur in bonis suis." "Qui habet
substanciam huius mundi et videt fratrem suum
necessitatem habere et clauserit viscera sua ab eo,
quomodo caritas Dei manet in ipso?" Non enim
proximum suum diligit sicut seipsum—quem inedia
sinit perimi, egestate consumi; neque Deum diligit
super omnia—cui prefert aurum, preponit argentum.

In Ecclesias-
tico

Iohannes in
Epistola

[15] QUOD AVARICIA DICATUR YDOLORUM SERVITUS

Recte diffinit Apostolus: "Avaricia est idolorum
servitus." Sicut enim ydolatra servit symulachro, sic
avarus servit thesauro. Nam ille cultum ydolatrie
diligenter amplificat, et iste cumulum pecunie libenter augmentat. Ille cum omni diligencia colit symulachrum, et iste cum omni cura custodit thesaurum.
Ille spem ponit in ydolatria, et iste spem constituit in
pecunia. Ille timet mutilare symulachrum, et iste
timet minuere thesaurum.

[16] DE QUIBUSDAM PROPRIETATIBUS AVARI

Avarus ad petendum promtus, ad dandum tardus, ad
negandum frontuosus. Si quid expendit, totum amit-
tit. Tristis, querulus, et morosus, sollicitus, suspirat;
dubius, heret; invitus, inpendit. Magnificat datum,

163

giving; he gives in order to get, but does not get in order to give. He is liberal with a stranger's property, but miserly with his own. He empties his gullet in order to fill his coffer; he reduces his body in order to enlarge his wealth. "He has a hand shut to giving, but stretched out for accepting"; closed to giving, but open for receiving. But "the riches of the unjust shall be dried up like a river," because he who accumulates wickedly scatters quickly. It is a just judgment that what comes from evil comes to evil, and what does not proceed from good does not move towards good. Therefore the avaricious man has ruination in the life that is now and is to come.

[17] OF GLUTTONY

"The beginning of man's life is water and bread and clothing and a house to cover shame." But now the fruits of trees are not sufficient for gluttons, nor the varieties of vegetables, nor the roots of plants, nor the fish of the sea, nor the beasts of the earth, nor the birds of the sky, but they seek for paints, compare aromas, nurse fattened birds, catch the plump ones, which are carefully prepared by the skill of the cooks, which are splendidly presented by the ceremony of the waiters. One grinds and strains, another mixes and prepares, turns substance into accident, changes nature into art, so that satiety turns into hunger, squeamishness recovers an appetite; to stimulate gluttony, not to sustain nature; not fill a need, but to satisfy a desire. Yet the pleasure of gluttony is so brief that as to the size of the place it is scarcely four inches, as to length of time scarcely as many moments. Moderation is condemned, and

invitus invictus *some MSS.* 5 set et C¹⁰C¹⁴C¹⁸; *om* L³¹. non *above line* L³¹. lucratur lucretur L³¹. 7 adimpleat impleat *most MSS incl* C³C¹⁴C¹⁸L³¹Ro. 7–8 extenuat eximat C¹⁸; exterminat Pa⁸Re³T². 8 lucrum opes C¹⁴C¹⁸. extendat ostendat C¹⁰; recondat C¹⁴; rotondat C¹⁸. 8–9 ad . . . collectam collectam ad dandum L³¹. 9 set *om* L³¹. accipiendum C¹⁰; recipiendum *most MSS incl* C³Ro; capiendum ArL⁶Re³T². 10 dandum errogandum C¹⁴C¹⁸. 9–10 ad (2nd) . . . apertam *om* L³¹. 10 set *om* C¹⁰. 11 iniustorum invictorum L³¹. sicut quasi C¹⁰C¹⁴C¹⁸L³¹. sicut . . . siccabuntur siccabuntur quasi fluvius L³¹. 12 qui quod C¹⁰C¹⁴C¹⁸. cito subito C¹⁸. 13 que quod C¹⁰C¹⁴C¹⁸L³¹. proveniunt provenit C¹⁰C¹⁴L³¹; pervenit C¹⁸. 13–14 perveniant perveniat C¹⁰C¹⁴C¹⁸; proveniat L³¹. 14 accedat excedat C¹⁸; attendat ArRe³T². 15 ergo *om* C¹⁰C¹⁴C¹⁸L³¹. habet . . . vite dampnacionem huius vite habet C¹⁰C¹⁴L³¹; dampnacionem vite habet C¹⁸; damnationem habet vite *most MSS incl* Ro. 16 future in futuro C¹⁰; in futuro C¹⁸.

II.17: 1 Inicium Sufficerent C¹⁸; Sufficiunt L³⁷. aqua . . . panis *trans many MSS incl* C¹⁰C¹⁴C¹⁸L³¹. 3 gulosis non sufficiunt non sufficiunt gulosis L³¹. 3–5 nec (all) non *most MSS incl* C³C¹⁰Ro; et *for 1st* C¹⁴C¹⁸; non *for 2nd and 5th* C¹⁴; non *for 2nd* C¹⁸; non *all but first* L³¹. 3 genera grana *some MSS.* 5 querunt queruntur *most MSS incl* C³L³¹Ro. 6 comparant comparantur *most MSS incl* C³C¹⁰C¹⁴L³¹Ro; comparatur C¹⁸. nutriunt nutriuntur *most MSS incl* C³C¹⁰C¹⁴L³¹Ro. capiunt obesa capiuntur obesa *most MSS incl* C³Ro; obesa capiuntur C¹⁰C¹⁸L³¹; obesa comparantur C¹⁴; adquiruntur offensa D¹; bestie capiuntur O²⁴; obesa capiuntur et cibaria delicata L⁶. 7 coquantur coquuntur *many MSS incl* RoL³¹. 8 parentur parantur *many MSS incl* Ro. 8–9 contundit et colat contendit et colant C¹⁸. 10 saturitas securitas *corrected to* saturitas C¹⁴; satietas L³¹. 11 transeat crescat C¹⁴C¹⁸; transit L³¹D²L³L²⁷L⁴¹Ru¹. ut et C¹⁰L³¹; *om* C¹⁴C¹⁸. appetitum in appetitum L³¹. 12 irritandam irritandum *most MSS incl* C³C¹⁰C¹⁴C¹⁸L³¹; irrigandum *some MSS.* gulam gulam non ad sustinendam gulam C¹⁸. sustentandam -tan- *above line* L²⁰; sustentandum *most MSS incl* C³C¹⁰Ro, *with* -tan- *above line* C¹⁴; sustinendum C¹⁸. 14 explendam explendam pro cum fames constat magno fastidium O²⁶. Ceterum Ecce C¹⁸. breve brevis *most MSS incl* C³C¹⁰C¹⁴C¹⁸L³¹Ro. 16 totidem quatuor C¹⁰L³¹; quatuor *but with* vel totidem *above line* C¹⁴. 16–17 Contempnitur mediocritas *trans*

set vilificat dandum; dat ut lucretur, set non lucratur
ut det. Largus in alieno, set avarus in proprio.
Gulam evacuat ut archam adimpleat; corpus / extenuat ut lucrum extendat. "Manum habet ad dandum collectam, set ad accipiendum porrectam"; ad
dandum clausam, set ad recipiendum apertam. Porro
"substancie iniustorum sicut fluvius siccabuntur,"
quia qui male congregat cito dispergit. Iustum iudicium ut que de malo proveniunt ad malum perveniant, nec accedat ad bonum quod non procedit ex
bono. Avarus ergo habet dampnacionem vite que
nunc est et future.

f. 94v
In Ecclesias-
tico

In Ecclesias-
tico

[17] DE GULA

"Inicium vite hominis aqua et panis et vestimentum
et domus protegens turpitudinem." Nunc autem
gulosis non sufficiunt fructus arborum, nec genera
leguminum, nec radices herbarum, nec pisces maris,
nec bestie terre, nec aves celi, set querunt pigmenta,
comparant aromata, nutriunt altilia, capiunt obesa,
que studiose coquantur arte cocorum, que laute
parentur officio ministrorum. Alius contundit et
colat, alius confundit et conficit, substanciam vertit
in accidens, naturam mutat in artem, ut saturitas
transeat in esuriem, ut fastidium revocet appetitum;
ad irritandam gulam, non ad sustentandam naturam;
non ad necessitatem supplendam, set ad aviditatem
explendam. Ceterum tam breve est gule voluptas ut
spacio loci vix sit quatuor digitorum, spacio tempo-
ris vix sit totidem momentorum. Contempnitur
mediocritas, et superfluitas affectatur. In diversitate

In Ecclesias-
tico

superfluity is pursued. The appetite knows no limit in diversity of foods and variety of tastes, and greediness exceeds measure. But then the stomach is weighed down, the mind is disturbed, the intellect is overcome; thence not prosperity and health, but sickness and death. Hear the opinion of the wise man on this: "Be not greedy in any feasting, and pour not out thyself upon any meat; for in many meats there will be sickness, and by surfeiting many have perished." "Meat for the belly and the belly for the meats: but God shall destroy both it and them."

[18] EXAMPLES AGAINST GLUTTONY

Gluttony demands a costly tribute, but it returns the smallest value, because the more delicate the foods are, the more stinking the excrements are. What goes in vilely comes out vilely, expelling a horrible wind above and below, and emitting an abominable sound. Gluttony closed paradise, sold the birth-right, hanged the baker, beheaded the Baptist. Nabuzardan, chief of cooks, burned the temple and destroyed all Jerusalem. At the banquet Baltasar saw the hand writing against him: "Mane, Thecel, Phares," and he was killed by the Chaldeans the same night. "The people sat down to eat and drink, and they rose up to play," but "yet their meat was in their mouth, and the wrath of God came upon them." "They that were feeding delicately died in the streets." The rich man who "feasted sumptuously every day" "was buried in hell."

[19] OF DRUNKENNESS

What is more unsightly than a drunkard, in whose mouth is a stench, in whose body a trembling; who utters foolish things, betrays secrets; whose reason is

---

C^{10}C^{14}C^{18}L^{31}. 18 **varietate** veritate C^9. **saporum** verborum et saporum L^{31}; verborum AuBuGoILmMu^{5}O^{5}O^{18}Pa^{9}Pa^{11}Pa^{15}; saporum vel ferculorum *above line* C^{14}; ferculorum O^{17}U^4; soporum C^9. **aviditas** ariditas C^{3}Ro. 21 **mors** mors requiretur *above line* C^{14}. 22 **super . . . sapientis** sentenciam sapientis super hoc L^{31}. 25 **obierunt** perierunt et obierunt L^{31}L^{41}LaO^9; perierunt *many MSS incl* C^{14}C^{18}; abierunt BuLmPa^{9}Pa^{11}. 26 **Deus . . . destruet** hunc et hanc Deus destruet C^{14}C^{18}L^{31}.

II.18: *Title* De Exemplo Contra Gulam C^3; *om* C^{18}. 2 **quia** et C^{14}C^{18}L^{31}. **quanto** quanto plus BuGoLmMu^{1}Pa^{5}Pa^{9}Pa^{11}, *one word later* IMu^5. **sunt** *om* C^{14}C^{18}. **tanto** tanto magis C^{10}L^{31}. 3 **Turpiter** Turpius *most MSS incl* C^{3}C^{10}C^{14}C^{18}L^{31}Ro. 6 **pistorem** pastorem C^{18}. 8 **templum** templum Dei C^{14}C^{18}. **Ierusalem totam** *trans* L^{31}. 10 **Thechel** *corrected from* hechel L^{20}. **Phares** Phares quod sonat numerus apensio divisio C^{10}L^{31}; Phares quod sonat numera appende divide C^{14}C^{18}. 11 **Chaldeis** Chaldeis ministris regis C^{10}C^{14}C^{18}; Caldeis ministros regis L^{31}. 13 **erant** erat *most MSS incl* C^3 L^{31}. 15 **viis** viciis C^{10}; viis suis *above line* C^{14}. **epulabatur** vescebatur C^3. 16 **inferno** infernum L^{31}.

II.19: 1 **est** *om most MSS incl* C^{3}C^{10}C^{14}C^{18}L^{31}Ro; potus L^{6}Ru^{1}Wo^2. 2 **promit** promittit *many MSS incl* L^{31}; promittit C^{14} *but with* sive promit *above line*. **cui** cuius Gloss

166

ciborum et varietate saporum aviditas nescit modum, et voracitas excedit mensuram. Set inde gra-
20 vatur stomachus, turbatur sensus, opprimitur intellectus; inde non salus et sanitas, set morbus et mors.
Audi super hoc sentenciam sapientis: "Noli avidus In Ecclesias-
tico
esse in omni epulacione, et non te effundas super
omnem escam; in multis enim escis erit infirmitas, et
25 propter crapulam multi / obierunt." "Esca ventri et f. 95
Apostolus
venter escis: Deus autem et hunc et has destruet."

[18] EXEMPLA CONTRA GULAM

Gula carum tributum exigit, set vilissimum reddit,
quia quanto sunt delicaciora cibaria, tanto fetidiora
sunt stercora. Turpiter egerit quod turpiter ingerit,
superius et inferius horribilem flatum exprimens, et
5 abominabilem sonum emittens. Gula paradisum In Genesi
clausit, primogenita vendidit, suspendit pistorem, Marcus
decollavit Baptistam. Nabuzardan, princeps co- Regum
corum, templum incendit et Ierusalem totam evertit. Balthasar in convivio manum contra se scriben- In Daniele
10 tem aspexit: "Mane, Thechel, Phares," et eadem
nocte interfectus est a Chaldeis. "Sedit populus In Exodo
manducare et bibere, et surrexerunt ludere," set
"adhuc esce eorum erant in ore ipsorum, et ira Dei
ascendit super eos." "Qui vescebantur voluptuose In Trenis
15 interierunt in viis." Dives ille qui "epulabatur co- In Luca
tidie splendide" "sepultus est in inferno."

[19] DE EBRIETATE

Quid turpius ebrioso, cui fetor est in ore, tremor in
corpore; qui promit stulta, prodit occulta; cui mens

taken away, whose face is transformed? "For there is no secret where drunkenness reigneth." "Whom have the well filled cups not made well spoken?" Then wine does not suffice, nor cider, nor beer, but mead, syrup, spiced wine are eagerly prepared with great labor, with not a little care, with the greatest expense. But after that there are fights and brawls, disputes and quarrels. "For wine drunken with excess," as the wise man says, "raiseth quarrel and wrath and many ruins." And Osee: "Fornication and wine and drunkenness take away the understanding." Therefore the Apostle says: "Avoid wine, wherein is luxury." And Solomon: "Wine is an inebriating thing and drunkenness riotous." The son of Rechab and the son of Zachary did not drink wine or cider or anything that could inebriate.

[20] EXAMPLES AGAINST DRUNKENNESS

Drunkenness exposed the private parts, committed incest, killed the son of the king, strangled the head of the army. What Solomon says is therefore true: "They that give themselves to drinking and that club together shall be consumed." And Isaias: "Woe to you that rise up early in the morning to follow drunkenness and to drink till the evening in order to be inflamed with wine. The harp and the lyre and the timbrel and the pipe and wine are in your feasts." "Woe to you that are mighty at drinking wine and stout men at mixing drunkenness." "Behold joy and gladness, killing calves and slaying rams, eating flesh and drinking wine. Let us eat and drink, for tomorrow we die. And it will be revealed to my ears, says the Lord of Hosts, 'if this iniquity

and M²Ma⁴Ph³Wr². 3 **Nullum** Malum L³¹. **enim** enim latet Gloss *and* L³¹; enim est *some MSS.* 4 **quem** quod L³¹. 5 **disertum** desertum C³; desertum et multi pulices quem non fecere misertum *in margin* C¹⁴; discretum C⁹. **non** *(3rd)* cum L³¹. 6 **sicera** *preceded by* ci *marked for expunction in* L²⁰; cisera *some MSS.* **non cervisia** non servicia C¹⁸; *om* L³¹. **conficitur** confiscitur L³¹. 7–8 **non . . . maximo** magna sumptu non modico *most MSS incl* C³C¹⁰C¹⁴C¹⁸L³¹Ro. 8 **contenciones** contemptiones Ro. **et** *om many MSS incl* C¹⁰L³¹; ire C¹⁴C¹⁸. 9 **multum** *corrected from* multatum *in* L²⁰. 10 **sapiens** Salomon C¹⁰C¹⁴C¹⁸ L³¹. 9–10 **multum . . . sapiens** ut ait Salomon multum potatum L³¹. 10–11 **ruinas multas** ruinam multam *many MSS incl* C³; invidias multas L³¹. 11 **Fornicacio** Fornicationes ex eo sunt *many MSS incl* C³; *om* C¹⁸L³¹; *above line* C¹⁴. **et** *(1st) om* C¹⁰C¹⁴C¹⁸L³¹. 12 **ebrietas** ebrietates C¹⁴. **auferunt cor** aufert cor C¹⁰; alisunt cor C⁹; edificat I; aufert *or* auferunt cor populi *a few MSS.* **Propterea** Propter quod C¹⁰C¹⁴C¹⁸L³¹. **dicit** ait L³¹. 13 **in quo** quod C¹⁸. 14 **res** res est *many MSS incl* C³C¹⁰C¹⁸L³¹; est res C¹⁴. **tumultuosa** tumultuosa res *in margin* C¹⁴; multuosa L³¹. **Filius** Filii *most MSS incl* C³C¹⁰C¹⁴C¹⁸L³¹Ro. 15 **Rechab** Iacob C¹⁰L³¹; Rachel C¹⁴R. **filius** filii C¹⁰C¹⁴; *om* L³¹. 16 **poterat** potest L³¹. **biberunt** bibebant C¹⁴C¹⁸.

II.20: *Title* De Exemplo Contra Ebrietatem C³. 1 **verenda** verecundia C¹⁴; verecunda C¹⁸L³¹; verenda Noe *many MSS incl* Ro. **commisit** misit C³. 3 **Salomon ait** *trans* C¹⁰C¹⁴C¹⁸L³¹. 3–4 **et dantes** et vacantes C³; et vocantes *most MSS incl* C¹⁰; cum vacantibus C¹⁸; in vocantibus L³¹. 4 **symbolum** simbola *most MSS incl* C³C¹⁰ C¹⁴C¹⁸L³¹Ro; cimbalis BuIMu⁵Pa⁹Pa¹¹; cybaris L³³Pa⁵, *corrected from* cymbalis Go; cibis AuLm. **consumentur** consumuntur *most MSS incl* C³C¹⁴E¹; consumitur L³¹. **Et** *om* C¹⁰C¹⁴C¹⁸L³¹. 5 **consurgitis** surgitis C¹⁰. **ebrietatem sectandam** miscendam ebrietatem C¹⁰C¹⁸L³¹. 5–6 **potandum** ad potandum L³¹. 6 **vesperum** vesperam *nearly every MS incl* C³C¹⁰C¹⁴C¹⁸L³¹Ro. 7 **et** *(1st) om* C¹⁰C¹⁴C¹⁸. **tympanum . . . tibia** *trans* L³¹. **tibia** tuba C¹Re³T¹T². 9 **miscendam** sectandam C¹⁰L³¹. 10 **leticia** leticiam L³¹. **et** *(2nd) om* C¹⁰C¹⁴C¹⁸L³¹. 11–12 **Comedamus** Commendamus C¹⁸. 12 **revelabitur** revelata est *most MSS incl* C³C¹⁰C¹⁴C¹⁸Ro; revelata L³¹. 13 **auribus . . . Dominus** in auribus meis vox

alienatur, facies transformatur? "Nullum enim secretum ubi regnat ebrietas." "Fecundi calices quém
5   non fecere disertum?" Porro non sufficit vinum, non
sicera, non cervisia, set studiose conficitur mulsum,
syropus, claretum labore multo, sollicitudine non
modica, sumptu maximo. Set inde contenciones et
rixe, lites et iurgia. "Vinum enim multum pota-   In Ecclesias-
tico
10 tum," ut ait sapiens, "irritacionem et iram et ruinas
multas facit." Et Osee: "Fornicacio et vinum et
ebrietas auferunt cor." Propterea dicit Apostolus:
"Fugite vinum, in quo est luxuria." Et Salomon:
"Ebriosa res vinum / et tumultuosa ebrietas." Filius   f. 95v
Ieremias
15 Rechab et filius Zacharie vinum et siceram et omne
quod inebriare poterat non biberunt.

[20] EXEMPLA CONTRA EBRIETATEM

Ebrietas verenda nudavit, incestum commisit, filium
regis occidit, principem exercitus iugulavit. Verum
est ergo quod Salomon ait: "Vacantes potibus et   Salomon
dantes symbolum consumentur." Et Ysaias: "Ve qui   Ysaias
5   consurgitis mane ad ebrietatem sectandam et potandum usque ad vesperum ut vino estuetis. Cythara et
lyra et tympanum et tibia et vinum in conviviis
vestris." "Ve qui potentes estis ad bibendum vinum
et viri fortes ad miscendam ebrietatem." "Ecce
10 gaudium et leticia, occidere vitulos et iugulare
arietes, comedere carnes et bibere vinum. Comedamus et bibamus, cras enim moriemur. Et revelabitur
auribus meis, dicit Dominus Exercituum, 'si dimit-

169

shall be forgiven you till you die'." "Woe to the crown of pride of Ephraim." "The priests and the prophets have been ignorant of judgment." O shame, when the blessing was asked of a certain father at the reciting of the gospel reading, he is reported to have said in a high voice, belching forth the inebriation of the day before and the drunkenness of the night: "May the King of the Angels bless the drink of his servants."

[21] OF LUST

A foul mother produces a fouler daughter. For it is just that "he that is filthy may be filthy still." "They are all adulterers, like an oven heated by the baker. The princes began to be mad with wine." "For a richly filled belly willingly embraces Venus." O extreme foulness of desire, which not only weakens, but debilitates the body; not only defiles the soul, but pollutes the person. "For every sin that a man doth is without his body, but he that committeth fornication sinneth against his own body." Desire and wantonness always precede it, stench and filth always attend, sorrow and repentance always follow. "For the lips of a harlot are like a honeycomb dropping, and her throat is smoother than oil; but her end is as bitter as wormwood and sharp as a two-edged sword."

[22] OF THE UNIVERSALITY OF LUST

The enemy is a familiar, living not far away, but nearby, not outside, but inside; for "his force is in his loins, and his strength in the navel of his belly." It

Domini *many MSS incl* C³; in auribus nostris vox Domini C¹⁰C¹⁸; in auribus vestris hec vox Domini C¹⁴; in auribus Domini L³¹; in auribus vestris vox Domini *most MSS.* 13-14 **dimittetur** dimittatur C¹⁰C¹⁴C¹⁸L³¹. 14 **moriamini** moriamur L³¹. 15 **Sacerdos** Sacerdotes C¹⁸. 16 **nescierunt** nescierunt ebrietatem L³¹. **a vino** animo E¹. 17 **iudicium** iudicia C¹⁸; Dominum O³¹. 17-18 **pudor** dolor C¹⁰C¹⁴L³¹. 18 **leccionem** *om* L³¹. 19 **patre** presbitero BuD¹GoLmO²¹Pa⁵Pa⁸Pa⁹Pa¹¹; priore C¹Es². **peteretur** petebatur L³¹. **hesternam** nocturnam C¹⁰C¹⁴C¹⁸L³¹. 20 **et nocturnam** et *above line expunged, then both words added in margin* L²⁰; nocturnam *om* C¹⁰C¹⁴C¹⁸L³¹. **eructuans** *om* L³¹. 21 **servorum** servorum dixisse L³¹Ph¹.

II.21: 1 **Porro** *om* C¹⁰C¹⁸L³¹; *in margin* C¹⁴. **filiam** puerum C¹⁴; ebrietas filiam L³¹. 3 **adulterantes** adulatores Re³T². 3-4 **succensus a coquente** accensus a coquente C¹⁰; a coquente C¹⁴; coquente accensus C¹⁸; a coquente succensus L³¹. 4 **a vino** animo *many MSS.* 4-5 **Venter . . . amplexatur** Venter enim mero estuans de facili spumat in libidinem C¹⁴, enim *om* C¹⁸; *original lines added in margin of* C¹⁴. 5 **opipatus** opipare satur *most MSS incl* C³L³¹; opere satur C¹⁰; opido sat *both in margin* C¹⁴; *many variants incl* eorum oppiparum, opiparetur, oppresatus, saturatur, saturatus, vino saturatus, opipare id est splendide satur. 6 **extrema** externa Pa⁴. **libidinis** veneris Pa⁵. 7 **set** set eciam Gloss *and* L³¹Bv²C⁴C⁵C¹⁹C²²EvL²⁷O⁷Pa¹⁵Ru². 9 **suum** *om many MSS incl* C¹⁰C¹⁴C¹⁸L³¹. 11 **ardor et** *om* C¹⁴. 12 **comitantur** concomitantur C¹⁸. 12-13 **semper . . . penitencia** semper . . . penitencia *post* et cetera Gloss; pena et dolor sequuntur semper C¹⁴C¹⁸L³¹; penitencia et dolor secuntur semper E¹, *followed by* Boetius Quid dicam de voluptatibus seculi quarum appetitus anxietas sacietas vero penitencia L⁹L¹⁴, *also in* E¹ *but not a group reading, in margin* L⁴⁵. 13 **enim** *om* C¹⁴C¹⁸L³¹. 14 **oleo . . . eius** guttur eius oleo C¹⁰. 15 **autem** *om* C¹⁰C¹⁴C¹⁸L³¹. **illius** *corrected from* eius *in* L²⁰; eius *many MSS incl* C¹⁴C¹⁸. **sicut** quasi C¹⁰C¹⁴C¹⁸L³¹.

II.22: 1 **Familiaris . . . inimicus** Ipsa est familiaris inimicus L³¹. 2 **eius** eius est C¹⁴C¹⁸. 3 **lumbis** uberibus L⁴⁰. **est** eius *most MSS incl* C³C¹⁰C¹⁴C¹⁸L³¹V². **illius** *in margin*

tetur hec iniquitas vobis donec moriamini'." "Ve
15 corone superbie Effraym." "Sacerdos et propheta
nescierunt pre ebrietate: absorti sunt a vino, nescierunt videntem, ignoraverunt iudicium." Proh pudor, cum ad pronunciandam evangelicam leccionem
a quodam patre benedictio peteretur, hesternam
20 crapulam et nocturnam ebrietatem eructuans, fertur
alta voce dixisse: "Potum servorum suorum benedicat Rex Angelorum."

[21] DE LUXURIA

Porro turpis mater filiam generat turpiorem. Iustum   In Apocalipsi
est enim ut "qui in sordibus est sordescat adhuc."
"Omnes adulterantes, quasi clibanus succensus a   Osee
coquente. Ceperunt principes furere a vino." "Ven-
5 ter enim opipatus libenter Venerem amplexatur." O
extrema libidinis turpitudo, que non solum effeminat, set corpus enervat; non solum maculat animam,
set fedat personam. "Omne namque peccatum   Apostolus
quodcumque / fecerit homo extra corpus suum est,   f. 96
10 qui autem fornicatur in corpus suum peccat." Semper illam precedunt ardor et petulancia, semper
comitantur fetor et immundicia, semper secuntur
dolor et penitencia. "Favus enim distillans labia   Salomon
meretricis, et nitidius oleo guttur eius; novissima
15 autem illius amara sicut absinthium et acuta quasi
gladius biceps."

[22] DE GENERALITATE LUXURIE

Familiaris est inimicus, habitans non procul, set
prope, non exterius, set interius; nam "virtus eius in

171

is never put to flight except when it is avoided, never killed except when it is weakened. It requires freedom and abundance for its cause, but for its effect it finds the skill and the opportunity. It corrupts every age, confounds each sex, dissolves every order, overthrows every rank. For it attacks the old and the young, men and women, the learned and the simple, the higher and the lower, finally even priests, who embrace Venus at night, worship the Virgin in the morning. Disgraceful to mention, but most disgraceful to do, let it be allowed to be mentioned in order that it not be pleasing to be done: at night they arouse the son of Venus on a bed, in the morning they offer the Son of the Virgin on an altar.

[23] OF THE DIVERSE KINDS OF LUST

Who is able to set forth sufficiently the many kinds of lust? For it overthrew Pentapolis along with the adjoining region, destroyed Sichem along with its people, killed Juda's sons Her and Onan, stabbed the Jew and the Madianite woman with a dagger, annihilated the tribe of Benjamin for the wife of the Levite, destroyed in war the sons of Heli the priest; it killed Urias, murdered Amnon, stoned the elders; it cursed Ruben, seduced Samson, corrupted Solomon. What is read is therefore true: "Many have perished by the beauty of a woman." For "wine and women make wise men fall off." It "hath cast

L[20]; eius *most MSS incl* C[10]C[18]L[31]V[2]; *om* C[14]. 5 **mactatur** debilitatur C[18]. **cum** cum caro C[14]C[18]. 6 **libertatem** liberalitatem C[10]C[14]C[18]. **reperit** recipit C[10]C[14]C[18]; exigit Wo[2]. 7 **adiacenciam** ad iactanciam C[3]; iactanciam C[10]C[14]C[18]L[31]. 8 **omnem** *(1st)* hec omnem C[10]C[18]. **sexum** sensum C[3]C[10]C[14]C[18]. 12 **amplexantur** amplexuntur C[3]; amplexantur et C[10]C[14]C[18]L[31]. 13 **dictu set** dictu turpius auditu C[10]C[14]C[18]L[31]. 14 **ut** id quod C[18]. **filium** filiam C[14]C[18]. 15 **Virginis** hominis L[17]O[31].

II.23: 1-2 **Quis . . . explicare** Item sunt enim sodomite raptores immundi fornicatores incestuosi molles seu raptores et huiusmodi Bn. 1 **luxurie** eius *most MSS incl* C[3]C[10]C[14]C[18]L[31]Ro. 2 **enim** enim fornicatores MoO[25]Re[3]T[2]. **adiacenti** adiacente L[31]. 3 **subvertit** submersit C[10]C[14]C[18]; subvertit raptores BnR; subvertit id est sodomitas C[3]; scilicet sodomitas *near this point in many MSS.* **Sychem** Sichem raptorem Re[3]T[2]; Sichem fornicatem raptorem Bm[1]; Sichen stupratores *in margin* L[24]. **interemit** interemit scilicet sodomitas Du[2]; interemit immundos BnL[39]O[3], *above line* L[25]L[29]; scilicet raptores *near this point in many MSS.* **Her** molles Her O[21], molles *in margin* L[24]. 4 **Onam** Onam et Sellam L[31]. **percussit** percussit fornicatores L[39]O[21]RRe[3]T[2], *in margin* L[24], *above line* L[25]; percussit adulteros Bn; percussit scilicet immundos *many MSS.* **et** *(2nd)* id est C[3]. 5 **transfodit** transfodit stupratores O[21]R; transfodit adulteros *above line* L[29]; scilicet fornicatores *or* fornicantes *or* fornicationes *near this point in many MSS.* **tribum** triphum L[31]; tribum raptores *in margin* L[24]. **Beniamin** *final* -n *corrected from* -m L[20]; Beniamin in Iudeos scrupatores ArRe[3]T[1]T[2]; Beniamin invidos stupratores fornicatores et raptores Ph[1]O[25], *with Iuda for* invidos *and* id est *before* fornicatores Du[4]. 6 **delevit** delevit scilicet adulatores O[31]; delevit inmundos O[21]; delevit stupratores L[12], *above line* L[25]L[29]; scilicet adulteros *near this point in many MSS.* **Hely** Levi *a few MSS;* Hely adulteros *in margin* L[24]. 6-7 **prostravit** prostravit id est stupratores C[3]; prostravit scilicet stupratores *some MSS;* prostravit adulteros O[9]O[21]; prostravit adulteros immundos R. 7 **occidit** percussit Au[1]; percussit incestuosos O[21]; occidit incestuosos *above line* O[29], *in margin* Bv[2]; occidit Etheum percussit Mu[5]. **interfecit** interfecit incestuosos *many MSS incl* C[3], *in margin* L[24]; molles *(above line)* interfecit L[25]. 7-8 **presbiteros** populos C[10]; molles presbiteros L[39], molles *above line* L[29]; sacerdotes *many MSS.* 8 **hec** *om* C[14]L[31]. **Ruben** urbem *a few MSS;* Ruben inmundos *in margin* L[24]. 9 **seduxit Salomonem** *om* L[31]. **ergo** *om* C[10]C[14]C[18]L[31]. 10 **perierunt** obierunt C[10]. 11 **Nam** *om* C[10]C[14]C[18]. **faciunt** fanc *(sic)* L[31]. 11-12 **sapientes**

lumbis est, et fortitudo illius in umbilico ventris
eius." Nunquam fugatur nisi cum fugitur, nunquam
5   mactatur nisi cum maceratur. Ad causam exigit
libertatem et habundanciam, set reperit ad effectum
facultatem et adiacenciam. Hec omnem etatem corrumpit, omnem sexum confundit, omnem ordinem
solvit, omnem gradum pervertit. Invadit enim senes
10 et iuvenes, mares et feminas, prudentes et simplices,
superiores et inferiores, ad extremum eciam sacerdotes, qui nocte Venerem amplexantur, mane Vir-
ginem venerantur. Turpe dictu, set turpissimum
actu, dici liceat ut agi non libeat: nocte filium
15 Veneris agitant in cubili, mane Filium Virginis of-
ferunt in altari.

[23] DE DIVERSIS SPECIEBUS LUXURIE

Quis luxurie multiplices species sufficienter valeat
explicare? Hec enim Pentapolim cum adiacenti re-   Sodomitas
gione subvertit, Sychem cum populo interemit, Her   Raptores
et Onam filios Iude percussit, Iudeum et Madianiti-   Immundos
5   dem pugione transfodit, tribum Beniamin pro uxore   Stupratores
Levite delevit, filios Hely sacerdotis in bello pro-   Adulteros
stravit; hec Uriam occidit, Amon interfecit, / pres-   Incestuosos
biteros lapidavit; hec Ruben maledixit, Sansonem   f. 96v
seduxit, Salomonem pervertit. Verum est ergo quod
10 legitur: "Propter speciem mulieris multi perierunt."   In Ecclesias-
Nam "vinum et mulieres apostatare faciunt sa-   tico

173

down many wounded, and the strongest have been slain by it; its house is the woe of hell, reaching even to the inner chambers of death." It weakens the powers, diminishes the senses, consumes days, squanders wealth.

[24] OF INTERCOURSE AGAINST NATURE

This causes a shameful metamorphosis, which the Apostle is not embarrassed to name: "For this cause," he says, "God delivered them up to shameful affections. For their women have changed the natural use into that which is against nature. And in like manner the men, leaving the natural use of woman, have burned in their lusts one towards another, men with men, working that which is filthy." What is filthier than this filth? What more criminal than this crime? In the law the copulation of a male with a male and the intercourse of a man with a beast are joined as equals. For thus it is read in Leviticus: "Thou shalt not lie with mankind in womanly intercourse, because it is an abomination. Thou shalt not copulate with any beast, neither shalt thou be defiled with it." The same punishment is written down for each: "If anyone lie with a man in womanly intercourse, each hath committed an abomination; let them be put to death. He that shall copulate with a beast, let him be put to death; the beast also ye shall kill." He who has ears to hear, let him hear; on the contrary, he who is foolish, let him recover his senses.

[25] OF THE PUNISHMENT OF THIS CRIME

The punishment showed what this sin deserved: "For the Lord rained upon

sapientes et arguunt sensatos Ro, *in margin* C[14]; homines D[5]; hominem I; homines vel sapientes L[27]O[24]. 13 **quique** quoque C[10]. **ve** vie *nearly every MS incl* C[3]C[10]C[14]C[18]L[31]Ro. 14 **in interiora** inferiora *many MSS incl* C[3]C[10]C[14]C[18]L[31]. **mortis** montis C[3]; mortis ventris *above line* C[14]. 15 **sensus** sensum L[31]. **consumit** comminuit L[31]. 15-16 **effundit** confundit C[14]; diffundit C[18].

II.24: *Combined with II.23 in* L[31]. 1 **Hec** *om* C[10]L[31]; Nec C[18]. 1-2 **tamen** *om* C[14]C[18]. 2 **Apostolus** pluribus ArRe[3]T[2]. **non** *om* L[31]. 3 **tradidit** *in margin* L[20]. **illos** vos C[18]L[31]. **Deus** Dominus C[14]; *om* C[18]L[31]. **passiones** passionem C[14]. 4 **commutaverunt** mutaverunt C[14]; commutatem commutaverunt L[31]; transmutaverunt O[3]. 6-7 **relicto . . . masculi** *om* C[18]E[1]L[31]; *in margin* C[14]. 7 **exarserunt** exarserit C[3]; erraverunt *in margin* C[14]. **in** (2nd) *om most MSS incl* C[3]C[14]Ro. 8 **turpitudinem** turpiter C[18]; turpiter *corrected to* turpitudinem *above line* C[14]. **operantes** operantur C[18]L[31]; operantur *corrected to* operantes C[14]. **hac** ac C[14]C[18]. 10 **concubitus** coitus C[10]C[14]C[18]. 13 **femineo** feminino L[31]. 13-14 **quia . . . eo** *om* C[10]L[31]. 15 **Utrique** Uterque C[10]C[14]C[18]; Utrique enim L[31]. **par** pari C[10]. **subscribitur** subtribuitur C[3]; describitur C[10]C[14]L[31]. **dormierit** dormit C[14]C[18]. 16 **femineo** feminino L[31]. **uterque** utrique *most MSS incl* C[10]C[14]L[31]V[2]. 16-17 **operatus est nefas** operati sunt nephas *most MSS incl* C[3]C[10]C[14]C[18]Ro; sunt nephas operati L[31]. 17 **morte moriantur** morte moriatur C[3]; *om* C[10]L[31]. **iumento** iumento vel cum aliquo bruto C[14], *with* cum *omitted* C[18]. 18 **coierit** dormierit C[10]L[31].

II.25: *Title* Penitentia *for* Pena C[3]. 3 **a Domino** *expunged* C[14]; *om* L[31]V[2]. **celo**

pientes." Hec "multos vulneratos deiecit, et fortis-
simi quique interfecti sunt ab ea; ve inferi domus
eius, penetrantes in interiora mortis." Hec vires
15   enervat, sensus diminuit, dies consumit, opes effundit.

[24] DE COITU CONTRA NATURAM

Hec ignominiosam morphosym operatur, quam ta-
men Apostolus non confunditur nominare: "Prop-   Ad Romanos
terea," inquit, "tradidit illos Deus in passiones igno-
minie.   Nam   femine   eorum   commutaverunt
5   naturalem usum in eum qui est contra naturam.
Similiter et masculi, relicto naturali usu femine,
exarserunt in desideriis suis in invicem, masculi in
masculos, turpitudinem operantes." Quid hac tur-
pitudine turpius? Quid hoc crimine criminosius? In
10   lege quasi paria coniunguntur concubitus maris cum
masculo et coitus hominis cum iumento. Sic enim
legitur in Levitico: "Cum masculo non commisesebe-
ris coitu femineo, quia abominacio est. Cum omni
pecore non coibis, nec maculaberis cum eo."
15   Utrique par pena subscribitur: "Qui dormierit,"
inquit, "cum masculo coitu femineo, uterque operatus est nefas; morte moriantur. Qui cum iumento
coierit, morte moriatur; pecus quoque occidite."
Qui habet aures audiendi, audiat; immo, qui desipit,
20   resipiscat.

[25] DE PENA HUIUS SCELERIS

Pena docuit quid hec culpa promeruit: "Pluit enim   In Genesi
Dominus super Sodomam et Gomorram sulphur et

Sodom and Gomorrha brimstone and fire from the Lord out of heaven." The Lord did not wish to entrust the execution of this punishment to any of the angels or of men, but reserved to himself the avenging of this crime, according to this saying: "Vengeance is mine, and I will repay." And therefore the Lord rained from the Lord, that is to say from himself, not rain or dew, but brimstone and fire—brimstone because of or upon the stench of lust, fire upon the burning of desire—so that the punishment might be similar to the sin. Nor is "sent" said, but "rained," so that with the word itself he might indicate the magnitude and vastness of the punishment. His eye spared no one, but destroyed them all at the same time. He also changed the wife of Lot, who looked back, into a statue of salt; he turned not only the cities, but all the region around into a dead sea and a valley of salt. "It is therefore a fearful thing to fall into the hands of the living God": the greater the patience he shows of his long suffering, the harsher the vengeance he brings of his severity.

[26] OF THE AMBITIOUS MAN

And thus the covetous man gathers riches and the avaricious man preserves them, the gluttonous man tastes delights and the lustful man practices them, the ambitious man pursues honors and the proud man praises them. But the ambitious man is always fearful, always attentive, lest he say or do something that has power to displease in the eyes of men. He simulates humility, feigns honesty, exhibits affability, shows friendliness, follows and complies, honors everybody, inclines to all, frequents courts, visits magnates, rises and embraces, applauds and fawns. Well does he know that verse: "And if there is no dust, shake off none anyhow." He is prompt and eager where he might

dominico celo L³¹. **Noluit** Noluit enim C¹⁰C¹⁴C¹⁸L³¹. **cuiquam** cuidam L³¹. 5 **huius** huius pene huius L³¹Du³. 6 **reservavit** om L³¹. **Michi vindictam** Mea est ultio most MSS incl C³C¹⁰C¹⁴C¹⁸L³¹Ro. 7 **retribuam** retribuam dicit Dominus C¹⁰C¹⁴C¹⁸; retribuam dicit Deus L³¹; retribuam eis Ro. **Dominus** om C¹⁴; Deus L³¹. 7-8 **a Domino** a Domino de celo C¹⁰C¹⁴C¹⁸; de dominico celo L³¹. 8 **videlicet** a preceding id expunged L²⁰; scilicet C¹⁴; id est C¹⁸. **semetipso** seipso most MSS incl C³C¹⁰C¹⁸L³¹Ro. 9 **propter vel super** vel super in margin L²⁰; super most MSS incl C³C¹⁰C¹⁴C¹⁸Ro; om L³¹. 10 **super** om L³¹. 11 **similis esset** trans C¹⁸L³¹. 13 **pene notaret** trans C¹⁰C¹⁴C¹⁸L³¹. 15 **respexit** aspexit C¹⁴C¹⁸L³¹. 16-17 **circa regionem** regionem L³¹; regionem circumiacentem V². 17-18 **et . . . convertit** et vallem silvarum convertit many MSS incl C³; convertit et vallem salinarum E¹; convertit convallem salinarum L³¹. 18 **est igitur** est ergo C¹⁰L³¹; ergo est C¹⁴C¹⁸. 19 **maiorem . . . longanimitatis** sue longanimitatis maiorem C¹⁰C¹⁴C¹⁸L³¹.

II.26: 1 **Opes** Spes corrected to Opes C¹⁴; Spes some MSS. **itaque** ita C¹⁸; utique L³¹. **et** cupidus et AuGoILm. 2 **et** superbiam et BuGoLmPa⁵Pa⁹Pa¹¹; superbiam I. 3-4 **affectat . . . autem** affectat et superbus extollitur Ambiciosus C³; om C¹⁰; affectat C¹⁸; affectat also in C¹⁴, with the rest in margin; affectat Ambiciosus L³¹. 5 **in** om L³¹. 6 **valeat displicere** displiceat C¹⁴C¹⁸L³¹. 6-7 **Humilitatem . . . mentitur** Simulat honestatem mentitur humilitatem C¹⁰, with Similat for Simulat C¹⁴; Similis at honestatem mentitur humilitatem C¹⁸; Simulat humilitatem mentitur honestatem L³¹. 8 **subsequitur** sequitur C¹⁰C¹⁴C¹⁸L³¹. 11 **Bene** Unde many MSS incl C¹⁸L³¹. **nullus . . . pulvis** trans many MSS incl C³C¹⁰C¹⁴. 13 **tepidus** trepidus C¹⁴C¹⁸E¹. 15 **ut (2nd)** et C¹⁴C¹⁸E¹L³¹. 16

ignem a Domino de celo." Noluit Dominus cuiquam
angelorum vel hominum execucionem huius pene
committere, set sibi ipsi vindictam huius sceleris
reservavit, secundum illud: "Michi vindictam, et
ego retri- / -buam." Et ideo pluit Dominus a Domino, videlicet a semetipso, non imbrem vel rorem,
sed sulphur et ignem—sulphur propter vel super
fetorem luxurie, ignem super ardorem libidinis—
quatinus pena similis esset culpe. Nec "misisse"
dicitur, set "pluisse," quatinus ipso verbo magnitudinem et habundanciam pene notaret. Nemini pe-
percit oculus eius, set omnes simul extinxit. Uxorem
quoque Loth, que retro respexit, in statuam salis
mutavit; nec solum urbes, set omnem circa regionem in mare mortuum et vallem salinarum convertit. "Horrendum est igitur incidere in manus Dei
viventis": qui quanto maiorem sue longanimitatis
exhibet pacienciam, tanto duriorem sue severitatis
infert vindictam.

In Deutero-
nomio
f. 97

Apostolus

[26] DE AMBICIOSO

Opes itaque cupidus congregat et avarus conservat,
voluptates gulosus degustat et luxuriosus exercet,
honores ambiciosus affectat et superbus extollit.
Ambiciosus autem semper est pavidus, semper at-
tentus, ne quid dicat vel faciat quod in oculis hominum valeat displicere. Humilitatem simulat, honestatem mentitur, affabilitatem exhibet, benignitatem
ostendit, subsequitur et obsequitur, cunctos honorat,
universis inclinat, frequentat curias, visitat opti-
mates, assurgit et amplexatur, applaudit et adulatur.
Bene novit illud poeticum: "Et si nullus erit pulvis,
tamen excute nullum." Promptus et fervidus ubi

presume to please, negligent and lukewarm where he might expect to displease. He condemns evil things, detests injurious things, but approves and condemns different things with different people so that he will be judged capable, so that he will be reputed agreeable, so that he will be praised by all, so that he will be approved by each. And behold, he sustains a grave struggle within himself, and a hard conflict, while iniquity pushes his mind and ambition restrains his hand, and what the former suggests be done, the latter does not permit to be done. Yet the mother and the daughter, iniquity and ambition, conspire with each other: for the mother exists in the open, and the daughter does not resist in private. The one in fact demands for herself a public place, the other a secret place. The ambitious man bargains concerning the preeminence that he seeks, and says: "O when will he rule who is stern in justice, pious in mercy, who does not deviate for love or hate, who is not corrupted by request or reward, who trusts in the faithful and accedes to suppliants, who is humble and kind, generous and mild, constant and patient, wise and astute?"

[27] OF EXCESSIVE DESIRE

If by chance he does not profit by this practice, he turns to another. He calls Simon and comes to Giezi; through the latter he strives to gain from the former what he is not able to obtain by himself. He begs and promises, offers and pays. O shame! The favor that he was not able to get for nothing he strives to get by villainy. Nor does he stop with this, but pursues and violently seizes honor, and impudently snatches rank; he is puffed up by the voice of friends, by the support of neighbors, and by such a fire for domination, such a desire to be in authority, that he does not tremble at division, does not dread scandal. But leprosy struck Giezi, and Simon perished with his money;

laudetur laudem L31. **omnibus** hominibus *many MSS incl* C3C10; hominibus accipiat L31C21. 17 **singulis** cunctis C10C14L31. 17–18 **gravem . . . sustinet** gravem sustinet C10; sustinet gravem C18L31, *with* intus se *in margin* C14; gravem intus se sustinet *many MSS*. 18 **difficilemque** difficilem C18, *with* que *above line* C14. 19 **pulsat animum** *trans* L31. **manum** malum Du3Re3T2. 20 **illa** *om* C10. **faciendum** ad faciendum C10C14C18. **hec** hoc *many MSS incl* L31. 22 **iniquitas** iniquitas scilicet C10. **mater in aperto** in aperto mater C10C14C18L31. **subsistit** exigit C18. 23 **vero** ergo *most MSS incl* C3C10C14C18L31. **vendicat sibi** *trans* L31. 25 **ambit** arabit L17O31. 25–26 **quando principabitur** quando principabatur L31; quam principaliter C9. 26 **sit** est L31. 28 **corrumpatur** corrumpitur C10C14C18; corrumpitur L31. **credat fidelibus** credelibus L31. 29 **supplicibus** simplicibus *many MSS incl* C10C14C18L31. 30 **et (2nd)** *om* L31.

II.27: *Title* De Nimia Concupiscentia Ambitionis C3Ro, *with last two words trans* C18; De Fraude Ambiciosorum C10; De Fraude Ambicionis C14. 1 **forte** forsan *many MSS incl* C3C10L31. 2 **Advocat** Adducat L31. 3 **valet** prevalet *most MSS incl* C3C10C14C18L31. 4 **pudor** dolor C14C18E1L31. 5 **nephas** fas et nephas *most MSS incl* C3C10C14C18L31. 6 **adipisci nititur** *trans most MSS incl* C3C10C14L31Ro; adipisci contendit C18. **desistit** desinit C3. 6–7 **insistit . . . invadit** *trans* L31. 7 **impudenter** inprudenter *many MSS incl* C18L31BuGoILmPa9Pa11. **arripit** ambit C10C14C18L31; accipit *some MSS.* 8 **dignitatem** integritatem BuGoILmPa9Pa11. **suffragio** suffragia L31. 8–9 **subsidio propinquorum** presidio propinquorum *most MSS incl* C3Ro; *trans* C10C14C18L31. 9 **tantoque** tanto enim C14C18L31. **dominacionis** damnationis *many MSS;* donationis I. **inflatur** inflammatur *most MSS incl* C3C10C14C18L31Ro. **tanta** tantaque C10C14C18L31. 10 **presidendi** possidendi C18. 11 **et** *om* C10C14C18. 12 **autem** *om most MSS incl* C10C14C18L31Ro. 12–13 **complici-**

178

placere cognoverit, remissus et tepidus ubi putaverit
displicere. Improbat mala, detestatur iniqua, set alia
cum aliis probat et improbat ut iudicetur idoneus, ut
reputetur acceptus, ut laudetur ab omnibus, ut a
singulis approbetur. Et ecce, gravem intra se sustinet pugnam, difficilemque / conflictum, dum ini- f. 97v
quitas pulsat animum et ambicio continet manum,
et quod illa suggerit faciendum, hec fieri non per-
mittit. Colludunt tamen ad invicem mater et filia,
iniquitas et ambicio: nam mater in aperto subsistit,
et in occulto filia non resistit. Hec vero vendicat sibi
publicum, illa secretum. Ambiciosus libenter agit de
principatu quem ambit, et dicit: "O quando principabitur ille qui severus sit in iusticia, pius in misericordia, qui non deviet amore vel odio, qui non
corrumpatur prece vel precio, qui credat fidelibus et
adquiescat supplicibus, qui sit humilis et benignus,
largus et mansuetus, constans et patiens, sapiens et
astutus?"

[27] DE NIMIA CONCUPISCENCIA

Si forte hac arte non proficit, recurit ad aliam.
Advocat Symonem et accedit ad Gyezi; per hunc ab
illo nititur emere quod per se non valet optinere.
Supplicat et promittit, offert et tribuit. Proh pudor!
Graciam quam gratis adipisci non potuit per nephas
adipisci nititur. Nec desistit adhuc, set insistit et
invadit violenter honorem, et impudenter arripit
dignitatem; amicorum suffragio, subsidio propinquo-
rum, tantoque dominacionis inflatur ardore, tanta
libidine presidendi, ut scisma non horreat, scan-
dalum non formidet. Set Gyezi lepra percussit, et In Regum
In Actibus
Apostolorum
In Libro
Numeri
Symon periit cum pecunia; Chore autem cum com-

moreover fire consumed Core along with his accomplices; the earth swallowed up Dathan and Abiron alive. "And so let no one take the honor to himself but him that is called by God, like Aaron."

[28] AN EXAMPLE OF AN AMBITIOUS MAN

A clear example of ambition is found in Absalom, who, when he aspired to the kingdom, "made himself a chariot and horsemen and fifty men to run before him. And rising up early, Absalom stood by the entrance of the gate, and any man who had business to come to the king's judgment he called to him and said: 'Of what city art thou?' Answering, he said: 'I thy servant of a tribe of Israel'. Absalom answered him: 'Thy words seem to me just and good, but there is no man appointed by the king to hear thee'. And Absalom said: 'Who would make me judge over the land, that all that have business might come to me and I might judge them justly?' But when any man came to him and saluted him, he put forth his hand and, taking him, kissed him. And this he did to all Israel that came for judgment to be heard by the king, and he enticed the hearts of the men of Israel." And when Absalom had gone to Hebron, "he sent spies unto all the tribes of Israel, saying: 'As soon as you shall hear the sound of the trumpet, say ye: "King Absalom reigneth in Hebron"'." And "there was a strong conspiracy formed, and the people running together increased with Absalom."

bus -ci- *added above line* L^{20}. 13 **suis** *om most MSS incl* C^{3}Ro. **absumpsit** consumpsit C^{10}C^{14}C^{18}L^{31}; assumpsit *most MSS incl* Ro. **Dathan** C^{10}; et Dathan *most MSS incl* Ro C^3. 14 **itaque** quidem L^{31}. **assumat** sumat *many MSS incl* C^{14}.

II.28: *Title* Contra Fraudem Ambiciosorum C^{10}; Exempla Contra Ambicionem C^{14}. 1 **Liquidum** Si quid non C^{18}; Si quidem *many MSS incl* L^{31}. **ambicionis** ambitiosis C^3. 2-3 **currum** currus *many MSS incl* L^{31}V^2. 4 **consurgens** con- *above line* L^{20}. 4-5 **iuxta** intra L^{31}. 5 **virum** *om* C^{10}. **habebat** herebat C^{18}; hebat L^{31}. 6 **regis iudicium** *trans* C^{10}C^{14}C^{18}L^{31}. 6-7 **ad se et** ei C^{18}. 7-8 **respondens aiebat** respond*ebat* L^{31}. 8 **una** vera L^{31}. **ego** ego sum *most MSS incl* C^{3}C^{10}C^{14}C^{18}L^{31}Ro. 8-9 **Responditque** Respondebatque *most MSS incl* C^{3}Ro; Respondebat C^{10}C^{14}C^{18}L^{31}. 10 **iusti . . . boni** *trans most MSS incl* C^{3}C^{14}C^{18}L^{31}Ro. **te audiat** *trans* C^{14}C^{18}L^{31}. 11 **rege** lege L^{31}. **Dixitque** Dicebatque *most MSS incl* C^{3}C^{10}L^{31}; Et subiunxit C^{14}C^{18}; Dicebatque ei Ro. 11-12 **iudicem** iudicem vel principem *above line* C^{14}. 13 **negocium** negocium et iudicium C^{14}. **iudicem** iudicari L^{31}. **Set** Sed et C^3; Et C^{14}C^{18}. 13-14 **accederet** accederent C^{14}C^{18}E^{1}L^{31}; ascenderent *a few MSS*. 14 **homo** *om* C^{10}C^{14}C^{18}L^{31}. **salutaret** salutarent C^{10}C^{14}C^{18}L^{31}. **illum** C^{10}; eum *most MSS incl* C^{3}Ro; eum *corrected to* illum *above line* C^{14}. **extendebat** extendit C^{3}C^{10}C^{14}C^{18}L^{31}. 15 **et . . . illum** et apprehendens eum osculabatur C^3; *om* C^{10}; apprehendens deosculabatur C^{14}; et apprehendens eos deosculabatur C^{18}; et apprehendens osculabatur eos L^{31}; et apprehendens osculabatur eum *most MSS incl* V^2. 16 **Faciebatque hec** Faciebatque Absolon C^{10}; Hec faciebat Absolon C^{14}; Hoc faciebat Absalon C^{18}; Faciebat hec Absalon L^{31}. 16-18 **qui . . . Israel** *om* L^{31}. 16 **veniebat ad** habebat C^{10}C^{14}C^{18}. 17-18 **corda virorum** viros, *with* vel corda virorum *above line* C^{14}; vires C^{18}. 18 **Absalon** *a false start of* Abssi *for* Absalon *expunged* L^{20}. 19 **in . . . tribus** universis tribubus C^{10}C^{14}; universis tribus C^{18}; in omnibus tribubus L^{31}. 20 **ut** cum C^{10}C^{14}C^{18}L^{31}. 21 **Regnavit** Regnabit C^{18}. **Rex** *om nearly every MS incl* C^{3}C^{10}C^{14}C^{18}L^{31}Ro. 22 **coniuracio valida** *trans* C^{14}C^{18}; coniunctio valida L^{31}L^{23}. **populusque** et populus C^{14}C^{18}. **concurrens** occurrens C^{18}.

plicibus suis ignis absumpsit; Dathan et Abyron
terra vivos absorbuit. "Nullus itaque sibi assumat Ad Hebreos
15 honorem set qui vocatur a Deo, tanquam Aaron."

[28] EXEMPLUM DE AMBICIOSO

Liquidum ambicionis exemplum reperitur in Absa-
lone, qui, cum aspiraret ad regnum, "fecit sibi cur- In Regum
rum et equites et quinquaginta viros qui precederent
eum. Et mane consurgens, Absalon stabat iux-
5   ta / introitum porte, et omnem virum qui habebat f. 98
negocium ut veniret ad regis iudicium, vocabat ad se
et dicebat: 'De qua civitate es tu?' Qui, respondens,
aiebat: 'Ex una tribu Israel ego servus tuus'. Responditque ei Absalon: 'Videntur michi sermones tui
10 iusti et boni, set non est qui te audiat constitutus a
rege'. Dixitque Absalon: 'Quis me constituat iudicem super terram, ut ad me veniant omnes qui
habent negocium et iuste iudicem?' Set cum accederet ad eum homo et salutaret illum, extendebat
15 manum suam et, apprehendens, osculabatur illum.
Faciebatque hec omni Israeli qui veniebat ad iudicium ut audiretur a rege, et sollicitabat corda virorum Israel." Cumque abisset Absalon in Ebron,
"misit exploratores in universas tribus Israel, dicens:
20 'Statim ut audieritis clangorem buccine, dicite:
"Regnavit Rex Absalon in Ebron"'." Et "facta est
coniuracio valida, populusque concurrens augebatur
cum Absalon."

But assume that a man is raised up on high, is carried to the summit. His cares increase, his anxieties pile up, his fasts are extended, his sleepless periods are prolonged. Through these things his nature is corrupted, his spirit is weakened, his sleep is taken away, his appetite is lost, his strength is debilitated, his body is made thin. And thus failing in himself, he does not live half his days, but concludes a miserable life with a more miserable end. Whence occurs that verse: "Great things fall on themselves, and it was denied to the highest to stand long; they are raised up on high so that they may fall harder." But truer is that prophecy: "I have seen highly exalted" et cetera; and "I passed by and lo he was not" et cetera. "Before his days be full he shall perish; he shall be blasted as a vine in the first flower of its grape and as an olive tree casting its flower." Hear the opinion of the wise man on this: "The life of every powerful man is short."

[30] OF THE DIVERSE CHARACTERISTICS OF THE PROUD

Now as soon as the ambitious man has been promoted to an honor, he is inflated with pride and unbridled in boasting; nor does he care to be useful, but glories in being foremost; he presumes himself to be better because he perceives himself superior. But not status, but virtue makes a good man, not rank, but honesty. He disdains former friends, ignores acquaintances, becomes acquainted with strangers, despises old companions. He turns his face, raises his glance, straightens his neck, displays haughtiness, says grand things, thinks lofty things, does not tolerate being subordinate, strives to be foremost, hostile to superiors, oppressive to inferiors. He does not endure annoyances,

II.29: *Title* De Brevi et Misera Vita Magnatum C³C¹⁴; Brevis Est et Misera Vita Magnatum C¹⁰; De Brevitate Vite Magnatum C¹⁸; Quod Brevis Est et Misera Vita Magnatum Ro. 1 **provehatur** promoveatur C³; provehatur sive promoveatur *above line* C¹⁴. **ad** in L³¹. 2 **Cure** Statim cure *most MSS incl* C³C¹⁸L³¹Ro; Statum cure C¹⁰C¹⁴. **cumulantur** curantur L³¹. 4 **spiritus** sensus C¹⁴C¹⁸; *om* L³¹. **corripitur** corrumpitur *most MSS incl* C¹⁰C¹⁴C¹⁸Ro. 5 **debilitatur virtus** debilitantur vires L³¹. 6 **seipso** semetipso L³¹. 6-7 **non dimidiat** dimidiabit C¹⁴; indimidiat C¹⁸. 7 **miserabiliori** miserabili C¹⁰L³¹; miserabile C¹⁴. 8 **fine** fuce L³¹. **Unde** Verum *most MSS incl* C³L³¹Ro. **est** *om* C¹⁴C¹⁸. 9 **diu** diu set L³¹. 11 **autem** *om* C¹⁴C¹⁸. **propheticum** poeticum O²⁶Ru¹. **Vidi** Vidi impium *most MSS incl* C³C¹⁰C¹⁴C¹⁸L³¹Ro. 12 **cetera** elevatum sicut cedros Libani *most MSS incl* C³C¹⁰C¹⁴C¹⁸V², *with* super *for* sicut L³¹. **et (2nd)** *om most MSS incl* C³C¹⁰C¹⁴Ro. 12-13 **et cetera** quesivi eum et non est inventus locus eius *most MSS incl* C³C¹⁰Ro, eum *om* C¹⁴C¹⁸; locus eius inventus L³¹. 13 **eius** *om* C¹⁰; *above line* C¹⁴. **repleantur** repleatur C¹⁰C¹⁴. 15 **florem proiciens** producens florem C¹⁴C¹⁸L³¹, *with* vel proiciens *above line* C¹⁴; florem producens C²¹O¹⁶. 16 **potentis** potentatus *most MSS incl* C³C¹⁰C¹⁴C¹⁸L³¹Ro; pontificatus L¹⁷O³¹. **vita** est vita C¹⁴C¹⁸; vite L³¹.

II.30: *Title* Diversis *om* C¹⁴; *titles om from here to end of treatise* C¹⁸. 1 **promotus est** *trans* C¹⁰C¹⁴C¹⁸L³¹. 2-3 **effrenatur** refrenatur C³; exterminatur D¹. 3 **nec** non C¹⁴C¹⁸. 4 **se** super L³¹L²⁸Pa¹⁵. **esse** *om most MSS incl* Ro. **quia** qui C¹⁴; eo, *with* quod *in margin* C¹⁸. **se cernit** *trans most MSS incl* C³C¹⁰C¹⁴C¹⁸Ro; cernit se esse L³¹. 5 **Set** Ad C¹⁰C¹⁴C¹⁸L³¹; At *most MSS incl* Ro. **non facit** *trans most MSS incl* C¹⁰C¹⁴C¹⁸Ro. 6 **dedignatur** dedignantur L³¹. 7 **extraneos** hesternos *most MSS incl* C³C¹⁴C¹⁸L³¹; externos *some MSS*. **novit** *om most MSS incl* C³C¹⁰C¹⁴C¹⁸L³¹Ro; amat *a few MSS*. **antiquos** antiquos extraneos diligit *in margin* C¹⁴; et antiquos L³¹; amicis L¹⁷O³¹. 8 **attollit** *om* C³; extollit *most MSS incl* C¹⁰C¹⁴C¹⁸L³¹Ro. 11 **Molesta** Molestiam C¹⁰C¹⁴C¹⁸; Molestia L³¹. 11-12 **concepta** contempta C³C¹⁰L³¹; contemptum C¹⁴C¹⁸; contenta *some MSS*.

[29] QUAM BREVIS ET MISERA VITA MAGNATUM

Sed esto sullimetur in altum, provehatur ad sum-
mum. Cure succrescunt, sollicitudines cumulantur,
extenduntur ieiunia, vigilie producuntur. Ex quibus
natura corrumpitur, spiritus infirmatur, corripitur
5 sompnus, amittitur appetitus, debilitatur virtus, corpus attenuatur. Et sic in seipso deficiens, non dimidiat dies suos, set miserabilem vitam miserabiliori
fine concludit. Unde est illud poeticum: "In se
magna ruunt, summisque negatum est stare diu;
10 tolluntur in altum ut lapsu graviore ruant." Verius
est autem illud propheticum: "Vidi superexalta-   In Psalmo
tum" et cetera; et / "transivi et ecce non erat" et   f. 98v
cetera. "Antequam dies eius repleantur peribit;
ledetur quasi vinea in primo flore botrus eius et sicut Iob
15 oliva florem proiciens." Audi super hoc sentenciam   In Ecclesias-
sapientis: "Omnis potentis brevis vita."   tico

[30] DE DIVERSIS PROPRIETATIBUS SUPERBORUM

Statim autem ut ambiciosus promotus est ad honorem, in superbiam extollitur et in iactanciam effrenatur; nec curat prodesse, set gloriatur preesse;
presumit se esse meliorem quia se cernit superiorem.
5 Set bonum non facit gradus, set virtus, non dignitas,
set honestas. Priores dedignatur amicos, notos ignorat, extraneos novit, comites contempnit antiquos.
Vultum avertit, visum attollit, cervicem erigit, fas-
tum ostendit, grandia loquitur, sullimia meditatur,
10 subesse non patitur, preesse molitur, prelatis infes-
tus, subditis honerosus. Molesta non suffert, con-

does not defer his thoughts; he is rash and bold, haughty and arrogant, disagreeable and rude.

[31] OF THE PRIDE AND FALL OF LUCIFER

O pride, intolerable to all, odious to everybody, among all vices you are always first, you are always last. For every sin is committed when you approach, is repudiated when you withdraw. For it is written: "Pride is the beginning of all sin," "the firstborn death." For among the very first beginnings of things it set up the created against the Creator, angel against God. But without delay it cast him down because he did not continue in the truth; it cast him down from innocence into sin, from delights into miseries, from sublime heaven into murky air. Hear the prophet: "How art thou fallen, Lucifer, who didst rise in the morning? Thou saidst in thy heart: 'I will ascend into heaven; I will exalt my throne above the stars of God; I will sit in the mountain of the covenant, in the sides of the north; I will ascend above the height of the clouds; I will be like the Most High'." "Thou wast the seat of resemblance, full of wisdom and perfect in beauty; thou wast in the pleasures of the paradise of God. Every precious stone was thy covering: the sardius, the topaz, the jasper, the chrysolite, the onyx, the beryl, the sapphire, the carbuncle, the emerald; gold the work of thy beauty. Thou a cherub stretched out and protecting, and I set thee in the holy mountain of God. Thou hast walked in the midst of the stones of fire, perfect in thy ways from the day of thy creation until iniquity was found in thee. Thou hast sinned, and I cast thee out from the mountain of God. Thy heart was lifted up with thy beauty, and I have cast thee to the ground." "The cedars in the paradise of God were not higher than he. The fir trees did not compare to his top; the plane trees were

II.31: 1 **O** *om most MSS incl* C³C¹⁰C¹⁴C¹⁸L³¹V². **importabilis** inportabilis est L³¹. 2 **semper es prima** semper eius ultima prima C³; es semper prima C¹⁰L³¹; es prima semper C¹⁸. **tu** *om* C¹⁰C¹⁴C¹⁸L³¹. **es** *om* C¹⁴C¹⁸. 3 **accedente** ascendente C¹⁸. 3–4 **committitur** accedit C¹⁰C¹⁸L³¹, *with* sive committitur *above line* C¹⁴. 4 **dimittitur** recedit C¹⁰C¹⁸L³¹, *with* sive dimittitur *above line* C¹⁴. **enim** *om* C¹⁰C¹⁴C¹⁸L³¹. 5 **peccati** peccati est *most MSS incl* C³C¹⁴C¹⁸Ro. **primogenita** primogenita eius C¹⁴C¹⁸; o primogenita L³¹; primogenita est *some MSS*. 6 **primordia rerum** *trans most MSS incl* C³C¹⁰C¹⁴L³¹Ro; ire primordia C¹⁸. 8 **eum** *a superfluous line above* -u- *expunged* L²⁰. **deiecit** *om most MSS incl* C³C¹⁰C¹⁴C¹⁸L³¹Ro. 11 **caliginosum** *corrected in* L²⁰, *perhaps from* caligniosum; caliginosum illum decrusit C¹⁴, illum *om* C¹⁸. **Quomodo** Quando C³. **cecidisti** cecidit L³¹; cecidisti de celo *some MSS*. 12 **corde** ore C¹⁰L³¹. 13 **In . . . conscendam** In celum ascendam *most MSS incl* C³C¹⁴V²; Concendam in celum L³¹. **Dei** celi *most MSS incl* C¹⁰C¹⁴C¹⁸L³¹. 14 **testamenti** celesti L³¹. 14–15 **lateribus** latere C¹⁴C¹⁸. 17 **similitudinis** similitudinis Dei C¹⁴C¹⁸. **in** *om most MSS incl* C³C¹⁰C¹⁴C¹⁸Ro. 18 **paradisi** *om* C³L³¹. 19 **operimentum tuum** operimentum eius L³¹, *with* suum *above line;* ornamentum tuum D¹. 20 **carbunculus** carbunculus et *most MSS incl* C³C¹⁰C¹⁴C¹⁸. 21 **aurum** durum D¹. **opus** omne AuGoIPa¹⁵; omnes Mu⁵. **tui** tui et foramina tua in die qua conditus es preparata sunt *some MSS*. **cherub** cherubin *many MSS incl* C³C¹⁰C¹⁴C¹⁸L³¹. 22 **et** *om* C¹⁰C¹⁴C¹⁸L³¹. 24 **iniquitas in te** in te iniquitas C¹⁰; in te iniquitas et C¹⁴C¹⁸L³¹. 25 **eieci** eiecisti C¹⁰C¹⁴C¹⁸L³¹. **monte** monte sancto C¹⁴C¹⁸. 26 **et** *om* L³¹. **proieci** proiecisti L³¹. 28 **non equaverunt** non equaverunt se C¹⁸; non adequaverunt Ro; nequiverunt L¹⁷O¹⁰O³¹. 29 **eius** illius *most MSS incl* C³C¹⁰C¹⁴C¹⁸

cepta non differt; preceps et audax, gloriosus et
arrogans, gravis et importunus.

[31] DE SUPERBIA ET CASU LUCIFERI

O superbia, cunctis importabilis, omnibus odiosa,
inter omnia vicia tu semper es prima, tu semper es
ultima. Nam omne peccatum te accedente committitur, te recedente dimittitur. Scriptum est enim:
5 "Inicium omnis peccati superbia," "primogenita   Iob
mors." Hec enim inter ipsa primordia rerum creatu-
ram contra Creatorem erexit, angelum contra
Deum. Set eum absque mora deiecit quoniam in
veritate non stetit; deiecit ab innocencia in pecca-
10 tum, a deliciis in miserias, a celo empireo in aerem
caliginosum. Audi prophetam: "Quomodo cecidisti,   Ysaias
Lucifer, qui mane oriebaris? Qui dicebas in corde
tuo: 'In celum conscendam; super astra Dei exaltabo
solium meum; sedebo in monte testamenti, in lateri-
15 bus aquilo- / -nis; ascendam super altitudinem   f. 99
nubium; similis ero Altissimo'." "Tu signaculum   Ezechiel
similitudinis, plenus sapiencia et perfectus in decore;
in deliciis paradisi Dei fuisti. Omnis lapis preciosus
operimentum tuum: sardius, topazius, iaspis, crisoli-
20 tus, onix, berillus, saphirus, carbunculus, smaragdus;
aurum opus decoris tui. Tu cherub extensus et
protegens, et posui te in monte sancto Dei. In medio
lapidum ignitorum ambulasti, perfectus in viis tuis a
die condicionis tue donec inventa est iniquitas in te.
25 Peccasti, et eieci te de monte Dei. Elevatum est cor
tuum in decore tuo, et in terram proieci te." "Cedri
non fuerunt alciores illo in paradiso Dei. Abietes
non equaverunt ad summitatem eius; platani non
fuerunt equales frondibus eius. Omne lignum pre-

185

not equal to his branches. No precious tree of paradise was like him and his beauty, for God made him beautiful with many thick branches." "He is king over all the children of pride." He is "a great red dragon, having seven heads and ten horns, and on his heads seven diadems, whose tail drew the third part of the stars of heaven and cast them to the earth." "And that great dragon was cast out, that old serpent, who is called the devil and Satan, who seduceth the whole world, and he was cast unto the earth, and his angels were thrown down with him." Truth also says about him: "I saw Satan like lightning falling from heaven." For "everyone that exalteth himself shall be humbled and he that humbleth himself shall be exalted."

[32] OF THE ARROGANCE OF MEN

O proud presumption, presumptuous pride, which not only wished to make the angels equal to God, but presumed to deify man! It then pushed down those whom it had raised up, and humbled those whom it had exalted. Hence God said to the prophet: "Son of man, say to the prince of Tyre: 'Thus saith the Lord God: because thy heart is lifted up as the heart of God and thou hast said, "I am God," whereas thou art a man and not God, therefore I will bring upon thee the strongest of the nations, and they shall kill thee, and thou shalt die the death of them that are slain'." Nabuchodonosor, because he proudly boasted of his power and said: "'Is not this Babylon, which I have built for myself in the seat of my kingdom, in the strength of my power, and in the glory of my excellence?' While the word was yet in the king's mouth, a voice came down from heaven: 'To thee it is said, King Nabuchodonosor: thy kingdom passeth from thee, and they shall cast thee out from among men, and thy dwelling shall be with cattle and wild beasts; thou shalt eat grass like an

Ro. 31 **eius** illius L^{31}. **fecit eum Dominus** fecit eum *most MSS incl* C^{3}C^{10}L^{31}; fecerat illum C^{14}C^{18}; feci eum Ro. 32 **condensis frondibus** condensis frondibus tandem corruit C^{14}; tandem cum frondibus suis corruit C^{18}; tandem cum frondibus L^{31}. 33-34 **rufus** ruftus L^{31}; hyspidus Mu^5; visus Pa^{10}. 34 **decem** *om* L^{31}. 35 **suis** *om many MSS incl* C^{3}C^{10}C^{14}C^{18}L^{31}. 37 **ille draco** *trans most MSS incl* C^{3}C^{10}C^{14}C^{18}L^{31}Ro. 38 **vocabatur** vocatur *most MSS incl* C^{10}C^{14}C^{18}L^{31}V^2. 39 **seducit** seduxit C^3. **orbem** mundum C^{18}L^{31}ArC^{11}Du^{4}L^{41}L^{44}Ma^{2}O^7. 40 **et (2nd)** *om most MSS incl* C^{3}C^{10}C^{14}C^{18}L^{31}. 41 **quasi** sicut C^{10}C^{14}C^{18}L^{31}. 42 **omnis** *om* C^{14}C^{18}L^{31}. 42-43 **exaltat humiliabitur . . . humiliat exaltabitur** *trans* C^{10}C^{14}C^{18}.

II.32: *Title* Humana *for* Hominum C^3. 1 **O . . . superbia** Superba presumptio C^3; O quam presumptuosa est superbia immo presumpcio superba C^{14}C^{18}; O superbia presumptuosa presumpcio superba L^{31}; O *om many MSS incl* C^{10}V^2. 2 **angelos Deo** angelos L^{31}; homines Deo BuGoLmPa^{9}Pa^{11}; angelos Dei *a few MSS.* **set** set eciam L^{31}. 4 **humiliavit** humiliat C^{14}. **ad** per Ro. 6 **pro** *om nearly every MS incl* C^{3}C^{10}C^{14}C^{18}Ro. 7 **Deus** Deus enim C^{10}. 8 **et** *om* L^{31}. 9 **interficient** interficiam C^3. 10 **in** *om* C^{10}. 10-11 **quia potenciam** qui superbiam BuGoLmPa^{9}Pa^{11}. 12 **Babilon** civitas C^{10}C^{18}L^{31}; civitas, *with* Babilon *above line* C^{14}; Ierusalem Bv^1. **michi** *om most MSS incl* C^{3}C^{10}C^{14}C^{18}L^{31}. **regni** regni mei C^{14}L^{31}, *corrected from* regni Dei C^{18}. 13 **in (1st)** *om* L^{31}. **in gloria** vigilia Re^{3}T^2. 14 **regis** eius C^{14}; regis *in* C^{18}, *but an earlier* eius, *after* sermo, *expunged.* 15 **ruit** irruit C^{10}L^{31}; irruit dicens C^{14}C^{18}. **Tibi dicitur** Sibi dicens C^3; Tibi dico L^{31}BoBs D^{4}Er^{2}L^4. **regnum** regnum tuum Ro, *above line* C^{14}. 16 **transit** transiit *many MSS incl* C^{3}C^{18}; transibit *a few MSS;* Deus celi transfert EvRu^2. **a** ad *corrected to* a C^{14}; ad L^{31}. **te eicient** eicient te C^3; te eiciet C^{10}C^{14}C^{18}; eiciet te L^{31}. 16-17 **bestiis . . . feris** *trans* C^{10}C^{14}L^{31}. 19 **dominatur** C^{10}; dominetur *most MSS incl* C^{3}V^2. 20 **dat** det *most MSS incl*

186

ciosum paradisi non est assimilatum illi et pulcritu-
dini eius, quoniam speciosum fecit eum Dominus in
multis condensis frondibus." "Ipse est rex super Iob
omnes filios superbie." Ipse est "draco magnus ru- Apocalipsis
fus, habens capita septem et cornua decem, et in
capitibus suis septem diademata, cuius cauda trahe-
bat terciam partem stellarum celi et misit illas in
terram." "Et proiectus est ille draco magnus, serpens antiquus, qui vocabatur diabolus et Sathanas,
qui seducit universum orbem, et proiectus est in
terram, et angeli eius cum eo missi sunt." De quo et
Veritas ait: "Videbam Sathanam quasi fulgur de Lucas
celo cadentem." Nam "omnis qui se exaltat humiliabitur et qui *se humiliat exaltabitur.*"

[32] DE ARROGANCIA HOMINUM

O superba presumpcio, presumptuosa superbia, que
non solum angelos Deo voluit adequare, set homines
presumpsit deificare! Porro, quos erexit depressit, et
quos exaltavit humiliavit. Hinc ait Dominus ad
prophetam: "Fili hominis, dic principi Tyri: 'Hec Ezechiel
dicit / Dominus Deus: pro eo quod elevatum est cor f. 99v
tuum quasi cor Dei et dixisti, "Deus ego sum," cum
sis homo et non Deus, iccirco ego adducam super te
robustissimos gencium, et interficient te, et morieris
in interitu occisorum'." Nabugodonosor, quia poten- Daniel
ciam suam superbe iactavit et ait: "'Nonne hec est
Babilon, quam ego edificavi michi in domum regni,
in robore fortitudinis mee, et in gloria decoris mei?'
Cum adhuc sermo esset in ore regis, vox de celo
ruit: 'Tibi dicitur, Nabugodonosor Rex: regnum
transit a te, et ab hominibus te eicient, et cum bestiis
et feris erit habitacio tua; fenum quasi bos comedes,

ox, and seven times shall pass over thee till thou know that the Most High ruleth in the kingdom of men and giveth it to whomsoever he will'. The same hour the word is fulfilled upon Nabuchodonosor." Whence it is true what is read: "Man when he was in honor did not understand; he is compared to senseless beasts, and is become like to them." Pride overturned the tower and confounded language, brought Goliath down and hanged Aman, killed Nicanor and destroyed Antiochus, drowned Pharao and slew Sennacherib. "God overturneth the thrones of proud princes and maketh the roots of proud nations to wither."

[33] OF THE ABOMINATION OF PRIDE

How detestable is pride the Lord himself attests through the prophet: "The Lord God hath sworn by his own soul, saith the Lord God of Hosts: 'I detest the pride of Jacob'." And "the Lord hath sworn against the pride of Jacob: 'Surely I will never forget all their works'." Whence among "the six things which the Lord hateth, and the seventh which his soul detesteth," Solomon puts first "haughty eyes," that is, pride. And Isaias: "The day of the Lord of Hosts shall be upon one that is proud and highminded and upon everyone that is arrogant, and he shall be humbled; and upon all the tall and lofty cedars of Libanus, and upon all the oaks of Basan, and upon all the high mountains, and upon every high tower, and upon every fenced wall, and the loftiness of men shall be bowed down, and the haughtiness of men shall be humbled." "Therefore hath hell enlarged her soul and opened her mouth without any bound, and their high and glorious ones shall go down into it." "The Lord of Hosts

C³C¹⁰L³¹Ro; dabit C¹⁴C¹⁸. 20-21 **completur sermo** sermo completus est *most MSS incl* C³C¹⁰C¹⁴C¹⁸Ro; sermo complevit L³¹D⁵O¹⁸. 21 **Unde** *om most MSS incl* C³C¹⁰C¹⁴ C¹⁸L³¹Ro. 22 **est** est ergo *most MSS incl* C³C¹⁰C¹⁴C¹⁸Ro. 23-24 **comparatus . . . illis** et cetera C¹⁴C¹⁸. 23 **est** *om* L³¹. 24 **turrem** lignum L¹⁷O¹⁰O³¹. 24-25 **linguam** linguas L³¹; lignum *a few MSS.* 25 **confudit** confundit *most MSS incl* C¹⁴C¹⁸Ro. **Goliam** Goliath *most MSS incl* C³C¹⁰C¹⁸L³¹. 26 **peremit** pervertit C¹⁴. 26-27 **Antiochum** *Greek rough-breathing sign over* i L²⁰. 27-28 **interemit** interfecit L³¹. 28 **destruit Deus** *om* C¹⁰L³¹. 29 **superbarum** superbiencium C¹⁴C¹⁸. **arefacit** arefecit *most MSS incl* C³C¹⁰C¹⁴C¹⁸L³¹.

    II.33: 1 **detestabilis** detestabile L³¹. **ipse** *om* L³¹. 3 **Deus** *om most MSS.* 4 **Iacob** *om* C³C¹⁸. 5 **superbia** superbiam *many MSS incl* C³L³¹V². **ad** in *many MSS incl* L³¹. 6 **omnia** *om* C¹⁰C¹⁸L³¹; *above line* C¹⁴. **Unde** Unum C³. **inter illa** in Parabolis L³¹. **sex** sex sunt C¹⁰L³¹. 7 **Dominus odit** odit Deus C¹⁴C¹⁸; *trans* L³¹. 8 **Salomon** *om* L³¹. 11 **et** *(1st)* *om* C¹⁰C¹⁴C¹⁸L³¹. 12 **erectas** erectos C¹⁰C¹⁸L³¹. 18-19 **os . . . termino** absque mora os suum BuGoILmMu⁵Pa⁹Pa¹¹. 19 **descendunt** descendent *most MSS incl* C³C¹⁰C¹⁸L³¹V²; descendens *corrected to* descendent C¹⁴. **gloriosique** et gloriosi C¹⁴C¹⁸; gloriosi L³¹. **eius**

et septem tempora mutabuntur super te donec scias
quod Excelsus dominatur in regno hominum et
20 cuicumque voluerit dat illud'. Eadem hora completur sermo super Nabugodonosor." Unde verum
est quod legitur: "Homo cum in honore esset non
intellexit; *comparatus* est *iumentis* insi*pientibus, et simi-*
lis factus est illis." Superbia turrem evertit et lin-
25 guam confudit, prostravit Goliam et suspendit
Amon, interfecit Nichanorem et peremit Antiochum, Pharaonem submersit et Sennacherib interemit.
"Sedes ducum superborum destruit Deus et
radices gencium superbarum arefacit."

In Psalmo

In Ecclesias-
tico

[33] DE ABOMINACIONE SUPERBIE

Quam detestabilis sit superbia Dominus ipse per
prophetam testatur: "Iuravit Dominus Deus in
anima sua, dicit Dominus Deus Exercituum: 'Detes-
tor ego superbiam Iacob'." Et "Iuravit Dominus in
5 superbia Iacob: 'Si oblitus fuero usque ad finem
omnia opera eorum'." Unde inter "illa sex que
Dominus odit, et septimum quod detestatur anima
eius," Salomon primum ponit "oculos sullimes," id
est, superbiam. Et Ysaias: "Dies Domini Exerci-
10 tuum super omnem superbum et excelsum et super
omnem arrogantem, et humiliabitur; et super omnes
cedros Li- / -bani sullimes et erectas, et super
omnes quercus Basan, et super omnes montes excel-
sos, et super omnes colles elevatos, et super omnem
15 turrim excelsam, et super omnem murum munitum,
et incurvabitur sullimitas hominum, et humiliabitur
altitudo virorum." "Propterea dilatavit infernus
animam suam et aperuit os suum absque ullo termino, et descendunt sullimes gloriosique eius ad

Amos

In Parabolis

f. 100

hath designed it to pull down the pride of all glory." Job also says: "If his pride mount up even to heaven and his head touch the clouds, in the end he shall be destroyed like a dunghill."

[34] AGAINST THE ARROGANCE OF THE PROUD

Nearly every bad man loves a man similar to himself, but the proud man hates an exalted man. Whence Solomon: "Among the proud there are always contentions," and "where pride is, there also shall be reproach." The proud man desires unusual things, loathes the usual things. He considers it a great thing if he deigns to speak, very great if he rises and embraces. He believes that his rank has gained more from him than he from his rank. He will never use the affection of fatherly feeling but always the power of lordship. His pride and his disdain and his arrogance are greater than his courage. Let him turn over in his mind what is read in the gospel: "There was a strife among the disciples of Jesus which of them should seem to be the greater, and Jesus said to them: 'The kings of the gentiles lord it over them, and they that have power among them are called beneficent. But you not so, but he that is the greater among you, he shall be as the younger and he that is the leader as he that serveth'." And Peter, the chief of the apostles: "Not as lording it over the clergy, but being made a pattern of the flock from the heart." "The earth is the Lord's and the fullness thereof" et cetera. There is therefore one God; others are not lords, but servants, to whom lordship is forbidden and service is appointed. Hear the wise man on this: "If they have made thee ruler, be not lifted up, but be among them as one of them."

om C¹⁰C¹⁴C¹⁸L³¹. 20 **cogitavit** cogitabit L³¹. 20–21 **destrueret** detraheret *most MSS incl* C³C¹⁴C¹⁸L³¹Ro; detraherent C¹⁰. 22 **celum** nubes C¹⁰C¹⁴C¹⁸L³¹. 23 **tetigerit** detegerit C¹⁸. 23–24 **perdetur** putrescat vel perdetur C³L³⁵Pa¹⁰, *with* putrescet vel *above line* L²⁹; perdetur vel putrescat *in margin* C¹⁴.

II.34: *Title* De Proprietatibus Arrogancium C¹⁴. 1 **diligit . . . similem** sibi diligit similem C¹⁰; sibi similes diligit C¹⁴C¹⁸; sibi similem diligit set L³¹. **superbus** *corrected from* superbum L³¹. 2 **autem** aut C¹⁸; *om* L³¹. **elatum** elatum sive elevatum *above line* C¹⁴. 3 **et** (*1st*) *om* C¹⁰C¹⁴C¹⁸L³¹. **ibi** ibi erit C³. 5 **dignetur** *a preceding* videtur *expunged in* L³¹. 6 **si surgat** non assurgat C¹⁸; si surgit *many MSS incl* V². **amplexetur** amplexatur V². 7 **ipso** illo C¹⁰C¹⁴C¹⁸L³¹. 8 **uti** ita L³¹. **affectu . . . dominationis** *most MSS incl* C³C¹⁰C¹⁸L³¹Ro, *whole passage in margin* C¹⁴. 9–10 **indignacio . . . arrogancia** *trans most MSS incl* C³C¹⁰C¹⁴C¹⁸L³¹V². 10 **fortitudo** sollicitudo L³¹. **Revolvat** Revolve L³¹. 11 **contencio** convencio C⁹; contemptio La. 13 **Reges** C¹⁰; Principes *most MSS incl* C³Ro. 13–14 **dominantur . . . vocantur** et cetera C¹⁴C¹⁸. 14 **inter eos** inter illos C³; super eos *most MSS incl* C¹⁰L³¹Ro. 15 **erit** fiat C¹⁸. 16 **iunior** minor *many MSS incl* C¹⁴; minister Bt¹L³⁵Pa¹⁰. **est** *om most MSS incl* C³C¹⁴L³¹Ro; et C¹⁸. 17–18 **dominantes in clero** in clero dominantes C¹⁰C¹⁴C¹⁸L³¹. 18 **in clero** in choro Ma²Pa¹²Pa¹³; Iudeo C⁹; in Deo O⁹; in oculo O³¹. **forma** fortes L⁹, *also* E¹ *but not a group reading.* **facti** facti sicut L³¹. **animo** anima L³¹. 19 **et cetera** orbis terrarum et universi qui habitant in eo *most MSS incl* C³C¹⁰Ro; orbis C¹⁴; orbis terrarum et cetera L³¹. 20 **ergo** *om* L³¹. **Deus** Dominus L³¹. **unus** C¹⁰; et unus est *most MSS incl* C³C¹⁴C¹⁸; unus est L³¹Ro. **Dominus** Deus L³¹. 21 **interdicitur** interdum C³; impenditur L¹⁷O³¹. 21–22 **dominium et indicitur** *om* C¹⁸L³¹. 22 **indicitur** interdicitur C³C¹⁰C¹⁴; inducitur L¹⁷O³¹. 23 **posuerunt** constituerunt C¹⁴C¹⁸. 24 **ipsis** illis *most MSS incl* C¹⁰C¹⁴C¹⁸L³¹Ro.

20 eum." "Dominus Exercituum cogitavit hoc ut destrueret superbiam omnis glorie." Iob quoque dicit:
"Si ascenderit usque ad celum superbia et caput eius
nubes tetigerit, quasi sterquilineum in fine perdetur."

[34] CONTRA ARROGANCIAM SUPERBORUM

Omnis fere viciosus diligit sibi similem, superbus
autem odit elatum. Unde Salomon: "Inter superbos   In Parabolis
semper sunt iurgia," et "ubi fuerit superbia, ibi et
contumelia." Superbus insolita gestit, consueta fas-
5 tidit. Magnum reputat si loqui dignetur, maximum
si surgat et amplexetur. Estimat plus dignitatem ab
ipso quam ipsum assecutum ex dignitate. Nunquam
vult uti paternitatis affectu, set semper dominacionis
imperio. Superbia eius et indignacio eius et arrogan-   Ysaias
10 cia eius plus quam fortitudo eius. Revolvat in animo
quod legitur in evangelio: "Facta est contencio inter   Lucas
discipulos Iesu quis eorum videretur esse maior, et
ait illis Iesus: 'Reges gencium dominantur eorum, et
qui potestatem habent inter eos benefici vocantur.
15 Vos autem non sic, set qui maior est inter vos, erit
sicut iunior et qui precessor est sicut ministrator'."
Et Petrus, apostolorum magister: "Non quasi do-   In Epistola
minantes in clero, set forma facti gregis ex animo."·   Canonica
"Domini est terra et plenitudo eius" et cetera. Unus   In Psalmo
20 est ergo Deus, unus Dominus; ceteri non sunt domini, set ministri, quibus interdicitur dominium et
indicitur / ministerium. Audi super hoc sapientem: f. 100v
"Rectorem te posuerunt, noli extolli, set esto in illis   In Ecclesias-
quasi unus ex ipsis."   tico

191

The sons of Zebedee, who through the intervention of their mother requested an honor of Christ: "Say," she says, "that these my two sons may sit, the one on thy right and the other on thy left, in thy kingdom," were sad to hear: "You know not what you ask." For one arrives at the kingdom not through an honor, but through difficulty. Whence the Lord adds: "It is not mine to give to you." It is indeed "mine" to give, but not "to you," that is, to the ambitious, as you are. Moreover although all power is from God, still the proud man does not reign from God, according to that prophetical saying: "They have reigned, but not by me; they have been princes, and I knew them not."

[36] OF THE CHARACTERISTICS OF THE ARROGANT

The proud man loves "the first chairs in the synagogues, the first places at feasts, salutations in the market place, and to be called rabbi by men." He wishes to be called not by the name of his person, but by the name of his rank; he wishes to be honored not as a man, but as God. He sits elevated, he walks exalted, he wishes everyone to rise for him, each to bow. Once a certain philosopher, wishing to mock the arrogance of a certain king, when he saw him sitting elevated on the royal throne, worshipped him humbly stretched out on the ground, and immediately, going up uninvited, sat down beside the king. The king, greatly astonished because he knew him to be a philosopher, inquired why he had done this. The philosopher replied: "Either you are a god or a man: if you are a god, I must worship you; if a man, I can sit beside you."

II.35: *Title* De Arrogancia C^{14}. 2 **Dic inquit** dicentis Dic C^{14}C^{18}. 3 **ad dexteram** a dextris C^{14}C^{18}; ad d L^{31}. **et** *om* L^{31}. 3-4 **ad sinistram** a sinistris C^{14}; a s C^{18}; ad s L^{31}. 4 **tuam** *om* C^{3}C^{14}C^{18}L^{31}. 5 **set onere** *om* L^{31}. 6 **subdit** subdidit C^{14}; scribit C^9. 7 **est quidem** *trans many MSS incl* C^{3}C^{10}C^{14}C^{18}L^{31}. 10 **non . . . Deo** *trans* C^{14}C^{18}L^{31}, *with* ex *corrected from a above line* C^{14}. 11 **set** et *most MSS incl* C^{3}C^{10}C^{14}C^{18}. 12 **extiterunt** constiterunt C^{14}C^{18}; extinnxerunt L^{31}; exciderunt L^{40}; exciterunt *a few MSS*.

II.36: 1-2 **primos** primus L^{31}. 2 **recubitus** incubitus L^{17}O^{31}. **cenis** cenis et L^{31}. 3-4 **nomine** *om* C^{14}C^{18}. 5 **adorari** honorari *most MSS incl* C^{3}C^{14}C^{18}L^{31}Ro; honorari sed C^{10}. 7-8 **cuiusdam . . . arroganciam** arrogantiam cuiusdam regis *most MSS incl* C^{3}C^{10}C^{14}C^{18}L^{31}Ro. 8 **eludere** elidere C^{18}; illudere *many MSS incl* C^{14}. 9 **suppliciter** pronus C^3. 12 **nosset** non nosset C^{10}C^{14}; nosceret *some MSS*; novisset L^{17}O^{31}. **eum** eum esse *most MSS incl* C^{3}C^{14}C^{18}L^{31}; illum esse *many MSS incl* Ro. **quare** quid *most MSS incl* C^{3}C^{10}C^{14}C^{18}Ro. 13 **inquisivit** exquisivit *most MSS incl* C^{3}C^{10}L^{31}Ro; requisivit C^{14}C^{18}. **vero** ergo *most MSS incl* C^{3}C^{10}C^{14}C^{18}L^{31}Ro. **Aut** *om* C^{10}C^{14}C^{18}L^{31}. 14 **homo (1st)** L^{31} *ends with this word at the bottom of f. 183v, with catchwords* si Deus *at very bottom of the page*. **es** *om most MSS incl* C^{3}C^{10}C^{14}C^{18}Ro. 15 **racionem** responsionem Ro. 17 **debuisti** debuisse

[35] CONTRA FRAUDEM AMBICIOSORUM

Filii Zebedei, qui per interventum matris honorem
postulaverunt a Christo: "Dic," inquit, "ut sedeant   Matheus
hii duo filii mei, unus ad dexteram et alius ad
sinistram tuam, in regno tuo," meruerunt audire:
5 "Nescitis quid petatis." Non enim honore, set onere
pervenitur ad regnum. Unde Dominus subdit: "Non
est meum dare vobis." "Meum" est quidem dare, set
non "vobis," id est, ambiciosis, quales vos estis.
Licet autem omnis potestas a Deo sit, superbus
10 tamen non regnat ex Deo, secundum illud propheticum: "Ipsi regnaverunt, set non ex me; principes   Osee
extiterunt, et non cognovi eos."

[36] DE PROPRIETATIBUS ARROGANCIUM

Superbus amat "primas cathedras in synagogis, primos recubitus in cenis, salutaciones in foro, et vocari
ab hominibus rabi." Non nomine persone, set nomine fortune vult appellari; non ut homo, set ut
5 Deus vult adorari. Sedet sullimis, incedit excelsus,
vult sibi omnes assurgere, singulos inclinare. Porro
philosophus quidam, volens cuiusdam regis arroganciam eludere, cum vidisset eum in throno regali
sedere sullimem, prostratus in terram suppliciter
10 adoravit et confestim, non invitatus ascendens, iuxta
regem consedit. Quod rex, vehementer admirans eo
quod nosset eum philosophum, quare hoc egerit
inquisivit. Philosophus vero respondit: "Aut deus es
aut homo: si deus es, debui te adorare; si homo,
15 potui iuxta te sedere." Rex autem, racionem con-

But the king, turning the reasoning against the philosopher, retorted: "On the contrary, if I am a man, you must not worship me; if I am a god, you must not sit beside me." The former replied wisely, but the latter parried skillfully.

[37] OF SUPERFLUOUS CLOTHING

God made aprons for our first parents after their sin, and it is said by Christ to Christians: "Have not two coats." But according to the counsel of John: "He that hath two coats, let him give one to him that hath none." But the proud man, so that he may seem magnificent, endeavors to be clothed with two, to be covered with soft fabrics, to be adorned with precious things. But what is a man adorned with precious things but a whited sepulcher without, yet filled with filthiness within? Blue cloth and purple cloth, scarlet cloth and linen rot in the slime; gold and silver, precious stones and gems become dirty in the mud. Rank and power lie unattractively in the dust; honor and glory sit unbecomingly in the ashes. Why therefore, proud man, do you expand your phylacteries and enlarge your hems? That rich man "who was clothed in purple and linen was buried in hell." Dina, daughter of the patriarch Jacob, remained a virgin until she went out, as Josephus says, to buy an ornament from the women of the province; but when she went out, Sichem, son of King Hemor, raped her. Holofernes, who was sitting under "a canopy that was woven of purple and gold and emerald and precious stones," was killed by Judith, who, since she had made use of a haircloth before, then took the clothing of delight. Hear the counsel of the wise man on this: "Glory not in apparel at any time." And the Apostle: "Not with costly attire." "Let it not be the outward plaiting of the hair, or the wearing of gold, or the care of apparel."

C[14]. **sum** *om many MSS incl* C[3]Ro. 18-19 **respondit** sedit C[3]; reddit C[9]. 19 **elusit** illum eludit C[10]; eum illusit, *with* illusit *probably corrected from* eludit C[14]; eum elisit C[18]; illusit *a few MSS;* concludit C[2].

II.37: *Title* De Superfluo Cultu Superborum C[14]; Ornatu *for* Cultu Re[3]T[2]. 3 **habeatis** habebitis *most MSS incl* C[3]C[10]. 4 **unam non habenti** non habenti unam C[14]Ro; unam *om* C[18]. 5 **autem** *om* C[14]C[18]. 6 **vestiri** uti C[18]. 6-7 **ornari . . . preciosis** *om* C[18]. 9 **coccus** coctus C[14]C[18]. 9-10 **putrescunt** putrescit C[18]. 11 **sordescunt** surdescant C[18]. **male iacent** materiale iacet C[18]. 12 **male** materiale C[18]. **sedent** sordent C[10]; sedunt C[18]. 16 **emeret** *om here and added after* provincialium C[10]C[14]C[18]. 17 **ornamentum** ornatum *many MSS incl* C[10]V[2]. **mulierem** *om* C[10]. 18 **exivit** exiret C[18]. **Sichem** *om* C[10]C[18]; *above line* C[14]. 19 **Emor** Amon *some MSS.* 20 **canopeo** canopio indutus vestimento *above line* C[18]. **ex** *om* C[18]. 22-23 **tunc ornatum** ornatus C[14]. 23 **hoc** *om* C[14]. 24 **consilium** sentenciam V[2]. **ne glorieris** negligeris *some MSS.* 25 **Non** Ne C[18]. 26 **Non** Nec *most MSS incl* C[3]C[10]C[14]C[18]Ro. **extrinsecus** intrinsecus C[3].

vertens contra philosophum, intulit: "Immo, si
homo sum, non debuisti me adorare; si deus sum,
non debuisti iuxta me sedere." / Sapienter iste re- f. 101
spondit, set ille prudenter elusit.

[37] DE SUPERFLUO CULTU

Primis parentibus fecit Deus perizomata post pecca- In Genesi
tum, et a Christo dicitur Christianis: " 'Non duas
tunicas habeatis'." Set iuxta Iohannis consilium:
" 'Qui habet duas tunicas, det unam non habenti'."
5 Superbus autem, ut magnificus videatur, satagit
vestiri duplicibus, indui mollibus, preciosis ornari.
Set quid est homo preciosis ornatus nisi sepulchrum Matheus
foris dealbatum, intus autem plenum spurcicia? Iacinctus et purpura, coccus et bissus in limo putres-
10 cunt; aurum et argentum, lapides et gemme in luto
sordescunt. Dignitas et potestas male iacent in pulvere; honor et gloria male sedent in cinere. Quid
ergo, superbe, philacteria dilatas et magnificas fim-
brias? Dives ille "qui induebatur purpura et bisso, Lucas
15 sepultus est in inferno." Dina, filia patriarche Iacob, In Iosepho
antequam egrederetur, ut ait Iosephus, ut emeret
ornamentum mulierum provincialium virgo per-
mansit; cum autem exivit, Sichem, filius Regis
Emor, eam violenter oppressit. Olofernes, qui sede- Iudith
20 bat "in canopeo quod erat ex purpura et auro et
smaragdo et lapidibus preciosis intextum," iugulatus
est a Iudith, que, cum prius uteretur cilicio, tunc
ornatum iocunditatis assumpsit. Audi super hoc
consilium sapientis: "In vestitu ne glorieris In Ecclesias-
25 unquam." Et Apostolus: "Non in veste preciosa." tico
"Non sit extrinsecus capillatura, aut circumdacio Petrus in
auri, aut vestimentorum cultus." Epistola

195

Consider what the Lord threatens through the prophet against superfluous ornament: "Because the daughters of Sion are haughty and have walked with stretched out necks and wanton glances of their eyes, the Lord will make bald the crown of the head of the daughters of Sion and will discover their hair. In that day the Lord will take away the ornament of shoes and little moons and chains and necklaces and bracelets and bodkins and leg-bands and tablets and little scent-bottles and cloaks and fine linen and earrings and jewels hanging on the forehead and changes of apparel and crisping pins and looking-glasses and lawns and headbands and veils. And instead of a sweet smell there will be a stench, and instead of a girdle a cord, and instead of curled hair baldness, and instead of a stomacher haircloth." Behold, a just penalty will be rendered for the crime, so that they will be punished in the thing with which they have sinned. Hear yet another prophet on these matters: "O Tyre, fine broidered linen from Egypt was woven for thy sail; blue and purple from the islands of Elisa were made thy covering. They exchanged for her price teeth of ivory. They set forth a precious stone and purple and broidered works and fine linen and silk and scarlet in her market. The men of Dedan were thy merchants in tapestry for sitting, and thou wast replenished and glorified exceedingly. But now thou art destroyed in the sea and thy riches in the depths of the waters; thou art brought to nothing, and thou shalt never be any more."

[39] THAT MORE IS ATTRIBUTED TO CLOTHES THAN TO VIRTUES

When a certain philosopher had approached the palace of a prince in contemptible clothing and, after knocking for a long time, had not been admitted,

---

II.38: 1 **Attende** Attendite C^{14}C^{18}; Audi L^{40}U^4; Contendit C^9. **ornatum** ornamentum C^3. 2 **prophetam** prophetam dicens C^{14}C^{18}. 6 **ornamentum** ornatum *most MSS incl* C^{10}C^{14}C^{18}V^2. 7 **lunulas** iniurias L^{17}O^{31}. **armillas** armillas et mitras *most MSS incl* C^{3}C^{10}C^{14}C^{18}Ro. 8 **perichelidas et murenulas** *om* C^{14}C^{18}. **et (3rd)** *om* C^{10}C^{14}C^{18}. 8-9 **olfactoriola** olfactoria *most MSS incl* C^{3}C^{10}C^{14}C^{18}. 9 **pallia et lintheamina et** *om here and added in l. 10 after* mutatoria et *most MSS incl* C^{3}C^{10}C^{14}C^{18}Ro. **inaures et** in aures eciam in C^{14}; in auros et C^{18}; lauros et L^{17}O^{31}. 10 **pendentes** pendentes et perichelides et murenulos C^{14}C^{18}. 14 **iusta . . . pena** ista pena redditur C^3. 15 **peccaverant** peccaverunt *most MSS incl* C^{3}C^{14}C^{18}V^2. 16 **audi** *om* C^{18}. 17 **tibi** *om* C^{10}. **velum** celum *a few MSS*. 18 **insulis** *om* C^{18}. 19 **eburneos** eburneos et ebeninos *most MSS incl* C^{3}C^{10}C^{14}C^{18}Ro. **commutaverunt** mutaverunt C^3; eam mutaverunt BuGoILmPa^{9}Pa^{11}. **suo** tuo *most MSS incl* C^{3}C^{10}C^{14}C^{18}Ro. 21 **coccum** coctum C^{14}C^{18}; crocum D^6; cortam C^9. **suo** *corrected from* tuo L^{20}; tuo *most MSS incl* C^{3}C^{10}C^{14}C^{18}Ro. 22 **Dedan** Dederunt C^{3}C^{18}. **tapetibus** capitibus *many MSS*. **sedendum** fodiendum C^3; videndum L^{17}. 23 **es (2nd)** *om many MSS incl* C^{3}C^{14}. **nunc** tunc C^{18}. 25 **deducta** redacta *many MSS incl* C^3. **es** sunt Ro. **usque** *om* C^{18}.

[38] CONTRA SUPERFLUUM ORNATUM

Attende quid contra superfluum ornatum commi-
netur Dominus per prophetam: "Pro eo quod ele-
vate sunt filie Syon et ambulaverunt extento collo et
nutibus oculorum ibant, decalvabit Dominus verti-
5 cem filiarum Syon et crinem earum nudabit. In
die / illa auferet Dominus ornamentum calciamen-
torum et lunulas et torques et monilia et armillas et
discriminalia et perichelidas et murenulas et olfactoriola et pallia et lintheamina et inaures et anulos et
10 gemmas in fronte pendentes et mutatoria et acus et
specula et sindones et vittas et theristra. Et erit pro
suavi odore fetor, et pro zona funiculus, et pro
crispanti crine calvicium, et pro fascia pectorali
cilicium." Ecce, iusta redditur pena pro culpa, ut in
15 eo puniantur in quo peccaverant. Adhuc super his
audi alium prophetam: "O Tyre, bissus varia de
Egypto texta est tibi in velum; iacinctus et purpura
de insulis Elisa facta sunt operimentum tuum.
Dentes eburneos commutaverunt in precio suo.
20 Gemmam et purpuram et scutulata et bissum et
sericum et coccum proposuerunt in mercato suo.
Dedan institores tui in tapetibus ad sedendum, et
repleta es et glorificata es nimis. Set nunc contrita es
in mari et in profundis aquarum opes tue; ad nichi-
25 lum deducta es, et non eris usque in perpetuum."

[39] QUOD PLUS DEFERTUR VESTIBUS QUAM VIRTUTIBUS

Cum quidam philosophus in habitu contemptibili
principis aulam adisset et, diu pulsans, non fuisset

197

but as often as he had tried to enter, so often had he happened to be repulsed, he changed his clothing and put on splendid dress: then at the first call the way was open for his coming. Proceeding to the prince, he began reverently to kiss the cloak that he was wearing. The prince, wondering at this, inquired why he was doing it. The philosopher replied: "I honor the thing giving honor, because what my virtue was not capable of, my clothing obtained." O vanity of vanities, more honor is given to clothes than to virtues, more to beauty than to integrity.

[40] OF THE PAINTING OF COLORS

An artificial appearance is put on, and the natural appearance is covered over, as if the ingenuity of man could surpass the skill of the Creator. Not so, not so. "Consider," he says, "the lilies of the field, how they grow; they labor not, neither do they spin. But I say to you that not even Solomon in all his glory was arrayed as one of these." Far be it for a counterfeit color to be comparable to a natural one: indeed on the contrary, when the face is painted with a counterfeit color, the countenance is spoiled by an abominable stench. "All things are vanity, every man living." For what is more vain than to comb the locks, smooth the hair, color the cheeks, smear the face, lengthen the eyebrows, when indeed "favor is deceitful and beauty vain"? "All flesh is grass, and all the glory thereof as the flower of the grass," "for it shortly withers away as grass and as the greens of herbs quickly falls." But in order that I may exclude the adornment of the person lest I seem to inflame minds more in malice than in truth, what is more vain than to adorn a table with embroidered cloths, knives with handles of ivory, gold vessels, silver plate, bowls and napkins, singers, dishes, trays, spoons, forks, saltcellars, basins,

II.39: 3 **admissus** exauditus C[10]C[14]C[18]. 4 **repelli** eum repelli C[3]. 6 **principem** principis pedes Ro; principem *corrected to* principis *and* pedes *added above line* C[14]. 8 **cur** quid *most MSS incl* C[3]C[10]C[14]C[18]Ro. **hoc** *above line* L[20]. **ageret** egerit C[3]. **inquisivit** exquisivit *most MSS incl* C[3]C[10]C[14]C[18]Ro; requisivit EvRu[2]. 9 **vero** ergo *most MSS incl* C[3]Ro; *om* C[14]C[18]E[1]. **Honorantem** Honorantem me *many MSS incl* C[14]C[18]. 10 **quia** et C[10]. 11 **honoris** hominis C[10]. **defertur** differtur C[3]; refertur L[40]. 12 **venustati** vestimento C[10]C[18]; vestimento, *with* sive venustati *in margin* C[14]; distincto N.

II.40: *Title* De Ornatu Persone Mense et Domus Ro; *many variants for* Fucacione *incl* Fricacione, Fuscacione, Sophisticatione vel Fucatione, Suffocatione; De Fuscacione Oculorum L[9] *and* E[1] *but not a group reading.* 1 **Artificialis** Artificiis ArRe[3]T[2]; Tristificialis C[9]. **superducitur** superdudicitur C[18]; *many variants incl* superdicitur, subducitur, superinducitur. **et . . . obducitur** *om* C[3]C[18]. **obducitur** *many variants incl* obduitur, obdividitur, obliviscitur. 2 **naturalis** naturali C[3]. **superet** superat C[3]; separat D[6]. 3 **inquit** *om* C[14]C[18]. 4-5 **neque nent** Amen C[3]; vivent C[18]. 5 **quoniam nec** quod non C[14]C[18]. 7 **adulterinus** alterius *many MSS incl* C[3]. 8 **fucatur** fuscatur *most MSS incl* C[3]C[10]C[18]Ro; fuscatus C[14]. 12 **quando quidem** cum tamen huiusmodi C[14]C[18]. 12-13 **fallax** vana *many MSS incl* C[3]. 13 **gracia** gloria *most MSS incl* C[3]C[10]C[18]. 14 **feni** agri *some MSS.* 15 **arescit** arescet *many MSS incl* C[10]C[18]; ares C[14]; arescent Ro. **sicut** tanquam C[10]C[18]; quem ad modum *many MSS.* 16 **cadit** cadet *many MSS incl* C[18]; decident *many MSS incl* V[2]; de C[14]. 17 **preteream** pertranseam C[10]C[14]; transeam C[18]. **malignius** malignius pocius C[10]C[14]C[18]. 17-18 **videar . . . succendere** videar subcensere C[3]; aliquos succendere videar C[14]C[18]; aliquos succendere E[1]; videar aliquos succensere *most MSS incl* Ro. 20 **vasellis** vasculis V[2]. **argenteis** aureis C[18]. **nappis** mappis *many MSS.* **vocalibus** vocalibus et *most MSS incl* C[3]C[14]C[18]; *om* C[10]; varalibus et Ro; bucalibus et C[23]D[1]Pa[8]. 21 **gradalibus** gracilibus I. 21-22 **scutellis . . . urceolis** et

admissus, set quociens temptasset ingredi, tociens
contigisset repelli, mutavit habitum et assumpsit
5 ornatum: tunc ad primam vocem aditus patuit veni-
enti. Qui procedens ad principem, pallium quod
gestabat cepit venerabiliter osculari. Super quo
princeps, admirans, cur hoc ageret inquisivit. Phi-
losciphus vero respondit: "Honorantem honoro,
10 quia quod virtus non potuit, vestis obtinuit." O
vanitas vanitatum, plus honoris defertur vestibus
quam virtutibus, plus venustati quam honestati. /

Artificialis species superducitur, et facies obducitur
naturalis, tanquam hominis artificium artem superet
Creatoris. Non sic, non sic. "Considerate," inquit,
"lilia agri, quomodo crescunt; non laborant, neque
5 nent. Dico autem vobis quoniam nec Salomon in
omni gloria sua coopertus est sicut unum ex istis."
Absit ut adulterinus color comparabilis sit nativo:
quin immo, cum facies adulterino colore fucatur, os
abominabili fetore corrumpitur. "Universa vanitas,
10 omnis homo vivens." Quid enim vanius quam pec-
tere crines, planare cesariem, tingere genas, unguere
faciem, producere supercilia, quando quidem "fallax sit gracia et vana pulcritudo"? "Omnis caro
fenum, et omnis gloria eius quasi flos feni," "quo-
15 niam tanquam fenum velociter arescit et sicut olera
herbarum cito cadit." Ut autem ornatum persone
preteream ne malignius quam verius videar animos
succendere, quid vanius quam ornare mensam man-
tilibus picturatis, cultellis ebore manicatis, vasis
20 aureis, vasellis argenteis, cuppis et nappis, vocalibus,
gradalibus, scutellis, coclearibus, furcinulis, salariis,

199

pitchers, boxes, and fans? What use is it to paint rooms, decorate poles, curtain an entrance, cover a floor, arrange a bed puffed with down, covered with silks, enclosed with curtains or even a canopy? For it is written: "When a man shall die, he shall take nothing away, nor shall his glory descend with him."

There is no one who can boast about the purity of his heart, because "in many things we all offend," and "if we say that we have no sin, we deceive ourselves, and the truth is not in us." Who is he who can say even this with the Apostle: "I am not conscious to myself of anything, but I am not hereby justified"? "Who is he and we will praise him?" "Behold among the saints none is unchangeable, the heavens are not pure in his sight," "and in his angels he found wickedness." "How much more is man abominable and unprofitable, who drinketh iniquity like water?" "It repented God that he had made man on the earth, seeing that the wickedness of men was great on the earth and that all the thought of man's heart was bent upon evil at every opportunity, and therefore, being touched inwardly with sorrow of heart, destroyed man whom he had created." Moreover wickedness has flourished, and the charity of many has grown cold. "They have all gone aside; they have become unprofitable together" et cetera. Nearly the whole life of mortals is filled with mortal sins, so that hardly anyone can be found who does not stray towards evil, who does not return to his vomit, who does not rot in his own dung, whereas instead they boast "when they have done evil and rejoice in

between each of the three pairs of words in most MSS incl C³C¹⁴C¹⁸Ro; et *between the second only* C¹⁰. 22 **bacilibus** hostilibus C⁹. **flabellis** favellis C¹⁰C¹⁴C¹⁸. **Quid** Qui C¹⁸. 24 **lectum** saccum C¹⁸. 25 **inflatum plumis** *trans* C¹⁴C¹⁸. 26 **canopeo** canopati C¹⁸. 26-27 **Homo . . . omnia** Non cum morietur accipiet hec omnia *nearly every MS incl* C³Ro, hec *and* omnia *trans* C¹⁴, hec *om* C¹⁸E¹. 27 **neque** neque simul *most MSS incl* C³Ro. 28 **gloria** gloria domus *many MSS incl* C¹⁰C¹⁸; Deus gloria C¹⁴; omnis gloria domus ArRe³T². **eius** eius Explicit Liber Secundus Ro, *followed by table of contents to Book III entitled* Incipiunt Capitula Tertii Libri.
      II.41: **Title** *om* C³ *because this chapter is included in the preceding one*; De Labe Interiori C¹⁰; De Labore Interiori C¹⁴; Incipit Liber Tertius de Damnabili Humane Dissolutionis Ingressu (Egressu *in table of contents*) Ro (*see Introduction, pp. 51-52, 53*). 3 **quia** quod C¹⁸. **nosmetipsos** nos ipsos *most MSS incl* C³C¹⁰C¹⁴C¹⁸Ro. 4 **est qui** *om* C¹⁸. 5 **vel . . . valeat** valeat illud dicere C¹⁴; valeat dicere illud C¹⁸; velit illud dicere V²; vel valeat dicere Pa⁹Pa¹¹. 6 **set non** non tamen *most MSS incl* C³Ro; nec tamen C¹⁰C¹⁴C¹⁸. 9 **eius** suis *most MSS incl* C³C¹⁰C¹⁴C¹⁸Ro. **repperit** repperit Deus C¹⁰C¹⁴C¹⁸. 10-11 **et . . . homo** homo et inutilis *many MSS incl* C¹⁴C¹⁸Ro. 11-12 **Penituit** Penituit ergo *nearly every MS incl* C³C¹⁰Ro, *above line* C¹⁴. 12 **quod . . . fecisset** fecisse hominem C³; quod fecisset hominem *many MSS incl* C¹⁰C¹⁴C¹⁸. 13 **hominum** *om* C¹⁰; *added in margin* C¹⁴. **cuncta** cuncta ergo C¹⁴C¹⁸. 14 **est** C¹⁰; *om most MSS incl* C³C¹⁴Ro. 15 **et ideo** *om* C¹⁰C¹⁴C¹⁸. **tactus** tactus ergo Deus C¹⁴C¹⁸. **cordis** *om* C³. 16 **quem** quod C¹⁸. **creavit** creaverat C³. **Porro** Porro ubi C¹⁸. 17 **malicia** iniquitas *most MSS incl* C³Ro; nequicia C¹⁰C¹⁴C¹⁸. **et** *om* C¹⁴C¹⁸. **multorum** nullorum C¹⁸. 18 **et cetera** non est qui faciat bonum non est usque ad unum *most MSS incl* C³C¹⁰C¹⁴Ro; *om* C¹⁸. 19 **pene vita** *trans* C¹⁰C¹⁴C¹⁸. **mortalibus** *om* C³. 20 **deivet** *spelled* *deviet *in nearly every MS incl* C³C¹⁰C¹⁴C¹⁸Ro. 21 **revertatur** vertatur C¹⁴C¹⁸. **ad vomitum** admonitum C¹⁸. 21-22 **computrescat** putrescat *most MSS incl* C³C¹⁰C¹⁴C¹⁸. 22 **stercore** stercore suo Ro. **cum** quin *most MSS incl* C³C¹⁰C¹⁴C¹⁸; qui Ro. **gloriantur** glorientur C¹⁴. 23 **exultant**

bacilibus, urceolis, capsulis, et flabellis? Quid prodest pingere cameras, ditare perticas, palliare vesti-
bulum, substernere pavimentum, componere lectum
25 inflatum plumis, opertum sericis, obductum cortinis
aut etiam canopeo? Scriptum est enim: "Homo cum
interierit, non sumet omnia, *neque descendet cum eo*
gloria eius."

[41] QUOD NEMO DE SE GLORIETUR

Non est qui de cordis mundicia valeat gloriari,
quoniam "in multis offendimus omnes," et "si dixerimus quia peccatum non habemus, nosmetipsos
seducimus, et veritas in nobis non est." Quis est qui
5 vel illud dicere valeat cum Apostolo: "Nichil michi
conscius sum, set non in hoc iustificatus sum?"
"Quis est / hic et laudabimus eum?" "Ecce inter   f. 102v
sanctos nemo est immutabilis, celi non sunt mundi in
conspectu eius," "et in angelis eius repperit pravita-
10 tem." "Quanto magis abominabilis est et inutilis
homo, qui bibit quasi aquam iniquitatem?" "Peni-
tuit Deum quod hominem fecisset in terra, eo quod
multa esset malicia hominum super terram et cuncta
cogitacio hominis omni tempore ad malum est in-
15 tenta, et ideo, tactus dolore cordis intrinsecus, delevit hominem quem creavit." Porro superhabundavit
malicia, et refriguit caritas multorum. "Omnes de-
clinaverunt; simul inutiles facti sunt" et cetera. Tota
pene vita mortalium mortalibus est plena peccatis,
20 ut vix valeat inveniri qui non deivet ad sinistram,
qui non revertatur ad vomitum, qui non computres-
cat in stercore, cum pocius gloriantur "cum male-

most wicked things." "Being filled with all iniquity, malice, fornication, avarice, wickedness, full of envy, murder, contention, deceit, malignity, whisperers, detractors, hateful to God, contumelious, proud, haughty, inventors of evil things, disobedient to parents, foolish, dissolute, without affection, without fidelity, without mercy." This world is filled with such and worse by far; for it abounds with heretics, schismatics, traitors, tyrants, simoniacs, hypocrites, the ambitious, the covetous, robbers, plunderers, the violent, extortioners, usurers, forgers, the ungodly, the sacrilegious, betrayers, liars, flatterers, deceivers, babblers, the crafty, gluttons, drunkards, adulterers, the incestuous, the effeminate, the impure, the lazy, the negligent, the vain, the wasteful, the impetuous, the angry, the impatient, the inconstant, sorcerers, soothsayers, perjurers, those who blind, the presumptuous, the arrogant, the unbelieving, the desperate, finally those caught in all vices combined. But "as smoke vanisheth they shall vanish, and as wax melteth before the fire, so shall the wicked perish."

exultent C10C14; exultavit C18. **25 homicidio** homicidiis *most MSS incl* C3C10C14C18Ro. **30 multo** *om most MSS incl* C3C10C14C18Ro. **est** *om most MSS incl* C3C10C14C18Ro. **31-40 hereticis . . . desperatis** et *between each pair of words in nearly every MS incl* C3C10C14C18Ro. **33 violentis** vinolentis C3. **exactoribus** execratoribus C10; extractoribus C14C18. **33-34 usurariis** usurariis gulosis C18. **34 falsariis** ebriosis C18. **35 adulatoribus** adulteratoribus C18. **36 gulosis ebriosis** *om* C18. **37 prodigis** profugis C14C18. **39-40 periuris . . . arrogantibus** *om* C10C14C18. **39 execatis** execratis *most MSS incl* C3Ro. **40 incredulis** incrudelis *a few MSS.* **deinde** demum *most MSS incl* C3C10C14C18Ro. **41 irretitis** irretiti C14C18. **sicut deficit** sic deficient C3. **42 deficient . . . cera** *om* C10C18; *in margin* C14, *with* deficiant *for* deficient. **sic** ita *many MSS incl* C3. **42-43 peccatores peribunt** peccatores peribunt a facie Dei C3; pereant peccatores a facie Dei *many MSS incl* C14E1V2; peribunt peccatores a facie Dei C18. **43 peribunt** *followed by table of contents to Book III in* L20 *(on f. 103), entitled* Incipiunt Capitula Tercie Partis; *two chapters follow in* Ro, *for which see Appendix III.*

fecerint et exultant in rebus pessimis." "Repleti
omni iniquitate, malicia, fornicacione, avaricia, ne-
25 quicia, pleni invidia, homicidio, contencione, dolo,
malignitate, susurrones, detractores, Deo odibiles,
contumeliosi, superbi, elati, inventores malorum,
parentibus non obedientes, insipientes, incompositi,
sine affectione, absque federe, sine misericordia."
30 Talibus et multo peioribus mundus iste repletus est;
habundat enim hereticis, scismaticis, perfidis, tyran-
nis, symoniacis, ypocritis, ambiciosis, cupidis, rap-
toribus, predonibus, violentis, exactoribus, usurariis, falsariis, impiis, sacrilegis, proditoribus,
35 mendacibus, adulatoribus, fallacibus, garrulis, ver-
sutis, gulosis, ebriosis, adulteris, incestuosis, mollibus, immundis, pigris, negligentibus, vanis, prodigis,
impetuosis, iracundis, impacientibus, inconstantibus,
veneficis, auguribus, periuris, excecatis, presumptu-
40 osis, arrogantibus, incredulis, / desperatis, deinde   f. 103
universis viciis irretitis. Porro "sicut deficit fumus
deficient, et sicut fluit cera a facie ignis, sic peccatores peribunt."

THE THIRD PART

[1] OF THE ROTTENNESS OF CORPSES

"His spirit shall go forth, and he shall return into his earth; in that day all their thoughts shall perish." O how many and how great the things mortals plan on account of the uncertainty of wordly foreknowledge, but at the moment of sudden death the things that they had planned suddenly disappear. "I am taken away like the shadow when it declineth, and I am shaken off as locusts." Therefore the spirit does not go forth willing, but unwilling, because it gives up with sorrow what it possessed with love, and whether it wishes or not, a limit has been set for it that cannot be gone beyond, at which earth shall return to earth. For it is written: "Earth thou art, and into earth thou shalt return." Certainly it is natural that something made of matter should be dissolved into matter. "He shall therefore take away their breath, and they shall fail, and shall return to their dust." But when man shall die, he shall inherit beasts, serpents, and worms. "For they shall all sleep in the dust, and worms shall cover them." "For the worm shall eat them up as a garment, and the moth shall consume them as wool." "I am to be consumed as rottenness and as a garment that is moth-eaten." "I have said to rottenness, 'Thou art my father'; to worms, 'my mother and my sister'." "Man is rottenness, and his son a worm." How foul the father, how vile the mother, how abominable the sister! For man is conceived of blood made rotten by the fire of lust; in the end worms stand by his body like mourners. Alive, he brings forth lice and tapeworms; dead, he will beget worms and flies. Alive, he produces dung and vomit; dead, he produces rottenness and stench. Alive, he fattens one man;

III: *Title* Incipit Liber Tertius de Putredine Cadaverum C³; Tercia Pars de Putredine Cadaverum C¹⁴; *om* Ro.

III.1: *Title* *no separate title to* III.1 *in* C³C¹⁴. 1 **Exibit** Exibit ergo C¹⁰. **eius** *om* C¹⁰; meus C¹⁴. 3 **quot et** *om* C¹⁰. **provisionis** promissionis C¹⁴C¹⁸. 4 **sub repentine** sub repente C¹⁰C¹⁴C¹⁸; sub repentino V²; subrecte L¹⁷; subrepte O³¹. 5 **repente** cuncta C¹⁰C¹⁴C¹⁸; repente cuncta *most MSS incl* C³Ro. **cogitaverant** cogitaverunt C¹⁴; cogitant V². 6 **cum** que C¹⁴C¹⁸. **ablatus sum** ablati sunt *many MSS*. **ablatus . . . sum** ablati sunt et excussi sunt *many MSS incl* C³C¹⁴C¹⁸. 7 **spiritus** spiritus eius C¹⁴C¹⁸. 8 **dimittet** amittet *many MSS incl* C¹⁴C¹⁸; dimittit V². **que** quod *most MSS incl* C¹⁰C¹⁴C¹⁸. **amore** gaudio C¹⁸. 9 **et velit** at velit *most MSS incl* C³Ro; velit an C¹⁰; an velit an C¹⁴; velit C¹⁸. **ei** *om* C³C¹⁸. **qui** que C¹⁸. 10 **potest** poterit *most MSS incl* C³C¹⁰C¹⁴C¹⁸Ro. **quo** qua C¹⁸. **revertetur** revertatur C¹⁰. 11 **enim** *om* C¹⁴C¹⁸. 12 **Naturale** Navitale C¹⁸. **siquidem** quidem C¹⁴C¹⁸. **materiatum** materialiter C¹⁸. 13 **resolvatur** revertatur C¹⁰C¹⁴C¹⁸; dissolvatur *many MSS incl* Ro. 13-14 **et deficient** inde C¹⁰; et deficiant C¹⁸. 14 **suum** *om* C¹⁰. 15-16 **bestias . . . vermes** vermes et serpentes C¹⁰C¹⁸; vermes bestias et serpentes C¹⁴. 16 **dormient** dormiunt C¹⁰; dormiant C¹⁸. 18 **comedet eos vermis** commedent vermes C¹⁸. 22-23 **filius eius** filius hominis C³; et filius hominis *most MSS incl* C¹⁰C¹⁴C¹⁸Ro. 24 **Conceptus** *corrected from* Contemptus C¹⁸. **enim** *om most MSS incl* C¹⁰C¹⁴C¹⁸V². 26 **cadaveri** cadaveri tam musce C³, *in margin* C¹⁴. **quasi** quam C¹⁸; quasi *expunged and* quam *added in margin* C¹⁴. **assistent** assistunt C¹⁴. 27 **gignit** genuit *most MSS incl* C³C¹⁰C¹⁴C¹⁸Ro. 28 **producit** produxit *most MSS incl* C³C¹⁸Ro. 29 **producit** producet *most MSS incl* C³Ro; *om* C¹⁰. **putredinem** pudorem ArRe³T². 30 **unicum**

TERCIA PARS

[1] DE PUTREDINE CADAVERUM

"Exibit spiritus eius, et revertetur in terram suam; In Psalmo
in illa die peribunt omnes cogitaciones eorum." O
quot et quanta mortales de mundane provisionis
incertitudine cogitant, set sub repentine mortis arti-
5 culo repente que cogitaverant evanescunt. "Sicut In Psalmo
umbra cum declinat ablatus sum, et excussus sum
sicut locusta." Exibit ergo spiritus non voluntarius,
set invitus, quia cum dolore dimittet que cum amore
possedit, et velit nolit, constitutus est ei terminus qui
10 preteriri non potest, in quo terra revertetur in
terram. Scriptum est enim: "Terra es, et in terram In Genesi
ibis." Naturale siquidem est ut materiatum in materiam resolvatur. "Auferet ergo spiritum eorum, et In Psalmo
deficient, et in pulverem suum revertentur." Cum In Ecclesias-
tico
15 autem morietur homo, hereditabit bestias, serpen-
tes, et vermes. "Omnes enim in pulvere dormient, Iob
et vermes operient eos." / "Sicut vestimen- f. 103v
Ysaias
tum sic comedet eos vermis, et sicut lanam sic
devorabit eos tinea." "Quasi putredo consumendus
20 sum et quasi vestimentum quod commeditur a
tinea." "Putredini dixi, 'Pater meus es; mater mea Iob
et soror mea', vermibus." "Homo putredo, filius
eius vermis." Quam turpis pater, quam vilis mater,
quam abominabilis soror! Conceptus est enim homo
25 de sanguine per ardorem libidinis putrefacto; cuius
tandem cadaveri quasi funebres vermes assistent.
Vivus, gignit pediculos et lumbricos; mortuus, generabit vermes et muscas. Vivus, producit stercus et

dead, he will fatten many worms. What, then, is more foul smelling than a human corpse? What more horrible than a dead man? He whose embrace was most pleasing in life will indeed be a disgusting sight in death. What good, therefore, are riches? What good sumptuous food? What good delicacies? They will not free from death, will not defend from the worm, will not take away from the stench. He who was lately sitting glorious on the throne now lies despised in the grave; he who was lately shining splendid in the palace is now slighted naked in the tomb; he who was lately filling himself with delicacies in the dining hall is now consumed by worms in the sepulcher.

[2] OF THE SAD MEMORY OF THE DAMNED

"The vengeance on the flesh of the ungodly is worm and fire." Each one double: an interior one that gnaws and burns the heart, an exterior one that gnaws and burns the body. "Their worm," he says, "shall not die, and the fire shall not be quenched." "The Lord will give fire and worms into their flesh that they may burn and may feel forever." The worm of conscience will torture in three ways: it will weaken with memory, it will disturb with repentance, it will torment with anguish. "For they shall come with fear at the thought of their sins, and their iniquities shall stand against them opposite," saying: "What hath pride profited us, and what advantage hath the boasting of riches brought us? All those things are passed away like a shadow, like a ship that passeth through the waves whereof, when it is gone by, the trace cannot be found." Thus also us: having been born, we immediately cease to be; indeed we can show no sign of virtue, but are consumed in our own evil. With great confusion they will reflect upon what they have done with

unum C^{14}C^{18}. **inpinguat** inpugnavit C^3; inpinguabat C^{14}; inpugnavit *corrected to* inpinguavit C^{18}; inpinguavit *most MSS incl* V^2. 31 **inpinguabit** inpugnabit C^3; generabit BuLmPa^{5}Pa^{9}Pa^{11}, *corrected from* impinguabit Go. **ergo** igitur C^3; enim C^{10}; est C^{14}C^{18}. 33 **gratissimus** gravissimus *a few MSS.* **erat amplexus** erat C^{10}C^{18}; amplexus erat in terra C^{14}. 33-34 **molestus . . . morte** eciam aspectus eius molestus erit in morte C^{10}; et aspectus erit molestus in morte C^{14}; aspectus terribilis erit in morte infectus C^{18}; horribilis *for* molestus *a few MSS.* 35 **delicie** honores C^3; honores Divitie enim *many MSS incl* Ro; delicie, *with* honores *and* divicie *in margin* C^{14}. 36 **non defendent** non defendunt C^{18}; epule non defendent *many MSS incl* Ro, epule *in margin* C^{14}. **verme** putredine C^{14}C^{18}. **non eripient** honores non eripient *many MSS incl* Ro, honores *in margin* C^{14}. 37-38 **sedebat . . . modo** *om here but added later, before* vescebatur *in ll. 39-40* C^{10}C^{14}C^{18}. 39 **sordet nudus** sordet C^3; sedet nudus *some MSS.*

III.2: 1 **impii** vipera C^{10}; impie C^{14}C^{18}; cornupeta L^{17}O^{31}. **vermis . . . ignis** *trans* C^{10}C^{14}C^{18}. 2-3 **qui (2nd) . . . corpus** *om* C^{18}. 3 **corpus** cor C^{14}. 4 **ignis** ignis racionis C^{10}; ignis inquit eorum C^{14}C^{18}. 4-5 **Dominus** Deus C^{10}C^{14}C^{18}. 6 **usque** *om* C^{3}C^{14}C^{18}. **sempiternum** eternum C^{14}C^{18}. **Vermis** Virtus E^1. 7 **tripliciter** triplex C^{18}. **lacerabit** laborabit C^{10}. **memoria** memoriam eorum C^{10}. 7-8 **penitencia** pena *many MSS incl* C^3; prudenciam C^{10}. 8 **angustia** iusticia vel angustia C^{14}C^{18}. **enim** *om many MSS incl* C^{3}C^{10}. 8-9 **cogitacione** cogitacionem C^{10}; cogitacionibus C^{14}C^{18}; memoriam EvRu^2. 9 **suorum** *above line* L^{20}. **timidi** timidi vel stimuli *above line* C^{14}. **et** *om* C^{14}C^{18}. **transducent** transducet *most MSS incl* C^{3}C^{10}C^{14}C^{18}. 10 **illos** eos C^{10}C^{14}C^{18}. **iniquitates** iniquitas *most MSS incl* C^{3}C^{10}C^{14}C^{18}Ro. 11 **profuit nobis** *trans* C^{14}C^{18}. **et** *om* C^{14}C^{18}. 12 **contulit nobis** *trans* C^{14}C^{18}. **omnia illa** *trans most MSS incl* C^{3}C^{10}C^{18}Ro. 13 **tanquam** quasi C^{10}C^{18}; sicut C^{14}. **sicut** et quasi C^{14}; et sicut C^{18}; qui C^{18}. **pertransit** pertransiit C^{18}; per C^{14}. 14 **aquam** undam C^{18}. **cuius** quam C^3. **preterierit** pertransierit C^{10}C^{14}C^{18}. **non** et ideo C^{18}. **invenire** inventum C^{10}C^{14}C^{18}. 15 **vestigium** vestigium eius

vomitum; mortuus, producit putredinem et fetorem.
30 Vivus, hominem unicum inpinguat; mortuus, vermes
plurimos inpinguabit. Quid ergo fetidius humano
cadavere? Quid horribilius homine mortuo? Cuius
gratissimus erat amplexus in vita molestus erit
eciam aspectus in morte. Quid, ergo, prosunt divi-
35 cie? Quid epule? Quid delicie? Non liberabunt a
morte, non defendent a verme, non eripient a fetore.
Qui modo sedebat gloriosus in throno modo iacet
despectus in tumulo; qui modo fulgebat ornatus in
aula modo sordet nudus in tumba; qui modo vesce-
40 batur deliciis in cenaculo modo consumitur a vermibus in sepulchro.

[2] DE TRISTI MEMORIA DAMPNATORUM

"Vindicta carnis impii vermis et ignis." Uterque In Ecclesias-tico
duplex: interior qui rodit et urit cor, exterior qui
rodit et urit corpus. "Vermis," inquit, "eorum non Ysaias
morietur, et ignis non extinguetur." "Dabit Domi- In Iudicum
5 nus ignem et vermes in carnes eorum ut urantur et
senciant usque in sempiternum." Vermis consciencie
tripliciter lacerabit: affliget memoria, turbabit penitencia, torquebit angustia. "Venient enim in cogi- In Libro Sapi-encie
tacione peccatorum suorum timidi, et transducent
10 illos ex adverso iniqui- / -tates eorum," dicentes: f. 104
"Quid profuit nobis superbia, et iactancia diviciarum quid contulit nobis? Transierunt omnia illa
tanquam umbra, sicut navis que pertransit fluctuan-
tem aquam cuius, cum preterierit, non est invenire
15 vestigium." Sic et nos: nati, continuo desinimus esse;
virtutis quidem nullum signum valemus ostendere,
set in malignitate nostra consumpti sumus. Cum
ingenti turbacione recogitabunt que cum nimia de-

excessive delight, so that the prick of memory torments into punishment those whom the sting of wickedness has goaded into sin.

[3] OF THE USELESS REPENTANCE OF THE CONDEMNED

They will say within themselves, doing penance: "We have erred from the way of truth, and the light of justice hath not shined into us." "Then shall they begin to say to the mountains: 'Fall upon us'; and to the hills: 'Cover us'." They will repent to the point of punishment, but will not repent to the point of forgiveness. For it is just that those who would not when they could cannot when they wish, for God gave them an opportunity for repentance and they wasted it. For that reason the rich man who was tormented in the flame said to Abraham: "'I beseech thee, father, that thou wouldst send Lazarus to my father's house. For I have five brethren, that he may testify unto them, lest they also come into this place of torments'. When Abraham said to him: 'They have Moses and the prophets; let them hear them', he said: 'No, father Abraham, but if one went to them from the dead, they will do penance'." He himself was also doing penance in hell, but because he knew it to be useless, he asked that it be reported to his brothers so that they might do fruitful penance in this life, because it is good for a man to repent when he is able to sin.

[4] OF THE UNSPEAKABLE ANGUISH OF THE DAMNED

"These seeing it shall be troubled with terrible fear, groaning for anguish of spirit and saying: 'These are they whom we had some time in derision and for a parable of reproach; we fools esteemed their life madness and their end without honor. Behold how they are numbered among the children of God

C^3. 16 **quidem** *om many MSS incl* C^{18}Ro. 18 **recogitabunt** cogitabunt C^{14}. 18-19 **delectacione** cogitatione C^3. 19 **gesserunt** gesserint C^{18}. **pungat** pungnat (*for* pugnat?) C^{14}.

III.3: 1 **Dicent** Dicunt C^{18}. **intra** inter C^{3}C^{14}C^{18}. 4 **collibus** colles C^{14}C^{18}. **Operite** Operire C^3; Cooperite C^{10}C^{18}. **set** et C^{14}C^{18}. 5 **conterentur** convertentur *most MSS incl* C^{3}E^{1}Ro; revertentur C^{14}C^{18}. **que** qui C^3; quia *most MSS incl* C^{10}C^{14}C^{18}. 7 **Deus eis** *trans most MSS incl* C^{3}E^{1}Ro; illis Deus C^{14}; eis C^{18}. 8 **Propterea** Ipse C^{18}. **ille** *om* C^{10}C^{14}C^{18}. 10-12 **Habeo . . . tormentorum** et cetera C^{14}C^{18}. 11 **ut . . . illis** *om many MSS incl* C^{3}C^{10}. 12 **Cui cum** Cum enim C^{10}; Cum autem C^{14}; Cum et C^{18}. 15 **eos** illos C^{3}C^{14}C^{18}. 17 **rogabat** rogavit C^{10}C^{14}C^{18}. 20 **potest . . . peccare** potest peccare C^3; ipse ex sui facultate potest peccare vel penitenciam agere C^{14}; ipse ex sui facultate peccare potest vel penitenciam temporalem portare C^{18}; potest ipse portare E^1.

III.4: *Title* De Ineffabili Angustia Reproborum vel Dampnatorum C^3. 1-2 **pre . . . gementes** gementes pre angustia spiritus *most MSS incl* C^{3}C^{10}C^{14}C^{18}Ro. 3 **derisum** desiderium Re^{3}T^2. 4 **illorum** *om many MSS incl* C^3. 8 **gloriam** glorias C^3. **beatorum**

lectacione gesserunt, ut stimulus memorie pungat ad
20 penam quos aculeus nequicie stimulavit ad culpam.

[3] DE INUTILI PENITENCIA REPROBORUM

Dicent intra se, penitenciam agentes: "Erravimus a In Libro Sapiencie
via veritatis, et iusticie lumen non illuxit nobis."
"Tunc incipient dicere montibus: 'Cadite super nos'; Lucas
et collibus: 'Operite nos'." Penitebunt ad penam, set
5 non conterentur ad veniam. Iustum est enim ut que
noluerunt cum potuerunt cum velint non possint,
dedit enim Deus eis locum penitencie et ipsi abusi
sunt eo. Propterea dives ille qui cruciabatur in
flamma dicebat ad Abraham: "'Rogo te, pater, ut Lucas
10 mittas Lazarum in domum patris mei. Habeo enim
quinque fratres, ut testetur illis, ne et ipsi veniant in
hunc locum tormentorum'. Cui cum Abraham re-
spondisset: 'Habent Moysen et prophetas; audiant
illos', subiunxit: 'Non, pater Abraham, set si quis ex
15 mortuis ierit ad eos, penitenciam agent'." Agebat et
ipse penitenciam in inferno, set quia cognoscebat
illam inutilem, rogabat ut annunciaretur hoc fratribus quatinus agerent penitenciam in hoc seculo
fructuosam, quia tunc prodest homini penitere cum
20 potest ipse peccare.

[4] DE INEFFABILI ANGUSTIA DAMPNATORUM /

"Videntes turbabuntur timore horribili, pre angus- f. 104v
tia spiritus gementes et dicentes: 'Hii sunt quos
aliquando habuimus in derisum et in similitudinem
improperii; nos insensati vitam illorum estimabamus
5 insaniam et finem illorum sine honore. Ecce quo-

and their lot is among the saints'." The punishment of the wicked will be to look upon the glory of the blessed, although perhaps after the end of judgment. The blessed may indeed see the condemned in torments, according to this saying: "The just shall rejoice when he shall see the revenge on the ungodly." But the condemned may not see the blessed in glory, according to this saying: "Let the wicked be taken away lest he see the glory of God." "Such things as these the sinners said in hell, for the hope of the wicked is as dust which is blown away with the wind, and as a thin froth which is dispersed by the storm, and as a smoke scattered abroad by the wind, and as the remembrance of a guest of one day."

[5] OF HELL FIRE

The fire of hell is neither fed by wood nor kindled by blowing, but was created inextinguishable by God from the beginning of the world. It is written: "A fire that is not kindled shall devour him." It is believed, moreover, to be under the earth, according to the prophetic saying: "Hell below was in an uproar to meet thee at thy coming." But indeed every place is penal for the condemned, who always carry a torture with them and encounter a torment confronting them everywhere. "I will bring forth," he says, "a fire from the midst of thee, to devour thee." But the fire of hell will always blaze and never be visible, always burn and never consume, always trouble and never cease. For there is in hell the greatest obscurity of darkness, an immense harshness of torments, an infinite immensity of miseries. "Bind," he says, "his hands and feet; cast him into the exterior darkness; there shall be weeping and gnashing of teeth." Individual members will undergo torments appropriate to their own sins, so that people are punished in the member with which they have sinned. For it is written: "By what things a man sinneth, by the same also is he

bonorum $C^{10}C^{14}C^{18}$; beatorum C^3. **finem** diem many MSS incl $C^{10}C^{14}C^{18}$. 9 **Beati** Sancti $C^{10}C^{14}C^{18}$. **sint** sunt most MSS incl $C^{10}C^{14}$Ro; s C^3. 11 **visuri non sint** non sunt visuri most MSS incl $C^3C^{10}C^{14}C^{18}$Ro. 12 **beatos** bonos C^{14}; beatos C^3. 13 **dicent** dicunt C^{18}. 17 **memoria hospitis** hospes C^3. diei one chapter follows in Ro, for which see Appendix III.

III.5: 3 **Scriptum est** om C^3; Sicut scriptum est Ro. **eos** eum most MSS incl $C^{10}C^{14}C^{18}V^2$. 4 **autem** et $C^{14}C^{18}$. 6 **occursu** occursum most MSS incl $C^3C^{10}C^{14}C^{18}$Ro. **tui** sui C^{14}. **et** om many MSS incl $C^3C^{10}C^{14}C^{18}$. 7 **qui** quia most MSS incl $C^3C^{10}C^{14}C^{18}$. 7-8 **secum deferunt** trans $C^{10}C^{14}C^{18}$. 10-11 **et . . . lucebit** om C^{10}. 11 **uret** exuret many MSS incl $C^3C^{14}C^{18}$. 13-14 **immensa . . . acerbitas** om C^{18}. 14 **miseriarum** miserorum C^{10}. 14-15 **immensitas** eternitas most MSS incl $C^3C^{10}C^{14}C^{18}$Ro. 15 **manibus . . . pedibus** trans most MSS incl C^3C^{10}. 16 **mittite** proicite C^{10}. 19 **peccaverunt** peccave-

modo computati sunt inter filios Dei et inter sanctos sors illorum est'." Supplicium erit malorum intueri gloriam beatorum, licet forte post finem iudicii. Beati quidem visuri sint reprobos in tormentis,

10 secundum illud: "Letabitur iustus cum viderit vindictam impiorum." Reprobi vero visuri non sint beatos in gloria, secundum illud: "Tollatur impius ne videat gloriam Dei." "Talia dicent in inferno peccatores, quoniam spes impii tanquam lanugo est

15 que a vento tollitur, et tanquam spuma gracilis que a procella dispergitur, et tanquam fumus a vento diffusus, et tanquam memoria hospitis unius diei."

In Psalmo

Ysaias

In Libro Sapi-
encie

[5] DE IGNE GEHENNALI

Ignis gehenne nec lignis nutritur nec flatu succendi-
tur, set a Deo creatus est inextinguibilis ab origine mundi. Scriptum est: "Devorabit eos ignis qui non succenditur." Creditur, autem, esse sub terris, se-

5 cundum illud propheticum: "Infernus subter con-
turbatus est in occursu adventus tui." Set et omnis locus reprobis est penalis, qui semper secum deferunt cruciatum et ubique contra se tormentum incur-
runt. "Producam," inquit, "ignem de medio tui, qui

10 comedet te." Ignis autem gehenne semper ardebit et nunquam lucebit, semper uret et nunquam consu-
met, semper afficiet et nunquam deficiet. Est enim apud inferos summa tenebrarum obscuritas, immensa penarum acerbitas, infinita miseriarum im-

15 mensitas. "Ligatis," inquit, "manibus et pedibus; mittite eum in tenebras exteriores; ibi erit fle- /- tus et stridor dencium." Singula menbra pro suis peccatis propria sustinebunt tormenta, ut in eo puniantur in quo peccaverunt. Scriptum est enim: "Per que

Iob

Ysaias

Ezechiel

Matheus
f. 105

Salomon

211

tormented." Thus he who sinned with the tongue was tortured in the tongue. Because of this he cried: "Father Abraham, have mercy on me and send Lazarus that he may dip the tip of his finger in water to cool my tongue, for I am tormented in this flame."

[6] OF INFERNAL DARKNESS

The condemned are in fact wrapped not only in exterior but also in interior darkness, because they are devoid of spiritual as well as corporeal light. For it is written: "Let the wicked be taken away lest he see the glory of God," who alone will then be "in everlasting light." For the condemned will suffer so much anguish in their punishments that they will hardly be able to contemplate anything except the punishments, but "will direct the power of their thoughts to the place where they feel the force of their pains." A certain student is actually said to have appeared after death to his teacher. When the teacher had perceived that he was damned, he asked of him if any "questions" were deliberated in hell. He is said to have replied that in hell only what is not a punishment is inquired into. But in addition Solomon says: "Neither work nor reason nor wisdom shall be in hell, whither thou art hastening." For there will be among the condemned so much forgetfulness of the mind, so much blindness of the intellect, so much confusion of the reason that rarely or never can they rise to think anything about God, still less can they take a breath to confess. For "from the dead," as from one who is not, "praise perisheth." For it is written: "The dead shall not praise thee, Lord, nor any of them that go down to hell." "Hell shall not confess to thee, neither shall death praise thee."

rant C³. 20 **hec** hoc C¹⁸. **torquetur** torquebunt C³; torquebitur C¹⁴C¹⁸. 21 **lingua** *(1st)* in lingua *many MSS incl* C¹⁰C¹⁴C¹⁸. **in . . . cruciabatur** cruciabantur in lingua C³; torquebatur in lingua C¹⁰C¹⁴; *om* C¹⁸; *trans most MSS incl* Ro. 22 **ipse clamabat** clamabat C¹⁰; clamabat ipse dives C¹⁴C¹⁸. 24-25 **flamma** flamma Per digitum intelligitur operatio digitis enim operamur Quasi diceret Si minimum operum Lazari haberem minorem penam sentirem V², *in margin* C¹⁴ *with* dicent *for* diceret *and* digitum *for* operum.

III.6: **Title** Inferni *for* Infernalibus C³C¹⁰C¹⁴Ro. 2 **quia** quorum C¹⁸. 5 **lucem eternam** lucem sempiternam *most MSS incl* C³Ro; vitam eternam C¹⁴E¹; eternam vitam C¹⁸. **enim** autem *most MSS incl* C³C¹⁰C¹⁴C¹⁸Ro. 7 **valeant** valebunt C³. **preter penas** preter penam C¹⁴; propter penam V². 8-9 **quidam discipulus** *trans most MSS incl* C³C¹⁰C¹⁴C¹⁸Ro. 9 **magistro** magistro suo C³, *above line* C¹⁴. 10 **intellexisset** intellexisse C¹⁸. **esse** *om* C³. 11 **quesivit** que sunt C¹⁸, *corrected to* quesivit C¹⁴. **apud** ad C¹⁸. 13 **queri . . . pena** nichil esse nisi penam C³; nichil esse nisi solummodo penam C¹⁸, *with* penam *corrected to* pena C¹⁴. **et** *om many MSS incl* C¹⁸V². 14 **racio** oracio C¹⁰. **sapiencia** scientia nec sapientia *most MSS incl* C³C¹⁰C¹⁴C¹⁸; sapientia nec scientia Ro. 15 **in reprobis** reprobis *many MSS incl* C¹⁴C¹⁸; improbis *some MSS.* 16-17 **confusio** concussio EvRu². 18 **nedum** nec C³; nec Deo L¹⁷O³¹. **ad** *om* C¹⁸. 20 **non est** periit C¹⁰; perit C¹⁸. 21-22 **neque . . . infernum** et cetera C¹⁸. 22 **Nec** Non *most MSS incl* C³C¹⁰C¹⁴C¹⁸Ro.

peccat homo, per hec et torquetur." Unde qui
lingua peccaverat in lingua cruciabatur. Propter
quod ipse clamabat: "Pater Abraham, miserere mei   Lucas
et mitte Lazarum ut intingat extremum digiti sui in aqua
ut refrigeret linguam meam, quia crucior in hac flamma."

[6] DE TENEBRIS INFERNALIBUS

Reprobi vero non solum exterioribus set etiam interi-
oribus tenebris involventur, quia spirituali pariter
et corporali luce carebunt. Scriptum est enim: "Tol-   Ysaias
latur impius ne videat gloriam Dei," qui solus tunc
erit "in lucem eternam." Tantam enim in penis
reprobi tolerabunt angustiam ut vix aliquid cogitare
valeant preter penas, set "illuc dirigent impetum
cogitacionis ubi sencient vim doloris." Sane quidam
discipulus fertur apparuisse magistro post mortem.
Quem cum magister intellexisset esse dampnatum,
quesivit ab eo si alique questiones apud inferos
verterentur. Qui dicitur respondisse apud inferos
queri quid solummodo non sit pena. Set et Salomon
ait: "Nec opus nec racio nec sapiencia est apud
inferos, quo tu properas." Erit enim in reprobis
tanta mentis oblivio, tanta cecitas animi, tanta confusio racionis ut raro vel nunquam ad cogitandum
quicquam de Deo possint assurgere, nedum ad confitendum valeant respirare. Nam "a mortuo," tanquam ab eo qui non est, "perit confessio." Scriptum
est enim: "Non mortui laudabunt te, Domine, neque   In Psalmo
omnes qui descendunt in infernum." "Nec infernus
confitebitur tibi, neque mors laudabit te."

"Suffer me," says Job, "that I may lament my sorrow a little before I go, and return no more, to a land that is dark and covered with the mist of death, a land of misery and darkness, where the shadow of death, and no order, but everlasting horror dwelleth." There will indeed be order in the quantity of punishments, because "with what measure you mete, it shall be measured to you again," so that they who have sinned in greater measure are punished in greater measure. "For the mighty shall suffer torments mightily." But there will be no order in the quality of things, because "they will pass from the snow waters to excessive heat," so that the sudden exchange of opposites causes a greater torment. I have learned from experience that a person who has been burned, if he is immediately subjected to cold waters, will feel a more burning torture.

[8] OF THE UNFAILING SUPPLY OF TORMENTS

"They are laid in hell like sheep; death shall feed upon them." This saying is from the resemblance of the beasts of burden, who do not tear out the grass by the roots, but pull only the tops, so that the grass grows again for fodder. Thus also the ungodly, as if consumed by death, will revive to death so that they are forever dying. "Thus the liver of Tityus, unconsumed and always growing again, will not perish, so that it can perish many times." Then will death be undying; then will the dead live who are dead to life. They who have had and lost life will seek and not find death. Hear John in the Apocalypse, saying: "In those days men shall seek death and shall not find it, and they shall desire to die, and death shall fly from them." O death, how sweet you would be to

III. 7: *Title* De Conversione Penarum C³Ro; Confessione *for* Confusione Re³T². 1 **dicit Iob** Domine C¹⁰C¹⁸, *with* dicit Iob *above line* C¹⁴. 2 **et non revertar** *om many MSS incl* C³C¹⁰C¹⁸. 4 **et tenebrarum** *om* C¹⁸. 5 **quidem** quidam C¹⁸. 5–6 **erit** *om* C¹⁴C¹⁸. 7 **fueritis** fuerint C³. **vobis** eis C³. **ut** unde C¹⁸. 7–8 **gravius** graviter C¹⁰C¹⁴C¹⁸. 8 **peccaverunt** peccaverit C¹⁴C¹⁸E¹. **gravius** graviter C¹⁴. **puniantur** puniatur C¹⁰C¹⁴C¹⁸. 9 **patientur** et ertientur C³; tollerabunt C¹⁴C¹⁸. 9–10 **in qualitate** in quantitate *many MSS incl* C³; equalitate C¹⁸E¹. 10 **rerum quia** elementorum quia ignis exuret et non lucebit ut serviat ad tormentum non ad consolationem et EvRu². 11 **nimium** nimium et de nimio ardore ad frigus intollerabile EvRu². **subita** subito C¹⁰. 12 **inferat** inferet C¹⁴. 13 **frigidis statim** frigidum statim *most MSS incl* C³C¹⁰C¹⁴; frigus statim C¹⁸; frigidum Ro. **adhibeatur** adhibeat *most MSS incl* C³C¹⁰C¹⁴C¹⁸Ro.

III.8: *Title* Dampnatorum *for* Tormentorum C¹⁰; De Infidencia Dampnatorum C¹⁴; De Diffidentia Damnatorum Ro. 1 **depascet** depascit C¹⁴; d C¹⁸. 2 **eos** ei C¹⁸. **autem** *om most MSS incl* C³C¹⁰C¹⁴C¹⁸Ro. 3–4 **summitates solummodo** *trans many MSS incl* C¹⁴ C¹⁸. 4 **iterum** interim C¹⁴. **renascantur** nascantur C¹⁸. 5–6 **reviviscent** reviviscunt C¹⁸. 6 **Sic** Unde poeta Sic C¹⁴C¹⁸. 8 **sepe** *om* C¹⁸. **perire** venire C³. 9 **qui** *om* C³; quia *most MSS.* 13 **et (1st)** *om most MSS incl* C¹⁰C¹⁴C¹⁸. **desiderabunt** desiderabunt homines

[7] DE CONFUSIONE PENARUM

"Dimitte me," dicit Iob, "ut plangam paululum
do*lorem* m*eum* antequam va*dam,* et non re*vertar,* ad
te*rram* te*nebrosam* et o*pertam* m*ortis* c*aligine,* te*rram*
m*iserie* et te*nebrarum,* ubi u*mbra* m*ortis* et n*ullus* or*do,*
5 set sem*piternus* hor*ror* inhabitat." Ordo quidem e-
rit / in quantitate penarum, quoniam "in qua men-   f. 105v
sura mensi fueritis, remecietur vobis," ut qui gravius peccaverunt, gravius puniantur. "Potentes enim
potenter tormenta patientur." Set ordo non erit in
10 qualitate rerum, quia "de aquis nivium transibunt ad   Iob
calorem nimium," ut subita contrariorum mutatio
graviorem inferat cruciatum. Experimento cognovi
quod adustus, si frigidis statim adhibeatur, arden-
ciorem senciet cruciatum.

[8] DE INDEFICIENCIA TORMENTORUM

"Sicut oves in inferno positi sunt; mors depascet   In Psalmo
eos." Dictum est autem hoc a simili iumentorum,
que non radicitus herbas evellunt, set summitates
solummodo carpunt, ut iterum herbe renascantur ad
5 pastum. Sic et impii, quasi morte depasti, reviviscent ad mortem ut eternaliter moriantur. "Sic in-   Ovidius
consumptum Ticii semperque renascens non perit,
ut possit sepe perire iecur." Tunc erit mors immortalis; tunc vivent morti qui vite sunt mortui. Que-
10 rent mortem et non invenient qui vitam habuerunt et
perdiderunt. Audi Iohannem in Apocalipsi, dicentem: "In diebus illis querent homines mortem et non
invenient eam, et desiderabunt mori, et fugiet mors
ab illis." O mors, quam dulcis esses quibus tam

those to whom you were so bitter; they who violently hated you alone will eagerly desire you alone.

[9] WHY THE CONDEMNED WILL NEVER BE FREED FROM PUNISHMENT

Let ńo one flatter himself and say that "God will not be angry in the end, nor will he threaten forever," but "his tender mercies are over all his works," because when he is angry, he does not "forget to show mercy," nor does he hate any of the things that he has made. Assuming in proof of this error what the Lord says through the prophet: "They shall be gathered together as in the gathering of one bundle into the pit, and they shall be shut up in prison, and after many days they shall be visited." For man sinned in time; God will therefore not punish all men in eternity. O vain hope, o false presumption! "He shall not believe, being vainly deceived by error, that he may be redeemed with any price," "because in hell there is no redemption." Therefore sinners shall be gathered into a pit and shut up in a prison, namely in hell, in which they will be tortured without their bodies up to the day of judgment, and after many days, namely after they rise with their bodies on the last day, they will be visited not with salvation but with vengeance, because after the day of judgment they will be punished more severely. Thus also is it said elsewhere: "I will visit their iniquities with a rod and their sins with stripes." God is therefore temporarily angry with those who are saved, for "he scourgeth every son whom he receiveth." From these things it is accepted: "He will not always be angry" et cetera. But with the condemned God is eternally angry, for it is just that what sin the ungodly man commits in his eternity God punishes in his. ·For although the capability of sinning may

C³. 14 **illis** ipsis C³; eis *most MSS incl* C¹⁴C¹⁸Ro. 15 **solam** solum C¹⁴C¹⁸. 16 **oderunt** oderunt O mors quam dura quam trista sunt tua iura T²Re³.

III.9: *Title* Cur *for* Quod C³C¹⁴Ro; Quare *for* Quod C¹⁰; Libentur *for* Liberabuntur C¹⁰; Penis *for* Pena C³C¹⁰C¹⁴Ro. 1 **Nullus** Nullus ergo *many MSS incl* C³; Nullus igitur *most MSS incl* C¹⁰C¹⁴C¹⁸V². **sibi** sic C³. **Deus** *om* C¹⁴. 1-2 **non in finem** in finem non C¹⁰C¹⁴C¹⁸. 2 **irascetur** irasceretur C¹⁸. 3 **opera** ossa C¹⁸. 4 **iratus est non** *om* C¹⁸. **est** fuerit C¹⁴. **obliviscitur** obliviscetur C³. 5 **odit** odivit *most MSS incl* C³C¹⁰C¹⁴C¹⁸Ro. 6 **Dominus** Deus C¹⁰. 7 **in** *(1st)* *om* C¹⁴C¹⁸. **fascis** falcis C³. 8 **carcerem** carcere *most MSS incl* C¹⁰C¹⁴. 9 **visitabuntur** visitabuntur non ad salutem C¹⁰; vivificabuntur non ad salutem C¹⁴; iustificabuntur C⁴C⁵. **peccavit** peccat C¹⁰C¹⁴C¹⁸; pecunie ArRe³T². 10 **omnes** Deus *most MSS incl* C³C¹⁸; Dominus C¹⁰C¹⁴; *om* Ro. **puniet** punit C¹⁸. 14 **peccatores in lacum** in lacum peccatores C¹⁰C¹⁸. 15 **carcere** carcerem *most MSS incl* C³Ro. 16 **corporibus** opibus Re³T². 16-17 **usque . . . dies** *om* C¹⁸. 16 **ad** in *most MSS incl* C¹⁰C¹⁴V². 17 **postquam videlicet** *om* C¹⁰C¹⁸; visitabuntur postquam videlicet V². 17-18 **resurgent cum corporibus** in corporibus resurgent C¹⁰C¹⁴; resurgunt C¹⁸; resurgent cum opibus ArRe³T². 18 **visitabuntur** *corrected to* vivificabuntur C¹⁴. 20 **punientur** puniantur C³C¹⁸. **dicitur** *om* C¹⁰C¹⁸. 21-22 **et . . . eorum** et cetera C¹⁸. 23 **flagellat** flagellat Pater C¹⁰C¹⁴; flagellat Deus C¹⁸. 24-25 **et cetera** neque in eternum comminabitur *many MSS incl* C¹⁴; *om* C¹⁸V². 25 **autem . . . irascitur** vero irascitur C¹⁴E¹; vero irascitur Deus C¹⁸. 26-27 **in . . . eterno** prevaricatur eterno in suo C¹⁴C¹⁸. 27 **suo** suo eterno C³C¹⁴C¹⁸. 28 **ipse tamen** *trans* C¹⁰C¹⁴C¹⁸. 29 **peccandi** peccati C³;

15 amara fuisti; te solam desideranter optabunt qui te
solam vehementer oderunt.

[9] QUOD REPROBI NUNQUAM LIBERABUNTUR A PENA

Nullus sibi blandiatur et dicat quia "Deus non in   In Psalmo
finem irascetur, neque in eternum indignabitur," set
"miseraciones eius super omnia opera eius," quia
cum iratus est, non "obliviscitur misereri," nec
5   quicquam eorum que fecit odit. Assumens in argu-
mentum erroris quod ait Dominus per prophetam:
"Congregabuntur in congregacione unius fascis in
lacum, et clauden- / -tur in carcerem, et post mul-   f. 106
tos dies visitabuntur." Homo namque peccavit ad
10 tempus; non ergo omnes puniet in eternum. O spes
inanis, o falsa presumpcio! "Non credat, frustra
errore deceptus, quod aliquo precio redimendus
sit," "quoniam in inferno nulla est redempcio."
Congregabuntur ergo peccatores in lacum et clau-   Ysaias
15 dentur in carcere, scilicet in inferno, in quo sine
corporibus usque ad diem iudicii torquebuntur, et
post multos dies, postquam videlicet resurgent cum
corporibus in novissimo die, visitabuntur non ad
salutem set ad vindictam, quia post diem iudicii
20 gravius punientur. Sic et alibi dicitur: "Visitabo in   In Psalmo
virga iniquitates eorum et in ver*beribus peccata
eorum.*" Predestinatis ergo Deus irascitur temporali-
ter, quia "flagellat omnem filium quem recipit." De
quibus illud accipitur: "Non in finem irascetur" et
25 cetera. Reprobis autem Deus irascitur eternaliter,
quia iustum est ut quod impius in suo prevaricatur
eterno Deus ulciscatur in suo. Nam licet peccandi
facultas illum dimittat, ipse tamen non dimittit

217

abandon him, still he does not abandon the desire for sinning. For it is written: "The pride of them that hate thee ascendeth continually." The condemned will not be humbled, having already despaired of forgiveness, but the evil of hatred will grow so much in them that they wish him not to exist at all through whom they know themselves to exist so unhappily. They will curse the Most High and blaspheme the Most Excellent, complaining that he is evil who created them for punishment and is never inclined to forgiveness. Hear John in the Apocalypse, saying: "Great hail came down from heaven upon men, and men blasphemed God for the plague of the hail because it was exceeding great." The will of the damned person therefore, though it lose the effect of its power, will still have its fondness for evil, and will itself be a punishment in hell that was a sin in the world, although perhaps even there it may be a sin, but not deserving of punishment. The ungodly man therefore, because he will always have in him the guilt of sin, will always feel the torment of punishment confronting him, because what he himself did not cancel out through repentance God will not forgive through pardon. "It therefore pertains to the great justice of the Judge that they are never free from punishment in hell who never wished to be free from sin in this life. They would therefore have wished, if they could, to live without end so that they might have been able to sin without end. For they show that they always desire to live in sin who never cease to sin while they live."

[10] TESTIMONIES OF ETERNAL PUNISHMENTS

"Which of you," says Isaias, "can dwell with everlasting burnings?" "These shall be as smoke in my anger, a fire burning all the day." "Day and night it shall not be quenched, but the smoke thereof shall go up forever." Jeremias: "I will bring an everlasting reproach upon you and a perpetual shame which

peccandi quia si semper viveret semper vellet peccare EvRu². 31 **iam tam** C¹⁸. 32 **in** . . . **tantum** tantum in illis *most MSS incl* C³Ro; tantum in illum C¹⁰C¹⁴; in Deum C¹⁸. **tantum excrescet** excrescet tantum *marked for trans* L²⁰. **excrescet** exercetur C¹⁰; exercebitur C¹⁴C¹⁸. **ut velint** velit C¹⁸. 33 **per** propter C¹⁸. **infeliciter** feliciter C¹⁸. 34 **esse** esse dampnatos C¹⁰; esse dampnandos C¹⁴C¹⁸. **Maledicent** Maledicunt C¹⁸. 35 **conquerentes** et querentes C¹⁴. **esse** *om many MSS incl* C³C¹⁰C¹⁸. **qui** quia *many MSS incl* C³. 36 **illos** eos *most MSS incl* C³C¹⁰C¹⁴C¹⁸V². **inclinatur** inclinetur *most MSS incl* C³C¹⁰C¹⁴C¹⁸. 38 **descendit** descendet C¹⁸. 38-39 **blasphemaverunt** blasphemabunt C¹⁸. 39 **grandinis** *om* C¹⁰C¹⁸. 40 **vehementer** nimis C¹⁰C¹⁴C¹⁸. **Voluntas** Voluptas *many MSS incl* C³. 41 **potestatis** *om* C³; peccatis C¹⁴. 42 **tamen** cum C¹⁸. 44 **forsitan et** et forsan C¹⁰; forsitan C¹⁴; *trans* C¹⁸; forsan et *most MSS incl* Ro. **peccatum sit** *trans* C¹⁰C¹⁴; erit peccatum C¹⁸. 45 **semper** *om* C¹⁰C¹⁸. **habebit** habebat *many MSS incl* C¹⁰C¹⁸Ro; habet C¹⁴. 45-46 **in** . . . **culpa** reatum ad culpam *corrected to* reatum ex culpa C¹⁸. 46 **semper** *om* C³C¹⁸. **contra se** se esse V². 48 **remittet** remittit C³C¹⁴. 48-54 **Ad** . . . **vivunt** *om* C³. 49 **ut** si C¹⁰C¹⁴. 49-50 **careant in gehenna** eciam gehennali careant C¹⁰C¹⁴C¹⁸. 51 **hac** *om most MSS incl* C¹⁰C¹⁴C¹⁸Ro. **itaque** C¹⁰; utique *most MSS incl* Ro. 51-52 **potuissent** possent C¹⁰; possunt C¹⁸. 52 **sine** . . . **vivere** vivere sine fine C¹⁰C¹⁴C¹⁸. **potuissent** possent C¹⁸. **sine fine** *om* C¹⁰C¹⁸. **peccare** peccare dum viverent C¹⁴; peccasse C¹⁸. 53-54 **Ostendunt** . . . **peccare** *om* C¹⁰C¹⁸. 54 **vivunt** viverent C¹⁰C¹⁸.

III.10: *Title* Testimonia *om* C¹⁰. 1 **de vobis** *om* C¹⁰C¹⁸. 2 **Isti** Istis C¹⁴C¹⁸. **erunt** . . . **fumus** fumus erunt *most MSS incl* C³Ro; erunt ignis C¹⁰; fumus erit C¹⁴; erit fumus C¹⁸. 3 **in** *om* C¹⁸. **Die ac nocte** Nocte et die *most MSS incl* C³C¹⁰C¹⁴Ro; Nocte dieque C¹⁸. 4 **eius** eius usque C¹⁰C¹⁴C¹⁸. 5-6 **Dabo** . . . **eternam** *om* C¹⁰. 5 **vos** *om* C¹⁸. 6 **in** *om most*

voluntatem peccandi. Scriptum est enim: "Superbia In Psalmo
30 eorum qui te oderunt ascendit semper." Non humi-
liabuntur reprobi, iam desperati de venia, set malig-
nitas odii in illis tantum excrescet ut velint illum
omnino non esse per quem sciunt se tam infeliciter
esse. Maledicent Altissimo et blasphemabunt Excel-
35 sum, conquerentes eum esse malignum qui creavit
illos ad penam et nunquam inclinatur ad veniam.
Audi Iohannem in Apocalipsi, dicentem: "Grando
magna descendit de celo in homines, et blasphemaverunt homines Deum propter plagam grandinis quo-
40 niam magna facta est vehementer." Voluntas ergo
dampnati, licet amiserit potestatis effectum, semper
/ tamen habebit malignitatis affectum, et ipsa erit f. 106v
in inferno supplicium que fuerat in mundo peccatum, licet forsitan et ibi peccatum sit, set non meri-
45 tum pene. Impius ergo, quia semper habebit in se
reatum ex culpa, semper senciet contra se cruciatum
ex pena, quia quod ipse per penitenciam non delevit
Deus per indulgenciam non remittet. "Ad magnam
ergo pertinet iusticiam Iudicantis ut nunquam ca-
50 reant in gehenna supplicio qui nunquam voluerunt in
hac vita carere peccato. Voluissent itaque, si potuissent, sine fine vivere ut potuissent sine fine peccare.
Ostendunt enim quod in peccato semper vivere
cupiunt qui nunquam desinunt peccare dum vivunt."

[10] TESTIMONIA DE SUPPLICIIS ETERNALIBUS

"Quis," inquit Ysaias, "poterit habitare de vobis
cum ardoribus sempiternis?" "Isti erunt quasi fumus
in furore meo, ignis ardens tota die." "Die ac nocte
non extinguetur, set ascendet fumus eius in sempi-
5 ternum." Ieremias: "Dabo vos in obprobrium sem-

shall never be forgotten." Daniel: "Those that sleep in the dust of the earth shall awake, some unto life everlasting, others unto reproach to see it always." Solomon: "When the wicked man is dead, there shall be no hope for him." For this man his damnation will come immediately, and he will be destroyed suddenly, nor will he have a remedy besides. John the apostle: "If any man shall adore the beast and his image, he shall drink of the wine of the wrath of God and shall be tormented with fire and brimstone; and the smoke of his torments shall ascend up forever and ever, neither will he have rest day and night who has adored the beast and his image." Truth confirms this, who will tersely condemn the damned in judgment: "Depart, you cursed, into everlasting fire, which was prepared for the devil and his angels." If according to divine judgment "in the mouth of two or three witnesses every word stands," by how much more will the word of propounded truth stand firm in the mouth of so many and such great men.

[11] OF THE DAY OF JUDGMENT

"Behold, the day of the Lord shall come, cruel and full of indignation and of wrath and fury, to lay the land desolate and to destroy the sinners thereof out of it, for the stars of heaven and their brightness shall not display their light, the sun shall be darkened in his rising, and the moon shall not shine with her light. And I will visit evils upon the world and their own iniquity against the wicked, and I will make the pride of infidels to cease and will bring down the arrogance of the mighty." The Lord says: "Therefore shall all hands be faint, and every heart of man shall melt and shall be broken. Grippings and pains shall take hold of sinners; they shall be in pain as a woman in labor. Everyone

MSS incl C³C¹⁴C¹⁸Ro. 7 **oblivione** in oblivione C¹⁰. **dormient** dormiunt C¹⁰C¹⁴C¹⁸; dormierunt V². 8 **terre** terra in C¹⁰C¹⁴C¹⁸. 9 **obprobrium** obprobrium sempiternam C¹⁴. **videant** vivant C¹⁰C¹⁴C¹⁸. 10 **eo** illo C¹⁰C¹⁴. 11 **extemplo** exemplo many MSS. **perdicio** petitio C³. 12 **apostolus** above line C¹⁴; om C¹⁸. 13 **et** vel C¹⁰C¹⁴C¹⁸. 14 **bibet** om C¹⁸. **Dei** dicitur C¹⁸. 15 **eius** C¹⁰; om most MSS incl C³C¹⁸Ro. 16 **nec** non C³C¹⁸. 17 **et** vel C¹⁴C¹⁸. 18 **sentencialiter** sentenciabit et C¹⁰C¹⁴; om V². 19 **reprobabit** reprobabit dicens C¹⁴C¹⁸Ro. 19-20 **in . . . eius** et cetera C¹⁸. 20 **preparatus** propria C³; paratus V². 21-22 **testium** om C¹⁰C¹⁸. 22 **stat** stet in C³; stet most MSS incl C¹⁰C¹⁴C¹⁸Ro. **in ore** testimonio C¹⁰C¹⁸. 23 **virorum de** om C¹⁰; virorum testimonio de C¹⁴. **proposita** posita C¹⁰; in posita C¹⁸. **veritate** vita D¹.

III.11: *Title* De Magno Die Iudicii C¹⁴. 1-2 **plenus indignacionis** trans most MSS incl C³C¹⁰C¹⁴C¹⁸Ro. 2 **et** (*1st*) om C¹⁴C¹⁸. 4 **stelle** splendor C³. **earum** stellarum C³. **non** om C¹⁰. **expandent** expandunt C¹⁴. 5 **suum** om C¹⁸. **obtenebrabitur** obtenebratus C³; obtenebratus est most MSS incl C¹⁰Ro; obscuratus est C¹⁴C¹⁸. 8 **quiescere** requiescere V². 9 **Dicit Dominus** om most MSS incl C³C¹⁰C¹⁴C¹⁸Ro; contra omnes L¹⁷O³¹. 11 **contabescet** tabescet most MSS incl C³C¹⁰C¹⁴C¹⁸Ro. 12 **peccatores** om most MSS incl C³Ro; eos C¹⁰; eos et C¹⁴C¹⁸. **quasi . . . dolebunt** om C¹⁰. 14-15 **dies** (*3rd*) . . . **angustie**

piternum et in ignominiam eternam que nunquam
oblivione delebitur." Daniel: "Qui dormient in
terre pulvere evigilabunt, alii in vitam eternam, alii
in obprobrium ut videant semper." Salomon: "Mortuo homine impio, nulla spes erit de eo." Huic
extemplo veniet perdicio sua, et subito contereretur,
nec habebit ultra medicinam. Iohannes apostolus:
"Si quis adoraverit bestiam et ymaginem eius, hic
bibet de vino ire Dei et cruciabitur igne et sulphure;
et fumus tormentorum eius ascendet in secula seculorum, nec habebit requiem die ac nocte qui adoraverit bestiam et ymaginem eius." Confirmat hoc
Veritas, que dampnandos in iudicio sentencialiter
reprobabit: "Ite, maledicti, in ignem eternum, qui
preparatus est diabolo et angelis eius." Si secundum
divinum / iudicium "in ore duorum vel trium testium stat omne verbum," quanto magis in ore tot et
tantorum virorum de proposita veritate constabit.

f. 107
In Deutero-
nomio

[11] DE DIE IUDICII

"Ecce, dies Domini veniet, crudelis et plenus indignacionis et ire et furoris, ad ponendam terram in
solitudinem et peccatores eius conterendos de ea,
quoniam stelle celi et splendor earum non expandent
lumen suum, obtenebrabitur sol in ortu suo, et luna
non splendebit in lumine suo. Et visitabo super
orbem mala et contra impios iniquitatem eorum, et
quiescere faciam superbiam infidelium et arrogancium forcium humiliabo." Dicit Dominus: "Propter
hoc omnes manus dissolventur, et omne cor hominis
contabescet et conteretur. Torciones et dolores te-
nebunt peccatores; quasi parturiens dolebunt. Unusquisque ad proximum suum stupebit, facies com-

shall be amazed at his neighbor, their countenances as faces burnt." "That day, a day of wrath, a day of tribulation and distress, a day of calamity and misery, a day of darkness and obscurity, a day of cloud and whirlwinds, a day of the trumpet and alarms, for the Lord shall make a speedy destruction of all them that dwell in the land." "And that day shall come suddenly as a snare upon all that sit upon the face of the earth," for "as lightning cometh out of the east and appeareth even unto the west, so shall the coming of the Son of Man be." "For the day of the Lord shall so come as a thief in the night. For when they shall say 'Peace and security', then shall sudden destruction come upon them, as the pain upon her that is with child, and they shall not escape."

[12] OF THE TRIBULATION THAT PRECEDES

"Great tribulation," however, "such as hath not been from the beginning of the world until now, neither shall be," will precede. "And unless those days had been shortened, no flesh should be saved." "For nation shall rise against nation, and kingdom against kingdom, and there shall be great earthquakes in divers places and pestilences and famines and terrors from heaven and tempests." "And there shall be signs in the sun and the moon and the stars, and upon the earth distress of nations by reason of the confusion of the roaring of the sea and of the waves, with men withering away for fear and expectation of what shall come upon the whole world." "There shall arise false Christs and false prophets, and they shall show great signs and wonders to deceive, if possible, even the elect." "Then the man of sin shall be revealed, the son of perdition, who opposeth and is lifted up above all that is called or worshipped God, so that he sitteth in the temple of God, showing himself as if he were God," "whom God shall kill with the spirit of his mouth." "Elias the prophet,"

om C^3. **dies *(3rd)*** . . . **dies *(2nd)*** *om* C^{10}C^{14}C^{18}. 15 **miserie** miserie dies tribulacionis et angustie C^{14}C^{18}. 15–16 **dies *(2nd)*** . . . **caliginis** *om* C^{10}. 17 **quia** quia cum C^{10}. 17–18 **consummacionem cum festinacione** cum consumatione C^{10}. 18 **faciet** veniet C^{10}; sencient L^8; vanet Ma^3. **Dominus** Deus C^{10}C^{14}C^{18}. 18–19 **terram** super terram C^{10}C^{14}C^{18}. 19 **repentina** dies illa repentina C^{10}C^{14}; *om* C^{18}. **dies illa** *om* C^{14}. 20 **omnes** omnibus C^{10}. **sedent** sedunt C^{18}. **terre** C^{10}; omnis terre *most MSS incl* C^{3}Ro; universe terre *a few MSS*. 21 **fulgur** *om* C^3. **exit** erit C^{14}C^{18}. **ab** in C^{10}C^{14}C^{18}. **apparet** patet C^3; apparebit C^{14}; paret *some MSS*. 22 **occidentem** occidentes C^3. 23 **in** . . . **ita** de nocte C^{10}C^{14}; ita de nocte C^{18}. 24 **veniet** *om* C^{18}. 25 **eis** *om* C^{10}C^{18}. **dolor** dolorem C^{10}C^{18}. 25–26 **in** . . . **habenti** in utero habent C^{10}; in utero C^{14}; habebunt in utero C^{18}.

III.12: 1 **tribulacio magna** *trans* C^{10}C^{14}C^{18}. 1–2 **nunquam** non C^{14}C^{18}. 2 **neque** nec C^{10}; non C^{18}. 3 **fuissent breviati** *trans most MSS incl* C^{3}Ro; abreviati fuissent C^{10}C^{18}; abbreviati essent C^{14}; abbreviasset Dominus EvRu^2. **illi dies** *trans most MSS incl* C^{3}C^{10}C^{14}C^{18}Ro. 5 **terremotus** . . . **erunt** erunt terremotus C^{10}C^{14}C^{18}. 6–7 **fames** . . . **et *(1st)*** *om* C^{18}. 6 **terroresque de celo** *om* C^{10}. 7–8 **et stellis** *om* C^{10}C^{18}; et in stellis C^{14}. 8 **terris** terra C^{3}C^{18}; ter C^{10}C^{14}. **gencium** hominum *many MSS incl* C^3. 9–11 **arescentibus** . . . **orbi** *om* C^{10}. 10 **supervenient** superveniet C^{18}; superve C^{14}. 12 **signa** signa magna *most MSS incl* C^{3}Ro; signa multa C^{10}C^{14}C^{18}. 13 **inducantur** ducantur C^{18}. 15 **super** supra C^{10}C^{14}C^{18}. **dicitur** dicitur Deus *many MSS incl* C^{14}C^{18}. **aut** aut quod *many MSS incl* C^{14}C^{18}E^1. 16 **Deus** *om many MSS incl* C^{18}. 17 **Deus *(2nd)*** Dominus Iesus *most MSS incl* C^{3}C^{10}C^{14}C^{18}Ro. 18 **propheta** *om* C^{10}C^{18}. 18–19 **priusquam** antequam C^{14}. 19 **veniat**

buste vultus eorum." "Dies illa, dies ire, dies tribulacionis et angustie, dies calamitatis et miserie, dies
tenebrarum et caliginis, dies nebule et turbinis, dies
tube et clangoris, quia consummacionem cum festinacione faciet Dominus cunctis habitantibus terram." "Et superveniet repentina dies illa tanquam Lucas
laqueus in omnes qui sedent super faciem terre,"
quoniam "sicut fulgur exit ab oriente et apparet Matheus
usque in occidentem, ita erit adventus Filii Homi-
nis." "Dies enim Domini sicut fur in nocte ita Ad Tessaloni-
censes
veniet. Cum dixerint 'Pax et securitas', tunc repen-
tinus eis superveniet interitus, sicut dolor in utero
habenti, et non effugient."

[12] DE PRECEDENTE TRIBULACIONE

Precedet, autem, "tribulacio magna, qualis nun- Matheus
quam fuit ab inicio mundi usque modo, neque fiet.
Et nisi fuissent breviati illi dies, non fieret salva
omnis caro." "Surget enim gens contra gentem, et
regnum adversus regnum, et terremotus magni erunt
per loca et pestilencie et fames terroresque / de celo f. 107v
et tempestates." "Et erunt signa in sole et luna et
stellis, et in terris pressura gencium pre confusione
sonitus maris et fluctuum, arescentibus hominibus
pre timore et expectacione que supervenient uni-
verso orbi." "Surgent pseudochristi et pseudopro-
phete, et dabunt signa et prodigia ut in errorem
inducantur, si fieri potest, eciam electi." "Tunc Ad Tessaloni-
censes
revelabitur homo peccati, filius perdicionis, qui
adversatur et extollitur super omne quod dicitur aut
colitur Deus, ita ut in templo Dei sedeat, ostendens
se tanquam sit Deus," "quem Deus interficiet spiritu
oris sui." Mittetur, autem, "Helyas propheta prius- Malachias

223

however, will be sent "before the great and dreadful day of the Lord cometh, and he shall turn the hearts of the fathers to the children and the hearts of the children to the fathers." With him will come Enoch, "and they shall prophesy a thousand two hundred sixty days clothed in sackcloth." "And when they shall have finished their testimony, the beast that ascendeth out of the abyss shall make war against them and shall overcome them and kill them. And their bodies shall lie in the streets of the great city where their Lord was crucified." "And after three days and a half the spirit of life shall enter into them."

[13] HOW HE WILL COME TO JUDGE

"And immediately after the tribulation of those days, the sun shall be darkened, and the moon shall not give her light, and the stars shall fall from heaven, and the powers of the heavens shall be moved; and then shall appear the sign of the Son of Man in heaven. And then shall all tribes of the earth mourn." "Kings, princes, and tribunes, the rich and the strong and every bondman and every freeman shall hide themselves in the dens and in the rocks of mountains, and they shall say to the mountains and the rocks: 'Fall upon us and hide us from the face of him that sitteth upon the throne and from the wrath of the Lamb, for the great day of their wrath will come, and who shall be able to stand?'" "And he shall send his angels with a trumpet and a great voice, and they shall gather together his elect from the four winds of heaven, from the farthest parts of the heavens to the utmost bounds of them." Then "the Lord himself shall come down from heaven with commandment and with the voice of an archangel and with the trumpet of God." And "all that are in the graves shall hear the voice of the Son of God, and they that have done good things shall come forth unto the resurrection of life, but they that have done evil unto the resurrection of judgment." "Death and hell shall give up their dead that were in them," and "every eye shall see, and they also that pierced him," "the Son of Man coming in the clouds of heaven with great

... **Domini** veniat dies *many MSS incl* C[3]; dies Domini veniat C[10]; veniet dies Domini C[18]. **magnus** magis C[18]. 20–21 **corda ... patres** ad *corrected from* in L[20]; cor patrum ad filios et cor filiorum ad patres *many MSS incl* C[3]; corda filiorum ad patres et corda patrum ad filios C[14]C[18]E[1]; corda patrum in filios et cor filiorum ad patres eorum V[2]. 24 **adversus** contra C[18]. **illos** *(both)* eos *many MSS incl* C[10]C[14]C[18]. 25 **occidet** tradet C[10]. 26 **Dominus** Deus C[10]C[14]C[18]. 28 **eos** eis C[10]C[14]C[18].

III.13: **Title** De Die Iudicii C[3]; De Iusticia Iudicis C[10]; De Potencia et Iusto Iudicio C[14]; Qualiter Veniet Dominus ad Iudicium Ro; De Signis Precedentibus BuGoLm Pa[5]Pa[9]Pa[11]. 3 **celorum** earum C[18]. 5 **se** *om* C[14]; super se *many MSS incl* Ro. **tribus** fines C[10]C[14]. **Reges** Reges et *most MSS incl* C[3]C[10]C[14]C[18]V[2]. 6 **et** *(1st) om* C[10]C[14]C[18]. **tribuni** tribuni et *most MSS incl* C[3]C[10]C[14]C[18]. **divites** duces C[18]; principes C[9]. **fortes et** *om* C[10]C[14]C[18]. 6–7 **servus ... liber** *trans* C[10]C[14]C[18]. 7 **abscondent** abscondunt C[18]. **speluncis** sepulcris C[14]. **petris** cavernis C[14]C[18]. 8 **dicent** dicunt C[18]. 8–9 **et** *(2nd) ... et (1st) om* C[3]. 9 **et ... nos** *om* C[14]C[18]. **super thronum** in trono C[10]C[18]; in throno abscondite nos C[14]. 10 **quoniam** quem C[18]. **venit** veniet *many MSS incl* C[3]C[14]C[18]. **ire** *om* C[10]C[18]. **ipsorum** impiorum *many MSS incl* C[3]C[14]C[18]Ro. 11 **mittet** nutret C[18]. **suos** *om* C[10]. 13 **suos** eius *most MSS incl* C[3]C[10]Ro. **celi** celi et C[14]C[18]. 15 **in tuba** veritu C[18]. 16 **qui in** *om* C[18]. **monumentis** monumento C[3]. 17 **procedent** procedant C[18]. 19 **mortuos suos** *trans* C[10]. 21 **in ... celi** *om* C[10]C[14]C[18]. 22 **magna** multa *many MSS incl*

quam veniat dies Domini magnus et horribilis, et
20 convertet corda patrum in filios et corda filiorum ad
patres." Cum quo veniet Enoch, "et prophetabunt
diebus mille ducentis sexaginta amicti saccis." "Et
cum finierint testimonium suum, bestia que ascendet
de abysso faciet adversus illos bellum et vincet illos
25 et occidet. Et corpora eorum iacebunt in plateis
civitatis magne ubi Dominus illorum crucifixus est."
"Et post tres dies et dimidium spiritus vite intrabit
in eos."

[13] QUOMODO VENIET IUDICATURUS

"Statim autem post tribulacionem dierum illorum,
sol obscurabitur, et luna non dabit lumen suum, et
stelle cadent de celo, et virtutes celorum movebun-
tur; et tunc apparebit signum Filii Hominis in celo.
5 Et plangent se omnes tribus terre." "Reges, prin-   In Apocalipsi
cipes, et tribuni, divites et fortes et omnis servus et
liber abscondent se in speluncis et in petris mon-
cium, et dicent montibus et petris: 'Cadite super nos
et abscondite nos a facie Sedentis super thronum et
10 ab ira Agni, quoniam venit dies magnus ire ipsorum,
et quis poterit stare?'" "Et mittet an- / -gelos suos   Matheus
cum tuba et voce magna, et congregabunt electos   f. 108
suos a quatuor ventis celi, a summis celorum usque
ad terminos eorum." Tunc "ipse Dominus in iussu et   Ad Tessaloni-
15 in voce archangeli et in tuba Dei descendet de celo."   censes
Et "omnes qui in monumentis sunt audient vocem
Filii Dei, et procedent boni in resurrectionem vite,
mali vero in resurrectionem iudicii." "Mors et   In Apocalipsi
infernus dabunt mortuos suos qui in ipsis erunt," et
20 "videbit omnis oculus, et qui eum pupugerunt,"
"Filium Hominis venientem in nubibus celi cum

225

power and majesty." The Lord, however, will come to judgment not only with the angels but also with the senators of the land of his people. "Her husband was honorable in the gates when he sat among the senators of the land." For indeed they themselves will also sit "on twelve seats judging the twelve tribes of Israel." "I beheld," he says, "till thrones were placed and the Ancient of Days sat. His garment was white as snow, and the hair of his head like clean wool, his throne like flames of fire, the wheels of it a burning fire. A swift stream of fire issued forth from before him. Thousands of thousands ministered to him, and ten times a hundred thousand stood before him." "Our God shall come manifestly, our God, and shall not keep silence; a fire shall burn before him, and a mighty trumpet round about him." "Clouds and darkness are round about him, justice and judgment the establishment of his throne." "He shall call heaven from above to judge his people." For "all nations shall be gathered together before him, and he shall separate them one from another, as the shepherd the sheep from the goats; and he shall set the sheep on the right, but the goats on the left."

[14] OF THE POWER, WISDOM, AND JUSTICE OF THE JUDGE

O how great will be the fear and the trembling then; how great will be the weeping and the moaning! For if "the pillars of heaven tremble at and dread his coming," and "the angels of peace shall weep bitterly," then what will sinners do? "If the just man shall scarcely be saved, where shall the ungodly and the sinner appear?" For that reason the prophet called out: "Enter not into judgment with thy servant, Lord, for in thy sight no man living shall be justified." "For if thou, Lord, wilt mark iniquities, Lord, who shall stand it?" Who would not fear the most powerful, wisest, most just Judge—the most

C³. 23 **solum** solus C¹⁰C¹⁸, *corrected to* solum C¹⁴. **cum angelis** *om* C¹⁰C¹⁸; *above line* C¹⁴. **et** *om* C¹⁰C¹⁴C¹⁸. **cum** in C¹⁴. 24 **senatoribus** senioribus C¹⁴C¹⁸. **terre** *om most MSS incl* C¹⁰C¹⁴C¹⁸Ro. **populi sui** *om* C³; populi sui scilicet cum angelis suis C¹⁰. 24–25 **Nobilis . . . terre** *om* C¹⁸; *in margin* C¹⁴. **vir eius** *om most MSS incl* C³Ro. 25 **terre** populi sui C¹⁰. 26 **etenim** *om many MSS incl* C³C¹⁰C¹⁴C¹⁸; enim *most MSS incl* Ro. 27 **inquit** inquit Daniel C¹⁰C¹⁴C¹⁸. 28 **sedit** *a preceding* sedebit *expunged* L²⁰; sedebit C¹⁴. 30 **capitis** *om* C¹⁸. **quasi (2nd)** C¹⁰; *om most MSS incl* C³Ro. 31 **rote . . . ignis** *om* C¹⁰C¹⁸; *in margin* C¹⁴. **accensus** accensi C¹⁴C¹⁸, *with* accensus *in margin* C¹⁴. **Fluvius** Fumus C¹⁸. 32 **egrediebatur** egredietur C¹⁰. 33 **ministrabant** ministrabunt C¹⁸. **centena** milies centena *many MSS incl* C³; *om* C¹⁰. **assistebant** assistent C¹⁸. 35 **exardescet** ardebit C³. 36–38 **Nubes . . . eius** *om here and added after* suum *in line 39* C¹⁴E¹, *with* eius *om* C¹⁸, *with* conspectu *for* circuitu *some group MSS.* 37 **correctio** preparacio V². 38 **Et** *om* C³C¹⁰C¹⁴C¹⁸. **advocavit** advocabit C³. **desursum** desursum et terram *most MSS incl* C³C¹⁴C¹⁸V²; desuper C¹⁰. **discerneret** discernat *most MSS incl* C³C¹⁰C¹⁴C¹⁸Ro. 39 **Nam** Tunc Ro. 40 **gentes** reges omnes gentes servient ei C¹⁰C¹⁴C¹⁸. **ab** ad *most MSS incl* V². 41 **pastor** pastor segregat *most MSS incl* C³C¹⁰C¹⁴C¹⁸Ro. **statuet** statuet quidem *most MSS incl* C³C¹⁰Ro; statuit C¹⁸.

III.14: *Title* De Potentia Sapientia Iustitia et Iudicio C³; *om* C¹⁰ *because III.14 incl in III.13;* De Potencia Iudicis C¹⁴; et Sapientia *for* Sapiencia Ro. 1 **O** *om* C¹⁰C¹⁸. **tunc erit** *trans* C¹⁴C¹⁸. **quantus (2nd)** quantus tunc *many MSS incl* C¹⁰Ro. 2 **si** *om* C³. 2–3 **contremiscunt** contremescent C¹⁴. 3 **pavent** pavescent C³; pavescunt Ro. **adventum eius** *om* C¹⁰C¹⁸; *above line* C¹⁴; adventum filii hominis BuGoLmPa⁵Pa⁹Pa¹¹Pa¹⁵. 5–6 **parebunt** apparebunt C¹⁴C¹⁸. 6 **Propterea** *corrected probably from* Propheta L²⁰. **clamabat** clamat *many MSS incl* C¹⁴Ro. **Non** Ne *many MSS incl* C¹⁰V². 7 **Domine** *om many MSS incl* C³C¹⁰C¹⁴C¹⁸Ro. 10 **Quis** C¹⁰; Quis enim *most MSS incl* C³Ro. **timeat** timet C¹⁰.

virtute magna et maiestate." Veniet, autem, Dominus ad iudicium non solum cum angelis set et cum
senatoribus terre populi sui. "Nobilis in portis vir   Salomon
25 eius quando sederit cum senatoribus terre." Sede-
bunt etenim et ipsi "super sedes duodecim iudicantes   Marcus
duodecim tribus Israel." "Aspiciebam," inquit,   Daniel
"donec throni positi sunt et Antiquus Dierum sedit.
Vestimentum eius quasi nix candidum, et capilli
30 capitis eius quasi lana munda, thronus eius quasi
flamme ignis, rote eius ignis accensus. Fluvius igneus
rapidusque egrediebatur a facie eius. Milia milium
ministrabant ei, et decies centena milia assistebant
ei." "Deus noster manifeste veniet, Deus noster, et   David
35 non silebit; ignis in conspectu eius exardescet, et in
circuitu eius tempestas valida." "Nubes et caligo in
circuitu eius, iusticia et iudicium correctio sedis
eius." "Et advocavit celum desursum ut discerneret
populum suum." Nam "congregabuntur ante eum   Matheus
40 omnes gentes, et separabit eos ab invicem, sicut
pastor oves ab hedis; et statuet oves a dextris, hedos
autem a sinistris."

[14] DE POTENCIA, SAPIENCIA, ET IUSTICIA IUDICIS

O quantus tunc erit timor et tremor; quantus erit   f. 108v
fletus et gemitus! Nam si "columpne celi contremis-   Iob
cunt et pavent adventum eius," et "angeli pacis
amare flebunt," peccatores autem quid facient? "Si   In Epistola
                                                      Canonica
5 iustus vix salvabitur, impius et peccator ubi parebunt?" Propterea clamabat propheta: "Non intres in   David
iudicium cum servo tuo, Domine, quia non iustificabitur
in conspectu tuo omnis vivens." "Si enim iniquitates
observaveris, Domine, Domine, quis sustinebit?"
10 Quis non timeat Iudicem potentissimum, sapientissi-

227

powerful whom no one can escape, the wisest from whom no one can hide, the most just whom no one can corrupt or reproach? "If strength be demanded, he is most strong," wise in heart and strong in might; "if equity of judgment, no man dare bear witness for me. If I would justify myself, my own mouth shall condemn me; he shall prove me wicked although I should be simple." "He spoke, and they were made; he commanded, and they were created." "He calls the stars, and they say: 'Here we are'." "He maketh his angels spirits and his ministers a burning fire," whose "will absolutely nothing resists," for whom "no word is impossible," to whom "every knee shall be bowed of those that are in heaven, on earth, and under the earth." Consequently no one can escape him, as the prophet says: "If I ascend into heaven, thou art there; if I descend into hell, thou art present." "He searcheth the reins and hearts," to whose "eyes all things are naked and open," who "measures the drops of rain and the sand of the sea," "the Lord a God of all knowledge," prescient of all things and conscious of individual things, secret inquisitor of all secret things. Consequently no one can hide from him, as the Apostle says: "There is no creature invisible in his sight." He is a "just judge, strong and long-suffering," who does not turn aside from the path of righteousness "for entreaty or reward" or love or hatred, but always going the right way "passes no evil unpunished, leaves no good unrewarded." Consequently no one can reproach him, according to what the psalmist says: "Thou wilt render to each man according to his works."

Iudicem potentissimum *trans* $C^{14}C^{18}E^1$. 11 **iustissimum** et iustissimum *most MSS incl* $C^{10}C^{14}C^{18}$Ro. 12 **effugere . . . potest** *om* $C^{10}C^{14}C^{18}$. 13 **latere . . . potest** *om* C^3. 13-14 **corrumpere vel corripere** corrumpere *most MSS incl* C^3Ro; corrumpere sapientissimum quem nemo potest decipere $C^{10}C^{14}$, *with* corripere *for* corrumpere C^{18}. 14 **queritur** queratur C^{14}. 16 **pro me** *om* C^{14}. **testimonium reddere** *trans* C^{10}. 17 **condempnabit** contempnabit C^{18}. 18 **pravum . . . fuero** et si simplex fuero pravum me condempnabit C^{10}; si simplex fuero pravum me comprobabit $C^{14}C^{18}$. 19-20 **ipse (2nd) . . . sunt** *om* C^{10}. 19 **ipse (2nd)** omnia *many MSS incl* C^3; *om* C^{18}. 20 **sunt** sunt universa *some MSS*. **vocat** vocavit C^{18}. 22 **ignem urentem** flammam ignis $C^{10}C^{14}$. 23 **est** *om* C^{18}. 25 **ergo** *om many MSS incl* $C^{10}C^{14}C^{18}V^2$. 25-26 **sicut dicit** C^{10}; dicente *most MSS incl* C^3Ro. 26 **illuc** illic *most MSS incl* $C^{10}C^{14}$Ro; il C^3C^{18}. 28 **renes . . . corda** *trans* $C^{10}C^{14}$. **cuius oculis** cui C^3. 29 **harenam** arenas $C^{14}C^{18}$. 30 **Dominus** Dominus est C^3; et Dominus C^{18}. **prescius** prescius futurorum *above line* C^{14}. 31 **et** *om* C^{10}. **occultus** cognitor C^3; occultor C^{10}; *om* $C^{14}C^{18}$. 32 **ergo** *om many MSS incl* $C^{10}C^{14}C^{18}V^2$. 33 **dicit Apostolus** *trans* $C^{10}C^{14}C^{18}$. **Non est ulla** Non nulla C^3; Non est $C^{14}C^{18}$, *with* ulla *above line* C^{14}; Nulla *many MSS incl* V^2. 34 **eius** Dei $C^{14}C^{18}$. **Ipse** Ipse enim C^{10}; Ipse eciam $C^{14}C^{18}$. 35 **longanimis** longanimus $C^{14}C^{18}$. **nec . . . nec** nunc . . . vel C^{18}. 36 **nec (2nd)** vel C^{18}. 37 **recta** regia *most MSS incl* $C^3C^{10}C^{14}C^{18}$Ro. 39 **corripere** corrumpere *most MSS incl* $C^3C^{10}C^{14}C^{18}$Ro. 40 **ait** inquit *most MSS incl* C^3Ro. **singulis** unicuique C^{18}. **secundum** iuxta C^{18}. 41 **eorum** sua C^{14}.

mum, iustissimum—potentissimum quem nemo potest effugere, sapientissimum quem nemo potest
latere, iustissimum quem nemo potest corrumpere
vel corripere? "Si fortitudo queritur, robustissimus   Iob
15 est," sapiens corde et fortis robore; "si equitas
iudicii, nemo audet pro me testimonium reddere. Si
iustificare me voluero, os meum condempnabit me;
pravum me comprobabit etiam si simplex fuero."
"Ipse dixit, et facta sunt; ipse mandavit, et creata
20 sunt." "Qui vocat stellas et dicunt: 'Assumus'."
"Qui facit angelos suos spiritus et ministros suos
ignem urentem," cuius "voluntati nichil omnino
resistit," cui "nullum verbum est impossibile," cui
"flectitur omne genu celestium, terrestrium, et in-
25 fernorum." Hunc ergo nemo potest effugere, sicut
dicit propheta: "Si ascendero in celum, tu illuc es; si   David
descendero ad infernum, ades." "Ipse scrutatur
renes et corda," cuius "oculis omnia nuda sunt et
aperta," qui "pluvie guttas et harenam maris di-
30 numerat," "Deus scienciarum Dominus," prescius
omnium et conscius singulorum, occultus occul-
torum omnium indagator. Hunc ergo nemo potest
latere, sicut dicit Apostolus: "Non est ulla creatura   Ad Hebreos
invisibilis in conspectu eius." Ipse est "iudex / ius-   f. 109
35 tus, fortis et longanimis," qui "nec prece nec precio" nec amore nec odio declinat a semita rectitudi-
nis, set via recta semper incedens, "nullum malum
preterit impunitum, nullum bonum irremuneratum
relinquit." Hunc ergo nemo potest corripere, iuxta
40 quod ait psalmista: "Tu reddes singulis secundum
opera eorum."

But who would not fear that trial in which the same man will be the accuser and the advocate and the judge? For he will accuse when he says: "I was hungry, and you gave me not to eat; I was thirsty, and you gave me not to drink." He will advocate when he adds: "As long as you did it not to one of these least, neither did you do it to me." He will judge when he concludes: "Depart from me, you cursed, into everlasting fire." Witnesses will not be necessary in this judgment because "the hidden things of darkness" will then be exposed. "For nothing is hid that shall not be revealed." "Then the books will be opened, and the dead will be judged by those things which were written in the books according to their works." How great will be the shame among the sinners! How great the confusion when their most abominable crimes will be plainly exposed to all! "Blessed are they whose iniquities are forgiven and whose sins are covered." From that sentence he will never be able to be challenged because "the Father hath given all judgment to the Son," "he that openeth and no man shutteth, shutteth and no man openeth." "For the mouth of the Lord hath spoken it."

[16] THAT NOTHING SHALL BENEFIT THE DAMNED

Then riches will not benefit, nor honors protect, nor friends support. For it is written: "Their silver and gold shall not be able to deliver them in the day of the wrath of the Lord." "The kings of the earth shall weep and wail when they see the smoke of the burning," "for fear of its torments." "What therefore will ye do in the day of visitation and calamity which cometh from afar? To whom will ye flee for help?" "Everyone shall bear his own burden."

III.15: *Title* De Dei Noticia Re³T². 1 **timeat** timet C¹⁰; timebit C¹⁴C¹⁸. **in quo** ubi C¹⁸. 2 **Accusabit** Accusator C³. 3 **et** sitivi C³. 4 **dedistis** dedisti C¹⁴C¹⁸. **sitivi . . . michi** vel C³. 5 **de** ex *many MSS incl* C¹⁴C¹⁸. **minimis** minoribus *most MSS incl* C³C¹⁰. 6 **his** meis *many MSS incl* C¹⁴C¹⁸. **nec . . . fecistis** et cetera C¹⁴C¹⁸. 6-7 **Discedite a me** Ite C¹⁸. 7 **maledicti** maligni C¹⁰. 8 **testes . . . iudicio** in illo iudicio testes C¹⁰C¹⁴C¹⁸. 9 **abscondita** absedita C³. 10 **reveletur** revelabitur *most MSS incl* C³C¹⁰. **libri** libri conscientiarum Ro. 12 **eorum** eorum tribue illis et cetera C¹⁴, *with* illorum *for* eorum C¹⁸. **Quantus** Quantus tunc C¹⁰C¹⁴C¹⁸. 14 **cunctis erunt** *trans* C¹⁴C¹⁸. 15-16 **iniquitates . . . peccata** et cetera C¹⁸. 16-17 **nunquam** nusquam *many MSS incl* C³C¹⁸; nunquid *many MSS incl* C¹⁴. 17 **provocari** appellari non C¹⁴; appellari hec C¹⁸. 18 **dedit** dabit C¹⁰. **aperit** *(2nd) om* C¹⁸.

III.16: *Title* Prodit *for* Proderit C³; Quod *om* C³C¹⁰. 1 **non** nichil C¹⁰C¹⁴C¹⁸. **proderunt** proderunt dampnandis C¹⁰C¹⁴C¹⁸. 1-2 **nec (both)** non *most MSS incl* C¹⁰C¹⁴C¹⁸Ro. 2-3 **Argentum** Argentum eorum *most MSS incl* C³Ro. 4 **plangent** plangent super se omnes C¹⁰C¹⁴C¹⁸. 5 **viderint** videbunt C³. 8 **onus** bonus Re³T². 10 **O**

[15] DE DIVINO IUDICIO

Quis autem non timeat illud examen in quo idem
erit accusator et advocatus et iudex? Accusabit enim
cum dicet: "Esurivi, et non dedistis michi mandu-   Matheus
care; sitivi, et non dedistis michi bibere." Advocabit
5 cum subdet: "Quamdiu non fecistis uni de minimis
his, nec michi fecistis." Iudicabit cum inferet: "Discedite a me, maledicti, in ignem eternum." Non
erunt testes in illo iudicio necessarii quia tunc mani-
festa erunt "abscondita tenebrarum." "Nichil enim
10 occultum quod non reveletur." "Tunc libri erunt   In Apocalipsi
aperti, et iudicabuntur mortui ex his que scripta sunt
in libris secundum opera eorum." Quantus erit
pudor in peccatoribus! Quanta confusio cum eorum
nefandissima crimina cunctis erunt liquido mani-
15 festa! "Beati quorum remisse sunt iniquitates et   In Psalmo
quorum tecta sunt peccata." Ab illa sentencia nunquam poterit provocari quia "Pater omne iudicium   In Iohanne
dedit Filio," "qui claudit et nemo aperit, aperit et
nemo claudit." "Os enim Domini locutum est."

[16] QUOD NICHIL PRODERIT DAMPNANDIS

Tunc non proderunt opes, nec defendent honores,
nec suffragabuntur amici. Scriptum est enim: "Argentum eorum et aurum non valebit liberare eos in   Ezechiel
die furoris Domini." "Flebunt et plangent reges   In Apocalipsi
5 terre cum viderint fumum incendii," "propter timorem tormentorum eius." "Quid ergo facietis in   Ysaias
die visitacionis et calamitatis de longe venientis? Ad
cuius fugietis auxilium?" / "Unusquisque onus   f. 109v

231

"The soul that sins, the same shall die." O severe judgment, in which not only of deeds, but "of every idle word that men have spoken, they shall render an account," in which the debt will be exacted with interest up to the last farthing. "Who therefore will be able to flee from the wrath to come?" "Therefore the Son of Man shall send his angels, and they shall gather out of his kingdom all scandals and them that work iniquity"; they shall bind them in bundles for burning "and shall cast them into the furnace of glowing fire. There shall be weeping" and moaning, wailing and shrieking, grief and torment, gnashing and shouting, fear and trembling, labor and pain, fire and stench, darkness and anxiety, anguish and harshness, calamity and want, distress and sorrow, oblivion and confusion, tortures and pains, bitternesses and terrors, hunger and thirst, cold and heat, brimstone and fire burning forever and ever.

Here Ends the Book of the Misery of the Human Condition Published by Lotario, Cardinal-Deacon of Saints Sergius and Bachius, Who Was Afterwards Called Pope Innocent the Third.

Erit enim C[14]; Erit et C[18]. 11 **lucuti** *spelled* locuti *nearly every MS incl* C[3]C[10]C[14]C[18]Ro. 13 **ad** in C[18]. **exigetur** exiget C[18]. 14 **poterit fugere** *trans most MSS incl* C[3]C[10]C[14]C[18] V[2]. 14-15 **a . . . ira** ab ira ventura *most MSS incl* C[3]C[10]. 15 **ergo** enim C[10]C[14]; *om* C[18]. 16 **eius** suo C[10]C[14]C[18]. 16-17 **eos . . . iniquitatem** *om* C[10]C[14]C[18]. 17 **in** *om most MSS incl* C[3]C[10]C[14]C[18]Ro. 19 **Ibi** Ubi C[18]. **et** *(1st)* et stridor dentium Ro. **eiulatus** *om many MSS incl* C[10]C[18]. 21-23 **obscuritas . . . egestes** calamitas et egestas obscuritas et asperitas C[10]; calamitas et egestas obscuritas et anxietas acerbitas et asperitas C[14]C[18]. 23-24 **torciones** terrores, *with* et terrores *om later* C[10]. 25 **sitis** sites C[14]. **sulphur** fulgur C[14]. 26 **seculorum** seculorum Amen C[3]; seculorum a quibus nos eruat Iesus Christus Dominus noster Rex noster Iudex noster cum venerit iudicare vivos mortuos et seculum per ignem Amen C[14]; ab istis liberet nos Pater et Filius et Spiritus Sanctus Amen Amen Amen C[18].

Colophon om C[3]C[10]C[18]Ro; *table of contents to all books, divided into books and without title, in* C[14], *followed by* Expliciunt Capitula Tractatus Domine Pape Innocencius Tercius de Contemptu Mundi.

suum portabit." "Anima que peccaverit, ipsa morie-
10 tur." O districtum iudicium, in quo non solum de
factis, set "de omni verbo ocioso quodcumque lucuti   Matheus
fuerint homines, reddituri sunt racionem," in quo
usque ad novissimum quadrantem exigetur debitum
cum usuris. "Quis ergo poterit fugere a ventura
15 ira?" "Mittet ergo Filius Hominis angelos suos, et
colligent de regno eius omnia scandala et eos qui
faciunt iniquitatem"; alligabunt in fasciculos ad
comburendum "et mittent eos in caminum ignis
ardentis. Ibi erit fletus" et gemitus, eiulatus et
20 ululatus, luctus et cruciatus, stridor et clamor, timor
et tremor, labor et dolor, ardor et fetor, obscuritas
et anxietas, acerbitas et asperitas, calamitas et egestas, angustia et tristicia, oblivio et confusio, torciones et punctiones, amaritudines et terrores, fames
25 et sitis, frigus et cauma, sulphur et ignis ardens in
secula seculorum.

Explicit Liber de Miseria Condicionis Humane Editus a Lothario, Diacono-Cardinali Sanctorum Sergii
et Bachii, Qui Postea Innocencius Papa Tercius
Appellatus Est.

APPENDICES

APPENDIX I:
MANUSCRIPTS OF THE *DE MISERIA*

This list contains manuscripts that contain all or part of a Latin *De Miseria*. The list could of course be expanded by the addition of works that quote from the *De Miseria*, especially those like Richard Lavynham's *Litel Tretys on the Seven Deadly Sins* or Nicholas Eymerich's *Correctorius Correctorii* that quote large portions of the text, and translations, like Eustache Deschamps's French translation (in Paris, Bibl. Nat., MSS. fr. 840 and fr. 20029), that include parts of the Latin text, but it has seemed unnecessary to do so. In all such cases, however, I have examined the Latin quotations for readings that might be similar to those in the glosses to the Man of Law's Tale and in British Library, MS. Royal 8 F.xiv but have found nothing that would shed any light on Chaucer's text of the *De Miseria*.

As I have indicated earlier (Introduction, nn. 167, 168), * beside a manuscript means that I have collated it and † that I have not been able to examine it. All sigils are in alphabetical order except those standing for manuscripts from London libraries. I have given provenances or medieval locations where they are known for all manuscripts now in British libraries and British provenances or medieval locations where known for all manuscripts not in British libraries. I have added notes on manuscripts that are fragments or condensations or that contain excerpts or that omit large portions of the text (at least ten chapters), but these notes are not intended to be complete. For fuller descriptions of the manuscripts used in this edition, see the Introduction, pp. 55-62.

A   * Aberystwyth, Wales. National Library of Wales, Peniarth 335, ff. 91-103v, first half of 14th c. Britain.

Ad   Admont, Austria. Stiftsbibliothek, 163, ff. 215v-34v, 15th c.
         346, ff. 77-87, 14th c.
         724, ff. 60-81v, 14th c. Contains only through Book II, chap. 21.
         782, ff. 123-39, 13th c.

Alba Julia, Rumania. Biblioteca Batthyaneum, 64, ff. 68-84v, 15th c.

Amiens, France. Bibliothèque Municipale, 481, ff. 63-102v, 14th c.

Angers, France. Bibl. Mun., 319, ff. 64-71, 15th c. Extracts.
         403, ff. 19v-38, 14th c.

Arezzo, Italy. Biblioteca della Fraternità di S. Maria, 396, ff. 145-47, 15th c. Contains only through Book I, chap. 16.

Arras, France. Bibl. Mun., 456, ff. 3-39v, 14th c.

Ar   *   757, ff. 83-98v, 15th c. Begins in Book I, chap. 28.
              770, ff. 85-96, 13th c.
              944, ff. 72-84, 13th c.
              971, ff. 144-71v, 14th c.
       Assisi, Italy. Bibl. Communale, 575, ff. 83-99, end of 14th c.
Au   * Auxerre, France. Bibl. Mun., 7, ff. 105-16v, 13th c.
Av¹ * Avignon, France. Musée Calvet, 302, ff. 3-51v, 14th c.
Av² *   592, ff. 99-104, 13th c. Ends in Book I, chap. 17.
B   * Baltimore, Maryland, U.S.A. Walters Art Gallery, W. 348, ff. 1-60, ca. 1450.
       Bamberg, West Germany. Staatsbibl., Patr. 53, ff. 87-143v, 15th c.
             Theol. 106, ff. 96-113, 15th c.
             Theol. 108, ff. 353-76, 15th c.
Ba   Theol. 127, ff. 293-96v, 15th c. Excerpts.
       Barcelona, Spain. Archivo de la Corona de Aragón, San Cugat 45, ff. 26-57, 14th c.
             San Cugat 64, ff. 1-4v, 24v-44v, 14th c. Contains through Book II, chap. 32, and Book III, chaps. 2-12.
       Basel, Switzerland. Universitätsbibl., A IX 70a, ff. 11-27v, 15th c.
Be   * Berlin (East). Deutsche Staatsbibl., Phillipps 1904 (lat. 147), ff. 151v-73, end of 13th c. Battle Abbey. Omits from Book I, chap. 11 to Book II, chap. 24.
Bl¹ * Berlin (West). Staatsbibl. der Stiftung Preussischer Kulturbesitz, theol. lat. fol. 39 (lat. 391), ff. 1v-25v, 14th c.
Bl² *   theol. lat. fol. 39a (lat. 392), ff. 1-15v, 14th c.
Bl³ *   theol. lat. fol. 240 (lat. 484), ff. 201v-19, 15th c.
Bl⁴ *   theol. lat. qu. 64 (lat. 568), ff. 90v-123, 15th c.
Bl⁵ *   theol. lat. qu. 70 (lat. 424), ff. 107-23v, 14th c.
       Bern, Switzerland. Burgerbibl., 152, ff. 1-10, 13th-14th c.
       Besançon, France. Bibl. Mun., 208, ff. 3-41v, 1337.
             220, ff. 189-208v, 14th c. Text ends in Book III, chap. 7.
Bm¹ * Birmingham, England. University Library, 6/iii/36 (formerly Phillipps 2866), ff. 1-46v, 15th c. France (Paris, Carthusians).
Bm² *   6/iii/36 (formerly Phillipps 2866), ff. 49v-67v, 15th c. France (Paris, Carthusians).
Bn   * Blickling, Norfolk, England. Blickling Hall Library, 6849, ff. 125v-65v, second half of 15th c. France.
       Bonn, West Germany. Universitäts Bibl., 730, ff. 224-38v, 15th c.
Bo   * Bordeaux, France. Bibl. Mun., 331, ff. 86v-107, 1409.
       Boston, Massachusetts, U.S.A. Gardner Museum, 12, f. 55v, 15th c. Fragment.
Bs   *   Public Library, 13, ff. 97-122, 1448.
Bt¹ * Bourges, France. Bibl. Mun., 160, ff. 22-100v, 15th c.
Bt² *   161, ff. 1-44v, 15th c.
       Bratislava, Czechoslovakia. Archív mesta Bratislavy, E.L. 16, ff. 178-79, 14th c. Text ends in Book I, chap. 4.
Bu   * Braunschweig, West Germany. Stadtbibl., 163, ff. 177-88, 14th-15th c.

Bv¹　*　Bristol, England. Library of the Roman Catholic Bishopric of Clifton, 6, ff. 1–32v, 15th c. Germany (Erfurt, Carthusians).

Bv²　*　　　University Library, D.M.268, ff. 1–56, 14th c. France (Rodez, Franciscans).

　　　Brno, Czechoslovakia. Universitní Knihovna, 70, ff. 35–60v, 15th c.
Bw　　　A. 51, ff. 148–60v, 1402-3.

　　　Bruges, Belgium. Bibl. Mun., 303, ff. 138–71v, 13th c.
　　　　　390, ff. 1–21v, 14th c.

Bz¹　　　Brussels, Belgium. Bibl. Royale, 1138–59 (2058), ff. 91v–107, 15th c.
　　　　　1338–41 (372), ff. 40v–50v, 14th c.
　　　　　2146–54 (2060), ff. 49–82v, 1430.

Bz²　*　　　2653–62 (2057), ff. 1–31, 14th c.
　　　　　12065–68 (1911), ff. 115v–36v, 14th c.
　　　　　14720 (2059), ff. 7–29v, 15th c.
　　　　　19944–45 (2222), f. 216v, 15th c. Fragment.
　　　　　21532–35 (485), ff. 147–68v, 13th–14th c.
　　　　　II-2433 (1341), ff. 104–31v, 1470.

　　　Budapest, Hungary. Egyetemi Könyvtár, 59, ff. 231v–55v, 15th c.
　　　　　75, ff. 463–72, 15th c.

　　　Cambrai, France. Bibl. Mun., 253, ff. 1–19v, 13th c.
　　　　　260, ff. 2–27v, 14th–15th c.

C¹　*　Cambridge, England. Corpus Christi College, 63, ff. 47–56v, 13th c.
　　　Canterbury Cathedral.
C²　*　　　433, ff. 73v–91, 13th–14th c. Wenlock, Cluniac Priory of St. Milburga.
C³　*　　　459, ff. 1–22v, 13th c. Peterborough Abbey.
C⁴　*　　　500, ff. 36v–49, 14th–15th c.
C⁵　*　　　518, ff. 95–109v, 14th c.
C⁶　*　　　Emmanuel College, 27, ff. 34–44, 13th c. Sompting Parish Church.
C⁷　*　　　Gonville and Caius College, 61, pp. 9–64, late 13th c.
C⁸　*　　　105, third flyleaf r–v, 14th–15th c. Fragment.
C⁹　*　　　349, ff. 137–44, 13th–14th c. Begins at end of Book I, chap. 10.
C¹⁰　*　　　Magdalene College, F.4.15, ff. 1–22, 13th c. Stamford, Franciscan Convent.
C¹¹　*　　　Pembroke College, 225, ff. 24–29, early 13th c. Reading Abbey.
C¹²　*　　　230, ff. 65–80v, late 14th–15th c. Pembroke College.
C¹³　*　　　Peterhouse, 218, ff. 166v–82v, 15th c.
C¹⁴　*　　　219, ff. 1–20v, 14th c.
C¹⁵　*　　　255, ff. 40–49, early 13th c.
C¹⁶　*　　　St. John's College, 111, ff. 67–105v, early 13th c.
C¹⁷　*　　　Trinity College, 1133, ff. 38v–43, 13th c. Excerpts.
C¹⁸　*　　　University Library, Dd.1.21, ff. 147v–51v, early 14th c. England.
C¹⁹　*　　　Dd.4.54, ff. 213v–23v, 227r–v, 14th c. Condensation.
C²⁰　*　　　Gg.1.31, ff. 2–62, 14th c.
C²¹　*　　　Ll.1.15, ff. 83–99, 14th c.
C²²　*　　　Addl. 3305, ff. 23–46, 15th c. Germany.

C²³   *   Addl. 6191, ff. 488–513v, late 15th c. Germany (Strasbourg).
Ca   * Carcassonne, France. Bibl. Mun., 30, ff. 87–109v, 15th c.
Cc   Carpentras, France. Bibl. Mun., 31, ff. 143–52, 14th c.
          690, ff. 111r–v, 126r–v, 15th c. Fragment.
          1277, ff. 1–43v, 15th c.
Ch   * Charleville, France. Bibl. Mun., 22, ff. 28–37, 14th c.
       Chartres, France. Bibl. Mun., 419, ff. 28v–47, 15th c. Badly damaged in World War II; on microfilm at Institut de Recherche et d'Histoire des Textes, Paris.
Ci   * Chicago, Illinois, U.S.A. University Library, 478, ff. 1–39v, 15th c.
       Cologne, West Germany. Erzbischöfliche Diözesanbibl., 71, ff. 66–70, 1425. Contains Book III only.
       Copenhagen, Denmark. Kongelige Bibliotek, Add. 49 fol. (formerly at Universitetsbibl.), ff. 166–82, ca. 1431.
          Fabric. 89, 4° (formerly at Universitetsbibl.), ff. 25v–51, 15th c.
          Gl. kgl. Saml. 3393, 8°, ff. 149–96, 14th c.
       Douai, France. Bibl. Mun., 400, ff. 1–22, 1480.
          457, ff. 226–50v, 15th c.
          537, ff. 255–75, 14th c.
D¹   * Dublin, Ireland. Trinity College, 97, ff. 242–53, 14th c. Abbey of St. Thomas near Dublin.
D²   *   195, ff. 1–19, second half of 14th c. Italy.
D³   *   301, ff. 194v–204, 14th c. Probably England.
D⁴   *   312, ff. 28–46v, second half of 14th c. Condensation. England.
D⁵   *   332, ff. 57v–71, end of 13th c. York, Abbey of St. Mary.
D⁶   *   514, ff. 183–204v, 13th–14th c. Canterbury, Abbey of St. Augustine.
Du¹ * Durham, England. Cathedral Library, A.IV.29, ff. 150–61v, ca. 1300. Ends in Book II, chap. 19.
Du² *   B.III.18, ff. 100–24, end of 14th c. Durham.
Du³ *   B.IV.28, ff. 101–8v, 13th c. Durham.
Du⁴ *   Hunter 30, pp. 115–33, 14th c.
E¹   * Edinburgh, Scotland. University Library, 107, ff. 1–28v, late 13th c. Probably English.
E²   *   331, ff. 158–62, 15th c. Extracts. Germany (Erfurt, Carthusians).
Eg   Eger, Hungary. Főegyházmegyei Könyvtar, B.X.45, ff. 51–83, 15th c.
   † Engelberg, Switzerland. Stiftsbibl., 258, ff. 185–202, 15th c.
Er¹   Erfurt, East Germany. Wissenschaftliche Allgemeinbibl. CA 2° 6, ff. 150–65, end of 13th c.
          CA 4° 50, ff. 114–30, ca. 1395.
          CA 4° 77, ff. 298–319, end of 13th c.
Er²   *   CA 4° 116, ff. 156–70, 14th–15th c.
          CA 4° 128, ff. 130–36v, end of 13th c. Begins in Book II, chap. 17.
       Erlangen, West Germany. Universitätsbibl., 546, ff. 59–81, 15th c.
Es¹   El Escorial, Spain. Real Biblioteca, e.IV.20, ff. 2–30, 14th c.
Es²   *   I.III.7, ff. 59v–71v, 13th c. England.
          K.III.24, ff. 2–32v, 14th c.

	L.III.15, ff. 178-204, 13th c.
Es³	O.I.8, ff. 1-9, 14th c.
	Q.III.20, ff. 139-47v, 13th c.
	R.II.14, ff. 25-29v, 13th c. Begins in Book II, chap. 28.

Ev * Evreux, France. Bibl. Mun., 23, ff. 96-132, 13th c.

Florence, Italy. Bibl. Medicea Laurenziana, Ashburnham 142, ff. 138v-55v, 15th c. Contains only through Book II, chap. 24.

    Ashburnham 182, ff. 1-54, 15th c.

    Ashburnham 1919, ff. 1-32v, 14th c.

    Gaddian. 145, ff. 1-33, 15th c.

    Plut. 12.27, ff. 39-51, 13th c.

    Plut. 18 dext.7, ff. 222-32v, 13th c.

    Plut. 19.29, ff. 109-31, 14th-15th c.

    Plut. 21.17, ff. 1-79, 1489.

    Plut. 89 sup.90, ff. 97-112, 16th c. Book III only.

    Strozzi 29, ff. 1-10, 13th c.

   Bibl. Nazionale Centrale, II.IX.48, ff. 85-100, 14th c.

    Conv. soppr. D.7.1888, ff. 1-20v, 14th c.

    Conv. soppr. D.8.119, ff. 1-8v, 74v-76v, 15th c. Contains only Book I, chaps. 1-6, and Book III.

    Conv. soppr. H.9.1562, ff. 1-26, 14th c.

   Bibl. Riccardiana, 352, ff. 1-14v, 15th c.

F	824, ff. 22-39, 15th c.

Frankfurt am Main, West Germany. Stadt- und Universitätsbibl., Barth. 98, ff. 10-23v, 15th c.

    Praed. 77, ff. 242-58, 1435.

    Praed. 176, ff. 3-29, mid-15th c. Condensation.

Fulda, West Germany. Hessische Landesbibl., Aa 49, ff. 34v-45v, 12th-13th c.

Gdańsk, Poland. Biblioteka Gdańska Polskiej Akademii Nauk, 1956, ff. 2-11, 15th c. Omits from Book I, chap. 9 to Book II, chap. 1.

G	1963, ff. 100v-119v, 15th c.
	Mar. F 283, ff. 81v-98, 15th c.

Giessen, West Germany. Universitäts-Bibl., 706, ff. 2-20, 15th-16th c.

    802, ff. 243-56v, 1429.

Gi	853, ff. 206-38v, 1470.
Gl	* Gloucester, England. Cathedral Library, 27, ff. 23-47, 14th c. England.

Gotha, East Germany. Forschungsbibl., Chart. 261, ff. 1-28v, 15th c.

Go	* Membr. I 123, ff. 50-61, beginning of 14th c.
Gr	Graz, Austria. Universitätsbibl., 704, ff. 54-69, 14th c.
	1468, ff. 119v-34, 13th c.
H¹	* The Hague, Netherlands. Koninklijke Bibliotheek, 128 F 17, ff. 1-58v, 15th c.
H²	* Museum Meermanno-Westreenianum, 119, ff. 114-27, first half of 15th c.

Hamburg, West Germany. Staats- und Universitätsbibl., theol. 1160, pp. 649-92, 16th c. (now at the Deutsche Staatsbibl. in East Berlin).

Hannover, West Germany. Niedersächsisches Landesbibl., 38, ff. 5–17, 15th c.

Harburg über Donauwörth, West Germany. Fürstlich Oettingen-Wallerstein'sche Bibl. und Kunstsammlung, I, 2, 4°, 28, ff. 61–68v, 14th c. Ends in Book II, chap. 16.

    II, 1, 2°, 5, ff. 125v–48v, 15th c.

    II, 1, 2°, 52, ff. 126–40, 1438.

    II, 1, 2°, 137, ff. 1–52, 15th c.

Heiligenkreuz, Austria. Stiftsbibl., 207, ff. 40–49v, 13th c.

Innsbruck, Austria. Universitätsbibl., 65, ff. 97–113v, 15th c.

    71, ff. 220v–42, 15th c.

I   *   942, ff. 51–66, 13th c.

Jena, East Germany. Friedrich-Schiller-Universitätsbibl., El.q.7, ff. 2–22, 15th c.

J * Jerusalem, Israel. Jewish National and University Library, Yahuda Var. 11 (formerly Phillipps 437), ff. 1–7v, 13th c. Ends in Book I, chap. 17.

Klagenfurt, Austria. Bischöfliche Bibl., XXIX.d.17, ff. 117–70, 16th c.

    Studienbibl., Pap.-HS. 45, ff. 1–17, 1439. Ends in Book II, chap. 28.

    Pap.-HS. 109, ff. 205–15v, 13th c. Begins in Book I, chap. 6.

Klosterneuberg, Austria. Bibl. Can. Reg. S. Augustini, 187, ff. 129–46, 1458.

    194, ff. 170v–90v, 15th c.

    265, ff. 121–37v, 14th c.

    428, ff. 217–32, 15th c.

Krakow, Poland. Bibl. Jagiellońska, 1221 (AA II 18), ff. 120–36v, 1452.

    1398 (DD XIV 10), ff. 90v–107v, 15th c.

    1422 (AA III 13), ff. 32v–57v, 14th c.

    2538 (DD XIX 4), ff. 104v–35v, 14th c.

    Przyb. 181/66, ff. 2–9v, 14th c.

Kremsmünster, Austria. Stiftsbibl., 56, ff. 1–22, 14th c.

Kreuzenstein (Burg) near Leobendorf, Austria. Burgbibl., 5668, ff. 172–81v, 15th c.

Lambach, Austria. Stiftsbibl., chart. 281, ff. 76–103, 15th c.

    membr. XCI, ff. 74–88v, 13th–14th c.

La * Laon, France. Bibl. Mun., 179, ff. 108–19, 13th c.

    272, ff. 91v–108, 15th c.

Lawrence, Kansas, U.S.A. University of Kansas Library, Y 119 (formerly Phillipps 3984), ff. 1–34, 14th c.

Le * Leicester, England. City of Leicester Museums and Art Gallery, 10D34, Vol. 10, ff. 27–33v, late 14th or early 15th c. Condensation.

Leipzig, East Germany. Karl-Marx-Universitätsbibl., 439, ff. 1–17, 13th c.

    534, ff. 121–35v, beginning of 15th c.

Lm * Le Mans, France. Bibl. Mun., 197, ff. 3–50, 15th c.

Léon, Spain. Bibl. de S. Isidoro, XXX, ff. 2–29, 14th c.

Lilienfeld, Austria. Stiftsbibl., 124, ff. 113–31v, 14th c.

145, ff. 87–97v, 13th c.

Linz, Austria. Studienbibl., 401, ff. 162–83v, 15th c.

488, ff. 183v–88v, 13th c.

Lisbon, Portugal. Biblioteca Nacional, Alcobacenses 380, ff. 14–31, late 13th–early 14th c.

L¹ * London, England. British Library, Arundel 332, ff. 136–57v, 13th c. Durham Cathedral.

L² * Burney 253, ff. 1–33, 14th c.

L³ * Burney 356, pp. 230–63, beginning of 15th c.

L⁴ * Cotton Vespasian D. XIII, ff. 98–112, 13th c. England.

L⁵ * Harley 275, ff. 53–66, 15th c.

L⁶ * Harley 323, ff. 89–99v, 13th c.

L⁷ * Harley 325, ff. 9–29, 13th c.

L⁸ * Harley 337, ff. 54–65v, early 14th c.

L⁹ * Harley 979, ff. 50–72v, 13th c. Reading Abbey.

L¹⁰ * Harley 1037, ff. 135–47, 13th c.

L¹¹ * Harley 1659, preliminary folios, 13th c. Contains only through Book I, chap. 14. Worcester Cathedral.

L¹² * Harley 3227, ff. 47v–83, 15th c.

L¹³ * Harley 3852, ff. 1–16, 15th c. Ends in Book II, chap. 4.

L¹⁴ * Harley 3923, ff. 57–64v, 14th c.

L¹⁵ * Harley 4736, ff. 94–128, 15th–16th c.

L¹⁶ * Harley 4887, ff. 23–32, 15th c.

L¹⁷ * Harley 4987, ff. 98v–113v, 15th c.

L¹⁸ * Harley 5234, ff. 114–22, 13th c. Durham Cathedral.

L¹⁹ * Harley 5235, ff. 116v–22, 13th c. Condensation.

L²⁰ * Lansdowne 358, ff. 78–109v, first half of 13th c. Battle Abbey.

L²¹ * Royal 4 B.viii, ff. 248–55, 13th c. Lincoln, Gilbertine Priory.

L²² * Royal 5 A.viii, ff. 87–108, 13th c. Bury St. Edmunds.

L²³ * Royal 5 C.vi, ff. 87–97, 14th c. Worcester Cathedral.

L²⁴ * Royal 5 E.xxi, ff. 7–23v, 14th c.

L²⁵ * Royal 7 D.xvii, ff. 184–212, 13th–14th c. Sheen, Charterhouse.

L²⁶ * Royal 7 D.xxi, ff. 4–38v, beginning of 14th c. Westminster Abbey.

L²⁷ * Royal 7 E.x, ff. 1–24, first half of 14th c.

L²⁸ * Royal 8 A.xxi, ff. 104v–14, 13th c.

L²⁹ * Royal 8 C.vii, ff. 127v–49, 15th c.

L³⁰ * Royal 8 D.xx, ff. 2–12, beginning of 13th c. Spalding Priory.

L³¹ * Royal 8 F.xiv, ff. 180v–83v, first half of 13th c. (after 1237). Bury St. Edmunds. Text ends in Book II, chap. 36

L³² * Royal 13 A.iv, ff. 90–100, 13th c. Begins in Book II, chap. 3.

L³³ * Royal 13 A.xiv, ff. 117v–29, 13th–early 14th c. Most of Book II omitted. Ireland.

L³⁴ * Sloane 1613, ff. 52v–70v, 14th c. Condensation.

L³⁵ * Sloane 2275, ff, 218v–29v, 14th c.

L³⁶ * Addl. 6716, ff. 82–96v, 15th c.

L³⁷ * Addl. 11760, ff. 25–49, 15th c.

L^{38} *   Addl. 15237, ff. 57-78, 15th c.
L^{39} *   Addl. 18318, ff. 18-31, 14th c. Germany (Altenburg Monastery).
L^{40} *   Addl. 33957, ff. 51-73v, 15th c.
L^{41} *   Addl. 38119, ff. 56-67, 1378. Germany.
L^{42} *   Addl. 57533, ff. 65v-80v, late 12th-early 13th c.
L^{43} *   Gray's Inn, 7, ff. 138v-47v, 13th c. Chester, Franciscan Convent.
L^{44} *   Lambeth Palace, 144, ff. 91v-102v, 14th c. Canterbury, Abbey of St. Augustine.
L^{45} *   366, ff. 62v-80v, late 12th-early 13th c.
L^{46} *   388, ff. 164-96, 13th-14th c. Lanthony, Gloucestershire.
L^{47} *   500, ff. 87-138v, 15th c.
        Lucca, Italy. Bibl. Statale, 2110, ff. 87-111v, 13th c.
        Lyon, France. Bibl. du Palais des Arts, 28, f. 155v, 15th c. (now at the Bibl. Mun.). Book I, chap. 1 only.
M^1 Madrid, Spain. Bibl. Nacional, 93, pp. 1-67, 1432.
        411, ff. 1-26, 13th c.
        501, ff. 1-19, 13th c.
        4402, ff. 75v, 80v, 15th c. Excerpts.
M^2 8121, ff. 1-42v, 15th c.
        8854, ff. 1-28, 1418.
        9465, ff. 99-144v, 168-69v, 15th c.
        9481, ff. 8v-10, 22-67, 14th-15th c.
        Vitrina 25-7, ff. 96-114v, 1432.
        Real Academia de la Historia, Aemilianensis 14, ff. 281-301v, 13th c.
        Mainz, West Germany. Stadtbibl., I 48, ff. 2-17v, second quarter of 14th c.
Ma^1 I 62, ff. 5-22v, first quarter of 15th c.
Ma^2 *   I 109, ff. 51-80, 1472.
            I 146, ff. 38-61v, second half of 14th c.
Ma^3 *   I 240, ff. 125-37v, ca. 1400.
            I 300, ff. 255-62, first half of 15th c. Book III only.
            II 171, ff. 121-44, first quarter of 15th c.
Ma^4 II 238, ff. 218-45v, last half of 15th c.
            II 318, ff. 61-66, beginning of 15th c. Contains only through Book I, chap. 18.
        Manchester, England. John Rylands Library, lat. 125, f. 16, late 13th-early 14th c. Fragment: alphabetical table to the *De Miseria*.
        Maria Saal, Austria. Archiv des Collegiatstiftes, 1, ff. 197-207v, 1456.
        Melk, Austria. Stiftsbibl., 386 (339. F 39), ff. 56v-69v, 14th c.
Me   634 (915. Q 51), ff. 49-69, 14th c.
        803,2 (807. O 44,2), pp. 317-62, 15th c.
        978 (822. P 8), ff. 96-116, 14th-15th c.
        Merseberg, East Germany. Domstiftsbibl., 31, ff. 72-97, 15th c.
        50, ff. 89-110v, 15th c.
        79, ff. 63-77v, 15th c.
        131, ff. 123-40v, 1357.

Mf   * Metz, France. Bibl. Mun., 479, ff. 49–70v, beginning of 14th c.

       Milan, Italy. Bibl. Ambrosiana, A 65 inf., ff. 41v–50, 13th c.

                C 14 inf., ff. 75–96v, 1457.

                D 36 inf., ff. 1–22v, 14th c.

                D 46 sup., ff. 127–37, 13th c. Contains only through Book I, chap. 26.

                D 97 inf., ff. 1–15v, 14th c.

                O 3 sup., ff. 231v–46v, 13th c.

                P 117 sup., ff. 176–79, 15th c. Condensation.

Mi   + 48 sup., ff. 9–74, beginning of 13th c.

Mn   Modena, Italy. Bibl. Estense, α.0.6.24 (Lat. 189), ff. 1–26v, 15th c.

                γ.Y.5.16 (Camp. App. 1248), ff. 1–15, 14th c.

       Mogila, Poland. Bibl. O. O. Cystersów, 623 (1463), ff. 112–31v, 15th c.

       Mons, Belgium. Bibl. Publique, 18/111, ff. 201–10v, 13th c.

                58/116, ff. 41v–62, 13th c.

       Montserrat, Spain. Abadia de Montserrat, 1075, ff. 98–120v, 15th c.

Mo * Moulins, France. Bibl. Mun., 39, ff. 1–33, 14th c.

       Munich, West Germany. Bayerische Staatsbibl., Cgm 660, ff. 100–115, 1448–1475.

Mu[1] *   Clm 213, ff. 168v–69v, 207v–8v, 13th c.

                Clm 2611, ff. 107–23, 13th c.

                Clm 3042, ff. 131–44v, 1468.

                Clm 3115, ff. 161v–85, 15th c.

                Clm 3221, ff. 10v–29v, 14th c.

                Clm 3334, ff. 88v–116, 1477–79.

                Clm 3686, ff. 228–41, 14th c.

                Clm 3812, ff. 186v–210, 15th c.

                Clm 4350, f. 83, 14th c. Fragment.

                Clm 4589, ff. 108v–35, 13th c.

                Clm 4753, ff. 234–71v, 1470.

                Clm 5409, ff. 71–91v, 15th c.

                Clm 6808, ff. 124–53, 1473.

                Clm 7565, ff. 170–93, 15th c.

                Clm 7624, ff. 1–8, 13th c.

Mu[2]   Clm 7705, ff. 88–94v, 15th c. Omits from Book I, chap. 29 to Book II, chap. 37.

Mu[3]   Clm 8377, ff. 88–108, 15th c.

                Clm 8961, ff. 186–229, 15th c.

                Clm 9583, ff. 226–38v, 15th c.

                Clm 9716, ff. 261–77v, 15th c.

Mu[4] *   Clm 9726, ff. 34v–69v, 15th c.

                Clm 9806, ff. 154v–93, 15th c.

Mu[5] *   Clm 11723, ff. 50–66v, 15th c.

                Clm 14142, ff. 133–47, 15th c.

                Clm 14243, ff. 244–57v, 1415–24.

                Clm 14347, ff. 155–80, 1430–31.

                Clm 15126, ff. 143–47v, 15th c. Contains only through Book I, chap. 29.

Clm 15173, ff. 235–63v, 15th c.

Clm 15183, ff. 158–83v, 15th c.

Clm 15548, ff. 258–79, 1469.

Clm 15722, ff. 1–14v, 1390.

Clm 17105, ff. 82v–95, beginning of 13th c.

Mu⁶   *   Clm 17287, ff. 163–98v, 15th c.

Clm 18358, ff. 347–65, 15th c.

Clm 18379, ff. 1–9v, 13th c.

Clm 18539b, ff. 44v–67, 13th c.

Clm 19130, ff. 76v–139v, 14th c.

Clm 19535, ff. 1–17v, 1427.

Clm 21075, ff. 313–21, 15th c. Text ends in Book II, chap. 20.

Clm 21103, ff. 144–66, 15th c. Omits some chapters in Book II.

Clm 21576, ff. 2v–55v, 13th c.

Clm 21702, ff. 101–21, 15th c.

Clm 23449, ff. 79v–110v, 15th c.

Clm 23974, ff. 1–16v, 1478 (the former Clm 29176 is now part
of this MS.).

Clm 26645, ff. 160–73v, 15th c. Ends in Book III, chap. 5.

Clm 26936, ff. 85–107, 15th c.

Clm 28635, ff. 1–16, 15th c.

Namur, Belgium. Bibl. de la Société Archéologique de Namur, 24, ff.
17v–23, 15th c.

Nantes, France. Musée Thomas Dobrée, VI, ff. 1–47v, beginning of
13th c.

Naples, Italy. Bibl. Nazionale, I.H.38, ff. 186–211, 15th c.

IV.G.25, ff. 31–44, beginning of 13th c. Condensation; text
ends in Book II, chap. 39.

VII.E.2, ff. 213–21, 15th c.

VII.G.49, ff. 137v–68v, 14th c.

VII.G.58, ff. 39–68v. 14th c.

N   *   Newbury, Berkshire, England. Library of H. W. Edwards, Tollemache
L.J.I., ff. 28–71v, 15th c. England.

Ne   *   New York, New York, U.S.A. Pierpont Morgan Library, M.A.842, ff.
308–29v, 15th–16th c. Text ends in Book II, chap. 25.

Novara, Italy. Bibl. Capitolare, LX, ff. 1–11, beginning of 13th c.

Nürnberg, West Germany. Stadtbibl., Cent.IV, 76, ff. 1–17, 13th c.

Oporto, Portugal. Bibl. Publica Municipal, 102, ff. 87–107, 13th c.

O¹   *   Oxford, England. Bodleian Library, Ashmole 360, f. 148v, 13th c.
Excerpts. Bodmin, Franciscan Convent.

O²   *   Ashmole 751, ff. 137v–40, end of 14th c. Condensation.

O³   *   Bodley 122, ff. 136–58, first half of 15th c. England.

O⁴   *   Bodley 133, ff. 106–19v, first half of 13th c. Windsor Chapel.

O⁵   *   Bodley 798, ff. 143v–55v, last quarter of 14th c. England.

O⁶   *   Bodley 844, ff. 70–86v, 15th c. Omits from Book I, chap. 28
through Book II, chap. 31; text ends in Book III, chap. 8.

O⁷   *   Can. Lat. Pat. 44, ff. 81–107v, 14th c.

O⁸   *   Can. Misc. 95, ff. 139–74, 13th–14th c. Italy (near Verona).

O[9]   *   Can. Misc. 335, ff. 32-63v, 15th c.
O[10]   *   Digby 149, ff. 74-87v, 13th c.
O[11]   *   Digby 173, ff. 1-9, 13th c. Salisbury Cathedral.
O[12]   *   Laud Misc. 80, ff. 98-116v, 13th c. Germany (Mainz, Carthusians).
O[13]   *   Laud Misc. 112, ff. 46-52, 13th c. Ely Cathedral.
O[14]   *   Laud Misc. 322, ff. 4-52v, beginning of 15th c. Condensation.
O[15]   *   Laud Misc. 378, ff. 53v-55v, 14th c. Condensation. Germany (Mainz, Carthusians).
O[16]   *   Laud Misc. 426, ff. 247-68, 15th c. Germany (Regensburg, Carthusians).
O[17]   *   Laud Misc. 515, ff. 3v-38v, beginning of 13th c. Waltham Abbey.
O[18]   *   Laud Misc. 527, ff. 265-80v, late 12th-14th c.
O[19]   *   Rawlinson A.363, ff. 19-28, 13th c. Omits most of Book III. Staindrop Hospital.
O[20]   *   Rawlinson A.423, ff. 7-13, 15th c. Text begins in Book II, chap. 31.
O[21]   *   Rawlinson C.22, pp. 241-77, 13th c. Text ends in Book III, chap. 4.
O[22]   *   Rawlinson C.269, ff. 19v-47v, 15th c. Canterbury Cathedral.
O[23]   *   Rawlinson C.317, ff. 5v-10, 13th c. Book I only. Cockersand Abbey.
O[24]   *   Rawlinson C.504, ff. 1-26, 13th c. Bardney Abbey.
O[25]   *   Rawlinson C.536, ff. 1-37, end of 14th c. Italy.
O[26]   *   Rawlinson C.780, ff. 87-115, 14th-15th c. Worcester, Dominican Convent.
O[27]   *   Selden Supra 74, ff. 102v-19, second half of 13th c. England.
O[28]   *   Brasenose College, 15, ff. 42v-49, 15th c. Condensation. Syon Abbey.
O[29]   *   Christ Church, 91, ff. 196-203v, end of 13th-15th c. Crediton Collegiate Church.
O[30]   *   Corpus Christi College, 155, ff. 49v-81v, 15th c. Rievaulx Abbey.
O[31]   *   Magdalen College, 109, ff. 82v-97, 15th c. At Magdalen in the Middle Ages.
O[32]   *   Merton College, 249, ff. 12-29v, 13th c. At Merton by late 14th c.
O[33]   *   Trinity College, 18, ff. 33-37v, 13th-14th c. Selections. Ashridge, House of Bonshommes of B.V.M.

Padova, Italy. Bibl. Universitaria, 739, ff. 33-71v, 166-74, 1453.

P   *   1305, ff. 1-23v, 14th c.

Paris, France. Bibl. de l'Arsenal, 495, ff. 61-80, 14th c.

Bibl. Mazarine, 646, ff. 125-68, 1399.

980, ff. 1-24, 13th-14th c.

995, ff. 1-53, 1455.

Bibl. Nationale, Baluze 379, f. 226, second half of 17th c. Excerpt: "De Poenis Inferni," an extra chapter often appended to the *De Miseria.*

Pa[1]   fr. 24870, pp. 10-42, 13th c.

		lat. 455, ff. 40–43v, 13th c.
		lat. 2042, ff. 180–82, 14th c. Condensation.
		lat. 2049, ff. 85v–98v, 14th–15th c.
		lat. 2568, ff. 27v–37, end of 13th–14th c.
Pa²		lat. 2708, ff. 136v–68, 15th c.
		lat. 3239, ff. 23v–30, 32–33, 13th c. Excerpts.
		lat. 3265A, ff. 92v–93, beginning of 16th c. Fragment.
Pa³		lat. 3267, ff. 37–54v, 55–56, second half of 14th c.
		lat. 3464, ff. 61–90v, 14th c.
Pa⁴	*	lat. 3487A, ff. 86–96v, 14th c.

Pa² lat. 2708, ff. 136v–68, 15th c.
     lat. 3239, ff. 23v–30, 32–33, 13th c. Excerpts.
     lat. 3265A, ff. 92v–93, beginning of 16th c. Fragment.
Pa³ lat. 3267, ff. 37–54v, 55–56, second half of 14th c.
     lat. 3464, ff. 61–90v, 14th c.
Pa⁴ * lat. 3487A, ff. 86–96v, 14th c.
     lat. 3611, ff. 1–28v, 14th c.
     lat. 3612, ff. 1–14v, 14th c.
     lat. 3612A, ff. 1–40, end of 14th c.
     lat. 3613, ff. 1v–104v, 15th c.
Pa⁵ * lat. 3697, ff. 94–162, 14th c.
Pa⁶ * lat. 3768, ff. 83–99, 13th c.
     lat. 4289, ff. 69–88, 14th c.
     lat. 5151, ff. 113v–36v, 14th c.
     lat. 5698, ff. 93–106, 15th c.
     lat. 7420, ff. 77–94, 13th c.
     lat. 9581, ff. 1–18v, 15th c.
     lat. 10635, ff. 1–37v, 1477.
Pa⁷ * lat. 12387, ff. 37–45v, 13th c.
     lat. 13333, ff. 136–41v, 13th c. Contains only through Book II,
        chap. 7.
     lat. 13430, ff. 1–49v, 14th c.
Pa⁸ * lat. 13431, ff. 1–19, 14th c.
     lat. 13444, ff. 69–97v, 13th c.
Pa⁹ * lat. 14444, ff. 175v–87, end of 12th c.
     lat. 14880, ff. 95–110v, 13th c.
Pa¹⁰ * lat. 15700, ff. 20v–33, 14th c. England.
Pa¹¹ * lat. 15737, ff. 44–55v, 13th c.
     lat. 15988, pp. 77–94, 13th c.
Pa¹² * lat. 16331, ff. 180v–98, 13th c.
Pa¹³ * lat. 16490, ff. 205–17v, 14th c.
Pa¹⁴ * lat. 16875, pp. 135–80, 13th c.
     lat. 17534, ff. 99–103, 14th c. Extracts.
     lat. 18123, ff. 3–40v, 13th c.
     lat. 18531, ff. 17–40v, 13th c. Part of Book III omitted.
     lat. nouv. acq. 559, ff. 14–38, 15th c.
Pa¹⁵ * Bibl. Ste.-Geneviève, 80, ff. 2–24v, 13th c.
     1199, ff. 112–22v, 13th c.
     1643, ff. 19–56, 14th c.
     2785, ff. 130–41v, 13th c.
Pavia, Italy. Bibl. Universitaria, Aldini 124, ff. 73–96v, 14th or 15th c.
     Aldini 167, ff. 33v–39, 15th or 16th c. Condensation.
Perugia, Italy. Bibl. Comunale Augusta, I 52, ff. 63–75v, 1511. Contains Book I only.

Pesaro, Italy. Bibl. Oliveriana, 1101, ff. 23-53v, 15th c.
Ph¹ * Philadelphia, Pennsylvania, U.S.A. Free Library, J. F. Lewis 84, ff. 135-69v, 14th c. England.
Ph² *   University of Pennsylvania Library, Lat. 55, ff. 62-70, 13th c.
Ph³ *   Lat. 90, ff. 14-42, 15th c.
       Poitiers, France. Bibl. Mun., 228, ff. 1-58, 15th c.
Po   255, ff. 33-81v, 15th c.
       Prague, Czechoslovakia. Metropolitní Kapituli, 153 A. LXXIX.6, ff. 9-23v, 1388.
       473 C. XLVI, ff. 215-30v, 14th c.
       513 C. LXXXII, ff. 1-14, last half of 14th c.
Pr¹   583 D. XVII, ff. 171v-97, 1435.
       637 D. LXXI, ff. 1-9v, 14th c.
Pr²   639 D. LXXIII, ff. 42-68, first half of 15th c.
       642 D. LXXVI, ff. 53-70v, 14th c.
       826 E. LXV, ff. 187v-204, 1436.
       872 F. XXV, ff. 206-37v, last half of 15th c.
       1531 N. VII, ff. 19v-23, first half of 15th c. Book III only.
       1535 N. XI, f. 191, last half of 15th c. Excerpt.
       1567 N. XLIII, ff. 21-32, first half of 14th c.
       Národní Muzeum, X A 10, ff. 99v-111v, 14th-15th c.
       XII B 4, ff. 180v-93v, 15th c.
       XII E 6, ff. 131-44v, 14th c.
       XIII D 28, ff. 54-71v, 1467.
       XIII F 2, ff. 174-98, 14th c.
       XIV C 9, ff. 147-61, 14th c.
Pr³   Universitní Knihovna, I C 45, ff. 179-95, 15th c.
       I D 29, ff. 3v-15v, 1476-77.
       I G 2, ff. 1-28, 14th c.
       III C 8, ff. 60-71v, 14th-15th c.
       III D 23, ff. 157-72, 14th-15th c.
       IV A 14, ff. 202-11, 1372-78.
       IV C 3, ff. 124v-31v, 14th c. Text ends in Book II, chap. 10.
       V G 10, ff. 104-17v, 14th-15th c.
Pr⁴   VI A 5, ff. 11-24, 14th-15th c.
       VIII B 30, ff. 128-42, 14th c.
       IX B 7, ff. 288v-305v, 15th c.
       IX B 9, ff. 235-48, 15th c.
       XII E 13, ff. 1-24v, 15th c.
       XII F 18, ff. 260-88, 1475.
       XIII F 21, ff. 1-22v, 15th c.
       XIII G 18, ff. 180-83, 15th c. Excerpts.
       XIV D 6, ff. 71-86v, 15th c.
       XIV D 7, ff. 198v-216, 15th c. Condensation.
       XIV D 23, ff. 97-111v, 14th c.
Pr⁵   XIV F 5, ff. 49-64, 14th c.
       XX A 11 (formerly Admont 372), ff. 1, 57-63v, 13th c.
       XXIII D 174 (formerly Lobkowitz 587), ff. 22-37v, 15th c.

		adlig. 40. G. 8, ff. 10v–41, 15th c.
Pr⁶		Osek 33, ff. 136v–49, 14th c.
R	*	Reading, England. Library of Mrs. M. R. Ormerod, Phillipps 788, ff. 1–83v, 15th c.

Regensburg, West Germany. Bibl. des Kollegiatstiftes u. L. Frau zur Alten Kappelle, 1809, ff. 372–76, 15th c. Excerpts.

Re¹		Reims, France. Bibl. Mun., 66, ff. 31–55v, 14th c.
Re²		456, ff. 72v–82, beginning of 14th c.
Re³	*	457, ff. 26–45v, beginning of 15th c.
		466, ff. 1–29, 15th c.
		564, ff. 12–49v, 15th c.
		768, ff. 213–28v, 15th c.

Ri		Ripon, England. Ripon Cathedral, 10, ff. 1–2v, 13th c. Fragments.
Rl	*	Rock Island, Illinois, U.S.A. Augustana College, 2, pp. 1–36, 15th c.

Rodez, France. Bibl. Mun., 60, ff. 1–19v, 15th c. Omits from Book II, chap. 4, to Book III, chap. 2.

Rome, Italy. Bibl. Angelica, 492, ff. 26v–37, 14th c.

Bibl. Nazionale, Sessor. 149, ff. 58–65v, 13th c. Text ends in Book II, chap. 9.

Sessor. 289, ff. 41v–73, 15th c.

Sessor. 297, ff. 139–47v, 15th c. Text ends in Book I, chap. 17.

Bibl. Vallicelliana, B. 75, ff. 73v–79v, 13th c. Text ends in Book II, chap. 29.

Ro	*	F. 26, ff. 66–86v, late 12th c.
		Rouen, France. Bibl. Mun., A204 (625), ff. 39–48, 13th c.
		A454 (671), ff. 266–95, 13th–14th c.
Ru¹	*	A526 (677), ff. 50v–92v, 14th c.
Ru²	*	U136 (1468), ff. 280v–94v, 13th c.
S¹	*	Saint Omer, France. Bibl. Mun., 59, ff. 34v–43, 14th c.
S²	*	283, ff. 1–22, 15th c.
S³	*	297, ff. 1–40, 15th c.
S⁴	*	347, ff. 158–69, 15th c.

Salamanca, Spain. Bibl. Universitaria, 2.146 (formerly 2K5 at Real Bibl. in Madrid), ff. 37–51v, 13th c.

Salzburg, Austria. Universitätsbibl., M II 88, ff. 107–22v, 15th c.

M II 143, ff. 233–43, 15th c.

Sankt Florian, Austria. Stiftsbibl., XI.71, ff. 157–70v, 14th c.

XI.124, ff. 34–39v, 14th c.

XI.126, ff. 212v–23, 14th c.

XI.149, ff. 1–13v, 14th c.

XI.228, ff. 84–104, 15th c.

Sankt Paul im Lavanttal, Austria. Archiv des Benediktinerstiftes, 117/3, ff. 108–31v, 13th–14th c. Condensation.

Sankt Pölten, Austria. Diöcesanbibl., San Hippolytensis 27, ff. 301–16, 15th c.

San Marino, California, U.S.A. Henry E. Huntington Library, HM 1068, flyleaf, 15th c. Fragment.

Sa	*	HM 19914, ff. 189–200, 14th c. England.

Schlägl, Austria. Bibl. Canoniae Plagensis, 219 (823,230), ff. 36-64, 15th c.

Se   Seitenstetten, Austria. Stiftsbibl., 78, ff. 149-96, 15th c.
        248, ff. 1-17, 15th c.
        251, ff. 87-100, 15th c.

† Sigüenza, Spain. Catedral, 9, Item 6, 13th c.
Soissons, France. Bibl. Mun., 130, f. 116, 15th c. Excerpt.
Stockholm, Sweden. Kungliga Biblioteket, Holm. A 206, ff. 264-77v, 15th c.

So * Stonyhurst, England. Stonyhurst College, A.VI.32, ff. 91v-104, 14th c. Condensation.

St   Strasbourg, France. Bibl. Universitaire, 70, ff. 22v-42, 1462.

Stuttgart, West Germany. Württembergische Landesbibl., HB I 5, ff. 142-63v, 1460-64.
        HB I 70, ff. 108-12, 13th c. Text ends in Book I, chap. 27.
        HB III 45, ff. 300-316, 1463.
        theol. et phil. fol. 131, ff. 270-301, 15th c.
        theol. et phil. quart. 22, ff. 297v-331v, 15th c.

Su   Subiaco, Italy. Monasterio di S. Scolastica, CCLXXVII, ff. 210v-25v, 1438.

Sy * Sydney, Australia. University Library, Nicholson 27, ff. 1-47, 15th c.
Torino, Italy. Bibl. Nazionale, D VI 45, ff. 1-38, 14th c.
        E VI 16, ff. 413-37v, 14th c.
        H V 17, ff. 1-58v, 15th c.
Tours, France. Bibl. Mun., 405, ff. 149-70, 14th c.
        473, ff. 167-78v, 14th c.
Trebon, Czechoslovakia. Národní Archiv, 21, ff. 107-19v, 15th c.
Trier, West Germany. Bistumsarchiv, 54 (from the former Dombibl.), ff. 1-59v, 15th c.
        Bischöfliches Priesterseminar, 71, ff. 18v-52v, 15th c.
        Stadtarchiv, 1166/468, ff. 31-38v, 15th c.
        Stadtbibl., 41/1017, ff. 98-100v, 14th c. Selections.
        132/1197, ff. 49-75, 15th c.
        300/1973, ff. 160-64v, beginning of 15th c. Contains only through Book I, chap. 17.
        628/860, ff. 1-30v, 15th c.
        731/894, ff. 241-62v, 1458.

T¹ * Troyes, France. Bibl. Mun., 831, ff. 115v-30, 14th c.
T² *   1032, ff. 53-91, 14th c.
        1721, ff. 1-29, 13th c.
Überlingen, West Germany. Leopold-Sophien-Bibl., 18, ff. 146-58v, 15th c.

U¹ * Uppsala, Sweden. Universitetsbibl., C 77, ff. 9-34v, 15th c.
U² *   C 176, ff. 243-69, 15th c.
U³ *   C 199, ff. 2-22v, 14th c.
U⁴ *   C 226, ff. 16-38, 15th c.
U⁵ *   C 233, ff. 1-40, 14th c.

U⁶   *   C 237, ff. 157v–81v, 14th c.
U⁷   *   C 241, ff. 1–29, 14th c.
U⁸   *   C 565, ff. 24–34, 14th c.
Ut¹   * Utrecht, Netherlands. Bibl. der Rijksuniversiteit, 206 (eccl. 174), ff. 87–104v, 14th–15th c.
Ut²   *   263 (eccl. 30), ff. 229–38, 14th c.
               317 (eccl. 359), ff. 47–68v, 14th c.
      † Valencia, Spain. Catedral, 158, ff. 1–11, 15th c.
        Valenciennes, France. Bibl. Mun., 242, ff. 1–16v, 14th c.
        Vatican City, Vatican. Bibl. Apostolica Vaticana, Barber. lat. 704, ff. 167–77v, 14th c.
               Ferraioli 707, ff. 1–95v, 15th c.
               Ottob. lat. 22, ff. 1–32v, 15th c.
               Ottob. lat. 33, ff. 1–29v, 15th c.
               Ottob. lat. 49, ff. 34–57v, beginning of 15th c.
               Ottob. lat. 128, ff. 38–44, beginning of 13th c. Parts of Books II and III omitted.
               Ottob. lat. 433, ff. 144–93, 15th–16th c.
               Ottob. lat. 825, ff. 1–38, 15th c.
               Ottob. lat. 1472, ff. 71–81v, 14th c.
               Palat. lat. 396, ff. 1–23, 15th c.
               Palat. lat. 397, ff. 2–14, 1438.
               Palat. lat. 482, ff. 139–47v, beginning of 15th c.
V¹   Palat. lat. 1284, ff. 129r–v, 137v–42v, 15th c. Text ends in Book II, chap. 37.
               Palat. lat. 1880, ff. 1–43, late 15th–early 16th c.
V²   *   Regin. lat. 71, ff. 1–33v, beginning of 13th c.
               Regin. lat. 261, ff. 74v–99v, 15th c.
               Rossiano 398, ff. 69v–77v, 15th c. Contains through Book II, chap. 14, only.
               Rossiano 647, pp. 1–89, 1451.
V³   Rossiano 1024, ff. 122v–55v, 15th c.
               Urbin. lat. 604, ff. 99–137, 1516.
               Vat. lat. 696, ff. 1–32v, 15th c.
               Vat. lat. 1042, ff. 119–40v, 13th–14th c.
               Vat. lat. 1248, ff. 165–89, 13th c.
               Vat. lat. 2206, ff. 82v–83v, 13th c. Text ends in Book I, chap. 10.
               Vat. lat. 2590, ff. 63v–69v, beginning of 14th c.
               Vat. lat. 2699, ff. 61–73, 14th c.
               Vat. lat. 3759, ff. 71–85, 14th c.
V⁴   Vat. lat. 4363, ff. 116–24v, 13th c.
        Venice, Italy. Bibl. Nazionale Marciana, Lat. III,27 (2769), ff. 22v–44v, 1414.
               Lat. III,159 (2624), ff. 89–123, 15th c.
               Lat. VI,174 (3021), ff. 142–59, 14th c.
               Lat. XIV,273 (4346), ff. 117–35, 15th c.

Lat. Z,74 (1866), ff. 81v–88v, 14th c. Contains Book I only.

† Vercelli, Italy. Archivio Capitolare, 132, ff. 96–98, 14th c.

Vienna, Austria. Oesterreichische Nationalbibl., 322, ff. 64–93, 15th c.

566, ff. 120–41v, 14th c.

813, ff. 131–64, 13th–14th c.

876, ff. 1–25, 14th c.

1030, ff. 108–29, 14th c.

1075, ff. 1–29v, 14th c.

1165, ff. 1–55v, 14th c.

1345, ff. 1–34, 14th c.

1357, ff. 1–24v, 14th c.

1540, ff. 88–110, 13th c.

2216, ff. 119–30, 14th c.

4013, ff. 15–39, 15th c.

4180, ff. 192–93, 15th c. Excerpts.

4241, ff. 332v–50v, 14th–15th c.

Vi   4253, ff. 34v–45v, 15th c.

4477, ff. 14–27v, 15th c.

12529, ff. 41–76v, 14th c.

12538, ff. 177–87v, 14th c.

13822, ff. 176–210v, 1443.

Series nova 3618, f. 31v, 14th–15th c. Excerpt.

Schottenstift, 231, ff. 75–99v, 13th c.

293, ff. 32v–51, 14th c.

311, ff. 277v–92v, 15th c.

Vorau, Austria. Chorherrenstift, 112 (CCXXVIII), ff. 73–90v, 15th c.

304 (XX), ff. 77v–99, 13th c.

W   Wertheim, West Germany. Evangelische Kirchenbibl., 45, ff. 61–79v, 15th c.

Wilhering, Austria. Stiftsbibl., IX.63, ff. 105–25, 15th c.

Wolfenbüttel, West Germany. Herzog-August-Bibl., Aug. 2° 75.3, ff. 1–16, 1431.

Gud. lat. 233, f. 2, 15th c. Selections.

Helmst. 353, ff. 88–108v, 15th c.

Helmst. 615, ff. 100–113, 15th c.

Helmst. 1230, ff. 19–124, 15th c.

Wo[1] * Worcester, England. Worcester Cathedral, F. 117, ff. 80–95v, 13th–13th/14th c. Worcester.

Wo[2] *   F. 152, ff. 26v–33, 14th c. Worcester.

Wroclaw, Poland. Bibl. Uniwersytecka, I F 157, ff. 241v–58, 1449.

I F 253, ff. 26–39v, second half of 15th c.

I F 259, ff. 162–72, first half of 15th c.

I F 293, ff. 97–119, first half of 15th c.

I F 309, ff. 112v–31, first half of 14th c.

Wr[1]   I F 334, ff. 242–55v, first half of 15th c.

I F 631, ff. 144–61v, second half of 14th c.

I O 23, ff. 26–68v, first half of 15th c.

Wr²   I Q 276, ff. 303–32v, 15th c.
           I Q 348, ff. 254r–v, 264r–v, 14th c. Contains through Book I,
        chap. 4, only.
           II Q 12, ff. 25–36, end of 14th c.
           IV F 58, ff. 1–12v, second half of 15th c.
           IV O 7, ff. 120–23, second half of 15th c. Text ends in Book I,
        chap. 5.
           IV Q 72, ff. 1–25v, second half of 13th c.
           IV Q 158, ff. 153–89v, first half of 15th c.
           Görlitz 46, ff. 49–65v, 15th c.
           Milich 12,88/9421, ff. 178–231, 15th c.
           Milich 47/9425, ff. 129–45, 14th c.
           Milich 73/7797, ff. 1–16v, 15th c.
Würzburg, West Germany. Universitätsbibl., ch. f. 52, ff. 233–36v,
    15th c. Excerpts.
           ch. f. 86, ff. 221–38v, 14th c.
           ch. f. 135, ff. 216–30, 15th c.
           ch. f. 186, ff. 249–60, 14th c.
           ch. f. 193, ff. 228v–43v, mid-14th c.
           p. th. f. 127b, ff. 152v–62v, 14th c.
Zurich, Switzerland. Zentralbibl., C 151, ff. 1v–65, 15th c. Omits from
    Book II, chap. 16, to Book III, original chap. 2.

APPENDIX II:
THE TEXTUAL RELATIONSHIPS OF L^{31}

L^{31} belongs to a group of manuscripts that contain a large number of readings that are consistently and strikingly different from Lotario's original (both as reconstructed by Maccarrone and as represented in Ro and V^2, the manuscripts closest to Lotario's original in the critical apparatus to the present edition). The group contains the following manuscripts:

Au	Auxerre, Bibliothèque Municipale, 7
C^1	Cambridge, Corpus Christi College, 63
C^2	Cambridge, Corpus Christi College, 433
C^9	Cambridge, Gonville and Caius College, 349
C^{10}	Cambridge, Magdalene College, F.4.15
C^{18}	Cambridge, University Library, Dd.1.21
D^6	Dublin, Trinity College, 514
E^1	Edinburgh, University Library, 107
Es^2	Escorial, Real Biblioteca, I.III.7
Ev	Evreux, Bibliothèque Municipale, 23
L^9	London, British Library, Harley 979
L^{17}	London, British Library, Harley 4987
L^{24}	London, British Library, Royal 5 E.xxi
L^{25}	London, British Library, Royal 7 D.xvii
L^{29}	London, British Library, Royal 8 C.vii
L^{31}	London, British Library, Royal 8 F.xiv
L^{35}	London, British Library, Sloane 2275
L^{36}	London, British Library, Addl. 6716
L^{40}	London, British Library, Addl. 33957
L^{45}	London, Lambeth Palace, 366
La	Laon, Bibliothèque Municipale, 179
N	Newbury, Library of H. W. Edwards, Tollemache L.J.I.
O^{10}	Oxford, Bodleian Library, Digby 149
O^{13}	Oxford, Bodleian Library, Laud Misc. 112
O^{19}	Oxford, Bodleian Library, Rawlinson A.363
O^{31}	Oxford, Magdalen College, 109
Pa^4	Paris, Bibliothèque Nationale, lat. 3487A
Pa^6	Paris, Bibliothèque Nationale, lat. 3768
Pa^{10}	Paris, Bibliothèque Nationale, lat. 15700

Ru²   Rouen, Bibliothèque Municipale, U136 (1468)
Sa   San Marino, Henry E. Huntington Library, HM 19914
Wo²   Worcester, Cathedral, F. 117

In addition to these thirty-two manuscripts, there are four others that must also be included but that are special cases:

C¹⁴   Cambridge, Peterhouse, 219
C¹⁷   Cambridge, Trinity College, 1133
L⁸   London, British Library, Harley 337
O²⁰   Oxford, Bodleian Library, Rawlinson A.423

C¹⁴ is part of the group in Books II and III but has only eleven of twenty-eight readings in Book I. It would be misleading, however, to omit it from the list because the greater part of I is part of the group: from I.13 to the end of the book it has ten of seventeen group readings; from the beginning through I.12 it has almost no group readings and is presumably from a different textual tradition. C¹⁷ contains miscellaneous parts of the *De Miseria* (I.1, 8, the last half of 9, 10-12; II.18 and 20; III.1,15-16), but all exhibit group readings. The *De Miseria* in L⁸ is a combination of two different texts in two different hands: the first contains from the beginning of the treatise to the middle of I.17 and from II.5 to the end and is not part of the group; the second contains from I.18 to the beginning of II.6 and is part of the group. O²⁰ does not begin until II.31 and then omits various sections (II.33-37; III.6-9, 13-15) but is part of the group throughout.

The evidence for the group, which is presented at the end of this Appendix, is extensive but is not always exclusive; that is, not every manuscript in the group has all the readings that distinguish the group, and often manuscripts outside the group have group readings. This situation is to be expected, for a number of reasons. First, with a work as popular as the *De Miseria,* there is bound to be a great deal of contamination, either conflation of two or more manuscripts or correction of one manuscript from another. Maccarrone, for instance, found that there was so much contamination in copies of the work ("inter se commixta et contaminata sunt"), even in the early stages of transmission, that it was impossible to reconstruct Lotario's original by the genealogical method.[1] Such contamination is, of course, greatly magnified by the time the work reaches Chaucer, in England, nearly two hundred years later. Second, in a work as full of commonplaces and in such a well-known, well-defined genre as the *De Miseria,* there will be much conscious variation, that is, the supplying by scribes of words and phrases that they know by heart for ones in their exemplars.

255

Third, as in the transmission of all medieval texts, one finds a great deal of unconscious, or mechanical, scribal copying along well defined lines.[2] The important point to be made about the group manuscripts, however, is that, with a few exceptions, they consistently have the readings in question.[3]

The great majority of the nongroup manuscripts that appear with the group do so only a few times, and their readings are doubtless the result of coincident scribal variation, either conscious or unconscious. Other manuscripts, however, persist in having readings similar to the group readings, and these are probably either conflations of a group manuscript and a nongroup manuscript, or manuscripts corrected from group manuscripts, or possibly earlier stages of the group before its appearance in Britain. Because I am concerned here with the relationship between L^{31} and Chaucer's text of the *De Miseria* and because none of these manuscripts has close similarities to L^{31} outside of the group readings, it is unnecessary to undertake a detailed examination of each of them, but a brief survey of them all is in order.[4] Some manuscripts are part of the group in one or more books: L^{43} from the beginning of Book I into chapter 9, but not at all from there on; O^{26} in I, and very close in II; D^{4} in II (through II.21 only), though it also has a number of the group readings in the early part of I; L^{6} and Ma^{3} in II and III, but not in I; L^{5} in III, where it shows a textual tradition different from that in I and II; L^{22}, O^{24}, Pa^{14}, and Ru^{1} in III. Go, I, and Mu^{5} exhibit a similar pattern: either part of the group or extremely close in I, and close in II and III; to a lesser extent, the same pattern appears in the related manuscripts Bu, Lm, Pa^{9}, and Pa^{11}. Re^{3} and T^{2} are part of the group in I, and close in II, but not at all in III (Ar, though it does not begin until I.28, is to be added here because it is closely related to Re^{3} and T^{2}). L^{7} is interesting because it is a corrected manuscript in which the group readings appear above the lines. O^{6} is not part of the group in I, and omits from I.27 to II.32 but has many of the group readings in III before breaking off in III.8. Other manuscripts, though not part of the group, are close, or fairly close, in one or more of the three books: $BsD^{1}Er^{2}L^{14}O^{21}O^{23}Pa^{5}Pa^{8}Pa^{15}$.

The large group of manuscripts is interesting in its own right, and a great many observations could be made about it, but I will confine myself to remarks that are germane to the purpose at hand: to determine the relationship of L^{31} and the glosses and ultimately Chaucer's text of the *De Miseria*. First of all, it must be emphasized that the large group is just that—a group—and not a consistently homogeneous genetic family. There is a great deal of contamination, especially among the nongroup but related manuscripts, that would be impossible to sort out adequately, and there are variational groups of two, three, and more manuscripts within the large group that may or may not be genetic.[5] If I were attempting to reconstruct Lotario's original, I would certainly analyze the group and its members in detail. For the moment I am interested in showing only that a large group exists and that L^{31} is a member of it.

Second, in addition to the evidence for the existence of the group presented below, there are two strong corroborating pieces of evidence. First, in all group manuscripts except nine ($C^{14}C^{17}C^{18}L^{8}L^{31}L^{36}O^{10}$ $O^{19}O^{20}$), Book III, chapters 13 and 14 are combined to form a single long chapter with a new title, "De Iusticia Iudicis." Of the exceptions, C^{17}, L^{8}, and O^{20} are special cases, none of these manuscripts having III.13 or III.14 as part of their texts; L^{31}, O^{10}, and O^{19} all break off before the end and thus do not exhibit these two chapters; only C^{14}, C^{18}, and L^{36} are therefore true exceptions, and they may be mixed texts. Fifteen other manuscripts have this combination, of which 9 are among the possibly contaminated manuscripts ($BuGoIL^{5}L^{14}Mu^{5}Pa^{9}$ $Pa^{11}Ru^{1}$); this leaves only 6 manuscripts ($C^{7}L^{2}L^{29}L^{46}Mu^{1}Se$) out of the more than 600 remaining manuscripts to show coincident variation, which is a strong argument for the combination as a group characteristic. The second piece of corroborating evidence is the main title to the work. All but 10 group manuscripts ($AuC^{17}C^{18}L^{8}L^{36}NO^{19}$ $O^{20}Pa^{6}Pa^{10}$) have *De Contemptu Mundi,* either separately or in combination, and of these ten Au has no meaningful title of any kind; L^{8} is one of the special cases, with its early chapters not part of the group; the title in N is a later addition, the original text not having a title; O^{19} and O^{20} begin imperfectly, but both have a variety of *De Contemptu Mundi* in their colophons; and C^{17} and Pa^{10} lack the prologue, appearing to have derived their main titles from the title to Book I, chapter 1: "De Miseria Hominis."[6] This leaves only three true exceptions ($C^{18}L^{36}Pa^{6}$), and even one of these, Pa^{6}, has *De Contemptu Mundi* in its colophon; the other two may be mixed texts.

Third, the distribution and provenances (where known) of the group manuscripts, as well as of those manuscripts that are probably either contaminated or earlier stages of the group, are of interest to the history of the medieval transmission of the *De Miseria* and may shed some light, if not on Chaucer's manuscript, at least on the manuscript tradition in Britain in the late fourteenth century. None of the manuscripts is from an Italian library or can be traced to Italy, where Lotario wrote his treatise. Only a few are from German or Austrian libraries: Bu (provenance: probably the Braunschweig Franziskanerkloster), Er^{2}, Go, I (provenance: Kartäuserkloster Schnals), Ma^{3} (provenance: Mainz, Carthusians), and Mu^{5} (provenance: Polling Canons), to which can be added Bs, which was written in Germany (Rüden). A

257

larger number are now in French libraries—18 (of which 7 are definitely part of the group throughout) out of a possible 109; there is very little evidence as to the specific provenances of these manuscripts in the printed catalogues, but one can assume, I think, that most, if not all, of them were written in France (Pa[10] is an exception, having been written in England). The other 39 (29 definitely in the group; 10 in some way related) are from either British or Irish libraries (of the 3 Irish manuscripts, one—D[6]—is from Canterbury, Abbey of St. Augustine, and another—D[4]—has an English provenance; the British manuscripts, so far as one can ascertain, are of either definitely or presumably British provenance) or were written in England (Es[2] and Sa). To put it another way, of the 115 manuscripts that I have termed "British," 30, or just over one-quarter, are definitely part of the group throughout. In short, it would appear that as the text of the *De Miseria* progressed farther and farther from its place of origin, it had a greater chance to become like the group to which L[31] belongs. If these figures are at all representative of the actual situation, in theory one out of every four manuscripts in existence in late-fourteenth-century Britain, when Chaucer began to translate the *De Miseria*, was a group manuscript (or more than one out of every three when the related manuscripts are included).[7]

Finally and most importantly, what is the status of L[31] and what is its place in the manuscript tradition? The first observation to be made is that some of the differences between L[31] and the glosses and between L[31] and the original for the nonglossed passages can be accounted for by reference to the group readings. Two variants in L[31] as against original readings in the glosses—*deduxit* for *duxit* and *compassio* for *passio* (I.20)[8]—are readings peculiar to the group. Others, not listed in the evidence below, are part of the extensive corroborative evidence for the group: the change of word order reflected in L[31]'s "pena et dolor secuntur semper" (II.21) appears in three-quarters of the group manuscripts and in only six manuscripts outside the group; *non* for *ne* (I.21), though it is a common scribal substitution and appears in many of the manuscripts that I have collated, can be found in all but two of the group manuscripts. In L[31]'s version of Book I, chapter 14, for which there is no gloss,[9] the additions of "proximum Deum eo" and "iniquum quod non recte dividicat" are probably the attempt by the scribe to grapple with the puzzling addition in his exemplar of "proximum criminatur malignum Deum eo," which is a group reading. In addition, a number of the other differences between L[31] and the original for the nonglossed passages are corroborative readings for the group: the omission of *petit* (I.14), *quia* for *quod* (I.14), *subvenit* for *subveniat* (I.14), the transposition of *pauper* and *odiosus erit* (I.14), the omission of *et* (I.14), *Audi* for *Adverte* (I.14), *et* for *ut* (II.17).

The remaining differences are of three kinds. Some are in a great many of the manuscripts that I have collated: the omission of *enim* (I.14), the omission of the two *et*'s (I.14.4 and 5), the addition of *et* (I.14.9), *irritandum* for *irritandam* (II.17); these are of course very common scribal changes. Some are in a few manuscripts: the addition of *ut* (I.21), *sit* for *sis* (I.21), *promittit* for *promit* (II.19), the addition of *et* (I.14.2), *transit* for *transeat* (II.17). Peculiar to L^{31} are misreadings like the following: *Malum* for *Nullum* (II.19), *reate* for *reatus* (I.20), *alia* for *aliqua* (I.20), the transposition of *cruciantur* and *premuntur* (I.14), *confurditur* for *confunditur* (I.14), *causeatur* for *causatur* (I.14), *amcii* for *amici* (I.14), *satietas* for *saturitas* (II.17). Most of these misreadings are doubtless the result of the carelessness of the scribe, or the scribe of his exemplar—a carelessness that is apparent on every folio of the manuscript, as a glance at the readings in the critical apparatus will make clear.

As for the place of L^{31} in the manuscript tradition, it is closest to C^{18}, another group manuscript. After I had finished collating the group manuscripts, I checked 336 nongroup readings that seemed at first glance to be peculiar to L^{31} with the rest of the group manuscripts to determine which one was closest. C^{18} had 78 readings, or over 23 percent; its nearest competitor was C^{14}, with 48 readings, or over 14 percent. No other group manuscript had more than 21 readings (C^{9}). After I had collated the other manuscripts, I discovered that 141 of the 336 readings were common to a great many manuscripts, but even omitting those, it was clear that no nongroup manuscript was as close to L^{31} as C^{18} (with 38 out of 195 readings, or nearly 20 percent). C^{14} was still the closest competitor (with 23 readings, or nearly 12 percent), but no other manuscript had more than 12 readings, or about half of C^{14}'s total.

Though some of the readings shared by L^{31} and C^{18} are common scribal errors, and in some others L^{31} and C^{18} do not stand alone against the rest of the manuscripts, it is important that (1) there are so many similarities between the two manuscripts—too many to be ascribed to chance; (2) when other manuscripts do join L^{31} and C^{18} in their readings, they are usually very few in number and exhibit no consistent pattern; and (3) L^{31} and C^{18} agree against all the other collated manuscripts in a few readings:

I.1.24 addition of *brevius sive;* I.2.10 **recognoscet** *se agnoscet;* I.10.13 **super filios** *filiis;* I.28.4 **Ierusalem (Ierosolimis)** *Ierosolimam;* II.20.4 **dantes** *vocantibus (vacantibus* C^{18}); II.24.3 **tradidit illos Deus** *tradidit vos;* II.31.32 **condensis frondibus** *tandem cum frondibus.*[10]

The rest of the evidence for C^{18}-L^{31} can be divided into two groups. In the first group are fairly striking readings shared by no more than ten (or approximately 5 percent) of the collated manuscripts:

I.6.6 **Hinc enim** *Hinc est quod* (+3); I.11.12 **sudoribus** *laboribus* (+9); I.11.18 **multa** *plura* (+1); I.12.16 addition of *agunt* (+7); I.23.21 **plurime** *plures* (+2); II.12.11-12 **et nichil . . . suis** *et cetera* (+5); II.28.15 **illum (eum)** *eos* (+4); II.31.39 **orbem** *mundum* (+7).

The second group consists of common scribal changes, either unique to C¹⁸–L³¹ or shared by no more than ten manuscripts (I give line numbers only):¹¹

Addition: II.3.22 (+1). Substitutions: I.1.25; I.9.9 (+1); I.17.25. Transpositions: I.10.10-11; I.16.14 (+5). Omissions: I.26.4; II.2.11; II.3.15 (+4); II.8.2 (+8); II.13.5 (+9); II.34.21-22.

Because of its closeness to L³¹, it is important to determine the affiliations of C¹⁸ before continuing with the relationship of L³¹ to Chaucer's manuscript. C¹⁸ forms a genetic group with C¹⁴, after C¹⁸ the closest manuscript to L³¹. Of all the manuscripts I have collated, the pair C¹⁴–C¹⁸ is more closely, and more strikingly, related than any other pair or group of manuscripts. The evidence is extensive, and, as it can easily be seen in the critical apparatus, it is unnecessary to present all of it here. The most important readings (50), unique to the two manuscripts, are as follows:¹²

I.16.67 **Propter** *Ob;* I.18.2 **Insidiaitur undique** *sint (fuit* C¹⁴) *videlicet qui insidiantur semper;* I.18.3 **demon et** *hii scilicet;* I.18.4 **et caro . . . viciis** *Demon caro;* I.18.5 addition of *demon cum viciis;* I.18.29 **et volucres** *et eciam volucres nobis insidiantur;* I.21.4 **Noverat** *Nam novit;* I.23.29 **regrediatur** *revertatur;* I.24.5 addition of *operatur;* I.28.12 **fatigabat** *vexabat;* I.28.24 **urgemur** *perurgemur;* I.28.31 **concepto** *precepto;* I.28.36 **quamvis animi** *et interim ora eorum;* II.1.11-12 **iactanciam** *vanam gloriam;* II.2.3 addition of *in hoc seculo;* II.3.5 addition of *unde ipsi non;* II.4.42 **parvum audietis** *pauperem audies ut divitem parvum;* II.7.5 **est** *efficitur;* II.16.8 **lucrum extendat** *opes recondat (rotondat* C¹⁸); II.16.10 **dandum** *errogandum;* II.17.11 **transeat** *crescat;* II.18.10 addition of *quod sonat numera appende divide;* II.21.4-5 **Venter . . . amplexatur** *Venter enim mero estuans de facili spumat in libidinem (enim* omitted C¹⁸); II.22.5 addition of *caro;* II.24.17 addition of *vel cum aliquo bruto (cum* omitted C¹⁸); II.28.11 **Dixitque (Dicebatque)** *Et subiunxit;* II.28.17-18 **corda virorum** *viros (vires* C¹⁸); II.29.4 **spiritus** *sensus;* II.31.11 addition of *decrusit;* II.31.31 **fecit (feci) eum** *fecerat illum;* II.31.32 addition of *corruit;* II.32.1 **O . . . superbia** *O quam presumptuosa est superbia immo presumpcio superba;* II.32.15 addition of *dicens;* II.32.29 **superbarum** *superbiencium;* II.35.2 **Dic inquit** *dicentis Dic;* II.38.2 addition of *dicens;* II.40.12 **quando quidem** *cum tamen huiusmodi;* II.41.15 addition of *ergo Deus;* II.41.37 **prodigis** *profugis;* III.1.36 **verme** *putredine;* III.2.8 addition of *iusticia;* III.3.20 **potest . . . peccare** *ipse ex sui facultate peccare potest vel penitenciam temporalem portare* (in C¹⁴ transposition of *peccare* and *potest,* and *agere* for *temporalem portare*); III.5.22 addition of *dives;* III.6.13 **queri . . . pena** *nichil esse nisi solummodo penam;* III.7.9 **patientur** *tollerabunt;* III.8.6 addition of *Unde poeta;* III.13.7 **petris** *cavernis*; III.15.12 addition of *tribue illis*; III.15.17 **provocari** *appellari*; III.16.10 **O** *Erit*.

In addition, there are thirty-seven striking readings shared by no more than five group manuscripts, fifty-four somewhat less striking readings unique to C^{14}–C^{18}, and seventy-one common scribal changes, either unique to C^{14}–C^{18} or shared by no more than five group manuscripts. Because there are individual peculiarities in each manuscript, the most important of which are omissions, that preclude copying one from the other, the simplest way to express the relationship of the two manuscripts is by radiation from a common ancestor:[13]

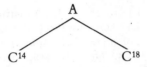

When one looks at the pattern of group readings in the two manuscripts, however, the situation is quite different. In addition to not having as many as most other manuscripts, they differ in 31 of the 101 readings at the end of this Appendix—a pattern that is confirmed and even emphasized when one looks at the extensive corroborative evidence for the group, much of it consisting of less striking readings than those presented below. The greatest differences are in the first twelve chapters of Book I, where C^{14} has almost no group readings, but the shifting pattern can be seen throughout the text. When two manuscripts as similar as C^{14} and C^{18} in their basic texts have such different patterns of readings from a well-attested group like the one presented below, they must be contaminated. The contamination is most simply and most economically explained by assuming the conflation of a base text containing the readings that characterize the genetic group C^{14}–C^{18} with a group manuscript containing the group readings written in the margins or between the lines, so that the scribe of C^{14} would have added some group readings to his text and the scribe of C^{18} would have added others.[14] Thus:

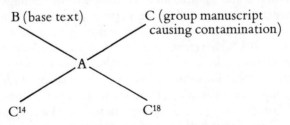

In addition to C^{18}–L^{31} and C^{14}–C^{18}, there appears to be a group

C^{14}–C^{18}–L^{31}, though not quite as persuasive as C^{18}–L^{31} and not nearly as persistent as C^{14}–C^{18}. The striking readings, in which the three manuscripts agree against all the other collated manuscripts, are as follows:

I.27.12 **immane** *terribile*; II.5.25 **aures Domini** *auribus Dei*; II.17.26 **Deus . . . destruet** *hunc et hanc Deus destruet*; II.24.8 **operantes** *operantur*; II.29.15 **florem proiciens** *producens florem*; II.31.32 addition of *tandem*.

The rest of the evidence for C^{14}–C^{18}–L^{31} can be divided into two categories. The first of these consists of additions and substitutions, either unique to the three manuscripts or shared by no more than ten (or approximately 5 percent) of the collated manuscripts:

I.1.25 **quodque** *et quod*; I.15.10 **et** *sed*; I.15.18 **enim** *autem*; (+2); I.15.26 **in-sompnes** *in sompnos* (+3); I.17.11 *sint* for *sunt* (+2); I.17.18 **et sicut** *sic eciam* (*sicut eciam* C^{18}); I.21.13 addition of *ut* (+2); I.22.4 **quia** *quoniam* (+4); II.2.6 **in** *ad* (+2); II.3.13 **eius** *vestri* (+2); II.4.42 **Nec** *Non* (+6); II.18.2 **quia** *et* (+3); II.25.15 **respexit** *aspexit* (+9); II.26.6 **valeat displicere** *displiceat* (+3); II.27.9 **tantoque** *tanto enim* (+1); II.31.24 addition of *et*.

In the second category are transpositions and omissions, either unique to C^{14}–C^{18}–L^{31} or shared by no more than ten manuscripts (I give line numbers only):

Transpositions: I.16.3 and 64 (+3); I.18.2 (+5); I.28.44–45 (+5); I.29.1; II.5.12 (+6); II.26.17–18; II.28.10 (+5); II.34.1 (+1); II.35.10 (+1). Omissions: I.18.23 (+3); I.21.5–6 (+1), 7 (+8), and 8; II.3.14 (+6); II.4.28 (+5); II.11.1 (+4); II.19.11 (+3); II.26.3; II.31.42 (+3).

Thus:

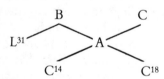

L^{31}, however, in addition to its similarities to the base strain of C^{14}–C^{18}, is a group manuscript, but it will be seen from the evidence below that it does not exhibit as many group readings as most of the other manuscripts and that the pattern of group readings is different from that in either C^{14} or C^{18} (thirty divergences from C^{14} and twenty from C^{18}). Is L^{31}, therefore, also a contaminated manuscript? The available evidence, which is of two kinds, indicates that it is.

First, L^{31} exhibits conflation of its base strain with readings from the group. For example, (1) at I.9.12 L^{31} has "amplius et plurimum erit." Lotario's original as reconstructed by Maccarrone has "amplius eorum," and about half the nongroup manuscripts that I have collated retain this reading, though both the manuscript used for this edition and Ro have "plurimum eorum." The group, however, has "plurimum erit" at this point, and it appears that L^{31} has combined the *amplius* that was probably in the base strain with the group reading. (2) The manuscript used for this edition and probably Lotario's original (though Maccarrone doubts it, p. xlii, printing instead "LX ... LXX") have "Pauci nunc ad quadraginta, paucissimi ad sexaginta annos perveniunt" at I.9.16-17. Most group manuscripts, but very few nongroup manuscripts, have "quadraginta...quinquaginta"(or "xl...l"). L^{31} has "xl ... l vel xlx," probably showing conflation of the two strains, with *xlx* a slip for *lx* made under the influence of the preceding *xl.* (3) At I.25.6-7 the manuscript used for this edition has "nam intolerabilis est propter passionis acerbitatem" (as in Lotario's original, except that there one finds *intolerabile* for *intolerabilis),* whereas the group omits the clause at this point but adds it later, after *necessitatem,* with *est* omitted. L^{31} has "et intollerabilis est propter" in line 5, but it is expunged, and it is possible that the scribe began to anticipate the original clause but then realized that it should be omitted here, expunged it, and added it later at the place where it appears in the group. (4) At I.27.8 both the manuscript used for this edition and Lotario's original have *excoriantur,* whereas the group has *excecantur* (item 27 in the list at the end of this Appendix): L^{31} has both *excoriantur* and *excetantur.* (5) At II.17.18 both Lotario's original as reconstructed by Maccarrone and the manuscript used for this edition have *saporum.* One group manuscript (Au), seven contaminated manuscripts that are definitely part of the group in II (BuGoILmMu^{5}Pa^{9}Pa^{11}), and only three others of the collated manuscripts (O^{5}O^{18}Pa^{15}) have *verborum* for *saporum.* L^{31} appears to show conflation here, with its "verborum et saporum," and the con-flation may indicate the nature of the group strain in L^{31}.[15]

Secondly, as W. W. Greg observes, "collation and 'correction' are confined to some of the more striking variants. This will show itself on analysis either by the sporadic appearance of anomalous groupings, or by those involving the more important variants consistently pointing in one direction, and those involving the minor variants consistently in another . . . where conflation is suspected, the value of variants as an indication of ancestry is in inverse proportion to their intrinsic impor-tance. To the herd of dull commonplace readings we must look for the genetic source of the text, to the more interesting and striking for the source of the contamination."[16] The rule involving the "herd of dull commonplace readings" is controversial, and George Kane, for exam-ple, justifiably questions its reliability as "a source of evidence for genetic relation," especially in Middle English manuscripts where one finds a great deal of coincident variation.[17] On the basis of my expe-rience with the manuscripts of the *De Miseria,* however, I would suggest that in general coincident variation is not as prevalent in Latin manuscripts as in Middle English manuscripts (perhaps because scribes tried to copy more faithfully in their second language, Latin, than in their native languages); moreover, that "herd of dull commonplace readings" is a somewhat misleading phrase when one is trying to determine the direction of contamination ("readings that do not catch a scribe's eye," while less colorful, is more accurate); that, when contamination is obvious, that is, when readings from one textual tradition are written in the margins or between the lines of a text from another tradition, such correction, or "contamination," is almost never the substitution of one "commonplace" reading for another; and that therefore, when one finds the retention of "readings that do not catch a scribe's eye" in a manuscript that exhibits signs of conflation, we can determine the direction of contamination with some confidence.

L^{31} preserves the nonstriking readings from its base, or nongroup, strain in the following readings from the list of evidence at the end of this Appendix: 2, 4, 5, 14, 16, 36, 55, 60. There is, however, a great deal of corroborative evidence for the group which has not been included in the list, partly because it would add unnecessarily to the bulk and partly because it does not divide itself as neatly (probably on account of coincident variation) into group versus nongroup manuscripts as the readings I have listed, which are, in general, rather striking readings. But the corroborative evidence can be seen by comparing C^{10} and E^{1}, the representatives of the group in the critical apparatus, with the manuscript used for this edition. Specifically, the places where L^{31} retains the nonstriking readings of its base strain are: I.2.24; I.8.1-2; I.9.30-31; I.10.10; I.11.12 and 21; I.12.7; I.15.11; I.16.7, 26, 51 (2), 56, and 68; I.18.29; I.23.8; I.25.4, 5, and 6; II.1.1; II.3.14; II.4.28 and 35; II.6.3 and 7; II.14.10; II.16.16; II.20.5; II.21.3-4 and 14; II.23.11; II.24.15; II.26.13 and 20; II.27.11; II.28.19; II.29.2; II.32.10; II.36.5 and 12.

The conclusion to be drawn from both the conflation and the retention of many nonstriking, nongroup readings is that L^{31} is a contaminated manuscript, with its base strain similar to that in C^{14} and C^{18} and with the contamination deriving from a group manuscript (D). Thus:

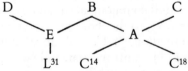

I recognize that claiming contamination is often an easy solution to the problem of obscured manuscript affiliations, but with a work as popular as the *De Miseria*, in which we know there was a great deal of contamination, even at the early stages of copying, it is a priori a likely solution. In addition, the evidence from the manuscripts in question—C^{14}, C^{18}, and L^{31}—seems to me strongly in favor of contamination. The way in which each manuscript was contaminated is less certain, but the nature of the readings in L^{31} and the differing patterns of group readings in C^{14} and C^{18} make it probable that the contamination came from a group manuscript in each case.[18]

Moreover, to see as contaminated certain manuscripts that appear to be part of the group helps to reconfirm the status of the group. It will be seen from the figures at the end of the list of evidence that the following manuscripts have fewer group readings than the others in one or more of the three books: Au, C^{14}, C^{18}, L^{31}, L^{36}, L^{40}, and Wo^2. Three of these seven manuscripts—C^{14}, C^{18}, and L^{31}—are almost certainly contaminated. If the other four are also contaminated (the shifting relationships of L^{36} and L^{40} seem to argue for contamination; Au has close similarities to a number of probably contaminated continental manuscripts, as I pointed out in note 5; the status of Wo^2 is unclear, though it too has similarities to a probably contaminated manuscript, L^6, in Books II and III), the result is a great deal of homogeneity among the remaining manuscripts of the group.[19] That is not to say that they all derive from a single manuscript, or even that all the British manuscripts derive from a single manuscript that came into Britain early in the transmission of the *De Miseria*—from what we know of the copying of manuscripts, that possibility would be very slight indeed—but that they are all very faithful preservers of the group textual tradition, with individual characteristics and groupings among themselves to be sure but with little or no sign of contamination.

There remains the crucial question of the relationship of L^{31} to Chaucer's glosses to the Man of Law's Tale, and the answer to it also bears out the likelihood that L^{31} is a contaminated manuscript. Given our earlier conclusions—(1) that both L^{31} and the glosses, in contrast to all other manuscripts that I have examined (that is, all but 4 of the 672), have the three additions (*Audi ergo, latet, eciam*) that are reflected in Chaucer's translations, (2) that the glosses retain the original readings so often whereas L^{31} belongs much of the time to a different, and well-attested, textual tradition, and (3) that L^{31} exhibits both conflation of the two traditions and the retention of nonstriking readings from the original tradition—the only reasonable explanation for the differences between L^{31} and the glosses is that L^{31} is a contaminated manuscript. If we assume, and I think we must in the absence of any evidence to the contrary, that the glosses were copied directly from the manuscript in Chaucer's possession, then the relationship of that manuscript, the glosses, and L^{31} must be:[20]

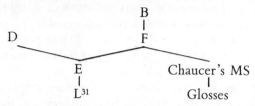

The following list contains the main evidence for the large group of manuscripts discussed above. The evidence consists almost entirely of additions and substitutions; I include a few important transpositions but no omissions. There is a great deal of additional, corroborative evidence for the group—insignificant additions and substitutions, transpositions, omissions, readings shared by a number of nongroup manuscripts, etc.—that is not given here but that can be found in the critical apparatus wherever the sigil C^{10} or the sigil E^1 appears. Readers familiar with scribal habits will recognize how many of the group readings originated—in repetitions, anticipations, recollections, and the like—and the origins doubtless explain why random manuscripts so often appear with the group manuscripts, but the importance of the list is the frequency and the consistency with which certain manuscripts exhibit the readings.

The list is based on my collations of 208, or approximately 30 percent, of the 672 extant manuscripts. These 208, which are asterisked in Appendix I, were chosen after a preliminary checking, for group readings, of all but 4 (marked with † in Appendix I) of the manuscripts and include all manuscripts in British and Irish libraries, all manuscripts with definite, probable, or possible British provenances, all non-British manuscripts that contained some of the group readings, and a sampling of other non-British manuscripts. I have collated all 208 manuscripts to the point at which L^{31} breaks off (Book II, chapter 36); from there on I have collated all manuscripts in British and Irish libraries, all manuscripts with British provenances, and all other manuscripts that bore some relationship to the group manuscripts in the earlier part.

The entries take the following form: book, chapter, and line numbers in the present edition; lemma in boldface type (except for additions), as in L^{20}, the manuscript used for the edition, followed by the reading in Lotario's original (as found in either Ro or V^2), in parentheses, when it differs from the reading in L^{20}; variant group reading, as in C^{10} or E^1; list of manuscripts, with sigils taken from

Appendix I; variations on the group reading, followed by the manuscripts containing them. The list is not a complete record of every reading in every manuscript that I have collated (the nature of this investigation does not warrant such a record, though the data is available for anyone who wishes to see it): I have ignored slight differences in spelling, capitalization, and word order, and have recorded only the group readings themselves, variations on the group readings, and other readings that shed some light on the group readings. I have listed every manuscript that contained a reading in any form and at any time, for example, when an original reading was corrected to the group reading, or when a group reading was expunged and another added. This principle applies especially to C^{14}, a group manuscript which has been corrected from a nongroup manuscript above the line and, primarily, in the margins; L^7, which has group readings as corrections above the line; and L^{25}, a group manuscript which is often corrected, over erasures, from a nongroup manuscript. The designation *both* is reserved for manuscripts which have both readings as part of their base text, usually joined with *vel* or *sive*.

Following the list of readings is a chart showing the numbers of readings various manuscripts have in each book. In order to keep the chart to a manageable size, I have given figures only for those manuscripts that have more than five readings in any book. For convenience in placing L^{31}, which breaks off in Book II, chapter 36, I have based my figures for II on II.1–36 and for III on II.37 through the last chapter of III. Please note that the following manuscripts do not contain a complete text: $ArC^9C^{17}C^{19}D^4L^{31}O^6O^{19}O^{20}O^{21}O^{23}$; see above, pp. 255–57, and Appendix I for details.

1. I.2.1: **hominem** *Adam* $Au Bu C^1 C^2 C^{10} C^{18} D^6 E^1 Es^2 Ev Go I L^7 L^9 L^{17} L^{22} L^{24} L^{25} L^{29} L^{31} L^{36} L^{40} L^{43} L^{45} La Mu^5 N O^{10} O^{14} O^{19} O^{26} O^{31} Pa^4 Pa^5 Pa^6 Pa^9 Pa^{11} Re^3 Ru^2 Sa T^2$; both Av^2

2. I.2.8: **valebit** *audebit* $Au Bu C^1 C^2 C^{10} C^{18} C^{19} D^4 D^5 D^6 Es^2 Ev Go I L^{11} L^{17} L^{24} L^{25} L^{36} L^{43} L^{45} La Lm Mu^5 O^{10} O^{13} O^{19} O^{22} O^{31} Pa^4 Pa^6 Pa^9 Pa^{11} Pa^{15} Re^3 Ru^2 Sa T^2 Wo^2$

3. I.2.15: transposition of lines 16–20 and 20–22 $C^1 C^2 C^{10} C^{18} D^4 D^6 E^1 Es^2 Ev L^9 L^{17} L^{24} L^{25} L^{29} L^{31} L^{35} L^{36} L^{40} L^{43} L^{45} La N O^{10} O^{13} O^{14} O^{19} O^{26} O^{31} Pa^4 Pa^6 Pa^{10} Pa^{14} Re^3 Ru^2 Sa T^2 Wo^2$

4. I.3.2: **semine** *corpore* $C^1 C^2 C^{10} D^4 D^6 E^1 Es^2 Ev L^9 L^{17} L^{24} L^{25} L^{29} L^{35} L^{36} L^{40} L^{43} L^{45} La N O^{10} O^{13} O^{19} O^{26} O^{31} Pa^4 Pa^6 Pa^{10} Ru^2 Sa$; both $Re^3 T^2$

5. I.4.3: **femina** *corpore* $Au Bu C^1 C^2 C^{10} C^{18} C^{19} D^4 D^6 E^1 Es^2 Ev Go I L^9 L^{17} L^{22} L^{24} L^{26} L^{29} L^{36} L^{40} L^{43} L^{45} La Lm Mu^5 N O^{10} O^{13} O^{14} O^{26} O^{31} Pa^4 Pa^5 Pa^6 Pa^9 Pa^{11} Pa^{12} Pa^{15} Ru^2 Sa Wo^2$

6. I.4.8: addition of *et cibo* $Bs C^1 C^2 C^{10} C^{14} D^4 D^6 E^1 Er^2 Es^2 Ev L^4 L^7 L^{11} L^{22} L^{24} L^{25} L^{29} L^{35} L^{36} L^{40} L^{43} L^{45} La Ma^3 O^{10} O^{13} O^{14} O^{19} O^{24} O^{26} Pa^4 Pa^6 Pa^{10} Re^3 Ru^2 Sa T^2 Wo^2$

7. I.6.6: addition of *prima parens nostra dicebatur* Bs C^{1}C^{2}C^{10}C^{19}D^{6}E^{1}Er^{2}Es^{2}Ev L^{7}L^{9}L^{11}L^{17}L^{22}L^{24}L^{25}L^{29}L^{31}L^{34}L^{35}L^{36}L^{40}L^{43}L^{45}LaNO^{10}O^{13}O^{14}O^{19}O^{26}O^{31}Pa^{4}Pa^{5}Pa^6 Pa^{10}Re^{3}Ru^{1}Ru^{2}SaT^{2}Wo^2; *prima parens dicebatur* C^{18}; *post parens* Pa^{14}

8. I.7.6: **indutus** *non nudus* AuBsC^{1}C^{2}C^{10}C^{18}D^{4}D^{6}E^{1}Er^{2}Es^{2}EvL^{9}L^{17}L^{24}L^{25} L^{26}L^{29}L^{31}L^{35}L^{36}L^{40}L^{43}L^{45}La NO^{10}O^{13}O^{19}O^{26}O^{31}Pa^{4}Pa^{6}Pa^{10}Re^{3}Ru^{2}SaT^{2}Wo^2; *nudus* AuAv^{2}BuC^{15}Du^{2}GoIL^{13}LmMu^{5}NeO^{30}Pa^{5}Pa^{9}Pa^{11}SyU^3

9. I.7.10: **eius** *filii sui* AuBeBuC^{1}C^{2}C^{10}C^{18}D^{1}D^{6}Du^{3}E^{1}Es^{2}EvGoIL^{9}L^{11}L^{14} L^{15}L^{17}L^{21}L^{24}L^{25}L^{29}L^{31}L^{36}L^{40}L^{43}L^{45}LaMu^{5}NO^{6}O^{10}O^{13}O^{19}O^{23}O^{26}O^{31}Pa^{4}Pa^{5}Pa^{6}Pa^9 Pa^{11}Pa^{14}Pa^{15}Re^{3}Ru^{2}SaT^{2}U^{4}U^{6}U^7; *filii tui* Wo^2; *filium suum* L^{26}L^{35}LmPa^{10}; *filium eius* Bz^{2}ChL^{13}Pa^{12}Pa^{13}

10. I.12.25: addition of *filios et filias* BsC^{1}C^{2}C^{9}C^{10}C^{17}C^{18}D^{4}D^{6}E^{1}Er^{2}Es^{2}EvL^7 L^{9}L^{17}L^{21}L^{22}L^{24}L^{25}L^{29}L^{31}L^{35}L^{40}L^{45}LaNO^{10}O^{13}O^{19}O^{26}O^{31}Pa^{4}Pa^{6}Pa^{10}Re^{3}Ru^{2}SaT^2

11. I.12.34: addition of *opera* AuBz^{2}C^{1}C^{2}C^{9}C^{10}C^{17}D^{1}D^{4}D^{6}E^{1}Es^{2}EvH^{1}L^{9}L^{17} L^{24}L^{25}L^{29}L^{31}L^{35}L^{36}L^{40}L^{45}La NO^{6}O^{10}O^{13}O^{19}O^{23}O^{26}O^{31}Pa^{4}Pa^{6}Pa^{8}Pa^{10}Pa^{14}Re^{3}Ru^1 Ru^{2}SaT^2

12. I.14.7: addition of *proximum criminatur malignum Deum eo* BsC^{1}C^{2}C^{9}C^{10} C^{18}C^{19}D^{1}D^{4}D^{6}E^{1}Er^{2}Es^{2}EvL^{9}L^{17}L^{24}L^{25}L^{35}L^{36}L^{40}L^{45}LaNO^{10}O^{13}O^{19}O^{23}O^{26}O^{31}P Pa^{4}Pa^{6}Re^{3}Ru^{2}SaT^2; *proximum criminatur malignum Deum causatur* C^{14}; *proximum Deum eo* L^{31}; *eo* AuH^{1}L^{11}Pa^{8}Wo^2

13. I.15.7: addition of *namque* C^{1}C^{2}C^{9}C^{10}C^{14}C^{18}C^{19}D^{1}D^{6}E^{1}Es^{2}EvL^{7}L^{9}L^{17} L^{24}L^{25}L^{29}L^{31}L^{35}L^{36}L^{40}L^{45}LaMa^{3}NO^{10}O^{13}O^{19}O^{23}O^{26}O^{31}PPa^{4}Pa^{6}Pa^{8}Pa^{10}Re^{3}Ru^{2}Sa T^{2}Wo^2

14. I.15.13: **oportet** *contingat (-et, -it)* AuBuC^{1}C^{2}C^{9}C^{10}C^{14}C^{18}C^{19}D^{6}E^{1}Es^2 EvGoIL^{6}L^{9}L^{17}L^{24}L^{25}L^{29}L^{35}L^{40}L^{45}LaLmMoMu^{1}Mu^{5}NO^{10}O^{13}O^{19}O^{26}O^{31}Pa^{4}Pa^6 Pa^{9}Pa^{10}Pa^{11}Ru^{2}SaWo^2; both L^{47}O^{30}

15. I.15.19: addition of *semper* AuBsBuC^{1}C^{2}C^{9}C^{10}C^{14}C^{18}C^{19}C^{21}D^{1}D^{6}E^{1}Er^2 Es^{2}EvGoIL^{9}L^{17}L^{21}L^{24}L^{25}L^{29}L^{31}L^{35}L^{36}L^{40}L^{45}LaLmMu^{5}NO^{10}O^{13}O^{19}O^{23}O^{26}O^{31}P Pa^{4}Pa^{6}Pa^{9}Pa^{10}Pa^{11}Pa^{12}Pa^{15}Re^{3}Ru^{2}SaT^{2}Wo^2

16. I.16.15: addition of *vestram* Bm^{1}C^{1}C^{2}C^{9}C^{10}C^{21}D^{6}E^{1}Es^{2}EvGoIL^{9}L^{14}L^{15} L^{17}L^{25}L^{26}L^{29}L^{35}L^{40}L^{45}LaMu^{5}NO^{6}O^{10}O^{13}O^{19}O^{26}O^{31}Pa^{4}Pa^{5}Pa^{6}Pa^{9}Pa^{10}Pa^{14}Ru^{1}Ru^2 SaWo^2; *nostram* L^{24}

17. I.16.67-68: **ita est** *est talis* C^{1}C^{2}C^{9}C^{10}C^{18}D^{6}E^{1}Er^{2}Es^{2}EvL^{9}L^{17}L^{21}L^{24}L^{25}L^{29} L^{35}L^{36}L^{40}L^{45}La NO^{10}O^{13}O^{19}O^{26}O^{31}Pa^{4}Pa^{6}Pa^{10}Pa^{14}Re^{3}Ru^{1}Ru^{2}SaT^{2}Wo^2; *talis est* BsL^{31}O^{23}PPa^8

18. I.17.19: addition of *ideo* C^{1}C^{2}C^{9}C^{10}C^{14}C^{18}D^{1}D^{6}Es^{2}L^{9}L^{21}L^{24}L^{25}L^{29}L^{31}L^{34} L^{35}L^{36}L^{40}L^{45}LaNO^{10}O^{13}O^{19}O^{23}O^{26}O^{31}Pa^{4}Pa^{6}Pa^{10}Re^{3}Ru^{2}SaT^2

19. I.18.23: **Insidiatur** *Ingrediatur* AuBuC^{2}C^{9}C^{10}EvGoIL^{9}L^{17}L^{22}L^{24}L^{29}L^{35}L^{40} L^{45}LmMu^{1}Mu^{5}NO^{10}O^{13}O^{19}O^{26}O^{31}Pa^{4}Pa^{5}Pa^{6}Pa^{9}Pa^{10}Pa^{11}Ru^{1}Ru^{2}SaWo^2; *Egrediatur* C^{1}E^{1}Es^{2}La

20. I.19.1: **corpore mortis** *morte corporis* AuBuC^{1}C^{10}D^{1}D^{6}Es^{2}EvGoIL^{7}L^{8}L^9 L^{22}L^{24}L^{25}L^{29}L^{35}L^{36}L^{45}LaLmMu^{1}Mu^{4}NO^{13}O^{18}O^{23}O^{26}Pa^{4}Pa^{6}Pa^{9}Pa^{10}Pa^{11}Pa^{14}Pa^{15} Ru^{1}Ru^{2}SaWo^2; both Pa^5; *carcere corporis* Bl^{2}Mu^{5}Pa^{12}Pa^{13}Ph^2

21. I.20.1: **duxerit (duxit)** *deduxit* AuBuC^{1}C^{2}C^{9}C^{10}C^{14}C^{18}C^{21}D^{1}D^{3}D^{6}E^1 Es^{2}EvGoIL^{7}L^{9}L^{14}L^{15}L^{17}L^{24}L^{25}L^{29}L^{31}L^{35}L^{36}L^{40}L^{45}L^{47}LaLmMu^{1}Mu^{5}NO^{10}O^{13}O^{19} O^{24}O^{26}O^{30}O^{31}PPa^{4}Pa^{6}Pa^{9}Pa^{10}Pa^{11}Pa^{15}Re^{3}Ru^{1}Ru^{2}T^{2}Wo^2

22. I.20.6: **passio** *compassio* AuBsBuC^{1}C^{2}C^{9}C^{14}C^{18}C^{21}D^{1}D^{3}D^{6}E^{1}Er^{2}Es^{2}L^7 L^{8}L^{9}L^{17}L^{25}L^{29}L^{31}L^{35}L^{36}L^{40}L^{45}La Lm Ma^{3}Mu^{1}Mu^{5}NO^{10}O^{13}O^{19}O^{23}O^{26}O^{31}Pa^{4}Pa^5 Pa^{6}Pa^{9}Pa^{10}Pa^{11}Re^{3}Ru^{1}Ru^{2}T^{2}Wo^2; both L^{47}O^{21}O^{30}

23. I.23.24: **per illusiones** *pollutiones* Au Bs Bz^2 C^1 C^2 C^9 C^{10} C^{18} D^1 D^6 E^1 Er^2 Es^2 Ev IL^8 L^9 L^{17} L^{24} L^{25} L^{29} L^{31} L^{35} L^{40} L^{45} La Mu^1 Mu^5 O^{10} O^{13} O^{19} O^{23} O^{26} O^{31} Pa^4 Pa^6 Pa^8 Pa^{10} Pa^{14} Re^3 Ru^2 Sa T^2 Wo^2; both C^4; *pollucionibus* Bu Go Lm O^6 Pa^9 Pa^{11} Pa^{15}; *per polluciones* C^{14}

24. I.23.24: addition of *ex quibus* Au Bs C^1 C^2 C^9 C^{10} C^{18} D^1 D^6 E^1 Er^2 Es^2 Ev L^8 L^9 L^{17} L^{24} L^{25} L^{29} L^{31} L^{35} L^{40} L^{45} La O^{10} O^{13} O^{19} O^{23} O^{26} O^{31} P Pa^4 Pa^6 Pa^8 Pa^{10} Re^3 Ru^2 Sa T^2

25. I.23.24: **caro** *corpus* Au Bo C^1 C^2 C^9 C^{10} C^{18} D^1 D^6 E^1 Es^2 Ev IL^8 L^9 L^{24} L^{25} L^{29} L^{31} L^{35} L^{36} L^{40} L^{45} La Mu^5 NO^{10} O^{13} O^{19} O^{23} O^{26} P Pa^4 Pa^6 Pa^8 Pa^{10} Re^3 Ru^1 Ru^2 Sa T^2 Wo^2

26. I.25.3: **tolerare** *sustinere* Bl^5 C^1 C^2 C^9 C^{10} C^{14} C^{18} C^{23} Ca D^1 D^6 E^1 Es^2 Ev L^8 L^9 L^{17} L^{24} L^{25} L^{29} L^{31} L^{35} L^{36} L^{40} L^{45} La N Ne O^{10} O^{13} O^{19} O^{23} O^{26} O^{31} Pa^4 Pa^6 Pa^{10} Re^3 Ru^1 Ru^2 Sa T^2 U^1 U^5 Wo^2

27. I.27.8: **excoriantur** *excecantur* Bs C^1 C^2 C^9 C^{10} C^{18} D^1 D^6 E^1 Es^2 Ev L^9 L^{17} L^{24} L^{25} L^{29} L^{35} L^{45} La Mu^5 NO^{10} O^{13} O^{19} O^{23} O^{26} O^{31} Pa^4 Pa^5 Pa^6 Pa^{10} Pa^{14} Ru^1 Ru^2 Wo^2; both L^{31} L^{36}; *execrantur* Bu Go I Pa^9 Pa^{11}

28. I.28.11: **ex indignacione** *indignatio* Bs Bt^1 C^1 C^2 C^9 C^{10} C^{14} C^{18} C^{21} D^6 E^1 Er^2 Es^2 Ev L^9 L^{17} L^{22} L^{24} L^{25} L^{29} L^{31} L^{35} L^{36} L^{40} L^{45} La Ma^3 NO^{10} O^{13} O^{19} O^{24} O^{26} O^{31} Pa^4 Pa^6 Pa^8 Pa^{10} Pa^{14} Ru^2 Sa

29. II.2.7: **malorum** *viciorum* Bs C^1 C^2 C^9 C^{10} C^{14} C^{18} D^1 D^6 E^1 Er^2 Es^2 Ev Go IL^9 L^{15} L^{17} L^{24} L^{25} L^{29} L^{31} L^{35} L^{40} L^{45} L^{47} La Mu^5 NO^{10} O^{13} O^{21} O^{24} O^{26} O^{30} O^{31} Pa^4 Pa^6 Pa^{10} Pa^{15} Ru^2 Sa; both D^4 O^{32}

30. II.3.12: **eius** *vestri* Au C^1 C^2 C^9 C^{10} C^{14} C^{18} D^4 D^6 E^1 Es^2 Ev Go IL^7 L^8 L^{14} L^{17} L^{22} L^{24} L^{25} L^{31} L^{36} L^{40} L^{45} La Ma^3 Mu^5 O^{10} O^{13} O^{19} O^{31} Pa^4 Pa^6 Pa^{15} Ru^2 Wo^2; both L^9

31. II.3.12: **rapientes** *rapaces* Ar Au C^1 C^2 C^9 C^{10} C^{14} C^{18} D^4 D^6 E^1 Es^2 Ev Go IL^8 L^9 L^{17} L^{24} L^{31} L^{36} L^{40} L^{45} La Mu^5 O^{10} O^{13} O^{19} O^{31} Pa^4 Pa^6 Pa^{13} Pa^{15} Re^3 Ru^2 T^2 Wo^2; both Bo Bz^2 GlL^{44} O^{16} O^{26} O^{30}

32. II.4.4: **animas** *vitas* (in a transposition) C^1 C^2 C^9 C^{10} C^{18} D^4 D^6 E^1 Es^2 L^8 L^9 L^{17} L^{24} L^{25} L^{29} L^{31} L^{35} L^{45} La NO^{10} O^{13} O^{19} O^{31} Pa^4 Pa^6 Pa^{10} Sa Wo^2

33. II.4.31: **vir** *unus* Au Bu C^1 C^2 C^{10} D^4 D^5 D^6 E^1 Ev Go IL^8 L^9 L^{17} L^{24} L^{25} L^{29} L^{31} L^{35} L^{36} L^{45} La Lm Mu^1 NO^5 O^{10} O^{17} O^{19} O^{26} O^{31} Pa^4 Pa^6 Pa^9 Pa^{10} Pa^{11} Ru^2 Sa; both Pa^{15} Wo^2

34. II.4.41: **Nulla** *Non* Au C^1 C^2 C^9 C^{10} C^{14} C^{18} D^4 D^6 E^1 Es^2 Ev L^8 L^9 L^{17} L^{24} L^{25} L^{29} L^{31} L^{35} L^{36} L^{45} La NO^{10} O^{13} O^{19} O^{26} O^{31} Pa^4 Pa^6 Pa^{10} Ru^2 Sa Wo^2

35. II.4.42: addition of *tibi* Au C^1 C^2 C^9 C^{10} C^{14} C^{18} D^4 D^6 E^1 Es^2 Ev L^8 L^9 L^{17} L^{24} L^{25} L^{29} L^{31} L^{35} L^{36} L^{45} La O^{10} O^{13} O^{19} O^{26} O^{31} Pa^4 Pa^6 Pa^{10} Ru^2 Sa Wo^2

36. II.5.7: addition of *quod* Au C^1 C^2 C^4 C^5 C^{10} C^{21} D^4 D^6 E^1 Ev L^9 L^{14} L^{17} L^{22} L^{24} L^{25} L^{29} L^{35} L^{36} L^{38} L^{45} L^{47} La NO^{10} O^{13} O^{19} O^{26} O^{30} O^{31} O^{32} Pa^4 Pa^6 Pa^{10} Pa^{15} Re^3 Ru^2 Sa T^2 Wo^2

37. II.5.8–9: **pecuniam** *lucrum* Au C^1 C^2 C^9 C^{10} C^{18} D^4 E^1 Es^2 Ev L^8 L^9 L^{17} L^{24} L^{25} L^{29} L^{31} L^{35} L^{36} L^{45} La NO^{10} O^{13} O^{19} O^{26} O^{31} Pa^4 Pa^6 Pa^{10} Ru^2 Sa

38. II.5.17: **ululantes** *eiulantes* Bu C^1 C^2 C^9 C^{10} C^{18} D^1 D^4 D^6 E^1 Es^2 Ev Go IL^8 L^9 L^{17} L^{24} L^{25} L^{29} L^{31} L^{35} L^{45} La Lm Mu^1 Mu^5 NO^{10} O^{13} O^{19} O^{21} O^{26} O^{31} Pa^4 Pa^5 Pa^6 Pa^8 Pa^9 Pa^{10} Pa^{11} Pa^{15} Ru^2 Sa Wo^2

39. II.7.3: **adhuc** *semper* Ar Au C^1 C^2 C^9 C^{10} C^{18} D^1 D^3 D^4 D^6 E^1 Es^2 Ev L^9 L^{15} L^{17} L^{24} L^{25} L^{29} L^{31} L^{35} L^{36} L^{45} La Ma^3 O^{10} O^{13} O^{19} O^{26} O^{31} Pa^4 Pa^6 Pa^{10} Re^3 Ru^2 Sa T^2 Wo^2; both L^{47} O^{21} O^{30} O^{32}

40. II.8.6: **plurimum** *multum* Au Bu Bv^1 C^1 C^2 C^5 C^9 C^{10} C^{14} C^{18} D^3 D^4 D^6 E^1 Es^2 Ev Go IL^9 L^{14} L^{17} L^{24} L^{25} L^{29} L^{31} L^{34} L^{35} L^{36} L^{45} La Lm Ma^2 Ma^3 Mu^1 Mu^5 NO^{10} O^{13} O^{14} O^{19} O^{31} Pa^4 Pa^5 Pa^6 Pa^9 Pa^{10} Pa^{11} Pa^{15} Ru^2 Sa Wo^2

41. II.8.9: **itaque** *mundi* C^1 C^2 C^9 C^{10} C^{18} D^4 D^6 E^1 Es^2 Ev L^9 L^{14} L^{24} L^{25} L^{29} L^{31} L^{35} L^{36} L^{45} La NO^{10} O^{13} O^{19} O^{26} Pa^4 Pa^6 Pa^{10} Ru^2 Sa Wo^2; both L^{15}

42. II.10.14: addition of *immo potius usque ad sui terminum loci* $Bt^1C^2ChDu^2E^1$ $EvL^9L^{21}L^{25}L^{29}L^{35}L^{36}L^{40}L^{45}L^{47}LaO^{10}O^{13}O^{30}O^{32}Pa^4Pa^6Pa^{12}Pa^{13}Ru^2Wo^2$; addition, but with *sine* for *sui* $C^1C^{10}D^6Es^2L^{24}$

43. II.10.16: addition of *thesaurorum et* $ArBsC^1C^2C^9C^{10}C^{14}D^3D^6E^1Er^2Es^2Ev$ $IL^7L^9L^{14}L^{15}L^{17}L^{24}L^{25}L^{29}L^{31}L^{35}L^{40}L^{45}L^{47}LaMu^5NO^{10}O^{13}O^{19}O^{24}O^{30}O^{31}O^{32}Pa^4Pa^6$ $Pa^{10}Pa^{14}Re^3Ru^2SaT^2Wo^2$

44. II.11.5: **rectus** *iustus* $ArBt^2C^1C^2C^9C^{10}C^{11}D^6E^1Es^2EvL^9L^{24}L^{29}L^{31}L^{35}L^{36}$ $L^{40}L^{45}LaNO^{10}O^{13}Pa^4Pa^6Pa^{10}Re^3Ru^2SaT^2$; both Bn

45. II.11.11: **psalmiste** *prophete* $AuBuBv^2Bz^2C^1C^2C^9C^{10}C^{14}C^{18}C^{20}D^6E^1Es^2$ $GoIL^6L^9L^{14}L^{24}L^{25}L^{29}L^{31}L^{32}L^{35}L^{36}L^{40}L^{43}L^{44}L^{45}LaMu^5NO^{10}O^{13}O^{14}O^{19}O^{27}Pa^4Pa^5$ $Pa^6Pa^9Pa^{10}Pa^{11}Ru^2Sa$; both Bm^2

46. II.12.8-9: **repetetur (repetent)** *recederet* $ArAuC^1C^2C^{10}D^4D^6E^1Es^2EvL^9$ $L^{17}L^{24}L^{29}L^{35}L^{40}L^{45}LmMa^3NO^{10}O^{13}O^{21}O^{26}O^{31}Pa^4Pa^6Pa^{10}Ru^2Sa$; *recederent* L^6; *recedet* $Du^2L^{25}L^{37}Re^3T^2$; *recedent* C^9Wo^2; *recesserit* O^{19}

47. II.12.17: **Set** *Ecce* $ArC^1C^2C^9C^{10}C^{14}C^{18}D^4D^6E^1Es^2EvL^6L^9L^{17}L^{24}L^{25}L^{29}$ $L^{31}L^{35}L^{36}L^{37}L^{40}L^{45}LaMa^3NO^{10}O^{13}O^{19}O^{31}Pa^4Pa^6Pa^{10}Re^3Ru^2T^2Wo^2$

48. II.13.2: addition of *nam* $ArAuBuC^1C^2C^9C^{10}C^{14}D^4D^6E^1Es^2EvGoIL^6L^9$ $L^{14}L^{15}L^{17}L^{22}L^{24}L^{25}L^{29}L^{35}L^{36}L^{40}L^{45}L^{47}LaLmMa^3Mu^5NO^{10}O^{13}O^{19}O^{26}O^{30}O^{31}Pa^4$ $Pa^5Pa^6Pa^9Pa^{10}Pa^{11}Re^3Ru^2SaT^2Wo^2$; *namque* L^{31}

49. II.14.1: **undis** *media unda* $AuC^1C^2C^9C^{10}C^{14}C^{18}D^4D^6E^1Es^2EvIL^6L^9L^{17}L^{24}$ $L^{25}L^{29}L^{31}L^{35}L^{36}L^{40}L^{45}LaMu^5NO^{10}O^{13}O^{19}O^{24}O^{31}Pa^4Pa^6Pa^{10}Ru^2SaWo^2$; *mediis* Pa^{14}

50. II.15.4-5: **libenter** *studiose* $C^1C^2C^9C^{10}C^{14}C^{18}D^4D^6E^1Es^2EvGoL^6L^9L^{17}$ $L^{22}L^{24}L^{25}L^{29}L^{31}L^{35}L^{36}L^{40}L^{45}LaMa^3NO^{10}O^{13}O^{19}O^{24}O^{31}Pa^4Pa^6Pa^{10}Pa^{14}Ru^2Sa$ Wo^2; both $L^{15}L^{47}$

51. II.16.15: addition of *huius* $BsC^1C^2C^9C^{10}C^{14}D^4D^6E^1Er^2Es^2EvGoL^3L^6L^9$ $L^{14}L^{17}L^{24}L^{25}L^{31}L^{36}L^{40}L^{41}L^{45}LaMa^3O^{10}O^{13}O^{19}O^{24}O^{31}Pa^4Pa^6Ru^2Sa$

52. II.17.16: **totidem** *quatuor* $C^1C^2C^9C^{10}C^{14}C^{19}D^4D^6E^1Es^2EvL^6L^9L^{10}L^{17}L^{22}$ $L^{24}L^{25}L^{29}L^{31}L^{35}L^{36}L^{37}L^{40}L^{45}LaMa^3NO^{10}O^{13}O^{19}O^{24}O^{26}O^{31}Pa^4Pa^6Pa^{10}Ru^2SaWo^2$

53. II.18.2: addition of *magis* $ArBuC^1C^2C^9C^{10}C^{17}D^1D^4D^6E^1Es^2EvGoIL^6L^9$ $L^{14}L^{17}L^{22}L^{24}L^{25}L^{29}L^{31}L^{35}L^{36}L^{40}L^{45}L^{47}LaLmMa^3Mu^5NO^{10}O^{13}O^{21}O^{24}O^{30}O^{31}Pa^4$ $Pa^5Pa^6Pa^8Pa^9Pa^{10}Pa^{11}Pa^{14}Pa^{15}Re^3Ru^2SaT^2$

54. II.18.11: addition of *ministris regis* $ArAuC^1C^2C^9C^{10}C^{14}C^{17}C^{18}D^1D^6E^1$ $Es^2EvL^6L^9L^{14}L^{17}L^{21}L^{22}L^{24}L^{25}L^{29}L^{31}L^{35}L^{36}L^{40}L^{45}L^{47}Ma^3NO^{10}O^{13}O^{19}O^{24}O^{26}O^{30}$ $O^{31}Pa^4Pa^5Pa^6Pa^8Pa^{10}Re^3Ru^2SaT^2Wo^2$; *ministris* $BuGoIMu^1Pa^9Pa^{11}$; *ministris suis* Lm

55. II.18.15: **viis** *viciis* $BsC^1C^9C^{10}C^{17}C^{21}D^6E^1Er^2Es^2EvL^9L^{17}L^{21}L^{22}L^{24}L^{25}L^{29}$ $L^{35}L^{36}L^{40}L^{45}LaMa^3NO^{10}O^{13}O^{19}O^{26}O^{31}Pa^4Pa^6Pa^{10}Ru^2Sa$

56. II.19.15: **Rechab** *Iacob* $ArC^1C^2C^9C^{10}C^{21}D^6E^1Es^2L^9L^{14}L^{17}L^{22}L^{24}L^{25}L^{29}$ $L^{31}L^{35}L^{36}L^{40}L^{45}LaMa^3NO^{10}O^{13}O^{19}O^{26}O^{31}Pa^4Pa^{10}Pa^{14}Re^3SaT^2$

57. II.20.5: **sectandam** *miscendam* $ArAuBsBuC^1C^2C^9C^{10}C^{17}C^{18}D^1D^4D^6E^1$ $Er^2Es^2EvGoIL^6L^9L^{17}L^{24}L^{29}L^{31}L^{35}L^{40}L^{45}LaMa^3NO^{10}O^{13}O^{19}O^{21}O^{31}Pa^4Pa^6Pa^8Pa^{10}$ $Pa^{14}Pa^{15}Re^3Ru^2SaT^2Wo^2$; both L^{21}

58. II.20.9: **miscendam** *sectandam* $ArAuBsC^1C^2C^9C^{10}C^{17}D^1D^4E^1Er^2Es^2Ev$ $GoIL^6L^9L^{17}L^{24}L^{29}L^{31}L^{35}L^{40}L^{45}LaMa^3NO^{10}O^{13}O^{19}O^{26}O^{31}Pa^4Pa^6Pa^8Pa^{10}Pa^{14}Re^3$ $Ru^2SaT^2Wo^2$

59. II.23.7-8: **presbiteros** *populos* $AuC^1C^2C^9C^{10}D^6E^1Es^2EvIL^6L^9L^{14}L^{17}L^{22}$ $L^{24}L^{36}L^{40}L^{45}LaMa^3O^{10}O^{19}O^{24}O^{31}Pa^4Pa^6Ru^2SaWo^2$; *populum* Mu^5

60. II.24.10: **concubitus** *coitus* $C^1C^2C^9C^{10}C^{14}C^{18}D^1D^3D^6Du^4E^1Es^2EvL^4L^9$ $L^{17}L^{24}L^{25}L^{29}L^{35}L^{36}L^{40}L^{45}LaMa^3MoNO^{10}O^{13}O^{19}O^{21}O^{24}O^{31}Pa^4Pa^6Pa^8Pa^{10}Ph^1Ru^2$ SaT^1

61. II.25.7: addition of *dicit Dominus* $ArAuBuC^1C^2C^9C^{10}C^{14}C^{18}D^1D^3D^6E^1$ $Es^2EvGoIL^6L^9L^{14}L^{17}L^{23}L^{24}L^{25}L^{29}L^{35}L^{36}L^{40}L^{45}LaLmMa^3Mu^1Mu^5O^{10}O^{19}O^{21}O^{26}$ $O^{31}Pa^4Pa^5Pa^6Pa^8Pa^9Pa^{10}Pa^{11}Pa^{14}Pa^{15}Re^3Ru^2SaT^2Wo^2$; *dicit Deus* $L^{31}N$; *inquit Dominus* L^7

62. II.26.17: **singulis** *cunctis* $AuBuC^1C^2C^9C^{10}C^{14}C^{18}D^1D^3D^6E^1Es^2EvGoIL^6L^9$ $L^{14}L^{17}L^{24}L^{25}L^{29}L^{31}L^{35}L^{36}L^{40}L^{45}LaLmMa^3Mu^1Mu^5NO^{10}O^{13}O^{19}O^{21}O^{31}PPa^4Pa^5$ $Pa^6Pa^8Pa^9Pa^{10}Pa^{11}Ru^2SaWo^2$; both $O^{16}Pa^{15}$

63. II.27.7: **arripit** *ambit* $C^1C^2C^9C^{10}C^{14}C^{18}D^3D^6E^1Es^2EvL^7L^9L^{15}L^{17}L^{22}L^{24}$ $L^{25}L^{29}L^{31}L^{35}L^{36}L^{45}L^{47}LaMa^3NO^{10}O^{13}O^{19}O^{24}O^{26}O^{30}O^{31}Pa^4Pa^6Pa^{10}Ru^2$

64. II.27.8: **subsidio (presidio)** *subsidio* $ArAuC^1C^2C^9C^{10}C^{14}C^{18}D^1D^3D^6E^1$ $Es^2EvL^6L^9L^{14}L^{17}L^{20}L^{23}L^{24}L^{25}L^{26}L^{29}L^{31}L^{35}L^{36}L^{40}L^{45}LaMa^3NO^5O^{10}O^{13}O^{19}O^{24}O^{31}$ $PPa^4Pa^6Pa^8Pa^{10}Re^3Ru^2SaT^2U^4Wo^2$

65. II.28.16: addition of *Absolon* $C^1C^2C^9C^{10}C^{14}C^{18}D^1D^6E^1Es^2L^6L^9L^{14}L^{17}L^{22}$ $L^{24}L^{25}L^{29}L^{31}L^{35}L^{36}L^{40}L^{45}LaMa^3NO^{10}O^{13}O^{19}O^{21}O^{24}O^{26}O^{31}PPa^4Pa^6Pa^8Pa^{10}Sa$ Wo^2

66. II.31.3–4: **committitur** *accedit* $C^1C^2C^9C^{10}C^{14}C^{18}D^6E^1Es^2EvL^6L^9L^{14}L^{17}$ $L^{25}L^{28}L^{29}L^{31}L^{35}L^{36}L^{40}L^{45}LaMa^3NO^{10}O^{13}O^{19}O^{31}Pa^4Pa^6Pa^{10}Ru^2SaWo^2$; *accendente* for *committitur te* L^{24}

67. II.31.4: **dimittitur** *recedit* $ArC^1C^2C^9C^{10}C^{14}C^{18}E^1Es^2EvL^6L^9L^{14}L^{17}L^{22}L^{24}$ $L^{25}L^{28}L^{29}L^{31}L^{35}L^{36}L^{40}L^{45}LaMa^3NO^{10}O^{13}O^{19}O^{31}Pa^4Pa^6Pa^{10}Re^3Ru^2SaT^2Wo^2$

68. II.31.12: **corde** *ore* $C^1C^{10}D^6E^1Es^2L^9L^{14}L^{17}L^{24}L^{25}L^{31}L^{36}L^{40}L^{45}LaMa^3O^{10}$ $O^{13}O^{19}O^{20}O^{24}O^{31}Pa^4Sa$

69. II.32.12: **Babilon** *civitas* $ArC^1C^2C^9C^{10}C^{14}C^{18}D^6E^1Es^2L^9L^{14}L^{17}L^{24}L^{25}L^{29}$ $L^{31}L^{40}L^{45}LaMa^3NO^{10}O^{13}O^{19}O^{20}O^{24}O^{31}Pa^4Pa^6Re^3SaT^2$; both $AuBz^2CaD^1L^{35}L^{36}$ $O^{21}PPa^8Pa^{10}Pa^{14}Ru^1$

70. II.33.22: **celum** *nubes* $C^1C^2C^9C^{10}C^{14}C^{18}D^6E^1Es^2L^9L^{14}L^{17}L^{24}L^{25}L^{29}L^{31}L^{35}$ $L^{36}L^{40}L^{45}NO^{10}O^{13}O^{19}O^{20}O^{24}O^{31}Pa^4Pa^6Pa^{10}Pa^{14}Ru^1Sa$

71. II.39.3: **admissus** *exauditus* $BuC^1C^2C^9C^{10}C^{14}C^{18}D^6E^1Es^2EvL^6L^7L^9L^{17}$ $L^{24}L^{25}L^{29}L^{35}L^{36}L^{40}L^{45}LaMa^3NO^6O^{10}O^{13}O^{19}O^{20}Pa^4Pa^6Pa^{10}Pa^{14}Ru^1Ru^2SaWo^2$; both $ArRe^3T^2$; *auditus* $O^{24}O^{31}$

72. II.39.11: **honoris** *hominis* $AuC^1C^2C^9C^{10}D^6E^1Es^2L^7L^{17}L^{24}L^{35}L^{40}Ma^3Mu^5$ $NO^{10}O^{13}O^{19}O^{20}O^{31}Pa^4Pa^6Pa^{10}Pa^{14}Ru^1Sa$

73. II.39.12: **venustati** *vestimento* $Bm^1Bv^1C^1C^2C^9C^{10}C^{14}C^{18}C^{21}D^6E^1Es^2$ $EvL^6L^7L^9L^{17}L^{22}L^{24}L^{29}L^{35}L^{40}L^{45}LaMa^3O^{10}O^{13}O^{19}O^{24}O^{26}O^{31}Pa^4Pa^6Pa^{10}Ru^2Sa$ Wo^2; *vestimenti* $IL^{25}Mu^5$; *vestimentis* C^{16}

74. II.40.17: **preteream** *pertranseam* $C^1C^2C^9C^{10}C^{14}D^1D^6E^1Es^2L^6L^9L^{17}L^{24}L^{25}$ $L^{29}L^{36}L^{40}L^{45}LaMa^3NO^{10}O^{13}O^{19}O^{21}O^{24}O^{31}Pa^4Pa^6Pa^8Pa^{14}Ru^1Ru^2SaWo^2$; both C^6; *transeam* $AuC^{18}EvL^{35}O^{20}Pa^{10}$; *preteream vel transeam* O^{30}; *preteritum vel transeam* C^{13}

75. II.40.17: addition of *pocius* $Bm^1Bv^1C^1C^2C^6C^9C^{10}C^{13}C^{14}C^{18}D^6E^1Es^2Ev$ $L^6L^7L^9L^{17}L^{21}L^{22}L^{24}L^{25}L^{29}L^{35}L^{36}L^{40}L^{45}LaMa^3NO^{10}O^{13}O^{19}O^{20}O^{24}O^{26}O^{30}O^{31}O^{32}$ $Pa^4Pa^6Pa^{10}Pa^{14}Ru^1Ru^2SaWo^2$

76. II.41.17: **malicia (iniquitas)** *nequicia* $AuC^1C^2C^9C^{10}C^{14}C^{18}D^1D^5D^6E^1$ $Es^2EvGoIL^5L^6L^9L^{17}L^{22}L^{24}L^{25}L^{29}L^{35}L^{40}L^{45}LaO^6O^{10}O^{13}O^{16}O^{18}O^{19}O^{20}O^{21}O^{24}O^{31}$ $Pa^4Pa^6Pa^{10}Ru^1Ru^2SaWo^2$

77. III.1.13: **resolvatur (dissolvatur)** *revertatur* $AuBuC^1C^2C^9C^{10}C^{14}C^{17}C^{18}$ $D^6E^1Es^2EvGoIL^2L^5L^6L^9L^{17}L^{22}L^{25}L^{29}L^{30}L^{35}L^{36}L^{40}L^{43}L^{45}LaLmMa^3Mu^5NO^6O^7$ $O^{10}O^{13}O^{19}O^{24}O^{31}Pa^4Pa^6Pa^9Pa^{10}Pa^{11}Ru^1Ru^2SaWo^2$

78. III.1.13-14: **et deficient** *inde* $C^2C^9C^{10}C^{17}E^1EvL^5L^9L^{17}L^{29}L^{35}L^{40}L^{45}La$ $Ma^3NO^{10}O^{13}O^{19}O^{31}Pa^4Pa^6Pa^{10}Ru^2Sa$

79. III.2.1: **impii** *vipera* $C^1C^2C^9C^{10}C^{21}D^1D^6E^1Es^2EvL^6L^9L^{40}L^{45}LaMa^3O^6$ $O^{10}O^{13}Pa^4Pa^6Ru^1Ru^2Sa$

80. III.2.4: addition of *racionis* $AuC^2C^9C^{10}D^6E^1Er^2GoIL^7L^9L^{12}L^{17}L^{22}L^{24}L^{25}$ $L^{40}L^{45}LaMa^3Mu^5O^{10}O^{13}O^{24}O^{31}Pa^4Pa^{14}Ru^1SaU^4$

81. III.2.7: **lacerabit** *laborabit* $AuBv^2C^1C^2C^9C^{10}C^{16}C^{23}D^6E^1Es^2EvGoIL^4L^6$ $L^7L^9L^{17}L^{21}L^{24}L^{28}L^{40}L^{45}LaMa^3Mu^5O^{10}O^{12}O^{13}O^{17}O^{18}O^{20}O^{31}Pa^4Pa^6Pa^{10}Pa^{14}Pa^{15}$ $Ru^2SaU^4;$ both O^6

82. III.2.7: addition of *eorum* $AuBsBuC^1C^2C^6C^9C^{10}C^{13}D^6E^1Er^2Es^2EvGo$ $IL^6L^9L^{17}L^{22}L^{24}L^{28}L^{40}L^{45}L^{47}LaLmMa^3Mu^1Mu^5O^{10}O^{13}O^{20}O^{30}O^{31}Pa^4Pa^6Pa^{11}Pa^{14}$ $Ru^1Ru^2SaWo^2$

83. III.2.7-8: **penitencia** *prudenciam* $AuBsC^1C^2C^9C^{10}D^6E^1Er^2Es^2EvGoIL^9$ $L^{17}L^{21}L^{22}L^{24}L^{36}L^{40}L^{45}LaMa^3Mu^5O^5O^6O^{10}O^{13}O^{17}O^{18}O^{24}O^{31}Pa^4Pa^6Pa^{14}Ru^1Ru^2Sa$ U^4

84. III.2.14: **preterierit** *pertransierit* $AuC^1C^2C^9C^{10}C^{14}C^{18}D^3D^6E^1Es^2EvL^5L^6$ $L^9L^{17}L^{22}L^{24}L^{25}L^{28}L^{29}L^{35}L^{36}L^{37}L^{40}L^{45}LaMu^5NO^{10}O^{13}O^{20}O^{24}O^{27}O^{31}Pa^4Pa^5Pa^6Pa^{10}$ $Pa^{15}Ru^1Ru^2SaWo^2;$ *pertransiit* $BuC^4C^5GoILmMu^1Pa^9Pa^{11};$ *transierit* $L^{44}Ma^3O^6$

85. III.4.9: **Beati** *Sancti* $AuC^1C^2C^9C^{10}C^{14}C^{18}D^6E^1Es^2EvL^5L^6L^9L^{17}L^{24}L^{25}L^{29}$ $L^{35}L^{36}L^{40}L^{45}LaMa^3NO^6O^{10}O^{13}O^{20}O^{24}O^{31}Pa^4Pa^6Pa^{10}Ru^2SaWo^2;$ *Sanctorum* L^{26}

86. III.5.16: **mittite** *proicite* $AuC^1C^2C^7C^9C^{10}D^3D^6Du^3Es^2EvL^5L^6L^{15}L^{17}L^{24}$ $L^{25}L^{29}L^{35}L^{36}L^{40}L^{45}LaNO^{10}O^{13}O^{20}O^{24}O^{31}Pa^4Pa^6Pa^{10}Pa^{14}Ru^1Ru^2Wo^2$

87. III.5.21: **cruciabatur** *torquebatur* $C^1C^2C^9C^{10}C^{14}D^3D^6E^1Es^2EvL^5L^6L^9L^{17}$ $L^{24}L^{25}L^{29}L^{35}L^{36}L^{40}L^{45}LaMa^3NO^{10}O^{13}O^{20}O^{24}O^{31}Pa^4Pa^6Ru^1Ru^2Sa$

88. III.9.9: addition of *non ad salutem* $AuBsC^1C^2C^9C^{10}C^{14}D^1D^3D^6E^1Er^2Es^2$ $EvL^5L^6L^7L^9L^{17}L^{21}L^{22}L^{24}L^{25}L^{29}L^{35}L^{40}L^{45}LaMa^3NO^{24}O^{31}Pa^4Pa^6Pa^8Pa^{10}Ru^1Ru^2Sa;$ *non ad seculum* $O^{10};$ *non ad celum* O^{13}

89. III.9.23: addition of *Pater* $ArAuBv^2C^1C^2C^9C^{10}C^{14}D^6E^1Es^2EvIL^5L^7L^9$ $L^{17}L^{22}L^{24}L^{25}L^{29}L^{35}L^{36}L^{40}L^{45}LaMa^3NO^{10}O^{12}O^{13}O^{24}O^{26}O^{31}Pa^4Pa^6Pa^{10}Pa^{14}Re^3Ru^2$ $SaT^2;$ *Deus Pater* $D^1;$ *Deus* $Bz^2C^{18}L^{28}$

90. III.9.34: addition of *dampnatos* $AuC^1C^2C^9C^{10}E^1Es^2EvL^5L^6L^7L^9L^{22}L^{24}L^{25}$ $L^{29}L^{35}L^{40}L^{45}LaMa^3NO^{10}O^{13}O^{24}O^{25}O^{26}Pa^4Pa^5Pa^6Pa^{10}Ru^1Ru^2Wo^2;$ *dampnandos* $Bv^1Bz^2C^{14}C^{18}D^6Du^2L^{17}L^{32}O^{31}Pa^{14}$

91. III.9.40: **vehementer** *nimis* $AuC^1C^2C^9C^{10}C^{14}C^{18}D^6E^1Es^2EvL^5L^6L^9L^{17}$ $L^{22}L^{24}L^{25}L^{29}L^{35}L^{36}L^{40}L^{45}LaMa^3NO^{13}O^{24}O^{31}Pa^4Pa^6Pa^{10}Ru^2SaWo^2;$ both $L^{47}O^{30}$

92. III.10.2: **fumus** *ignis* $ArAuBsC^1C^2C^6C^9C^{10}C^{13}D^6E^1Er^2Es^2EvL^5L^9L^{17}$ $L^{24}L^{25}L^{29}L^{36}L^{40}L^{45}L^{47}LaMa^3NO^{13}O^{26}O^{30}O^{31}O^{32}Pa^4Pa^6Re^3Ru^2SaT^2;$ both Pa^{14}

93. III.10.22: **in ore** *testimonio* $AuC^1C^2C^9C^{10}C^{18}D^6E^1Es^2L^5L^7L^9L^{17}L^{24}L^{25}L^{29}$ $L^{35}L^{36}L^{40}L^{45}Ma^3O^{13}O^{20}O^{31}Pa^4Pa^6Pa^{10}SaWo^2;$ *testimonium* $BsLa;$ *testimonium in ore* $Du^2Gl;$ *in ore*, with *testimonio* later, after *virorum* $C^{14};$ *in ore testimoniorum* $O^{24};$ *testificacio* $EvRu^2;$ *testacio* Ru^1

94. III.11.12: **peccatores** *eos* $AuC^1C^2C^6C^9C^{10}C^{13}C^{14}C^{18}D^3D^6E^1Es^2EvL^5L^7$ $L^9L^{15}L^{17}L^{22}L^{24}L^{25}L^{29}L^{35}L^{36}L^{40}L^{45}L^{47}LaMa^3NO^{10}O^{13}O^{24}O^{26}O^{30}O^{31}O^{32}Pa^4Pa^5Pa^6$ $Pa^{10}Pa^{14}Ru^1Ru^2SaWo^2$

95. III.11.18: **faciet** *veniet* $AuC^1C^2C^9C^{10}D^6E^1Es^2EvGoIL^5L^6L^7L^9L^{17}L^{22}L^{24}$

$L^{29}L^{35}L^{36}L^{40}L^{45}$LaMu^{5}NO^{13}O^{24}O^{31}Pa^{4}Pa^{5}Pa^{10}Ru^{1}Ru^2; *venit* Pa^{6}Wo^2; *vanet* Ma^3

96. III.12.12: **signa (signa magna)** *signa multa* Be Bs BuC^{1}C^{2}C^{9}C^{10}C^{14}C^{18} D^{1}D^{6}E^{1}Es^{2}EvGoIL^{5}L^{6}L^{9}L^{17}L^{22}L^{24}L^{25}L^{29}L^{35}L^{40}L^{45}LaLmNO^{13}O^{20}O^{24}O^{31}Pa^{4}Pa^6 Pa^{10}Pa^{15}Ru^{2}SaWo^2

97. III.13.5: **tribus** *fines* AuC^{1}C^{2}C^{4}C^{5}C^{9}C^{10}C^{12}C^{14}D^{3}D^{6}E^{1}Es^{2}EvGoIL^{5}L^9 L^{22}L^{24}L^{25}L^{29}L^{35}L^{36}L^{40}L^{45}LaMa^{3}Mu^{5}NO^{13}O^{24}Pa^{4}Pa^{6}Pa^{10}Pa^{14}Ru^{1}Ru^{2}SaWo^3

98. III.13.40: addition of *reges omnes* AuBsBuC^{1}C^{2}C^{9}C^{10}C^{14}C^{15}C^{18}D^{6}E^{1}Er^2 Es^{2}GoIL^{5}L^{7}L^{9}L^{17}L^{22}L^{24}L^{29}L^{35}L^{36}L^{40}L^{45}LaLmMa^{3}Mu^{5}NO^{13}O^{24}O^{26}O^{31}Pa^{4}Pa^{5}Pa^6 Pa^{9}Pa^{10}Pa^{11}Pa^{14}Pa^{15}Ru^{1}Sa

99. III.13.40: addition of *servient ei* AuBs BuC^{1}C^{2}C^{9}C^{10}C^{14}C^{18}D^{6}E^{1}Er^{2}Es^2 GoIL^{5}L^{7}L^{9}L^{17}L^{22}L^{24}L^{25}L^{29}L^{35}L^{36}L^{40}L^{45}LaLmMa^{3}Mu^{1}Mu^{5}NO^{13}O^{24}O^{26}O^{31}Pa^{4}Pa^5 Pa^{6}Pa^{9}Pa^{10}Pa^{11}Pa^{14}Ru^{1}Sa

100. III.14.18: **comprobabit** *condempnabit* (in a transposition) AuC^{1}C^{2}C^{6}C^9 C^{10}C^{13}D^{6}E^{1}Es^{2}EvL^{5}L^{6}L^{8}L^{17}L^{22}L^{24}L^{25}L^{29}L^{30}L^{32}L^{35}L^{36}L^{40}L^{45}L^{47}LaNO^{13}O^{24}O^{26}O^{30} O^{31}Pa^{4}Pa^{6}Pa^{10}Ru^{1}Ru^{2}SaWo^2

101. III.14.22: **ignem urentem** *flammam ignis* AuBnBt^{2}C^{1}C^{2}C^{9}C^{10}C^{14}C^{22} D^{1}D^{6}E^{1}Es^{2}EvL^{2}L^{4}L^{5}L^{6}L^{9}L^{17}L^{24}L^{25}L^{29}L^{35}L^{36}L^{39}L^{45}L^{46}LaNO^{7}O^{13}O^{22}O^{24}O^{26}O^{29} O^{31}Pa^{4}Pa^{6}Pa^{8}Pa^{10}Pa^{14}Ru^{2}Sa; both Ru^1

	I (28 readings)	II (42 readings)	III (31 readings)		I (28 readings)	II (42 readings)	III (31 readings)
Ar	—	16	3	L^5	0	0	21
Au	15	22	24	L^6	1	19	20
Bs	12	6	8	L^7	8	4	14
Bu	13	10	7	L^8	6	8	1
C^1	28	41	29	L^9	27	41	28
C^2	27	40	31	L^{14}	3	21	0
C^9	17	38	29	L^{15}	3	7	2
C^{10}	27	42	31	L^{17}	24	38	29
C^{13}	0	0	6	L^{22}	8	13	19
C^{14}	11	25	20	L^{24}	27	41	29
C^{18}	22	26	16	L^{25}	26	38	22
C^{19}	7	1	0	L^{29}	26	37	25
D^1	14	13	7	L^{31}	20	36	—
D^3	2	8	6	L^{35}	25	37	25
D^4	9	24	0	L^{36}	22	35	20
D^6	27	39	29	L^{40}	26	32	30
E^1	25	42	30	L^{43}	9	0	1
Er^2	11	6	7	L^{45}	28	42	30
Es^2	27	40	29	L^{47}	3	10	5
Ev	26	34	27	La	28	39	30
Go	13	16	12	Lm	11	9	6
I	14	18	12	Ma^3	4	26	26

	I (28 readings)	II (42 readings)	III (31 readings)		I (28 readings)	II (42 readings)	III (31 readings)
Mu¹	6	6	3	Pa⁴	28	42	31
Mu⁵	15	14	11	Pa⁵	10	8	6
N	24	34	23	Pa⁶	28	40	30
O⁶	4	—	8	Pa⁸	7	11	3
O¹⁰	27	42	21	Pa⁹	14	9	4
O¹³	27	39	31	Pa¹⁰	24	36	25
O¹⁹	27	38	8	Pa¹¹	12	9	5
O²⁰	—	4	13	Pa¹⁴	10	10	17
O²¹	1	11	2	Pa¹⁵	7	11	4
O²³	14	—	—	Re³	21	17	3
O²⁴	3	16	25	Ru¹	10	2	23
O²⁶	27	20	10	Ru²	28	36	27
O³⁰	4	10	7	Sa	25	37	28
O³¹	25	37	29	T²	21	17	3
P	7	4	0	Wo²	20	29	18

NOTES TO APPENDIX II

1. Maccarrone, p. xxiii. Manly and Rickert found the same situation with the popular Canterbury Tales (see vol. 2 of The Text of the Canterbury Tales, passim), as did George Kane with Piers Plowman (see his introduction, passim, to Piers Plowman: The A Version [London: Athlone Press, 1960]). The Roman de la Rose and the Divina Commedia are in the same category (see Brusendorff, The Chaucer Tradition, pp. 62–63). Paul Maas has a general statement on the subject in his Textual Criticism, trans. Barbara Flower (Oxford: Clarendon Press, 1958), p. 48.

2. See, for example, Kane's introduction, pt. 4: "Editorial Resources and Methods"; Eugene Vinaver, "Principles of Textual Emendation," in Studies in French Language and Mediaeval Literature Presented to Professor Mildred K. Pope (Manchester: Manchester University Press, 1939), pp. 351–69; Ludwig Bieler, "The Grammarian's Craft: An Introduction to Textual Criticism," Classical Folia: Studies in the Christian Perpetuation of the Classics, 10 (1956), 28–32.

3. My policy has been to designate as group manuscripts only those that have more than 50 percent of the group readings in each of the three books of the De Miseria, as this both gives a clearer picture of the group than, for instance, 50 percent of the total readings and makes the placing of L³¹, which omits from towards the end of Book II, chap. 36 to the end, more convenient. See, further, the figures at the end of the list of evidence and the discussion of contaminated manuscripts below, p. 256. It is important not to be too dogmatic about the manuscripts that comprise the group. It is clear from the figures as well as from my own examination of the other readings that the

great majority of the manuscripts in the group are very closely related to each other, probably all derived *ultimately* from a single exemplar. A few of the manuscripts, however, are not so closely related—Au, C^{14}, C^{18}, L^{31}, L^{36}, Wo^2, for example—and may either stand in some less direct relationship with the others or be contaminated. See below, pp. 261-65, for a fuller discussion of three of these manuscripts—C^{14}, C^{18}, and L^{31}.

4. For the sake of convenience I have included in this list only manuscripts that show more than 25 percent of the group readings in any book or that otherwise show signs of being closely related to the group. As will be clear from the figures at the end of the list of evidence, other manuscripts may have some relationship to the group, though not a close one: for example, $C^{13}C^{19}D^3L^{15}L^{47}Mu^1O^{30}P$. Probably they show contamination, which one expects with a text as frequently copied as the *De Miseria*.

5. This is what Kane found with the manuscripts of the A-version of *Piers Plowman* (see pp. 55, 81-82, 112-114, et passim in pt. 3 of his introduction, "Classification of the Manuscripts"). Three of the variational groups will be discussed below, pp. 259-64: C^{14}-C^{18}, C^{18}-L^{31}, and C^{14}-C^{18}-L^{31}. Without going into details about others, among the group manuscripts, C^1 and Es^2 are nearly identical; L^{17} and O^{31} are very close; Ev and Ru^2 are very close, with La often joining them; E^1 and L^9 are very close, with L^{45} joining them at times; L^{35} and Pa^{10} are close; and Wo^2 is joined by L^6, a nongroup but related manuscript, in Books II and III. Among the nongroup but related manuscripts, Re^3 and T^2 are nearly identical, and Ar is very closely related to them; D^1 and O^{23} are closely related in Book I, which is all that O^{23} contains; Pa^9 and Pa^{11} are very close, and are often joined by Bu, Go, and Lm; I and Mu^5 are often together, and in addition show similarities to Au, a group manuscript, and to Bu, Go, Lm, Pa^9, and Pa^{11}. Though I am aware of the dangers inherent in trying to call small variational groups genetic (see, for example, Kane, pp. 81-85), it is still probably of some significance that there are so many interrelationships among these nongroup manuscripts, especially the continental ones, bearing out the likelihood that they are contaminated and confirming what I say below, pp. 257-58, that the group is more narrowly confined near the place of origin of the *De Miseria* and more widespread farther away, especially in Britain.

6. See above, pp. 25-27.

7. See Introduction, n. 170, for the way in which I have determined "British" manuscripts. The presumed dates of the extant manuscripts do not change the figures: if anything, there is a larger percentage of group manuscripts among the thirteenth- and fourteenth-century manuscripts than among the fifteenth-century manuscripts. Of the eighteen French manuscripts, only three are fifteenth century (and none of the seven definite group manuscripts); by contrast, only two of the seven manuscripts now in German and Austrian libraries or written in Germany are from before the end of the fourteenth century, perhaps giving support to the view that these manuscripts are contaminated.

8. See discussion above, pp. 46-47.

9. For the nonglossed passages, see above, pp. 47-49.

10. For this last reading see also the evidence for C^{14}-C^{18}-L^{31}, below, p.

275

262. Here and following in this Appendix the lemma is the reading in the text of this edition; when the reading in Lotario's original (as found in Ro or V²) differs, I have put it in parentheses following the lemma.

11. In the two preceding lists and in the one following I count no readings that are shared by C¹⁴, C¹⁸, and L³¹, for which see below, p. 262. Readings common to C¹⁸ and L³¹ that are shared by more than ten manuscripts can be found at I.7.2, I.8.9, II.3.24, II.10.11, II.12.19, II.25.11, II.26.11, II.27.7.

12. C¹⁴ was corrected later, the correction taking the form of additions in a hand different from that of the original scribe, both in the margins and above the lines, from a nongroup manuscript. For the purpose of this comparison between C¹⁴ and C¹⁸, however, it would be misleading to use the corrected readings: only the original readings in C¹⁴ are used. For C¹⁴–C¹⁸ the readings were compared with all other group and contaminated manuscripts; for C¹⁸–L³¹, and for C¹⁴–C¹⁸–L³¹ (below, pp. 261–62), the readings were compared with all other collated manuscripts. As with C¹⁸–L³¹, the manuscripts that share the C¹⁴–C¹⁸ and C¹⁴–C¹⁸–L³¹ readings exhibit no consistent pattern.

13. See, for example, Archibald A. Hill. "Some Postulates for Distributional Study of Texts," *Studies in Bibliography*, 3 (1950–51), 89–90, and Maas, pp. 5–6, 7, 44.

14. The conflation can be seen in other ways, especially in C¹⁸. For example, at I.4.13 a corroborative piece of evidence for the group is *iubetur* for *precipitur*: C¹⁸ has "iubetur . . . precipitur"; another piece of corroborative evidence for the group is *quam* for *qui* at II.5.23: C¹⁸ has "quam qui"; a third piece of corroborative evidence for the group is at II.8.3–9—the omission of "divicie . . . mundi" followed by the later addition of "Opposita sunt esse divitem et egenum": C¹⁸ both retains the earlier reading and adds the later one. C¹⁸ may also show conflation at I.4.8, where it adds "ex semine," as do all group manuscripts, but retains *seminis,* which most group manuscripts omit (though a few other manuscripts do the same); and at I.19.3, where it adds "qui non vult educi de carcere," perhaps under the influence of the group correction in his exemplar, and then crosses it out. C¹⁴ shows conflation at I.23.24, where the group has *pollutiones* for "per illusiones": C¹⁴ has *polluciones* as well, but in addition retains the *per* from the original phrase; and at III.10.22, where the group has *testimonio* for *in ore:* C¹⁴ retains *in ore,* but adds *testimonio* a few words later. C¹⁴ may show conflation at III.9.52–54, where the group skips from one *peccare* to the next and then substitutes *viverent* for *vivunt:* C¹⁴ adds "dum viverent" after the first *peccare* but in addition retains the following sentence (including *vivut,* a mistake for *vivunt*).

My explanation, or theory, of the relationships between C¹⁴ and C¹⁸ is of course not the only one that "saves the appearances." C¹⁴ and C¹⁸ might have had exemplars contaminated separately by a group manuscript (the same or different) at a stage intermediate between B and each manuscript; or one manuscript could have been copied from an incompletely corrected exemplar whereas the other could have been copied later, from the same exemplar completely corrected; or C¹⁴ might exhibit in its first twelve chapters a manuscript tradition different from that in C¹⁸ and in the rest of its own text.

However, the best theory is the one that "saves the appearances" with the fewest possible assumptions: mine does this, whereas the others do not, and that is the most we can expect of a theory until new evidence is discovered to refute it.

15. L^{31} may also show conflation at I.11.10 with "dolorem et laborem," at I.19.8 with "dolebit et lugebit," and at II.17.25 with "perierunt et obierunt," though these passages do not involve the group. The first and the third, however, are passages from the Bible, which were particularly susceptible to change by scribes; in addition, for the first passage, the words *laborem* and *dolorem* are often found together (and, in fact, are a few lines earlier in the same chapter), and for the second, *dolebit* may have been repeated from five words earlier. The third passage may reflect the base strain, with *perierunt,* of C^{14}-C^{18}-L^{31}. Other possible signs of contamination, consistent with the state called conflation, can be found at the following places, where L^{31} retains an important reading that the group omits: I.4.6; I.12.7 and 17–18; I.13.4–5; I.16.9 and 53; I.22.8–9; II.1.10–11; II.2.6; II.14.7; II.16.2–3; II.28.15.

16. *The Calculus of Variants: An Essay on Textual Criticism* (Oxford: Clarendon Press, 1927), p. 57.

17. Kane, p. 59. Manly and Rickert experienced the difficulties involved in separating the original strain from the contaminated strain in some of the manuscripts of the *Canterbury Tales,* especially the first 1740 lines of the Knight's Tale in the Fitzwilliam MS., but their thinking on the matter is similar to Greg's (see *The Text of the Canterbury Tales,* vol. 2, 25–27, 113–16).

18. The simplest and most economical stemma would not include a hypothetical manuscript E—the E position would be filled by L^{31} itself—but that would assume that the scribe of L^{31} himself copied from two exemplars at the same time, and from what we know of scribal habits that would have been an unusual procedure. Contamination usually occurs when a scribe copies from a manuscript that has been corrected (in the margins, between the lines, or over erasures) from a manuscript of different descent, the readings by correction becoming indistinguishable from the original readings in the new copy (see, e.g., Manly and Rickert, vol. 2, 24–25; Greg, pp. 56–57; Maas, p. 8). It is more likely, therefore, that a corrected manuscript was intermediary between B and D, and L^{31}, and I have indicated it by E.

As with all reconstructions of this sort, there are questions which neither the stemma nor the available evidence can answer: for example, (1) were C and D the same manuscript (the law of probabilities and some of the evidence for conflation in C^{14}, C^{18}, and L^{31} would seem to argue against it); (2) were C and D (one or both) themselves contaminated (the most that can be said, I think, is that the extant manuscripts C^{14}, C^{18}, and L^{31} are contaminated); (3) could either C or D be identified with one of the extant group manuscripts or with one of the extant contaminated manuscripts (the fact of contamination itself makes this question unanswerable)? (4) Nor can the stemma reveal the answer to the interesting question of why L^{31} is closer to C^{18} than to C^{14}, though, if I am right in my analysis of the relationship between C^{14} and C^{18} (p. 261 above), it is almost certain that the conflated manuscript A would have contained "corrections" of B other than just those that characterize the group, and the explanation may be that C^{18} chose the uncorrected reading (that is, the reading that derives from B and that could also be reflected in L^{31}) more often than C^{14}. It must be emphasized that one need not accept the groups C^{18}-L^{31} or C^{14}-C^{18}-L^{31} in order to discover the relationships of L^{31}, the glosses, and Chaucer's manuscript: the purpose of bringing C^{14} and C^{18} into the discussion at all is to show how one could reconstruct Chaucer's manuscript, for which see Introduction, pp. 49-51.

19. The reconfirmation can also be seen in the two pieces of corroborating evidence for the group on p. 257. The three exceptions to the first are C^{14}, C^{18}, and L^{36}; the exceptions to the second include C^{18} and L^{36}.

20. As with the preceding stemma, I have assumed a hypothetical manuscript F where the simplest and most economical assumption would have been to fill the F position with Chaucer's manuscript, and I have done so because without it we would have to assume that most of the differences between B and L^{31} either originated in the glosses or were the result of correction, by E or L^{31}, of either D or Chaucer's manuscript. Neither one of these assumptions is impossible, but I think the first is unlikely if we believe, as I do, that the glosses were written by Chaucer himself or by a scribe working under his direction; against the second is the fact that so many of the corrections would have been commonplace substitutions (*quippe* for *igitur, cui* for *cuius, sonitum* for *sonum*)—precisely the kind of substitution a correcting scribe would have been unlikely to make. If my stemma is correct, it means that the additions "Audi ergo," *latet, post,* probably *eciam* originated in F, that the common substitutions (*igitur, cuius, sonum*; also *dileccione*) probably originated in Chaucer's manuscript, and that the omissions originated either in Chaucer's manuscript or the glosses (probably the latter, as the nature of a gloss is to omit nonessential words); it also means that, when the extant manuscripts C^{14}, C^{18}, and L^{31} agree against the glosses, as they do, for example, in having *ut* after "Salubre consilium" in I.21, we must assume that F had the same reading and that the difference between the extant manuscripts and the glosses (in this case an omission) originated either in Chaucer's manuscript or in the glosses.

I am aware that my stemma, like most stemmata, especially of popular texts, assumes a number of hypothetical manuscripts. I see no way out of this difficulty. However, I have assumed, with Greg (pp. 2-4), that the hypothetical manuscripts are in fact "inferential," that is, the "latest exclusive common ancestors" of the groups in question, and, as I observed in n. 18, it is possible that at least C and D (one or both) might be identified with extant manuscripts (though not A, B, E, and F). Moreover, we must assume that all families of medieval manuscripts have been decimated, and this would be especially true of British manuscripts of the *De Miseria* because of the dissolution of the monasteries, where, if one can judge from the provenances of the extant manuscripts, the work had its greatest popularity.

APPENDIX III: ADDITIONAL CHAPTERS FROM THE *DE MISERIA*

As I indicated in the Introduction, pp. 51-52, the original chapters 2, 3, and 8 of Lotario's Book III (as reconstructed by Maccarrone) are omitted in over two-thirds of the extant manuscripts and in over 90 percent of the British manuscripts and would therefore not appear in a typical manuscript of the *De Miseria* as it circulated in the Middle Ages. I append these three chapters here so that one can reconstruct Lotario's original in full and see its fate in the process of transmission.

As with the text of this edition, I have chosen my text for these three chapters from among the manuscripts of demonstrably or presumably British provenance. Thirteen British manuscripts contain one or more of the three chapters: $C^4C^5C^{12}C^{20}Du^2Du^4L^{23}O^{14}O^{18}O^{20}Ph^1RWo^1$. Of these, ten can be eliminated: five ($C^{20}Du^4O^{14}O^{18}Wo^1$) omit one of the three chapters; two (Du^2R) have an abbreviated version of the original III.3, joined, without title, to the original III.2 (see Maccarrone's discussion, pp. xxv-xxvi); three ($C^4C^5L^{23}$) combine the full version of III.3 with III.2, thus showing no title, and make many changes in what is presumably the original text, especially L^{23}, which adds a long passage to each of the three chapters. Of the three remaining ($C^{12}Ph^1O^{20}$), the related manuscripts C^{12} and Ph^1 are superior to O^{20}, which has a very erratic text and is part of the large group of manuscripts discussed in Appendix II. It is difficult to choose between C^{12} and Ph^1, but C^{12} retains a slightly more accurate version of the presumed original, and I have therefore chosen it. C^{12} is a manuscript of the late fourteenth or early fifteenth century, written in Anglicana Formata, and was presumably at Pembroke College, Cambridge, in the late Middle Ages.

I have followed the same editorial principles as for L^{20}, the manuscript used for this edition (see Introduction, pp. 54-55). In the critical apparatus I have recorded variant readings from O^{20}, Ph^1, Ro, and V^2 (the last two the manuscripts judged by Maccarrone to have been closest to Lotario's original). I have recorded all substantive variants (see Introduction, p. 59), but have recorded nonsubstantive variants only when they are shared by two or more manuscripts or when two or more manuscripts have separate variants. The arrangement of the critical apparatus is the same as in the main part of this edition (see Introduction, pp. 63-64). The first two chapters, originally III.2 and 3 (and thus in Ro), would have come between II.41 and III.1 of this edition;

the third, originally III.8 (and thus in Ro), would have come between III.4 and 5 of this edition. In C^{12} and Ph^1 they are III.1, 2, and 6 respectively; in V^2 they are III.2 (containing the original chapters 2 and 3 combined into one) and 7; in O^{20} chapters and books are not numbered.

a) DE DOLORIBUS QUOS MALI PACIUNTUR

Mali siquidem quatuor dolores in morte paciuntur. Primus dolor est angustia corporea, tanta et tam gravis quanta vel qualis nec fuit, nec est in presenti vita ante dissolucionem illam. Que in quibusdam, etsi ne moribus, apparet pre nimio dolore seipsos dissipantibus. Fortis
5 enim et intemperabilis est violencia quando nexus illi et fizicales nodi inter corpus et animam disrumpuntur. Unde propheta, lamentando, ait in Psalmo: "Circumdederunt me dolores mortis." Dixit "circum*dederunt*" quia non est membrum nec articulus in corpore quin penitus involvatur illo inexplicabili dolore. Secundus dolor est
10 quando, iam plene diffatigato corpore et suis exhausto viribus, anima multo liberius videt tunc omnia in momento occurrere omnia opera sua bona vel mala que fecit, que omnia reducuntur ante oculos interiores. Dolor iste tantus est et retractio ista tam gravis est quod anima plurimum turbata cogitur quasi seipsam odisse. Unde dicitur
15 in Psalmo: "Torrentes iniquitatis contur*baverunt* me." Nota: "torrentes iniquitatis" cum multo impetu veniunt et videntur dirruere omnia; ita in morte videbit malus omnia subito ante que fecit opera bona vel mala. Tercius dolor est quando anima incipit tam iusto die iudicare et sibi pro iniquitatibus suis singularia omnia et debita
20 gehenne tormenta videt iminere. Unde dicitur in Psalmo: "Circum-

a) *Title* Mali *om* O^{20}; De . . . Paciuntur in Morte O^{20}Ph^{1}RoV^2. 2 **tanta** animata O^{20}. **quanta vel** quam talis O^{20}; quanta et Ph^1. 2-3 **nec est** *om* O^{20}. 3-4 **etsi ne moribus** et sine moribus Ph^1; etsi non in omnibus O^{20}RoV^2. 4 **dissipantibus** discrepantibus O^{20}; discerpentibus V^{2}Ro. 5 **intemperabilis** incomparabilis O^{20} Ph^{1}RoV^2. **fizicales** philosophi tales O^{20}. 6 **disrumpuntur** corrumpunt O^{20}. 7 **in Psalmo** *om* O^{20}RoV^2. **Dixit** Nota O^{20}RoV^2. 8 **quia** me O^{20}RoV^2; me dolores mortis quia Ph^1. **non est** *om* Ph^1. 9 **quin penitus** quod penitus O^{20}; quod penitus non RoV^2. 10 **viribus** corpore viribus Ro; virtutibus corpore O^{20}; corpore virilibus V^2. 11 **anima . . . videt** dandam multo liberatus vides O^{20}. **omnia** *(1st)* *om* O^{20}Ph^{1}RoV^2. 12 **reducuntur** reconduntur Ph^1. 13 **ista tam** ita O^{20}. 14 **turbata** turbatur V^2. **odisse** adisse O^{20}. 15 **in Psalmo** *om* O^{20}RoV^2. **Torrentes . . . Nota** *om* O^{20}. 17 **ante que** *trans* O^{20}Ph^{1}RoV^2. 18 **incipit** iam incipit O^{20}RoV^2. 18-19 **iusto die iudicare** iuste diiudicare RoV^2; iuste dividi dare O^{20}; iuste dividicare Ph^1. 19 **pro** in O^{20}RoV^2. **omnia** *om* O^{20}V^2. 20 **tormenta** *om* V^2. **videt** videtur Ro. **in Psalmo** *om* O^{20}RoV^2. 21 **mortis et inferni** mortis O^{20}Ph^{1}V^2; inferni Ro.

dederunt me dolores mortis et inferni" et cetera. Quartus dolor est
quod anima, adhuc in corpore posita, videt spiritus malignos ad
rapiendum se paratos, ubi tantus dolor est et timor quod misera
anime, licet extincta, quamdiu potest refugiat et tempus sue captivi-
25 tatis redimat antequam de corpore exeat.

b) DE ADVENTU CHRISTI AD DIEM MORTIS CUIUSLIBET HOMINIS

Videt eciam tam bonus quam malus, antequam egrediatur de corpore, Christum in cruce positum. Malus ut ad confusionem erubes-
cat se non esse redemptum sanguine Christi, sua culpa exigente.
Unde de malis dicitur in Evangelio: "Viderunt in quem pupuge-
5 runt," quod intelligitur de adventu Christi ad iudicium et de adventu
ad diem mortis bonis ut videant exultacionem. Habemus ex verbis
Apostoli, qui ait: "Usque in diem adventus Domini nostri Iesu
Christi": id est, usque in diem mortis, quando apparet tam bonis
quam malis Christus in cruce positus. Et ipse Christus de Iohanne
10 evangelista ait: "Sic eum volo manere donec veniam," id est, in
virginitate perseverantem donec veniam ad obitum eius. Quatuor
namque leguntur adventus Christi. Duo visibiles: primus in mundum, secundus ad iudicium. Et duo invisibiles: primus in mentem
per graciam, unde in Evangelio: "Ad eum veniemus et mansionem
15 apud eum faciemus"; secundus in obitu cuiuslibet fidelis, unde
Iohannes in Apocalipsi: "Veni, Domine Iesu." Unde dicitur obitus,
quia obviam venit ei Christus.

22 **quod** quando O²⁰Ph¹RoV². 24 **extincta** extracta O²⁰; extractura V². 25 **redimat**
redimat que O²⁰.

b) *Title om* V² *because this chapter is combined with the preceding, as in many MSS (see
Maccarrone, pp. xxv-xxvii);* Christi *om and ante for* ad O²⁰; Cuiuslibet Hominis *om* Ph¹. 1
Videt Vidi O²⁰; Videat Ph¹; Viderit Ro. **antequam** antequam anima O²⁰V². 2
Christum *om* O²⁰. **ut ad confusionem** ad confusionem ut RoV²; ad confessionem ut
O²⁰. 4-6 **Unde . . . mortis** *om* V². 4 **in Evangelio** *om* O²⁰Ro. **Viderunt** Videbunt
O²⁰Ph¹Ro. 4-5 **pupugerunt** pupugerunt vel transfixerunt O²⁰. 5 **Christi** *om* O²⁰Ro. 6
bonis bonus O²⁰Ph¹RoV². **ut videant** ergo videt ad O²⁰; vero videt Ph¹; vero videt ad
RoV². **Habemus** Sed habemus O²⁰Ro; Et hoc habemus V². 7 **Usque** Vel O²⁰. 7-8
Domini . . . est eius V². 9-17 **Et . . . Christus** *om* V² *and many MSS (see Maccarrone, pp.*
xxv-xxvii). 10 **id est** sic O²⁰; et Ph¹; sic id est Ro. 11 **perseverantem** permanente O²⁰.
12-13 **primus in mundum** in carne primus O²⁰Ro; primus in mente Ph¹. 13 **secundus**
ad indicium ad indicium secundus in obitu cuiuslibet fidelis Ph¹. 14 **in Evangelio** *om*
O²⁰Ro. 15 **secundus . . . cuiuslibet** alius . . . uniuscuiusque O²⁰; alter . . . uniuscuiusque Ro. 16 **Iohannes in Apocalipsi** Iohannes O²⁰Ro; Iob in Apocalipsi Ph¹.
Domine *om* Ph¹.

Pene autem infernales diverse secundum diversa peccata sunt. Prima
pena est ignis, secunda est frigus, et de hiis dixit Deus: "Erit fletus et
stridor dencium" propter frigus. Tercia erit fetor. De hiis tribus
dicitur in Psalmo: "Ignis, sulphur, et spiritus procell*arum*." Quarta
5 vermes indeficientes, unde Ysaias: "Vermis eorum non morietur, et
ignis non extinguetur." Quinta mallei percuciencium, unde dicit in
Ysaia: "Parata sunt iudicia blasphematoribus et percucientes malleis
stultorum corpora" et cetera. Sexta tenebre palpabiles exteriores et
interiores, unde Iob: "Terra miserie et tenebrarum, ubi um*bra*
10 mor*tis*" et cetera; et alibi: "Vadam ad terram tenebrosam et oper-
tam mortis caligene"; et in Psalmo: "Non videbit lumen"; et alibi:
"Impii in tenebris conticissent." Septima confusio peccatorum: sicut
enim legitur, "Tunc erunt libri aperti," id est, consciencie hominis
et erunt omnes consciencie manifeste. Octava horribilis visio de-
15 monum, qui videbuntur in excussione sintillarum de igne ascenden-
cium. Nona ignee cathene, quibus impii constringuntur membris.
Prima per concupiscenciam est; secunda malinosorum; tercia luxu-
riosorum; quarta invidorum et odium habencium; quinta eorum qui
in hoc seculo flagello non meruerunt castigari, quia "exacerbave-
20 runt Dominum peccatores et secundum multitudinem iniquitatem
suarum non querent"; sexta eorum qui, in tenebris ambulantes ad
lumen verum, venire contempserunt; septima confitencium peccata
sua et penitenciam contempnencium; octava illorum in seculo liben-

---

c) *Title* De . . . Inferni Eterni Ph¹. 1 **diverse** *om* Ph¹Ro. **diverse . . . sunt** sicut
diversa peccata sunt sunt diverse O²⁰. 2 **dixit** dicit O²⁰Ph¹RoV². **Deus** Dominus O²⁰Ph¹
RoV². **Erit** Ibi erit O²⁰Ro; Ibi V². 3 **dencium** dencium Fletus propter fumum ignis
stridor dencium V². **propter** per O²⁰. **Tercia** Tercia pena O²⁰V². 4 **in Psalmo** *om*
O²⁰RoV². 5 **Ysaias** dicitur O²⁰RoV². 5-6 **morietur . . . non** *om* V². 6 **mallei** flagella
O²⁰V²; salegra Ph¹; flagra Ro. 6-7 **dicit in Ysaia** dicitur O²⁰V²; dicit Ysaias Ph¹; dicitur
Isai Ro. 7 **malleis** mallei Ph¹V²; malleum O²⁰; mallea Ro. 8 **corpora et cetera**
corporibus O²⁰Ph¹RoV². 9 **Iob** illud O²⁰RoV². 10-11 **et alibi . . . caligene** *om* V². 11 **in
Psalmo** illud In eternum O²⁰RoV²; in Psalmo In eternum Ph¹. **alibi** illud V². 12 **Impii**
Alii Ph¹. 12-13 **sicut . . . Tunc** Tunc enim ut legitur RoV²; Tunc enim viriliter O²⁰. 13
libri alibi Ph¹. **id est** *om* Ph¹Ro. **hominis** hominum O²⁰Ph¹Ro; homini V². 14 **erunt** et
erunt Ph¹. **omnes** omnibus O²⁰RoV²; omnibus consciencie Ph¹. 15 **qui** que O²⁰.
videbuntur videbitur O²⁰; videbunt Ro. **excussione** excusationem Ph¹. 16 **constringuntur membris** singuli membris astringentur O²⁰; singulis menbris astringuntur Ro,
with astringentur V². 17 **malinosorum** maleficiorum O²⁰. 18 **invidorum** invidio-
sorum O²⁰; Iudeorum Ph¹. **et . . . habencium** homicidium et hereticum O²⁰. 19
flagello per flagella O²⁰RoV². 19-20 **exacerbaverunt . . . peccatores** exacerbavit . . .
peccator O²⁰RoV². 20-21 **iniquitatem suarum** ire sua O²⁰RoV². 22 **verum** verum
scilicet Christum O²⁰; ad Christum V². 23 **et penitenciam** in penitencia O²⁰. 23-24 **in**

ter vident mala et faciunt; nona qui per delicias suas sunt defluxi, qui
25 ambulant in deliciis suis et in concupiscenciis suis.

. . . **libenter** libenter in hoc seculo V²; in hoc seculo O²⁰Ro; in hoc seculo libenter Ph¹.
24 **nona** nona eorum O²⁰RoV²; nona illorum Ph¹. **delicias suas** singula vicia O²⁰Ph¹
RoV². 25 **deliciis** desideriis O²⁰Ph¹Ro; semitis V². **in . . . suis** eunt post concupiscen-
cias suas O²⁰RoV².

NOTES TO THE TEXT

NOTES TO THE TEXT

In keeping with the policies and aims of the Chaucer Library, these notes to the text of the *De Miseria* deal exclusively with sources and textual matters. For the books of the Bible, from which the bulk of the *De Miseria* is drawn, I have used abbreviations (in English); in addition to these, I have used only three: "Cf." to indicate that words in the *De Miseria* are reminiscent of certain words in a source, usually the Bible, but are not quoted directly from the source; "See" to indicate that a certain source, almost always biblical, is intended but that it has no verbal similarities to the passage in the *De Miseria*; and "*PL*" to indicate that a source can be found in the well-known *Patrologia Latina* by J. P. Migne (1844–1868). Nagy and Maccarrone (see Introduction, n. 2) mention a number of possible sources for general ideas in the *De Miseria*, but in these notes I have cited a source only if there is a verbal connection between it and the corresponding passage in the *De Miseria*. I have not, however, considered it necessary to indicate the sources either of verbal commonplaces (for example, "O vanitas vanitatum" at II.39.10–11) or of allusions to well-known biblical personages in a nonnarrative context (for example, Adam at I.3.1–2). In checking quotations from the Bible I have used *Biblia Sacra Vulgatae Editionis Sixti V Pont. Max. Iussu Recognita et Clementis VIII Auctoritate Edita,* 2nd ed. ([Turin]: Marietti, 1965) and for quotations from classical Latin writers the appropriate volumes of the Loeb Classics; for all others I have given full bibliographical information in the notes.

The textual notes have been kept to a minimum. Readers familiar with scribal habits in general will recognize how many of the readings, both in L^{20} and, primarily, in the manuscripts in the critical apparatus, originated. I have not considered it necessary to comment on these habits or on abbreviations that might have given rise to variant readings (for example, *secretum* from *ferreum* in L^{31} at I.24.8). The textual notes deal primarily with scribal practices in L^{20} and in the manuscripts mentioned in the critical apparatus.

TITLE

Neither Ro nor V^2 has Lotario's original title: in Ro there is no original title, a postmedieval hand adding *De Miseria Humanae Vitae . . . de Mundi Contemptu* at the top of the first page of text; the title in V^2 is *Incipit Liber Lotharius ab Actoris Nomine Vocatus.* See further, Introduction, pp. 20, 51.

PREFACIO

For the possible origin of this distinction in L^{20}, see Introduction, p. 52.

PRIMA PARS

I.1   1-3: Jer. 20:18.
         7-9: Job 3:11-12.
         9-10: Isa. 9:5.
         11-12: Jer. 20:17.
         12-13: Job 10:19.
           14: Cf. Jer. 9:1.

I.2   1-2: Gen. 2:7.
         10-13: Eccles. 3:19-20.
         16-18: Job 10:9.
         18-19: Gen. 3:19.
         19-20: Job 30:19.

I.3   1: In Ro chap. 3 begins as in Lotario's original as reconstructed
by Maccarrone—that is, at l. 13 with the title *De Conceptione
Infantis*—and in the table of contents to Book I this is the only title
given for chap. 3. In the margin next to this line, however, the
rubricator of Ro has added the title *De Vitio Conceptionis*. There is no
evidence for the origin of this title—whether it came from another
manuscript, or whether the rubricator created it himself, or whether it
is based on a direction given by Lotario—but it indicates that very
early in the transmission of the text a marginal notation was elevated
to the status of a separate chapter heading, which appears in nearly 80
percent of the extant manuscripts. It is not clear why the original title
to chap. 3 disappears, but it is interesting that some manuscripts still
retain both titles and divide the present chap. 3 into two: a new, shorter
one containing ll. 1-12 and the original, longer one beginning at l. 13.
See also Introduction, p. 52.
         5-6: Job 14:4. The addition in BuGoLmPa⁵Pa⁹Pa¹¹ is a continua-
tion of the same verse.
         6-7: Job 15:14.
         8-9: Ps. 50:7.
         41-43: Cf. Peter Lombard's *Sententie* II, Dist. xxx, *PL*, 192, col. 1060.
         45-46: 1 John 1:8.
         49-51: Rom. 5:12.
         51-53: Jer. 31:29; quoted in Ezech. 18:2, which may be a more likely
source in view of the possibility that I.4.10-12 are indebted to Ezech. 18;
cf. also the marginal note in L²⁰.

I.4   4-7: Isidore, *Etymologie* XI.i.141, *PL*, 82, col. 414.
         10-12: See Ezech. 18:6, 13.
         12-15: See Lev. 12.

287

I.5   1-2: Job 3:20.

I.6   3-4: Quoted by Odo of Cheriton in similar form in one of his sermons, according to Léopold Hervieux in *Les Fabulistes latins* (Paris: Librairie de Firmin-Didot et Cie., 1896), IV: *Eudes de Cheriton et ses dérivés*, 351.

        4: The scribe of L[20] may simply have passed over Lotario's pun—"nisi eu a"—after the second *Eva*, but it is also possible that he may have omitted it because he was not amused by it. I have added the word *syllable* to the following sentence to compensate for the omission. For another example of the possibility that the scribe was not attuned to Lotario's style—this time his rhetoric—see II.41.31-41 and accompanying note.

        7-8: Gen. 3:16.

        10-11: Cf. Gen. 35:18.

        11-13: See I Kings 4:20-21. The additions in L[31]CiH[1]Sa at l. 13 are doubtless indebted ultimately to vv. 21 and 22. *N* spellings of *Hichaboth* at l. 13 are characteristic of group MSS, with *Nichaboth* the most common form of the word; *H* spellings are characteristic of most other MSS.

        13-16: John 16:21.

I.7   2-3: Job 1:21.

        4-5: 1 Tim. 6:7.

        9-11: Gen. 38:29.

I.8   8-9: Matt. 7:18.

        13-15: Cf. Job 13:25.

I.9   1-2: See Gen. 5:5-14.

        3-6: Gen. 6:3.

        10-12: Ps. 89:10.

        12-13: Job 10:20.

        13-14: Job 7:6.

        15-16: Job 14:1; in most MSS the quotation continues through v. 2.

        17-29: The scribe who wrote the marginal *Gregorius*, and perhaps Lotario as well, must have been thinking of Gregory's *Homilia* I.i (on Luke 21:25-32), in *PL*, 76, esp. col. 1080, but the ideas expressed have a long history, going back to Horace's *Ars Poetica* 169-74. See George R. Coffman, "Old Age from Horace to Chaucer Some Literary Affinities and Adventures of an Idea," *Speculum*, 9 (1934), 249-58 et passim.

        29-30: Ultimately Horace, *Ars Poetica* 169; the quotation often appears by itself in the Middle Ages: see Hans Walther, *Carmina Medii Aevi Posterioris Latina*, II: *Proverbia Sententiaeque Latinitatis Medii Aevi*, 2 (Göttingen: Vandenhoeck & Ruprecht, 1964), item 15428. The addition in C[14]Er[2]L[22]O[21] is from ll. 170-71.

I.10   1-2: Job 5:7.
               2-4: Eccles. 2:23.
               7-8: Eccles. 1:2.
               11: Eccles. 1:17.
          11-14: Ecclus. 40:1.

I.11   6-10: Eccles. 1:17-18.
          16-18: Wisd. 9:15.
          19-20: Eccles. 1:8.
          20-24: Eccles. 8:16-17.
          24-26: Ps. 63:7-8.
          26-27: Prov. 25:27.
          30-31: Eccles. 7:30.

I.12   9: One often finds an intrusive *n* in words with *-gn-* in Latin and French manuscripts. The scribe of L³¹ is usually very careful to distinguish *n* and *u* and both here and at l. 25 the form is clearly *lingna*. The ambiguity of *n/u* in connection with the intrusive *n*, however, doubtless accounts for the form *lingua*, which appears in some manuscripts. L³¹'s *toneunt* in this same line—with the abbreviation *tõeunt*—is probably ultimately a misreading of *tondunt* or *tondent* (*tondeo* 'clip, shear'). Cf. *quam ora* at I.15.12 for a similar probable misreading of a *d*.
          21-37: Eccles. 2:4-9, 11.

I.13   8-10: Job 10:15.

I.14   6: Because of the abbreviation—*cēatur*—in L³¹, it may be that the scribe of this manuscript first thought *creatur* after *Deum* and conflated that with *causatur* in his own writing of the word.
          10-11: Ecclus. 40:29.
          11-12: Prov. 14:20.
          12: Prov. 15:15.
       13: The form *amcii* in L³¹ was produced by inserting the minim omitted earlier in *amci* at the wrong place. Thus, the confusion in *causeatur* at l. 6, and the dittography in *criminanatur* at ll. 7-8 seem to indicate that the usually very careful scribe of L³¹ was nodding or was in some way distracted during the copying of this chapter.
          12-14: Prov. 19:7.
       14-15: Ultimately Ovid, *Tristia* I.ix.5-6, though in a form identical to one that is often found in the Middle Ages: see Walther, II, 1 (1963), item 4165.
          26: Matt. 6:21.

I.15   5: Ultimately Horace, *Epistles* I.ii.14, though this quotation is often found by itself in the Middle Ages: see Walther, II, 4 (1966), item 25272.

5-7: Ecclus. 13:23.

7-8: Cf. Gregory, *Moralia* XXI.xv.22, *PL*, 76, col. 203 or *Regula Pastoralis* II.vi, *PL*, 77, col. 34.

12: Juvenal, *Satires* V.2. The reading *quam ora* in L³¹—with the abbreviation *quā*—is probably ultimately a misreading of the original *quadra*. Cf. *toneunt* at I.12.9.

23-25: Cf. Ps. 18:3.

I.16   2-3: See Josue 15:63.

3-4: Ultimately Horace, *Epistles* I.x.24, though often found by itself in the Middle Ages: see Walther, II, 3 (1965), item 15938.

4-6: Matt. 19:11-12.

6-10: See Exod. 28:2-4, 40-43.

11-14: 1 Cor. 7:5.

14-15: 1 Cor. 7:9.

20-24: 2 Kings 11:2-4.

24-25: 1 Cor. 7:33.

28-29: 1 Cor. 7:28.

33-34: A well-known proverb in the later Middle Ages, though I have not seen it in this form in any work prior to the *De Miseria*. Chaucer himself quoted it, from Lotario via the French translation of Albertano of Brescia's *Liber Consolationis et Consilii* (1246), in *Melibee* B² 2276; also in the Wife of Bath's Prologue 278-280; and cf. Parson's Tale 631.

34-57: Ultimately from St. Jerome, *Adversus Jovinianum*, I.xlvii, *PL*, 23, col. 289, though the wording in the *De Miseria*, especially from l. 37 on, is quite different. Chap. xlvii, which is quoted from the *Liber Aureolus de Nuptiis* of Theophrastus, circulated separately during the Middle Ages, appearing, for example, in Peter Abelard's *Theologia Christiana* II (ca. 1124) and in John of Salisbury's *Policraticus* VIII.xi (1159) as well as in antifeminist compilations, for which see Robert A. Pratt, "Jankyn's Book of Wikked Wyves: Medieval Antimatrimonial Propaganda in the Universities," *AnM*, 3 (1962), 6, 9, et passim.

57-60: Cf. Matt. 5:32.

60-62: Cf. 1 Cor. 7:11.

63-64: Prov. 18:22.

67-68: Matt. 19:10.

71: Gen. 2:24.

I.17   1-2: Wisd. 11:17.

2: L³¹ has *c̃ic̃iis* in the margin next to the misreading *vermss*, in the same hand as the text. The most likely reading of this difficult form is probably *cerviciis* (a mistake for *cervicibus*?), but the case is not right, and it may be that the scribe was attempting to correct *vermss* but added too many strokes and an extra minim to the word.

2-4: Cf. Isa. 66:24 and Mark 9:43, 45.

4-6: Job 4:8-9.

11-13: Horace, *Epistles* I.ii.57-59. Both quotations are often found separately in the Middle Ages: see Walther, II, 2, items 12788 and 12756a respectively.

    15-21: Rom. 1:21, 24, 28.
    21-22: 2 Tim. 3:12.
    22-29: Heb. 11:36-38.
    29-34: 2 Cor. 11:26-27.
       34: Luke 9:23.
    35-36: Cf. Gal. 5:24 and 6:14.
    36-38: Heb. 13:14.
    39-40: Ps. 118:19.
    40-42: Ps. 38:13-14.
    42-44: Ps. 119:5-6.
    44-46: 2 Cor. 11:29.
    47-48: See Josue 15:16-20 and Judges 1:12-15.

I.18
      1: Job 7:1.
    6-7: Gal. 5:17.
    7-10: Eph. 6:12.
   10-12: 1 Pet. 5:8.
     13: Cf. Jer. 9:21.
   13-14: Cf. Lam. 3:51.
   14-15: Wisd. 5:21.
   15-17: Luke 21:10-11. As noted in the margin of L[20], there is a version of this passage in Matt. (24:7), but the wording in the *De Miseria* is closer to the version in Luke.
   20-23: Gen. 3:17-19.
   23-24: Ps. 79:14.
   30-31: Gen. 1:28.
   33-34: Deut. 32:24.

I.19
    1-2: Rom. 7:24.
    4-5: Ps. 141:8.
    7-8: Job 14:22.

I.20
    8-9: Ultimately Juvenal, *Satires* VI.165, though the quotation often appears by itself in the Middle Ages: see Walther, II, 4, item 26260.
   10-11: Ecclus. 18:26.
   11-12: Job 20:2.
   12-15: Job 21:12-13.

I.21
    4-5: Prov. 14:13.
    6-7: Job 1:13.
    7-10: Job 1:19.
   10-11: Job 30:31.
   12-13: Eccles. 7:3.
   13-14: Ecclus. 11:27.
   14-15: Ecclus. 7:40.

I.22   Title: C³ clearly has *in* rather than *vi-*, and I doubt that it was intended to be joined to the next word. *Incivilitate* does make sense in this context, but the abbreviation is almost certainly the one for *Civitate*. The difficulty of course is surely caused ultimately by a misreading of *Vicinitate*.

    4: Ecclus. 14:12.

    5-6: Ps. 89:4.

    12-14: Eccles. 4:2-3.

I.23   10-14: Job 4:13-15.

    15-17: Job 7:13-14.

    17-20: See Dan. 2:1.

    26-29: Deut. 23:10-11, the attribution in Lotario's text notwithstanding; cf. Lev. 15.

I.24   7: Ultimately Ovid, *Heroides* I.12, though the quotation often appears by itself in the Middle Ages: see Walther, II, 4, item 26666.

    12-15: Cf. John 11:33.

    15-16: For this line and for the clause omitted in L²⁰—"Forsitan . . . est"—cf. Robert of Melun on 1 Thess. 4:13 in his *Questiones de Epistolis Pauli, Oeuvres de Robert de Melun,* ed. Raymond M. Martin (Louvain: "Spicilegium Sacrum Lovaniense" Bureaux, 1938), 2, 270.

I.25   11-12: The idea of man as a *microcosmus,* or *minor mundus*, a reflection of the *megacosmus*, or *maior mundus*, has a long history, going back to Plato's *Timaeus,* but was particularly popular in the twelfth century. Bernard Silvester's *Cosmographia* is probably the best-known medieval treatment of the idea, and the variants in AuL³⁵Pa¹⁰ may reflect Bernard's words at the beginning of the *Cosmographia.* For a recent summary of the tradition see Brian Stock's *Myth and Science in the Twelfth Century* (Princeton: Princeton University Press, 1972), pp. 275-76, 197-207 passim, and n. 70 on p. 197.

I.26   3-4: Prov. 27:1.

    5-8: Eccles. 9:12.

I.27   9-12: Jer. 15:2.

I.28   1-46: The story is ultimately from Flavius Josephus, *De Bello Judaico* VI.iii, but in a form nearly identical with that in John of Salisbury's *Policraticus* II.vi. See *Flavii Josephi Opera,* ed. G. Dindorfius (Paris: Editoribus Firmin-Didot et Sociis, 1929), 2, 286-87 and *Ioannis Saresberiensis Episcopi Carnotensis Policratici,* ed. C. C. I. Webb (Oxford: Clarendon Press, 1909), 1, 79-81.

I.29   2: 1 Cor. 10:12.

    7-8: Job 12:4-5.

SECUNDA PARS

II.1   Title: Though the title to Book II in Maccarrone's reconstruction of Lotario's original and in most of the manuscripts that retain some form of the presumed original title contains *Conditionis*, it may be that *Conversationis*, as in Ro, is more likely because of the distinction made by Lotario at I.1.15-17: "condicionis . . . conversacionis . . . dissolucionis," and that is what I have entered in the critical apparatus. *Conditionis* could be easily explained as a scribal substitution under the influence of the title to the whole work, *De Miseria Humane Conditionis*. Cf. the note to the title of II.41.

    4-7: 1 John 2:15-16.

II.2   1-2: Ecclus. 10:9-10.

    3-7: 1 Tim. 6:9-10.

    11: The scribe of L³¹ probably intended to produce the reading in many group manuscripts, *immanet*, but omitted -ne- by mistake.

II.3   2-4: Isa. 1:23.

    5: Part of the original line was doubtless omitted because the scribe's eye jumped from one *iudicant amore* to the next, with the *non* later expunged because it was in conflict with "Non . . . retribuciones."

    6: L³¹ may provide the clue to the addition of *retribucionis* in a number of manuscripts: the word is directly under the *retribuciones* in the preceding line. If *retribuciones* was originally the word added, perhaps it was changed to the genitive during the process of transmission in order to fit in with *largicionem*.

    8-9: The marginal *Ysaias* refers to the same passage that is quoted in ll. 2-4.

    12-13: Ezech. 22:27.

    13-15: Mich. 3:11.

    16-22: Deut. 16:18-20.

II.4   2-4: Isa. 5:20.

    4-5: Ezech. 13:19.

    12-13: Cf. Matt. 6:22.

    13-15: Cf. 1 Cor. 5:6.

    21-24: Ecclus. 13:28-29.

    25-26: Cf. Job 19:7.

    30-37: James 2:2-4.

    38-41: Jer. 5:27-28.

    41-44: Deut. 1:17.

    44-45: Rom. 2:11.

II.5   7: Matt. 10:8.

9-12: Matt. 16:26.
12-15: Ps. 48:8-10.
16-25: James 5:1-4.
26-28: Matt. 6:19.

II.6   5-6: Ecclus. 14:9.
6-8: Eccles. 5:9.
9-10: Prov. 30:15.
10-11: Ultimately Juvenal, *Satires* XIV.139, though the line is often found by itself in the Middle Ages: see Walther, II, 1, item 3731.

II.7   4-5: Cf. 1 Cor. 6:17.
9-10: Cf. 2 Cor. 6:14-15.
11: Cf. Matt. 6:24.

II.8   6-7: Cf. Eccles. 5:10.
9: Following *egenum* in Lotario's presumed original is a quatrain that circulated widely in the Middle Ages: see Walther, II, 1, item 3913.

II.9   2-4: See Num. 22, esp. v. 25.
4-6: See Josue 7.
6-7: See 3 Kings 21.
7-8: See 4 Kings 5.
9-10: See Matt. 27:5.
10-12: See Acts 5:1-10.
12-16: Zach. 9:3-4.

II.10   1-2: Ecclus. 8:3.
2-3: Ecclus. 31:5.
3-5: Ps. 72:12.
6-7: Matt. 10:9.
7-9: Cf. Matt. 19:24.
12: Acts 3:6.
12-14: Isa. 5:8.
14-16: Isa. 2:7.
16-17: Isa. 57:17.

II.11   2: There is a splotch over the words "opulentus . . . tamen" in L^{31} that makes it impossible to read anything between the *l* in *opulentus* and the $\bar{n}$ abbreviation in *tamen*. If the ending on *opulentus* is not abbreviated, there is no room for *Et*; cf. $C^{14}C^{18}$ in the critical apparatus.
3-4: Gen. 15:6.
4-6: Job 1:8.
7-8: 2 Cor. 6:10.
9-10: Ps. 61:11.

11-12: Ps. 33:11.
16-18: Jer. 6:13.

II.12 5-8: Luke 12:18.
    8-9: Luke 12:20.
     10: Cf. Ps. 38:7.
    10-12: Ps. 75:6.
    12-14: Job 27:19.
    14-17: Ps. 48:17-18.
    17-19: Ps. 48:11-12.
    20-21: Ecclus. 14:4.

II.13 2-4: Job 14:2.
    5-6: Cf. 1 Tim. 6:8.
    9-13: Matt. 6:31-33.
    13-14: Ps. 36:25.

II.14 1: Appears to be ultimately a conflation of Horace, *Satires* I.i.68 and *Epistles* I.ii.56. There are similar passages in Walther (esp. II, 5 [1967], item 31043), but not with the same wording as the one in question here.
    4-6: Prov. 13:7.
    12-14: Ecclus. 14:3.
    14-15: Ecclus. 14:5.
    15-18: 1 John 3:17.

II.15 1-2: Col. 3:5.

II.16 8-9: Cf. Ecclus. 4:36.
    11: Ecclus. 40:13.

II.17 1-2: Ecclus. 29:28.
    22-25: Ecclus. 37:32-34.
    25-26: 1 Cor. 6:13.

II.18 5-7: The examples are from Gen. 3, 25, 40, and Mark 6 respectively.
    7-9: See 4 Kings 25:8-10.
    9-11: See Dan. 5. The quotation is from Dan. 5:25, and the addition after *Phares* in group manuscripts is a distillation of Dan. 5:26-28.
    11-12: Exod. 32:6; quoted in 1 Cor. 10:7.
    13-14: Ps. 77:30-31.
    14-15: Lam. 4:5.
    15-16: Luke 16:19, 22.

II.19 3-4: Prov. 31:4.

4-5: Ultimately Horace, *Epistles* I.v.19, though the line is often found by itself in the Middle Ages: see Walther, II, 2, item 8903.

9-11: Ecclus. 31:38.

11-12: Osee 4:11.

13: Cf. Eph. 5:18.

14: Prov. 20:1.

14-16: See Jer. 35 passim and Luke 1:15.

II.20   1-2: The examples are from Gen. 9, 19; 2 Kings 13; and Jth. 13 respectively.

3-4: Prov. 23:21.

4-8: Isa. 5:11-12.

8-9: Isa. 5:22.

9-14: Isa. 22:13-14.

14-15: Isa. 28:1.

15-17: Isa. 28:7.

21-22: Cf. the table blessing for a little evening dinner on fast days in the Monastic Breviary: "Collationem servorum suorum benedicat Christus Rex Angelorum." The edition I have used is *Breviarium Monasticum . . . pro Omnibus sub Regula S. Patris Benedicti Militantibus*, 2nd ed. (Malines: H. Dessain, 1933).

II.21   2: Apoc. 22:11.

3-4: Osee 7:4-5.

4-5: I have not been able to find the source of this couplet. It must also have puzzled the scribes, for, as the critical apparatus makes clear, *opipare satur* (Lotario's presumed reading) caused great confusion. I assume the scribe of L[20] thought either *opimatus* or *opiparus* but wrote *opipatus*.

8-10: 1 Cor. 6:18.

13-16: Prov. 5:3-4.

II.22   2-4: Job 40:11.

II.23   2-9: These examples can be found in Gen. 19, 34, 38; Num. 25; Judges 19-20; 1 Kings 2 and 4; 2 Kings 11 and 13; Dan. 13; Gen. 49; Judges 14; and 3 Kings 11 respectively. There is great confusion among a group of manuscripts (nearly all of them related to C[3]) that contain, in the text or in the margin, the six words that appear in the margin of L[20], and I suspect that the confusion can be traced ultimately to a scribe's (or, more likely, scribes') adding the marginal words in his exemplar to the text he was writing but not knowing exactly where they were intended to go.

10: Ecclus. 9:9.

11-12: Ecclus. 19:2. The form *fanc* in L[31] is probably a misabbreviation of *faciunt*, perhaps with *n* inserted under the influence of the following nasal.

12-14: Prov. 7:26-27.

II.24   2–8: Rom. 1:26–27.
        12–14: Lev. 18:22–23.
        15–18: Lev. 20:13, 15.

II.25   1–3: Gen. 19:24.
        6–7: Cf. Deut. 32:35.
        7–18: See Gen. 19:24–29.
        18–19: Heb. 10:31.

II.26   11–12: Ovid, *Ars Amatoria* I.151; quoted by Peter Cantor, *Verbum Abbreviatum* xlv, *PL*, 205, col. 141.

II.27   11–14: The examples are from 4 Kings 5, Acts 8, Num. 26, and Deut. 11 respectively.
        14–15: Cf. Heb. 5:4.

II.28   2–18: 2 Kings 15:1–6.
        19–21: 2 Kings 15:10.
        21–23: 2 Kings 15:12.

II.29   8: The word in L[31] is definitely not *fine*. It is probably *fuce* 'with deceit' or perhaps *fute* 'in vain'.
        8–10: Lucan, *De Bello Civili* I.81 ("In . . . ruunt") and 70–71 ("summisque . . . diu"); Claudian, *In Rufinum* I.22–23 ("tolluntur . . . ruant"). Walther has entries for all three quotations, with the first and third appearing together in one manuscript; because Lotario seems to think of the three as one ("poeticum"), he may have found them together in his source.
        11–13: Ps. 36:35–36.
        13–15: Job 15:32–33.
        16: Ecclus. 10:11.

II.31   5: Ecclus. 10:15.
        5–6: Job 18:13.
        11–16: Isa. 14:12–14.
        16–26: Ezech. 28:12–17.
        26–32: Ezech. 31:8–9.
        32–33: Job 41:25.
        33–37: Apoc. 12:3–4.
        37–40: Apoc. 12:9.
        41–42: Luke 10:18.
        42–43: Luke 14:11 and 18:14.

II.32   5–10: Ezech. 28:2, 6–8.
        11–21: Dan. 4:27–30.
        22–24: Ps. 48:13.
        24: The marginal "In Ecclesiastico" in fact refers to the quotation in ll. 28–29.

24-28: The examples are taken from Gen. 11; 1 Kings 17; Esther 7; 2 Mach. 15, 9; Exod. 14; and 4 Kings 19 respectively.
28-29: Ecclus. 10:17-18.

II.33   2-4: Amos 6:8.
     4-6: Amos 8:7.
     6-8: Prov. 6:16-17.
    9-17: Isa. 2:12-15, 17.
    17-20: Isa. 5:14.
    20-21: Isa. 23:9.
    22-24: Job 20:6-7.

II.34   2-3: Prov. 13:10.
     3-4: Prov. 11:2.
    11-16: Luke 22:24-26.
    17-18: 1 Pet. 5:3.
      19: Ps. 23:1.
    23-24: Ecclus. 32:1.

II.35   2-4: Matt. 20:21.
      5: Matt. 20:22.
     6-7: Matt. 20:23.
    11-12: Osee 8:4.

II.36   1-3: Matt. 23:6-7.
    6-19: I do not know the immediate source of this exemplum, but it appears to be a variant of one in Frederic C. Tubach's *Index Exemplorum: A Handbook of Medieval Religious Tales*, FFC 204 (Helsinki: Suomalainen Tiedeakatemia, 1969), p. 227, item 2091; in one of the two versions that Tubach cites Magister Jordanus uses words similar to those in the *De Miseria* in addressing King Roger of Sicily: "An Deus es an homo. . . ."

II.37   1-2: See Gen. 3:21.
     2-3: Luke 9:3.
      4: Luke 3:11.
     7-8: Cf. Matt. 23:27.
    12-14: Cf. Matt. 23:5.
    14-15: Luke 16:19, 22.
    15-19: See Gen. 34:1-2, though nothing corresponds to "emeret ornamentum" (or "emeret ornatum," as in V²): Dina simply goes out to see the women ("videret mulieres"). In Flavius Josephus's *Antiquitates Judaicae* I.xxi, Dina goes out to see the women's clothes, or ornaments ("ad visendum cultum"), but there is no mention of her acquiring, or buying, them, as in the *De Miseria* (*Emeret*), and Lotario may have been working from another source or a variant of this one. See *Flavii Josephi Opera* (Paris: Editoribus Firmin-Didot et Sociis, 1929), 1, 38-39.

20-23: Jth. 10:19; see also 10:1-3 and 13:10.
24-25: Ecclus. 11:4.
   25: 1 Tim. 2:9.
26-27: 1 Pet. 3:3.

II.38   2-14: Isa. 3:16-24.
16-25: Ezech. 27:7, 15-16, 20, 25, 34, 36.

II.39   1-10: A popular exemplum in the Middle Ages: see Tubach, p. 90, item 1113; also told of Homer and of Peter Abelard at a monastery. Cf. also the biblical passage at II.4.30-37.

II.40   3-6: Matt. 6:28-29.
9-10: Ps. 38:6.
12-13: Prov. 31:30.
13-14: Isa. 40:6.
14-16: Ps. 36:2.
   26: From this point on the scribe writes both *etiam* and *eciam* and in general is less careful than he has been up to this point in distinguishing *t* and *c* before *i* plus a vowel. My sense of his new practice is that he is still very careful with *t* and *c* in important words (with two exceptions: *patientur* and *mutatio* at III.7.9 and 11) but that, in familiar, common words, he is less careful, writing *t* or *c* as he wishes. Cf., for example, the occurrences of *etiam/eciam* from here to the end of the treatise, or *Nec* at III.6.22, in which the *c* looks almost like a *t*.
26-28: Ps. 48:18.

II.41   Title: Though the title to II.41 (originally Book III) in Maccarrone's reconstruction of Lotario's original and in most of the manuscripts that retain some form of the presumed original title contains *Conditionis*, it may be that *Dissolutionis*, as in Ro, is more likely because of the distinction made by Lotario at I.1.15-17, and that is what I have entered in the critical apparatus. Cf. the note to the title of Book II. Ro's *Ingressu* is surely an error for *Egressu*, which appears correctly in the table of contents to Book III.
   2: James 3:2.
2-4: 1 John 1:8.
5-6: 1 Cor. 4:4.
   7: Ecclus. 31:9.
7-9: Job 15:15.
9-10: Job 4:18.
10-11: Job 15:16.
11-16: Gen. 6:5-7.
16-17: Cf. Matt. 24:12.
17-18: Ps. 13:3.
   20: L[20] has a stroke over the first minim of *deivet*, which is easily explained as a scribal error. On the other hand, the scribe of L[20] is very accurate and does not make such mistakes, and it may be that because

the shape of the stroke is slightly different from others in the manuscript and because the ink with which it is written is now not quite the same color as that of the base text, someone other than the original scribe made this "correction" to clear up the ambiguity produced by three minims written together.

22–23: Prov. 2:14.

23–29: Rom. 1:29–31.

31–41: The scribe of L[20], or of his exemplar, omits all of Lotario's *et*'s between pairs in this section. The scribe may have omitted them under the influence of the preceding passage (ll. 23–29), but it is also possible that he was not attuned to Lotario's rhetoric and to the effect the listing of pairs rather than isolated words would have. Cf. I.6.4 and accompanying note.

41–43: Ps. 67:3.

TERCIA PARS

III.1
    1–2: Ps. 145:4.
    5–7: Ps. 108:23.
    9–10: Cf. Job 14:5.
    11–12: Cf. Gen. 3:19.
    13–14: Ps. 103:29.
    14–16: See Ecclus. 19:3.
    16–17: Job 21:26.
    17–19: Isa. 51:8.
    19–21: Job 13:28.
    21–22: Job 17:14.
    22–23: Job 25:6.

III.2
    1: Ecclus. 7:19.
    3–4: Isa. 66:24.
    4–6: Jth. 16:21.
    8–10: Wisd. 4:20.
    11–15: Wisd. 5:8–10.

III.3
    1–2: Wisd. 5:6.
    3–4: Luke 23:30.
    9–12: Luke 16:27–28.
    12–15: Luke 16:29–30.

III.4
    1–7: Wisd. 5:2–5.
    10–11: Ps. 57:11.
    12–13: Cf. Isa. 26:10.
    13–17: Wisd. 5:14–15.

III.5
    3–4: Job 20:26.

5–6: Isa. 14:9.
9–10: Ezech. 28:18.
15–17: Matt. 22:13.
19–20: Wisd. 11:17.
22–25: Luke 16:24.

III.6   3–4: Cf. Isa. 26:10.
      5: Isa. 60:19.
      7–8: Cf. Peter Lombard, *Sententie* IV, Dist. L, *PL*, 192, col. 961.
      14–15: Eccles. 9:10.
      19–20: Ecclus. 17:26.
      21–22: Ps. 113:17.
      22–23: Isa. 38:18.

III.7   1–5: Job 10:20–22.
      6–7: Matt. 7:2.
      8–9: Wisd. 6:7.
      10–11: Job 24:19.

III.8   1–2: Ps. 48:15.
      6–8: Ovid, *Epistolae ex Ponto* I.ii.39–40.
      12–14: Apoc. 9:6.

III.9   1–2: Ps. 102:9.
      3: Ps. 144:9.
      4: Ps. 76:10.
      7–9: Isa. 24:22.
      11–13: Job 15:31.
      13: Response to Lesson vii of the Third Nocturn of the Office of the Dead in both the Roman and the Monastic Breviaries: "Quia in inferno nulla est redemptio, miserere mei, Deus, et salva me." The edition of the Roman Breviary that I have used is *The Hours of the Divine Office in English and Latin,* 3 (Collegeville: The Liturgical Press, 1964). For the Monastic Breviary see the note to II.20.21–22.
      14–20: The marginal *Ysaias* refers to the same passage that is quoted in ll. 7–9.
      20–22: Ps. 88:33.
      23: Heb. 12:6.
      24–25: Ps. 102:9.
      29–30: Ps. 73:23.
      37–40: Apoc. 16:21.
      48–54: Gregory, *Dialogi* IV.44, *PL*, 77, col. 404.

III.10   1–2: Isa. 33:14.
      2–3: Isa. 65:5.
      3–5: Isa. 34:10.
      5–7: Jer. 23:40.

　　　　7-9: Dan. 12:2.
　　　　9-10: Prov. 11:7.
　　　　13-17: Apoc. 14:9-11.
　　　　19-20: Matt. 25:41.
　　　　21-22: Deut. 19:15; quoted in Matt. 18:16 and, in similar form, in 2
Cor. 13:1.

III.11　　　1-9: Isa. 13:9-11.
　　　　9-14: Isa. 13:7-8.
　　　　14-19: Soph. 1:15-16, 18.
　　　　19-20: Luke 21:34-35.
　　　　21-23: Matt. 24:27.
　　　　23-26: 1 Thess. 5:2-3.

III.12　　　1-4: Matt. 24:21-22.
　　　　4-7: Luke 21:10-11.
　　　　7-11: Luke 21:25-26.
　　　　11-13: Matt. 24:24.
　　　　13-17: 2 Thess. 2:3-4.
　　　　17-18: 2 Thess. 2:8.
　　　　18-21: Mal. 4:5-6.
　　　　21-22: Apoc. 11:3.
　　　　22-26: Apoc. 11:7-8.
　　　　27-28: Apoc. 11:11.

III.13　　　1-5: Matt. 24:29-30.
　　　　5-11: Apoc. 6:15-17.
　　　　11-14: Matt. 24:31.
　　　　14-15: 1 Thess. 4:15.
　　　　16-18: John 5:28-29.
　　　　18-19: Apoc. 20:13.
　　　　　20: Apoc. 1:7.
　　　　21-22: Luke 21:27, probably conflated with Matt. 26:64.
　　　　24-25: Prov. 31:23.
　　　　26-27: Matt. 19:28.
　　　　27-34: Dan. 7:9-10.
　　　　34-36: Ps. 49:3.
　　　　36-38: Ps. 96:2.
　　　　38-39: Ps. 49:4.
　　　　39-42: Matt. 25:32-33.

III.14　　　2-3: Job 26:11.
　　　　3-4: Isa. 33:7.
　　　　4-6: 1 Pet. 4:18.
　　　　6-8: Ps. 142:2.
　　　　8-9: Ps. 129:3.
　　　　14-18: Job 9:19-21.

19–20: Ps. 148:5.
   20: Cf. Bar. 3:35.
21–22: Ps. 103:4.
22–23: Cf. Rom. 9:19.
   23: Cf. Luke 1:37.
24–25: Phil. 2:10.
26–27: Ps. 138:8.
27–28: Cf. Apoc. 2:23.
28–29: Heb. 4:13.
29–30: Cf. Ecclus. 1:2.
   30: 1 Kings 2:3.
33–34: Heb. 4:13.
34–35: Cf. Ps. 7:12.
35–36: Cf. Walther, II, 2, items 16237c and 16237d.
37–39: Often cited in the Middle Ages, in Peter Lombard's *Sententie,* Peter of Poitiers's *Sententie,* and other works (see *Sententiae Petri Pictaviensis,* 2, eds. P. S. Moore, J. N. Garvin, and M. Dulong [Notre Dame: University of Notre Dame, 1954], 54–55, n. to lines 182–183); see also Introduction, n. 34.
40–41: Ps. 61:12.

III.15   3–4: Matt. 25:42.
       5–6: Matt. 25:45.
       6–7: Matt. 25:41.
         9: 1 Cor. 4:5.
     9–10: Matt. 10:26.
   10–12: Cf. Apoc. 20:12.
   15–16: Ps. 31:1.
   17–18: John 5:22.
   18–19: Apoc. 3:7.
      19: Isa. 58:14.

III.16   2–4: Ezech. 7:19.
      4–5: Apoc. 18:9.
      5–6: Apoc. 18:15.
      6–8: Isa. 10:3.
      8–9: Gal. 6:5.
    9–10: Ezech. 18:20.
  11–12: Cf. Matt. 12:36.
  14–15: Cf. Matt. 3:7 and Luke 3:7.
  15–19: Matt. 13:41–42.
     26: An additional chapter, entitled *De Proprietatibus Romanorum,* taken from St. Bernard's *De Consideratione* IV.ii, follows in Ro, V², and a few other manuscripts. For the text of this chapter see *PL*, 182, cols. 774–75, beginning with "Ante omnia sapientes" and ending with "malignissimi proditores"; see also Maccarrone, p. xxx.